DATE DUE

DE 20 '96			
DC 9 '97			
OC 30 '98			
DE 8 '98			
MY 24 '99			
NO 7 '00			
MY 2 '09			

DEMCO 38-296

EIGHTH EDITION

Labor Relations

Arthur A. Sloane
University of Delaware

Fred Witney
Indiana University

Prentice Hall, Englewood Cliffs, New Jersey 07632

Library of Congress Cataloging-in-Publication Data

Sloane, Arthur A.
    Labor relations / Arthur A. Sloane, Fred Witney. - 8th ed.
    Includes bibliographical references and index.
    ISBN 0-13-521600-1
    1. Industrial relations-United States.   2. Collective bargaining-
    United States.   I. Witney, Fred.   II. Title.
    HD8072.S6185   1994
    331.8-dc20   93-10895
                                          CIP

Acquisitions editor: *Valerie Ashton / Natalie Anderson*
Assistant editor: *Lisamarie Brassini*
Editorial assistant: *Diane Peirano*
Editorial/production supervision: *Elaine Lynch*
Copy editor: *Mary Louise Byrd*
Interior design: *Suzanne Behnke*
Cover design: *Suzanne Behnke*
Cover photograph: *Theo Rudnak / Renard Represents, Inc.*
Prepress buyer: *Trudy Pisciotti*
Manufacturing buyer: *Patrice Fraccio*

Prentice-Hall International (UK) Limited, London
Prentice-Hall of Australia Pty. Limited, Sydney
Prentice-Hall Canada Inc., Toronto
Prentice-Hall Hispanoamericana, S.A., Mexico
Prentice-Hall of India Private Limited, New Delhi
Prentice-Hall of Japan, Inc., Tokyo
Simon & Schuster Asia Pte. Ltd., Singapore
Editora Prentice-Hall do Brasil, Ltda.,Rio de Janeiro

To Louise, Amy, and Laura
and Ruth, Billy, and Ann

Contents

PART II   THE ENVIRONMENTAL FRAMEWORK

PART III   COLLECTIVE BARGAINING

6 *Administration of the Agreement* *259*

7 *Wage Issues under Collective Bargaining* *326*

10 *Administrative Issues under Collective Bargaining* 485

Preface

There are no prerequisites to this book beyond an interest in labor-management relations. We have designed it to serve as an aid to all readers who desire a basic understanding of unionism in its natural habitat. With such a thrust, however, the volume focuses on certain areas, necessarily minimizing the treatment of others.

Labor Relations brings in, for example, sufficient economic material to allow a fundamental appreciation of the union-management process and stops at that point. Throughout, we have tried to implement our belief that all the various topic treatments should be short enough to be interesting while at the same time long enough to do justice to the subject. On the other hand, our offering in no way restricts itself to what is commonly described as collective bargaining. Its focus is on the negotiation and administration of labor agreements, with emphasis on the more significant bargaining issues as they now appear between the covers of the contracts. Further, our own teaching experiences have shown us that these topics cannot profitably be studied in isolation. Labor relations, in the sense in which we use the term, can best be viewed as an interaction between two organizations—management and the labor union—and the parties to this interaction are always subject to various, often complex, environmental influences. Only after the reader gains an understanding of the evolving management and labor institutions, and only after the environment surrounding their interactional process has been appreciated, can he or she attempt to understand bargaining itself in any satisfactory way.

The book consequently begins with a broad overview of the general nature of the labor-management relationship as it currently exists in the United States (Part I). It then moves to a survey of the historical, legal, and structural environments that so greatly influence contractual contents and labor relations behavior (Part II). Finally, it presents a close examination of the negotiation, administration, and major contents of the labor agreement itself (Part III).

Through description, analysis, discussion questions, and, in the later part of this volume, selected arbitration cases drawn from our own experiences, we hope to impart understanding of all these aspects of labor relations.

Numerous changes—primarily additions, although all of the chapters have been given some streamlining—mark this eighth edition. Even in the three years since the seventh edition, developments in the field have warranted the inclusion of new material on the issue of permanent replacements for strikers, unions and hospital employees, changes in the Teamsters Union, health insurance, worker participation programs, the Civil Rights Act of 1991, and recent developments in labor law (among other new topics). We have also substantially enlarged upon our treatment of such subjects as labor relations consultants, unions in politics, contract negotiations, concessionary bargaining, the Occupational Safety and Health Act, pensions, and plant closings. And we have updated the discussion of a host of other topics ranging from union membership to minorities and women in labor unions.

Nine recent arbitration cases are presented, in addition to three cases retained from the seventh edition. Each chapter now begins with an outline of its key contents and concludes with two "managerial" minicases, many of them with ethical dimensions. And many new visual aids are included, as are a significantly revised bibliography and an amended mock negotiation problem.

Nonetheless, we have exercised self-restraint in the rewriting. Only changes that can be defended on the grounds of general improvement of *Labor Relations* have been incorporated. We are strong believers in the old Puritan dictum that "nothing should ever be said that doesn't improve upon silence" and we also share with the late Calvin Coolidge the conviction that "if you don't say anything, no one will ever call upon you to repeat it."

Acknowledgments

When a book has reached the stage of an eighth edition, it stands indebted to so many people that individual acknowledgment is futile. As in the case of the prior editions, students, friends from the ranks of both management and labor, and colleagues at other educational institutions have offered constructive suggestions and we have implemented a host of them. Rita M. Beasley, who cheerfully and competently provided many helpful services on behalf of this volume, does deserve a special citation, however, as does her daughter, Amy C. Beasley, who ably compiled the index. Nor can the contributions of two outstanding Prentice Hall staffers—Assistant Editor Lisamarie Brassini and Production Editor Elaine Lynch—go unrecognized.

Arthur A. Sloane

Fred Witney

Organized Labor and the Management Community: An Overview

Our society has historically placed a high premium on property rights. Because of this, and perhaps also because the American soil has nurtured a breed of highly individualistic and aggressive managers, employers in this country have accepted unionism through the years approximately as well as nature tolerates a vacuum.

Symbolic of management sentiments in the mid-nineteenth century, for example, were the comments of the editors of the *New York Journal of Commerce* relating to current demands of the printers in that locality:

> Who but a miserable craven-hearted man, would permit himself to be subjected to such rules, extending even to the number of apprentices he may employ, and the manner in which they shall be bound to him, to the kind of work which shall be performed in his own office at particular hours of the day, and to the sex of the persons employed, however separated into different apartments or buildings?...It is marvelous to us how any employer, having the soul of a man within him, can submit to such degradation.[1]

Five decades later, George F. Baer, president of the Philadelphia and Reading Railroad, relied on God rather than ridicule in setting forth views that were no less representative of many employers of *his* time. In a 1903 letter, Baer replied to a citizen who had requested him "as a Christian gentleman" to make concessions to the striking workers on his railroad, as follows:

> I see you are evidently biased in your religious views in favor of the right of the working man to control a business in which he has no other interest than to secure fair wages for the work he does. I beg of you not to be discouraged. The rights and interests of the laboring man will be protected and cared for, not by the labor agitators, but by the Christian men to whom God in His infinite wisdom has given control of the property interests of the country.[2]

Sinclair Lewis used fictional satire to make his points, but real-life counterparts of his small-town businessman George F. Babbitt were sufficiently in supply to make *Babbitt* an instant success when it was published in 1922. Babbitt's opinions on the subject of organized labor were forthright, if not entirely consistent:

> A good labor union is of value because it keeps out radical unions, which would destroy property. No one ought to be forced to belong to a union, however. All labor agitators who try to force men to join a union should be hanged. In fact, just between ourselves, there oughtn't to be any unions allowed at all; and as it's the best way of fighting the unions, every businessman ought to belong to an employer's association and to the Chamber of Commerce. In union there is strength. So any selfish hog who doesn't join the Chamber of Commerce ought to be forced to.[3]

In our own day, management views on the subject are considerably more sophisticated and far less emotion-laden. Major changes have affected the employment relationship and contributed to the lessening of overt anti-unionism. The findings of industrial sociology and applied psychology have led to an employee-centered management approach that was unknown to an earlier era. Far greater worker expectations have been fostered by a new social climate derived from the ending of mass immigration, growing levels of education, and the spread of the world's most ambitious communications network. The old-time owner-manager, holding a major or exclusive proprietary interest in his business, has now been substantially displaced. He has been succeeded by the hired administrator, oriented toward management as a profession, as much an employee as the people far below in the organizational hierarchy, and increasingly aware that profitability is not the only test of performance today (and that community responsibilities are also prime considerations). Finally, the right of workers to organize and bargain collectively, free of employer restraint or coercion, has been protected by statute since the mid-1930s.

In this new setting, progress in union-management relations has undeniably been made. Violence in labor disputes has all but disappeared. The incidence of strikes has been almost steadily decreasing, and strikes now consume a minuscule portion of total working time—in the neighborhood of one tenth of 1 percent in most recent years. A greater willingness by both parties to resort to facts rather than to power or emotion as a basis for bargaining is in evidence. And, indeed, unions have now been completely accepted by some managers, with outspoken attacks on organized labor in general being relatively rare from *any* employer quarter.

For all these developments, however, unions are still far from welcome in the eyes of the employer community. If the attacks are more muted and less belligerent than they were, they nonetheless exist on a wide scale. Three decades ago, one observer summed up what he saw as the modal situation at that time in words that are wholly appropriate even now:

> Even if the manager does not view the union as a gang, he often still feels that (unions) strike a discordant note in the happy home. Once there, unrest develops. A peer group outside the home becomes more important to the children than the parents; the father's powers are challenged; the child begins to think his goals are not synonymous with those of the parents (he may even want his allowance raised); and, perhaps worst of all, he wants to have his voice heard in how the home should be run.[4]

In the face of this management enmity, on the other hand, unionism has shown absolutely no tendency to retreat. Owing primarily to the inroads of changing technology and the resulting employment decline, as well as to changing market demands affecting manufacturing, organized labor has, it is true, lost some of its membership in recent years, both in absolute and in relative terms. And despite some claims that the fast-growing white collar sector will soon become more hospitable to collective bargaining, it is equally true that union penetration in this area thus far has fallen considerably short of its potential. But it is no less a matter of record that almost six times as many workers are union members today as was the case in 1932, and it is quite apparent that the 17 million employees who currently constitute the labor movement in this country exhibit no notable signs of disenchantment with it. Whatever one's speculation about the problems awaiting unionism as the nature of our labor force changes (and, as will be shown, the speculation is both optimistic and pessimistic from the union viewpoint), the labor union seems to be very much here to stay.

In this introductory chapter, then, we shall want to examine several questions. Why do workers, apparently in complete disregard of their employers' wishes, join and remain in unions? Why, for that matter (beyond the extremely general reasons suggested by the preceding paragraphs), do employers so steadfastly continue to oppose the concept of unionism? Assuming that managers have no choice other than to deal with a labor organization, what alternative methods for this collective bargaining are open to them? And what, if any, trends in their concrete dealings with unions have managements exhibited in recent years? Before we discuss these questions, however, we must assess the current status and strategic power of the American labor movement itself.

THE STATE OF THE UNIONS TODAY

Completely reliable statistics relating to union membership in this country have never been available. Some unions in reporting their figures have traditionally exaggerated, to gain respect and influence for the union itself within the total labor movement, to make the union officers look better by showing a rise in enrollments during their term of office, or merely to hide a loss of membership. Other unions have been known to report fewer members than they actually have, for financial reasons (for example, to avoid paying per capita taxes to labor federations to which they may belong, particularly the American Federation of Labor—Congress of Industrial Organizations) or because of bookkeeping practices that exclude workers currently on strike (or those on layoff from work) from the list of present members.

The figure of 17 million workers that was offered earlier as constituting the present extent of union organization is commonly accepted as an appropriate one, however. This total includes, according to the best current estimates of the U.S. Bureau of Labor Statistics, some 10.7 million union members in private industry and 6.3 million government workers. It excludes the approximately 1.5 million Canadians who belong to internationals with headquarters in the United States. It also excludes the more than 2.2 million U.S. wage and salary employees, over half of them in the governmental sector, who are represented at their workplaces by a union but who are not union members: Not being required to join a union as a condition of continued employment in their cases, they have for a variety of reasons chosen not to do so. Nor do the BLS estimates include union members who are currently unemployed.

In 1993, the 17 million in the unionized work force represented about 16.4 percent of all U.S. workers, a statistic that was down appreciably from the 24.7 percent of the nation's labor force that unions had represented only a quarter century earlier, but that still allowed organized labor significant influence in at least some sectors.

Close to 40 percent of all employees in federal, state, and local government is, for example, now in the ranks of unions. And in the vitally important private-sector worlds of transportation and public utilities, the union proportion is a reasonably impressive 33 percent. Other major private industries with above-average union membership percentages are construction and manufacturing (almost 25 percent in each case) and mining (18 percent).[5]

More specifically, about 35 percent of the nation's blue collar workers, those whose job duties are primarily manual in nature, continues to be represented by unions. And in some blue collar bastions the nonunionist is a relative rarity. The great majority of manual workers in such "smoke-stack" industries as automobiles and steel, for example, carry union cards (and, generally speaking, take considerable pride in their unions. The United Steelworkers of America, for example, operates a rather lucrative side business in selling the USWA rings depicted in Exhibit 1-1, and other blue collar unions can point to comparable membership loyalty.) The same can be said for their counterparts in aerospace, rubber, agricultural implements, the needle trades, paper, and brewing. Organization also covers a substantial, if somewhat lesser, percentage of the blue collar employees in the printing, oil, chemical, electrical, electronic, pharmaceutical, and shoe industries and in the increasingly vital world of communications.

States and cities with a high percentage of their workers in all of these industries show, not surprisingly, a high proportion of unionized employees. Indeed, five states alone—New York, California, Pennsylvania, Illinois, and Ohio—account for almost half of all union members in this country (while employing just over one third of the U.S. nonagricultural work force). There are, in fact, more union members in New York alone than there are in eleven southern states, including Texas, combined. And Washington, Michigan, and Massachusetts also have ratios of union membership to nonagricultural employment that place them well above the national average. Several major cities, too, that are comparatively dependent on the industries cited—Pittsburgh, Detroit, and Seattle, among others—currently have at least 90 percent of their manufacturing-plant workers covered by union contract. On the other hand, states and cities without large representation from these industries tend to show considerably lower figures: In both North Carolina and South Carolina, less than 7 percent of the nonagricultural labor force belongs to a union and anyone who wagers that a random work group in Charlotte or Charleston (or Jacksonville or New Orleans, for that matter) is a nonunion one is very likely going to win.[6]

Union strength, then, is highly concentrated in areas that are strategic to our economy. If organized labor has thus far been notably unsuccessful

EXHIBIT 1–1

Source: Steelabor, August, 1987, back cover.

in its attempt to organize such white collar (and fast-growing) sectors as trade, services, and finance, and such remaining pockets of nonunionism in manufacturing as the textile industry, unions *have* been cordially greeted by the workers in much of large-scale industry. Indeed, the labor movement today bargains with many of the most influential managements in the country, those that regularly take the lead in price and wage movements. From trucking, whose importance to the nation is such that the American Trucking Associations can boast in its motto "If you got it, a truck brought it," to the focal points of any advanced industrialized nation in durable goods production, unions are important. They have power, accordingly, where the possession of power is particularly significant.

Titles do not always accurately portray the kind of worker represented by a union. Teachers in Oklahoma City belong to the Laborers Union, for example, and taxicab drivers in Chicago are members of the Seafarers' International Union. And the United Automobile Workers currently represents secretaries at Columbia University (as well as teaching assistants at the University of California, lawyers in Detroit, writers at New York's *The Village Voice,* and several hundred other white collar groups). But official names are at least generally indicative, and a reading of the names of the nine largest 1993 internationals as offered in the accompanying table gives further evidence of the importance of blue collarites to labor.

Union	Members
Teamsters	1,400,000
State, County and Municipal Employees	1,200,000
Food and Commercial Workers	999,000
Service Employees	881,000
Automobile Workers	840,000
Electrical Workers*	800,000
Carpenters	615,000
Machinists	550,000
American Federation of Teachers	550,000

*International Brotherhood of Elecrical Workers.
Source: Authors' estimates based on data published by the U.S. Department of Labor.

Of these nine largest unions (which collectively today account for almost 46 percent of all union members), only four appear even from their names to be outside of labor's main blue collar mold, and in three of these four cases this is somewhat misleading. Many State, County and Municipal Employee members perform such definitely blue collar assignments as stock handling and pothole patching. The United Food and Commercial Workers represents mainly manual workers. And there are more janitors and related custodial employees in the Service Employees than there are anything else. (Most members of the American Federation of Teachers do, on the other hand, teach.)

WHITE COLLAR EMPLOYEES

If the labor movement is predominantly a blue collar one, however, this is no longer true of the U.S. labor force itself. In 1956, the number of white collar workers exceeded that of blue collar workers in this country for the first time in our nation's history. And the gap has been steadily widening ever since. The service sectors—including trade, finance, and government—have continued to expand, while the blue collar sectors—particularly manufacturing, mining, and transportation—have actually, in the face of improved technologies and changing consumer demands, shown employment declines.

A mid-1980s report of the AFL-CIO itself was both accurate and, from labor's viewpoint, gloomy:

> ...the growth of the work force has occurred, and will continue to occur, principally in those sectors of the economy that have not traditionally been highly organized. Manufacturing and construction, for example, currently account for 50 percent of the AFL-CIO's membership, but these sectors have declined relative to others and currently employ only 22 percent of the civilian work force. In contrast, the service sector...has had, and will continue to have, the largest growth. During the 1970s, about 90 percent of all new jobs were added in service organizations. By 1990, service industries will employ almost three-quarters of the labor force. Yet, less than 10 percent of the service sector is organized, and only 20 percent of the AFL-CIO membership is in unions representing workers primarily in the service industries.[7]

The trend has continued in the years since. Less than 16 percent of workers in U.S. industry are now employed in manufacturing, as compared with some 23 percent two decades ago, while that graphic symbol of the nation's service sector, the McDonald's hamburger empire, has expanded to the point where it employs more than five times as many workers as does USX (formerly United States Steel). In fact, employment in the iron and steel industry, which peaked at 952,000 in 1957, had fallen to not much more than half that total by the 1990s, whereas jobs in automobiles, chemicals, apparel, and many other older industries, while often taking longer to peak (and in many cases not actually doing so until the late 1970s), had demonstrated similar decline by then. Whether or not smoke-stack America was actually in its sunset years at the time of this writing, most experts *believed* that it was and that all the grim employment trends would only continue.

More than any other factor, this changing complexion of the labor force has given organized labor cause for concern. Its inability to recruit white collar workers on any significant scale has been primarily responsible for its slippage from representing just under 25 percent of the labor force to its above-noted position of representing closer to 16 percent. Unless it can do far better than it has to date in organizing the nation's millions of clerical, sales, professional-technical, and other employees, it will by simple mathematical logic see the percentage drop even more, perhaps to the 13 or 14 percent level.

This is not to say, of course, that unions do not exert a major collective bargaining influence on behalf of some groups of white collar workers. Such white collar types as musicians and actors have for years been willing joiners of labor organizations. In recent years, two unions in particular have shown significant gains in this quarter: the State, County and Municipal Employees, whose estimated 1.2 million members (as noted) now make it one of the largest labor organizations in the country; and the American Federation of Teachers, which grew from 60,000 members in 1960 to over nine times that number three decades later. Also exhibiting no small amount of organizational success have been the Postal Workers and the Letter Carriers (each with current memberships in the vicinity of 350,000). Some 125,000 college faculty members and 40,000 physicians, too, are in the ranks of unions at the present time, as are almost 50,000 engineers and several thousand lawyers. Nurses on the East and West Coasts are far more often bargained for collectively than they are not.

In addition, as even the most casual follower of the news must be fully aware, professional athletes in all major league sports are not only nowadays collectively bargained for, as essentially none of them were a relatively few years ago, but they have in all of these sports but basketball engaged in notable work stoppages. The 800 members of the Major League Baseball Players Association struck their twenty-six owners for fifty days in 1981, wiping out a third of that year's schedule; they conducted a second strike in 1985 (although it lasted a mere two days); and in 1990 they participated in a third collective bargaining impasse—in this case delaying spring training by some three weeks. In 1982, the National Football League's Players Association, with some 1,500 members, went head to head with the owners in its sport in an eight-week suspension of play and waged a second strike, a three-week stoppage, in 1987. In 1992, the almost 600 members of the National Hockey League Players Association struck their league for the first time in seventy-five years, for ten days.

For all of this, there has been no particularly impressive change in total union penetration of the white collar field in recent years. In 1956, some 2.42 million white collar workers were in unions; a decade later, the figure had risen only to approximately 2.7 million, despite the growth of this sector by several million more jobs, to over 26 million by the late 1960s. And by 1993, with an even more rapid growth in total white collar employment in the intervening years, the union rolls had advanced only to about the 5 million mark, a point clearly far short of the saturation level. Nor had even these modest gains of organized labor been evenly spread throughout the white collar world. Most of them had been gained strictly from the public-service sector, where, as we shall see, in many cases favorable legislation had made the enrollment of new members both comparatively easy and comparatively meaningless: In Texas, for example, public-sector unions can neither bargain collectively for wages nor—even in the case of teachers' unions—strike, and any resemblance between these labor organizations and, say, the Teamsters in Michigan is strictly coincidental.

SOME PROBABLE EXPLANATIONS

Why has the white collar world been so relatively unreceptive to the union organizer when its blue collar counterpart has been so hospitable? Among the many explanations for labor's general failure to date in penetrating the

White Collar Frontier, the following may well be the most accurate. Taken collectively, they also constitute some rather formidable grounds for union pessimism in the years ahead.

1. The public has in recent years been inundated with news of seemingly irresponsible union strikes and commensurately unstatesmanlike settlements, union leaders' criminality, and featherbedding situations. The resulting poor image of the labor movement, as conveyed by the mass media, may well have alienated hundreds of thousands—and, conceivably, even millions—of potential white collar union joiners. In an age when even the occupant of the White House can be determined by public image, this factor—although it is not only unquantifiable but even basically unprovable—cannot be overlooked.

This topic should in any event receive far more attention than it has heretofore been given. Certainly, as has long been observed by thoughtful students of labor relations, unions most often get into the headlines for activities that cover them with discredit. A union leader's criminality will invariably do the trick. And so, too, will news of any seemingly irresponsible union strike, or almost any charge, if made with sufficient vigor, that unionized employees are receiving pay for work that is not performed (or "featherbedding").

Thus, there may well be significant numbers in the general population who believe that "Construction Strike Threat Looms" is a regular, if somewhat repetitious, column appearing in their local newspaper. (*Looms,* from all available evidence, is the only verb utilized in such situations, a phenomenon similar to that pertaining to "Prison Riots," which can only be "Quelled"—or for that matter "Last Minute Settlements," which can do only one thing to strikes, namely, "Avert" them.) And one can only guess at how many Americans think that "Featherbedding" is part of the official job designation of the "Railroad Firemen." It is also true, as the late A. J. Liebling once commented, that the public is regularly informed that "Labor *Demands*" but that "Management *Offers*"; and few can argue with a further observation of this famous journalist that when General Motors workers go out on strike for more wages, this is major news throughout the nation (if not the world), whereas the president of General Motors takes his considerably larger income home quietly.

From labor's point of view there is, of course, an intrinsic unfairness in such a factor. It is conflict, as more than one media member has observed, that makes the headlines. The large majority of union agreements that are peacefully renegotiated year after year go virtually unnoticed by the reporters of the news, but the few strikes of any dimensions are treated with the journalistic zeal of a Tolstoy. The overwhelming proportion of union officials continue to lead their lives in full compliance with the laws of the land, but this seems insignificant to the news compilers in the face of the conviction of a single general president of the International Brotherhood of Teamsters: Four of the last six holders of that position have been indicted and three—including the celebrated Jimmy Hoffa—went to jail; it is understandable, if ironic, that these developments received substantial media coverage. It is no less ironic that at least Hoffa continues to be a household word in the 1990s, albeit most often through the vehicle of generally tasteless jokes that appear to circulate as widely today as they did in the immediate aftermath of his 1975 disappearance (e.g., "Question: Who was the last person ever to see Jimmy Hoffa? Answer: Jacques Cousteau") while few people could name the current IBT president if their lives depended on it. And charges that unions demand pay for work that is not performed totally dwarf the large body of evidence that featherbedding is engaged in by only a small segment of unionized employees.

Yet what editor can justify headlines proclaiming that "Local 109 of the American Federation of Musicians Is a Very Statesmanlike Local," that "Business Agent Duffy Gabrilowitz of the Plumbers Union Is One Hundred Percent Honest," or that "Management Says That Flight Attendants Are Giving a Fair Day's Work for a Fair Day's Pay"? Only, we suspect, a journalist with a strongly developed suicidal urge. Accordingly, the large segment of the population that allows its opinions of unionism to be molded only by those labor activities receiving wide publicity is understandably— if, for organized labor, unfortunately—less than enthusiastic about the institution. An incalculable but undoubtedly formidable number of white collar workers—unlike their blue collar counterparts, who are generally in a better position by virtue of proximity to perceive strengths as well as weaknesses in unionism—fall into this population category.

2.   The labor movement has in recent years been distinguished in the main by uninspiring, rather bureaucratic leadership that seems only dimly aware of the white collar problem and totally unimaginative about discovering any solutions. The complaint of labor scholar J. B. S. Hardman that "superannuated leaders, who have outlived their usefulness, are probably met more frequently in the labor movement than in any other militant social movement,"[8] although it was made many years ago and intended to apply exclusively to the late 1920s, could fit into any typical outsider's critique of labor's current performance without doing violence to the basic theme.

Nor has this condition entirely escaped the attention of labor leaders themselves. There are many more top leaders in their sixties now than there are septuagenarians and octogenarians, and the observation once made by a United Automobile Worker secretary-treasurer that "some of the board members of some of the unions, when they have a board meeting, they look like a collection of a wax museum" no longer basically applies. But there is still much validity to the charge made by the UAW when it withdrew from the AFL-CIO some years ago in a now-concluded dispute with its leadership, that the federation "has become isolated from the mainstream and too often acts like a comfortable, complacent custodian of the status quo."[9]

For those who continue to believe strongly in the potential of the labor movement as a force for accomplishment in our society, there is something quite sad about the current state of union leadership. All the trappings of success surround it—as Raskin could accurately point out, "The hair shirt has given way to white-on-white broadcloth, imported fabrics, and custom tailoring"[10]—and the expense-account perquisites of labor's major officials are totally indistinguishable in their lavishness from those of the leaders of the business community. But somewhere in the transformation from crusader for the underdog to accepted member of the Establishment, both the sense of mission and the creative spark to implement it seem to have been severely dampened by affluence. The senior citizens who constitute the bulk of current labor leadership appear, in short, to be resting quite comfortably on their hard-earned laurels, lacking motivation to reenter the organizational arena and expend the energy, money, and, perhaps above all, imagination that are required by such an elusive potential constituency as the white collar sector. Wilfrid Sheed's thoughts are relevant: "The widespread impression that Labor consists of aging white men guarding their gains may be an exaggeration verging on libel; but it is widespread."[11] And so, too, are those of a union staff aide: "[Union leaders are] too worried about appearances, about losing battles instead of trying new things, and they spend too much time talking to each other at...receptions."[12]

Sheed's "widespread impression" may not be so close to libel, either, at least as far as labor's attitude toward the declining percentage of union members is concerned. On this topic, AFL-CIO president George Meany could observe in the 1970s that

> to me, it doesn't mean a thing. I have no concern about it, because the history of the trade union movement has shown that when organized workers were a very, very tiny percentage of the work force, they still accomplished and did things that were important for the entire work force. The unorganized portions of the work forces have no power for the simple reason that they're not organized.[13]

And Meany's successor as AFL-CIO chief executive, Lane Kirkland, could elaborate as follows:

> Frankly, I don't care whether the salesmen are organized. If they want to be organized, fine. If they don't I don't feel any ideological compulsion to organize them. I don't feel any compulsion to organize foremen, plant managers, advertising men, hustlers, what have you.[14]

3. White collar workers possess certain unique general properties that may tend to work against unionization in any event.

a. White collar employees have long felt superior to their blue collar counterparts and have tended to believe that joining a union (an institution traditionally associated with manual workers) would decrease their occupational prestige. This goes well beyond the issue of labor's currently poor image cited above. A certain autonomy at work, however little it may be in many cases, is imparted to the holder of the white collar job as it is not to the factory or construction worker. Prior educational achievements, modes of dress and language, relative cleanliness of the work situations, and even job locations within the enterprise also typically give the white collar jobholder much more in common with management than with the blue collar employee. Income based on salary rather than wages further weakens the potential bonds between the two submanagerial classes. Nor, clearly, can the sheer fact that society generally looks down upon manual work and places its premium upon mentally challenging employment be disregarded in explaining the superiority complex of the white collarite.

In an economy such as ours—where for most people the more basic needs have now been relatively well satisfied—the role of such status considerations can be considerable. To ask the white collar worker to identify by unionization with the steel worker, truck driver, and hod carrier—and to follow in the traditions of Samuel Gompers or John L. Lewis (to say nothing of the leadership of the Teamsters or of former Mine Worker president Tony Boyle, of whom it was once said that he could immeasurably increase the moral level in a room simply by leaving it) is consequently, by its very nature, no small undertaking.

b. However tenuous it may be, white collar workers can at least perceive some opportunity to advance into managerial ranks, whereas blue collar employees are typically limited in their most optimistic advancement goal to the "gray area" of the foremanship. Unlike the wearers of the white collar, the blue collar workers sense (usually quite accurately) that educational and social deficiencies have combined to limit their promotional avenues within the industrial world, and they can adjust to the fact that they are permanently destined to be apart from and directed by the managerial class. Since such a fate is often not nearly as clear to the white collar workers (partially for the reasons cited in the previous paragraphs), they are understandably more reluctant to join the ranks of unionism and thus support what is potentially a major constraint on employer freedom of action.

c. The considerably higher proportion of women in white collar work than in blue collar work has served as a dampening force for organization. By and large, women have always been notoriously poor candidates for unionism. In many cases until now (although the situation is changing), the job has been thought of as temporary—either premarital or to supplement the family breadwinner's paycheck (often on a sporadic basis)—and, consequently, the union's argument of long-run job security has had little appeal. In other cases—perhaps as high as 25 percent at the time of this writing—the job is a part-time one, also to the detriment of the union organizer. Nor can the labor movement's traditional aura of militant masculinity be eliminated as a possible causal factor in explaining the female response to organizational attempts. ("There's no way we're going to attract them," one concerned union leader has said, "with the tank-top, tattoo, tough guy image.")

d. Finally, many white collar workers with professional identifications—engineers, college professors, and institutionally employed doctors, for example—continue to believe that for them there is still much more to be gained from individual bargaining with their employer than from any form of collective bargaining. Viewing the latter as an automatic opponent of individual merit rewards, they tend to perceive the relatively few unionists within their professions as either mediocrities in need of such group support, or masochists.

SOME GROUNDS FOR UNION OPTIMISM

If it is thus tempting to begin sounding the death knell for the labor movement on the grounds that its failure to penetrate the critical White Collar Frontier can be explained by a combination of factors that seem to be at least collectively insurmountable, realism dictates that several other factors also be pondered. And these additional considerations can lead one to an entirely different conclusion regarding the future of organized labor in the white collar area.

1. The same newsprint, television, and radio announcements that have brought news of union misdoings to the white collar population have also informed this primarily nonunion audience of highly impressive income improvements in the unionized sector. For example, few nonunionists are entirely unaware of the gains in the relatively heavily organized construction sector that by 1993 were adding $4.50 per hour and more to the wages of skilled craft workers over the next three years, or in many cases almost as much as the monies received as *total* hourly wages by workers in wholesale and retail trade, finance, insurance, real estate, and many other parts of the white collar world. The imminence of a situation where the lowest wage for even a common laborer in the construction industry would soon be some $30,000 or more could only have been received with considerable envy by the unrepresented insurance-company debit agent whose current earnings, despite his college degree, placed him at not much more than two thirds of this figure. And knowledge of the fact that substantial overtime opportunities at hefty premiums were also available to such unionists—as they were most frequently not to white collar workers—could only increase the latter's flow of adrenalin.

In fairness, it must be recognized that the historically overtight labor markets and fractionalized bargaining structure of construction have made it a labor union extreme from the viewpoint of wage aggrandizement. It is also true that workers in this sector were sometimes paying a significant penalty in recent years for the munificence of their earlier settlements: They were not always employed, their labor costs having made their employers noncompetitive with nonunion contractors. But the kind of invidious comparisons engendered by the construction totals clearly extends to other situations.

At the time of this writing, for example, the median weekly earnings of unionized workers across all industries according to the U.S. Department of Labor was $497, as against $372 for nonunion members nationwide. These figures reflected, primarily, the simple fact that unionists were in well-paying blue collar jobs, of course, but they at least hinted at the possibility that these jobs could have *been* well paying because they were in fact so often bargained for collectively.

Nor can the white collar population indefinitely be expected to be indifferent to truck-driver incomes (symbolically, the *International Teamster* magazine could report some years ago that "recently a professor at ivy-covered Williams College in New England returned to the Teamsters as an over-the-road driver because he could double his salary at Williams")[15] and to various other highly remunerated (and overwhelmingly unionized) workers such as longshoremen, tool and die makers, and airline mechanics. For that matter, San Francisco sanitation workers were receiving more than $30,000 in annual base wages alone in the early 1990s, and this figure, even though far from the poverty level, paled by comparison with the more than $33,000 contractually guaranteed to Port of New York Authority longshoremen, whether or not there was any work for them.[16] And not one of the 140,000 United Parcel Service drivers—unionists all—was making less than $31,000 as this section was being written, with many of these employees earning considerably above that figure.

The responsibility for the relatively high standards of living involved here certainly does not rest completely with unionism. Clearly, one must also examine such a variety of other factors as skill levels, industrial ability to pay, imperfections in the product market, and industrial productivity (among others) in explaining these wage levels. And one can readily cite such unionized areas as the boot and shoe industry and the meatpacking industry, where the overall situation often allows no real wage improvement at all and, consequently, none is received by organized labor.

But the hazards of accepting the more impressive union bargaining totals at their face value are not particularly relevant in this context. Misleadingly or not, such dollar amounts often symbolize in a highly visible fashion the ability of unionism to effect dramatic wage gains. And, as the gap between the incomes of the blue collar and white collar worlds continues to widen, a greater willingness to consider union membership may conceivably be the result. Indeed, appreciation of the fact that snobbishness neither purchases groceries nor pays the rent seems already to have accounted for some of the increased willingness of at least teachers and nurses to undertake such a consideration.

2. The definite upsurge in unionism among government employees—although probably attributable far more to enabling legislation than to any pronounced rank-and-file militancy—is combining with the (lesser) emergence of collective bargaining in other white collar areas to gradually weaken the nonmember's traditional association of organized labor with manual work. As previously implied, the process is still an excruciatingly slow one from labor's viewpoint. But the growing presence of these higher-status, better-educated federal civil servants and state employees (to say nothing of the previously mentioned college faculty members, physicians, engineers, lawyers, and nurses) in union ranks can only be expected to erode the older images in time. Whether this psychological change will be sufficient in itself to win over more than a fraction of the untapped white collar market for the labor movement is another question. But, certainly, one of the grounds for labor's failure until now will have been dissipated.

3. It is probably also only a question of time before considerably more aggressive, imaginative, and empathetic leadership than organized labor now possesses comes to the fore, which would also make widespread white collar unionization more likely.

For all the apparent apathy and conservatism at the highest levels of labor, there is no dearth of people in the second and third tiers of union leadership who exhibit these more positive characteristics. Far more attuned to the aspirations and values of our increasingly sophisticated labor force than are their currently more influential colleagues, they have become more and more frustrated by labor's lack of progress in recent years. They fully appreciate the necessity for an immense outpouring of financial, institutional, and personal effort in the quest for the white collarite. And they exhibit no lack of ideas as to how such unionization can be effected, even advocating wholly different organizational structures to attain this goal, should these become necessary. The vicissitudes of union politics clearly ensure that not all, or even many, of these leaders will ever actually achieve ascendancy in the labor movement. Those who do, however, will undoubtedly abet the chances of white collar unionism.

4. Finally, the working conditions of white collar employment are themselves now changing in a direction that may weaken both the superiority complex and promanagement proclivity of the white collar wearer.

The very individuality of white collar work is itself now disappearing from much of the industrial scene. An accelerating trend toward organizational bigness has already combined with the demands of technological efficiency to make cogs in vast interdependent machines of many clerks, computer operators, technicians, and even engineers, rather than allowing them to remain as individuals working alone or in comfortably small groups in these categories. White collar workers, no less than blue collar ones, are increasingly becoming bureaucratized. More and more, as a general statement, they are the victims of routine. Ever larger numbers of their jobs have become less desirable. Blue collar workers by no means covet white collar positions as they once did.

In the years ahead, all of this should only accelerate. The advance of technology, in various forms from word-processing equipment to elaborate computerized design systems, is now proceeding at a faster rate in offices than in factory atmospheres, and many of the analytical and decision-making challenges once allowed the white collarite are slowly disappearing as it does so. The enormous productivity gains that such new developments have brought about have also caused, quite justifiably, considerable job uncertainty and can of course also generate a definite decrease in the economic value of job skills. (Indeed, the Bureau of Labor Statistics has estimated that between 1979 and 1990 well over 1 million white collar workers—many of them, of course, in the smokestack industries—did lose their jobs because of plant shutdowns and changing economics.) Awareness that remote computer terminals can remove the work from the office altogether and assign it to such homebound subcontractors as mothers of small children and the physically handicapped is hardly cause for celebration among currently employed white collar workers. Nor is a common prediction that the computer (since it constitutes an indefensible luxury if allowed to be idle) may even force many white collar employees into one of the thus far most distinguishing features of factory work, shift work. It does not seem overly rash to assume that these changes could radically alter the complacent self-image of the white collar wearers by blurring the traditional perceived differences between the nature of their work and that of their blue collar counterparts.

And, in such an atmosphere, it may well be that the white collar workers' longstanding feeling of affinity with management as well as their sense of self-actualization on the job will also evaporate, to the point of rendering the white collarites far more susceptible than they have been in the past to the overtures of the union organizer.

Thus a case can be made for either position. It is difficult to deny that future white collar unionization does face great obstacles. But it is probably no less advisable to hedge one's bets before writing off organized labor as an institution doomed to an ultimate slow death because, having long ago captured the now-shrinking blue collar market, it has realized its only natural potential. If the grounds for union optimism as expressed above must necessarily remain speculative, nonetheless there are enough of them and there is sufficient logic to each of them to justify at least some amount of hopefulness on the part of the labor movement.

LABOR'S PRESENT STRATEGIC POWER

Other formidable obstacles also confront organized labor today. It is undeniable that unions have in recent years fallen from public favor, owing perhaps above all to various public exposures of corruption at the top levels of a few but nonetheless highly visible unions, and also to their own bargaining excesses. These latter topics will be discussed on subsequent pages. Here, it is relevant to note that the publicity involved, temporary or not, has cost the labor movement thousands of friends among the general public (and, presumably, in the ranks of potential union members): In one major study of the 1990s,[17] only 60 percent of the American people showed themselves as being favorable to unions, a figure that represented a significant decrease from 1967 (when the comparable statistic was 66 percent) and 1959 (when it was 76 percent). A Gallup Poll not long ago revealed that the public ranked labor leaders next to last—just above car salesmen—in terms of ethics and honesty.[18] And the last major strike in which unions received a meaningful amount of public support may well have been one that took place when Richard Nixon was in his first term as president: the nationwide stoppage of the postal workers in 1970.

Labor's fall from popular grace has also led to restrictive federal and state legislation that can in some ways be construed as "antilabor" (see Chapter 3).

Finally, labor has been handicapped, too, by such current factors as the national trend to smaller, decentralized plants, resulting in more-personalized worker treatment; industry's present tendency to locate new plants in smaller, semirural, and often southern communities, climates not conducive to a hearty reception for the union; and the growing levels of income across the nation, stripping some of the effect of union promises of a "living wage." Nor can the stiff competition from foreign companies with their markedly lower labor costs that American employers now face be ignored by unions.

Yet, for all these adverse factors, it is still of some relevance for anyone who attempts to predict the labor movement's future that in the unions' almost two centuries on the American scene, they have faced even greater obstacles than these and have ultimately surmounted them. As Chapter 2 relates, the history of U.S. labor is in many ways a study of triumph over economic, social, and political adversity.

However one views organized labor's future, its present strategic power cannot be denied. The labor movement's concentration of membership in the economy's most vital sectors has meant that the less than one fifth of the labor force that bargains collectively has been an extremely influential minority. One may not agree with the newspaper headlines that a particular strike has "paralyzed the economy," but it appears to be an acceptable generalization that the wages or salaries and other conditions of employment for much of the remaining portion of the labor force are regularly affected to some degree by the unionized segment.

Thus, if the exact future dimensions and membership totals of organized labor are today in some doubt, the importance of collective bargaining is not. Nor can one dispute labor's staying power, given the labor movement's deep penetration into virtually all the traditional parts of our economy and its continuing hold upon these areas. "Our obituary has been written at least once for every year of labor's history, and at least that many causes of death have been diagnosed, gleefully or scornfully, depending on the diagnostician," AFL-CIO chief executive Kirkland has quite accurately pointed out.[19] And if modern managers are unhappy with unionism, realism dictates not that they wait for it to vanish from the scene, but that they apply their efforts toward improving the collective bargaining process by which they—and all of us—are so likely to be directly affected.

WHY WORKERS JOIN UNIONS

Questions concerning human behavior do not lend themselves to simple answers, for the subject itself is a highly complex one. "Why do workers join unions?" clearly falls within this category.

In his widely accepted theory of motivation, however, the late psychologist A. H. Maslow has provided us with helpful hints, although the theory itself relates to the whole population of human beings rather than merely to those who have seen fit to take out union membership.[20]

Maslow portrays man (a category that presumably also encompasses "woman") as a "perpetually wanting animal," driven to put forth effort (in other words, to work) by his desire to satisfy certain of his needs. To Maslow, these needs or wants can logically be thought of in terms of a hierarchy, for only one type of need is active at any given time. Only when the lowest and most basic of the needs in this hierarchy has been relatively well satisfied will each higher need become, in turn, operative. Thus, it is the *unsatisfied* need that actively motivates man's behavior. Once a need is more or less gratified, man's conduct is determined by new, higher needs, which up until then have failed to motivate simply because man's attention has been devoted to satisfying his more pressing, lower needs. And the process is for most mortals unending, since few people can ever expect to satisfy, even minimally, all their needs.

At the lowest level in this Need Hierarchy, but paramount in importance until they are satisfied, are the *physiological* needs, particularly those for food, water, clothing, and shelter. "Man lives by bread alone, when there is no bread"; in other words, any higher needs he may have are inoperative when he is suffering from extreme hunger, for man's full attention must then necessarily be focused on this single need. But when the need for food and the other physiological essentials is fairly well satisfied, less basic or higher needs in the hierarchy start to dominate man's behavior, or to motivate him.

Thus, needs for *safety*—for protection against arbitrary deprivation, danger, and threat—take over as prime human motivators once man is eating regularly and sufficiently and is adequately clothed and sheltered. This is true because (1) a satisfied need is no longer a motivator of behavior, yet (2) man continues to be driven by needs, and (3) the safety needs are the next most logical candidates, beyond the physiological ones, to do this driving.

What happens when the safety needs have also been relatively satisfied, so that both the lowest need levels no longer require man's attention? In Maslow's scheme of things, the *social* needs—for belonging, association, and acceptance by one's fellows—now are dominant, and man puts forth effort to satisfy this newly activated type of want.

Still higher needs that ultimately emerge to dominate man's consciousness, always assuming that the needs below them have been gratified, are in turn *self-esteem* needs, especially for self-respect and self-confidence; *status* needs, for recognition, approval, and prestige; and finally, *self-fulfillment* needs, for realization of one's own potential and for being as creative as possible.

All this constitutes an oversimplification of Maslow's Need Hierarchy. Maslow himself qualified his concept in several ways, although only one of his reservations is important enough for our purposes to warrant inclusion here: He recognized that not all people follow the pattern depicted and that both desires and satisfactions vary with the individual.

Even in the capsule form presented above, however, Maslow's contribution is of aid in explaining why workers join unions. The many research findings that now exist on this latter topic[21] basically agree that all employees endeavor to gratify needs and wants that are important to them, because of dissatisfaction with the extent to which these needs and desires have been met. They also agree that, while what is "important" among these needs and wants varies with the individual employee, much of the answer depends upon what has already been satisfied either within the working environment or outside it. Many of these studies also support Maslow's hierarchy for the majority of workers in approximately the order of needs indicated by Maslow.

It should not be surprising that dissatisfaction with the extent of phys-iological need gratification is no longer a dominant reason for joining unions in this country. In our relatively affluent economy, few people who are working have any great difficulty in satisfying at least the most basic of these needs. In an earlier day, before the advent of minimum wage laws and other forms of legal protection, this was not as true, and, as has already been suggested, union promises of a "living wage" were of great appeal to many workers. However, those members of the labor force who today are frustrated in trying to satisfy their minimal needs for food, clothing, and shelter are those who are *unemployed,* not the most logical candidates for union membership. The research substantiates the downplaying of the role of physiological needs rather conclusively. Significantly, one of the most thorough of the studies found that not one employee out of 114 workers in a large industrial local union became a union member primarily for this purpose.[22] (This is hardly to say that union members have lost interest in higher wages and other economic improvements. As will be shown later, the desire for these benefits persists as strongly as ever. The point is, however, that this desire now stems from higher need activation. Money can satisfy more than just the physiological needs.)

On the other hand, research suggests that dissatisfaction with the extent of gratification of (1) safety, (2) social, and (3) self-esteem needs—in ap-proximately that order—has motivated many workers to join unions. To a lesser extent, status and self-fulfillment needs have also led to union membership.

Unions are uniquely equipped, in the eyes of thousands of workers, to gratify safety needs. If very few of the 200,000 labor-management contracts currently in force in the United States are identical, at least this much can be said for virtually all of them: They are generally arrived at through *compromise,* and they define in writing the "rules of the game" that have been *mutually agreed upon* to cover the terms and conditions of employ-ment of *all* represented workers for a specific future period of time. The union thus acts as an equal partner in the bilateral establishment of what has been called a "system of industrial jurisprudence." And in the interests of minimizing conflict among the workers it represents, it strives to inject uniformity of treatment—particularly in the area of job protection—into the contract.

Union membership can consequently provide workers with some assur-ance against arbitrary management actions. The union can be expected to push for curbs against what it calls "management discrimination and favoritism" in, for example, job assignment, promotional opportunity, and even continued employment. However well-meaning are a management's intentions, the employer cannot guarantee that it will not at times act arbitrarily, for in the absence of such checks as the union places on its actions, it is always acting unilaterally. Satisfaction of the safety needs—in the form of considerable protection against arbitrary deprivation, danger, and threat—is thus offered by the union in its stress on uniformity of treatment for all workers. Many employees, particularly after they have perceived "arbitrary" action by management representatives, have found the appeal irresistible.

The social needs are also known to be important, if secondary, motivators of union membership. Especially where the work itself must be performed in geographically scattered locations (as in many forms of railroad employment, truck driving, or letter-carrying) or where the technology of the work minimizes on-the-job social interaction (as on the automobile assembly line), the local union can serve the function of a club, allowing the formation of close friendships built around a common purpose. But even when the work is not so structured, local unions foster a feeling of identification with those of like interests, often in pronounced contrast to the impersonality of the large organization in which the worker may be employed. Increasingly, unions have capitalized upon their ability to help satisfy social needs. As the latter have become more important to members of the labor force (not only because of the declining frustration of the lower needs but also because general leisure time has increased), unions have become increasingly ambitious in sponsoring such activities as vacation retreats, athletic facilities, and adult education programs "for members only." But unions have never been reluctant to publicize the social bonds they allow: It is not by accident that internal union correspondence has traditionally been closed by the greeting "Fraternally yours," that the official titles of many unions have always included the word "Brotherhood," and that several labor organizations continue to refer to their local unions as "lodges."

Social *pressure* has also been instrumental in causing workers to join unions. Employees often admit that the disapproval of their colleagues would result from their not signing union application cards. Normally, the disapproval is only implied. One study, for example, unearthed such explanations from workers who had joined unions as "I can't think of a good reason, except everybody else was in it," and "I suppose I joined in order to jump in line with the majority." On occasion, however, the pressure has been considerably more visible, as witness this quotation from the same study: "They approached you, kept after you, hounded you. To get them off my neck, I joined."[23]

Other workers, at higher levels, have explained their union membership as being attributable mainly to their desire to ensure that they will have a direct voice, through union election procedures, in decisions that affect them in their working environment. Such employees tend to participate actively in union affairs and to use rather freely such phrases as "I wanted to have a voice in the system." The underlying rationale of this behavior is a clear one: Managements do not normally put questions relating to employment conditions to worker vote; unions, however imperfectly, purport to be democratic institutions. To these workers, representation by a labor organization has appeared to offer the best hope in our complex, interdependent, and ever-larger-unit industrial society that their human dignity will not be completely crushed. On this basis, self-esteem needs can, at least to some extent, be appeased.

Finally, a relatively few other employees have found in the union an opportunity for realization of their highest needs—for status and self-fulfillment. They have joined with the hope of gaining and retaining positions of authority within the union officer hierarchy. For the employee with leadership ambitions, but with educational or other deficiencies that would

otherwise condemn that employee to a life of prestige-lacking and un-
challenging work, opportunities for further need satisfaction are thus
provided.

Unionization, then, results from a broad network of worker needs. The
needs for safety, social affiliation, and, to a lesser extent, self-esteem
appear to be of primary importance to employees in contemporary America.
And it would appear that these needs are being relatively well met by unions,
or workers would have exercised their legally granted option of voting out
unions in far greater measure than they have done.

This in no way minimizes the role of money and other economic benefits,
for these—which unions have not been reluctant to seek, even with their
members' incomes at today's high levels—are as noted earlier clearly
related to needs beyond the physiological. Health insurance and pensions
lend protection against deprivation, for example, and wages themselves can
increase not only safety but status. But it does emphasize the role of
protection against arbitrary treatment, formal group affiliation beyond the
framework of the company, and—for some workers—an opportunity for
participation in "the system." By definition, management can never itself
satisfy either of the first two worker needs. Thus far, in unionized establishments, it has failed to satisfy employees on the last ground.

WHY MANAGERS RESIST UNIONS

Some time ago, after years of successfully withstanding union organization
attempts, a small-scale New York City dress manufacturer discovered that
a majority of his workers had finally become union members. Immediately
thereafter, these employees struck for increased job security and improved
pension benefits. On the very first morning of the strike, the
manufacturer's wife—who was also the firm's bookkeeper—reported to
work at her customary hour of 8 A.M. She was amazed to see her husband
out on the picket line, addressing the strikers as follows: "Sam, you stand
over there; Harry, you stand eight yards in back of Sam; and Leo, you come
over here, eight yards behind Harry." The puzzled woman posed the natural
question, "Jack, what on earth are you doing?" And the manufacturer
replied, "I want they should right away know who's boss!"

The outcome of this particular labor-management struggle is unknown.
But the episode nonetheless furnishes a clue as to one reason why managers
are considerably less than enthusiastic about unions. As we have already
seen, collective bargaining necessarily decreases the area of management
discretion. Every contractual concession to the union subtracts from the
scope that the management has for taking action on its own. As Bakke
observed many years ago, "A union is an employer-regulating device. It
seeks to regulate the discretion of employers...at every point where their
action affects the welfare of the men.[24] Yet it is the manager who tends to
be held ultimately responsible for the success or failure of the business,
and not the union. Hence, employers feel it essential that they reserve for

themselves the authority to make all major decisions, including those the union might construe to be affecting "the welfare of the men." In short, they feel that they must still be allowed to remain, on all counts, "the boss."

Behind such a sentiment is a managerial awareness, continuously reinforced for all administrators of profit-making institutions by day-to-day realities, that management hardly owes its exclusive allegiance to its employees. Clearly, employee needs are important and, for that matter, can be ignored for any length of time only with complete disregard for the continued solvency of the enterprise. But exactly the same can be said of the pressures exerted on management by the firm's customers, stockholders, competitors, and suppliers. Were these pressures not opposing ones, management's job would be far easier than it is. But because there are so many points of conflict, an aggressive union can make the managerial role a highly difficult one.

The desire to retain decision-making authority is by no means, however, strictly attributable to a managerial desire for peace of mind. Unions undoubtedly do add to the personal unhappiness and consequent morale problems of managers, but the resistance to unionism is often based also on a genuine and deep concern for the welfare of society. Countless managers believe that only if management remains free to operate without union-imposed restrictions can American business continue to advance. And only through such progress, they believe, can it provide employment for our rapidly growing labor force, let this nation compete successfully in world markets, and increase general living standards. By decreasing company flexibility (in the form of work-method controls, decreased workloads, increased stress on the seniority criterion in the allocation of labor, and various other ways), it is argued, unions endanger the efficiency upon which continued industrial progress depends. And this is no less true, managers contend, just because these union demands are made in the name of such euphemistic goals as "job security," "equitability," and "democracy in the workplace."

Admittedly, even in the absence of unionism, management's ability to make decisions in the employee-relations area is not an unlimited one. A widespread network of federal, state, and community legislation now governs minimum wages, hours of work, discrimination, safety and health, and a host of other aspects of employee life with complete impartiality as to whether or not the regulated firms are organized or nonunion. Moreover, where employers encounter tight labor markets (those in which new employees are difficult to recruit), they tend to accommodate at least their more visible personnel practices—wages and other economic benefits, in particular—to what the market demands. Finally, the prevalent values of our times must always be considered. The mores of society have an important influence on employers. And it is a hallmark of our ever more sophisticated society that workers expect to be governed by progressive personnel policies that are based on objective standards whenever possible. Most nonunion firms have attempted to conform to these values no less actively than have most unionized enterprises.

The fact remains, however, that managers who are not bound by the restrictions of labor agreements, and who do not have to anticipate the possibility of their every action in the employee relations sphere being challenged by worker representatives through the grievance procedure, have considerably more latitude for decision making than do their counterparts at unionized companies. One need not in any way sympathize with the management fear of unionism to understand this fear. Given the importance of the decision-making prerogative to managements, the managerial resistance to labor organizations—whether it stems directly from management self-interest or from a concern for the welfare of society—can at least be appreciated.

If the previous paragraphs help to explain the major reasons for management's jaundiced view of the labor union, they do not acknowledge other reasons that frequently bolster this view. There are, undoubtedly, several such reasons.

In the first place, many employers tend to look upon the union as an *outsider,* with no justifiable basis for interfering in the relationship between the management and its employees. The local union, with which the firm is most apt to engage in direct dealings, typically represents workers of many competitive companies, and hence by definition it cannot have the best interests of any particular firm at heart. Worse yet, runs this charge, the local is often part of a large, geographically distant international or national union, by which it is closely controlled, and thus is not allowed to give adequate consideration to unique problems within its locality.[25] Beyond this, the union (whether local, international, or some intermediate body) has objectives and aspirations that are very different from those of the particular employer: Where the latter seeks to maximize profits within certain limits, the union seeks such goals as the maximization of its own membership and of its general bargaining power. These are objectives that the management can at best greet with apathy and at worst (when the pursuit of such goals is "subsidized" by the management in the form of its own concessions to the union) can view only with unhappiness.

Second, the manager may look upon the union as a *troublemaker,* bent upon building cleavages between management and workers where none would otherwise exist. Even aside from the previously noted fact that the union grievance procedure allows all management actions affecting areas delineated in the labor contract to be challenged, and therefore regularly provides an opportunity for controversy that is normally absent in nonunion situations, there is some truth in this charge. Particularly where the union occupies an insecure status (in the absence, for example, of the union shop), its leaders may find it essential to solicit grievances in order to keep the employees willing to pay union dues. But even where the labor organization does have such security, grievances may still be encouraged by union officials and for several logical reasons: Ongoing grievances can later be dropped in return for management concessions; individual union leaders can point to a record of effective grievance handling as they seek to rise within the union hierarchy; and unpopular managers can be displaced if *their* superiors are sufficiently uneasy about high grievance rates within their units. And, of course, union representatives may simply prefer to have management—or, if need be, an arbitrator—deny the grievance rather than do it themselves: Managers and arbitrators do not have to stand for reelection and can more easily afford to incur worker wrath.

Third, many managers view unions as *underminers of employee loyalty* to the company. In order to understand this point of view, one does not have to fully embrace the philosophy that high worker motivation levels depend upon appreciative employees who view the employer as a benefactor and work for him to a great extent out of gratitude. It is sufficient for the reader to imagine the reactions of any employer who has prided himself on providing good wages and working conditions and showing a personal concern for the individual problems of his employees upon learning that a majority of his work force has suddenly decided to "go union." This employer may use such epithets as "ingrates" in speaking of his own employees, but it is more likely that the union itself will bear the brunt of his censure. It is human nature to attribute one's defeats to forces beyond one's own control ("an irresponsible union misleading our employees and turning them against management") rather than to factors looked upon as controllable ("employee attitudes"). The previously cited fact that management can *never* itself provide either full protection against arbitrary treatment or formal group affiliation independent of the employer is overlooked by managers at such moments. So, too, is a silver lining in the situation—namely, that it is entirely possible for workers to have dual loyalties, to the union *and* to the employer.[26] In at least the early stages of the union-management relationship, unions may be resisted for having subverted employee allegiance fully as much as they are opposed on the other grounds that have been noted.

A fourth root of tension may arise simply because the previously discussed *reputation* of the labor movement has preceded the arrival of unionism in the place. This has been a particularly influential factor in the resistance of some managers to collective bargaining in the recent past. Not being forced to deal with a union until now and, primarily because of this freedom, knowing little more about labor unions than they have been told by the mass media, such relatively unsophisticated employers have been alarmed by the widely publicized reports of irresponsible union strikes, union-leader criminality, and featherbedding charges that have found their way onto newspaper front pages and television screens over the past decade. These managers have asked, in effect, "How can you expect us to welcome an institution whose representatives engage in such activities?" To them, the old joke, "How many Teamsters does it take to screw in a light bulb?' 'Ten. You got a problem with that?'" is anchored to a solid foundation of fact.

Fifth, and rounding out the list of major causes of the corporate executive's opposition to organized labor, are the *major values of the labor movement* as these are perceived by management. Some of these values—a stress on seniority, work-method controls, and decreased workloads—have already been mentioned in the context of "threats to decision making." There are, however, many other such shared union values that rankle management at least as much.

"Security," for example, has far more favorable connotations to unionists than it does to employer representatives. Higher managers by definition have a history of successful achievement behind them and hence are willing to take chances because they are relatively optimistic as to the outcome. The average union member, feeling that the probabilities of his success in risk taking are low, and, indeed, often believing that he is running in a race that is fixed, presses the union leadership to obtain even greater protection for him in his *current* job.

"Democracy" is a hallmark of the union value structure, and union representatives who bargain with managements are usually elected, as indicated, through a process that at least claims to be democratic. Managers, whose hierarchy is based on merit and experience, are thus forced to bargain, often on issues with major ramifications for the organization, with unionists who may have no better credentials for their role than the possession of a plurality of votes in a popularity poll.

And where the management representative speaks glowingly of "individualism" and declares that America's economic triumphs have been based on it, the union sees itself as part of a social movement and places a premium on "group consciousness."

As for "efficiency," which scores high on the management scale of values, to the union it smacks of a callous disregard for worker dignity and even worker health. Accordingly, it is something to be regarded with deep suspicion by employee representatives and to be resisted whenever resistance is practicable.

(To this list of reasons why employers resist unionism, a desire for *status* in the managerial community could probably be added. It is, in certain management circles, quite a mark of distinction to be able to stay what is typically nowadays called "union-free." And while such a reason is somewhat less visible and thus less demonstrable than are the reasons outlined in the body of this section, such nonunion employers as IBM, Texas Instruments, Eastman Kodak, Delta Airlines, and DuPont regularly support its existence by proudly citing the fact that they have not as yet been vulnerable to any appreciable unionization. DuPont has been nothing if not enthusiastic in pointing out that national unions have succeeded in only 13 out of almost 250 representation elections there since 1940, for example, and Delta's chairman is given to the use of such declarations as "If we ever become unionized, this will be because we've made mistakes.")

Such comments as those above, as with our treatment of "Why Workers Join Unions," can be offered only as generalizations. For a specific union-management relationship, the value differences may hardly be as pronounced; the writers are personally familiar, for that matter, with several relationships in which the unions seem to place far higher values on ability and efficiency than do the managements. Such value conflicts as the ones enumerated are, however, quite genuine in many union-management situations and thus represent the realities of labor relations rather than its stereotypes. As such, they serve to reinforce management's opposition to unionism, however much this opposition may be anchored to such other reasons as the decision-making issue.

LABOR RELATIONS CONSULTANTS

Increasingly, in recent years, employers have succumbed to an urge to use "labor relations consultants," who are usually either lawyers or psychologists, to prevent a union from gaining bargaining rights or to get rid of an established union through a decertification election (about which more will be said in Chapter 3).

Informed estimates place the number of such consulting firms at an absolute minimum of 1,000, with at least five times that number of individuals directly involved in what unions bitterly call "union busting" and many employers contend is merely the providing of assistance to employees who genuinely want a nonunion environment. The AFL-CIO itself believes that a staggering 75 percent of all managements now turn to these consultants expressly to gain help in thwarting unionization and that they pay them over $100 million each year. Others would place these latter figures at lower, although still significant levels.

Some members of this new growth industry at times advise their employer-clients to engage in activities that are quite illegal under national labor policy, such as placing agents in the workplace to spy on employees; harassing and discharging union members; avoiding the hiring of blacks (who are—in the opinion of at least one practitioner in this line of work—"more prone to unionization than whites"); and initiating decertification elections. Others guide managements in engaging in bad-faith, uncompromising bargaining so as to provoke a strike in which the employer can replace unionized employees with a nonunion work force.

Some labor relations consultants are also adept at helping their management clients thwart union organizing drives by the blunt device of firing workers who seem to be particularly active in such drives. Even if the union takes such cases to court, time is definitely on the employer's side here. The cases can, with appeals, take up to five years for resolution and even with an ultimate union victory the dismissed workers may no longer be available to return to their jobs. One-on-one meetings with workers and arguments that a union is an unnecessary third party will also often frustrate a union-organizing drive.

Consultants also have been known to suggest to relevant clients that a company that purchases another company can legally get around recognizing the seller's union simply by hiring less than a majority of the seller's employees. And their expertise is also at times provided to employers who wish to legally move their unionized work to their nonunion facilities (some of which have been newly created for just this purpose). Given the current state of labor relations law, as Chapter 3 will explain in much more detail, consultants have a wide area of lawful tactics and strategies to place at their clients' disposal and by no means need move beyond what public policy allows in order to be effective.

In addition to providing such personalized services, some consultants hold seminars open to all comers for a fee. Favored topics here are "Making

Unions Unnecessary," "Avoiding Unions," and "Putting the Union Organizer on the Defensive." Members of the profession also produce a wide
variety of articles, books, and cassettes that find a lucrative market among
antiunion managements. For at least some of the consultants, it's nice work
if you can get it: Six-figure annual incomes are not at all uncommon in this
specialized, controversial field.

(Exhibit 1-2 constitutes one union's far from subtle but perhaps understandable description of members of the profession. "You have to understand your opponent before you can win the fight," the labor
organization—the International Brotherhood of Teamsters—informed its
members in the article accompanying this artwork in the union's monthly
magazine. Exhibit 1-3 summarizes the thoughts of a vice president of the
Sheet Metal Workers regarding not only the consultants but also the
general current thrust of management-labor relations activities that the
growth of the consultants symbolizes.)

MANAGEMENT PHILOSOPHIES TOWARD UNIONS

Given the many different roots of management opposition and the perva-
siveness of so many of these, it is tempting to speculate that, deep in their
corporate hearts, the basic attitude of *most* business enterprises must be
one of intransigent hostility. Were this presumed attitude, in other words,
to be stated as an official policy, it would read approximately, "We seek to
weaken organized labor by any and all means at our command, to frustrate
it in its demands, to grant it nothing that is not absolutely necessary, and
under no circumstances to make any attempt at accepting the union as a
permanent part of our employee relations. If we adhere to this approach
consistently and with sufficient patience, our workers will see that the
union offers them nothing. And they will ultimately arise and vote the
union out at least as enthusiastically as they have voted it in."

There can be no denying that some executives do espouse this policy, as
above, and that at an earlier time in American labor history, many managers did so. The irony of contemporary labor relations, however, is that
despite management's continuing opposition to unionism, its use of consultants, and its constant resistance to new labor inroads, much of the employer community has substantially departed from such a provocative
stance. It has moved instead to what Lloyd Reynolds has called a "defensive
endurance" philosophy: "If this is what our workers want, I guess we'll have
to go along with it." In a word, the union is *accommodated*, however
unwelcome and even unpalatable its presence may be. Management remains ever on guard as to "matters of principle," seeks to prevent the union
from "intruding" in areas that are "the proper function of management,"
and frequently is highly critical of certain union actions. *But* the labor
organization is taken for granted, harmony with it is sought wherever
possible, and the employer can deal with the union on a day-to-day basis
without feeling that conciliation has made him a traitor to his class.

EXHIBIT 1–2

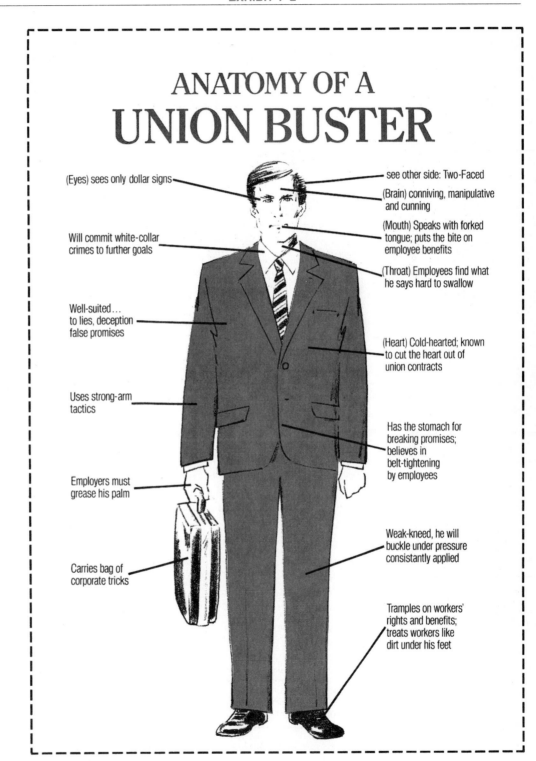

ANATOMY OF A
UNION BUSTER

(Eyes) sees only dollar signs

Will commit white-collar
crimes to further goals

Well-suited…
to lies, deception
false promises

Uses strong-arm
tactics

Employers must
grease his palm

Carries bag of
corporate tricks

see other side: Two-Faced

(Brain) conniving, manipulative
and cunning

(Mouth) Speaks with forked
tongue; puts the bite on
employee benefits

(Throat) Employees find what
he says hard to swallow

(Heart) Cold-hearted; known
to cut the heart out of
union contracts

Has the stomach for
breaking promises;
believes in
belt-tightening
by employees

Weak-kneed, he will
buckle under pressure
consistantly applied

Tramples on workers'
rights and benefits;
treats workers like
dirt under his feet

Source: International Teamster, July 1989, p. 17.

EXHIBIT 1–3

THE RIGHT TO STRIKE

For the past fifty years American Workers have used their right to withhold their labor as an effective economic weapon while their union contract was being negotiated during Collective Bargaining.

The threat of a strike resulted in most employers coming to the bargaining table, negotiating in good faith and in the vast majority of contracts a fair and equitable agreement was reached.

In 1935 the National Labor Relations Act, commonly referred to as the Wagner Act, was passed into law. The Wagner Act established the basic rights for workers to organize and defend themselves collectively. Included in these rights was the right to strike.

During 1938 the United States Supreme Court ruled on a case brought before them (NLRB vs Mackay Radio) wherein the court ruled that employers could permanently replace striking workers.

For over forty years labor and management resolved their disputes without management, except in very rare circumstances, implementing the hiring of permanent replacements.

However, in 1981, then President Ronald Reagan fired all striking Air Traffic Controllers and permanently replaced them with non-union strike breakers. Many employers throughout this country began using this tactic for busting unions.

The truth of the matter is that in many many circumstances the employer has been successful in achieving his initial goal.

That goal has been to bust the union or make it so ineffectual that it is only a question of time until a Decertification Petition is filed with the NLRB.

How do they do it?

Watch for these signs.

A few weeks, sometimes months, prior to your contract being opened for negotiations a new face shows up on the scene. He is generally introduced as a Production Consultant, Industrial Engineer, Efficiency Expert or some number of other titles.

In reality he is a Management Consultant hired by the employer to teach and instruct supervisors how to create an atmosphere within the shop of disunity among workers, criticism of the union stewards and union representatives.

One of their favorite tricks is to have the supervisors intentionally violate the Union Contract, force the filing of grievances then refuse to settle any grievance and attempt to put the blame on the union.

Another common trick is to hire a new employee (a professional who has been schooled by the Consultant) to work in the shop to complain about everything possible and blame the union.

You must also watch for a company who has never really concerned itself about the welfare of its employees who all of the sudden, just prior to contract negotiations, appear to develop a concern about you as an individual.

Then there is the most blatant and obvious tactic of all.

They come to the bargaining table and submit to the union's negotiating committee, contract proposal changes that they know cannot be acceptable to either you or your negotiating committee.

The proposals generally consist of items, such as drastic reductions in wages and benefits, as well as, language which renders the seniority and job protection clauses meaningless.

They then proceed to "surface bargain" and eventually wind up with a "last best and final" position they know the membership will reject and go on strike.

Next comes the permanent replacement workers (scabs). Many employers are now advertising in the local newspapers for *permanent* replacements *before* and *during* contract negotiations in anticipation of a strike.

Now that the employer has accomplished the first phase of his objective he moves to the second.

That is to prolong the strike until one of two objectives is obtained.

First: The membership becomes so disorganized and/or weakened by the length of the strike they "cave in" to management's position, thereby, destroying the effectiveness of the union.

Or:

Second: The strike is prolonged to a point where a Decertification Petition is filed with the NLRB and only the scabs are allowed to vote.

In either case management wins and the workers lose.

Is there an alternative?

The answer is very positive, YES!

In the next issue of the Journal I will cover what is being done to counteract employers who attempt to implement this type of program. ■

Richard J. Scott
Vice President For
Production Workers

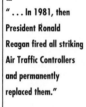

■
" . . . In 1981, then President Ronald Reagan fired all striking Air Traffic Controllers and permanently replaced them."

Source: Sheet Metal Workers Journal, August 1990, P. 8.

When people speak of "maturity" in labor relations, they are frequently thinking of this rapidly growing managerial posture—and organized labor's reciprocation of it.

A specific union-management relationship even today, however, need not necessarily be marked by *either* employer attitude depicted above. Variety is still the essence of our labor relations system, and so many variables can influence management policies that it is unrealistic to assume that the only possibilities are (1) intransigence and (2) accommodation. Variations in the abilities of managers to accurately understand the membership goals and leadership desires of the unions with which they are dealing, and in the skill with which employers have met these union aspirations—to say nothing of the nature of these goals and desires themselves—have led to a wide diversity of management positions. So, too, have variations in the managers' own relative degrees of security within the corporate framework, and the economic health of the employers involved. Obviously, variations in union attitudes may be highly relevant. And the same can be said of such other variables as the past labor relationships between the parties, the technological environments of both the industry and the employer, and even the role of the government, where this is a factor. Most of these topics will receive fuller treatment in later chapters of this book. Here it is pertinent to note the many grounds for differing attitudes toward unions among managerial groups.

Thus, although accommodation today is the dominant attitude in many relationships, having followed an era of intransigence, there are many variations on the theme of "management labor relations philosophies." And even among the more general of these different philosophies, at least six separate types (including the two above) can be distinguished.[27]

1. *Conflict,* or the intransigent, uncompromising attitude depicted previously, is now fast fading from the labor relations scene. Nonetheless, this attitude existed on a wide scale prior to World War II. Such a managerial stance arose to a great extent because many companies had been newly organized before that time, and because union organizational campaigns have never been notable for their sensitivity to personal feelings. Unions rarely resist the temptation in these circumstances to engage in negative stereotyping of those who run the organization. The top managers are painted as ruthless, greedy profiteers, ready to do almost anything to increase return on investment and wholly insensitive to the most obvious of human problems. Any actual incidents that might support such charges are, of course, produced as accompaniments to such charges, but lack of available evidence is not necessarily any obstacle at all.

The union, consequently, does more than "undermine employee loyalty to the company" at such a time; it frequently goes well beyond the borders of the factual and bruises management egos in the process. Add managerial fears of decision-making encroachments and of union values that are antithetical to those of management, as well as the other grounds for management's opposition to unionism on top of such an emotion-charged atmosphere, and it should not be surprising that many employers in the period immediately following their unionization embraced a philosophy of "no acceptance" of the union. Only in the face of the law and union power could unions extract concessions from such managements, and then only quite begrudgingly and on as temporary a basis as possible.

Some companies and an ever-growing number of public servants are, of course, even today among the newly organized. And it is in the labor relations of these, indeed, that one is most apt today to encounter the Conflict philosophy. But this managerial attitude is not confined to new bargaining relationships: A minority of long-organized companies also currently adheres to it, owing to changes in management personnel, changes in union personnel, or various other factors—including the particular management's sheer refusal to abandon the hope that if unions are never really accepted by their companies, they will eventually also lose acceptance from their worker-members. In recent years, various newspaper publishers throughout the country have seemed, to many observers, to epitomize this latter situation. So, too, have the owners and operators in the world of organized professional sports, most particularly baseball.

The mammoth Litton Industries, at least if allegations from the several unions that deal with it are to be believed, by repeatedly closing plants before unions can get in, and refusing to negotiate contracts even after unions have been successful in organizing Litton locations, has also represented the intransigent approach masterfully. Other deserving current nominees for the "Best Representative of a Conflict Philosophy Award" are Caterpillar Tractor, the world's largest construction equipment maker, and Allis-Chalmers, whose recent battles with the United Automobile Workers have been nothing if not nasty. A. T. Massey Coal Company, the nation's eighth largest coal producer with over $1 billion in sales, also merits inclusion on this list. (Exhibit 1-4 represents the far from positive view held toward Massey by the Mine Workers during a fifteen-month strike concluded a while ago. By the same token, during the walkout Massey management accused the union of "acts of terrorism" to force it to sign an agreement and announced that it would sue the Mine Workers for millions of dollars because of property damage and injuries to nonstriking employees caused by the union.)

Such an attitude does not lead to amicable labor relations. It can also be expected to foster union militancy, as the union reacts by engaging in various pressure tactics (often including slowdowns of production and sudden "wildcat" strikes) to gain through these means what it cannot hope to procure at the bargaining table. Finally, managements embracing a Conflict philosophy run a decided risk of being found in violation of the labor laws, particularly those involving "refusal to bargain" and discrimination against employees for the purpose of discouraging membership in a union.

It is primarily for these reasons that many Conflict philosophies have either been dismissed as realistic management alternatives in the first place or given way to:

2. An *Armed Truce* attitude. Here, employer representatives are motivated by approximately the following logic: "We are well aware that the vital interests of the employer and the union are poles apart, and that they

EXHIBIT 1–4

UMWA Members Deserve Better Than This

Fifty years ago, company-owned gun thugs were a common sight in the coalfields. Now, thanks to A. T. Massey Coal Co., they're making a comeback.

Massey has imported an army of hired guns into the mining regions of southern West Virginia and eastern Kentucky in an attempt to break the United Mine Workers of America.

Hundreds of UMWA members and supporters already have been arrested for protesting this danger to their families and communities.

They are facing potential fines, legal fees, court costs and other expenses which could total hundreds of thousands of dollars.

You Can Help

Rocky Peck, a rank-and-file UMWA member, has written and recorded two songs about the strike from his first-hand experience on the A. T. Massey picket line.

Now, that 45 rpm record, which contains the songs "UMWA" and "Hey, Mr. Massey," is available to UMWA members.

All proceeds will go to the **Miners Aid Fund,** which provides legal and financial assistance to UMWA members and supporters defending their jobs, their union and their constitutional rights.

To order copies of this UMWA record, fill out the coupon below and mail it in along with $3.95 (includes postage and handling) per copy to: **Miners Aid Fund,** c/o Office of the President, United Mine Workers of America, 900 15th St., N.W., Washington, D.C. 20005.

Further contributions to the **Miners Aid Fund** can also be sent to the above address.

Yes, I want to help defend the UMWA members and supporters arrested for defending their union. Please send me_____ copies of the "UMWA"/"Hey, Mr. Massey" 45. I enclose $_____ ($3.95 per record).

Make checks or money orders payable to the **Miners Aid Fund** and send to the address listed above. Please print clearly.

Name_____   Local union number_____
                         UMWA District_____
Address_____   Union or organization (if other
                         than UMWA)_____
City_____
State_____Zip_____   _____

Please allow six to eight weeks for delivery.

Source: United Mine Workers Journal, January 1986, p. 16.

always will be. But this doesn't mean that every action we take in our labor relations should be geared to weakening the union and thus forcing head-on conflict with it. Instead, since we can expect the union to firmly press to extend its fields of interest, our basic mission is to press, just as ambitiously, toward containing it within limits. We will honor the law immaculately, and therefore deal with the union without any subterfuges on the subject of wages, hours, and conditions of employment; but we will hold our bargaining practice strictly within the boundaries of these legal obligations and thus define our negotiation scope as rigidly as possible. Moreover, we will interpret any agreements emerging from these negotiations strictly and insist upon the union's observing, in its day-to-day conduct, its contractual obligations 100 percent."

What the management members (and those on the union side, too) really want here is, as Barbash has pointed out, a "workable adversary relationship," and because they do seek such a situation, they have *normalized* it.[28] Indeed, Barbash is hardly alone in believing that this adversary principle endures "because it reflects the objective reality of modern industrial organization—its competitiveness, its pervasive command-and-obey organization, and its zero-sum efficiency ethic, all of which by their nature pit participants against one another. We must not exclude the final possibility that there is something in the human psyche that infuses every human situation with latent aggressiveness."[29]

Even today, many union-management relationships have made no more progress than this. The union representatives return the feelings of their management counterparts, and the struggle for power goes on indefinitely. Wages, hours, and other rigidly construed employee-relations areas are dealt with as their issues arise, but the more crucial question of union security versus management rights, being insoluble in such an atmosphere, continually blocks more constructive dealings. With some justification, the General Electric Company has frequently been regarded as an excellent example of a company that has espoused this Armed Truce philosophy, at least until recently. The Timken Company, too, might be said to meet the criteria. ("If you need mercy, forget about it," a steelworker leader asserted with some bitterness a while ago. "You're not going to get it from Timken.")[30]

3. *Power Bargaining,* as an alternative, is more conducive to solving labor relations problems than is the Armed Truce approach. As is *not* the case under either Conflict or Armed Truce, managers in Power Bargaining can "accept" the union and, in fact, tend to pride themselves on their sense of "realism," which leaves them no choice but to acknowledge the union's power. (A prerequisite for this philosophy, obviously, is that the union *have* significant power.) By the same token, such executives press their own employer's bargaining power to the maximum that economic and other conditions at any one time allow. The managerial rationale is, more or less: "We face strong and deeply entrenched unions squarely and with an accurate perception of their power—and we accept them as sovereign spokespersons for their side. We are practical people and economic realists, not crusaders with naïve faith in idealistic trimmings. Our task is not to pursue the fruitless approach of directly opposing and limiting the union, but to increase and then use our own power to offset that of the other side where we can."

Might does not necessarily make right, but it can lead to agreement at the bargaining table. And on this basis it can be argued that continued controversy is minimized in Power Bargaining. However unenthusiastically, managements in such a relationship can live with their unions, for at least the short run, in most areas affecting employee relations.

On the other hand, any relationship focused upon a balance of power is a highly tenuous one. It always contains the danger of regression to one of the earlier approaches when the power ratios change. As such, Power Bargaining has not been widespread at any one time in American labor relations, although many industries marked by small employers and highly centralized unions have at one time or another seen it. In such cases, the employers have typically associated in an attempt at a united front to counter the union's strength.

In short, for the reasons indicated, most managements in the current economy view all three previous alternatives as unsatisfactory. Since, needless to say, their unions wholeheartedly agree with them on this point, the climate for a more harmonious relationship—in the form of Accommodation—exists.

4. *Accommodation,* however, is hardly the same as cooperation. As pointed out earlier, management remains constantly vigilant as to "principle" and, as does the union, clings to such values as "orbits of respective equities and privileges." In this regard, Accommodation differs little from Armed Truce. Moreover, the management gaze is still riveted upon the traditional agenda of collective bargaining—wages, hours, and conditions of employment—and there is a self-conscious employer unwillingness to discuss *officially* anything that cannot rather rigidly be construed as falling within these topics.

The property of Accommodation that makes it unique lies in the area of everyday practice rather than in formal declarations. Management regularly tries to "meet the union halfway," to conciliate informally whenever it can, and always to accept the fact that it and the union are mutually dependent institutions whose basic interests are identical (even if the employer given a choice of having a union around or not having one would seize upon the second option in a matter of seconds).

Such a definition in no way implies that the employer need go out of its way to *help* organized labor. Opposition to the concept of unionism in general may still remain the hallmark of management's philosophy. In an atmosphere of Accommodation, however, the roles of both emotion and raw power are minimized, in favor of management's *adjusting* to the union *as it is.* Extreme legalism in at least the basic areas of wages, hours, and conditions is supplanted by compromise, flexibility, and "toleration." As such, Accommodation constitutes a considerably more positive approach to labor relations than do any of the other alternatives.

There is ample evidence that the mainstream of American management has today entered the Accommodation stage in its dealings with unions. All the major automobile and steel employers now exhibit Accommodation characteristics—if not in every labor relations matter (subcontracting, production standards, and the possibility of plant shutdowns remain definite sticking-points, as we shall see), at least in the great bulk of them. And so, too, do most managements nowadays in such long-unionized industries as petroleum, construction, railroading, the airlines, trucking, rubber, and textiles. Not surprisingly, there is still wide variation in the nature and quality of contract administration among companies, and even among locations within the same company. But the growth of Accommodation has quite visibly resulted in the significant development of mutually acceptable policy and in more orderly day-to-day union-management relations, results that even the great diversity of labor relations cannot obscure. (Exhibit 1-5, drawn from the current national contract between General Motors and the United Automobile Workers, epitomizes Accommodation.)

EXHIBIT 1-5

Introduction

The management of General Motors recognizes that it cannot get along without labor any more than labor can get along without the management. Both are in the same business and the success of that business is vital to all concerned. This requires that both management and the employees work together to the end that the quality and cost of the product will prove increasingly satisfactory and attractive so that the business will be continuously successful.

General Motors holds that the basic interests of employers and employees are the same. However, at times employees and the management have different ideas on various matters affecting their relationship. The management of General Motors is convinced that there is no reason why these differences cannot be peacefully and satisfactorily adjusted by sincere and patient effort on both sides.

---

5. *Cooperation,* involving full acceptance of the union as an active partner in a formal plan, is for exactly that reason decidedly rare. It necessitates a management (as well as a union) that is willing to extend matters of everyday union-management relations beyond the traditional areas to such broader fields as technological change, waste, and business solvency. And this, in turn, calls for corporate executives who genuinely believe that unions can make definite and positive contributions to the success of the firm, through furnishing management with information it would not otherwise have, through winning over worker support for management goals, and in various other ways.

In a formal plan for Cooperation, the management supports not only the right but the *desirability* of union participation, and the union reciprocates by actively endorsing the employer's right and need for an adequate return on its investment. The two labor relations parties *jointly* deal with both personnel and production problems as they occur. Suggestions pertaining to cost reduction and productivity improvement are typically solicited from all worker levels. And whatever economic gains in increased efficiency may be realized from such cooperation projects are normally shared by the employer with the work force.

Most managements that have adopted this approach to labor relations have, by and large, been well publicized, either as participants in rather formalized Scanlon Plans or, as in the case of the Tennessee Valley Authority and the city of Jamestown, New York, independently. Also standing as a model of the cooperative rather than the adversarial relationship is the widely acclaimed and eminently successful joint venture between the UAW and General Motors-Toyota at New United Motors Manufacturing, Inc. (NUMMI) in Fremont, California. National Steel, which guarantees employment to its bargaining unit members and shares sensitive financial information with them (and whose Management Center facilities have been open to hourly workers for several years in an almost unprecedented show of togetherness), also belongs on this roster. But the very fact that so much publicity has been given to these cooperative approach plans graphically symbolizes how few they have been thus far. Moreover, the approach is still so incompatible with present-day management (and, often, union) value systems that most such plans have been implemented only as a last resort when the management was faced with a severe financial crisis. The word "cooperation" is frequently used in management addresses to worker groups, but in the manager's lexicon of today it obviously has a meaning that is considerably more restricted than the one depicted here.[31]

Nonetheless, it is safe to predict that labor-management cooperation will win more acceptance in the last years of the twentieth century. Fierce foreign and nonunion domestic competition are growing. The staggering multi-billion-dollar trade deficit of the United States stands as a genuine and compelling threat to jobs and business solvency. Management and union leadership will be forced to innovate in matters of labor relations to increase productivity so as to achieve the goals of job, union, and employer security.

Indeed, a labor agreement that was negotiated in 1992 by American Telephone and Telegraph and its two principal unions may well show the shape of things to come. Acknowledging competitive realities (Sprint and MCI in the United States are both essentially nonunion; and Fujitsu of Japan, Siemens of Germany, and Northern Telecom of Canada are all far less unionized than AT&T), the unions actually acknowledged the need for more layoffs than the new contract sanctioned. In a statement that could as readily have been made by AT&T's chairman of the board, the president of one of the two unions—Morton Bahr of the Communications Workers—told the media, "This is a company that is still top heavy. When we can't bid for a job because our operating costs are too high and someone underbids us, that's a problem."[32]

Both Bahr's union and the International Brotherhood of Electrical Workers accepted modest wage and pension improvements and generous opportunities for the retraining of workers no longer needed in their present positions in lieu of any meaningful protection against layoffs. The unions also won greater opportunities for organizing employees at AT&T's fast-growing Universal Credit Card division.

As different as each of the previous five approaches to labor relations is from the four others, there is a common denominator: Whichever one is selected is, subject to its ability to meet management goals, at the outset strictly the employer's business. Ultimately, a Conflict approach may lead to a strike involving government intervention, or an amassing of strength in a Power Bargaining situation may have other legal ramifications, and in any of the five cases, the union may, of course, react in such a way to make the approach unsuitable. The management can hardly do much with Accommodation if the union is Conflict oriented. But at least at the outset, the employer is perfectly free to experiment with any of the various approaches.

6. The same cannot be said of one other approach, *Collusion.* If, up until now, the enumerated management alternatives can be viewed as successively leading to more union-management harmony (from Conflict on the one hand to Cooperation on the other), this one can be looked upon as generating "too much harmony."

Under Collusion, employers have been known to bribe union officials to agree to bargaining table concessions and substandard (or "sweetheart") contracts, and sometimes to waive the formality of actually having a contract altogether. And these bribes have on occasion taken imaginative forms: interest-free loans, ownership interests (invariably disguised) in the company, and the placement of company insurance contracts with insurance agencies owned by the union officials.

But such activity has almost exclusively been confined to narrow sectors of local-market industries, with marginal and intensely competitive employers for whom a small difference in labor cost can mean the difference between solvency and insolvency, and where visibility to the public law-enforcement agencies is relatively slight. Having named the least ethical sectors of the garment trades, building trades, trucking, waterfront, and entertainment industries, one has almost exhausted the list.

LABOR RELATIONS IN THE PUBLIC SECTOR

If the unionized percentage of the total civilian labor force has registered some definite slippage in recent years, and if the figures from the overall white collar frontier in the recent past can be described as essentially unchanged, organized labor can point with satisfaction to its organizational successes in the fastest-growing employment sector of all, that of the public employee.

In 1940, according to the official figures of the U.S. Department of Labor, the nation's governmental work force at all levels (federal, state, and local) numbered 4.2 million, or 9.6 percent of total payroll employment. By 1960, the figure had exactly doubled, to 8.4 million. And, rising even more dramatically when compared with overall labor force figures, it reached the 12.5-million mark by the end of the 1960s. By 1976, it had climbed to almost 15 million (and over 18 percent of total payroll employment in the country), although this was to be its high-water mark for at least many years. After the late 1970s, negative reaction from the taxpayers to the rapid growth caused the figures to hit a plateau, albeit in no way to decrease. By 1993, there were slightly over 16 million such workers.

Undoubtedly, many factors explain the strong upward curve. But Loewenberg and Moskow seem to have their fingers on the foremost three of them in pointing out that (1) all else being equal, a growing population (the U.S. figures grew by 55 percent between 1940 and 1970, for example) requires an even larger growth in public services; (2) technological progress and relative affluence have produced a whole new gamut of challenges (for instance, air-lane regulations, water pollution, mass urban transport); and (3) changes in concepts of what government can do or should do vary over time, but generally in a more ambitious direction.[33]

No reliable figures for union membership among government employees are available for the period before 1956, when civil servants in the Bureau of Labor Statistics began collecting this kind of data. But where the BLS's information reveals 915,000 governmental unionists in 1956 (heavily concentrated in the federal service, and particularly among its postal, ship-yard, and arsenal employees), the same agency reported almost 1.5 million organized workers only eight years later, and by 1993 was estimating that somewhat over 6 million public employees—widely distributed throughout all levels of government and embracing a spectrum that included such disparate types as engineers, zookeepers, fire fighters, jail guards, teachers, sewage workers, and common laborers—were in union ranks.

Thus it should come as no surprise that the greatest rate of growth in the entire labor movement has occurred among unions that represent, either exclusively or primarily, public employees. The American Federation of State, County and Municipal Employees (AFSCME), gaining 1,000 new members a week in recent years and up to a total membership of some 1.2 million by 1993, as noted earlier (from only 210,000 in 1961), has until quite recently been the fastest-growing union in the nation. An almost comparable success story has been registered by the American Federation of Teachers, which increased (as also noted earlier) from 60,000 members in 1960 to 550,000 some three decades later. And the labor movement can also take considerable encouragement from the octupling of members recorded by the American Federation of Government Employees during the 1960s and 1970s, although the size of this organization—with little growth in its primary potential membership market of defense installations—has not shown this level of expansion in more recent years. In 1993, it had just under 220,000 members.

Even these statistics understate the degree of recent union penetration of the public sector, however. It was generally estimated at the time of this writing that at least another 3.5 million employees belonged to professional and civil service associations that were outside the official ranks of organized labor but in many cases distinguishable from bona fide unions only by their titles. Into this latter category would certainly fall the fast-growing and increasingly militant 2-million-member National Education Association, the heavy majority of whose members are now covered by collective bargaining agreements. So, too, would the Assembly of Government Employees (estimated strength of over 600,000 members in various state employee subunits), the American Nurses Association (representing the interests of almost 250,000 employees), and the Fraternal Order of Police (with over 150,000 members), all of these also having shown rapid rises in organizational size over the past few years.

One must freely acknowledge that organized labor still has a long way to go before its penetration of the public sector can be deemed to be anywhere near complete. Based only on official union-membership figures, the 6.3 million unionized public employees constitute less than 40 percent of the total membership potential. And even if all 3.5 million association members are included (and, as indicated above, not all of them should be, since an indeterminate although doubtless minority percentage of them are not bargained for collectively), the figure still comes to not much more than about 55 percent of the total public-sector employee population. It constitutes, in fact, the lowest percentage for public employees for any nation west of Berlin and is significantly lower than the comparable statistics for Great Britain, Sweden, Norway and Denmark (where over 80 percent of these employees are unionized), and even for our immediate neighbor to the north, Canada, where two thirds of the public-sector work force belongs to unions. But the gains of the recent past are nonetheless highly impressive and deserve exploration.

The Growth of Public-Sector Unionism: Some Explanations

In all likelihood, three factors have been particularly responsible for this new union thrust.

First and probably foremost, *legal developments* since 1960 have given organized labor both a protection and an encouragement that were previously conspicuous by their absence. At the federal level, a highly influential event was President John F. Kennedy's 1962 issuance of Executive Order 10988, constituting the first recognition ever on the part of the federal government that its employees were entitled to join unions and bargain collectively with the executive agencies for which they worked. Three types of union recognition were provided—informal, formal, and exclusive—depending upon the percentage of employees in the bargaining unit represented by the union. And, if the latter could gain exclusive recognition (by showing that it represented at least 10 percent of the employees involved and then being selected or designated by a majority of employees within the bargaining unit), the employing agency was compelled to meet and confer regularly with such a union on matters affecting personnel policy and practices and working conditions.

The order did remove many key topics from the scope of this collective bargaining—among them, mandatory union membership, agency budgetary negotiations, and new technology—and it had certain deficiencies in the dispute-settlement area (in case of a bargaining impasse, should mediation efforts fail, the only available procedure was an appeal to a higher level of the agency's own management). But E. O. 10988, nonetheless, by attempting to provide organizational and bargaining rights for employees of the federal government in essentially the same way as these rights had been established for employees in the private sector almost three decades earlier by the Wagner Act, provided a significant stimulus to union growth not just in the federal employee province but, in short order, also at the state and local government levels. As former President John F. Griner of the American Federation of Government Employees could succinctly observe, "No matter that the collective bargaining rights [under E. O. 10988] were modified, truncated, almost emasculated, E. O. 10988 was the...Magna Charta. The workers saw their opportunity. They grasped it. They joined the union in droves."[34]

The White House, moreover, liberalized its "Magna Charta" a very few years later. Richard M. Nixon's Executive Order 11491, effective as of January 1, 1970, abolished both informal and formal union recognition on the grounds that these two types had proved to have had little meaning. It provided, instead, that any union could gain exclusive recognition if selected by a majority of the bargaining unit employees in a secret-ballot election. It also created a three-member Federal Labor Relations Council to decide major policy matters and to administer and interpret the order itself, substituting these officials for the large potpourri of department heads who had handled—often quite inconsistently—these activities under E. O. 10988. And it gave the assistant secretary of labor for labor-management relations authority to settle disputes over the makeup of bargaining units and representation rights, to order and supervise elections, and to disqualify unions from recognition because of corrupt or undemocratic influences; formerly, these matters had been handled by the particular federal agency involved, and its ultimate judgment on them was not subject to appeal.

E. O. 11491 also established an impartial Federal Services Impasses Panel to settle disputes arising during contract negotiations, by final and binding arbitration if necessary. As stated above, the old order had provided for no such impartial procedure in the case of bargaining deadlocks (except for mediation), effectively placing unions at the ultimate mercy of the federal agency with which they were negotiating (and thus allowing one labor leader to compare the whole process to "a football game in which one side brings along the referee"). Since federal employees lack the right to strike, the new system for arbitration by neutrals seemed both equitable and realistic.

For all this liberalization contained in E. O. 11491, Congress in 1979 enacted a law that supplanted it. For many years, indeed since President Kennedy's original executive order, the government unions had pressured Congress to provide a *statutory* basis for the federal labor relations program, and their persistence paid off when Congress enacted the Civil Service Reform Act of 1978, Title VII of which superseded E. O. 11491 in January of the following year. Though it carried forward the basic rights and duties of federal employees and agencies as contained in the executive order, it made a number of important changes in the federal labor relations program. Functions formerly performed by the Federal Labor Relations Council and the assistant secretary of labor were lodged in an independent Federal Labor Relations Authority (FLRA). In large measure, the FLRA duplicates the functions of the National Labor Relations Board, which has jurisdiction in the private sector. By protecting the tenure of the members of the FLRA, and by making it independent from any existing federal agency, the law placed the new agency in a better position to administer objectively and effectively.

The new law also made a number of substantive changes. It expanded the scope of matters subject to negotiated grievance and arbitration procedures including, for the first time, employee discharge, demotion, and long-term suspensions. Upon a union's request, the federal agency involved is required to deduct dues of its members provided the employees sign the necessary dues checkoff authorization cards. And to balance the scales, official time (work time) may be used by employees representing the union in negotiations (including attendance at impasse settlement proceedings) to the extent that management officials are on paid time.

At the state level, although the influence of the developments in Washington can be clearly detected, the trend toward giving legal protection to civil servants in their efforts to organize and bargain collectively has been even more pronounced. Prior to the enactment of the Kennedy order, only one state, Wisconsin in 1959, had extended such a right to public employees. By the time of this writing, virtually all other states had sanctioned collective bargaining for at least some types of public workers. Indeed, some forty of them had enacted legislation conferring such protection upon all (or almost all) state and local employees, and laws in eight states (Alaska, Hawaii, Minnesota, Montana, Oregon, Pennsylvania, Vermont, and Wisconsin) even allowed—in different degrees—some strikes. Court decisions in three other states (Michigan, New Hampshire, and Rhode Island) had also effectively made the strike weapon a viable tool for some public workers in those jurisdictions.

And no signs of a reversal are on the horizon of either this trend or the significant increase in state and local employee-union membership that it has generated.

A *second* factor behind the explosion in public-sector unionism has been the public servant's increasing unhappiness as the *remuneration package has fallen* farther and farther *behind* that of private employment.

Wages in the two sectors had historically been quite comparable, but by the mid-1960s the gap, even going beyond that of the general union-non-union discrepancy already touched on in this chapter, was fully in evidence. As a general statement, public employees in these years earned from 10 to 30 percent less than their exact counterparts (whether these were electricians, laborers, stock clerks, or secretaries) in private industry, who perhaps worked down the street from them.[35]

Even more jarring to the civil servants, however, was the lag in working conditions underpinning this wage package, since these conditions had for years been far *superior* in the public sector. For their traditionally comparable pay, the public servants had been asked to work shorter hours (with appreciably more liberal holiday and vacation entitlements than their private counterparts), had been given a degree of job security that almost no other workers possessed, and could look forward to a pension entitlement that in most instances would dwarf that of private-industry employees—if, in fact, the latter even had a pension expectation. By the 1960s, all these relative advantages had eroded, as public-sector fringe benefits and working conditions saw little further liberalization, while these areas in private industry first caught up with and then slowly eclipsed the public emoluments. If the public employees were not completely disgruntled in the face of this development, they were certainly—to paraphrase the late P. G. Wodehouse—a long distance from being gruntled. Increasingly, they turned to their newly legalized avenue of collective bargaining to redress what was viewed as a clear injustice.

Third, and finally, one cannot disregard the *general spirit of the times* in explaining the rise of public unionism. These same growth years were marked throughout American society by a degree of social upheaval rare in the nation's history. No part of the established order was seemingly immune from attack, as blacks, Hispanics, women, gays, student activists, an increasingly broad spectrum of citizens opposed to the Vietnam War, and even older people organized—often, militantly—to exert in support of their respective causes a collective pressure that could hardly be over-looked. The results were, as in the case of the demands of minorities upon organized labor that will be dealt with in Chapter 2, generally mixed. But sufficient progress was certainly made to bring home to many public employees who had eschewed organization until that point the advantages to be gained by collective action.

To this trio of key explanations, readers might care to add others of their choosing: the increasing vulnerability to unionization of many public-sector managers because of archaic personnel policies; a fear on the part of government workers in the latter, inflation-dominated years of this period that their jobs would be the first to be eliminated in the face of growing taxpayer resistance to the higher costs of public administration; the chang-ing complexion of the government work force itself, with an ever-higher percentage of younger and often more aggressive jobholders; and perhaps the sheer numerical growth in public employees, making them a more tempting target for the union organizer. In any case, however, the reasons for the successes of labor in the public-employee arena appear at the very least to have been understandable. As such, they seem destined to continue, certainly for a while.

The Public-Employee Unionist: The Strike Issue

"If you treat public employees bad enough," said George Meany in 1974, on the occasion of the founding convention of the AFL-CIO's new Public Employee Department, "they'll go on strike and they'll get the support of the union movement." Meany, a man rarely accused of mincing words, also told the same audience that public workers involved in labor disputes should feel free to strike "any damn time you feel like going on strike."[36] This was not the first time that year that the (then) AFL-CIO chief executive had registered these sentiments. Nor did he depart from the views expressed by many other, if less influential, labor chieftains in advancing them. But the setting this time—the new department symbolized the conquests of the recent past by uniting under its aegis twenty-four AFL-CIO-affiliated unions representing more than 2 million workers— gave a special impact to his words.

Ironically, had Meany said exactly the same thing only a few years earlier, he would very likely have been either publicly vilified as a nihilistic demagogue or dismissed as a droll master of hyperbole (this being the same Meany who on an earlier occasion had offered his observation that "most college professors, when given a choice of publish or perish, tend to make the wrong decision"). For, throughout labor's long history in this country, public policy toward the public-sector strike had been clear, unequivocal, and resoundingly negative. Calvin Coolidge had deemed such work stoppages "anarchy": In a famous statement referring to the 1919 Boston police strike, he had also declared, "There is no right to strike against the public safety by anybody, anywhere, at any time": Franklin D. Roosevelt had called them "unthinkable"; relevant government regulations (including E. O. 11491) for federal employees had historically banned the public-worker strike; and as Barrett and Lobel have asserted, "In the mid-1960s, it would be accurate to say that public policy in all states clearly prohibited work stoppages of public employees by statute, court decision, or attorneys' general opinion."[37] Indeed, public-employee organizations themselves showed their general agreement with this constraint by including, in almost all cases, total bans on work stoppages in their own constitutions.

What was past was definitely not prologue in this case, however. If, prior to 1960, public-sector strikes were all but unknown, and if, even as late as 1960, only 36 such strikes were recorded, the 1970 totals showed 412 of them.[38] Strikes in the latter year included an unprecedented previously noted eight-day strike by the nation's postal employees (it was essentially over wages, leading one observer to comment that the government could end the stoppage by giving the strikers their wage increase, but mailing it to them) and another nationwide one by airport flight controllers. The trend was accelerating when Meany advanced his views on the subject, and it would not visibly diminish in the later years of the decade. An all-time record of 593 public-employee strikes actually took place in 1979, and as a publication of that year could assert, fairly enough in view of the reality so vividly communicated by the media:

> We may see firemen watching homes burn down as they pursue their labor relations goals, or nurses walking a picket line to achieve proper union recognition. Your local police may suddenly begin giving out traffic tickets for everything as they carry out a planned slowdown.... Sanitation workers might leave your garbage to pile up in your driveway, or the guards at the correctional facility might decide to withhold their services. It may be the postal employees who become reluctant to handle your mail unless collective bargaining works for them, or the teachers who carry out a strike action to effect an increase. There are a dozen other examples of the criticality of labor relations in the public sector.[39]

Yet the harsh punishments all but universally called for by the various laws were essentially being ignored by civic authorities. (For example, in the federal government, any striker is subject to up to five years in jail plus a fine and dismissal, but as A. H. Raskin has pointed out in speaking of the aforementioned postal and flight controllers' stoppages, "No striker ever got close to Leavenworth or Lewisburg,"[40] and no striker has since.) It was, indeed, in recognition of this fact—that except in the rarest of instances, the antistrike laws could be violated with impunity given the political realities—that the several states mentioned earlier had legalized the public strike for at least some workers. And, of potentially great significance, it was because of this awareness also that an increasing number of members of Congress appeared to be in basic agreement with the view of the new AFL-CIO department that *all* public-sector strikes except for those creating a demonstrable peril to the public health should be legalized.

On the other hand, not quite *every* public-sector strike has violated the laws with impunity. When the nation's 11,500 flight controllers waged a second strike eleven years later—in August 1981—President Ronald Reagan aggressively reacted by firing them and also by setting the wheels in motion for their union (the Professional Air Traffic Controllers Organization, or PATCO) to be removed as the controllers' legally recognized bargaining representative (as it ultimately was). PATCO, which displayed surprising ineptness in not trying to win support from other unions in advance of its stoppage and whose major demand (for higher wages than the controllers' current $35,000 to $40,000 annually and shorter hours) was not one calculated to win much support from outsiders anyhow, was hardly typical in any of its actions. But Reagan's actions were well received by a heavy majority of all Americans, and some experts thought that future political figures might heed a lesson here and act similarly in the years ahead. (A new union, the National Air Traffic Controllers Association, overwhelmingly won the right to represent the controllers in a 1987 representation election.)

Whatever happens, the next decade will presumably see a resolution of the inevitably emotion-laden issue of public-sector strikes. And, given the general ineffectuality of the present strike bans (PATCO notwithstanding), this resolution will quite probably be on the side of the right to strike except for (1) such clearly indispensable civil servants as police officers and firefighters and (2) cases in which the peril to health and safety is otherwise shown to exist; in these cases, most likely, binding arbitration by third parties will be utilized to resolve bargaining impasses.

Supporters of such a development—and in their ranks are many neutrals—contend that this right to strike would only recognize reality. They argue also that only the strike threat can guarantee that public officials will bargain in good faith. And they point out that the many private-sector unionists who perform jobs identical to those in the public arena (for example, transit employees, teachers, and maintenance workers), since they do have the right to strike, possess an inequitable bargaining advantage over their government counterparts.

Arguments on the negative (or antistrike) side focus on these factors: (1) In the private sector, the employer can counter the strike weapon with a lockout of his own, but he can hardly do this as a government official, and hence the legalized public strike would create a large labor relations imbalance; (2) public pressures on the public official to end a strike are infinitely greater than those on the private administrator, and thus the former is forced to capitulate more quickly, to the ultimate detriment of the community; and (3) the monopolistic nature of virtually all public-sector employment makes almost all of it "essential," and thus the public should be guaranteed against its legalized interruption.

Whatever the merits of these latter contentions and supplementary antistrike ones, the momentum definitely belonged to those taking the other side of the argument as this was being written.

Public Employees and Harder Times

Something that was far *less* to labor's liking was also happening in the public sector at the time of this writing, however. A combination of a widespread taxpayers' revolt, severe decreases in federal payments to state and local governments, and a definite animus on the part of citizens to perceived public employee excesses (symbolized, indeed, by the popularity of Reagan's PATCO actions) was taking a good deal of clout away from public-sector unions—ironically, even amid the improved prospects for their right to strike.

In 1978, embittered taxpayers in California—increasingly upset by ever-higher tax burdens and also mindful of the ravages of inflation on their own budgets—approved a severe limitation on the swollen property taxes in their state by voting by a landslide margin for a so-called Proposition 13. And the consequences of this popular referendum verdict—which was remarkable as much for its one-sidedness as for its direction—were rapidly assimilated across the nation as voters all over the country registered similar sentiments and politicians from Massachusetts to Montana found themselves with far fewer resources than they had previously been allocated to administer governmental services. Labor costs—typically accounting for 65 to 85 percent of governmental budgets—were obviously prime targets for diminution as it became painfully obvious to all public figures that standing up to union demands (even when these were perhaps warranted) would be a much more profitable course of action for them than would accommodating such demands.

When it took office in 1981, the Reagan administration compounded labor's woes by rapidly cutting almost $20 billion in federal payments to state and local governments for programs running the gamut from education to public employment. Coming on top of the Proposition 13 occurrences, the cuts were likened by one union leader to "the San Francisco fire on top of the earthquake." While in theory there was nothing to stop the state and local governments from making up for this federal niggardliness by raising revenue in other ways, in fact the latter course of action was rarely followed. Consequently, employment in government—until then, as mentioned above, one of the nation's great growth industries—no longer increased at all and even decreased in some places (if not on a national aggregate basis) in the 1980s and early 1990s.

Amid all of this taxpayer unwillingness to part with money and White House–engineered austerity, some amount of spine-stiffening by politicians in their dealings with public-sector unions was inevitable. And the generous settlements of earlier years were now replaced in short order by hard-nosed bargaining by governmental officials—something that may well have led the unions themselves to agree with Oscar Levant's dictum that "a politician is a person who will double-cross a bridge when he comes to it." But that was clearly what the public wanted. As one seasoned labor lawyer could comment regarding the Reagan administration's highly publicized firing of the PATCO strikers, it "just put the frosting on the cake. It was all public employers needed to hear because they were beginning to feel more confident anyway about their ability to deal with unions."[41] (Eleven years later, public-sector unions had hardly forgiven either Reagan or his vice president. They held George Bush no less responsible for the general antilabor animus and worked hard and, of course, successfully for the latter's Democratic opponent in 1992. Exhibit 1-6, a message from the president of the biggest public union to his constituents, is illustrative.)

The trend was an ominous one for labor, which initially chose to react by actively engaging in more strikes than ever, although by the late 1980s public resentment had caused some decrease in this activity in favor of union lobbying for new taxes around the country. This trend continued in the 1990s. But, given the basic union successes in public-sector bargaining in the pre-Proposition 13 years, there were grounds for union optimism, too. Under any conditions, it did not seem to be too much to hope that the current, newer, and not especially appealing situation would itself be replaced by a more responsible bargaining system, administered by parties whose maturity had been hastened by adversity, and fairer to all concerned.

SOME CONCLUDING THOUGHTS

It can be expected that managements will continue to oppose the concept of unionism and to resist new union inroads as energetically as ever, for the roots of this opposition are essentially rational ones as *judged by management values*. It also seems the safest of predictions that unions will continue to press for an ever-greater narrowing of the scope of management discretion, in the interests of obliging worker wants and needs as *they* view them. Indeed, in the years immediately ahead, the stresses between the parties seem destined to grow: The recent intensification of industrial price and technological competition (and, in the public sector, of severe budgetary pressures) has already pitted an accelerated employer search for greater efficiency against an equally determined union quest for increased job security.

Since a labor relations millennium is far distant, it is a certainty that occasional impasses will continue to be reached and that these will result in strike actions, as they have in the past.

EXHIBIT 1–6

"The delegates you send to AFSCME's 30th International Convention must lay out a new vision for a better and stronger America."

Our Vision for a Better America

In the two years since our last International Convention, the nation has begun to feel the full consequences of Reagan's and Bush's unfitness for national leadership. The economy is not the only thing that's gone to hell in a handbasket. Twelve years of ruinous fiscal policies, blind ideology, and contempt for ordinary people have imposed extraordinary strains in every area of American life.

Every one of you, the members of AFSCME, can attest to the misery and losses generated by policies designed to starve and vandalize the public sector at every level.

Today, nobody in American society works under greater stress than the men and women who provide public services and health care. You're up against layoffs, furloughs, and take-backs—and the job itself has become tougher as states and cities struggle to maintain essential services despite fewer dollars and greater need.

The damage goes across the board: Ask corrections officers about crowding, health workers about emergency rooms, social service workers about case loads, maintenance staffs about the condition of public facilities. Ask librarians, nurses, road crews, and drug counselors.

Public workers did not cause this epidemic of state and local fiscal crises. We are not the cause of falling tax revenues and crippled budgets. For all

EXHIBIT 1–6 (continued)

PRESIDENT'S COLUMN

A REPORT FROM GERALD W. McENTEE

of those things, we can look to the folly of Ronald Reagan and the empty ambition of George Bush. Both wanted a free ride for the rich, both coldly and deliberately turned their backs on the poor, the middle-class, and state and local governments. More than that: Reagan and Bush used all their skills to damn us for the trouble they created. They've come at public workers from every direction: from privatization to deregulation to union-bashing by right-wing mercenaries.

Sisters and Brothers, stupidity, greed, and zealotry have pushed our country to the economic and social brink, and we cannot recover until government at every level recognizes a shared responsibility to get us back on the tracks, until corporate America recognizes that there is something more important at stake in all of this than feeding the greed of chief executives, and until conservatives understand that without equity, tolerance, and fair taxation democracy cannot stand.

For more than two centuries America has traveled a road that set it apart, that made our land a beacon lighting up a world too often afflicted by tyranny and darkness. We have kept that beacon shining despite a terrible civil war, world wars, home-grown extremism, and human frailty. Time and time again we have paid for liberty and freedom with blood.

Now the damage caused by two successive Presidents who were captive of their rigid limitations has threatened everything America's striven to attain. In a time of trouble, the search is on for scapegoats, and public workers are not the only candidates—we are being joined by the poor and the homeless, by minorities and immigrants.

In these past two centuries, other nations and other experiments in governing how people live together have appeared, flowered, and vanished, but America has persevered to reach the last decade of the twentieth century. We have not traveled all this far to see the flame extinguished by fear, intolerance, and selfishness.

The delegates you send to AFSCME's 30th International Convention next month have a daunting task. They must do far more than set the course for this union for the next two years. This time, a time of danger, your delegates must lay out a new vision for a better and stronger America: for a nation recommitted to the principles of tolerance and fairness, recommitted to the well-being of every man, woman, and child, whatever their race, creed, color, or zip code.

When our nation enters the twenty-first century and that beacon is blazing as brightly as ever before, we want to be able to say, together, that the men and women of AFSCME showed America the way.

Source: *Public Employee*, May–June 1992, pp. 2–3.

There is both an irony and a serious threat for our system of free collective bargaining in the inevitability of future strikes. If labor relations progress has clearly been evident, the public has also increased its expectations in this area. It has become increasingly less tolerant of work stoppages, even as organized labor in its relatively weakened recent condition has engaged in fewer of these, and it regularly shows itself as favoring greater governmental control over union activities.

Despite an ever-deeper penetration of governmental regulations (described in Chapter 3 and elsewhere in the pages that follow), our labor relations system—the public-sector obviously excepted—has thus far essentially remained in private hands. This preference for private decision making is consistent with the dominant values of our society, particularly the maximum freedom of action for both individuals and organizations. But the possibility that a tripartite labor relations system, with the government as a full-fledged participant, will ultimately supplant the present bipartite system can never be overlooked. Whether or not what is still "free collective bargaining" will be allowed to continue will depend entirely on our current system's ability to continue its progress sufficiently to satisfy the increasingly high level of public expectation. There is still much room for improvement in the relations between organized labor and the management community, and this fact makes the whole system as it currently exists a vulnerable one.

DISCUSSION QUESTIONS

1. "No one except union officers and union staff members would suffer one iota if unions were to be outlawed in the United States, and enormous numbers of people would gain immeasurably if this should happen." Discuss.

2. "There is no reason on earth why lower and even middle managers should not consider joining a labor union, and it is really just a fluke that they, at least to date, have not." Comment fully.

3. "From the labor point of view, there is an intrinsic unfairness in the fact that it is essentially only conflict that attracts attention from the mass media." How valid, in your opinion, is this statement?

4. "The blue collar world is the only natural habitat of unionism in the United States, and union failures to date outside of this sector prove this statement conclusively." Do you agree? Why or why not?

5. "Managers resist unions for a variety of entirely logical and rational reasons, and thus they can be expected to continue this opposition indefinitely, since the reasons will presumably continue to be logical and rational." Comment, with specifics.

6. More than a few public officials in recent years have argued that any police officer, firefighter, or sanitation worker who goes out on strike in

defiance of the law should be fired on the spot. How does such a viewpoint accord with yours?

7. Under what, if any, circumstances, would you personally consider joining a union?

8. It has occasionally been argued that the United States is, in the words of a major rubber industry executive, "experiencing the cult of the individual." Do you accept this position and, if so, do you think that its continuation would significantly hurt labor's efforts in the years immediately ahead?

MINICASES

#1 The White Collar Union Organizer

"I have nothing against unions, mind you, but just give me one good reason why I should sign up with you," an office worker tells Office Employees International Union organizer Nancy Rogers.

"Anytime the production workers in this company get more money through their union, we nonunion folks in the office do too, simply because the management doesn't want us to be tempted to become unionists. In fact, we might even be getting just a little bit extra so as to guarantee that we don't get any funny ideas.

"And more than that, everybody knows that unions are really just for manual workers. It's not appropriate for white collar people like us to join them, which is why, except for a few malcontents, you just don't see office workers in unions. Maybe some day conditions will change here, but right now I don't see that it will help me in any way to be bargained for by some outside union lawyer or union leader. In fact, it might even hurt because unions, as we all know, want equal pay for equal work and have no rewards for individual merit. I don't want to boast, but I'm a very hard worker now. I'd be crazy to strain myself if we had a union contract."

If you were Rogers, what would say in response to this employee?

#2 An Overture from a Business Agent

"As you know, the labor contract for the three unionized taxi companies in this city expires on Saturday night," Taxi Drivers Union business agent Monty Everest reminds taxi company owner Herbert King, "and since the centralized negotiations with the three of you have now collapsed, it looks like a strike is inevitable.

"But we like you. You're a gentleman who's always treated us fairly and with sensitivity, just like your dad did. Tell you what. Just give me $10,000 in cash and we'll merely stop work at one—or possibly both—of your competitors under what we'll call a 'selective strike.' Your guys can continue working and all you'll have to do is match the new master contract once we've negotiated it with the other firms. Your revenue won't stop at all; you'll probably get plenty of new business while the strike is on; and—who knows?—maybe one or both of the others won't even be able to survive the work stoppage and you'll be the winner on a permanent basis. You've got everything to gain and nothing to lose."

As King, how would you react to such an overture?

NOTES

[1]*New York Journal of Commerce,* February 7, 1851, as quoted in Neil W. Chamberlain, *The Labor Sector* (New York: McGraw-Hill, 1965), p. 341.

[2]Herbert Harris, *American Labor* (New Haven, Conn.: Yale University Press, 1939), pp. 126–27.

[3]Sinclair Lewis, *Babbitt* (New York: Harcourt Brace Jovanovich, 1922), p. 44. (Rights for the British Commonwealth excluding Canada have been granted by Jonathan Cape Limited, Publishers, London, England, on behalf of the Estate of Sinclair Lewis.)

[4]Albert A. Blum, "Management Paternalism and Collective Bargaining," *Personnel Administration,* XXVI (January–February 1963), p. 38.

[5]Unofficial data furnished by U.S. Department of Labor, Bureau of Labor Statistics.

[6]*Ibid.*

[7]AFL-CIO, Committee on the Evolution of Work, *The Changing Situation of Workers and Their Unions* (Washington, D.C.: AFL-CIO, 1985), p. 8.

[8]J. B. S. Hardman, *American Labor Dynamics* (New York: Harcourt Brace, 1928), p. 95.

[9]*Business Week,* May 31, 1969, p. 77.

[10]A. H. Raskin, "The Unions and Their Wealth," *Atlantic Monthly,* April 1962, p. 89.

[11]Wilfrid Sheed, "What Ever Happened to the Labor Movement?" *Atlantic,* July 1973, p. 69.

[12]*Business Week,* August 17, 1981, p. 28.

[13]Haynes Johnson and Nick Kotz, *The Unions* (Washington, D.C.: Washington Post Co., 1972), p. 175.

[14]*Ibid.,* p. 176.

[15]*International Teamster,* September 1960, p. 16.

[16]Thus, many longshoremen might well go without work during slack periods for weeks or even months at a time and in some cases—if protected by enough security—more or less permanently while still drawing the pay.

[17]*Trade Union Advisor,* February 18, 1992, pp. 1–4.

[18]*Wall Street Journal,* February 21, 1985, p. 1.

[19]*New York Times,* October 27, 1985, Sec. E, p. 4.

[20]A. H. Maslow, *Motivation and Personality* (New York: Harper & Row, 1954).

[21]The most timeless of these studies are E. Wight Bakke, "To Join or Not to Join," in E. Wight Bakke, Clark Kerr, and Charles W. Anrod, eds., *Unions, Management and the Public* (New York: Harcourt Brace Jovanovich, 1960), pp. 79–85; and Joel Seidman, Jack London, and Bernard Karsh, "Why Workers Join Unions," in *Annals of the American Academy of Political and Social Science,* 274, no. 84 (March 1951). See also Henry S. Farber and Daniel H. Saks, "Why Workers Want Unions: The Role of Relative Wages and Job Characteristics," in *Journal of Political Economy,* 88, no. 21 (1980), pp. 349–69. Also instructive on the subject is Jeanne M. Brett's "Why Employees Want Unions," in Kendrith M. Rowland, Gerald R. Ferris, and Jay L. Sherman, *Current Issues in Personnel Management,* 2nd ed. (Boston: Allyn & Bacon, 1983).

[22]Seidman, London, and Karsh, "Why Workers Join Unions."

[23]*Ibid.*

[24]E. Wight Bakke, *Mutual Survival: The Goal of Unions and Management* (New York: Harper & Row, 1946), p. 7.

[25]Not all employers lament the "outside" aspects of unionization. Many prefer the more detached viewpoints of international union representatives who *are* removed from the tensions and political considerations involved in day-by-day local labor relations. Some managers welcome, in addition, the stabilization of labor terms among otherwise competitive employers that frequently accompanies wider-scale bargaining. The terms "international" and "national" are used interchangeably in this volume, as indeed they are used in practice.

[26]The most exhaustive study on the subject of "dual loyalties" is that of Father Theodore Purcell, conducted in the mid-1950s. Interviewing 202 workers in various departments at Swift and Company, he discovered that whereas at least 79 percent felt a definite allegiance to the union as an institution, 92 percent felt allegiance to the company. "Allegiance" was construed as an attitude of approval of the overall objectives of each institution, rather than strict loyalty. See Theodore V. Purcell, *Blue Collar Man* (Cambridge, Mass.: Harvard University Press, 1960); and also *The Worker Speaks His Mind on Company and Union* (Cambridge, Mass.: Harvard University Press, 1953), by the same author. More recently, a 1975 poll of several thousand Burlington Northern Railroad employees (made in this case by the management itself) showed that workers with a "favorable attitude" toward their union also had a favorable attitude toward their boss, to a very large extent.

[27]The late Benjamin M. Selekman was justifiably considered one of the foremost theoreticians in this field, although he generally portrayed "bargaining relationships" and not merely the management portion of these relationships. The exposition that follows bears a strong indebtedness to his work (although it departs from it on several major points), and particularly to his "Framework for Study of Cases in Labor Relations," in *Problems in Labor Relations,* 3rd ed., coauthored with S. H. Fuller, T. Kennedy, and J. M. Baitsell (New York: McGraw-Hill, 1964), pp. 1–11.

[28]Jack Barbash, "Values in Industrial Relations: The Case of the Adversary Principle," in *Proceedings of the Thirty-Third Annual Meeting, Industrial Relations Research Association,* September 5–7, 1980, p. 1.

[29]*Ibid.,* pp. 2–3.

[30]*Business Week,* November 9, 1981, p. 44.

[31]Chapter 9 will inspect another form of "cooperation": Quality of Work Life programs, whose ultimate acceptability to labor-management relations in general has yet to be determined.

[32]*Wall Street Journal,* March 4, 1992, p. A4.

[33]J. Joseph Loewenberg and Michael H. Moskow, *Collective Bargaining in Government* (Englewood Cliffs, N.J.: Prentice Hall, 1972), p. 3.

[34]*Ibid.,* p. 57.

[35]Thomas R. Brooks, *Toil and Trouble,* 2nd rev. ed. (New York: Dell, 1971), p. 306.

[36]*Wall Street Journal,* November 7, 1974, p. 29.

[37]Jerome T. Barrett and Ira B. Lobel, "Public Sector Strikes—Legislative and Court Treatment," *Monthly Labor Review,* 97, no. 9 (September 1974), p. 19.

[38]U.S. Department of Labor, Bureau of Labor Statistics, *Report 1727,* 1972.

[39]Marvin J. Levine and Eugene C. Hagburg, *Labor Relations in the Public Sector* (Salt Lake City: Brighton, 1979), p. xv.

[40]*New York Times,* September 22, 1974, Sec. E, p. 2.

[41]*Wall Street Journal,* November 30, 1981, p. 34.

SELECTED REFERENCES

Aaron, Benjamin, et al., eds., *Public-Sector Bargaining* (2nd ed.), Industrial Relations Research Association Series. Washington, D.C.: Bureau of National Affairs, 1988.

Bok, Derek C., and John T. Dunlop, *Labor and the American Community.* New York: Simon & Schuster, 1970.

Coleman, Charles J., *Managing Labor Relations in the Public Sector.* San Francisco: Jossey-Bass, 1990.

Dworkin, James B., *Owners versus Players: Baseball and Collective Bargaining.* Boston: Auburn House, 1981.

Freeman, Richard B., and James L. Medhoff, *What Do Unions Do?* New York: Basic Books, 1984.

Friedman, Allen, and Ted Schwarz, *Power and Greed.* New York: Franklin Watts, 1989.

Gagala, Ken, *Union Organizing and Staying Organized.* Reston, Va.: Reston, 1983.

Geoghegan, Thomas, *Which Side Are You On?* New York: Farrar, Straus & Giroux, 1991.

Hoerr, John P., *And the Wolf Finally Came, The Decline of the American Steel Industry.* Pittsburgh: University of Pittsburgh Press, 1988.

Kerr, Clark, and Paul D. Staudohar, eds., *Industrial Relations in a New Age.* San Francisco: Jossey-Bass, 1986.

Kochan, Thomas A., *Challenges and Choices Facing American Labor.* Cambridge, Mass.: MIT Press, 1985.

Lipset, Seymour Martin, ed., *Unions in Transition.* San Francisco: Institute for Contemporary Studies, 1986.

Nesbitt, Murray B., *Labor Relations in the Federal Government Service.* Washington, D.C.: Bureau of National Affairs, 1976.

Puette, William J., *Through Jaundiced Eyes: How the Media View Organized Labor.* Ithaca, N.Y.: ILR Press, Cornell University, 1992.

Quaglieri, Philip L., *America's Labor Leaders.* Lexington, Mass.: Lexington Books, 1989.

Shostak, Arthur B., *Robust Unionism: Innovation in the Labor Movement.* Ithaca, N.Y.: ILR Press, Cornell University, 1991.

Somers, Gerald G., ed., *Collective Bargaining: Contemporary American Experience.* Madison, Wis.: Industrial Relations Research Association, 1980.

Staudohar, Paul D., *The Sports Industry and Collective Bargaining.* Ithaca, N.Y.: ILR Press, Cornell University, 1986.

Sterrett, Grace, and Antone Aboud, *The Right to Strike in Public Employment* (2nd ed., rev.). Ithaca, N.Y.: ILR Press, Cornell University, 1982.

The Historical Framework

- Why the Great Depression generated notable gains for organized labor

- The rise of the Congress of Industrial Organizations as a rival to the AFL

- What World War II did and didn't do for the labor movement

- Factors behind the 1955 AFL-CIO merger

- Labor in the four decades since the merger

- The record of unions toward minorities

- Labor and the increasing self-awareness of women

As is true of other established disciplines, there is still some controversy as to the returns inherent in the study of history. For every Shakespeare asserting that "what is past is prologue," or a Santayana who proclaims that "those who do not understand history are condemned to repeat its mistakes," there is a Henry Ford declaring that "history is a pack of tricks that we play on the dead" and that the field is, in fact, "bunk."

No one can claim to understand present-day institutions, however, without having at least some basic knowledge of their roots. It would make a considerable difference to those who are either hopeful or fearful that labor unions will ultimately fade from the industrial scene, for example, if unions were purely a phenomenon of the last few years (and thus potentially destined for extinction when environmental conditions change), rather than being—as they are—organizations of relatively long standing in the economy. (Exhibit 2-1 indicates the ripe years of one union, as well as the UMWA's interest in its own antecedents; and, as the following pages will show, the Mine Workers are far from the oldest of American unions. Exhibit 2-2 shows an interest in *its* history by a somewhat less ancient labor organization, the Air Line Pilots Association.)

Similarly, only by recognizing what workers have expected of their unions in the past is one entitled even to begin to pass judgment on the present performance of organized labor. This chapter thus attempts to provide the reader with a necessary working knowledge of American labor history, as union membership rose (and sometimes fell) in the manner depicted in Exhibit 2-3.

EXHIBIT 2-1

You've Got To Know Where You've Been To Know Where You're Going

As UMWA members, we're proud of our history. Now, UMWA history comes alive in two new works celebrating the union's centennial.

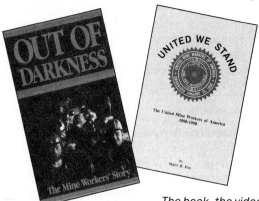

United We Stand: The United Mine Workers of America, 1890-1990 by Maier B. Fox is a complete history of the union's first 100 years. Exhaustively researched and six years in the making, this 600-page hardbound volume was introduced at the union's centennial convention in September, and now is available for sale to UMWA members and the public.

The book, the video and the soundtrack cassette are now available at special prices for union members.

Out of Darkness: The Mine Workers' Story is an exciting new video by Academy Award-winning director Barbara Kopple (*Harlan County, USA*) and award-winning video director and editor Bill Davis. Extensive historical film footage, photographs and first-hand accounts of events in our history from those who lived them are intertwined with dramatic sequences from the unprecedented fight at Pittston. Supplemented by an original soundtrack by Tom Juravich, this 100-minute video received a five-minute standing ovation at its September 17 premier at the UMWA centennial convention.

Yes, send me:

☐ **Out of Darkness**
(videocassette, VHS only)

☐ **Songs from *Out of Darkness***
(soundtrack cassette)

☐ **United We Stand**
(book)

Make checks and money orders payable to: ***The Labor History and Cultural Foundation***, and mail to:
P.O. Box 66500
Washington, D.C. 20035-6500

Enclosed is:
☐ $25 (all union members)
☐ $30 (other individuals and institutions)

☐ $12.50

☐ $20 (UMWA members only)
☐ $27.50 (other labor union members)
☐ $34.95 (individuals and institutions)

$ _____ Total enclosed
(Price includes shipping and handling)

Name _____

Local union _____ District _____

Address _____

_____

(allow four to six weeks for delivery)

Source: United Mine Workers Journal, November 1990, back cover.

EXHIBIT 2-2

Prints of *Air Line Pilot*'s 60th Anniversary cover and
the ALPA Code of Ethics, both suitable for
framing, are available for $4 each including
shipping and handling.

Send your requests to:
Air Line Pilot Cover, 535 Herndon Parkway
P.O. Box 1169, Herndon, VA 22070

Source: Air Line Pilot, July 1992, p. 56.

THE EIGHTEENTH CENTURY:
GENESIS OF THE AMERICAN LABOR MOVEMENT

If labor unions connote *permanent* employee associations that have as their primary goal the preservation or improvement of employment conditions, there were no such institutions in America until the closing years of the eighteenth century. Concerted actions of workers in the form of strikes and slowdowns were not unknown to the colonial period, but these disturbances were, without exception, spontaneous efforts. They were conducted on the spur of the moment over temporary grievances, such as withholding of wages. Generally unsuccessful, they were never undertaken by anything resembling permanent organizations.

EXHIBIT 2-3 Trade Union Membership in the United States for Selected Years

1836	300,000
1865	200,000
1878	50,000
1897	447,000
1904	2,073,000
1917	3,014,000
1920	5,100,000
1930	3,400,000
1933	2,973,000
1941	10,200,000
1953	16,300,000
1965	18,250,000
1975	22,200,000
1993 (est.)	17,000,000

Figures are based on data provided by the U.S. Bureau of Labor Statistics.

Given the dimensions of the labor movement today and the variety of seemingly compelling reasons why workers have attached themselves to it, this total absence of labor unions for well over a century calls for an immediate explanation.

In those years of simple handicraft organization, there were, in fact, at least four forces at work that served to weaken any motivation that workers might otherwise have had for joining together on a long-term basis.

In the first place, the market for the employer's product was both local and essentially noncompetitive. Workers were thus allowed close social ties with the owner, often performing their work in the owner's home. In addition, they could maintain a comparatively relaxed pace of production in such an atmosphere.

Second, both the laws of supply and demand and government regulations allowed employees a large measure of job security at this time. Labor of all kinds, and particularly skilled craft labor, was in short supply in the colonies. A series of colonial labor laws calling for apprenticeship service prior to many kinds of employment and carefully circumscribing the conditions under which employees could be discharged offered further protection to jobholders.

Third, the existence of ample cheap land in the West meant that the dissatisfied artisan or mechanic could always move on should either local adversity or the spirit of adventure strike. Many workers did migrate to the ever-expanding frontier, allowing even more advantageous employment conditions for those who remained: Incomes increased all the more in the East, to the point where, by some estimates, wages were twice those paid to workers in Britain.

Finally, the low ratio of labor to natural resources in the frontier nation helped ensure that price rises would lag behind the wage increases.

Ironically, however, the development of the frontier laid the groundwork for the birth of bona fide labor organizations. An expanded system of transportation built around canals and turnpikes was simultaneously linking the new nation's communities and allowing the capitalists of the late eighteenth century to enlarge their product markets into the beginnings of nationwide ones. The merchant who was unwilling or unable to respond to the challenge was left by the wayside as competitive pressures forced each businessperson to find cost-cutting devices in the newly unsheltered atmosphere. The more imaginative employers located such devices: To decrease labor costs, they introduced women and children to their workplaces, farmed out work to prison inmates, and generally cut the wages of males who remained in their employ. For good measure, they frequently increased the hours in the workday (at no increase in pay), minutely subdivided the work into more easily assimilated (but commensurately more repetitive and monotonous) operations, and hired aggressive overseers to enforce newly tightened work standards.

The less-skilled worker could react to these unwelcome changes by moving to the frontier. Not having invested much in the way of time or education in learning the current job, he or she might also attempt to move occupationally to more desirable kinds of work. The skilled worker, on the other hand, had mastered the craft through years of apprenticeship and was no longer occupationally mobile.

Some skilled craftsmen did move to the frontier. But the extension of the product market meant that their new masters were still not free to ignore labor cost-cutting methods; suits tailored in Ohio competed now with those made in Boston. Nor could the craftsmen count any longer on advancing into the class of masters themselves; the scope of manufacturing was necessarily greater, and to enter the employer ranks it now took capital on a scale not ordinarily available to most wage earners. Basically, the skilled workers' alternatives were to passively accept the wage cuts, the competition of nonapprenticed labor, and the harsh working conditions or to join in collective action against such employer innovations. Increasingly, by the end of the eighteenth century, they chose the latter course of action.

THE FIRST UNIONS AND THEIR LIMITED SUCCESSES

These early trade unions—individually encompassing shoemakers, printers, carpenters, tailors, and artisans of similar skill levels—waged blunt attacks on the changes brought about by the extension of markets. Their members agreed upon a wage level and pledged not to work for any employer who refused to pay this amount. They also bound themselves not to work alongside any employee who did not receive the basic minimum or who had not served the customary period of apprenticeship for the trade. In addition, most of these craft unions attempted to negotiate closed-shop agreements, whereby only those who were union members in the first place would be employed at all.

Generally proving themselves willing to strike, if need be, in support of their demands, the early unions were at times surprisingly successful in achieving them. And although work stoppages of the day were typically both peaceful and short in duration, the new worker aggressiveness they symbolized was sufficient to bring on considerable countervailing action from the employers.

The masters turned to two sources: organization in employers' associations and aid from the courts. Societies of otherwise competitive master masons, carpenters, shoemakers, printers, and other employers of skilled labor were quickly established in most urban areas where union activity was pronounced, for the purposes of holding down wages and destroying labor combinations wherever these existed. Attacking on a second front, the masters also turned to the judges and urged prosecution of their workers' organizations as illegal conspiracies in restraint of trade. The jurists were quickly convinced: The Journeyman Cordwainers (shoemakers) of Philadelphia were found guilty of joining in such a conspiracy by striking in 1806, and within the next decade a variety of similar court cases had also resulted in shattering defeats for the worker organizations. Not until 1842, indeed, with the famous *Commonwealth* v. *Hunt* decision in Massachusetts that strikes could be legal if they were undertaken for legal purposes, did the judges even begin to modify the harsh tenets of the "Cordwainer doctrine" when requested to rule on union affairs by employers.

If the criminal conspiracy doctrine and the varying successes of the employer associations crimped the growth of the incipient labor movement, moreover, an economic event temporarily sent unionism into almost total collapse. In 1819, a major nationwide depression occurred and, as was to be no less the case in later nineteenth-century periods of economic reversal, labor organizations could not withstand its effects. Union demands that might be translated into employer concessions when the demand for labor was high could be safely dismissed by the masters with jobs now at a premium. Employers once again cut rates with impunity and showed little hesitation in dismissing workers who had joined unions in earlier years. Under the circumstances, the worker cry was "Every man for himself," rather than "In union there is strength," and virtually no union could, or did, survive mass desertion.

REVIVAL, INNOVATION, AND DISILLUSIONMENT

The return of economic health to the country by late 1822 was paralleled by a revival of unionism. Their bargaining power restored, skilled employees in the trades that had previously been organized once again turned to union activity.

More significantly, the process of unionization now spread to new frontiers, both geographic and occupational. Aroused by the same merchant-capitalist threats to living standards and status that had previously given incentive for collective bargaining to their East Coast counterparts, craftsmen in such newly developed cities as Buffalo, Pittsburgh, Cincinnati, and Louisville established trade union locals at this time. And new (and widely publicized) victories of the skilled worker unions in both the older and newer cities had by the mid-1830s generated the formation of unions among such previously nonunion groups as stonecutters, hatters, and painters.

These years also saw other innovations made by organized labor. Prior to 1827, each local craft union had operated on its own as a totally separate organization. In that year, however, representatives of fifteen different trades in the city of Philadelphia formed the country's first central labor union, for joint action on a citywide basis. The original goal of the Philadelphia group was a ten-hour day for its trade union members, but this was soon displaced as a major demand: In 1828, the organization converted itself into a political party, endorsing "workingmen's candidates"—with only limited success—for public office.

Workingmen's parties were also organized in other eastern states in this period of Jacksonian democracy. Political associations of workers seeking such goals as universal free education and the abolition of imprisonment for debt arose in New York, Massachusetts, and Delaware. Most of their objectives were soon realized, but the workingmen's parties themselves— often torn by internal dissension and always confronted by competition from the two major national parties—were generally short lived.

The original form that the Philadelphia "city central" had taken—as a purely economic joint undertaking of several trade unions in a single city—had a more lasting influence on workers in other locations. Similar bodies were quickly set up throughout the East and, despite the frequent divergence of opinion among the various trades represented, showed remarkable staying power. By the mid-1830s, at least twelve cities had such "city centrals," most of which provided their affiliated local unions with financial and moral encouragement in times of strikes and coordinated such ancillary activities as the promotion of union-made goods.

Even the beginnings of national worker organization were attempted at this time. In 1834, delegates from the city centrals of several eastern cities met in New York to form the National Trades' Union. This pioneering workers' project quickly proved fruitless—industry had not yet itself significantly organized on a national basis and would not for three more decades—but the scope of the NTU's activities nonetheless symbolizes the ambitiousness of the worker representatives involved.

Indeed, the initiative displayed by leaders of both the city centrals and the local unions had led to impressive union membership totals by 1836. It has been estimated that there were in the country as a whole in that year 300,000 unionized workers, constituting 6.5 percent of the labor force.[1] One can only guess to what heights the total figures would have risen had not the following year brought a national economic depression that was even more severe than the business slump of 1819.

The hard times that began in 1837 were to last for almost thirteen years. In the face of them, trade union activity vanished almost as completely as it had two decades earlier. Moreover, a new factor now arose to compound union ills: The 1840s saw waves of immigrants—themselves often the victims of economic diversity in such countries as Ireland, Germany, and England—enter the United States. American business conditions by themselves had been sufficient to wipe out most unions of the day, but this new source of job competition and low wages ensured that not even the strongest of unions could endure.

Now so severely frustrated in their economic actions and distrustful of the free-enterprise system for having failed to safeguard their interests, some workers transferred their energies to a series of ambitious political schemes for redesigning the economy. "Associationists" set up socialistic agricultural communities; George Henry Evans preached the virtues of "land reform" through direct political action by workingmen ("Vote Yourself a Farm"); and still other advocates of a new social order promulgated producers' cooperatives—employee-owned industrial institutions—as the workingman's salvation.

None of these programs succeeded, however. As Dulles has observed, they did not "in any way meet the needs of labor. In spite of the enthusiastic propaganda, the answer to industrialization did not lie in an attempt to escape from it."[2]

THE LAYING OF THE FOUNDATION FOR MODERN UNIONISM AND SOME MIXED PERFORMANCES WITH IT

With the return of prosperity in 1850, unions once again became a factor to be reckoned with. Profiting from the past, they eschewed political diversions, concentrated on such now traditional goals as higher wages, shorter workdays, and increased job security and regained much of their former membership.

The first major national unions, often superseding the economic functions of the city centrals, were also established at this time. Although the "Golden Age" of American railroading still lay ahead, the construction of the first complex rail systems was now accelerating. As a result, not only were product markets once more widening but so too were labor markets, bringing workers within the same crafts and industries into direct economic competition with each other. National coordination to standardize wages, working conditions, membership rules, and bargaining demands was deemed necessary by labor leaders; the alternative was cutthroat competition among individual local unions, eager for new members and expanded work opportunities and therefore willing to undercut the terms of other locals (to the employer's distinct advantage). The International Typographical Union, the country's oldest permanent national, dates from 1852. By 1860, at least fifteen other crafts had organized on a national basis.

The 1861 advent of the Civil War brought a new spurt in union membership growth, to a post-1836 high of over 200,000 unionists by the end of hostilities in 1865. Some of this organizational success was due to the labor shortages brought on by military mobilization: The economy's demand for labor commensurately increased, thus enlarging labor's bargaining power and union economic gains. There were undoubtedly at least two other reasons, however: (1) wartime inflation always threatened to counteract the wage increases achieved by unions, and many workers (somewhat unsuccessfully) looked to collective bargaining as a force for staving off this menace; and (2) organized labor was further helped by the prolabor sentiments of President Lincoln, who firmly resisted employer and public pressure to intervene in the occasional wartime strikes and instead offered as his opinion that "labor is the superior of capital and deserves much the higher consideration."

At war's end, however, the labor movement still comprised less than 2 percent of the country's labor force (as against 6.5 percent in 1836) and had yet to make any real penetration into the factories of the land and their huge organizing potential. But the foundation for the unionism of the next seventy years had now been laid. Few skilled-worker types were totally unrepresented by unions in 1865: More than 200 local unions, individually encompassing such widely divergent craftsmen as cigar makers, plumbers, and barrel makers, were founded in the war years alone. In addition, the logical necessity of forming *national* unions had now been almost universally recognized by labor leaders, and some thirty new ones had been added to the several that had preceded the war. And labor had achieved, through Lincoln, at least a measure of government support for its right to strike.

Labor's momentum, moreover, was sustained in immediate postwar years. The war-generated nationwide prosperity continued virtually unabated until 1873 and, aided by its favorable economic conditions (as in earlier business booms), labor's bargaining strength again increased. New members were attracted by announcements of new union gains, but there were now also other reasons for the increased membership totals. The broader organizational foundations that had been laid prior to 1865, particularly in the multiplication of national unions, allowed both more efficient and more varied organizing campaigns. Moreover, the post–Civil War period unleashed formidable threats to the workingman in the form of (1) accelerated waves of immigrants (increasingly, now, from southern and eastern Europe) who were willing to work for low wages; (2) changing technology, with the machine downgrading many skill requirements and allowing the employer to substitute unskilled labor for craftsmen and women for men; and (3) the continued widening of the gap between wages and prices that had begun in the wartime years. Workers thus had more incentive to join in collective bargaining, and acted upon it.

On the other hand, not every union shared in these gains. Particularly unsuccessful, in fact, was the new Molders national union, whose embittered president, William Sylvis, now turned away from "pure and simple" collective bargaining to espouse cooperative foundries. He was totally convinced that workers "must adopt a system which will divide the *profits* of labor among those who produce them," and was soon instrumental in the establishment of a number of producers' cooperatives.

These undertakings proved no more successful than they had in the 1840s, however. By 1870, most of the worker-owned associations had been forced by competitive pressures to cut wages, hire lower-cost labor, and—in general—act very much like the management-run business that Sylvis had so lamented.

Sylvis then transferred his energies to a new organization, which had been founded in 1866. The National Labor Union, riding the crest of union optimism at the close of the war, constituted the first major attempt at uniting all national unions, city centrals, and locals into a single central federation of American labor since the ill-fated National Trades' Union of 1834. Its first leaders had unsuccessfully urged legislative enactment of the eight-hour working day. They had also sought, again without tangible success, such further political goals as currency reform and women's suffrage.

Sylvis drew the organization even further from economic action to such new political objectives as the reservation of public lands for actual settlers only and abolition of the convict labor system. But the National Labor Union could not sustain membership enthusiasm with a credo that was so far removed from worker pocketbooks; one by one, its constituent labor organizations deserted it, and by 1872 the NLU had passed from the scene.

The failures of the cooperative and political movements were harbingers of more wide-sweeping labor disasters. Business collapsed in 1873, beginning a new period of deep depression that lasted for more than five years. In its wake, most of the local unions (as well as the city centrals) once more disappeared. Many of the nationals fared no better, but the greater financial resources and more diversified memberships of these broader organizations did allow them to offer greater resistance to the slump; not only did eleven of the nationals, in fact, weather these years but eight new nationals were established during this time. Consequently, for the first time, a depression did not completely stop unionization. Nonetheless, five sixths of total union membership did erode in the 1873–1878 period; only 50,000 unionists remained in 1878.

Encouraged by the depression-caused weakening of unions, employers also turned—in the 1870s—to weapons of their own, in an all-out attack on what was left of organized labor. Acting both singly and through employer associations, they engaged in frequent lockouts, hired spies to ferret out union sympathizers, circulated the names of such sympathizers to fellow employers through so-called blacklists, summarily discharged labor "agitators," and engaged the services of strikebreakers on a widespread scale.

The results of these efforts varied. Most of the labor organizations that were strong enough to withstand the depression could also frustrate the employer onslaughts. But there was at least one notable effect of the management campaign. Retaliating in kind to the quality of employer opposition (as well as to the widespread unemployment of the times), both unionists and nonunionized workers engaged in actions that for bitterness and violence were unequaled in American history. A secret society of anthracite miners, the Molly Maguires, terrorized the coal fields of Pennsylvania in a series of widely publicized murders and acts of arson. Railroad strikes paralyzed transportation in such major cities as Baltimore, Pittsburgh, and Chicago and, with mob rule typically replacing organized leadership as these ran their course, were most often ended only with federal troops being called out to terminate mass pillaging and bloodshed. Public opinion was almost always hostile to such activities, and lacking this support the demonstrations could not succeed. It is probably also true that employers were more easily enabled, by the general resentment directed toward worker groups for these actions, to gain still another weapon in their battle against unions: The labor injunction, first applied by the courts during a railway strike at this time, was to be quite freely granted—as Chapter 3 will bring out—by the judges for more than five decades thereafter.

THE RISE AND FALL OF THE KNIGHTS OF LABOR

Prosperity finally returned to the country in 1878, and with it union growth once again resumed. Over the next ten years, sixty-two new national unions (or "international" unions, as many of these were now calling themselves, in recognition of their first penetration of the Canadian labor market) were established. Locals and city centrals also resumed their proliferation. Even more significantly, the early 1880s marked American labor's most notable attempt to form a single, huge "general" union, the Noble and Holy Order of the Knights of Labor.

The Knights had actually been established before the depression. In 1869, a group of tailors had founded the organization's first local in Philadelphia. Its avowed goal was "to initiate good men of all callings"—unionists as well as those not already in unions, craftsmen, and (unlike virtually all other labor organizations of the day) totally unskilled workers. It particularly desired such a broad base of membership to "eliminate the weakness and evils of isolated effort or association, and useless and crushing competition resulting therefrom." But the Knights' definition of "good men of all callings" was not all-inclusive; the founders specifically wanted "no drones, no lawyers, no bankers, no doctors, no professional politicians."

Surviving the depression as a secret society, the Knights abolished their assortment of rituals and passwords in the late 1870s and thenceforth openly recruited in all directions.

Such aggressiveness, combined with what now was the normal increase in union bargaining strength amid general economic prosperity, allowed a slow but steady growth of the order's membership. There were roughly 9,000 Knights in 1878 and over 70,000 by 1884. Then, following a major 1885 strike victory against the Wabash Railroad, the growth became spectacular. Workers of all conceivable types clamored for membership, and by mid-1886 there were 700,000 people in the wide-sweeping organization.

The aftermath of the Wabash strike was to be the high-water mark for the Knights, however. The leaders of the order proved wholly unable to cope with the gigantic membership increase, and as the new Knights sought to duplicate the Wabash triumph with one ill-timed and undisciplined strike after another, a steady stream of union defeats ensued. The very diversity of backgrounds among the members also drained the effectiveness of the organization: The old skilled trade unionists found little in common with the shopkeepers, farmers, and self-employed mechanics who shared membership with them, and they rapidly deserted the order. Nor did the presence of thousands of unskilled and semiskilled industrial workers, often of widely varying first-generation American backgrounds, add anything to group solidarity. Greatly discouraged by the schisms within their organization, many such workers soon followed the path set by the skilled tradesmen and left it.

Although each of the factors above was undoubtedly influential in the Knights' rapid decline after 1886—to 100,000 members by 1890 and to virtual extinction by 1900—still another factor was probably even more responsible for the fall of the order. The system of values held by the Knights' leadership was considerably at variance with the values of rank-and-file Knights. For all their diversity and essential lack of discipline, the latter could (employers and the self-employed always excepted) at least unite on the desirability of higher wages, shorter hours, and improved working conditions. Under Knights president Terrence V. Powderly, however, these goals were significantly minimized in favor of such "social" goals as the establishment of consumer and producer cooperatives, temperance, and land reform. Even the strike weapon, despite its great success against the Wabash management and its popular appeal to Knights' members, was viewed with disdain by Powderly to the end; he considered it both expensive and overly militant. Why was this Knight different from all other Knights? The historical records lack a definitive explanation. But whatever the reason the philosophical gap between leadership and followers was thus a wide one, and Powderly was forced to pay the supreme penalty for perpetuating it. Ultimately, he was left with no one to lead.

By the late 1880s, a wholly new organization—the American Federation of Labor—had won over the mainstream of the Knights' skilled-trade unionists, and the once vast array of other membership types, disillusioned, was again outside the ranks of organized labor.

THE FORMATION OF THE AFL AND ITS PRAGMATIC MASTER PLAN

Almost from its inception in 1881, the American Federation of Labor was a highly realistic, no-nonsense organization.

Even in that year, the more than 100 representatives of skilled-worker unions who gathered at Pittsburgh to form what was originally entitled the Federation of Organized Trades and Labor Unions included many dissident Knights, disenchanted with Powderly's "one big union" concept and political-action emphasis. The rebels were already convinced that the future of their highly skilled constituents lay completely outside the catchall Knights. They recognized that such craftsmen possessed considerably greater bargaining power than other, less-skilled types of Knights members because of their relative indispensability to employers. Consequently, they were anxious to exercise this power *directly* in union-management negotiations. Powderly's idealistic and somewhat hazy legislative goals might be appropriate for workers who could not better their lot in any other way. But the goals seemed to many FOTLU founders to be a poor substitute for strike threats and other forms of economic action when undertaken by unionists who were not so easily replaceable. Well versed in American labor history, these early advocates of an exclusive federation of craft unions were also well aware of the fates of earlier organizations that had subordinated economic goals to political ones.

However logical these arguments for a more homogeneous and "pure collective bargaining" federation of skilled craft unions may seem to present-day readers, the FOTLU was not immediately a smashing success. It was initially torn by both personality and philosophical schisms. More important, the built-in weaknesses of the Knights had not yet become widely apparent to the large body of American craftsmen; paradoxically, the craft confederation's ultimate triumph had to await the first real victories—and then the rapid downfall—of the Powderly organization.

Indeed, the basic issue that was to split irrevocably the craft unions from the Knights involved the jurisdiction of the national unions themselves. The dramatic spurt in Knights membership following the 1885 Wabash victory threatened to entirely submerge the craft "trade assemblies" and the parent national craft unions, which had thus far retained their separate identities within the order, in a throng of numerically superior semiskilled and unskilled workers. Nor would Powderly, never the compromiser and now at the pinnacle of his short-lived success, grant any assurances that the Knights would not violate the jurisdictions of the existing national unions. Rubbing salt into the nationals' wounds, the Knights' leadership even went so far now as to organize rival national unions and to try to absorb both these and the established nationals into the "mixed" assembly and the district structures of the order.

The rupture was soon complete. In 1886, representatives of twenty-five of the strongest national unions met at Columbus, Ohio, transformed the somewhat moribund FOTLU into the American Federation of Labor, unanimously elected Samuel Gompers of the Cigar Makers as the AFL's first president, and thereby ushered in a new era for the American labor movement. Despite their moment of glory, the Knights were soon to begin their rapid decline—with some of the impetus toward their dissolution, to be sure, being directly lent by the secession of the skilled-worker nationals. For the next fifty years, the basic tenets of the AFL were to remain unchallenged by the mainstream of labor in this country.

Samuel Gompers, the Jewish immigrant from England who was to continue as president of the federation for all except one of the next thirty-eight years,[3] has frequently been referred to as a supreme pragmatist, a leader convinced that any supposed "truth" was above all to be tested by its practical consequences. Careful consideration of the basic principles upon which he and his lieutenants launched the AFL does nothing to weaken the validity of this description. Essentially, Gompers had five such principles.

In the first place, the national unions were to be autonomous within the new federation: "The American Federation of Labor," Gompers proudly announced, "avoids the fatal rock upon which all previous attempts to effect the unity of the working class have split, by leaving to each body or affiliated organization the complete management of its own affairs, especially in its own particular trade affairs."[4] The leader of a highly successful national himself, Gompers felt particularly strongly that questions of admission, apprenticeship, bargaining policy, and the like should be left strictly to those directly involved with them.

Second, the AFL would charter only one national union in each trade jurisdiction. This concept of "exclusive jurisdiction" stemmed mainly from the unpleasant experiences of the nationals with rival unions chartered by the Knights. It was also, however, due to Gompers's deep concern that such competitive union situations would give the employer undue bargaining advantages by allowing him to pit one warring union against another.

Third, the AFL would at all costs avoid long-run reformist goals and concentrate instead only upon immediate wage-centered gains. As noted above, its founders were determined not to suffer the fates of earlier, reform-centered organizations: "We have no ultimate ends," asserted Gompers's colleague Adolph Strasser on the occasion of his testimony before a congressional committee at this time. "We are going on from day to day. We are fighting only for immediate objects—objects that can be realized in a few years."

Fourth, the federation would avoid any permanent alliances with the existing political parties and, instead, "reward labor's friends and punish labor's enemies." (A century later, these words had hardly been forgotten, as Exhibit 2-4, the handiwork of the journal of the Laborers Union, shows.) Gompers was willing, however, to accept help for the AFL from any quarter, with only one major exception: He had at one time been a Marxian Socialist, but familiarity had bred contempt and, long before 1886, he had permanently broken with his old colleagues. At the 1903 AFL convention, he was to announce to the relative handful of Socialists present: "Economically, you are unsound; socially, you are wrong; and industrially, you are an impossibility."[5] To the end, Gompers's philosophy was firmly embedded in the capitalistic system.

Finally, Gompers placed considerable reliance on the strike weapon as a legitimate and effective means of achieving the wages, hours, and conditions sought by his unionists. Shortly before his election to the AFL presidency in 1886, he had been one of the leaders of a general strike designed to obtain the eight-hour day. More than 300,000 workers had participated in this action, and almost two thirds of them had achieved their objective through it. Gompers's own Cigar Makers, too, had rarely hesitated to resort to strikes when bargaining impasses had been reached. And, generally speaking, these demonstrations of economic strength had also been successful.

Profiting from the lessons of history, Gompers's federation thus represented a realistic attempt to adjust to an economic system that had become deeply embedded in the United States. National union autonomy, exclusive jurisdiction, "pure and simple" collective bargaining, the avoidance of political entanglements, and the use of strikes where feasible—these proven sources of union strength were to be the hallmarks of the new unionism. The federation would provide the definition of jurisdictional boundaries for each national and give help to all such constituent unions

Exhibit 2–4

66Reward Our Friends, Punish Our Enemies!99

—*Samuel Gompers*

Register & Vote!

Source: The Laborer, July–August 1984, back cover.

in their organizing, bargaining, lobbying, and public relations endeavors. But it would otherwise allow a free hand to its national union members as they pursued their individual goals. And the stress was to be on the needs of skilled workers, not those of "good men of all callings," as the Knights had placed it: Some semiskilled and unskilled workers within a relatively few industries (such as mine workers and electricians, because of the strategic power of their national unions) were encouraged to join, but basically the AFL made no great efforts to organize workers with less than "skilled" callings and was to admit them only if they organized themselves and had no jurisdictional disputes with craft unions.

So successful did this master plan prove to be that it was not until the mid-1930s that its logic was in any way seriously questioned.

THE EARLY YEARS OF THE AFL AND SOME MIXED RESULTS

Even in the short run, the policies of the AFL were so attractive to the nationals that within a few years virtually all of them had become members of the new organization. Given this reception, the Gompers federation grew steadily, if not spectacularly: It counted 140,000 members in 1886; by 1889, the figure had risen to 278,000.

It is also noteworthy that the economic depression that swept the country between 1893 and 1896 did not drastically deplete union membership totals, as had been the case in earlier hard times. The new principles of Gompers, reflected at both the federation and national levels, gave labor significant staying power. Moreover, the now centralized control held by the nationals over their locals both lessened the danger that local monies would be dissipated in ill-advised strikes and provided the locals with what were normally sufficient funds for officially authorized strikes.

On the other hand, organized labor still had a severe problem to contend with in the 1890s: the deep desire of the nation's industrialists, now themselves strongly centralized in this era of trusts and other forms of consolidation, to regain unilateral control of employee affairs. Not since the 1870s had the forces of management been as determined, as formidable, or, particularly in the case of two widely heralded strikes of the time—waged against the predecessor of the United States Steel Corporation, the Carnegie Steel Company, at Homestead, Pennsylvania, in 1892 and against the Pullman Palace Car Company and various railroads in many places in 1894—as successful in opposing unionism. In both cases, each marked by considerable violence, the defeats were crushing ones for organized labor.

Other managers in turn, impressed by these two employer triumphs and at times alarmed by what they felt was the overly belligerent stance of the AFL unions, also became more aggressive in their battles with labor. Employers in the metal trades formed a Metal Trades Association to defeat the Machinists in their quest for a nine-hour day and then adopted a policy of "no outside interference" with their company operations. Builders in

Chicago, no less strongly united, completely ousted their workers' union representatives and regained full control of construction activities following a one-year 1899 strike. And the employers in the job foundry industry banded together in the National Founders' Association, which successfully terminated not only longstanding Molders Union work rules but, for all practical purposes, the existence of the union itself. In addition, the general public tended to be no more sympathetic, normally, to the aims of the labor movement; symbolically, the president of Harvard University, Charles W. Eliot, "went so far as to glorify the strikebreaker as an example of the finest type of American citizen whose liberty had to be protected at all costs."[6]

Despite all these adverse factors, union membership growth in this period was unparalleled. From 447,000 unionists in 1897, the figure increased almost fivefold to 2,073,000 in 1904—a rate of expansion that has never been equaled since. The figures reflect the national prosperity of the day and the success of many of the national unions (their problems notwithstanding) in organizing their official jurisdictions along the lines of the AFL principles.

But the labor movement could not indefinitely withstand the continuing employer opposition, now augmented by a series of devastating court injunctions on the one hand and rival union challenges from leftist workingmen's groups on the other. Total union membership dropped to 1,959,000 in 1906, and even its ultimate growth to 3,014,000 by 1917 was quite uneven and—considering the fact that 90 percent of the country's labor force still remained unorganized—unspectacular.

Intensified employer campaigns for the open (nonunion) shop, led by the National Association of Manufacturers, resulted in a number of notable union strike losses after 1904 in the meatpacking and shipping industries, among others. Violence often occurred—most drastically at the Colorado Fuel and Iron Company's Ludlow location, when in 1913 eleven children and two women were found burned to death in strikers' tents that the state militia, summoned by the company, had set afire. These were also the peak years of yellow-dog contracts (under which employees promised in writing never to engage in union activities); labor spies; immediate discharge of workers at the slightest evidence of union sympathies; and the use of federal, state, and local troops on a wholesale scale to safeguard company interests in the face of strike actions.

The courts, too, were not particularly restrained in their conduct toward unions. Injunctions banning specific union activities often appeared to unionists to be issued quite indiscriminately.

Still another threat to the established unions, in the years between 1904 and 1917, came from workers themselves. Sometimes impatient with what they considered to be the slow pace of AFL union gains, and sometimes wholly antagonistic toward the very system of capitalism, radical labor groups arose to challenge (without, as it turned out, very much success) the Gompers unions for membership and influence. This was the heyday of immigration into the United States—some 14 million newcomers, mainly from Europe, arrived in the first two decades of the twentieth century—and the European political socialism that many of the radical groups espoused found some recruits in this quarter.

Nonetheless, Gompers and the AFL could point with satisfaction to some signal gains, gains that rested to a great extent on the outstanding organizing and bargaining successes of a few specific AFL member nationals, particularly in the building trades, the ladies' garment industry, and coal mining. Ironically, two of these unions (the International Ladies' Garment Workers and the United Mine Workers) owed much of their new strength to membership policies that took in many semiskilled and even unskilled workers, although skilled-worker needs were still emphasized (and although both these unions were definite exceptions to AFL union practice in their actions).

The AFL's further grounds for satisfaction rested on another irony: Despite the continuation of the policy against active involvement in politics, AFL lobbying activities at both the federal and state levels had been instrumental in the enactment of significant progressive labor legislation. Among other such achievements, by 1917 some thirty states had introduced workmen's compensation systems covering industrial accidents, and almost as many had provided for maximum hours of work for women. On the federal level, the 1915 LaFollette Seamen's Act had greatly ameliorated conditions on both American vessels and foreign vessels in American ports, and the 1916 Owen-Keating Act had dealt a severe blow to child-labor abusers. But Gompers was destined not to be successful in what had appeared at first to be an even greater triumph: Although the Clayton Act of 1914 had seemed to exempt labor from antitrust laws and the penalties of the injunction, in 1921 the Supreme Court was to interpret the Clayton Act in such a way as to render it toothless in labor disputes.

WARTIME GAINS AND PEACETIME LOSSES

From 1917 to 1920, the time of World War I and the months of prosperity following it, the AFL grew rapidly. The 3 million workers in the AFL unions on the eve of the hostilities increased to 4.2 million by 1919 and 5.1 million only one year later.

During the war, military production, the curtailment of immigration, and the draft combined to create tight labor markets and thus gave unions considerable bargaining power and commensurate gains. Real wages for employees in manufacturing and transportation increased by more than 25 percent during the war.

Even more significantly, labor received for the first time official government support for its collective bargaining activities. The rights to organize and bargain collectively, free of employer discrimination for union activities, were granted AFL leaders by the Wilson administration for the length of the war.

But the immediate postwar months were even more conducive to union growth than the war years. The economy's production needs remained high, now to satisfy pent-up consumer demands, and the cost of living hit an all-time high. Company profits also burgeoned, freed of artificial wartime restraints. No longer obliged to honor the no-strike pledges, unions aggressively struck in pursuit of worker wages attuned to both profits and cost of living, and, with their bargaining power now so high, they generally succeeded. As in earlier times of demonstrated labor triumphs, victory brought further conquest: New recruits flocked into the labor movement to gain their share in prosperity through collective bargaining.

Despite this auspicious entrance into the 1920s, however, the decade was to be one of great failure for unionism. Total union membership rapidly dwindled from the 1920 peak of 5.1 million to 3.8 million three years later and, steadily if less dramatically declining even after this, hit a twelve-year low of 3.4 million at the close of the decade. The drop is even more remarkable given the fact that the economy generally continued to flourish during this period; in every prior era of national prosperity, unions had gained considerable ground.

Nonetheless, there were understandable reasons for the poor performance of unionism in the 1920s. A combination of five powerful factors, most of them as unprecedented as organized labor's boom-period decline, was now at work.

First, after the beginning of the decade, prices remained stable, and, with workers generally retaining their relatively high wage gains of the 1917–1920 period, the cries of labor organizers that only union membership could stave off real wage losses fell on deaf ears.

Second, employers throughout the nation not only returned to such measures for thwarting unionization as the yellow-dog contract and the immediate discharge of union "agitators" but now embarked on an extensive antiunion, open-shop propaganda campaign.

The campaign, typically conducted under the slogan of the "American Plan," portrayed unions as alien to the nation's individualistic spirit, restrictive of industrial efficiency, and frequently dominated by radical elements who did not have the best interests of America at heart. Particularly in regard to the last of these charges, the public appeared to be impressed: It was still mindful of the radical unions of a few years earlier, and now its attention was also called, freely by the newspapers, to the relatively few other significant leftist inroads into labor circles. To many citizens, too, organizations that could even remotely be construed as going against individualism and the free-enterprise system in this day of laissez-faire Republicanism were also highly un-American.

Third, but often tied into their "American Plan" participation, many companies introduced what became known as "welfare capitalism." Intending to demonstrate to their employees that unions were unnecessary (as well as dangerous), they established a wide variety of employee-benefit programs: elaborate profit-sharing plans, recreational facilities, dispensaries, cafeterias, and health and welfare systems of all kinds. Employee representation plans were also instituted, with workers thus being offered a voice on wages, hours, and conditions—the companies being thereby enabled to satisfy many grievances before they became major morale problems. Although the managements could withdraw the benefits at any time, and although the employee representatives normally had only "advisory" voices, union ills were undeniably compounded by these company moves.

In the fourth place, the courts proved themselves even less hospitable to labor unions than they had been in labor's dark days preceding World War I. Having denied in 1921 that the Clayton Act exempted unions from the antitrust laws and the injunction, the Supreme Court proceeded to invalidate an Arizona anti-injunction law the same year and then struck down state minimum-wage laws as violations of liberty of contract in 1923. Encouraged by the implied mandate from Washington, lower-court judges now issued injunctions more freely than ever.

Fifth, and finally, some of the union losses were due to unimaginative leadership in the labor movement itself. Gompers died in 1924, and his successor, William Green, lacked the aggressiveness and the imagination of the AFL's first president. Labor's troubles were clearly not to be viewed with equanimity, but Green and most of his AFL union leaders were nothing if not complacent.

On the eve of the Great Depression in late 1929, then, organized labor remained almost exclusively the province of the highly skilled worker minority, apathetic in the face of the loss of one third of its members in a single decade, militantly opposed by much of the employer community, severely crimped by judicial actions, and often suspected by the general public of possessing traits counter to the spirit of America. It appeared to have a superb future behind it.

THE GREAT DEPRESSION AND THE AFL'S RESURGENCE IN SPITE OF ITSELF

The stock-market collapse of October 1929 ushered in the most severe business downturn in the nation's history. Between 1929 and the Depression's lowest point in 1933, the gross national product dropped from over $104 billion to around $56 billion, and a staggering 24.9 percent of the country's civilian labor force was out of work by 1933, compared with an unemployment rate of only 3.2 percent in 1929.[7]

Figures specifically relating to organized labor were equally gloomy. Between 1929 and 1933, the average twelve-month membership loss rate for organized labor accelerated to 117,000, and by 1933 union membership stood at 2,973,000—only 200,000 above the 1916 level.[8]

Given this severe loss of dues-payers, plus the necessity of sustaining strikes against the inevitable wage cuts of workers still employed, it is not surprising that many unions soon became as impoverished as their constituents. Symbolically, Ulman reports that "one forlorn strike against a small steel mill had to be called off after the contents of the strikers' soup kitchen had been depleted by a group of hungry children."[9]

It is surprising, however, that the mood of the workers themselves seemed to be one of bewildered apathy. The atmosphere was now marked by constant mortgage foreclosures. It was characterized by the fear of starvation on the part of many of those not working and the fear of sudden unemployment on the part of many of those still employed. Virtually all remnants of welfare capitalism were being abruptly terminated. Under these conditions, one might have expected a reincarnation of organizations seeking to overthrow the capitalistic system that was now performing so poorly. Some workers did indeed turn to such radical movements as Communism, but, in general, the nation seemed to have been shocked into inaction.

It is still more surprising, even considering its uninspiring performance in meeting the challenge of the 1920s, that the leadership of the AFL did not noticeably change its policies in these dark days. Through 1932, Green and the AFL executive council remained opposed to unemployment compensation, old-age pensions, and minimum-wage legislation as constituting unwarranted state intervention. They asked only for increased public-works spending from the government. So far was the AFL from the pulse of the general community at this time that, although the great bulk of union officials were and had long been Democratic party supporters, it refused, with scrupulous official neutrality, to endorse either candidate in the 1932 presidential election that swept Democrat Franklin D. Roosevelt into office with what was then the largest margin in American history.

Roosevelt's one-sided victory symbolized the country's (if not the AFL's) willingness to grant the federal government more scope for participation in domestic affairs than it had ever been given before. The business community, upon which the nation had put such a premium during the prosperous years of the 1920s, was now both discredited and demoralized. It had become painfully apparent, too, to the millions who had been steeped in the values of American individualism, that the individual worker was comparatively helpless to influence the conditions of the employment environment. In short, the Depression allowed labor unions—which had been so greatly out of favor with the American people only a few years earlier—a golden opportunity for revival and growth, now with government encouragement.

Even before the election, such a climate had resulted in one notable gain for unions. The Norris-La Guardia Act of 1932 satisfied a demand Gompers had originally made in a petition to the President and Congress some twenty-six years earlier: The power of judges to issue injunctions in labor disputes on an almost unlimited basis was now revoked. Severe restrictions were placed on the conditions under which the courts could grant injunctions, and such orders could in no case be issued against certain otherwise legal union activities. In addition, the yellow-dog contract was declared unenforceable in federal courts.

The 1932 act marked a drastic change in public policy. Previously, except for the temporary support that unions received during World War I, collective bargaining had been severely hampered through judicial control. Now it was to be strongly encouraged, by legislative fiat and—after Roosevelt took office in early 1933—by executive support.

Roosevelt and the first "New Deal" Congress wasted little time in making known their sentiments. The National Industrial Recovery Act of mid-1933, in similar but stronger language than that already existing in the Norris-La Guardia Act, specifically guaranteed employees "the right to organize and bargain collectively through representatives of their own choosing...free from the interference, restraint or coercion of employers." Green, in what for him was unusual enthusiasm, immediately praised the act as giving "millions of workers throughout the nation...their charter of industrial freedom" and launched a moderate drive to expand AFL membership among craft workers. More remarkable, however, was the response to the NIRA by rank-and-file workers themselves: Almost overnight, thousands of laborers in such mass-production industries as steel, automobiles, rubber, and electrical manufacturing spontaneously formed their own locals and applied to the AFL for charters. By the end of 1933, the federation had gained more than a million new members.

The largest single gains at this time were registered by those established AFL internationals that had lost the most members during the 1920s and could capitalize upon the new climate in public policy to win back and expand their old clientele. Both the men's and women's clothing unions fell into this category. Most impressive of all, however, was the performance of the United Mine Workers under their aggressive president, John L. Lewis. Lewis dispatched dozens of capable organizers throughout the coal fields, had signs proclaiming that "President Roosevelt wants you to join the union" placed at the mine pits, and not only regained virtually all his former membership but organized many traditionally nonunion fields in the Southeast. There were 60,000 Mine Workers at the time of the NIRA's passage; six months later, the figure had grown to over 350,000.

The employers, however, did not remain docile in the face of this new union resurgence. Terming collective bargaining "collective bludgeoning," many of them responded to the NIRA by restoring or instituting the employee representation plans of the previous decade. Such "company unions," although bitterly assailed by bona fide unionists as circumventing the law's requirements concerning "employer interference," spread rapidly. By the spring of 1934, probably one quarter of all industrial workers were employed in plants that had them. Many other managements simply refused, the law notwithstanding, to recognize any labor organizations. On many occasions, this attitude led to outbreaks of violence, ultimately terminated by the police or by National Guard units.

The National Industrial Recovery Act was itself declared unconstitutional by the Supreme Court early in 1935, but Congress quickly replaced it with a law that was even more to labor's liking. The National Labor Relations Act, better known (after its principal draftsman in the Senate) as the Wagner Act, was far more explicit in what it expected of collective bargaining than was the NIRA, in two basic ways. First, it placed specific restrictions on what management could do, including an absolute ban on company-dominated unions. Second, it established the wishes of the employee majority as the basis for selection of a bargaining representative and provided that in cases of doubt as to a union's majority status, a secret-ballot election of the employees would determine whether or not the majority existed. To implement both provisions, it established a National Labor Relations Board, empowered not only to issue cease-and-desist orders against employers who violated the restrictions but also to determine appropriate bargaining units and conduct representation elections.

Considerably less than enthusiastic about the Wagner Act, many employers chose to ignore its provisions and hoped that it would suffer the same fate as the NIRA. They were to be disappointed: In 1937, the Supreme Court held that the 1935 act was fully constitutional.

THE CIO'S CHALLENGE TO THE AFL

Meanwhile, however, the AFL itself almost snatched defeat from the jaws of victory. The leaders of the federation clashed sharply as to the kind of reception that should be accorded the workers in steel, rubber, automobiles, and similar mass-production industries who had spontaneously organized in the wave of enthusiasm following the NIRA's passage. The federation had given these new locals the temporary status of "federal locals," which meant that they were directly affiliated with the AFL rather than with one of the established national unions. The workers involved, however, wanted to form their own national industrial unions covering all types of workers within their industries, regardless of occupation or skill level. And this, obviously, meant a radical departure from the fifty-year AFL tradition of discouraging nonskilled workers and essentially excluding noncraft unions (the mining and clothing industries, as noted earlier, always excepted because of their particular situations).

John L. Lewis, who had shown such initiative in expanding the ranks of his Mine Workers in the preceding months, led the fight for industrial unionism within the federation. Allied with Sidney Hillman of the Clothing Workers and David Dubinsky of the Ladies' Garment Workers, he argued that changing times had now made skilled-craft unionism obsolete, that the AFL could no longer speak with any political power as long as it confined itself to what was (with the acceleration of mechanization and the replacement of craftsmen by semiskilled machine operators) a steadily dwindling minority of the labor force, and that, should the federation fail to assert its leadership over the new unionists, rival federations would arise to fill the vacuum. Holding perhaps the greatest oratorical powers ever possessed by an American labor leader (and very possibly the only one to begin sentences with "Methinks"), Lewis ridiculed the AFL president for not being able to decide the issue: "Alas, poor Green. I knew him well. He wishes me to join him in fluttering procrastination, the while intoning *O tempora, O mores!*" Moreover, in a dramatic speech at the 1935 AFL Atlantic City convention, Lewis warned that should the federation fail to "heed this cry from Macedonia that comes from the hearts of men" and refuse to allow industrial unionism or to organize the millions still unorganized, "the enemies of labor will be encouraged and high wassail will prevail at the banquet tables of the mighty."

Lewis spoke to no avail. The convention was dominated by inveterate craft unionists, many of whom possibly believed that Macedonia was somewhere east of Akron and who at any rate were opposed to admitting what Teamster president Daniel Tobin described as "rubbish" mass-production laborers. The demands of industrial unionism were defeated by a convention vote of 18,024 to 10,933. And Lewis, never one to camouflage his emotions for the sake of good fellowship with his AFL colleagues, left Atlantic City only after landing a severe uppercut to the jaw of Carpenter Union president William L. Hutcheson in a fit of pique.

Within a month, Lewis had formed his own organization of industrial unionists. The Committee for Industrial Organization (known after 1938 as the Congress of Industrial Organizations) originally wanted only to "counsel and advise unorganized and newly organized groups of workers; to bring them under the banner and in affiliation with the American Federation of Labor."[10] But the AFL, having already made its sentiments so clear, was to deny the new organization the latter opportunity; almost immediately, Green's executive council suspended the CIO leaders for practicing "dual unionism" and ordered them to dissolve their group. When these actions failed to dissuade the CIO, the AFL took its strongest possible action and expelled all thirty-two national member unions.

Lewis and his fellow founders were spectacularly successful in realizing their objectives. Armed with ample loans from the rebel nationals, aggressive leadership, experienced organizers, and, above all, confidence that mass-production workers enthusiastically *wanted* unionism, the AFL offshoot was able to claim almost 4 million recruits as early as 1937.

By 1941, even more remarkable conquests had been registered. One by one, virtually all the giant corporations had recognized CIO-affiliated unions as bargaining agents for their employees: all the major automobile manufacturers, almost all companies of any size in the steel industry, the principal rubber producers, the larger oil companies, the major radio and electrical equipment makers, the important meatpackers of the country, the larger glassmakers, and many others. Smaller companies that had also been unionized in this period could at least take comfort in the fact that they were in good company.

Still, the CIO's organizing campaigns were not welcomed by many of these companies with open arms. United States Steel recognized the CIO's Steel Workers Organizing Committee without a contest in 1937 (ostensibly because it feared labor unrest at a time when business conditions were finally improving). But the other major steel producers unconditionally refused to deal with unionism, the law notwithstanding. In 1941, the National Labor Relations Board ordered these companies to recognize what had by then become the United Steelworkers of America, but four years of company intimidation, espionage, and militia-protected strikebreaking—highlighted by a Memorial Day 1937 clash between pickets and police that resulted in the deaths of ten workers, injuries to many more, and substantial damage to property—had then elapsed. (From this unpromising start, the Steelworkers were to go on to become one of the nation's major unions, of course, and while the organization's fiftieth anniversary in 1986 was marked by the same pessimism that surrounded other smokestack industries, pride in the union's many successes was also highly visible. See Exhibit 2-5. The same union, three years later, was also offering commem-

Exhibit   2–5

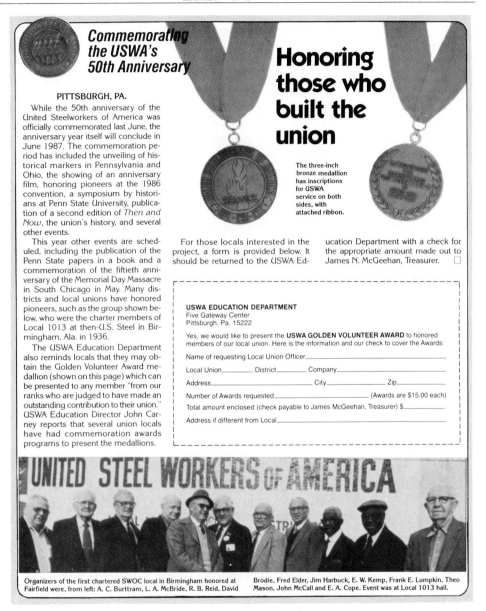

Commemorating the USWA's 50th Anniversary

PITTSBURGH, PA.

While the 50th anniversary of the United Steelworkers of America was officially commemorated last June, the anniversary year itself will conclude in June 1987. The commemoration period has included the unveiling of historical markers in Pennsylvania and Ohio, the showing of an anniversary film, honoring pioneers at the 1986 convention, a symposium by historians at Penn State University, publication of a second edition of *Then and Now*, the union's history, and several other events.

This year other events are scheduled, including the publication of the Penn State papers in a book and a commemoration of the fiftieth anniversary of the Memorial Day Massacre in South Chicago in May. Many districts and local unions have honored pioneers, such as the group shown below, who were the charter members of Local 1013 at then-U.S. Steel in Birmingham, Ala. in 1936.

The USWA Education Department also reminds locals that they may obtain the Golden Volunteer Award medallion (shown on this page) which can be presented to any member "from our ranks who are judged to have made an outstanding contribution to their union." USWA Education Director John Carney reports that several union locals have had commemoration awards programs to present the medallions.

Honoring those who built the union

The three-inch bronze medallion has inscriptions for USWA service on both sides, with attached ribbon.

For those locals interested in the project, a form is provided below. It should be returned to the USWA Education Department with a check for the appropriate amount made out to James N. McGeehan, Treasurer. ☐

USWA EDUCATION DEPARTMENT
Five Gateway Center
Pittsburgh, Pa. 15222

Yes, we would like to present the **USWA GOLDEN VOLUNTEER AWARD** to honored members of our local union. Here is the information and our check to cover the Awards:

Name of requesting Local Union Officer_____

Local Union_____ District_____ Company_____

Address_____ City_____ Zip_____

Number of Awards requested_____ (Awards are $15.00 each)

Total amount enclosed (check payable to James McGeehan, Treasurer) $_____.

Address if different from Local_____

Organizers of the first chartered SWOC local in Birmingham honored at Fairfield were, from left: A. C. Burttram, L. A. McBride, R. B. Reid, David Brodie, Fred Elder, Jim Harbuck, E. W. Kemp, Frank E. Lumpkin, Theo Mason, John McCall and E. A. Cope. Event was at Local 1013 hall.

Source: *Steelabor*, February 1987, back cover.

orative coins, as depicted in Exhibit 2-6, to its members at a discount and reporting that sales were brisk.)

The use of professional strikebreakers often served as a particularly potent employer weapon in these years. Such temporary payroll members were entrusted with such missions as the conveying of the impression that

EXHIBIT   2–6

Coin memorializes labor movement

The struggle of the American labor movement in the century since it took shape in the 1880s is symbolized by a silver coin available to USWA members at a discount.

The American Labor Movement Centennial Silver Eagle Commemorative coin was produced by Bill Hackworth of Prestonsburg, Ky., a United Mine Workers' member and Jobs With Justice organizer.

Each coin is 1.5 inches in diameter and has one ounce of .999 fine silver, mined and crafted by union members. Issued in a limited edition of 10,000, the coins are individually numbered. Proceeds will help fund the Jobs With Justice campaign.

The coin was issued at an initial price of $120, but it is available to USWA members until May 31 for $64.95 per coin, plus a shipping and handling charge of $3. VISA and MasterCard charges are accepted with a five percent credit charge.

To order a coin, send a check, money order or credit card information to Labor Concepts, P.O. Box 1356, Prestonburg, KY 41653.

Source: *Steelabor*, February–March, 1989, p. 23.

the struck organization was actually operating (to demoralize those out on strike) and the inciting of violence (to encourage the public authorities to take action against the unionists). In pursuit of the first goal the strikebreaker might, for example, burn paper in a plant furnace so that the smoke of the chimney would give the appearance of plant production. The driving of empty trucks to and from the plant was another frequently used ploy.

And these strikebreakers frequently adopted such tactics as the hurling of stones into picket lines and the spitting at strikers to provoke violence, facts that explain why such individuals were at times termed "agents provocateurs." If the strikers were goaded into counterviolence, as they often were, the state militia or National Guard—rarely friendly to labor organizations—could then be summoned to the scene.

It was not the most honorable kind of occupation, and many of its practitioners in fact possessed criminal records. As one of them—the well-known professional strikebreaker Sam "Chowderhead" Cohen—once commented about his own lengthy record of imprisonment, "You see, in this line of work they never asked for no references."[11]

But where there was a will on the part of unionists there was generally a way. In some industries, workers turned to "sit-down" strikes—protest stoppages in which the strikers remained at their places of work and were furnished with food by allies outside the plant. Such stoppages, now illegal as trespasses upon private property, were of considerable influence in gaining representation rights for the unions in the historically nonunion automobile, rubber, and glass industries.

Nor, more significantly, was the AFL itself placid in the face of its new competition. Abandoning its traditional lethargy, it now terminated its "craftsmen only" policy and chartered industrial unions of its own in every direction. AFL meatcutters emerged to challenge CIO packinghouse workers for members of all skill levels within the meatpacking industry. AFL papermill employees competed against CIO paper workers. AFL electricians tried to recruit the same workers, from all quarters of the electrical industry, as did the CIO electrical-union organizers. And the story was much the same in textiles and automobiles. Moreover, many of the long-established AFL unions now broadened their jurisdictions; most notable were the Teamsters, whose president had apparently become oblivious to his former charge that mass-production workers were "rubbish," and who now waged aggressive organizational campaigns among workers in the food and agricultural processing industries. Aided by the same favorable climates of worker opinion and public policy that had originally inspired Lewis, and now also helped by improving economic conditions, the AFL actually surpassed the CIO in membership by 1941. By that time, however, the CIO had paid its parent the supreme compliment: It had modified its framework to include craft unionism as well as industrial unionism, and the lines separating the two rival federations had become permanently clouded.

At the time of Pearl Harbor, in December 1941, total union membership stood at 10.2 million, compared with the fewer than 3 million members of only nine years earlier. The CIO itself—representing some 4.8 million workers at this time—was destined to achieve little further success, as measured by sheer membership statistics; it would enroll only 6 million employees at its zenith in 1947 and then gradually retreat before the onslaught of a further AFL counterattack. But if Lewis's organization failed to live up to its founder's expectations as the sole repository of future union leadership, neither could it in any satisfactory way be described as a failure. When America entered World War II in late 1941, the labor movement not only was a major force to be reckoned with but, for the first time, was to a great extent representative of the full spectrum of American workers. And for this situation, the CIO's challenge to the AFL's fifty years of dominance deserves no small amount of credit.

WORLD WAR II

As in the case of World War I, the years after Pearl Harbor saw a further increase in union strength. Although the country's economic conditions had improved considerably in the late 1930s, only after the start of hostilities and the acceleration of the draft did a tight labor market arise to weaken employer resistance to union demands.

Other factors favorable to organized labor were also present. The federal government, sympathetic enough with the goals of unionism for almost a decade, now went even further in its tangible support: In return for a no-strike pledge from both AFL and CIO leaders, labor was granted equal representation with management on the tripartite War Labor Board, the all-powerful institution that adjusted collective bargaining disputes during this period. It was also given an unprecedented form of union security—the still-utilized "maintenance of membership" arrangement, requiring all employees who are either union members when the labor contract is signed or who voluntarily join the union after this date to continue their membership for the length of the contract (subject to a short "escape" period).

Unions further profited in the membership area from the fast growth of such wartime industries as aircraft and shipbuilding and the reinvigoration of such now crucial sectors as steel, rubber, the electrical industry, and trucking. By the end of the war in 1945, union ranks had been increased by more than 4 million new workers, or by almost 40 percent.

By and large, labor honored its no-strike pledge during hostilities. However, with the cost of living continually rising, and with the War Labor Board nonetheless attempting to hold direct wages in check (not always successfully, and frequently at the cost of allowing such "nonwage" supplements as vacation, holiday, and lunch-period pay), the incidence of strikes did increase steadily after 1942. Particularly galling to the general public were several strikes by Lewis's own Mine Workers, all in direct defiance of President Roosevelt's orders and all given substantial publicity by the mass media. (If anything, however, the strikes only cemented Lewis's popularity with his constituents. Even now he remains a latter-day legend with coal miners who never knew him. Exhibit 2-7 is a page that appeared almost a half-century after these strikes in the major publication of the Mine Workers. Lewis is the portly gentleman standing at the lower left.)

Managers, themselves regaining much of their lost stature with the stress on war production at this time, could also point to other evidence that labor had become "too powerful." The competition between the AFL and CIO, officially postponed for the duration of the war, in practice continued almost unabated. Such rivalry on occasion temporarily curtailed plant output, as unions within the two federations resorted to "slowdowns" and "quickie strikes" to convince employers of their respective jurisdictional claims. Instances of worker "featherbedding"—the receipt of payment for unperformed work—marked several industries, notably construction. And members of the Communist party, originally welcomed by some CIO unions because of their demonstrated organizational ability, had now gained substantial influence if not effective control within several of these unions, including both the United Automobile Workers and the Electrical, Radio, and Machine Workers.

The public's attention was also called, by forces unhappy with the labor movement's rapid growth, to union political strength. The AFL had not yet abandoned its traditional policy of bipartisanship, but Lewis had led the CIO actively into political campaigning and had, in fact, resigned his federation presidency when the CIO rank and file had refused to bow to his wishes and vote for Republican Wendell Willkie in 1940. Under Lewis's successor, Philip Murray, and particularly through the direct efforts of Clothing Worker president Sidney Hillman, the CIO had become even more aggressive and influential—within the Democratic party. It now held considerable power within most northern Democratic state organizations, and such was its influence at the national Democratic level that when a fabricated story swept the country to the effect that Roosevelt had ordered his 1944 party convention to "clear everything with Sidney," it was widely believed. So effective had Hillman's CIO Political Action Committee become by this time that attacks upon it emanated from the highest of places: The Republican governor of Ohio claimed that the PAC was "trying to dominate our government with radical and Communistic schemes," and the

PORTAL TO PORTAL: As a result of the 1943 wartime strikes, some 500,000 miners won pay for time spent traveling from the mine mouth to the working face. The country's coal supply was never jeopardized, but the union was strongly criticized for striking a vital industry during wartime. The UMWA, led by President John L. Lewis, countered with an information campaign and refused to let the operators use the war as an excuse to further exploit them.

RANK-AND-FILE DISCIPLINE: During negotiations in 1941, President John L. Lewis calls for $1-per-day increase in wages for miners (above). In the fight for benefits, Lewis never went to the bargaining table alone— hundreds of thousands of miners gave him their undivided support. The wage and benefit victories achieved during Lewis' tenure as president from 1920 to 1960 were a direct result of rank-and-file solidarity and discipline. Across the country, miners would walk out of or return to the mines at his direction.

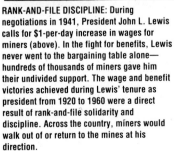

Source: *United Mine Workers Journal*, August–September 1990, p. 31.

House Un-American Activities Committee (with a membership unfriendly to Roosevelt) called it "a subversive...organization."[12]

The American man and woman in the street seemed to be impressed. By the end of the war in 1945, public opinion polls showed more than 67 percent of the respondents in favor of legislative curbs on union power.

PUBLIC REACTION AND PRIVATE MERGER

Organized labor fell even further from public favor in the immediate postwar period. Faced with income declines as overtime and other wartime pay supplements disappeared, with real wage decreases as prices rose in response to the huge pent-up consumer demand, and with layoffs as factories converted to peacetime production, workers struck as they had never done before. Although the violence of earlier-day labor unrest did not recur often, the year 1946 saw new highs established in terms of number of stoppages (4,985), number of employees involved (4.6 million), and person-days idle as a percentage of available working time (1.43). By the end of the year, noteworthy stoppages (many of them simultaneously) had occurred in virtually every sector of the economy, including the railroads, autos, steel, public utilities, and even public education.

Such strikes were not well received by a frequently inconvenienced public that had already voiced reservations about union strength. The sentiments that the Wagner Act and other public policies of the 1930s had been too "one-sided" in favor of labor grew rapidly and soon became compelling. In 1947, a newly elected Republican Congress passed, over President Truman's veto, the Taft-Hartley Act.

Taft-Hartley drastically amended the Wagner Act to give greater protection to both employers and individual employees. To the list of "unfair" labor practices already denied employers were added six "unfair" *union* practices, ranging from restraint or coercion of employees to featherbedding. Employees could now hold elections to decertify unions as well as to certify them. Provisions regulating certain internal affairs of unions, explicitly giving employers certain collective bargaining rights (particularly regarding "freedom of expression" concerning union organization), and sanctioning government intervention in the case of "national emergency strikes" were also enacted.

A fuller discussion of Taft-Hartley is reserved for later pages; however, it might be added here that the 1947 act was at least as controversial as the Wagner Act had been. Its proponents, consistent with the views of Senator Taft, asserted that it "reinjected an essential measure of justice into collective bargaining." Less friendly observers of Taft-Hartley, including the spokespeople of organized labor, were less happy and hurled such epithets as "slave labor act" at it. That the act has proved generally satisfactory to the majority of Americans, however, may be inferred from the fact that, almost a half-century later, Taft-Hartley, essentially unchanged from its original edition, remained the basic labor law of the land.

Speaking with the self-assurance always allowed one who can draw on hindsight, it is tempting to argue that the AFL-CIO merger of 1955 was inevitable. The issue that had led to the birth of the CIO was, as noted, blunted even by the late 1930s when the AFL rapidly chartered its own industrial unions and the CIO began to recognize craft unions as part of its structure. But another decade and a half was to elapse before merger became a reality, and significant differences still had to be bridged.

In the first place, the new unions that had been formed, first by the CIO and later by the AFL, were often meeting head-on in their quests for new members and enlarged jurisdiction. Any merged federation would have to resolve not only this kind of overlap but also the membership raiding that was frequently carried on by such rival unions. For a long while, compromise seemed impossible: The AFL tended to regard all jurisdictions as exclusively its own and to insist that the CIO unions be fully absorbed within its framework; on its part, the CIO strongly suggested that its affiliates would participate in a merger only if their existing jurisdictions were given official protection.

Second, the conservative AFL leaders displayed deep hostility toward the Communist-dominated unions within the CIO. Such unions reached a peak in the immediate postwar months, when a special report of the Research Institute of America listed eighteen of them in this category.

Finally, personalities played a role. Murray and Green were mutually suspicious leaders. Each was quite unwilling to take the initiative in any merger move that would involve subordination of influence to the other.

By 1955, however, most of these cleavages had been resolved. Murray, his patience with the Communist unions exhausted as they became more aggressive, had taken the lead in expelling most such unions from the CIO in 1949 and 1950. Virtually all other Communist-influenced unions, presumably taking the hint, had voluntarily left the federation shortly thereafter. Murray's move cost the CIO an estimated 1 million members, but new unions were quickly established to assume the old jurisdictions, and Murray claimed to have regained most of the lost membership within the next two years.

Further preparing the way for ultimate merger were the 1952 deaths of Murray and Green, both suddenly and only eleven days apart. The two successors—Walter Reuther of the United Auto Workers, for Murray, and AFL secretary-treasurer George Meany, for Green—were relatively divorced from the personal bitterness of the earlier presidents.

And beyond these factors were growing sentiments on the part of both AFL and CIO leaders that only a united labor movement could (1) stave off future laws of the Taft-Hartley variety, (2) avoid the jurisdictional squabbles that were increasingly sapping the treasuries of both federations, and (3) allow organized labor to reach significant new membership totals for the first time since 1947.

In December 1955, culminating two years of intensive negotiations between representatives of the two organizations, the AFL-CIO became a reality. The new constitution respected the "integrity of each affiliate," including both its "organizing jurisdiction" and its "established collective bargaining relationships." Consolidation of the rival unions was to be encouraged but was to be on a voluntary basis. And it was agreed that the new giant federation would issue charters "based upon a strict recognition that both craft and industrial unions are equal and necessary as methods of trade union organization." With the act of merger, the open warfare that had first revitalized and then damaged the labor movement passed from the scene.

ORGANIZED LABOR SINCE THE MERGER

Although some observers predicted that the original 15-million member-ship total (two thirds of it provided by the AFL) of the AFL-CIO would rapidly double, they were wrong. Four decades after the merger, the organization had fewer members than in 1955—some 14.3 million in 1993. As noted earlier in this book, the losses had not been confined merely to the federation, either. Labor had clearly been losing ground on all fronts in at least the latter part of this period. The shrinkage had taken it from the just under 25 percent of the nation's labor force that unions represented in 1970 to the 16.4 percent representation in 1993.

Several formidable obstacles undoubtedly serve to explain this situation. Paramount among them is, of course, the fact that blue collar workers, traditionally constituting that sector of the labor force most susceptible to the overtures of the union organizer, have now been substantially organized. And this sector has, it will be recalled, been declining as a source of jobs in recent years. It remains to be seen whether new approaches, fresh leadership, and environmental changes adversely affecting worker morale can gain for organized labor the allegiance of the growing white collar sector. As the statistics in the preceding chapter indicated, however, unions to date have not been spectacularly successful in recruiting this wave of the future.

Beyond this, labor's fall from public favor, which began in the 1940s and led initially to the enactment of Taft-Hartley, had yet to be arrested all these years later. Congressional disclosures of corruption in the Teamsters and several smaller unions in the late 1950s hardly improved labor's image. The AFL-CIO quickly expelled not just the Teamsters (who would not, in fact, be allowed to return until 1987) but all the offending unions. But the public seemed to be far more impressed by the disclosures than by the federation's reaction to them, as indeed had been the case following the CIO's expulsion of its Communist-dominated affiliates.

Union resistance to technological change, sometimes taking the form of featherbedding and insistence on the protection of jobs that seemed no longer to be needed (those of diesel firemen and certain airline and mari-time employees, for example), also was anything but calculated to regain widespread public support. Nor was it easy to generate sympathy outside the labor movement on behalf of plumbers who threatened to strike for wage rates in excess of $35 per hour, electricians demanding a twenty-hour workweek, and New York City transit workers seeking a 50 percent wage increase, a thirty-two-hour workweek, and some seventy-five other demands. These few examples were among the extremes; most unionists showed considerably more concern for the welfare of their industries in the post-merger years. But such actions as the ones illustrated, being more newsworthy, attracted more attention. It is conceivable that, through this combination of factors ranging from corruption to excessive demands, countless potential union members had been alienated.

The continuing lack of public confidence in unionism had also led, in the relatively recent past, to new legislation restricting labor's freedom of action. In particular, the Landrum-Griffin Act of 1959 stemmed from this climate and, directly, from the union-corruption revelations of Congress that were cited above. Among its other provisions, Landrum-Griffin guarantees union members a "Bill of Rights" that their unions cannot violate and requires officers of labor organizations to meet a wide and somewhat cumbersome variety of reporting and disclosure obligations. It also lays out specific ground rules for union elections, rules that have been deemed too inhibiting (as have most other parts of the act) by many labor leaders.

It is perhaps also true that labor's conspicuous recent lack of success has stemmed from the fact that the new breed of manager has acted a great deal more responsibly in employee relations, thereby making the organization considerably less vulnerable to unionization. Objective and essentially uniform standards for discipline, promotion, layoffs, recalls, and a host of other personnel areas have now all but totally replaced even the palest efforts at tyranny, and in the face of the change relatively few workers seem to feel the need for a collective bargaining agency as a curb on supervisory ruthlessness.

Whatever the reasons, it was obvious that organized labor could not count the four decades after the merger among its golden years and that many of the conditions that could explain unionism's lack of success in these years persisted at the end of this period.

UNIONISM AND THE MINORITY WORKER

Inevitably, in the late twentieth century, organized labor was also forced to devote considerable attention to an issue that was far less parochial in its thrust: the increasingly intense quest of the minority community for genuine equality of opportunity. Employment expectations that were initially (if indirectly) raised by the landmark Supreme Court school-desegregation decision of 1954 had been considerably heightened by the broad equal-employment-opportunities legislation of the Civil Rights Act of 1964. And since in subsequent years the gap between expectation and reality remained significant, the labor movement found itself under growing attack as frustrated blacks and other minorities charged it with bigotry and racism, collusion with an equally insensitive managerial community to exploit the minority worker, and total inadequacy in the field of integrative social action.

Not all minorities, of course, shared this dim opinion. The Urban League's highly respected Whitney Young undoubtedly echoed the sentiments of a significant sector of the black world in stating that "when we look at the whole picture, labor is strongly on the side of social justice and equal rights....All unions ought to be educating their members to the dangers of bigotry, and to the fact that racism damages white workers as well as blacks. But on the whole, organized labor is as good a friend of black efforts for equality as exists in our imperfect society."[13] Nor would objective minority-group members deny not only that AFL-CIO leadership, and particularly Meany and Reuther, had been in the forefront of efforts to enact the equal-employment-opportunities provisions into the Civil Rights Act of 1964 itself but that for a time these federation chieftains had waged this campaign almost entirely alone. As the head of the NAACP's Washington Bureau, Clarence Mitchell, could later testify in this regard, "Organized labor gave unfailing, consistent and massive support where it counted most....The members of organized labor were always present at the right time and in the right places."[14] And most blacks would presumably acknowledge that the approximately 3-million-member black contingent within the ranks of unionism by the 1990s constituted substantial progress from 1928, when black membership was 2.1 percent, and even from 1956, when the figure had climbed to 8.6 percent.[15] No authoritative figures have as yet been forthcoming for the nation's sizable Hispanic population, but there is no reason to think that progress in that fast-growing sector (its numbers rose five times as fast as the U.S. population in the 1980s and early 1990s and totaled almost 22 million by 1993) has not been commensurate.

To the growing body of minority militants, however, the Youngs and Mitchells could quickly be dismissed as Uncle Toms, whose laudatory statements only proved that they had been captured by the labor establishment. The militants irately pointed out that it was not until 1964, a full fifteen years after the armed forces started to integrate and ten years after the U.S. Supreme Court ordered desegregation in the public schools, that the last AFL-CIO affiliate struck down the "whites only" clause in its constitution.

In the black community at least, many blacks also argued that the significant numerical growth in black unionists in no way touched the heart of the problem—that even where the admissions bars were down, a highly disproportionate number of blacks' jobs were at the bottom of the skills ladder, situations shunned by whites and entirely lacking in career progression opportunities. Above all, these critics could point with considerable bitterness to the building trades, where many years after the passage of the Civil Rights Act, little more than 5 percent of all black apprentices were enrolled in skilled-craft training programs (the remainder being in the so-called "trowel trades"—general laborers, cement masons, and kindred occupations, whose pay scales averaged much less and whose status was lowest). This was an especially jarring situation to them, given the large number of projects financed with public money.

Thus, while minority-group militants—particularly black militants—had espoused picketing and (on occasion) disrupted production as a protest against alleged discrimination in the automobile, steel, and appliance sectors, it was in the nation's huge construction industry that the most potentially explosive confrontations occurred.

In the tension-packed year of 1969, especially notable and highly publicized black coalition protests had closed major construction projects in Chicago and Pittsburgh. Accompanied by some violence, these had generated union (and employer) pledges to hire and train black journeymen not only immediately but also in considerably greater numbers than ever before. Other cities also witnessed such direct action and a similar resolution of the action.

But the unlikely prospects for an amicable or imminent solving of the national construction employment issue had been accurately indicated by the enthusiastic reception accorded the president of the AFL-CIO Building and Construction Trades Department immediately after the Chicago and Pittsburgh confrontations. On this occasion, he defiantly declared to 300 cheering delegates at the department's convention, "We wish to make it clear that we do not favor acceptance of unreasonable demands....We should make it clear again that the conduct, curriculum, and control of our training programs are going to remain in the hands of our crafts and our contractors. They are not going to be turned over to any coalition."[16]

And vastly compounding the construction industry problem was the deeply embedded building trades tradition of restrictive membership, designed not only to limit competition for jobs and to increase the asking price for the existing members' performances of services but in part also to nurture a certain amount of father-son employment situations. In support of such goals, and also because much employment in the industry had been intermittent and seasonal, hiring had historically been done through the union hiring hall. Racial intolerance itself had, indeed, not often been easily provable in the face of these other exclusionary considerations—as, presumably, in the case of the Philadelphia building trades local whose leader some years ago countered black charges of discrimination with the outraged declaration that "we don't take in *any* new members, regardless of color."[17]

Adding a final complexity to the building trades issue, moreover, was the fact that, by craft union definition, journeymen cannot be created instantaneously. Skilled ironworkers, plumbers, electricians, steamfitters, and similarly highly remunerated workers by and large have emerged only after rigorous apprenticeship programs, often lasting five or more years (and paying relatively low trainee wages during the period). Only through this process, the unions had argued, could the high standards of the craft be upheld. To many minority-group members, who had long viewed much of the apprenticeship philosophy as primarily a restrictive device (racial or otherwise) anyhow, the unions owed the minority community considerable accelerated upgrading to journeymen status as compensation for years of total exclusion. To many whites already in unions, such a concession would greatly dilute the quality of craftsmanship and thus devastate morale among the present skilled-trades workers.

The gap separating the two positions was, consequently, a very large one. And given its dimensions, few observers predicted much success even from the federal government's much-heralded Philadelphia Plan, which was also implemented in 1969. This innovative concept established minority-group quotas for six building trades unions working on federal construction jobs in the Philadelphia area, beginning with a 4 percent quota in 1969 and scheduled to rise to a 19 percent average by 1973. It was, however, immediately assailed by unions and some contractors as an illegal system denying to other prospective employees equal protection of the Constitution, as a mechanism that would undermine the crafts and decrease the efficiency of building-trades work, and as an impractical device requiring the hiring of minorities either not available at all or unacceptable as employees if available. Ironically, civil rights groups also quickly attacked the plan as insufficient in ensuring jobs, and also as making no provisions for training or upgrading to journeyman status within the unions. They also viewed it negatively as being geared only to temporary employment.

Although plans similar to Philadelphia's had over the next dozen years been implemented in Atlanta, San Francisco, St. Louis, Camden, N.J., and Washington, D.C., as well as Chicago (although not Pittsburgh), support for the basic concept involved had long before steadily eroded. It had become a victim not only of the sharp attacks upon it from both sides but of a national white backlash in general. It had also been substantially weakened by the Nixon administration's preference in the 1970–1974 period for a voluntary approach to construction industry hiring. "It's best," said Secretary of Labor Peter J. Brennan in 1973, "when labor and management honestly agree on a plan and work together to make it succeed,"[18] and under the Nixon "hometown plan" approach to minority hiring, some seventy such plans—based on having labor, management, and minority leaders work out their own "goals and timetables" for integration—were implemented with mixed but generally very unimpressive results.

The deep national recessions culminating in 1975, 1983, and 1992, particularly severe ones for construction and ones whose further employment ramifications for minority-group members will be explored in the last chapter of this book, further dampened whatever optimism remained for significant building-trades job improvement on the part of minorities. And by the early 1990s, while some progress had obviously come about—overall, about 18 percent of all jobs in construction were then held by minority workers—minorities had not significantly increased their proportion of jobs in the *skilled* trades. Indeed, the national director of the NAACP could say in the late 1970s, in comparing this latter area with its situation regarding blacks several years earlier, "If it was bad then, it's worse now."[19] From all available evidence, there was nothing to give blacks or other minority-group members any additional encouragement at the time of this writing.

Nor were the building trades unique in having aroused the ire of minorities. Several of the railway brotherhoods continued even in the first years of the 1990s to show an almost total absence of blacks or Hispanics on their membership rosters (a situation that could primarily be explained by the strong southern historical ties of these unions), as did some printing and entertainment industry crafts and the Air Line Pilots Association. And black and Hispanic holders of major union-leadership posts, even in unions with substantial black and Hispanic memberships, remained conspicuous by their absence. The Teamsters and the Steelworkers, for example, had no blacks at all on their executive boards until the last years of the 1970s (when each union installed one) despite the large percentages of blacks in both of these large internationals; the Automobile Workers, over one-third black, could point to not much more progress, with only two blacks on their twenty-six-member board until recently (although one of these, Vice President Marc Stepp, was in charge of relations with the Chrysler Corporation and thus bargained for 90,000 UAW members); and the powerful, policy-making AFL-CIO Executive Council, with just three of its thirty-five members black, also remained a sea of white faces.

In fact, as these words were being written, there were only two black presidents of international unions, and one of these leaders headed a relatively small domain: Former Oakland Raiders football star Gene Upshaw was the top person in the Federation of Professional Athletes. The one large union with a black at its pinnacle was the almost 220,000-member American Federation of Government Employees: John N. Sturdivant was president of this increasingly influential collective bargaining representative of federal-sector workers, but as a major black top official he stood alone.

At that, twice as many blacks as Hispanics presided over the nation's unions, since only the charismatic chief executive of the United Farm Workers, Cesar Chavez, fell into the latter category. It is true, however, that one local union that was bigger than all but a relative handful of international unions—the 100,000-member New York City Local 1199 of the Drug, Hospital, and Health Care Employees—was also Hispanic-led. The bright and urbane Dennis Rivera occupied the latter slot, and many who observed him in action were predicting that he would go on to even higher office. Barely into his forties, he had attracted much favorable national attention (one union official had called him "maybe the best piece of talent around in the labor movement" and such influential publications as the *New York Times* and the *New Yorker* had made him the subject of lengthy, entirely positive profiles).

In all fairness, the problem of racism, at least as it involved the labor movement, should be viewed in perspective. Generally speaking, industrial unions had rarely practiced membership discrimination in either admission or job assignment. They had recognized that in most industries (as opposed to crafts) large numbers of blacks (and in some cases of Hispanics) already existed and that the price of discrimination in such a situation would be the sacrifice of organizing potential. Thus, even prior to the rise of the CIO, the needle trades unions and coal miners aggressively fought off efforts on the part of their more biased rank and file to restrict membership to whites, and essentially all industrial unions, following the great waves of organization in the 1930s, had espoused a policy of full equality regarding both admission and occupational level for minorities. The attitude of the AFL-CIO has already been cited, in reference to the 1964 Civil Rights Act, and it is no less a matter of record that the federation had consistently upheld as a cardinal principle ever since the 1955 merger "to encourage all workers without regard to race, creed, color, national origin or ancestry to share equally in the full benefits of union organization."[20] Nor can the effective alliances forged between labor and civil rights groups—which resulted most notably in improved conditions for black

Memphis, Tennessee, sanitation workers in 1968, and one year later (under the banner of "Union Power Plus Soul Power Equals Victory") union recognition and considerable economic betterment for black hospital employees in Charleston, South Carolina—be overlooked in any summary of this more positive side of labor's efforts.

It is also noteworthy that blacks (and other nonwhite workers, too, as they become an increasingly large part of the work force) are much more likely to be union members than are white workers. At present, almost 30 percent of all nonwhites are union members while only about 18 percent of whites are. Some of this simply reflects the fact that minorities fill more blue collar jobs proportionately than do whites, but there are also differences in desire. In one recent study, 34 percent of unorganized white blue collar workers said that they would vote for a union if given the opportunity, whereas a whopping 70 percent of nonwhite blue collarites said they would; and among white collar workers, the respective percentages were 26 and 67. Studies of union representation election voting, moreover, show that the chances of a minority-group member actually voting for a union are considerable higher than those of a white doing so.[21]

As Freeman and Medoff have asserted in regard to blacks, "The high proportion of blacks in organized labor suggests that union advances are especially likely to benefit blacks, as has been recognized by some black leaders." Not an unusual sentiment, they feel, is that of the executive director of a major center for black trade union studies, who has declared that blacks "have long understood trade unionism: They know it pays—and pays handsomely—to have a union card."[22] Most objective blacks and other minority-group members would probably agree with the sentiments of A. Philip Randolph Institute leader Norman Hill, who not long ago, after acknowledging that there were indeed more blacks in the upper (second and third) echelons of large unions than in the top ranks of large corporations, said of the progress to date, "I think it's still not what it should be, but it clearly is improving."[23]

Even the federation and industrial unions, however, have been unable to uproot occasional discriminatory practices within the lower levels of their hierarchies. The federation, as Chapter 4 will show, has limited powers over its affiliates and has stopped short of using its ultimate penalty of expulsion both out of consideration of "overkill" and because of a realistic fear that many craft unions might voluntarily leave the federation fold in sympathy with the disciplined organizations. And the elected leaders of local industrial unions have had much to lose and little to gain by fighting against racial prejudice where it does exist among their members at the lower levels. Again, however, the problem is nowhere near as blatant as in the case of the craft unions.

Perhaps it was asking too much of organized labor to exhibit a record that was above reproach in regard to its treatment of minority employees, considering that no other sector of our society had performed any better—or possibly, indeed, as well. But in view of the understandable unhappiness of the minority community with labor's performance to date, it was nonetheless obvious that this issue remained in the last years of the twentieth century, for unionism, a great one.

WOMEN IN LABOR UNIONS

Women make up some 35.2 percent of union membership in the United States[24] but hold only an estimated 14 percent of the leadership positions in their organizations; and even these statistics overstate how well they have done. Most of the positions are at the local as opposed to the national level, and even in locals the jobs are most often at the very bottom of the hierarchy, shop stewardships.

Until very recent years, indeed, the thirty-five-member AFL-CIO Executive Council, made up basically of the presidents of the major national unions affiliated with the federation, had remained an all-male province (and, as we know, almost an all-white one as well). And while three women now belong to this key governing body, one-third of even this modest total is accounted for by the holder of a secondary union position: Joyce D. Miller, one of more than a dozen vice presidents of the Amalgamated Clothing and Textile Workers and the first female awarded a seat on the Council (in 1980).

One of the two current chief executive exceptions is Susan Bianchi-Sand, president of the 33,000-member Association of Flight Attendants. She was elected to membership in 1989, presumably as something more than a token, but her union's saga also says something about labor's lack of receptivity to women's ambitions. Until 1984, the Flight Attendants were part of the Air Line Pilots Association, in which not so long ago women were called stewardesses, had to retire at age 32 (or when they got married), and although allowed to vote as ALPA members could not hold union office under that union's constitution. Her female predecessor was in fact actually denied an Executive Council seat when several such openings became vacant in late 1985, stunning many labor activists who had expected the Flight Attendant leader to win one of the positions easily. "You look up at that [Executive Council] podium," commmented one outraged onlooker on the occasion of that AFL-CIO action, "and all you see are old white men."[25]

The other female union president now sitting on the Council is Lenore Miller, leader of the 200,000-member Retail, Wholesale and Department Store Union. Elected in 1987, she was the first female chief executive council member. Until Bianchi-Sand came aboard two years later, she was also the only one. (Two other international unions, neither of them major by any standard, at the moment also have women at the top: the Screen Actors Guild and Actors' Equity.)

Nor is the story appreciably different, percentage-wise, for national union executive board memberships. Although almost one-third of all Teamster members are female, at this writing there had never been a woman on that huge union's seventeen-member board. And most other unions have not done much better in bringing women into their boardrooms.

Had women not become significantly more numerous both in the civilian labor force and within union ranks in the years since the merger, such statistics could well have been received with aplomb by all but perhaps the most militant of women. As it was, however, female unionists, according to Bureau of Labor Statistics figures, numbered just under 7 million by 1993, up from a meager 1.1 million in 1956. And in these same years, the female percentage of the total civilian labor force had risen from just over 30 percent to almost 47 percent. Justice had accordingly, in the eyes of many women, not been remotely rendered.

It had been in recognition of this lack of progress, and a deeply harbored belief that the masculine leaders of labor had not fought aggressively enough for higher wages and improved working conditions for their female constituents, that more than 3,000 women members from fifty-eight international unions had met at Chicago in 1974. In general agreement with the sentiments of one speaker that "the union presidents understand power,"[26] they had formed the Coalition of Labor Union Women (CLUW) to work within the union movement for change.

In particular, they had pledged that the new organization's objectives would focus upon increased union efforts to organize women workers; greater participation of women in union affairs, particularly in policy-making positions; positive action by unions against sex discrimination in pay, hiring, job classification, and promotion; and adequate child-care facilities. Not one union initially had specifically endorsed the new women's group. But the founders of CLUW had made it very clear that they harbored no thoughts of engaging in a direct confrontation with organized labor. "Working through the union" was the dominant theme of this convention, and no one questioned the declaration of the CLUW's new vice president, Addie Wyatt, that "our unions are not really our enemies, since we are the unions. Our real job is to see to it that our bosses respond in a more meaningful way to our needs." Nor was any challenge lodged to the assertion of another CLUW leader that "men aren't going to resign their posts. They're just going to have to make room for more people on the boards."[27]

Talk, as has been observed by many evaluators of it, is cheap. And twenty years later it still remained to be seen if all of this original oratory would lead to concrete results. CLUW itself (some of whose activities are noted in Exhibit 2-8) is still very much in business. Indeed, it has grown to sixty-five chapters, more than half of which have been formed since 1979 alone, and its most recent biennial convention drew delegates, alternates, observers, and visitors from twenty countries. But there is little to show that, for many unions, much has really changed at all in these years. For every union that is clearly devoting more concern to women than it has in the past (for example, the United Automobile Workers), there might well be another (such as the Ladies' Garment Workers or Joyce Miller's Amalgamated Clothing and Textile Workers, despite both unions' overwhelmingly female memberships) that appears to be far less aggressive in pursuing the interests of women than it once was.

Some overall progress has certainly been made, however. By all accounts CLUW was instrumental in converting the AFL-CIO from a stance of opposition to the Equal Rights Amendment to one of aggressive support. It also helped effect 1978 legislation forbidding employers to discriminate against pregnant employees and—although to date without success—has proven an energetic lobbyist (usually in tandem with other unionists) for federal actions effecting equal pay for "comparable" (as opposed to "identical") work. Even George Meany was sufficiently impressed to announce at

EXHIBIT 2–8

If you're trying to solve the mysteries of how to win job fairness & family security...

Try using these CLUWs.

Everyone knows that a secure family depends on a secure job with fair wages and working conditions. The psychological and emotional pressures of unemployment, low pay, and job discrimination often can lead to trouble at home.

Your union can do a lot to help. But it can't do everything alone. That's why there's a support organization of women and men that fights alongside your union to win the conditions at work that make for security at home. You need its help; it needs yours.

What is it? Try these CLUWs:

CLUW No. 1: Since its founding in 1974, this group has fought through your union to abolish sex- and race-based wage discrimination.

Forging Change For a New Generation of Families, Workers, & Unions.

CLUW No. 2: This organization leads the fight for decent child-care facilities for working parents. Without them, one or another spouse often is denied the right to a job.

CLUW No. 3: The more workers in our unions, the stronger we are at the bargaining table. Through its organizing efforts, this group has helped thousands of new workers join unions.

CLUW No. 4: Leadership counts. This group uses training and other programs to help women become active and advance to positions of leadership in their unions.

CLUW No. 5: What's won in bargaining can be lost in Congress. This group has worn a path to Capitol Hill and state legislatures to fight for pregnancy disability coverage, a decent minimum wage, pay equity, child care options, safe workplaces, and other laws that benefit all workers.

Still not sure of the solution? Here's a final CLUW — the *Coalition of Labor Union Women,* fighting for job equity and family security for over 10 years and growing stronger year by year.

CLUW's for you. And you can get with it. Contact your local union women's committee, your local CLUW chapter, or write CLUW, the Coalition of Labor Union Women, 15 Union Square, New York, N.Y. 10003.

Use This CLUW Card To Join Us Now!

COALITION OF LABOR UNION WOMEN
Application For National Membership

Name _____

Address _____

_____

Phone: (H) _____ (W) _____

International Union _____ Local Union _____

_____

FOR NATIONAL TREASURER'S USE ONLY

Membership Card No _____ Date Sent _____

_____
National Treasurer's Signature

National membership in CLUW is good for one full year from date of issuance of membership card by National Treasurer

I would like to join CLUW as a: (check one)

Regular Member—$20 (   )   Contributing Member—$25 (   )

Supporting Member—$50 (   )   Sustaining Member—$100 (   )

Retiree Member—$10 (   )

Position held in Union: _____
I am a member of a bona fide collective bargaining organization

_____
Signature

Attach your check to this card, enclose in envelope and mail to:

Gloria Johnson, Treasurer, CLUW
c/o IUE, 1126 16th St. NW
Wash., D.C. 20036

Source: *The Guild Reporter*, November 8, 1985, p. 6.

the 1977 CLUW convention that he had become "a closet feminist" and to tell his audience there that "if supporting a living wage for all workers makes a feminist, move over, sisters, I've been called a lot worse."[28] Milestones were achieved in 1983, when the Teamsters appointed a woman as their national director of organizing (Vicki Saporta, who as a 30-year-old Ivy Leaguer also was at variance with most other Teamster top officials in other ways), and in 1984, when the nation's third largest insurance company, Equitable Life Insurance Society, signed an initial labor contract covering its mostly female claims processors in Syracuse, New York. The latter accomplishment directly involved only fifty-four workers but many union watchers thought that it might well symbolize the shape of things to come in the huge, heavily female insurance industry. For that matter, it might also, they thought, be a harbinger of union successes in organizing the 20 million American female clerical workers.

On the other hand, tales of sexism among male union power-holders still abound. ("When we went shopping around for a union," one leader of a national organization devoted to organizing female office workers could report, "one [union] official said to us: 'If I had a girl here to do the typing, I'd have more time to organize women.'")[29] As indicated, the men have by no means actually made "room for more people on the boards." And since almost 85 percent of all female employees were still nonunionists in 1993, it is clear that the appeal of organized labor to women remains something short of irresistible.

Yet the increasing interest of women in their own jobs—not just through CLUW but through such other new organizations as the ambitious National Association of Working Women, which inspired the Dolly Parton movie *Nine to Five* and whose 12,000 members recently joined forces with the fast-growing Service Employees International Union in an attempt to sign up clerical workers—is nonetheless highly significant. If progress in recruiting women to date hardly justifies the verdict of one union organizer that "we're on a roll" and if even minimally prominent women labor leaders can still be counted on the fingers of one hand, the situation does seem to be changing. Women have now shown themselves, really for the first time in a sustained way, as being willing to engage in employment-improvement action on many fronts. As in the case of minorities' demands for more attention, it is clear in the 1990s that organized labor can now afford to ignore their increasing self-awareness only to its definite detriment. (Exhibit 2-9 shows in a page from a mid-1992 issue of the Screen Actors Guild's major publication one effort of a union to focus on women.)

SOME CONCLUDING THOUGHTS

At least one factor emerges clearly from a reading of United States labor history. And it suggests that the current reports of unionism's impending doom may be greatly exaggerated.

Organized labor has been surrounded by conditions at least as bleak as those confronting it today many times in its long history. And on each occasion it has proved equal to the challenge. It has fully recovered from disastrous economic depressions that at various times wiped out most of its membership. It has survived the inroads of reformers who temporarily succeeded in divorcing it almost entirely from its collective bargaining functions. It has overcome devastating victories won by employers, and formidable weapons in the hands of the courts. It has incurred deeply rooted public disfavor before, particularly in the 1870s and 1920s, and ultimately surmounted it. And at perhaps the two most critical junctures of all—(1) in the 1880s, with the rapid disintegration of the Knights and

EXHIBIT 2-9

ACTION

Women Working Together: Writers & Actresses Unite

Tired of stereotypes and slim supporting roles, female writers and actresses with production deals are joining forces to initiate new projects outside of the traditional development system.

The Women's Committees of the Writers Guild of America West and Screen Actors Guild launched the new WGA-SAG Access Program at the Nikko Hotel in Beverly Hills on April 1. The forum was jointly established to give female writers a more direct approach to actresses who produce, and to give those actresses a chance to discuss the kinds of material they are seeking.

According to WGA Women's Committee Chair Pamela Rosenberg, "We hope this access will create a more direct and mutually beneficial communication between the writing and acting communities. We want to promote the professional status of women and dispel the myth that there are no scripts with good female leads." Organizers said the event may be repeated once or twice a year.

In addition to the many writers who attended were performer-producers Geena Davis, Victoria Principal, Sally Kirkland and Sondra Locke, SAG President Barry Gordon, SAG Women's Committee Chair Christina Belford and WGA President Del Reisman.

"We are circumventing standard practices by opening direct communication between women writers and the actresses who can produce the projects," said Belford. "A lot of good projects by and for women get lost going through men's channels. If we can get the right script to the right woman, she can get the picture made."

Geena Davis agreed and called her experience with *Thelma and Louise* "extraordinary." She was particularly pleased that screenwriter Callie Khouri won the Oscar for her original script. Davis said, "It wasn't just a great role, it was a great adventure story for two women — and we need more of those. We're usually asked to fill supporting roles in men's adventures or to play some kind of psycho-demon-killer-bitch. Women need different kinds of roles."

Amy Jones, who wrote the screenplays for *Mystic Pizza* and the upcoming Demi Moore film *Indecent Proposal*, is often asked at pitch meetings, "Yes, yes, but who is the *male* lead?" She also said she has been asked to rewrite female roles in screenplays written by men, "as if we are a different species. Roles should be written for *people*, not for sex."

Victoria Principal observed that television is generally more receptive to women's stories than the theatrical market. "Advertisers know that more women are now controlling the family pocketbook, so they're sponsoring more stories of interest to women," she said. "I've been able to option scripts written for men and to rewrite the leading role as a woman. It's exciting to be here and see women networking and cultivating each other's talents — that's what men have been doing all along." ▥

Source: Screen Actor, Spring 1992, p. 19.

their "one big union" concept, and (2) on the eve of the Great Depression, when an apathetic AFL remained almost strictly interested in highly skilled workers despite mammoth membership losses and concerted attacks from without—a Gompers and a Lewis could emerge to lead unionism to heights previously thought unreachable.

It is entirely possible that labor's remarkable staying power has been due to the simple fact that to many workers, from the early nineteenth century to the present, there really has been no acceptable substitute for collective bargaining as a means of maintaining and improving employment conditions. Whatever its deficiencies, the labor union has offered millions of employees in our profit-minded society sufficient hope that their personal needs would be considered to warrant their taking out union membership. At the very least, these employees have concluded that the only theoretical alternative to collective bargaining—individual bargaining—has for them been no real alternative at all.

Thus, as the earliest pages of this book have indicated, the strongest of cases can be built that collective bargaining is here to stay—and most probably in the highly pragmatic "bread-and-butter" form from which its successes have always emanated, although presumably with some future structural changes to accommodate future institutional needs just as it has made these in the past.

From this it follows that we need to find, not an alternative to labor-management relations, but ways of *improving* the process that now exists. And the latter can be located only after we fully understand both this process and the framework in which it operates. Toward such understandings such a book as this is, of course, directed.

DISCUSSION QUESTIONS

1. "Without the rise of the merchant-capitalist in this country, there could have been no genuine labor movement." Comment.

2. It has been said that "unions are for capitalism for the same reason that fish are for water." Elaborate upon this statement, drawing from the historical record.

3. Explain the following paradox: Until relatively recent years, skilled workers who enjoyed comparatively high levels of income and status constituted the main source of union membership.

4. "If the Knights of Labor expired because it could not fulfill any function, the American Federation of Labor succeeded because it could admirably fulfill many functions." Elaborate, qualifying this statement if you believe that qualifications are needed.

5. One scholar of labor history has offered as his opinion that "even with the New Deal...union development experienced, not a marked muta-

tion, but a partial alteration and expansion in leadership, tactics, and jurisdiction. The adjustment in basic union philosophy was neither profound nor completely permanent." Do you agree?

6. If a Gompers and a Lewis could emerge to rescue unionism at critical times in the past, cannot a case be made that there is nothing basically wrong with organized labor today that imaginative leadership could not cure? Discuss fully.

7. "American unionism has very definitely been a war profiteer." Do you agree or disagree?

MINICASES

#1 The Frustrated Labor Historian

Dr. Horace P. Karastan, Distinguished Professor of Labor Relations History at the University and a widely recognized authority in his field, had readily accepted the invitation to speak at the upcoming winter banquet meeting of the Newspaper Owners' Roundtable. Forty-five minutes had seemed to him to be somewhat on the meager side to properly accommodate the topic that he had been asked to handle—"American Labor Union History from the Eighteenth Century to the Present." But thoughts of the considerable remuneration that he would receive for this brief stint allowed him to forget his compunctions and he approached the date of the banquet with his customary optimism.

Unexpectedly, and sadly from Karastan's point of view, the two speakers who preceded him at the microphone (a United States Congressman and a woman from the Internal Revenue Service) each consumed far more than the fifteen minutes that *they* had been allotted. And the professor, originally scheduled to be presented to the audience at 8:15 P.M., did not get the floor until 9:10 P.M. The last words that he heard the Roundtable program chairman use in introducing him were "whose topic for the next few minutes will be 'The Three Most Important Events in American Labor Union History.'"

What would you, if Dr. Karastan, now say to the audience—and why?

#2 A Vote of No Confidence

MEMORANDUM TO: Irving L. Grohmann, Chairman, Department of Business Administration

FROM: Harold O. West-Sackville, Associate Professor and Chairman, Departmental Curriculum Committee

SUBJECT: Proposed Abolition of Labor History Course

After considerable thought, some of it frankly quite painful, I have come to the conclusion that when subjected to any kind of close scrutiny a course in American Labor History such as our BA 487 falls short of justifying itself in our curriculum by some distance.

Enrollments, as you know, have never been particularly gratifying for this elective offering, but since neither person who has taught BA 487 has been known as a crowd-pleaser I don't attach too much weight to this factor by itself. What concerns me much more is the fact that in no way can our graduates *use* the information that they get in this course: unlike essentially anything else that we offer, there is simply *no practical value* in the material that is covered in this full-semester experience.

Not one of our other advanced courses in the Personnel area—Wage and Salary Administration, Selection, Manpower Planning, and Collective Bargaining itself—is open to such an indictment; in all cases, their carry-over to the real world is obvious. And the same can be said for all of our many offerings, both at the survey course and advanced course level, outside of Personnel—in Marketing, Production, Finance, Quantitative Business Analysis and General Management. They are nothing if not relevant to the everyday life of the manager.

BA 487 stands out as the exception like an orange in a bag full of apples. And while I write at this moment only as an individual in making known my desire to see it dropped from our curriculum, I intend to make such a recommendation to my full committee when we next meet (on October 21) and, hopefully, thereafter to our full faculty.

Thanks for the backing that I know I have from you in adopting this position.

Do you agree or disagree with Professor West-Sackville's sentiments?

NOTES

[1]Foster Rhea Dulles, *Labor in America,* 2nd rev. ed. (New York: Thomas Y. Crowell, 1960), p. 59.

[2]*Ibid.,* p. 81.

[3]In 1924, he lost his try for reelection by a narrow margin and had to wait a year before he could return to office.

[4]Philip Taft, *Organized Labor in American History* (New York: Harper & Row, 1964), p. 117.

[5]*AFL Convention Proceedings,* 1903, p. 198.

[6]Joseph G. Rayback, *A History of American Labor* (New York: Free Press, 1966), p. 215.

[7]Stanley Lebergott, *The Measurement and Behavior of Unemployment* (Princeton, N.J.: National Bureau of Economic Research, 1957), p. 215.

[8]Lloyd Ulman, *American Trade Unionism—Past and Present* (Berkeley, Calif.: Institute of Industrial Relations, 1961), p. 397.

[9]*Ibid.,* pp. 397–98.

[10]*Minutes of Committee for Industrial Organization,* Washington, D.C., November 9, 1935.

[11]R.R.R. Brooks, *When Labor Organizes* (New Haven: Yale University Press, 1937), p. 146.

[12]Rayback, *History of American Labor,* p. 386.

[13]"John Herling's Labor Letter," *Washington Daily News,* November 30, 1968, p. 4.

[14]Ray Marshall, *The Negro Worker* (New York: Random House, 1967), pp. 40–41.

[15]Derek C. Bok and John T. Dunlop, *Labor and the American Community* (New York: Simon & Schuster, 1970), p. 120.

[16]*Business Week,* September 27, 1969, p. 31.

[17]Marten Estey, *The Unions* (New York: Harcourt Brace Jovanovich, 1967), p. 68.

[18]*Business Week,* December 1, 1973, p. 86.

[19]*Washington Post,* February 20, 1977, Sec. F, p. 9.

[20]*AFL-CIO Constitution,* Article II, Sec. 4.

[21]See Richard B. Freeman and James L. Medoff, *What Do Unions Do?* (New York: Basic Books, 1984), pp. 29–30 for some documentation here.

[22]*Ibid.,* p. 30.

[23]*New York Times,* January 8, 1989, p. 4E.

[24]*Ibid., New York Times,* April 6, 1989, p. A30.

[25]*Wall Street Journal,* November 20, 1985, *op. cit.*

[26]*Business Week,* March 30, 1974, p. 102.

[27]*Ibid.*

[28]*New York Times,* October 19, 1977, p. 55.

[29]*New York Times,* March 29, 1981, Sec. F, p. 8.

SELECTED REFERENCES

Bernstein, Irving, *The Turbulent Years: A History of the American Worker, 1933–1941.* Boston: Houghton Mifflin, 1970.

Brooks, Thomas R., *Toil and Trouble: A History of American Labor* (2nd ed., rev.). New York: Delacorte Press, 1971.

Byerly, Victoria, *Hard Times Cotton Mill Girls.* Ithaca, N.Y.: ILR Press, Cornell University, 1986.

Finley, Joseph E., *The Corrupt Kingdom: The Rise and Fall of the United Mine Workers.* New York: Simon & Schuster, 1972.

Fraser, Steven, *Labor Will Rule: Sidney Hillman and the Rise of American Labor*. New York: Free Press, 1991.

Galenson, Walter, *The CIO Challenge to the AFL: A History of the American Labor Movement, 1935–1941*. Cambridge, Mass.: Harvard University Press, 1960.

Goldberg, Roberta, *Organizing Women Office Workers: Dissatisfaction, Consciousness, and Action*. New York: Praeger, 1983.

Gompers, Samuel, *Seventy Years of Life and Labor: An Autobiography*. Edited and introduced by Nick Salvatore. Ithaca, N.Y.: ILR Press, Cornell University, 1984.

Gould, William B., *Black Workers in White Unions*. Ithaca, N.Y.: ILR Press, Cornell University, 1977.

Goulden, Joseph C., *Meany*. New York: Atheneum, 1972.

Kingsolver, Barbara, *Holding the Line: Women in the Great Arizona Mine Strike of 1983*. Ithaca, N.Y.: ILR Press, Cornell University, 1989.

Larson, Simeon, and Bruce Nissen, eds., *Theories of the Labor Movement*. Detroit: Wayne University Press, 1986.

Nielsen, Georgia Panter, *From Sky Girl to Flight Attendant*. Ithaca, N.Y.: ILR Press, Cornell University, 1982.

Rayback, Joseph G., *A History of American Labor*. New York: Free Press, 1966.

Reuther, Victor G., *The Brothers Reuther and the Story of the UAW*. Boston: Houghton Mifflin, 1976.

Schacht, John N., *The Making of Telephone Unionism, 1920–1947*. New Brunswick, N.J.: Rutgers University Press, 1985.

Schnapper, M. B., *American Labor: A Pictorial Social History*. Washington, D.C.: Public Affairs Press, 1972.

Sexton, Patricia Cayo, *The New Nightingales: Hospital Workers, Unions, New Women's Issues*. New York: Enquiry Press, 1982.

Sloane, Arthur A., *Hoffa*. Cambridge, Mass.: MIT Press, 1991.

Wilson, Joseph F., *Tearing Down the Color Bar: A Documentary History of the Brotherhood of Sleeping Car Porters*. New York: Columbia University Press, 1989.

Zieger, Robert H., *American Workers, American Unions, 1920–1985*. Baltimore: Johns Hopkins University Press, 1986.

3

The Legal Framework

OUTLINE OF KEY CONTENTS

- A century and a half of judge-made law and why labor didn't like it
- The Norris-La Guardia Act of 1932 and the start of a new era for unionism
- The Wagner Act of 1935 and why the modern American labor movement can be said to have begun with it
- The Taft-Hartley Act of 1947 and the public's less positive sentiments toward unions
- The Landrum-Griffin Act of 1959 and yet another change in the thrust of labor law
- The Reagan-Bush labor legacy
- The new and controversial issue of permanent replacements for strikers

As previous pages have suggested, today's managers are hardly free to deal with unions in any way that they want. A growing body of federal and state laws and the judicial and administrative interpretations of these laws now govern the employer at virtually all points of contact with organized labor. Legislation today has much to say about management's role in union organizational campaigns and its bargaining procedures in negotiating contracts once a union has gained recognition. It is also outspoken about the acceptable contents of the employer's labor agreements, and even its actions in administering these agreements. As is also true of the union, whose conduct is at least equally regulated by public policy, the management can scarcely afford to be poorly informed in the area of labor law.

If the laws have become extensive, however, they have also become complex and often nebulous. Labor lawyers have been forced to undertake herculean tasks, not always successfully, in attempting to assess what is legal and what is not in the sphere of collective bargaining. And inconsistent interpretations of the labor statutes—stemming from the National Labor Relations Board, the various state and lower federal judiciaries, and the Supreme Court itself—continue to mark the field. There is, in fact, some justification for those who have termed the last major piece of federal labor legislation, the Landrum-Griffin Act of 1959, the "Lawyers' Full Employment Act."

But if it is impossible to state definitively the exact constraints on union-management relations that the law now imposes, at least what might appropriately be described as "currently useful generalizations" can be offered. Moreover, not only such basic principles but also their paths of development must be dealt with if the environment in which labor relations now operate is to be fully appreciated. If the lessons of labor history have greatly influenced the nature of the bargaining process as it exists today, the ever-greater thrust of the laws has had an equally pervasive effect.

THE ERA OF JUDICIAL CONTROL

In view of the present scope of labor legislation, it is somewhat ironic that little more than six decades ago, employers were virtually unrestrained by law from dealing with unions as they saw fit. There was, as we have seen, almost no statutory treatment of labor-management relations from the days of the American Revolution until the Great Depression of the 1930s. Instead, individual judges exercised public control over these relations. And the courts' view of union activities was, for the most part, as unsympathetic as was that of most businesspeople of the times.

The employers' traditional weapons for fighting labor organizations— formal and informal espionage, blacklists, and the very potent practice of discharging "agitators"—were normally left undisturbed by the judges. However, if the members of the judiciary believed that union activities were being conducted either for "illegal purposes" or by "illegal means," they were generous in extracting money damages from the unions and in ordering criminal prosecution of labor leaders.

The qualifications for "illegality" varied to some extent from court to court. In general, however, most aggressive union activities of the day—strikes to obtain agreements whereby the employer would employ only union members (the closed shop), picketing by "strangers" (those not in a direct superior-subordinate relationship with the employer), and the secondary boycott (the exercise of economic pressure against one company to force it to exert pressure on another company that is actually the subject of the union's concern)—were held to be illegal. Many courts went even further. Through the 1920s, such remarks as "Judicial actions against even peaceful picketing are merely declaratory of what has always been the law and the best practice in equity" flowed freely from the judges. And although it was President Calvin Coolidge who asserted that "the business of the United States is business," the remark could readily have emanated from most members of the judiciary well into the third decade of this century. The courts, viewing their primary role as that of protecting property rights, allied themselves with few exceptions squarely with the employer community to neutralize the economic power of organized labor.

Fully as welcome to employers, too, was the extensive court use of the injunction. This device, a judicial order calling for the cessation of certain actions deemed injurious and for which the other forms of court-provided relief appeared to be unsuitable remedies, was often invoked by the judges following employer requests for such intervention. To unionists, such restraining orders seemed to be issued quite indiscriminately. Even the relatively detached observer of legal history, however, would very likely conclude that it did not seem to take much to convince the judges that union activities should be curbed: The jurists issued their restraining decrees almost as reflex actions; and strikes, boycotts, picketing—virtually any form of union "self-help" activity—thus ran the risk of being abruptly ended if in any way present or imminent damage to the employer's property could be shown as being threatened.

THE NORRIS–LA GUARDIA ACT OF 1932

Despite its 1932 date, the Norris–La Guardia Act is of considerably more than historical interest. As is true of the later labor laws that will be discussed in this chapter, most of its provisions are still valid and continue today to govern labor relations in interstate commerce.

At the time of its passage, however, the act was particularly noteworthy. Not only did it constitute the first major interindustry federal legislation to be applied to collective bargaining, but—as stated earlier—it marked a significant change in public policy *from repression to strong encouragement of union activity.* Implemented in the final days of the Hoover administration, it owed its birth mainly to the widespread unemployment of the times and to a general recognition that only through bargaining collectively could many employees exercise any satisfactory influence on their working environments. It also stemmed, however, from popular sentiment that justice had not been served by allowing the courts their virtually unlimited authority to issue injunctions in labor disputes.

Accordingly, the act greatly narrowed the scope of the courts for issuing such injunctions. Peaceful picketing, peaceable assembly, organizational picketing, payment of strike benefits, and a host of other union economic weapons were now made nonenjoinable. Also enacted within the new law were procedural requirements for injunctions issued on other grounds.

Even more symbolic of the major shift in public policy was the act's assertion that it was now necessary for Congress to guarantee to the individual employee "full freedom of association, self-organization, and designation of representatives of his own choosing, to negotiate the terms and conditions of his employment…free from interference, restraint, or coercion of employers." All the federal labor laws passed since 1932 have embodied this same principle.

Nor was the new treatment of unionism destined to be confined only to the federal arena. Within a short period of time, twenty states (including almost all the major industrial ones) had independently created their own "little Norris–La-Guardia Acts" to govern labor relations in intrastate commerce.

Norris–La Guardia and its state counterparts did not by themselves, however, greatly stimulate union growth. They clearly expanded union freedoms and placed legal limits on judicial capriciousness, but they did little to restrain employers directly in their conduct toward collective bargaining. Only the previously cited "yellow-dog" contract arrangement, whereby managements had been able to require nonunion membership or activity as a condition of employment, was declared unenforceable by the 1932 act. Otherwise, employers remained at liberty to fight labor organizations by whatever means they could implement, despite the ambitious language of Norris–La Guardia.

THE WAGNER ACT OF 1935

It remained for the National Labor Relations Act of 1935, more commonly known as the Wagner Act, to alter this situation by putting teeth in the government's pledge to protect employee collective bargaining rights. The Wagner Act, it will be recalled, accomplished this through two basic methods: (1) It specifically banned five types of management action as constituting "unfair labor practices"; and (2) it set forth the principle of majority rule for the selection of employee bargaining representatives and provided that, should the employer express doubt as to the union's majority status, a secret-ballot election of the employees would determine if the majority existed. It also created an independent, quasi-judicial agency—the National Labor Relations Board (NLRB)—to provide the machinery for enforcing both these provisions. (Exhibits 3-1 and 3-2 constitute the key documents currently being used by the NLRB for these two activities, respectively. Exhibit 3-3, a cartoon that originally appeared in 1935, conveys organized labor's jubilation at the time of the Wagner Act's passage.)

EXHIBIT 3-1

FORM EXEMPT UNDER 44 U.S.C. 3512

FORM NLRB-501 (8-83)	UNITED STATES OF AMERICA NATIONAL LABOR RELATIONS BOARD **CHARGE AGAINST EMPLOYER**	**DO NOT WRITE IN THIS SPACE**	
		Case	Date Filed

INSTRUCTIONS: File an original and 4 copies of this charge with NLRB Regional Director for the region in which the alleged unfair labor practice occurred or is occurring.

1. EMPLOYER AGAINST WHOM CHARGE IS BROUGHT

a. Name of Employer		b. Number of workers employed
c. Address *(street, city, state, ZIP code)*	d. Employer Representative	e. Telephone No.
f. Type of Establishment *(factory, mine, wholesaler, etc.)*	g. Identify principal product or service	

h. The above-named employer has engaged in and is engaging in unfair labor practices within the meaning of section 8(a), subsections (1) and *(list subsections)* _____ of the National Labor Relations Act, and these unfair labor practices are unfair practices affecting commerce within the meaning of the Act.

2. Basis of the Charge *(be specific as to facts, names, addresses, plants involved, dates, places, etc.)*

By the above and other acts, the above-named employer has interfered with, restrained, and coerced employees in the exercise of the rights guaranteed in Section 7 of the Act

3. Full name of party filing charge *(if labor organization, give full name, including local name and number)*

4a. Address *(street and number, city, state, and ZIP code)*	4b. Telephone No.

5. Full name of national or international labor organization of which it is an affiliate or constituent unit *(to be filled in when charge is filed by a labor organization)*

6. DECLARATION

I declare that I have read the above charge and that the statements are true to the best of my knowledge and belief.

By _____   _____
     (signature of representative or person making charge)   *(title if any)*

Address _____   _____ _____
                                                        (Telephone No.)   *(date)*

WILLFUL FALSE STATEMENTS ON THIS CHARGE CAN BE PUNISHED BY FINE AND IMPRISONMENT
(U. S. CODE, TITLE 18, SECTION 1001)

EXHIBIT 3-2

FORM NLRB-652
(5-80)

UNITED STATES OF AMERICA
NATIONAL LABOR RELATIONS BOARD

STIPULATION FOR CERTIFICATION UPON CONSENT ELECTION

Pursuant to a petition duly filed under Section 9 of the National Labor Relations Act, as amended, and subject to the approval of the Regional Director for the National Labor Relations Board (herein called the Regional Director), the undersigned parties hereby agree that the petition is hereby amended to conform to this Stipulation and that the approval of this Stipulation constitutes a withdrawal of any Notice of Representation Hearing previously issued in this matter, and further AGREE AS FOLLOWS:

1. **SECRET BALLOT.**—An election by secret ballot shall be held under the supervision of the said Regional Director, among the employees of the undersigned Employer in the unit defined below, at the indicated time and place, to determine whether or not such employees desire to be represented for the purpose of collective bargaining by (one of) the undersigned labor organization(s). Said election shall be held in accordance with the National Labor Relations Act, the Board's Rules and Regulations, and the applicable procedures and policies of the Board.

2. **ELIGIBLE VOTERS.**—The eligible voters shall be those employees included within the unit described below, who were employed during the payroll period indicated below, and also employees who did not work during said payroll period because they were ill or on vacation or temporarily laid off, employees in the military services of the United States who appear in person at the polls, employees engaged in an economic strike which commenced less than 12 months before the election date and who retained their status as such during the eligibility period and their replacements, but *excluding* any employees who have since quit or been discharged for cause and employees engaged in a strike who have been discharged for cause since the commencement thereof, and who have not been rehired or reinstated prior to the date of the election, and employees engaged in an economic strike which commenced more than 12 months prior to the date of the election and who have been permanently replaced. At a date fixed by the Regional Director, the parties, as requested, will furnish to the Regional Director an accurate list of all the eligible voters, together with a list of the employees, if any, specifically excluded from eligibility.

3. **NOTICES OF ELECTION.**—The Regional Director shall prepare a Notice of Election and supply copies to the parties describing the manner and conduct of the election to be held and incorporating therein a sample ballot. The parties, upon the request of and at a time designated by the Regional Director, will post such Notice of Election at conspicuous and usual posting places easily accessible to the eligible voters.

4. **OBSERVERS.**—Each party hereto will be allowed to station an equal number of authorized observers, selected from among the nonsupervisory employees of the Employer, at the polling places during the election to assist in its conduct, to challenge the eligibility of voters, and to verify the tally.

5. **TALLY OF BALLOTS.**—As soon after the election as feasible, the votes shall be counted and tabulated by the Regional Director, or Board agent or agents. Upon the conclusion of the counting, the Regional Director shall furnish a Tally of Ballots to each of the parties.

6. **POSTELECTION AND RUNOFF PROCEDURE.**—All procedures subsequent to the conclusion of counting ballots shall be in conformity with the Board's Rules and Regulations.

7. **RECORD.**—The record in this case shall be governed by the appropriate provisions of the Board's Rules and Regulations and shall include this Stipulation. Hearing and notice thereof, Direction of Election, and the making of Findings of Fact and Conclusions of Law by the Board prior to the election are hereby expressly waived.

EXHIBIT 3–2 (continued)

8. COMMERCE.—The Employer is engaged in commerce within the meaning of Section 2 (6) and (7) of the National Labor Relations Act, and a question affecting commerce has arisen concerning the representation of employees within the meaning of Section 9 (c). *(Insert commerce facts.)*

9. WORDING ON THE BALLOT.—Where only one labor organization is signatory to this agreement, the name of the organization shall appear on the ballot and the choice shall be "Yes" or "No." In the event that more than one labor organization is signatory to this Stipulation, the choices on the ballot will appear in the wording indicated below and in the order enumerated below, reading from left to right on the ballot, or, if the occasion demands, from top to bottom. *(If more than one union is to appear on the ballot, any union may have its name removed from the ballot by the approval of the Regional Director of a timely request, in writing, to that effect.)*

First.

Second.

Third.

10. PAYROLL PERIOD FOR ELIGIBILITY · THE PERIOD ENDING_____**.**

11. DATE, HOURS, AND PLACE OF ELECTION.—

12. THE APPROPRIATE COLLECTIVE-BARGAINING UNIT.—

....	....
(Employer)	*(Name of Organization)*
By	By ....
(Name) *(Date)*	*(Name)* *(Date)*
....	....
(Title)	*(Title)*
Recommended:	
....	....
(Board Agent) *(Date)*	*(Name of other Organization)*
Date approved	By ....
	(Name) *(Date)*
....	....
Regional Director,	*(Title)*
National Labor Relations Board.	Case No. ....

EXHIBIT 3-3

Source: United Mine Workers Journal, June 1992, p. 6

Employer Unfair Labor Practices

The five employer unfair labor practices, deemed "statutory wrongs" (although not crimes) by Congress, have been modified to some small extent since 1935, as noted below. They remain, however, a significant part of the law of collective bargaining to this day, and they constitute an impressive quintet of "thou shalt nots" for employers who might otherwise be tempted to resort to the blunt tactics of prior eras in an effort to undermine unionism. The Wagner Act (1) deemed it "unfair" for managements to "interfere with, restrain, or coerce employees" in exercising their now legally sanctioned right of self-organization; (2) restrained management representatives from dominating or interfering with either the formation or the administration of labor unions; (3) prohibited employers from discriminating "in regard to hire or tenure of employment or any term or condition of employment to encourage or discourage membership in any labor organization"; (4) forbade employers to discharge or otherwise discriminate against employees simply because the latter had filed "unfair labor practice" charges or otherwise offered testimony against management actions under the act; and (5) made it an unfair labor practice for employers to refuse to bargain collectively with the duly chosen representatives of their employees.

In the years since 1935, the NLRB and the courts (to which board decisions can be appealed by either labor relations party) have had ample opportunity to make known their interpretations of all five of these provisions. In dealing with some of them, both public bodies have been quite consistent in their decisions, and what the framers of the Wagner Act had in mind is no longer seriously questioned by either management or union representatives. In other cases, however, the board members and judges have had some difficulty in issuing rulings that have been perceived by the labor relations parties as being compatible with prior rulings on the same subject. But the judges have at least generally proved themselves to be reluctant to reverse the original NLRB decisions when these have been appealed to the courts, and the inconsistencies would in most cases appear to stem more from the changing membership of the five-member board through the years and from inherent difficulties in the words of the laws themselves than from this "opportunity for appeal" factor.

Relatively clear-cut decisions have been rendered by the NLRB and courts in two of the five areas:

1. The interpreters of the Wagner Act have consistently held a wide variety of employer practices to be in violation of the "interfere with, restrain or coerce employees" section. Among other management actions, bribery of employees, company spy systems, blacklisting of union sympathizers, removal of an existing business to another location for the sole purpose of frustrating union activity, and promises by employers of wage increases or other special concessions to employees should the latter refrain from joining a union have all historically constituted "interference" contrary to the act. The same can be said of board and court treatment of employers who have threatened to isolate ("like a rotten apple," in one case) prounion workers, engaged in individual bargaining with employees represented by a union, or questioned employees concerning their union activities in such a way as to tend to restrain or coerce such employees. When satisfied that any such violations have occurred, the board has issued cease-and-desist orders against the guilty employer with no hesitation. And when it has found that employees have been discharged unlawfully in the process, the NLRB has most frequently required their reinstatement with full back pay.

Particularly in this area, the courts have proved unwilling, by and large, to reverse board decisions upon appeal, moreover, and the fact that failure to "cease and desist" after the courts have called for this action constitutes contempt of court has at times dissuaded employers from carrying an appeal to the courts in the first place. However, under normal circumstances, the employer who both refuses to comply with an adverse board order and decides not to appeal it (so as not to bring the matter to the court's attention) stands to gain little; the NLRB itself can be counted upon to take the initiative and ask the judges for an order calling for employer compliance with the original board decision.

2. The board and courts have also had no apparent difficulty in deciding what constitutes evidence of employer discrimination related to the fourth unfair labor practice. They long ago concluded that such management actions as the layoff of an employee shortly after his testimony before the board and the discharge of a woman worker immediately after her husband had filed unfair labor practice charges (on other grounds) against the company could be taken as discriminatory, and they have consistently ruled in this direction ever since. The board has further concluded, apparently also without much hesitation, that management's belief that charges filed by an employee are false in no way justifies its taking punitive action against the employee. On the other hand, considerably fewer cases have had to be decided concerning this fourth unfair practice than any of the others, presumably because employers have themselves recognized that violations here are normally quite obvious to all concerned and have therefore refrained from taking such action in the first place.

Interpretation seems to have been somewhat more difficult when the issues have involved the three other portions of the employer unfair labor practice section.

1. The restriction on employer discrimination "in regard to hire or tenure of employment or any term or condition of employment to encourage or discourage membership in any labor organization" has clearly made it unlawful for employers to force employees who are union members to accept less desirable job assignments than nonunionists, or to reduce the former type of employee's pay because of the union affiliation. Similarly, it is obvious that managements that demand renunciation of union membership as a condition of continued employment, or in order to be promoted within the nonsupervisory ranks, do so only at their peril. But the legality of other types of employer conduct has proved to be anything but as clear-cut.

Where, for example, there is conclusive evidence that an employee has falsified an employment application and thus failed to reveal a previous criminal record, can the person be properly discharged for this offense? Not always, according to at least one NLRB decision covering exactly this situation. Here, the board cited the company's "antiunion bias," its knowledge of the employee's union activities, and its treatment of nonunion employees who had committed comparable offenses, in deciding that the company's official reason for the discharge was only a pretext for discrimination against union members.[1] Cases of this kind have proved to be thorny ones for the board and the courts and have often caused considerable flows of adrenalin on the part of employers.

2. The proviso restraining management representatives from dominating or interfering with both the formation and the administration of labor unions—included because of Congress's unhappiness with the widespread creation of employer-influenced company unions in the years preceding 1935—has been the basis of much complex litigation since that date. Obviously, when an employer has control over the union sitting on the other side of the bargaining table, genuine collective bargaining cannot take place. But determining just when an employer has such control has proven to be no easy matter. Among specific management actions that the board and courts have looked unfavorably upon as evidence of employer control have been the following: the solicitation of union membership by supervisory employees, the employer's payment of membership dues for all employees joining the union, and an employer gift to a union of $400 and the right to operate a canteen that made a monthly profit—none of these managerial moves being especially notable for their subtlety. On the other hand, interpretations have found nothing unlawful in the mere fact that, for example, a labor organization limits its membership to employees of a single employer; the test for unfair practice pivots exclusively upon the question of which party *controls* the organization, and in a case such as this only much closer inspection can reveal whether or not the employer is in violation of the law.

3. The fact that the 1935 legislation said little more on the subject of an employer's "refusal to bargain collectively with the representatives of his employees" than can be gleaned from these words perhaps guaranteed that controversies would result from this last section of the Wagner Act's "Rights of Employees" section, and this has indeed been the case. As such new topics for potential bargaining as pensions, health insurance, seniority, and subcontracting have arisen in the years since 1935, the NLRB and courts have been freely called upon to make known their opinions as to what must be bargained by employers, and what need not be. The courts have also been asked for a more precise definition of "bargaining" itself than the act provided. The issue is still far from resolved, and with new possibilities for bargaining constantly emerging, perhaps it never fully will be. But the board and judicial decisions of the past six decades have at least ambitiously attempted to shed light on the scope for employer action in this area, and certain statements can now be made with some authority.

In brief, there are today many "mandatory" subjects of bargaining with which the employer must deal in good faith. Such subjects include wages; hours of employment; health insurance; pensions; safety practices; the grievance procedure; procedures for discharge, layoff, recall, and discipline; seniority; and subcontracting. Managers are not required to make concessions or agree to union proposals on any of these (or various other) subjects. They *are* obligated, however, to meet with the union at reasonable times and with the good-faith intention of reaching an agreement. On "nonmandatory" or "voluntary" subjects—those that are lawful but not easily related to "wages, hours and other conditions of employment"—employers are not so obligated and are free to refuse to bargain about them.

Where there is a duty to bargain, the employer must supply—upon union request—information that is "relevant and necessary" to allow the labor representatives to bargain "intelligently and effectively." The NLRB and courts have ruled, for example, that a union is entitled to information in the employer's possession concerning wage rates and increases, on the grounds that it cannot deal intelligently with the subject without such information. Similarly, if a management claims financial inability to honor the union's demands, it must stand ready to supply the union with authoritative proof of this inability. This principle, established in *Truitt*,[2] was weakened by the NLRB in a 1991 decision.[3] An employer refused to provide the union the opportunity to inspect its financial records when it demanded reduced wages and benefits. It did not plead poverty because it was actually making a profit. Reduced wages and benefits, contended the employer, were needed to meet prices of its competitors. The board ruled that as long as the employer did not say it could not afford to maintain the present wages and benefits structure, it could lawfully refuse to make its financial records available to the union. Reduction of labor costs to meet competition is not the same thing as pleading poverty, the ruling asserted. Needless to say, the union felt that the board's decision was highly unrealistic.

The employer's duty to bargain also entails the duty to refrain from taking unilateral action on the "mandatory" subjects. Companies that have announced a wage increase without consulting the employees' designated representatives, or have subcontracted work to another employer without allowing their own union a chance to bargain the matter, violate this portion of the law.

Yet the apparent finality of such remarks as these is highly deceptive. Not only is considerable uncertainty left as to what else is a "mandatory" subject for bargaining (beyond the specific topics cited and the few others that the NLRB and judges have thus far dealt with affirmatively) and what is "nonmandatory," but the question of what constitutes "the good-faith intention of reaching an agreement" on the employer's part is left an open one.

It remains to be seen what further subjects the board and courts will ultimately assign to the "mandatory" category. A union demand for moving allowances for workers transferred by the company? A proposal that all production workers be placed on a salaried basis, rather than being paid by the hour? A request by the labor organization that all foreign production of the company's product be terminated? Guarantees by the company that pension funds will be invested in low-cost housing for union employees? Each of these demands has been raised on several occasions in actual bargaining situations in recent years. Except for the first, company negotiators have been notably reluctant to accommodate any of them, or numerous similarly ambitious union proposals. Yet as Fleming, who has raised the possibility of all of them ultimately going before the interpreters of public policy, has pointed out, "In the changing and very real world of bargaining, all [of these and similar demands] may be close to the felt needs of the parties...[and] deciding which of [them] falls into the mandatory category will not be an easy task. Job security and internal union affairs pose extremely delicate issues."[4]

If disposition of such issues as these must thus await future board and court treatment, it at least appears safe to predict that the books have not yet closed on the list of "mandatory" topics; most of the subjects with which employers are now required to deal in good faith are themselves relative newcomers to such status, in fact.

Indeed, a previous edition of this book declared with absolute confidence that (among other situations forbidden them) unions could not make the prices charged by employers for food in plant cafeterias and vending machines subject to the bargaining process. A mere four years from the time that those words were written, the U.S. Supreme Court made them obsolete by ruling, in a case involving the Ford Motor Company, that employers could in fact be required to bargain over such prices (and related services, too). Speaking for the Court, Justice Byron White said that "the availability of food during working hours and the conditions under which it is to be consumed are matters of deep concern to workers, and one needn't strain to consider them to be among those 'conditions' of employment that should be subject to the mutual duty to bargain."[5] Nothing is guaranteed except change.

In 1989, the NLRB dealt with compulsory testing of employees for drugs and alcohol, a major problem of the industrial world. Two issues were resolved by the agency: whether testing of persons applying for a job and the testing of current employees are mandatory issues of collective bargaining. With respect to the former, the board ruled that preemployment testing is not a subject of mandatory bargaining.[6] Until job applicants are hired, they are not part of the bargaining unit or covered by the labor agreement. In the second type of case, the employer unilaterally established a policy under which any employee injured on the job was compelled to be tested for drugs and alcohol. Holding that the rule changed the terms and conditions of employment, the agency said testing of current employees is a mandatory issue of bargaining.[7] The clear purpose of the testing program was that employees failing the test would be disciplined, possibly discharged. Before implementing such a rule, the employer must bargain with the union.

The steadily increasing types of tests adopted by the board and courts for "good faith"—for example, whether or not employer delaying tactics were used in the bargaining, some evidence of management initiative in making counterproposals, and employer willingness to accommodate completely routine demands (such as the continued availability of plant parking spaces)—have often been attacked for their naïveté, if not for the spirit behind them. Anyone who thinks that such tests by themselves can definitively reveal whether or not "good faith" has actually occurred at the bargaining table would probably believe almost anything.

At the very least, however, it is obvious that in being forced to plug the existing gaps in the Wagner Act's "refusal to bargain" interpretations, representatives of public policy have projected themselves more and more into the labor-management arena in the years since 1935, perhaps to an extent that was never contemplated when the Wagner Act was passed. Understand, however, that though the law requires bargaining over mandatory issues, it does not require agreement. Should an impasse be reached, strikes and lockouts are perfectly legal. To require agreement would lead to a system of compulsory arbitration, a policy that would be anathema to labor, management, and others who believe in the free collective-bargaining system.

Employee Representation Elections

Despite all the interpretative difficulties that have been involved in the employer unfair labor practice provisions, the latter clearly were—and are—widesweeping in their implications for collective bargaining. However, they still represent an *indirect* approach to the protection of employee bargaining rights: By themselves, they restrict employer action in the labor relations area, but they say nothing explicit about the key question of initial union recognition.

The authors of the Wagner Act were well aware of this gap and proceeded to deal directly with the issue in another section of the act, that pertaining to the secret-ballot election. As noted previously, the NLRB was authorized to conduct such an election should the employer express doubt that a majority of its employees had chosen to be represented by any union at all. Prior to this time, a union could gain recognition from an unreceptive employer only through the successful use of such economic weapons as the strike and boycott.

As this part of the act now stands, the board can conduct a representation election if requested to do so by a single employee, by a group of employees, or by a labor organization acting for employees. In any of these three cases, the petition must be supported by "a substantial number of employees" who desire collective bargaining representation, and it must allege that the employer refuses to recognize such representation. Employers may also petition for such an election, presumably with the objective of proving that the employees do *not* desire union representation or for various reasons of scheduling strategy (such as trying to get the board to hold the election at the time least favorable to the union).

It is also possible for an election to involve two or more unions, each claiming "substantial" employee support. The employees then have the choice of voting for any of the unions on the ballot or for "no union." If none of these choices (including "no union") wins a majority of the votes cast, a runoff election is then conducted between the two choices that have received the highest number of votes. (Exhibit 3-4 shows the NLRB form now used for all such petitions.)

In administering this portion of the law, the NLRB itself ultimately framed a few further rules designed to foster labor relations stability. Should any union win an NLRB-conducted election and then execute a valid contract with the employer, rival unions may now not seek bargaining rights (through a subsequent election) for a period of three years following the effective date of the contract or for the length of the contract—whichever is the shorter. However, the victorious union is still not guaranteed its bargaining rights for this period of time: If the employees themselves have second thoughts about the desirability of retaining the union's services, they can—after one year—petition the NLRB for a decertification election. A majority vote in this election rescinds the union's bargaining agency.

Unions lose a majority of decertification elections, and the trend here is very much against them. In the first two years of Taft-Hartley's operation, they lost bargaining rights in 144 out of 229 such elections, thereby

EXHIBIT 3–4

FORM NLRB-502
(5-85)

FORM EXEMPT UNDER 44 U S C 3512

UNITED STATES GOVERNMENT
NATIONAL LABOR RELATIONS BOARD
PETITION

DO NOT WRITE IN THIS SPACE	
Case No.	Date Filed

INSTRUCTIONS: Submit an original and 4 copies of this Petition to the NLRB Regional Office in the Region in which the employer concerned is located. If more space is required for any one item, attach additional sheets, numbering item accordingly.

The Petitioner alleges that the following circumstances exist and requests that the National Labor Relations Board proceed under its proper authority pursuant to Section 9 of the National Labor Relations Act.

1. PURPOSE OF THIS PETITION *(If box RC, RM, or RD is checked and a charge under Section 8(b)(7) of the Act has been filed involving the Employer named herein, the statement following the description of the type of petition shall not be deemed made.)* **(Check One)**

☐ **RC-CERTIFICATION OF REPRESENTATIVE** - A substantial number of employees wish to be represented for purposes of collective bargaining by Petitioner and Petitioner desires to be certified as representative of the employees.

☐ **RM-REPRESENTATION (EMPLOYER PETITION)** - One or more individuals or labor organizations have presented a claim to Petitioner to be recognized as the representative of employees of Petitioner.

☐ **RD-DECERTIFICATION** - A substantial number of employees assert that the certified or currently recognized bargaining representative is no longer their representative.

☐ **UD-WITHDRAWAL OF UNION SHOP AUTHORITY** - Thirty percent (30%) or more of employees in a bargaining unit covered by an agreement between their employer and a labor organization desire that such authority be rescinded.

☐ **UC-UNIT CLARIFICATION** - A labor organization is currently recognized by Employer, but Petitioner seeks clarification of placement of certain employees: *(Check one)* ☐ In unit not previously certified. ☐ In unit previously certified in Case No. _____.

☐ **AC-AMENDMENT OF CERTIFICATION** - Petitioner seeks amendment of certification issued in Case No. _____ *Attach statement describing the specific amendment sought.*

2. Name of Employer	Employer Representative to contact	Telephone Number

3. Address(es) of Establishment(s) involved *(Street and number, city, State, ZIP code)*

4a. Type of Establishment *(Factory, mine, wholesaler, etc.)*	4b. Identify principal product or service

5. Unit Involved *(In UC petition, describe **present** bargaining unit and attach description of proposed clarification.)*	6a. Number of Employees in Unit:
Included	Present
	Proposed *(By UC/AC)*
Excluded	6b. Is this petition supported by 30% or more of the employees in the unit? * ____ Yes ____ No *Not applicable in RM, UC, and AC

(If you have checked box RC in 1 above, check and complete EITHER item 7a or 7b, whichever is applicable)

7a. ☐ Request for recognition as Bargaining Representative was made on *(Date)* _____ and Employer declined recognition on or about *(Date)* _____ *(If no reply received, so state).*

7b. ☐ Petitioner is currently recognized as Bargaining Representative and desires certification under the Act.

8. Name of Recognized or Certified Bargaining Agent *(If none, so state)*	Affiliation
Address and Telephone Number	Date of Recognition or Certification

9. Expiration Date of Current Contract, If any *(Month, Day, Year)*	10. If you have checked box UD in 1 above, show here the date of execution of agreement granting union shop *(Month, Day, and Year)*

11a. Is there now a strike or picketing at the Employer's establishment(s) Involved? Yes _____ No _____	11b. If so, approximately how many employees are participating?

11c. The Employer has been picketed by or on behalf of *(Insert Name)* _____, a labor organization, of *(Insert Address)* _____ Since *(Month, Day, Year)* _____.

12. Organizations or individuals other than Petitioner *(and other than those named in items 8 and 11c)*, which have claimed recognition as representatives and other organizations and individuals known to have a representative interest in any employees in unit described in item 5 above. *(If none, so state)*

Name	Affilation	Address	Date of Claim *(Required only if Petition is filed by Employer)*

I declare that I have read the above petition and that the statements are true to the best of my knowledge and belief.

_____
(Name of Petitioner and Affilation, if any)

By _____   _____
(Signature of Representative or person filing petition)   *(Title, if any)*

Address _____   _____
(Street and number, city, State, and ZIP Code)   *(Telephone Number)*

WILLFUL FALSE STATEMENTS ON THIS PETITION CAN BE PUNISHED BY FINE AND IMPRISONMENT (U. S. CODE, TITLE 18, SECTION 1001)

"winning" (in the sense of staving off defeat) some 37 percent of them. In 1970, according to the National Labor Relations Board's annual report for that year, they won only 30.2 percent of some 301 decertification elections. In 1980, an unprecedented total of 902 such contests took place, and workers voted for retention of the union in a mere 25 percent of them. By 1993, with just under 700 of these elections being held annually, unions were continuing to lose three out of four.[8] And since at this point organized labor was annually winning only about 45 percent of all *new* certification elections, or significantly fewer than the 55 percent certification victory record commonly registered until the 1970s, there was double cause for concern in the labor movement.

Employers cannot legally start the decertification process, but antiunion consultants are amply available—in fact, as noted earlier, they constitute a new growth industry by themselves—to help management make the environment "right" for decertification. Forcing the union to go out on a costly strike is only one example. And something of a process of contagion may also abet the changes of a given union being thrown out as this trend continues: Employers who become aware that a competitor across town or downstate has become nonunion may be encouraged to try and do, through decertification, the same.

Although winning an election has historically been the most common way for a union to secure bargaining rights, in about 1 percent of all union organizing campaigns, the NLRB has not insisted on the election being held. If a union gets a majority of the bargaining unit employees to sign union membership authorization cards and the employer then engages in a serious unfair labor practice (such as the discharging of union sympathizers), the election requirement is waived. The board's theory here is that the union would have won the election were it not for the employer's conduct. In 1969, the Supreme Court—agreeing with the theory—sustained it in *NLRB* v. *Gissel Packing Company.*[9]

For a time the NLRB certified unions even without demonstrating majority support when employers committed "outrageous and pervasive" unfair labor practices during the organizational campaign. In 1984, however, the Reagan board, in a case involving Gourmet Foods, abolished that policy, ruling that it would not grant bargaining rights under any circumstances unless a union signed up a majority of employees within the bargaining unit.[10]

As established by the Wagner Act, then, the scope of National Labor Relations Board activities was to be twofold. The board was charged with investigating employer unfair labor practices, and it was given the authority to conduct employee representation elections.

The NLRB's members (appointed by the President, subject to confirmation by the Senate) and its various regional officials outside Washington, even in their earliest years of existence, undertook both these assignments zealously. By 1947, they had processed almost 44,000 unfair labor practice cases, running the gamut in their decisions from dismissing complaints as having no merit to issuing cease-and-desist orders against guilty employers. In the area of representation cases, the board was even more active. Almost 60,000 such cases were dealt with between 1935 and 1947. In addition to determining whether or not elections should be held and conducting such elections if the answer was in the affirmative, the NLRB often had the further duty of deciding the type of unit appropriate for the particular labor relationship (such as employer, craft, or plant).

Although its activities were necessarily controversial, as was the act sanctioning them, there is general agreement today that in this twelve-year period the board performed its basic mission of protecting the right of employees to organize and bargain collectively quite creditably. Even at the time, many contemporaries had been impressed; as in the case of Norris–La Guardia, "little Wagner Acts" were soon enacted in many states to govern labor relations in intrastate commerce.

The modern labor movement in this country can, in fact, justifiably be said to have begun in 1935. Union membership totals boomed after that year, due in no small measure to the Wagner Act and its state counterparts. Other factors were, of course, also responsible: the improving economic climate, the generally liberal sentiments of the times, the keen competition between the American Federation of Labor and the newly born Committee for Industrial Organization, and dynamic union leadership. And it is equally true that prior legislation—not only Norris–La Guardia but also the ill-fated National Industrial Recovery Act of 1933—had paved the way for the new era and had independently led to much spontaneous union organization before 1935. But it is no less a fact that employers could still legally try to counteract unionism by almost any means except the yellow-dog contract and the arbitrary injunction process—up to and including sheer refusal to grant the union recognition under any circumstances—before the passage of the Wagner Act. It is extremely doubtful that organized labor could have grown as it did—from 3.6 million unionized workers in 1935 to more than 14 million by 1947—without the Wagner Act's protection.

Certainly public opinion as registered in Congress did not debate this last point. The average citizen gradually turned against unionism in the mid-1940s, blaming existing public policy for the union excesses of the times, most notably for the postwar strike waves. As the last chapter has described, this view ultimately became a compelling one: Congress overrode President Truman's veto and passed the Taft-Hartley Act of 1947, thereby stilling the cries that the Wagner Act had become too "one-sided" in favor of labor.

With the advent of Taft-Hartley, officially known as the Labor-Management Relations Act, a new period in public policy toward labor unions began: that of *modified encouragement coupled with regulation.*

Much as the Wagner Act was to a great extent designed to fill gaps in Norris–La Guardia, which nonetheless was not repealed and remains a part of the legal environment of collective bargaining to this day, Taft-Hartley amended but did not displace the Wagner Act. The Wagner Act, essentially as adjusted by the 1947 legislation, governs labor relations today.

Indeed, the old unfair employer practices were continued virtually word for word by the new legislation. The only significant changes were that the closed shop (and its requirements that all workers be union members at the time of their hiring) was no longer allowed and that the freedom of the parties to authorize the *union shop* (which, as noted earlier, allows the employer to hire anyone but provides that all new employees must join the union after a stipulated period of time) was somewhat narrowed. The intention of this amendment related to the third employer unfair labor practice: In its ban on employer hiring and job condition discrimination in order to encourage or discourage union membership, the Wagner Act *had* authorized employers to enter into union and closed-shop agreements. The changes clearly symbolized public policy's new attitude toward unions.

Far more indicative of the public's less enthusiastic sentiments toward unions, however, were those portions of Taft-Hartley that dealt with (1) *unfair union labor practices,* which were now enumerated and prohibited in the same way that the employer practices had been; (2) *the rights of employees as individuals,* as contrasted with those rights that employees now legally enjoyed as union members; (3) *the rights of employers,* a subject the Wagner Act had glossed over in its concentration on employer duties; and (4) *national emergency strikes.* To some extent, other major parts of the new law—those relating to internal union affairs, the termination or modification of existing labor contracts, and suits involving unions—also demonstrated a hardening of congressional attitudes toward labor organizations. We shall consider these various provisions separately.

Unfair Union Labor Practices

Going the framers of the Wagner Act one better, Taft-Hartley enumerated six labor practices that the unions were prohibited from engaging in. Labor organizations operating in interstate commerce were now officially obliged to refrain from (1) restraining or coercing employees in the exercise of their guaranteed rights to themselves refrain from "any and all" union activities; (2) causing an employer to discriminate in any way against an employee in order to encourage or discourage union membership; (3) refusing to bargain in good faith with their employer about wages, hours, and other employment conditions; (4) certain types of strikes and boycotts; (5) charging employees covered by union-shop agreements initiation fees or dues "in an amount which the board finds excessive or discriminatory under all the circumstances"; and (6) engaging in "featherbedding," the requirement of payment by the employer for services not performed. (Exhibit 3-5 illustrates the major document currently being used by the NLRB to enforce this portion of the law.)

As in the case of the unfair employer labor practices, interpretative difficulties have marked the subsequent treatment of some of those provis-

EXHIBIT 3–5

FORM EXEMPT UNDER
44 U.S.C. 3512

FORM NLRB-508
(5-81)

UNITED STATES OF AMERICA
NATIONAL LABOR RELATIONS BOARD
CHARGE AGAINST LABOR ORGANIZATION OR ITS AGENTS

DO NOT WRITE IN THIS SPACE

Case No.

Date Filed

INSTRUCTIONS: File and original and 3 copies of this charge and an additional copy for each organization, each local, and each individual named in item 1 with the NLRB Regional Director of the Region in which the alleged unfair labor practice occurred or is occurring.

1. LABOR ORGANIZATION OR ITS AGENTS AGAINST WHICH CHARGE IS BROUGHT

a. Name

b. Union Representative to Contact

c. Telephone No.

d. Address (street, city, state and ZIP code)

e. The above-named organization(s) or its agents has (have) engaged in and is (are) engaging in unfair labor practices within the meaning of section 8(b), subsection(s) _____ of the National Labor Relations Act, and these
(list subsections)
unfair labor practices are unfair labor practices affecting commerce within the meaning of the Act.

2. Basis of the Charge (be specific as to facts, names, addresses, plants involved, dates, places, etc.).

3. Name of Employer

4. Telephone No.

5. Location of Plant Involved (street, city, state and ZIP code)

6. Employer Representative to Contact

7. Type of Establishment (factory, mine, wholesaler, etc.)

8. Identify Principal Product or Service

9. No. of Workers Employed

10. Full Name of Party Filing Charge

11. Address of Party Filing Charge (street, city, state and ZIP code)

12. Telephone No.

13. DECLARATION

I declare that I have read the above charge and that the statements therein are true to the best of my knowledge and belief.

By _____
(signature of representative or person making charge)

_____
(title or office, if any)

Address _____

_____
(telephone number)

_____
(date)

WILLFULLY FALSE STATEMENTS ON THIS CHARGE CAN BE PUNISHED BY FINE AND IMPRISONMENT
(U. S. CODE, TITLE 18, SECTION 1001)

ions. In addition, the six unfair labor practices directed against unions appear to have varied considerably more widely than in the case of the Wagner Act employer provisions in their effects on labor relations practice.

Two of the six provisions have perhaps had the greatest influence on collective bargaining, and, undoubtedly a salutary one, in the years since the enactment of Taft-Hartley:

1. The ban on union restraint or coercion of employees in the exercise of their guaranteed bargaining rights, which also entails a union obligation to avoid coercion of employees who choose to refrain from collective bargaining altogether. What constitutes such restraint or coercion? The myriad of rulings rendered by the NLRB and courts since 1947 has at least indicated that such union actions as the following will always run the risk of being found "unfair": the stating to an antiunion employee that the employee will lose his job should the union gain recognition; the signing with an employer of an agreement that recognizes the union as exclusive bargaining representative when in fact it lacks majority employee support; and the issuing of patently false statements during a representation election campaign. Union picket-line violence, threats of reprisal against employees subpoenaed to testify against the union at NLRB hearings, and activities of a similar vein are also unlawful.

This first unfair union practice also extends to the coercion of the employer in the latter's selection of its own bargaining representative. Post-1947 rulings have stated, for example, that unions cannot refuse to deal with former union officers who represent employers or insist on meeting only with the owners of a company rather than with the company's attorney. On the other hand, unions have every right to demand that the employer representative with whom they deal have sufficient authority to make final decisions on behalf of the company; the interpreters of public policy have clearly understood that to have this any other way would be to frustrate the whole process of bargaining.

2. The Taft-Hartley provision that makes it unfair for a union to cause an employer to discriminate against an employee in order to influence union membership. There is a single exception to this prohibition: Under a valid union-shop agreement, the union may lawfully demand the discharge of an employee who fails to pay his or her initiation fee and periodic dues. Otherwise, however, unions must exercise complete self-control in this area. They cannot try to force employers to fire or otherwise penalize workers for any other reason, whether these reasons involve worker opposition to union policies, failure to attend union meetings, or refusal to join the union at all. Nor can a union lawfully seek to persuade an employer to grant hiring preference to employees who are satisfactory to the union. Subject only to the union-shop proviso, Taft-Hartley sought to place nonunion workers on a footing equal to that of union employees.

3. Occupying more or less middle ground in its degree of influence upon the labor relations process stands the third restriction on union practices, pertaining to union refusal to bargain. Here, clearly, Taft-Hartley extended to labor organizations the same obligation that the Wagner Act had already imposed on employers.

To many observers, the law's inclusion of this union bargaining provision has meant very little; unions can normally be expected to pursue bargaining rather than attempt to avoid it. Nevertheless, the NLRB has used it to some extent in the years since Taft-Hartley to narrow the scope of permissible union action. The board has, for example, found it unlawful under this section for a union to strike against an employer who has negotiated, and continues to negotiate, on a multiemployer basis, with the goal of forcing that employer to bargain independently. It has also found a union's refusal to bargain on an employer proposal for a written contract to violate this part of the law. To the employer community, in short, at least some inequities seem to have been corrected by this good-faith bargaining provision.

4. The fourth unfair union practice has given rise to considerable litigation. Indeed, of all six Taft-Hartley union prohibitions, the ban on certain types of strikes and boycotts has proven the most difficult to interpret. Even as "clarified" by Congress in 1959, this area remains a particularly murky one for labor lawyers.

Briefly, Section 8(b)(4) of the 1947 act prohibits unions from striking or boycotting if such actions have any of the following three objectives: (1) forcing an employer or self-employed person to join any labor or employer organization or to cease dealing with another employer (secondary boycott); (2) compelling recognition as employee bargaining agent for another employer without NLRB certification; (3) forcing an employer to assign particular work to a particular craft.

Particularly in regard to the secondary boycott provision, it does not take much imagination to predict where heated controversy could arise. To constitute a secondary boycott, the union's action must be waged against "another" employer, one who is entirely a neutral in the battle and is merely caught as a pawn in the union's battle with the real object of its concern. But when is the secondary employer really neutral and when is he an "ally" of the primary employer? The board has sometimes ruled against employers alleging themselves to be "secondary" ones on the grounds of common ownership with that of the "primary" employer and, again, when "struck work" has been turned over by primary employers to secondary ones. But board and court rulings here have not been entirely consonant.

In its other clauses, too, the Taft-Hartley strike and boycott provision has led to intense legal battles. When is a union, for example, unlawfully seeking recognition without NLRB certification and when is it merely picketing to protest undesirable working conditions (a normally legal action)? Is a union ever entitled to try to keep within its bargaining unit work that has traditionally been performed by the unit employees? On some occasions, but not all, the board has ruled that there is nothing wrong with this. The histories of post-1947 cases on these issues constitute a fascinating study in the making of fine distinctions. At least, however, the large incidence of litigation might indicate that the parties have not been able to totally overlook the new rights and responsibilities bestowed upon them by Taft-Hartley (whatever these might exactly be).

Last, and least in the magnitude of their effect, stand the relatively unenforceable provisions relating to union fees and dues, and to featherbedding.

5. The proscription against unions charging workers covered by union-shop agreements excessive or discriminatory dues or initiation fees included, it will be recalled, a stipulation that the NLRB could consider "all the circumstances" in determining discrimination or excess. Such circumstances, the wording of the Taft-Hartley Act continues, include "the practices and customs of labor organizations in the particular industry and the wages currently paid to the employees affected." Without further yardsticks and depending almost exclusively on the sentiments of individual employees rather than on irate employers for enforcement, this part of the act has had little practical value. In one of the relatively few such cases to come before it thus far, some years ago, the board ruled that increasing the initiation fee from $75 to $250 when other unions in the area charged only about one eighth of this amount was unlawful. In another case, it was held that the union's uniform requirement of a reinstatement fee for ex-members that was higher than the initiation fee for new members was *not* discriminatory under the act.

6. The sixth unfair labor practice for unions has proved even less influential in governing collective bargaining: Taft-Hartley's prohibition of unions from engaging in featherbedding. The board has ruled that this provision does not prevent labor organizations from seeking *actual* employment for their members, "even in situations where the employer does not want, does not need, and is not willing to accept such services." Mainly because of this interpretation, the antifeatherbedding provision has had few teeth; the union would be quite happy to have the work performed, and the question of need is irrelevant. Employer spokespersons for some industries, entertainment and the railroads in particular, have succeeded in convincing the public that their unwanted—but performing—workers are featherbedding, but under the interpretation of the law as this now exists they are engaging in inaccuracies.

Even these least influential of the six union prohibitions, however, clearly indicate the philosophy in back of Taft-Hartley—in the words of the late Senator Robert A. Taft, "simply to reduce special privileges granted to labor leaders."

The Rights of Employees as Individuals

In other areas, too, the act attempted to even the scales of collective bargaining and the alleged injustices of the 1935–1947 period.

Taft-Hartley, unlike the Wagner Act, recognized a need to protect the rights of individual employees against labor organizations. It explicitly amended the 1935 legislation to give a majority of the employees the right to refrain from, as well as engage in, collective bargaining activities. It also dealt more directly with the question of individual freedoms—even beyond its previously mentioned outlawing of the closed shop, union coercion, union-caused employer discrimination against employees, and excessive union fees.

Right-to-Work Legislation.   Perhaps most symbolically, Taft-Hartley provided that should any state wish to pass legislation more restrictive of union security than the union shop (or in other words, to outlaw labor contracts that make union membership a condition of retaining employment), the state was free to do so. Many states have proved themselves as so willing: Twenty-one states, mainly in the South and Southwest, now have so-called "right-to-work" legislation. Advocates of such laws, which will be discussed at greater length in Chapter 9, have claimed that compulsory unionism violates the basic American right of freedom of association; opponents of right-to-work laws have pointed out, among other arguments, that majority rule is inherent in our democratic procedure. There has thus far, however, been an impressive correlation between stands on this particular question and attitudes toward the values of unionism in general. People opposed to collective bargaining have favored right-to-work laws with amazing regularity. Pro-unionists seem to have been equally consistent in their attacks on such legislation. Although it is difficult, if not impossible, to measure objectively the labor relations effects of right-to-work laws, there is consensus on one point: Such laws make it more difficult to organize a union and to maintain one once formed. This condition tends to attract industry to right-to-work states to take advantage of a comparatively union-free work environment with lower wages and general conditions of employment.

Direct Presentation of Grievances.   Also designed to strengthen the rights of workers as individuals was a Taft-Hartley provision allowing any *employee* the *right to present grievances directly* to the employer without intervention of the union. The union's representative was to be given a chance to be present at such employer/employee meetings, but the normal grievance procedure (with the union actively participating) would thus be suspended. Few employees have thus far availed themselves of this opportunity: The action can clearly antagonize the union, and since the employer's action is normally being challenged by the grievance itself, the employee may have a formidable task ahead.

Restricted Dues Checkoff.   Finally, the act placed a major restriction on the fast-growing dues-checkoff arrangement. Through this device (which will also be discussed in more detail later), many employers had been deducting union dues from their employee's paychecks and remitting them to the union. Managements were thus spared the constant visits of dues-collecting union representatives at the workplace, and unions had found the checkoff to be an efficient means of collection. Under Taft-Hartley, the checkoff was to remain legal, but now only if the individual employee had given his or her own authorization in writing. Moreover, such an authorization could not be irrevocable for a period of more than one year. This restriction has hardly hampered the growth of the checkoff; today it is provided for in over 80 percent of all labor contracts, compared with an estimated 40 percent at the time of Taft-Hartley's passage. The new legal provision has undoubtedly minimized abuse of the checkoff mechanism, however. (Exhibit 3-6, drawn from the current labor agreement between the International Paper Company's Formed Fabrics Division and the United Paperworkers International Union, shows typical dues-checkoff language.)

ARTICLE 4

DEDUCTION OF UNION DUES

4.1 Deduction of Union Dues

Subject to the provisions of State and Federal laws, the Company agrees to make a payroll deduction of the normal monthly union dues and a one time union initiation fee, provided there is on file with the Company a copy of a voluntary authorization as shown below, properly filled out, signed by the employee and countersigned by an official of the local Union.

The payroll deduction of Union dues shall be made only on the second payday of each month.

The total amount collected shall be transmitted to the Local Union financial secretary, marked "For Deposit Only." The Local Union will be supplied each month with the names of its members from whose earnings Union dues have been deducted. The authorization of Union dues deduction shall be in the following form:

Form A

CHECK-OFF AUTHORIZATION

I hereby voluntarily assign to my Local Union affiliated with the United Paperworkers International Union from any wages earned or to be earned by me, the amount of my monthly membership dues and initiation fee in said Union.

I authorize and direct my employer to deduct such amounts from my pay each month and to remit the same to the order of the financial secretary of my Local Union in accordance with the terms of this Agreement.

This assignment, authorization and direction shall be irrevocable for a period of one year from the effective date of the Agreement, or until the termination date of said Agreement, whichever occurs sooner, and I further agree and direct that this assignment, authorization and direction shall be automatically renewed and shall be irrevocable for successive periods of one year each or for the period of each succeeding applicable collective bargaining Agreement with the Union whichever shall be shorter, unless written notice is given by me to the Company and the Union not more than thirty days or less than ten days prior to the expiration of each period of one year or of each applicable collective bargaining Agreement, whichever occurs sooner.

Date_____ Signature of Employee_____

Name[Print]_____ UPIU Local No._____

Address_____City and State_____

Social Security No. _____

Employed By_____ Department_____

Other Employee Rights

Employees have gained other rights based on the language of Taft-Hartley or by NLRB and court construction. *When a labor agreement requires membership in a union as a condition of employment,* and should a member protest the stance of the union in political elections or lobbying activities, the U.S. Supreme Court has held that the union must rebate to the member that proportion of his or her dues allocated for political purposes. The union member who supports the Republican candidate for political office, for example, has the right to have rebated the portion of dues spent for political purposes when the organization supports the Democratic candidate.

This dues rebate policy originally surfaced under the Supreme Court's interpretation of the Railway Labor Act,[11] but in 1988 the Court established the same rule for unionized employees covered by Taft-Hartley.[12] The new policy, however, could injure unions much more seriously than merely making dues rebates to political dissenters. In *Communications Workers,* the Supreme Court held that dues-paying nonunion employees (as in agency shop arrangements, explained in Chapter 9) can demand a rebate for *any* union expenditure not related strictly to collective bargaining.

Thus, union expenses for organizing, some publications, certain litigation, and educational functions are now placed in jeopardy. In addition, unions may no longer select an arbitrary figure—5 percent, for example—for rebate purposes, as some have done in the past. *Communications Workers* commands that unions keep detailed records specifying what portion of the dues is in fact spent for collective bargaining purposes and what part on unrelated activities. Should the policy be fully applied to funds spent on organizational campaigns, the impact could be serious for labor organizations. The degree of organization within an industry or trade has a direct bearing on the ability of unions to negotiate wages and working conditions.[13] It is hard to believe that organizational efforts do not constitute a collective bargaining activity.

Taft-Hartley confers a special benefit on professional employees, who under its terms are defined in part as those whose work is primarily intellectual in character and who utilize considerable judgment and discretion in the performance of their jobs.[14] When employees meet requirements of the definition, the NLRB must poll them in a special election to determine whether they desire to be represented by a rank-and-file union, by an organization composed exclusively of professionals, or by no union. Whatever their verdict, the board must comply with their wishes. Thus, the agency may not place professional employees in a bargaining unit composed of production and maintenance employees unless a majority of the professionals polled vote for that kind of representation. Over the years the NLRB has struggled with the definition of professional employees. It has held that a college degree does not necessarily place the person in the professional category, and by the same token the lack of a college degree does not automatically exclude the employee. Rather than formal educational achievement, what counts is the kind of work the employee actually performs on the job.[15] In the professional category, for example, the board has included non-college-trained plant engineers, time study specialists, and employees who estimate the needs and cost of material used by their employers. In the nonprofessional category, the NLRB has placed—not without some controversy—general accountants, newspaper journalists, radio announcers, singers, and continuity writers.

Finally, pursuant to a mandate incorporated in Taft-Hartley, the NLRB under certain circumstances permits craft employees (electricians, machinists, carpenters, plumbers) to break away from an industrial bargaining unit and establish their own unions. In each case, the NLRB will consider the specific situation involved before ruling on separate craft union representation.[16] In one case the agency denied separation of a group of craft employees from the production workers unit on the grounds that their work was closely integrated in the employees' operation.[17] That is, the work of the skilled employees was so highly integrated into the productive process that a strike of the skilled group would cause a shutdown of the entire plant. In another case the NLRB permitted a group of craft employees to break out of the industrial unit because the evidence demonstrated that their work was not closely integrated. Equally important was the fact that the industrial union did not represent the craft employees fairly in collective bargaining.[18] As expected, industrial unions because of loss of membership and employers because of the problems involved in dealing with many unions in the same plant normally argue that craft employees should not be separated. Despite these claims, however, under the proper set of circumstances the NLRB permits craft employees to select their own bargaining agent.

The Rights of Employers

In still a third area, Taft-Hartley circumscribed the union's freedom of action in its quest for industrial relations equity. In this case, it explicitly gave employers certain collective bargaining rights.

For example, although employers were still required to recognize and bargain with properly certified unions, they could now give full freedom of expression to their views concerning union organization, as long as there was "no threat of reprisal or force or promise of benefit." Thus an employer may now, when faced with a representation election, tell employees that in his opinion unions are worthless, dangerous to the economy, and immoral. An employer may even, generally speaking, hint that the permanent closing of the plant would be the possible aftermath of a union election victory and subsequent high union wage demands. Nor will an election be set aside, for that matter, if the employer plays upon the racial prejudices of the workers (should these exist) by describing the union's philosophy toward integration, or if the employer sets forth the union's record in regard to violence and corruption (should this record be vulnerable) and suggests that these characteristics would be logical consequences of the union's victory in that plant—although the board has attempted to draw the line here between dispassionate statements on the employer's part and inflammatory or emotional appeals.[19] An imaginative employer can, in fact, now engage in almost any amount of creative speaking (or writing) for employees' consumption. The only major restraint on the employer's conduct is that he must avoid threats, promises, coercion, and direct interference with the worker-voters in the reaching of their decision. Two lesser restrictions also govern, however: The employer may not hold a meeting with employees on company time within twenty-four hours of an election; and the employer may never urge employees individually at their homes or in the office to vote against the union (the board has held that the employer can lawfully do this only "at the employees' work area or in places where employees normally gather").

An employer may avoid these two minor restrictions by holding a "captive audience" meeting before the twenty-four-hour limit on company property and during working time. And the employer need not give equal time to the union to reply to the employer's statements.[20] At such meetings, with all the employees assembled, the employer by the use of representatives has an excellent opportunity to influence the vote in the impending election. In a case involving the J. P. Stevens Company, the NLRB moved further to protect the right of employers to hold effective captive audience meetings. At a Stevens meeting a number of employees sympathetic to the union got up and asked questions. When they refused to sit down and stop asking questions, the company discharged them and the NLRB subsequently sustained the discharges.[21]

In an effort to balance the opportunity of unions to reach the employee, the NLRB has ruled that within seven days after an election is scheduled the employer must make available to a regional director of the agency the names and addresses of the employees eligible to vote in the election. Then the list is furnished to the union.[22] In other words, instead of granting unions equal time at captive audience meetings, the agency has provided unions with an alternative method of contacting employees—home visitation and letter writing. However, unions claim that these techniques do not measure up to the effectiveness of the captive audience meeting. Undoubtedly the captive audience doctrine is one factor explaining why unions currently lose a majority of NLRB elections.

Taft-Hartley afforded employers additional benefits. Under the Wagner Act, foremen had the right to organize and bargain collectively under the protection of the statute. As rank-and-file employees they had the opportunity to utilize the facilities of the NLRB when employers discharged them for union activities or refused to recognize and bargain with their unions. When the U.S. Supreme Court affirmed their protection under the law, it said that the fact that foremen are "employees" for purposes of the Wagner Act "is too obvious to be labored."[23] Protected by the NLRB, the foremen's union movement grew to 32,000 members during World War II. Responding to employer pressure, however, Congress excluded foremen from the scope of the Taft-Hartley Act. Under the 1947 law the NLRB no longer has the authority to provide foremen with protection in their union activities. Employers may discharge foremen if they show an interest in union organization, and the employer is no longer legally required to recognize or bargain with foremen's unions. Stripped of legal protection, the foremen's union movement has virtually disappeared.

Subsequently, the U.S. Supreme Court held that all managers are excluded from the scope of Taft-Hartley;[24] and, for good measure, that faculty members at private universities (but not public ones, which do not come under Taft-Hartley)—since they are also "managers"—are similarly deprived of legal protection in *their* union activities.[25] In this latter decision, a 1980 one involving *Yeshiva University,* the high court refused to grant faculty members bargaining rights under the law on the basis of their professional status but instead sided with university administrators and took away the former's legal protection. The American Association of University Professors recently reported that *Yeshiva* has "virtually brought to a complete halt union organizing at private institutions,"[26] and this surprised absolutely no one.

In addition, under Taft-Hartley, employers may lock out their employees when an impasse occurs in collective bargaining. At times, employees are willing to work on a day-to-day basis after the labor agreement expires. This procedure offers the parties additional time to reach an agreement without a work stoppage. Under the law, however, the employer may use the lockout to shock employees into accepting management's last offer. Even if employees are willing to work after the contract expires, the employer may deny them this opportunity and lock them out of the plant. The only qualification on this right is that the employer must have engaged in good-faith collective bargaining prior to the lockout. What makes the employer's lockout right even more effective is that it is all right to continue to operate the plant with temporary replacements.[27] Under these circumstances, the locked-out employees are under pressure to capitulate to the employer's final contract offer. Such changes understandably were favorably received by the employer community.

National Emergency Strikes

Of most direct interest to the general public, but of practical meaning only to those employers whose labor relations can be interpreted as affecting the national health and safety, are the national-emergency strike provisions that were enacted in 1947. As in the case of most Taft-Hartley provisions, these remain unchanged to this day.

Sections 206 through 210 of the act provide for government intervention in the case of such emergencies. If the President of the United States believes that a threatened or actual strike affects "an entire industry or a substantial part thereof" in such a way as to "imperil the national health or safety," he is empowered to take certain carefully delineated action. He may appoint a board of inquiry to find out and report the facts regarding the dispute. The board is allowed subpoena authority and can thus compel the appearance of witnesses. It cannot, however, make recommendations for a settlement. On receiving the board's preliminary report, the President may apply, through the attorney general, for a court injunction restraining the strike for sixty days. If no settlement is reached during this time, the injunction can be extended for another twenty days, during which period the employees are to be polled in a secret-ballot election as to their willingness to accept the employer's last offer. The board is then to submit its final report to the President. Should the strike threat still exist after all these procedures, the President is authorized to submit a full report to Congress, "with such recommendations as he may see fit to make for consideration and appropriate action."

By 1993, the national emergency provisions of the law had been invoked thirty-four times and twenty-seven injunctions had been issued.[28] On five occasions the President did not elect to seek injunctions and twice federal district courts turned down the President on the grounds the strikes did not imperil the national health or safety. Much of the earlier excitement and controversy about this feature of Taft-Hartley has subsided. The last attempt to use it was in 1977 when a court refused President Carter's request for an injunction in a coal strike. An injunction was issued for the last time in 1972. The major explanation is attributable to the lessening of power of labor organizations within industries in which injunctions were previously issued. For example, in 1993, only about 20 percent of the coal industry was organized whereas in John L. Lewis's time it used to be about 80 percent. Given these circumstances, the national emergency dispute provisions of Taft-Hartley are more or less a relic of labor relations law.

Other Taft-Hartley Provisions

Taft-Hartley also devoted attention to *internal union affairs,* the first such regulation in American history. Its impetus came not only from the previously cited Communistic taints attached to several unions but also from the fact that, in the case of a few other labor organizations, lack of democratic procedures and financial irregularities (often involving employer wrongdoing as well) had become glaringly evident. Accordingly, the act set new conditions for unions thenceforth seeking to use the NLRB's services: (1) All union officers were obligated to file annual affidavits with the board, stating that they were not members of the Communist party; (2) certain financial and constitutional information had to be filed annually by unions with the secretary of labor; and (3) unions (as well as corporations) could no longer contribute funds for political purposes in connection with any federal election. The affidavit requirement, judged to be ineffective, was repealed in 1959. The other stipulations were allowed to remain in force until that date, when they were only slightly amended and then substantially enlarged upon (as further discussion will indicate). Essentially, aside from what unionists vocally termed a nuisance value, the provisions are notable for the first recognition of public policy that some internal regulation of the union as an institution was in the public interest—and as a harbinger of more such regulation to come.

Another Taft-Hartley provision that has upset some union leaders involves the *termination or modification of existing labor contracts.* Applicable to both labor organizations and employers, it requires the party seeking to end or change the agreement to give a sixty-day notice to the other party. The law further provides that, during this time period, the existing contract must be maintained without strikes or lockouts. In addition, the Federal Mediation and Conciliation Service and state mediation services are to be notified of the impending dispute thirty days after the serving of the notice. Workers striking in violation of this requirement lose all legal protection as "employees" in collective bargaining, although the law also asserts that "such loss of status for such employee shall terminate if and when he is reemployed" by the employer.

In some instances, leaders of labor organizations have found it both difficult and politically unpopular to restrain their constituents from violating this provision. Unionists have also, on occasion, frankly pointed out that the scheduling prerequisites for striking have deprived their organizations of some economic power, at least insofar as the element of surprise is concerned. Yet many representatives of both parties would undoubtedly agree that these provisions have let mediators intervene before it is too late to help and have generally aided in the resolution of disputes by allowing more time for thoughtful consideration of what is involved. From the point of view of the public interest, it is on this basis that the effectiveness of the notice provisions should be judged.

Section 301 of Taft-Hartley decreed that "*suits for violations of contracts* between an employer and a labor organization representing employees in an industry affecting commerce" could be brought directly by either party in any U.S. district court. Labor agreements, in short, were to be construed as being legally enforceable for the first time in American history. Damage suits are not calculated to increase mutual trust or offset misunderstandings between the parties in labor relations, however, and unions and managements have generally recognized this. Consequently, relatively few such suits have come to the courts in the years since this provision was enacted. Many contracts today, in fact, contain agreements *not* to sue, a perfectly legal dodge of Section 301. More will be said about this issue in Chapter 9.

Though employer suits against unions under Section 301 for violation of no-strike provisions have been comparatively infrequent, the U.S. Supreme Court has established some applicable policies. Only the union, and not individual members or officers, is liable for any damages assessed in court proceedings.[29] Also, a national union is not responsible for damages when its local unions engage in wildcat strikes, assuming that the national has neither provoked nor encouraged the illegal cessation of work.[30] Local unions do not normally have huge treasuries, and employers would much prefer to recover damages from the nationals. But absent specific contractual language allowing them to do the latter (something that national unions have understandably rarely agreed to), employers are simply out of luck in these situations.

Coverage of Private Hospitals

In 1974, Congress extended the coverage of Taft-Hartley to private nonprofit hospitals and nursing homes. This was no small matter. More than 3 million employees now work in almost 4,000 such nonprofit institutions and some 83 percent of all private hospitals in the United States are not operated for profit. Before 1974, only proprietary (profit-making) health-care institutions were covered by the National Labor Relations Act and thus came under the NLRB's jurisdiction.

But whatever benefit organized labor could derive from this change in organizing its large and rapidly growing worker market was not immediately apparent. Typically, the NLRB decided prospective bargaining units on a case-by-case basis and could be counted on to issue findings that lumped most occupational categories in a simple broad group for purposes of a potential union election.[31] Thus, such diverse worker types as salaried physicians, registered nurses, X-ray technicians, physical therapists, maintenance employees, and business office clerks would all be found to be part of a single "appropriate" unit. And hospital managements could rather readily play upon the lack of common identities to divide and conquer any union hopes of winning a representation election.

In 1989, however, a less conservative board concluded two years of hearings on this increasingly incendiary topic by ruling that thenceforth separate elections for each of eight private hospital groups could routinely be held. Doctors, registered nurses, all other professional employees, technicians, skilled maintenance workers, business office clerical employees, guards, and all other nonprofessionals could now each vote to have their own bargaining units, regardless of the wishes of the other groups.[32]

Hospital managements, through their umbrella American Hospital Association, immediately sued to overturn this union victory. They argued that the NLRB did not have the legal authority to do anything but decide such matters on a case-by-case basis. But their effort failed: In 1991, the Supreme Court unanimously affirmed the board action of two years earlier.[33] At the time of this writing, hospital unions—which had significantly stepped up their organizational efforts in the wake of the favorable judicial development—were quite optimistic about what they deemed to be the dawn of a new era.

AFL-CIO President Lane Kirkland has argued in this regard that

> fair and timely elections are essential for the law to fulfill its promise of freedom of choice on union representation.[34]

But hospital executives have warned in speaking of the 1991 ruling:

> The rule will mean that medical costs, already rising sharply, will increase even faster.[35]

Only time will tell which prophecy proves correct.

To avoid disturbing patients, hospital management can forbid the solicitation of union members and the distribution of union literature in patient rooms and other patient-care areas such as X-ray, operating, and therapy rooms even if the activity occurs during nonworking time. In contrast, within industry in general, employers may not forbid such union activities during nonworking time. The more difficult problem involves patient-access areas, such as hallways, gift shops, cafeterias, and visitors' lounges. So perplexing and controversial is this problem that the matter has been before the NLRB and the courts many times. Using two U.S. Supreme Court decisions as the authority, it would appear that unions may not solicit members in hospital corridors and in lounges on floors occupied by patients. However, unions may solicit in cafeterias, gift shops, and the main lobby even though patients may have access to them,[36] so long as they give ten days' advance notice.

With regard to the ten-day notice rule, the NLRB has applied the provision literally. Hospital employees who strike or picket without filing the notice may be discharged by the hospital. It does not matter whether or not the employees are represented by a union or whether or not the union had knowledge of their illegal conduct.[37]

In a highly controversial decision, the NLRB has held that hospital interns and resident physicians are excluded from the protection of Taft-Hartley.[38] It said that such persons are not "employees" within the meaning of the law but are students pursuing a graduate medical education. Though the nation's 12,000 interns and 48,000 residents receive salaries for their work, pay federal income taxes on their earnings, and devote a great deal of time to patient care, the agency held that they have no rights under Taft-Hartley. Should they strike for union recognition, being denied access to the NLRB election procedures, this NLRB policy may well prove not to be in the public interest.

Administrative Changes in the Law

Taft-Hartley also enlarged the NLRB from three to five members and, in the interests of a faster disposition of cases, authorized the board to delegate "any or all" of its powers to any group of three or more members. In addition, the office of independent General Counsel was created within the NLRB, to administer the prosecution of all unfair labor practices. This last change was made to satisfy the increasingly bitter charges (particularly from employers) that the same individuals had exercised both prosecution and judicial roles.

As the NLRB machinery now operates, the board members and General Counsel delegate most of their work in processing unfair labor practice charges and conducting representation elections to fifty-two regional, subregional, and resident offices scattered throughout the country.[39] Each office deals with these two issues as they arise in its particular geographic area. The General Counsel supervises the work of the offices, and the board members' efforts are thus saved for those issues appealed to it from the regional level. As will be recalled, board decisions can themselves be appealed to the courts (and ultimately to the Supreme Court).

From what has been said, it is obvious that the NLRB has considerable authority to apply the provisions of the law. What the legislation does is to establish broad guidelines, but it is up to the agency to apply the law to particular situations. In the vast majority of the cases, the courts have sustained the decisions of the board on the grounds that the agency possesses expertise that should be given full faith and credit by the judiciary. It follows, therefore, that how the law will be applied depends to a great extent on who sits on the board. It is a matter of common sense that Presidents will choose members who generally represent the socioeconomic philosophy of the nation's chief executive office, and thus, over the years, employers and unions alternately have been bitterly critical of board policies. In general, unions have criticized the policies of Republican-appointed NLRB members, and employers have displayed the same attitude toward the board when directed by appointees of Democratic chief executives. Possibly providing for permanent tenure for board members in the same manner as federal judges are appointed for life would be a more palatable arrangement for both sides.

As might have been expected, the Taft-Hartley Act generated considerable controversy. In the years immediately after its passage, labor leaders bitterly assailed the new law as being—in addition to a "slave labor act"—a punitive one, and invoked such statements in regard to its authors as "the forces of reaction in this country want a showdown with free American labor." Taft-Hartley supporters, on the other hand, frequently referred to the act as a "Magna Charta" for both employers and employees and widely praised its efforts to "equalize bargaining power." Unable to see any appropriateness in these latter remarks, spokespersons for organized labor, until roughly a decade ago, in turn responded by pressing for the repeal of the act—or occasionally, for its drastic amendment—in every session of Congress. Their complete failure to realize this goal and their recent unwillingness even to pursue it attests to the basic acceptance of Taft-Hartley's provisions in the recent past by the American public, as well as to labor's concern that an even less desirable law might be the outcome.

The framers of public policy themselves, however, did not long remain satisfied that existing labor legislation was fully adequate to uphold the public interest. In 1959, the national legislature passed another significant law, the Landrum-Griffin Act (officially, the Labor-Management Reporting and Disclosure Act). This act was the direct outgrowth of the unsatisfactory internal practices of a small but strategically located minority of unions, as revealed by Senate investigations, and it can be said to have marked the beginning of quite *detailed regulation* of internal union affairs, going far beyond the Taft-Hartley treatment of this subject.

Under Landrum-Griffin provisions, as noted earlier, union members are guaranteed a "Bill of Rights" that their unions cannot violate, officers of labor organizations must meet a variety of reporting and disclosure obligations, and the secretary of labor is charged with the investigation of relevant union misconduct.

The "Bill of Rights" for union members is an ambitious and wide-sweeping one. It provides for equality of rights concerning the nomination of candidates for union office, voting in elections, attendance at membership meetings, and participation in business transactions—all, however, "subject to reasonable" union rules. It lays down strict standards to ensure that increases in dues and fees are responsive to the desires of the union membership majority. It affirms the right of any member to sue the organization once "reasonable" hearing procedures within the union have been exhausted. It provides that no member may be fined, suspended, or otherwise disciplined by the union except for nonpayment of dues, unless the member has been granted such procedural safeguards as being served with written specific charges, given time to prepare a defense, and afforded a fair hearing. And it obligates union officers to furnish each of their members with a copy of the collective bargaining agreement, as well as full information concerning the Landrum-Griffin Act itself. In a 1989 case, the U.S. Supreme Court made it clear that the Bill of Rights section protects union members' right to free speech. An elected union representative was removed from office because he spoke out against a dues increase. Ruling the action illegal, the high court held that the union action violated the free speech guarantee of Landrum-Griffin.[40]

Not content to stop here in prescribing internal union conduct, the 1959 legislation laid out specific ground rules for *union elections*. National and international unions must now elect officers at least once every five years, either by secret ballot or at a convention of delegates chosen by secret ballot. Local unions are obligated to elect officers at least once every three years, exclusively by secret ballot. As for the conduct of these elections, they must be administered in full accordance with the union's constitution and bylaws, with all ballots and other relevant records being preserved for a period of one year. Every member in good standing is to be entitled to one vote, and all candidates are guaranteed the right to have an observer at the polls and at the ballot counting.

Landrum-Griffin also made it more difficult for national and international unions to place their subordinate bodies under *trusteeships* for purely political reasons. The trusteeship, or the termination of the member group's autonomy, has traditionally allowed labor organizations to correct constitutional violations or other clearly wrongful acts on the part of their locals. The Senate investigations preceding Landrum-Griffin had found, however, that this device was also being used by some unions as a weapon of the national or international officers to eliminate grassroots opposition per se. Accordingly, the act provided that trusteeships could be imposed only for one of four purposes: (1) to correct corruption or "financial malpractice"; (2) to assure the performance of collective bargaining duties; (3) to restore democratic procedures; and (4) to otherwise carry out the "legitimate objects" of the subordinate body. Moreover, the imposition of a trusteeship, together with the reasons for it, was now to be reported to the secretary of labor within thirty days, and every six months thereafter until the trusteeship was terminated.

The extent of Landrum-Griffin control of the internal affairs of unions is perhaps best illustrated by the act's policing of the kind of person who can serve as a union officer. Persons convicted of serious crimes (robbery, bribery, extortion, embezzlement, murder, rape, grand larceny, violation of narcotics laws, aggravated assault) are barred for a period of five years after conviction from holding any union position other than a clerical or custodial job. The period of exclusion may be shortened if the person's citizenship rights are fully restored before five years or if the U.S. Department of Justice decides that an exception should be made.

A fair question to ask is whether or not this policy should be applied to officers of other kinds of institutions, such as business, government, universities, and churches. On the surface, at least, it would appear that if government controls the moral character of union officers, it should apply the same policy across the board. To do otherwise makes it appear that union officers are being held to a higher standard of personal conduct than is required of, say, corporation officials. Should a corporation official who has been convicted of a serious crime, including violations of the nation's antitrust and pure food and drug laws, be treated in the same way as a union officer? This could be the subject for a lively debate in any student group.

To curb financial corruption, the law requires that union officers must each year file reports with the secretary of labor containing the purpose for which union funds are spent. The objective is to discourage union officers from using the organization's treasury for items of a personal nature. Since financial reports are made available to union members, they can learn whether or not their dues are being used in the interest of the membership. Should it be determined that a union officer has used union funds for personal items, the law authorizes court suits to recover the money from the officer. If a report is not filed, or if the information contained is not true, the responsible union officer is subject to criminal penalties. Outright embezzlement of union funds may also result in imprisonment and/or fines. In addition, all union officers must be bonded by a private bonding company in which the union has no interest.

Although most of Landrum-Griffin was aimed at union behavior, the act does include provisions that cover employer activities. Landrum-Griffin made employers responsible for reporting annually to the secretary of labor all company expenditures directed at influencing employee collective bargaining behavior. Employer bribery of union officers and other such blunt tactics had actually constituted federal crimes since the passage of Taft-Hartley, but the new act expanded the list of unlawful employer actions. Bribes by companies to their own employees so that they do not exercise their rights to organize and bargain collectively were added to the list of crimes. So, too, were many forms of employer payment aimed at procuring information on employee activities related to labor disputes. Violations by employers of their reporting obligations invite the same criminal penalties as are provided for union representatives. This provision, however, was weakened considerably by a 1989 decision of the federal appeals court for the District of Columbia.[41] When its employees were being organized, the employer hired a labor consultant for the purpose of defeating the union in the upcoming NLRB election. A federal district court directed the employer to report to the secretary of labor the amount of money paid to the consultant. However, the federal appeals court reversed the lower court, holding that the consultant only provided advice to the employer, and did not directly persuade the employees to reject the union.

In a way, the law attempted to fill the gap created by union-membership apathy. It can be argued that a more effective way to promote union democracy and financial responsibility is by active participation of members in union affairs. The members of any union, local or international, have it in their power to require that their organizations adhere to democratic procedures and financial responsibility through the existing internal machinery of their unions. It is debatable that the federal government should protect union members against abuse by the organization when these members are not particularly concerned as to how their unions in fact operate.

But few would now argue for repeal of the legislation. Even union opposition to Landrum-Griffin has subsided. Control of the internal affairs of unions by government is now an established feature. Possibly, no law will convert unions into models of democracy; still, the effect of the law has eliminated some of the more flagrant abuses of undemocratic practices and financial irresponsibility. For example, in 1969, the United Mine Workers held an election to choose their international officers. This was the first such national election ever conducted in this union in over forty years, and it is not likely that it would have been held in the absence of the law's requirements. Undoubtedly, too, the act has curtailed the activities of the comparatively small number of union officers who would regard the union's treasury as something to be used for their personal aggrandizement. Although there still exist some undemocratic practices and corruption in unions there have been fewer flagrant instances of such conduct since the passage of the legislation. If nothing else, the law has educated union officers as to their responsibilities to their members. To this extent, the law has apparently accomplished its major objectives, and does for union members what they have failed through apathy to do for themselves.

Landrum-Griffin—Title VII

Quite apart from regulating internal union affairs and imposing obligations on employers, Landrum-Griffin in Title VII made some important changes in the Taft-Hartley Act. It authorized the NLRB to decline cases involving small employers engaged in interstate commerce, and permitted the states to take jurisdiction of such cases. The theory here was that the NLRB should conserve its funds and staff for those cases that have a substantial impact on interstate commerce.

In letting the board decline the lesser cases, however, Title VII in effect entirely withdrew all legal protection for the employees of many small employers in their efforts to organize and bargain collectively: Many states simply do not have a law similar to Taft-Hartley and employees there since 1959 can quite lawfully be entirely ignored by their employers. Most managements have made full use of this opportunity.

Title VII also closed the so-called loopholes that developed under Taft-Hartley's secondary boycott provisions. As we have seen, one purpose of Taft-Hartley was to outlaw secondary boycotts. However, the NLRB and the courts permitted unions to engage in certain types of secondary boycott activity. The reason for this was the character of the language of the 1947 law that regulated these activities. Under the 1959 law, Congress adopted new language that generally closed these loopholes, and under the present state of affairs, a union's opportunity to engage in secondary boycott activities has virtually been eliminated.

As a matter of fact, there are only three conditions established by the Supreme Court under which unions may lawfully engage in secondary boycott activities. Union appeals to managers of neutral employers to cease doing business with the primary employer (the one with which the union has the actual dispute) are lawful provided they have the managerial discretion to grant the union appeal.[42] The high court has also held that a union may picket at the site of the secondary employer, say, a supermarket, to try to persuade the public not to purchase the product (apples in the actual case) produced by the employer with which the union has the primary dispute. Such picketing would be unlawful, however, should the union persuade the public not to purchase any products sold by the secondary employer. To be lawful, picketing may target only the product in question.[43]

In a 1988 case, *De Bartolo,* the Supreme Court unanimously established the third exception to the 1959 secondary boycott language.[44] De Bartolo, the owner of a large shopping mall in Tampa, Florida, hired a nonunion contractor to build a store within the mall. In retaliation, building trades unions distributed handbills (not picketing) at the mall's entrances requesting the public not to shop at any store located in the mall because of the "Mall's Ownership Contribution to Substandard Wages." De Bartolo charged that the unions were pressuring mall store tenants to stop doing business with him to force the mall owner to cease doing business with the nonunion contractor. Rejecting a Reagan board decision holding the union's action illegal, the high court said that the legislative history of Landrum-Griffin did not indicate that Congress intended to "proscribe peaceful handbilling, unaccompanied by picketing during a consumer boycott of a neutral employer."

Landrum-Griffin also outlawed the "hot-cargo" arrangement. Under a hot-cargo clause, an employer agrees with a union not to handle products of or otherwise deal with another employer involved in a labor dispute. Accordingly, the hot-cargo arrangement is a form of secondary boycott. The difference is that an employer agrees by contractual provision to engage in secondary boycotts upon receiving a signal from its union that another employer should be boycotted. Such arrangements are now illegal, and unions that force an employer to negotiate hot-cargo clauses engage in an unfair labor practice. For reasons peculiar to the nature of the construction and garment industries, however, Congress excepted these two industries from the hot-cargo proscription.

Title VII imposed another important restriction upon unions. It pinned down and controlled recognition and organizational picketing. At times, unions have found this kind of picketing effective to force employers to recognize unions and to persuade employees to join unions. Such picketing is particularly effective in a consumer business, such as a department store or a restaurant. A picket line thrown around a department store could persuade customers not to buy at the store, and this pressure could force the employer to recognize the union. Under Taft-Hartley, there was no restriction on this kind of picketing, and unions could picket for recognition and organizational purposes for an indefinite length of time.

Under the 1959 law, the opportunity for unions to picket for such purposes was sharply reduced. Such picketing activities now constitute an unfair labor practice if (1) the employer is lawfully recognizing another union; (2) a valid election has been conducted by the NLRB in the previous twelve months; or (3) no election petition has been filed with the NLRB within thirty days after the picketing began.

This provision is of particular importance to employers who want to be freed from the pressure of picketing. Thus, within thirty days after the start of the picketing, the union must file a petition for an election. If it loses the election, recognition and organizational picketing may not be engaged in for one year. Consequently, the opportunity of a union to picket for an indefinite period of time is eliminated.

However, there is one major qualification to this proscription. A union may picket for informational purposes after thirty days without filing an election petition. Informational picketing is defined by the law as the kind that advises the public that the employer involved does not employ members of the union or have a contract with it. Of course, the picket-sign legends must be truthful. For example, they may not state that the employer does not employ members of the union if in truth he does. Also, informational picketing, as distinct from recognition and organizational picketing, may not interfere with pickup and delivery of products at the site of the company being picketed.

PUBLIC POLICY IN RECENT YEARS

If the labor movement was something less than enthusiastic about Landrum-Griffin, moreover, it was to be absolutely incensed by what public policy would do to it in the 1980s and early 1990s. By the middle of the former decade, a major report of the AFL-CIO could assert that "the norm is that unions now face employers who are bent on avoiding unionization at all costs and who are left largely free to do so by a law that has proven to be impotent and a Labor Board that is inert."[45] And Federation President Lane Kirkland, going even farther, was regularly declaring in these years that it would not be a bad thing if the collective bargaining statutes were done away with altogether and the parties allowed to go back to their pre-Wagner Act "law of the jungle," as he called it. (Exhibit 3-7 conveys labor's general sentiments about the evenhandedness of government in the early 1990s.)

The four basic laws of collective bargaining—Norris–La Guardia, Wagner, Taft-Hartley, and Landrum-Griffin—had not, of course, changed a bit in these years. What had changed, as it often had in the past and

EXHIBIT 3-7

SOURCE: The Guild Reporter, January 10, 1992, p. 8

assuredly will in the future, was the makeup of the major interpreter of these laws, the NLRB. And a scant half decade after applauding a host of decisions rendered by the relatively liberal Jimmy Carter–era board, labor was in fact virtually united in its animosity toward the NLRB as controlled by appointees of Ronald Reagan and then George Bush.

Few opinions from unionists regarding the newly turned conservative board were notable for their moderation. The president of the AFL-CIO's largest member national, the United Food and Commercial Workers, had asked rhetorically, "If we cannot get fairness from the board, why fool with it?"[46] A staff attorney for the United Automobile Workers had given vent to his opinion that "the board is no longer a neutral agency. It's trying to give management the maximum amount of freedom."[47] The veteran general counsel of the International Ladies Garment Workers, to cite only one more of a myriad of markedly antiboard observers, had announced that "we're dealing with a board whose tilt to management is the most pronounced in my [thirty-one-year] experience."[48]

Such sentiments had been inspired by more than a dozen sharp reversals of prolabor Carter board precedents by the Reagan and Bush appointees.

Among other actions, the newer NLRB had ruled that employers could move work being performed by union workers to a nonunion facility during the life of a labor agreement that didn't specifically prohibit such a move. It had also declared that these employers need not bargain on the move at all even with such a specific prohibition if the move was due to factors other than labor cost considerations. In addition, the NLRB had reduced protection for employees that labor believed had been granted by the Wagner Act by holding that for an activity to be "concerted" and thus covered by that act at least two workers had to be involved. As noted earlier in this chapter, it had declared that it would no longer order an employer to bargain with a union unless the labor organization could prove that it represented a majority of the employees, even in the face of outrageous unfair labor practices by management.

Reversing other precedents of a few years earlier, the newer NLRB provided employers more leeway to interrogate individual employees about their union sympathies; curtailed the scope of the statute by refusing to certify a union composed of teachers in schools related to a religious organization, but not directly operated by the church or synagogue; made it more difficult to have an adverse arbitration decision reversed by the board when it previously deferred to arbitration; and, in cases which particularly irritated the labor movement, made it unlawful for unions to impose fines on employees who resigned from the unions before working during a strike, and refused unions the right to enforce bylaws forbidding union members to resign during a strike.

The courts had yet to rule on most of these NLRB actions, although union appeals had been lodged in many cases. Even in the case of the judges, however, one action had caused considerable union concern.

In early 1984, the Supreme Court had ruled unanimously in *Bildisco Manufacturing* that a company that had filed for bankruptcy could cancel its labor agreement without having to prove that the contract would cause it to go entirely broke. If the employer could show merely that the labor pact "unduly burdened" its prospects for recovery and that it had made "reasonable" efforts to bargain with the union for labor cost savings, it had no further relations obligations, said the court. Even in its weakened 1980s condition, labor had enough friends in Congress to reverse this rather one-sided decision a few months later, and employers now have to convince a bankruptcy court that they would go out of business without contract termination prior to being allowed such relief. The fact that the court decision could have been rendered in the first place, however, still rankled unionists some years later.

Only the severest of the prophets of doom in the labor movement expected such unfriendly public policy actions as these to continue indefinitely. As a matter of fact, after the initial Reagan appointees left the NLRB, as their five-year terms expired, the agency started to become more evenhanded. The major event was the resignation of Donald Dotson, a management attorney, who served as chair from 1983 until his term expired in late 1987. James M. Stephens, the new chair, immediately promised "a commitment to fairness and a belief in our system of peaceful industrial relations through law" and seemed to practice what he preached.

On the other hand, the board had not set aside the controversial decisions of the initial Reagan appointees, and the legacy of the Reagan NLRB remained a part of the nation's labor relations law through the era of George Bush.

In bestowing its various forms of protection on employee collective bargaining, the Wagner Act quite clearly allowed union members the right to strike without losing their jobs. Employers could not—and cannot—in *any* way punish striking union members, much less fire them, for taking such action.

But a mere three years after this landmark legislation was passed, a U.S. Supreme Court decision essentially negated this stricture. In 1938, the Court ruled that employers could hire permanent replacements for workers who were striking for "economic reasons" such as increased pay or benefits or for improved working conditions, as opposed to unfair labor practices. In such strikes as the former—and most strikes by far, of course, have significant wage-benefit-working condition components—managements can achieve exactly the same result as a mass discharge of their workers would have simply by awarding the jobs of the strikers to new employees. Only if the courts find that the employer has engaged in an unfair labor practice can the strikers regain their jobs and accrued pay. Otherwise, the most that a striking worker can hope for is a preferential claim to the job that he or she has lost *after* the replacement has retired or for some other reason vacated the position.

For more than four decades after 1938, the replacement-worker strategy was nonetheless used very sparingly by managements. Employers feared retaliation not only directly by organized labor but from unionized suppliers and prounion consumers. Considerations of public relations, community relations, the costs and uncertainties of recruiting and training the new workers, and even possible governmental intervention on the side of the striking union also acted as deterrents. Nor was the chance of violence by the strikers themselves to be casually dismissed. Between 1938 and 1981, only some 200 cases of permanent replacement action were officially recorded.[49]

It was the previously noted illegal strike of 11,500 air traffic controllers in mid-1981 and the then-President Ronald Reagan's immediate authorization of permanent replacements for these strikers that finally gave the policy a huge shot in the arm. Thenceforth, as Mine Worker President Richard L. Trumka has pointed out, "any businessman could...say, 'The President did it so it must be O.K.' "[50] With this extreme kind of action having come from the highest elected official in the land, employers no longer had to worry about governmental intervention on the side of organized labor in such situations—at least as long as friends like Reagan were in power.

Nor by the 1980s were managements oblivious to two other developments that were not only continuing but seemed to be accelerating. One was the declining influence of unions, making potential retaliation in cases of permanent replacement less likely. The other was a general wage stagnation in the economy; it was creating a sizable supply of nonunion workers who were making far less than the incomes realized by many of their unionized counterparts and who were therefore presumably quite able to be attracted to these bargaining unit positions should they become available.

In recent years, replacement workers have been hired with increasing frequency. Some of the companies embracing the tactic—Continental Airlines, the New York *Daily News,* Greyhound, Eastern Air Lines, and Boise Cascade, among many others—were in dire financial straits at the time and vehemently argued that they had no choice in the matter if they wished to survive. But other employers—most notably, Caterpillar, the world's largest manufacturer of construction equipment—have been quite profitable.

What's more, use of the weapon has often been surprisingly effective. Caterpillar's mere threat of hiring permanent replacements in 1992 broke a bitter five-month Automobile Worker strike within days. In Maine, International Paper had no trouble finding many more candidates for replacement jobs than were needed in 1987 and 1988, despite relatively low unemployment at the time and the fact the replacements were offered hourly rates that were less than 70 percent of what the strikers had been getting: Within two weeks of the strike's beginning, International Paper was bringing in permanent replacements in large numbers; by 1988, it had reduced its work force by almost 20 percent and abolished premium pay. Two years later, some 80 percent of the work force was made up of replacement workers.[51]

With such successes, the replacement strategy has gained a remarkable number of employer converts in the recent past. In 1985, 15 percent of 132 managements that experience strikes said that they would use permanent replacements.[52] In 1989, about 23 percent of such employers did.[53] (In both years, about 15 percent actually hired the replacements.) In a 1992 survey of a much larger group of employers (most of whom responded strictly hypothetically), 32 percent said that they would definitely replace the strikers and an additional 48 percent said that they would "consider" replacing their old employees to keep operating.[54]

Nor has organized labor been able to remove this very real threat by getting Congress to declare it, in the style of *Bildisco,* illegal. A labor-backed Workplace Fairness bill got the highest possible legislative priority from unions in the 1991–1992 session of the national legislature. But even its margin of victory in the House (247–182) was too small to override an expected veto by President George Bush. In the Senate, the bill's backers could not even muster the sixty votes needed to head off a Republican-led filibuster. (Exhibit 3-8 constitutes the summary of this voting as seen by the United Steelworkers' major magazine. The publication made it easy for its readers by recording votes as either "right" or "wrong.") At this writing, it appeared that labor would have to await the election of many more friends to national office—not, it would appear, excluding the White House—before it could breathe easily concerning this unwelcome new employer weapon.

EXHIBIT 3-8

STEELWORKERS IN WASHINGTON

House votes on scabs

247 right; 182 wrong

Three weeks after delegates to the USWA Legislative Conference marched across Capitol Hill to lobby for H.R.5 and S.55—the bills that would bar permanent replacement of striking workers—the House of Representatives voted on July 17 to adopt the House bill.

Here is a complete record of the House vote, as tallied by the AFL-CIO Taskforce on Workplace Fairness.

Those representatives who voted right should be thanked; those who voted wrong should be reminded they can correct their error by voting to override President Bush's expected veto of the bill.

ALABAMA

1. H. Callahan (R) .... W
2. W. Dickinson (R) .... W
3. G. Browder (D) .... R
4. T. Bevill (D) .... R
5. B. Cramer (D) .... R
6. Ben Erdreich (D) .... R
7. C. Harris, Jr. (D) ..... R

ALASKA

1. D. Young (R) .... R

ARIZONA

1. J. Rhodes III (R) ...... W
2. M. Udall (D) I
3. B. Stump (R) .... W
4. J. Kyl (R) .... W
5. J. Kolbe (R) .... W

ARKANSAS

1. B. Alexander (D) .... R
2. R. Thorton (D) .... R
3. J. Hammerschmidt (R) W
4. B. Anthony Jr. (D) ..... W

CALIFORNIA

1. F. Riggs (R) .... W
2. W. Herger (R) .... W
3. R. Matsui (D) .... A
4. V. Fazio (D) .... R
5. N. Pelosi (D) .... R
6. B. Boxer (D) .... R
7. G. Miller (D) .... R
8. R. Dellums (D) .... R
9. F. Stark (D) .... R
10. D. Edwards (D) .... R
11. T. Lantos (D) .... R
12. T. Campbell (R) .... W
13. N. Mineta (D) .... R
14. J. Doolittle (R) ...... W
15. G. Condit (D) .... R
16. L. Panetta (D) .... R
17. C. Dooley (R) .... R
18. R. Lehman (D) .... R
19. R. Lagomarsino (R) .... W
20. W. Thomas (R) .... W
21. E. Gallegly (R) .... W
22. C. Moorhead (R) .... W
23. A. Beilenson (D) ...... R
24. H. Waxman (D) .... R
25. E. Roybal (D) .... R
26. H. Berman (D) .... R
27. M. Levine (D) .... R
28. J. Dixon (D) .... R
29. M. Waters (D) .... R
30. M. Martinez (D) .... R
31. M. Dymally (D) .... R
32. G. Anderson (D) .... R
33. D. Dreier (R) .... W
34. E. Torres (D) .... R
35. J. Lewis (R) .... W
36. G. Brown, Jr. (D) ..... R
37. A. McCandless (R) ..... W
38. R. Dornan (R) .... W
39. W. Dannemeyer (R) ..... W
40. C. Cox (R) .... W
41. B. Lowery (R) .... W
42. D. Rohrabacher (R) .... W
43. R. Packard (R) .... W
44. R. Cunningham (R) ..... W
45. D. Hunter (R) .... W

COLORADO

1. P. Schroeder (D) .... R
2. D. Skaggs (D) .... R
3. B. Campbell (D) .... R
4. W. Allard (R) .... W
5. J. Hefley (R) .... W
6. D. Schaefer (R) .... W

CONNECTICUT

1. B. Kennelly (D) .... R
2. S. Gejdenson (D) .... R
3. R. De Lauro (D) .... R
4. C. Shays (R) .... W
5. G. Franks (R) .... W
6. N. Johnson (R) .... W

DELAWARE

1. T. Carper (D) .... R

FLORIDA

1. E. Hutto (D) .... W
2. P. Peterson (D) .... R
3. C. Bennett (D) .... R
4. C. James (R) .... W
5. B. McCollum (R) .... W
6. C. Stearns (R) .... W
7. S. Gibbons (D) .... W
8. C. Young (R) .... W
9. M. Bilirakis (R) .... W
10. A. Ireland (R) .... W
11. J. Bacchus (D) .... R
12. T. Lewis (R) .... W
13. P. Goss (R) .... W
14. H. Johnston (D) .... R
15. E. Shaw Jr. (R) .... W
16. L. Smith (D) .... R
17. W. Lehman (D) .... R
18. Ros-Lehtinen (R) ...... W
19. D. Fascell (D) .... R

GEORGIA

1. L. Thomas (D) .... W
2. C. Hatcher (D) .... W
3. R. Ray (D) .... W
4. B. Jones (D) .... R
5. J. Lewis (D) .... R
6. N. Gingrich (R) .... W
7. G. Darden (D) .... R
8. J. Rowland (D) .... W
9. E. Jenkins (D) .... W
10. D. Barnard Jr. (D) .... W

HAWAII

1. N. Abercrombie (D) ..... R
2. P. Mink (D) .... R

IDAHO

1. Larry LaRocco (D) ...... R
2. R. Stallings (D) .... R

ILLINOIS

1. C. Hayes (D) .... R
2. G. Savage (D) .... R
3. M. Russo (D) .... R
4. G. Sangmeister (D) ..... R
5. W. Lipinski (D) .... R
6. H. Hyde (D) .... W
7. C. Collins (D) .... R
8. D. Rostenkowski (D) .... R
9. S. Yates (D) .... R
10. J. Porter (R) .... W
11. F. Annunzio (D) .... R
12. P. Crane (R) .... W
13. H. Fawell (R) .... W
14. D. Hastert (R) .... W
15. Ewing (R) .... W
16. J. Cox (D) .... R
17. L. Evans (D) .... R
18. R. Michel (R) .... A
19. T. Bruce (D) .... R
20. R. Durbin (D) .... R
21. J. Costello (D) .... R
22. G. Poshard (D) .... R

INDIANA

1. P. Visclosky (D) .... R
2. P. Sharp (D) .... R
3. T. Roemer (D) .... R
4. J. Long (D) .... R
5. J. Jontz (D) .... R
6. D. Burton (R) .... W
7. J. Myers (R) .... W
8. F. McCloskey (D) .... R
9. L. Hamilton (D) .... R
10. A. Jacobs Jr. (D) ..... R

IOWA

1. J. Leach (R) .... W
2. J. Nussie (R) .... W
3. D. Nagle (D) .... R
4. N. Smith (D) .... R
5. J. Lightfoot (R) .... W
6. F. Grandy (R) .... W

KANSAS

1. P. Roberts (R) .... W
2. J. Slattery (D) .... R
3. J. Meyers (R) .... W
4. D. Glickman (D) .... R
5. D. Nichols (R) .... W

KENTUCKY

1. C. Hubbard Jr. (D) ..... R
2. W. Natcher (D) .... R
3. R. Mazzoli (D) .... R
4. J. Bunning (R) .... W
5. H. Rogers (R) .... W
6. L. Hopkins (R) .... W
7. C. Perkins (D) .... R

LOUISIANA

1. B. Livingston (R) ...... W
2. B. Jefferson (D) .... R
3. W. Tauzin (D) .... W
4. J. McCreary (R) .... W
5. J. Huckaby (D) .... W
6. R. Baker (R) .... W
7. J. Hayes (D) .... R
8. C. Holloway (R) .... W

MAINE

1. T. Andrews (D) .... R
2. O. Snowe (R) .... W

MARYLAND

1. W. Gilchrest (R) .... W
2. H. Bentley (R) .... R
3. B. Cardin (D) .... R
4. T. McMillen (D) .... R
5. S. Hoyer (D) .... R
6. B. Byron (D) .... R
7. K. Mfume (D) .... R
8. C. Morella (R) .... W

MASSACHUSETTS

1. J. Olver (D) .... R
2. R. Neal (D) .... R
3. J. D. Early (D) .... R
4. B. Frank (D) .... R
5. C. Atkins (D) .... R
6. N. Mavroules (D) .... R
7. E. Markey (D) .... R
8. J. Kennedy II (D) ...... R
9. J. Moakley (D) .... R
10. G. Studds (D) .... R
11. B. Donnelly (D) .... R

MICHIGAN

1. J. Conyers Jr. (D) ..... R
2. C. Pursell (R) .... W
3. H. Wolpe (D) .... R
4. F. Upton (R) .... W
5. P. Henry (R) .... W
6. B. Carr (D) .... R
7. D. Kildee (D) .... R
8. B. Traxler (D) .... R
9. G. Vander Jagt (R) ..... W
10. D. Camp (R) .... W
11. R. Davis (R) .... R
12. D. Bonior (D) .... R
13. B. Collins (D) .... R
14. D. Hertel (D) .... R
15. W. Ford (D) .... R
16. J. Dingell (D) .... R
17. S. Levin (D) .... R
18. W. Broomfield (R) ..... W

MINNESOTA

1. T. Penny (D) .... R
2. V. Weber (R) .... W
3. J. Ramstad (R) .... W
4. B. Vento (D) .... R
5. M. Sabo (D) .... R
6. G. Sikorski (D) .... R
7. C. Peterson (D) .... R
8. J. Oberstar (D) .... R

MISSISSIPPI

1. J. Whitten (D) .... W
2. M. Espy (D) .... R
3. G. Montgomery (D) ...... W
4. M. Parker (D) .... R
5. G. Taylor (D) .... W

MISSOURI

1. W. Clay (D) .... R
2. J. Horn (D) .... R
3. R. Gephardt (D) .... R
4. I. Skelton (D) .... R
5. A. Wheat (D) .... R
6. E. Coleman (R) .... W
7. M. Hancock (R) .... W
8. B. Emerson (R) .... W
9. H. Volkmer (D) .... R

MONTANA

1. P. Williams (D) .... R
2. R. Marlenee (R) .... W

NEBRASKA

1. D. Bereuter (R) .... W
2. P. Hoagland (D) .... R
3. B. Barrett (R) .... W

NEVADA

1. J. Bilbray (D) .... R
2. B. Vucanovich (R) ...... W

NEW HAMPSHIRE

1. B. Zeliff (R) .... W
2. D. Swett (D) .... R

NEW JERSEY

1. R. Andrews (D) .... R
2. W. Hughes (D) .... R
3. F. Pallone, Jr. (D) .... R
4. C. Smith (R) .... R
5. M. Roukema (R) .... W
6. B. Dwyer (D) .... R
7. M. Rinaldo (R) .... R
8. R. Roe (D) .... R
9. R. Torricelli (D) ...... R
10. D. Payne (D) .... R
11. D. Gallo (R) .... W
12. D. Zimmer (R) .... W
13. H. Saxton (R) .... W
14. F. Guarini (D) .... R

NEW MEXICO

1. S. Schiff (R) .... W
2. J. Skeen (R) .... W
3. B. Richardson (D) ...... R

NEW YORK

1. G. Hochbrueckner (D) ... R
2. T. Downey (D) .... R
3. R. Mrazek (D) .... R
4. N. Lent (R) .... W
5. R. McGrath (R) .... R
6. F. Flake (D) .... R
7. G. Ackerman (D) .... R
8. J. Scheuer (D) .... R
9. T. Manton (D) .... R
10. C. Schumer (D) .... R
11. E. Towns (D) .... R
12. M. Owens (D) .... R
13. S. Solarz (D) .... R
14. S. Molinari (R) .... W
15. B. Green (R) .... R
16. C. Rangel (D) .... R
17. T. Weiss (D) .... A
18. J. Serrano (D) .... R
19. E. Engel (D) .... R
20. N. Lowey (D) .... R
21. H. Fish Jr. (R) .... R
22. B. Gilman (R) .... R
23. M. McNulty (D) .... R
24. G. Solomon (R) .... R
25. S. Boehlert (R) .... R
26. D. Martin (R) .... W
27. J. Walsh (R) .... W
28. M. McHugh (D) .... R
29. F. Horton (R) .... R
30. L. Slaughter (D) ...... R
31. B. Paxon (R) .... W
32. J. LaFalce (D) .... R
33. H. Nowak (D) .... R
34. A. Houghton Jr. (R) ... W

N. CAROLINA

1. W. Jones (D) .... R
2. I. Valentine Jr. (D) ... W
3. H. Lancaster (D) .... W
4. D. Price (D) .... R
5. S. Neil (D) .... W
6. J. Coble (R) .... W
7. C. Rose (D) .... R
8. W. Hefner (D) .... R
9. A. McMillan (R) .... W
10. T. Ballenger (R) ...... W
11. C. Taylor (R) .... W

NORTH DAKOTA

1. B. Dorgan (D) .... R

OHIO

1. C. Luken (D) .... R
2. B. Gradison (R) .... W
3. T. Hall (D) .... R
4. M. Oxley (R) .... W
5. P. Gillmor (R) .... W
6. B. McEwen (R) .... W
7. D. Hobson (R) .... W
8. J. Boehner (R) .... W
9. M. Kaptur (D) .... R
10. C. E. Miller (R) ...... W
11. D. Eckart (D) .... R
12. J. Kasich (R) .... W
13. D. Pease (D) .... R
14. T. Sawyer (D) .... R
15. C. Wylie (R) .... W
16. R. Regula (R) .... R
17. J. Traficant (D) ...... R
18. D. Applegate (D) ...... R
19. E. Feighan (D) .... R
20. M. Oakar (D) .... R
21. L. Stokes (D) .... R

OKLAHOMA

1. J. Inhofe (R) .... W
2. M. Synar (D) .... R
3. B. Brewster (D) .... W
4. D. McCurdy (D) .... W
5. M. Edwards (R) .... W
6. G. English (D) .... W

OREGON

1. L. AuCoin (D) .... R
2. B. Smith (R) .... W
3. R. Wyden (D) .... R
4. P. DeFazio (D) .... R
5. M. Kopetski (D) .... R

PENNSYLVANIA

1. T. Foglietta (D) .... R
2. W. Gray III (D) .... R
3. R. Borski (D) .... R
4. J. Kolter (D) .... R
5. R. Schulze (R) .... W
6. G. Yatron (D) .... A
7. W. Weldon (R) .... R
8. P. Kostmayer (D) .... R
9. B. Schuster (R) .... W
10. J. McDade (R) .... R
11. P. Kanjorski (D) ...... R
12. J. Murtha (D) .... R
13. L. Coughlin (R) .... W
14. W. Coyne (D) .... R
15. D. Ritter (R) .... W
16. R. Walker (R) .... W
17. G. Gekas (R) .... W
18. R. Santoum (R) .... R
19. B. Gooding (R) .... W
20. J. Gaydos (D) .... R
21. T. Ridge (R) .... W
22. A. Murphy (D) .... R
23. W. Clinger Jr. (R) .... W

RHODE ISLAND

1. R. Machtley (R) .... W
2. J. Reed (D) .... R

S. CAROLINA

1. A. Ravenel, Jr. (R) .... W
2. F. Spence (R) .... W
3. B. Derrick (D) .... W
4. E. Patterson (D) .... W
5. J. Spratt (D) .... W
6. Robin Tallon (D) .... W

SOUTH DAKOTA

1. T. Johnston (D) .... R

TENNESSEE

1. J. Quilen (R) .... W
2. J. Duncan (R) .... W
3. M. Lloyd (D) .... R
4. J. Cooper (D) .... W
5. B. Clement (D) .... R
6. B. Gordon (D) .... R
7. D. Sundquist (R) .... W
8. J. Tanner (D) .... R
9. H. Ford (D) .... R

TEXAS

1. J. Chapman (D) .... R
2. C. Wilson (D) .... R
3. S. Johnson (R) .... W
4. R. Hall (D) .... W
5. J. Bryant (D) .... R
6. J. Barton (R) .... W
7. B. Archer (R) .... W
8. J. Fields (R) .... W
9. J. Brooks (D) .... R
10. J. Pickle (D) .... W
11. C. Edwards (D) .... R
12. P. Geren (D) .... W
13. B. Sarpalius (D) ...... R
14. G. Laughlin (D) .... R
15. E. de la Garza (D) .... R
16. R. Coleman (D) .... R
17. C. Stenholm (D) .... W
18. C. Washington (D) ..... R
19. L. Combest (R) .... W
20. H. Gonzalez (D) .... R
21. L. Smith (R) .... W
22. T. DeLay (R) .... W
23. A. Bustamante (D) ..... R
24. M. Frost (D) .... R
25. M. Andrews (D) .... R
26. D. Armey (R) .... W
27. S. Ortiz (D) .... W

UTAH

1. J. Hansen (R) .... W
2. W. Owens (D) .... R
3. B. Orton (D) .... R

VERMONT

1. B. Sanders (I) .... R

VIRGINIA

1. H. Bateman (R) .... W
2. O. Pickett (D) .... W
3. T. Bliley Jr. (R) ...... W
4. N. Sisisky (D) .... W
5. L. Payne (D) .... W
6. J. Olin (D) .... R
7. D. Slaughter (R) .... W
8. J. Moran (D) .... R
9. F. Boucher (D) .... R
10. F. Wolf (R) .... W

WASHINGTON

1. J. Miller (R) .... W
2. A. Swift (D) .... R
3. J. Unsoeld (D) .... R
4. S. Morrison (R) .... W
5. T. Foley (D) .... R
6. N. Dicks (D) .... R
7. J. McDermott (D) .... R
8. R. Chandler (R) .... W

WEST VIRGINIA

1. A. Mollohan (D) .... R
2. H. Staggers Jr. (D) .... R
3. B. Wise (D) .... R
4. N. Rahall II (D) .... R

WISCONSIN

1. Les Aspin (D) .... R
2. S. Klug (R) .... W
3. S. Gunderson (R) .... W
4. G. Kleczka (D) .... A
5. J. Moody (D) .... R
6. T. Petri (R) .... W
7. D. Obey (D) .... R
8. T. Roth (R) .... W
9. F. Sensenbrenner (R) ... W

WYOMING

1. C. Thomas (R) .... W

KEY

R = Voted right
W = Voted wrong
A = Absent, did not vote or make position known

July/August 1991/**Steelabor** 11

Source: *Steelabor,* July–August 1991, p. 11.

SOME CONCLUSIONS

What are some reasonably safe conclusions based on the long experience of public policy recited on these pages?

The first conclusion must be that public policy toward organized labor and collective bargaining, as indicated above, has changed significantly over the years. It has moved from legal repression to strong encouragement, then to modified encouragement coupled with regulation, and, finally, to detailed regulation of internal union affairs in an environment that unions see as increasingly antilabor. It seems a safe prediction not only that further shifts in this public policy can be expected, but also that these changes, as was not always the case in earlier times, will depend for this direction strictly on the acceptability of current union behavior to the American public.

This point is particularly important to the unionists of today. Especially since 1937, when it held the Wagner Act wholly constitutional, the Supreme Court has permitted the legislative branch of government the widest latitude to shape public policy. Congress and the state legislatures are judicially free to determine the elements of the framework of labor law. To most citizens, such a situation is only as it should be; our judiciary is expected to interpret law but not to make it, and we generally expect actions of the legislative branch to be voided only when the particular statute clearly and unmistakably violates the terms of the Constitution. But since today the polls, and not the courts, do constitute the forum in which our policies toward labor are determined, and since the public has in the recent past apparently increased its level of aspiration as to union behavior, labor organizations have been forced amid their adversity to become increasingly conscious of the images they project. Such a situation accounts to a great extent for the growing union stress on such nontraditional labor concerns as charity work, college scholarships, Scout troops, and Little League teams, which will be discussed in the next chapter. It also accounts for the entire labor movement's uneasiness whenever strikes arousing the public ire or such notable black marks as convictions of Teamster leaders occur. And it undoubtedly has been one major factor in leading to more maturity and self-restraint on the part of some labor leaders at the bargaining table. As Chapter 1 noted, however, whether this progress will continue sufficiently and in time to satisfy the increasingly high level of public expectation and thereby ward off further laws of the Taft-Hartley and Landrum-Griffin variety remains an unanswered question.

Second, every law since Norris–La Guardia has expanded the scope of government regulation of the labor-management arena. To the curbs on judicial capriciousness enacted in 1932 have been added, in turn, restrictions on employer conduct, limitations on union conduct, and governmental fiats closely regulating internal union affairs. Most of the other parts of the later laws—to cite but two examples, Taft-Hartley's modification of the Wagner Act's closed- and union-shop provisions and Landrum-Griffin's new conditions regarding the hot-cargo clauses—represent ever-finer qualifications of the freedom of action of both parties. Given both the electorate's impatience with the progress of collective bargaining and Congress's apparently deep-seated reluctance to decrease the scope covered by its laws, future legislation can be expected to move *further* in the direction of government intervention. This should hold true whether the future laws are enacted with the implicit goal of "helping" or of "hurting" unions.

Individual value judgments clearly determine the advisability of such a trend. But if one believes that stable and sound industrial relations can be achieved only in an environment of free collective bargaining, wherein labor and management—the parties that must live with each other on a day-to-day basis—are allowed to find mutually satisfactory answers to their industrial relations problems, there is cause for concern. Government policy that limits this freedom strikes at the very heart of the process.

This is not to say that the more recent labor statutes are entirely barren of provisions that are valuable additions to the law of labor relations. The unfair union labor practices relating to restraint and coercion of employees and to union-caused employer discrimination are clearly a move in the right direction. So, too, are Taft-Hartley's curbs on strikes and boycott activity engaged in at times by some unions for the objective of increasing the power of one union at the expense of other labor organizations, despite all the litigation that has surrounded these curbs since 1947. Nor does the requirement that unions bargain collectively embarrass anyone except the union leader who is uncooperative and recalcitrant.

At the same time, however, the government intervention in regard to such issues as union security, the checkoff, and the enforcement of the collective bargaining agreement (to cite but three), and the decreasing scope for union and management bargaining-table latitude in general, do raise the question of ultimate government control over *all* major industrial relations activities. For one who believes in "free collective bargaining," the increasing reach of the statutes may be steering labor policy in a very dangerous direction.

Third, even if one does conclude that the gains of our present dosage of government regulation outweigh its losses and inherent risks, this hardly proves that the current statutes and their interpretations constitute the most *appropriate* ones to meet each specific labor relations topic now being dealt with.

Finally, and probably also as an inevitable consequence of the increased coverage of public policy, labor laws have become anything but easy to comprehend. The inconsistent NLRB and judicial rulings that have plagued them in recent years may be based to some extent on philosophical and political differences, but they undeniably also stem from the built-in interpretative difficulties in the laws themselves.

What constitutes "refusal to bargain"? When are employers discriminating in regard to "hire or tenure of employment or any term or condition of employment" to influence union membership? What constitutes unlawful union recognition picketing? It is hard to disagree with the commonly heard lament of unionists and labor relations managers that it has become ever more risky to state definitively what is legal in bargaining relationships and what is not; and the most valuable information available to the management or labor union representative who is concerned with labor law may very possibly be the telephone number of an able labor attorney. But, given the dimensions of this law today, however unpalatable many of its tenets may be to one or the other party, and whatever dangers may be inherent in present trends, the managers and unionists who are *not* concerned with public policy remain so only at their peril.

DISCUSSION QUESTIONS

1. Why, do you think, did the courts so squarely ally themselves with the employer community and against organized labor from the days of the American Revolution until the Great Depression of the 1930s?

2. "The Norris–La Guardia Act conferred no new rights on workers. It merely adjusted an inherently inequitable situation." Comment.

3. How much truth do you feel lies in the statement that "there was great need for the Wagner Act...its sole defect lay in the fact that it was not slightly broadened from time to time to regulate a few union practices of dubious social value"?

4. It has been argued that whatever deficiencies may have accompanied the Taft-Hartley Act, it did "free workers from the tyrannical hold of union bosses." Do you agree?

5. Do you feel that the Wagner Act or the Taft-Hartley Act has been more influential in leading to the current status of organized labor in this country?

6. "In the last analysis, the public must judge the relative merits of the collective bargaining process." Discuss.

7. If all existing national labor legislation could instantly be erased and our statutory regulation could then be completely rewritten, what would you advocate as public policy governing labor relations—and why?

8. Whether or not you agree with the exact scope and specific wording of the present laws, do you consider these laws to be essentially equitable to both management and labor?

9. "If union members were to attend union meetings regularly and take an active role in the operation of the union, there would be no need for Landrum-Griffin." Defend your position, whatever it may be.

10. What do you believe to be the most important right that the Taft-Hartley Act offers (a) the employee, (b) the employer? In each case, defend your selection.

MINICASES

#1 A Question of Definition

After some professors at Deer Valley University show an interest in collective bargaining and invite a national representative of the American Association of University Professors to visit their campus and explain to them and their colleagues how to go about holding a union representation election, the university administration makes an announcement. The faculty members had better forget the whole thing, it says, because DVU is a "private institution" and the AAUP is consequently deprived of all legal protection in its unionizing activities.

The professors immediately circulate an irate written rejoinder, asserting that the university is not private but "state-related" and thus quite entitled to the coverage of the state's "little Taft-Hartley" labor law. The institution, they point out, currently derives one-quarter of its annual revenues from the state, and four of its twenty-eight trustees are appointed by the governor (the other twenty-four are designated by vote of the board of trustees itself).

Who, in your opinion, is right—and why?

#2 Alleged Union Paranoia

Two weeks before a scheduled union representation election, a supervisor drives three times past a union meeting that is attended by about eighty employees. After the union loses the election, by the wide margin of 140 to 63, it asks the NLRB to set the latter aside on the grounds that the supervisor's actions constituted an obvious attempt to find out who was at the meeting and thus an implicit "threat of reprisal," prohibited by Taft-Hartley. The management tells the board that the union is being "paranoid" and that the connection between the supervisor's driving and reprisal is far too tenuous to prove anything illegal. The supervisor, it says, was "simply curious" as to who was attending and how large the overall crowd was. And, it asserts, he drove by entirely on his own, in no way at the behest of his supervisors.

If you were on the NLRB, would you set aside the election? Why or why not?

NOTES

[1]*Photoswitch,* 99 NLRB 1366 (1962).

[2]*NLRB* v. *Truitt,* 351 U.S. 149 (1955).

[3]*Nielsen Lithographing,* 1991–92 CCH NLRB, 16, 992.

[4]Robben W. Fleming, "The Obligation to Bargain in Good Faith," in Joseph Shister et al., *Public Policy and Collective Bargaining* (New York: Harper & Row, 1962), p. 83; see also Guy Farmer, *Management Rights and Union Bargaining Power* (New York: Industrial Relations Counselors, 1965).

[5]*Ford Motor Company* v. *NLRB,* 441 U.S. 488 (1979).

[6]*Cowles Media Co. Star Tribune Division,* 295 NLRB No. 63 (1989).

[7]*Johnson-Bateman Co.,* 295 NLRB No. 26 (1989).

[8]National Labor Relations Board, *Annual Report,* 1992, p. 11.

[9]395 U.S. 575 (1969).

[10]270 NLRB 578 (1984).

[11]*Machinists* v. *Street,* 367 U.S. 740 (1961); *Brotherhood of Railway and Steamship Clerks* v. *Allen,* 373 U.S. 113 (1963). See also Benjamin J. Taylor and Fred Witney, *Labor Relations Law,* 4th ed. (Englewood Cliffs, N.J.: Prentice Hall, 1983), pp. 396–98.

[12]*Communication Workers* v. *Beck,* 86 Sup. Ct. 637 (June 29, 1988).

[13]In *Ellis* v. *Railway Clerks,* 466 U.S. 435 (1984), a railroad case, the Supreme Court held that organizing expenses are rebatable though it said that dissenters could not recover expenditures for union conventions, social activities, and certain publicity and litigation costs.

[14]Here is the complete definition of a professional employee: "any employee engaged in work (i) predominantly intellectual and varied in character as opposed to routine mental, manual, mechanical, or physical work; (ii) involving the consistent exercise of discretion and judgment in its performance; (iii) of such a character that the output produced or the result accomplished cannot be standardized in relation to a given period of time; (iv) requiring knowledge of an advanced type in a field of science or learning customarily acquired by a prolonged course of specialized intellectual instruction and study in an institution of higher learning or a hospital, as distinguished from a general academic education or from an apprenticeship or from training in the performance of routine mental, manual, or physical processes; or any employee, who (i) has completed the courses of specialized intellectual instruction and study described in clause (iv) or paragraph (a), and (ii) is performing related work under the supervision of a professional person to qualify himself to become a professional employee as defined in paragraph (a)."

[15]*Ryan Aeronautical Company,* 132 NLRB 1160 (1962).

[16]*Malinckrodt Chemical Works,* 162 NLRB 48 (1966).

[17]*Firestone Tire & Rubber Company,* 222 NLRB 1254 (1976).

[18]*Buddy L. Corporation,* 167 NLRB 808 (1967).

[19]For a fuller discussion of these and various related organizational matters, see Taylor and Witney, *Labor Relations Law,* Chapter 12.

[20]*Livingston Shirt,* 107 NLRB 400 (1953).

[21]*J. P. Stevens,* 219 NLRB 850 (1975).

[22]*Excelsior Underwear, Inc.,* 156 NLRB 1236 (1966). Sustained by U.S. Supreme Court in *NLRB* v. *Wyman Company,* 394 U.S. 759 (1969).

[23]*Packard Motor Car Company* v. *NLRB,* 67 Sup. Ct. 789 (1947).

[24]*NLRB* v. *Bell Aerospace Company,* 416 U.S. 267 (1974).

[25]*NLRB* v. *Yeshiva University,* 444 U.S. 672 (1980). This decision generated sharp criticism among faculty groups. See, for example, John William Gercacz and Charles E. Krider, "NLRB v. Yeshiva University: The End of Faculty Unions?" *Wake Forest Law Review,* 16, No. 6 (December 1980), 891–914; and American Association of University Professors, "The Yeshiva Decision," *Academe,* Bulletin of the AAUP, 66 (May 1980), pp. 188–97.

[26]American Association of University Professors, *Academe,* September–October 1987, p. 36.

[27]*Ottawa Silica,* 197 NLRB 53 (1972).

[28]Taylor and Witney, *Labor Relations Law,* p. 564.

[29]*Complete Auto Transit, Inc.* v. *Reis,* 451 U.S. 401 (1981).

[30]*Carbon Fuel* v. *United Mine Workers of America,* 444 U.S. 212 (1979).

[31]*St. Francis Hospital,* 271 NLRB 160 (1984).

[32]*Monthly Labor Review,* November 1988, p. 40.

[33]*American Hospital Association* v. *NLRB,* Case No. 90-97, April 23, 1991.

[34]*AFL-CIO News,* April 29, 1991.

[35]*New York Times,* April 24, 1991.

[36]*Beth Israel Hospital* v. *NLRB,* 434 U.S. 1033 (1978); *NLRB* v. *Baptist Hospital,* 440 U.S. 943 (1979).

[37]Office of the General Counsel (NLRB), Release No. 1385, March 27, 1975, p. 2.

[38]*Cedars-Sinai Medical Center,* 223 NLRB 251 (1976).

[39]National Labor Relations Board, "NLRB the First 50 Years. The Story of the National Labor Relations Board, 1935–1985," p. ix.

[40]*Sheet Metal Workers' Local 75* v. *Lynn,* 86 Sup. Ct. 1940, (January 17, 1989).

[41]*Auto Workers* v. *Dole,* CCA-DC No. 88-5109 (March 13, 1989).

[42]*NLRB* v. *Servette,* 377 U.S. 46 (1964).

[43]*NLRB* v. *Fruit & Vegetable Packers & Warehousemen, Local 706 et al. (Tree Fruits, Inc.),* 377 U.S. 58 (1964).

[44]*De Bartolo Corp.* v. *Florida Gulf Coast Trades Council,* 458 U.S. 568 (1988).

[45]"AFL-CIO, Committee on the Evolution of Work," *The Changing Situation of Workers and Their Unions* (Washington, D.C.: AFL-CIO, 1985), p. 10.

[46]*Business Week,* June 11, 1984, p. 122.

[47]*New York Times,* February 5, 1984, Sec. F, p. 4.

[48]*Wall Street Journal,* January 25, 1984, p. 35.

[49]*New York Times,* April 21, 1992, p. D2.

[50]*Ibid.,* January 27, 1991, p. 1.

[51]*Ibid.,* March 13, 1990, p. A24.

[52]*Ibid.,* January 27, 1991, p. 23.

[53]*Ibid.*

[54]*Wall Street Journal,* April 20, 1992, p. A3.

SELECTED REFERENCES

Ballace, Janice R., Allan Berkowitz, and Bruce D. Van Dusen, *The Landrum-Griffin Act.* Philadelphia: University of Pennsylvania, 1979.

Feldacker, Bruce S., *Labor Guide to Labor Law* (2nd ed.). Reston, Va.: Reston, 1983.

Flanagan, Robert, *Labor Relations and the Litigation Explosion.* Washington, D.C.: Brookings Institution, 1987.

Getman, Julius G., and Bertrand B. Pogrebin, *Labor Relations: The Basic Processes, Law and Practice.* Westbury, N.Y.: Foundation Press, 1988.

Goldman, Alvin L., *Labor Law and Industrial Relations in the U.S.A.* Washington, D.C.: Bureau of National Affairs, 1984.

Gould, William B., *A Primer on American Labor Law* (2nd ed.). Cambridge, Mass.: MIT Press, 1986.

Justice, Betty W., *Unions, Workers and the Law.* Washington, D.C.: Bureau of National Affairs, 1983.

Leslie, Douglas L., *Labor Law in a Nutshell* (2nd ed.). St. Paul, Minn.: West, 1986.

McKelvey, Jean T., ed., *The Changing Law of Fair Representation.* Ithaca, N.Y.: ILR Press, Cornell University, 1985.

McLaughlin, Doris B., and Anita W. Schoonmaker, *The Landrum-Griffin Act and Union Democracy.* Ann Arbor: University of Michigan Press, 1979.

Malin, Martin H., *Individual Rights Within the Union.* Washington, D.C.: Bureau of National Affairs, 1987.

Miller, Edward B., *An Administrative Appraisal of the NLRB* (3rd ed.). Philadelphia: University of Pennsylvania, 1981.

Morris, Charles J., ed., *American Labor Policy: A Critical Appraisal of the National Labor Relations Act.* Washington, D.C.: Bureau of National Affairs, 1987.

Schlossberg, Stephen I., and Judith A. Scott, *Organizing and the Law* (3rd ed.). Washington, D.C.: Bureau of National Affairs, 1983.

Swann, James P., Jr., *NLRB Elections: A Guidebook for Employers.* Washington, D.C.: Bureau of National Affairs, 1980.

Taylor, Benjamin J., and Fred Witney, *Labor Relations Law* (6th ed.). Englewood Cliffs, N.J.: Prentice Hall, 1992.

Union Behavior: Structure, Government, and Operation

OUTLINE OF KEY CONTENTS

- Why national unions do and sometimes don't belong to the AFL-CIO
- The somewhat complex structural organization of the AFL-CIO
- The major interests and activities of the AFL-CIO
- The relationship between national and local unions
- What national unions do beyond providing service to local unions
- How national unions are governed and why, even though they hardly grow rich on the salaries of their offices, national union officers generally like the work
- The government and basic characteristics of local unions
- The financial status of unions

Simplicity does not mark the structure of organized labor in the United States.

For example, the AFL-CIO is a federation that contains many different sectors exercising different duties and authority. Most of the 147 national or international unions in existence in the United States belong to the federation, although 58 of them do not. National unions, in turn, are themselves subdivided into regions or districts for more efficient management and administration. And although the vast majority of the country's approximately 50,000 local unions belong to national unions, several hundred of them do not and are commonly described as "independent" unions.[1] Finally, some unions are craft in character, others industrial, and some are both craft and industrial.

Because unions are not similar in terms of heritage, size, geographic location, the personalities of their officers, and the kinds of workers who are members, it should be expected that they will differ widely in terms not only of their governments but also of their day-to-day operations. Some (perhaps most notably the International Typographical Union, which is unique among unions in having an organized two-party system, and the Newspaper Guild) both before and after Landrum-Griffin have operated very democratically, whereas a few (including, until democratic procedures were forced upon them by a governmental consent decree in 1989, most segments of the International Brotherhood of Teamsters) have always maintained a highly autocratic system of internal government. Unions are different in terms of the intensity of their political activities, although events of the past few decades have made virtually all labor organizations conscious of a need to become relatively active in political campaigns and thus in influencing the selection of lawmakers. Some unions have engaged in considerably more "social" activities of the type alluded to earlier in this book than have others. Above all, unions vary in terms of their internal rules, dues and initiation fees, and qualifications for membership. Thus, although in the following pages an effort will be made to present a systematic analysis of union behavior, structure, and government, one should recognize that diversity rather than uniformity characterizes the American labor movement. We must be concerned with common principles and trends, but there are many exceptions to them.

THE AFL-CIO

Relationship to National Unions

The decision of the former AFL and CIO to unite forces into a consolidated AFL-CIO in 1955 was made by the affiliated national unions of the two federations; the officers of the AFL and the CIO did not themselves have the power to bring about such a consolidation. This observation demonstrates a very important principle of the structure of the American labor movement—the autonomy of the national unions. The federation can exist only as long as the national unions that belong to it agree to stay in this labor body.

In a sense, the relationship of the national unions to the federation compares closely with the relationship of member nations to the United Nations. No nation *must* belong to the United Nations; any nation *may* withdraw from the international organization at any time and for any reason whatsoever. Nor does the UN have the power to determine the internal government of any of its affiliates, its tax laws, its foreign policy, the size of its military establishment, and similar national specifications. Nations affiliate and remain members of the world body for the advantages that the organization allows in the pursuit of world peace, and for other purposes, but they continue to exercise absolute sovereignty in the conduct of their own affairs.

The same is true of the relationship of the AFL-CIO to its affiliated national unions. A union belongs to the federation because of the various advantages of affiliation, but the national union is autonomous in the conduct of its own affairs. Each union determines its own collective bargaining program, negotiates its contracts without the aid or intervention of the federation, sets its own level of dues and initiation fees, and may call strikes without any approval from the AFL-CIO; nor, conversely, can the federation prohibit a strike that an affiliated member desires to undertake.

Moreover, the federation cannot force a merger of two of its affiliates that have essentially the same jurisdiction. For example, the International Brotherhood of Electrical Workers of the old AFL and the International Union of Electronic Workers of the old CIO have what strikes the disinterested observer as virtually identical jurisdictions in manufacturing. It may seem logical that these two national unions should merge their forces, and in the process further consolidate with the smaller, independent United Electrical Workers; in fact, all three of these unions have in recent years discussed such a consolidation. To date, however, the conversations have produced no action, and perhaps they never will. As Jerry Wurf, late president of the American Federation of State, County and Municipal Employees, once observed:

> Mergers and consolidations are, of course, easier to talk about than to bring about. At stake are the bread-and-butter questions that always impede institutional change: What will happen to the elected officers, the paid staff, the local and regional structures, and the assets and traditions to which all unions, meek or mighty, cling? There still would be jobs and titles. But even the most selfless politician (and we labor leaders are, after all, political creatures) often sees himself as peerless when it comes to occupying a union presidency. The power, the payroll, the trappings—these are the real obstacles.[2]

On the other hand, two or even more unions within the AFL-CIO may merge voluntarily if they do desire to do so, and, since 1955, some eighty of them have. Most notable were the 1969 joining together of four of the five railroad operating brotherhoods into the 220,000-member United Transportation Union, now the largest AFL-CIO affiliate concerned solely with transportation, and the 1979 amalgamation of the Retail Clerks International Union and the Amalgamated Meat Cutters and Butcher Workmen into the 1.3 million-member United Food and Commercial Workers. Consolidations of some importance have also taken place in the past few years in printing, the postal service, chemicals, steel, and textiles.

Steadily rising administrative costs have motivated many of these merger actions; roughly fifty of the federation's eighty-nine national unions have fewer than 50,000 members and thus fall below what AFL-CIO officials have estimated to be the minimum dues-paying base necessary to support effective action while another thirty of the AFL-CIO affiliates have under 100,000 members and are also often hard-pressed for cash. In other cases, technological change or the changing desires of the marketplace have simply made a union obsolete, and the merger becomes a device to provide a respectable burial. Examples in this latter category would surely be the Cigar Makers, whose remaining 2,500 members merged with the Retail, Wholesale, and Department Store Workers in 1974, and the Sleeping Car Porters, who disappeared by merger into the Brotherhood of Railway and Airline Clerks four years later.

In still other situations, the growth of the managerial conglomerate—with ownership spanning several different product markets—has been the spur. The Tobacco Workers and Bakery and Confectionery Workers merger and the absorption by the Steelworkers of not only the Mine, Mill, and Smelter Workers but also the Aluminum Workers and District 50 of the Mine Workers can all be explained on this latter basis. The mergers were triggered by a desire to match the bargaining strength of employers whose own boundaries had themselves been significantly expanding. Obviously, such a multifaceted conglomerate as the LTV Corporation (to use only one example), which today controls—among other operations—Jones & Laughlin Steel, Youngstown Sheet and Tube, Kentron International, Lykes Bros. Steamship, Continental-Emsco, and Vought Corporation, could not be met on equal terms by narrowly jurisdictioned unionism.

All of these reasons have led to many mergers in recent years. Since 1956, there have been ninety-seven such combinings—forty of them since 1978. Not all of them involved the AFL-CIO, but the heavy majority did, and some observers of the trend now predict that within another decade the federation will be comprised of only fifteen to twenty large unions—perhaps one for the communications field, one for retailing, another single union for the metalworker trades, and so on.

It must be stressed again, however, that all mergers under the decentralized AFL-CIO system have been voluntary. The affiliated unions decide their own fates, and each of them can pursue its own objectives, conduct its own affairs, and devise what policies and programs it desires to follow without intervention by either the federation or any other national union. Least of all can any outsider compel the unions to merge.

Nor, for that matter, can the AFL-CIO compel them to *stay* merged. Although most mergers are permanent, some simply don't work out and, usually by mutual agreement of the merging parties, the arrangement terminates. In 1976, for example, the Pottery Workers merged with the Seafarers International Union in what many observers viewed as an unlikely wedding. Less than two years later, their differences too major to overcome, the two unions effected an institutional divorce. In 1982, the Pottery Workers, with barely 11,000 members at that point, merged with the 85,000-member Glass Bottle Blowers. When last heard from this time, they were happily married.

Enforcement of Federation Rules

The AFL-CIO constitution does contain certain rules of conduct that a national union must respect if it desires to remain a member of the federation. Each affiliate must pay to the federation a per capita tax of 27 cents per member per month. No union may "raid" the membership of any other affiliate, nor may it be officered by Communists, Fascists, or members of any other totalitarian group. Among other rules, an affiliate is obligated to conduct its affairs without regard to "race, creed, color, national origin, or ancestry." Each affiliate is further expected "to protect the labor movement from any and all corrupt influences."

The practical question immediately arises as to what powers the AFL-CIO may exercise when an affiliated national union does not comply with these and various other rules of the federation. If the AFL-CIO had wide-sweeping powers over the national unions, the federation officers could swiftly compel the errant union to correct its improper conduct. It could still belong to the federation, but its violation of the federation's constitution would be abruptly terminated.

The realities of the situation, however, are such that the federation is not empowered to correct violations by exercise of such power. It can do no more than suspend or expel a national union that persists in the violation of the federation's constitution.

The expulsion weapon has been used in several instances, but never rashly. Before the AFL-CIO expelled the Teamsters Union in 1957 to begin a separation that would endure for thirty years, for example, that union was put on notice that it stood in flagrant violation of the anticorruption provision of the federation's constitution. AFL-CIO officials instructed the Teamsters that they would face expulsion unless certain of their national officers were removed and the corrupt practices eliminated. Only when the Teamsters adamantly refused to comply did the AFL-CIO convert the threat into actuality and take the ultimate step of expelling the union from its ranks. And even though the UAW actually withdrew from the AFL-CIO in 1968 (and would not return until 1981) because of its claim that the AFL-CIO was not doing enough in organizational work and had not been militant enough in areas of social affairs, the federation technically expelled the UAW only on the entirely understandable ground that it had refused to pay its per capita dues.

Moreover, as a practical matter, the federation is compelled to use even this amount of authority sparingly and with discretion. The expulsion of the Teamsters was prompted by the corrupt practices of union officers who were highly visible to the public. The AFL-CIO could not tolerate such a situation in the light of the existing public clamor against dishonest union leadership and practices; it was fully aware that the retention of the Teamsters would reflect adversely on *every* affiliated union. One would be naïve, however, to believe that all unions scrupulously adhere to the letter and spirit of each rule incorporated in the federation's constitution. It is, for example, common knowledge that some affiliated unions still discriminate against minority group members, although—as has been noted earlier—in recent years progress has been made in eliminating such practices and although provisions of the Civil Rights Act of 1964 (which make it unlawful for unions to discriminate because of race, color, or creed) have further helped in this regard. Despite all this improvement, however, some unions still prohibit minorities from joining, fail to represent them fairly and equally in collective bargaining, and otherwise discriminate against them. Such practices, of course, conflict not only with legality but with the AFL-CIO constitutional proscription against racial discrimination. But the federation is faced with a major dilemma under such circumstances: If it were to expel each union found to be in any way discriminating, the size of the federation would be reduced and its influence as a labor body would be accordingly impaired. Indeed, to date no union has been expelled from the federation for racial discrimination; about all the federation officers have done has been to use moral suasion to deal with the problem. Such an approach has not yet been particularly effective in many cases, but to do more than this would jeopardize the entire federation.

Member-union autonomy is also evident from the ease with which national unions have left the federation voluntarily. Several affiliates—including the Mine Workers, Lithographers, and Radio and Television Directors—have pulled out of the larger body with impunity, saving their considerable per capita tax money in the process.

Why, then, *do* most national unions seek to belong to the federation? What do they get for their money?

Advantages of Affiliation

By far the chief benefit associated with membership is protection against "raiding." One provision of the AFL-CIO constitution states that "each such affiliate shall respect the established collective bargaining relationship of every other affiliate and no affiliate shall raid the established collective bargaining relationship of any other affiliate." This means that once an affiliated union gains bargaining rights with a management, no other union affiliated with the federation may attempt to dislodge the established union and place itself there instead. Such a stricture frees unions from the task of fighting off raids from sister unions of the federation. Time and money conserved in this way can be used to organize the unorganized or to devote to other union programs. Unions that violate the no-raiding provision of the constitution may realistically expect to be expelled from the AFL-CIO; and because mutual self-interest of all members is involved, the amount of raiding has in fact decreased sharply since the formation of the federation.

Thus, before a union withdraws voluntarily from the AFL-CIO or engages in conduct that could result in expulsion, the officers of the union must weigh the consequences of operating outside the federation as these consequences concern proneness to raiding. Such considerations have been particularly influential in maintaining AFL-CIO membership for most smaller and weaker nationals, whom protection against raids benefits to a greater degree than it does larger national unions. But considerations of the money, time, and energy involved in counterattacking raiding attempts have also convinced most larger nationals of the wisdom of continued federation membership.

Federation membership involves still other advantages. With the federation as the spearhead, the union movement has comparatively more power in the political and legislative affairs of the nation—a particularly influential consideration, given the thrust of the laws today—and labor's impact upon elections and congressional voting is correspondingly greater than if each national union went its own way. In addition, by coordinating political efforts, the federation can use union funds, and such other sources of political persuasion as letter-writing campaigns, more effectively. Moreover, the AFL-CIO helps national unions in organizing campaigns, although the nationals are expected to bear the chief responsibility for new organization. And affiliated national unions also receive some help from the federation in the areas of legal services, educational programs, research, and social activities.

On the other hand, in the best tradition of Gompers, the federation does not negotiate labor agreements for the affiliated national unions. It is not equipped to render such services; nor do the autonomous national unions desire such intervention. In only one way does a national union directly benefit on the collective bargaining front from its membership in the federation: A framework is provided whereby unions that bargain in the same industry or with the same company can consolidate their efforts. A large company such as General Electric, for example, bargains with many different unions, and affiliated unions that deal with General Electric can thus more easily adopt common collective bargaining goals (such as uniform expiration dates of labor agreements and the attainment of similar economic benefits) than would be the case without the availability of federation coordination; the joint bargaining endeavors over the past few decades of (most often) twelve major unions with General Electric (and subsequently with Westinghouse) have been in fact conducted under AFL-CIO auspices, through the coordinating efforts of the federation's increasingly active Industrial Union Department, and this has been true of several other joint union efforts, which are summarized in the next chapter under "Coordinated Bargaining."

Structure and Government of the AFL-CIO

As the chart on page 162 indicates, the supreme governing body of the federation is its *convention,* held once every two years. Each national union, regardless of size, may send one delegate to the convention, and unions

STRUCTURAL ORGANIZATION OF THE AFL-CIO

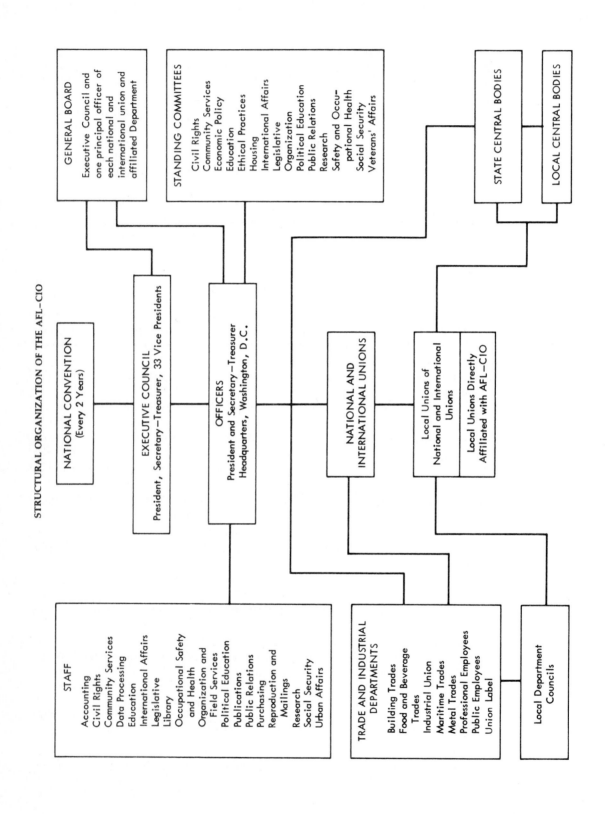

GENERAL BOARD

Executive Council and one principal officer of each national and international union and affiliated Department

STANDING COMMITTEES

Civil Rights
Community Services
Economic Policy
Education
Ethical Practices
Housing
International Affairs
Legislative
Organization
Political Education
Public Relations
Research
Safety and Occu-
pational Health
Social Security
Veterans' Affairs

STATE CENTRAL BODIES

LOCAL CENTRAL BODIES

NATIONAL CONVENTION
(Every 2 Years)

EXECUTIVE COUNCIL
President, Secretary−Treasurer, 33 Vice Presidents

OFFICERS
President and Secretary−Treasurer
Headquarters, Washington, D.C.

NATIONAL AND INTERNATIONAL UNIONS

Local Unions of National and International Unions

Local Unions Directly Affiliated with AFL−CIO

STAFF

Accounting
Civil Rights
Community Services
Data Processing
Education
International Affairs
Legislative
Library
Occupational Safety
and Health
Organization and
Field Services
Political Education
Publications
Public Relations
Purchasing
Reproduction and
Mailings
Research
Social Security
Urban Affairs

TRADE AND INDUSTRIAL DEPARTMENTS

Building Trades
Food and Beverage
Trades
Industrial Union
Maritime Trades
Metal Trades
Professional Employees
Public Employees
Union Label

Local Department Councils

with more than 4,000 members may send additional delegates in proportion to their size. Each national union delegate casts one vote for every member represented, an arrangement that allows larger unions, such as the Teamsters and the Food and Commercial Workers more influence in the affairs of the convention.

Financial expenses of the delegates are defrayed by their individual national unions and not by the federation. Such expenses can be quite high at times and may even dissuade nationals from sending their full quotas of delegates; the convention lasts two weeks, is held in first-rate hotels in a major city, and often involves considerable travel.

The convention reflects any convention of any large group. Federation officers are elected; amendments to the AFL-CIO constitution are proposed and at times adopted; committee reports are rendered; internal policies of the federation are deliberated and at times changed; and countless resolutions, ranging from purely trade-union affairs to such weighty topics as U.S. foreign policy, are voted upon. There are speakers and more speakers. Delegates must be able to sit for long periods and be capable of absorbing rhetoric that is, while occasionally inspirational, far more often soporific.

The decisions and policies adopted by the convention are implemented by the AFL-CIO *executive council,* composed of the president, secretary-treasurer, and thirty-three vice presidents of the federation. The vice presidents are elected at the convention and are usually selected from the presidents of the major affiliated national unions. Only the president of the federation and its secretary-treasurer devote full time to the affairs of the organization, however; the vice presidents meet with the executive council at least three times a year but remain as presidents of their own national unions.

Among its chief duties, the executive council interprets and applies the federation constitution; plays a "watchdog" role in legislative matters that affect the interests of workers and unions; assembles, through a full-time staff of legal and economic experts, the data needed for testimony before congressional committees; keeps in contact with the many federal agencies that have authority in the labor field; and ensures that the federation is kept free from corrupt or Communistic influences. If it suspects that a union or its officers are in violation of the federation's constitution, it may investigate the matter, and if it finds that the charges are valid, it may, by a two-thirds majority, vote to suspend the guilty union. It may also recommend the ultimate penalty of expulsion of the union, but only the full convention may actually expel the union from the federation.

The executive council also selects six of its membership who, along with the AFL-CIO president and secretary-treasurer, constitute the federation's *executive committee.* This smaller group meets every two months and has the major function of advising and counseling the president and secretary-treasurer on issues involving the federation and its policies. Only the president and the secretary-treasurer receive a salary for their duties. All other federation officers serve without salary, although they are compensated for their expenses when attending to federation business.

A fourth decision-making body within the federation is the AFL-CIO *general board,* which consists of all members of the executive council and one principal officer of each of the national unions and the affiliated departments (to be described below). Usually, the affiliated national union designates its chief officer as its representative to serve on the general board, which must meet at least once a year and may meet more often at the discretion of the federation's president. Its chief duty is to rule on all questions and issues referred to it by the executive council.

The federation constitution also requires that the president appoint a number of *standing committees,* and AFL-CIO custom dictates that each committee chairperson be president of a national union and that all members be active trade unionists. At present, such committees (which are in all cases supplied with full-time professional staffs) deal with such issues as civil rights, community services, economic policy, education, ethical practices, housing, international affairs, legislation, organization, political education, public relations, research, safety and occupational health, Social Security, and veterans' affairs. The federation's growing scope of interests is illustrated by the character of these committees, some of which are relatively new and virtually all of which clearly extend well beyond strictly trade union affairs.

Eight constitutional departments, trade and industrial groupings for unions with strong common interests, are currently in existence: Building Trades, Industrial Union, Maritime Trades, Metal Trades, Union Label, and—most recently—Professional Employees, Public Employees, and Food and Beverage Trades. National unions may belong to more than one of these departments, and many of them with memberships in two or more areas of interest do exactly that (for example, the International Brotherhood of Electrical Workers, with some members who work in the building trades and others who work in factories), but in each case the national is required to pay to the respective department a per capita tax based on the number of its members whose occupations or jobs fall under the department's jurisdiction. These dues are in addition to those the national union pays as a condition of belonging to the AFL-CIO.

Each department is concerned with problems of its particular industry. Such problems can involve collective bargaining issues, new organizational drives, legislative matters, or more specialized areas with which the unions of a particular branch of industry are uniquely confronted. The Union Label Department, for example, has as its primary objective the education of the consuming public with regard to the desirability of purchasing union-made goods. It is composed of all AFL-CIO affiliates that stress use of a union label to show that union members produced the product; to many union members, and to many supporters of unionism also, such a label is particularly persuasive before a purchase is made. (Exhibit 4-1 shows two efforts of this AFL-CIO unit.)

State and City Bodies

Even though most of the activities of the AFL-CIO are centered in Washington, the federation has also established state and city bodies to deal with problems at the state and municipal levels. There are now state bodies in each of the fifty states and one in Puerto Rico; on the city level, the federation has created city centrals in some 745 communities.

Note that these state and city central bodies are established *directly* by the AFL-CIO; they are not created by the national unions affiliated with the federation or by local unions that belong to these national unions. Local unions that belong to national unions affiliated with the AFL-CIO may join a state or a city central body, but the national union must be affiliated with the AFL-CIO; and should a national union be expelled from or withdraw voluntarily from the federation, its local unions lose membership in the state and city central bodies. Thus, when the Teamsters Union was expelled from the AFL-CIO, the locals of this union were likewise expelled from the state and city bodies.

Similar to the AFL-CIO, also, the state and city bodies have no executive power over their affiliated unions. They do not engage in collective bargaining, call or forbid strikes, or regulate the internal affairs of their affiliated local unions. Instead, the chief concern of the state and city bodies is

EXHIBIT 4–1

Courtesy of Union Label and Service Trades Department, AFL–CIO.

Exhibit 4–1 (continued)

DON'T BUY
National Boycotts Sanctioned by the AFL-CIO Executive Council

Ace Drill Corporation
Wire, jobber & letter drills, routers and steel bars
United Automobile, Aerospace & Agricultural Implement Workers of America Int'l Union

Austin Cablevision
Cable Television Providers
Communications Workers of America

Brown Corporation
Makes motor mounts, brackets, and dash assemblies for major auto makers, rubber companies, and farm appliance manufactuters.
Int'l. Union of Electronic, Electrical, Salaried, Machine and Furniture Workers

Brown & Sharpe Mfg. Co.
Measuring, cutting and machine tools and pumps
Int'l Association of Machinists and Aerospace Workers

Bruce Church, Inc.
Iceburg Lettuce: Red Coach, Friendly, Green Valley Farms, Lucky
United Farm Workers of America

California Table Grapes
Table grapes that do not bear the UFW union label on the carton or crate
United Farm Workers of America

Greyhound Lines, Incorporated
Intercity bus and charter services
Amalgamated Transit Union

Holly Farms
Chickens and processed poultry products
International Brotherhood of Teamsters

International Paper Company
Producer International and Hammermill bond, offset and writing paper and related products
United Paperworkers Int'l Union

Iron Age Protective Shoe Company
Work shoes
International Brotherhood of Teamsters

Kawasaki Rolling Stock, U.S.A.
Motorcycles
Transport Workers Union of America

Krueger International, Incorporated
Brand name chairs: Matrix, Poly, Dorsal, Vertebra, Stax, Afka, Modular, Auditorium and University Seating (for airports and auditoriums)
International Association of Machinists & Aerospace workers

Louisiana-Pacific Corp.
Brand name wood products: L-P Wolmanized, Cedartone, Waferwood, Fibrepine, Oro-Bord, Redex, Sidex, Ketchikan, Pabco, Xonolite
United Brotherhood of Carpenters and Joiners of America and Int'l Woodworkers of America

Mohawk Liqueur Corporation
Mohawk-labeled Gin, Rum, Peppermint Schnapps, and Cordials
Distillery, Wine and Allied Workers Int'l Union

R. J. Reynolds Tobacco Co.
Cigarettes: Camel, Winston, Salem, Doral, Vantage, More, Now, Real, Bright, Century, Sterling, YSL/Ritz; Smoking Tobaccos: Prince Albert, George Washington, Carter Hall, Apple, Madeira Mixture, Royal Comfort, Top, Our Advertiser; Little Cigars: Winchester
Bakery, Confection & Tobacco Workers Int'l Union

Rome Cable Corporation
Cables used in mining and construction industry
Int'l. Association of Machinists and Aerospace Workers

Shell Oil Company
Subsidary of Royal Shell (parent company of Shell South Africa); Gasoline, petroleum and natural gas products
AFL-CIO

Silo, Inc.
National retailers of electronic equipment and appliances
International Brotherhood of Teamsters

United States Playing Card Co.
Bee, Bicycle, Tally Ho, Aviator and Congress
Retail, Wholesale and Department Store Union

Union Label and Services Trades Department, AFL-CIO — June 1992 political and educational activities. They lobby for or against legislation, offer testimony before state legislative committees, and promote political candidates favored by organized labor. Almost all state organizations now hold schools for representatives of their affiliated unions—the classes being taught by union officials, university instructors, government officials, and, on some occasions, representatives of the business community. The city bodies, in addition to participating in similar legislative and educational activities, engage in a wide variety of community service work—promoting the United Way, Red Cross, and similar community projects, among other endeavors. In many cities and towns, such bodies have sponsored Boy Scout and Girl Scout troops and Little League baseball teams, as well as art institutes, musical events, day-care centers, and even the purchase of Seeing-Eye dogs for blind people. Although genuine altruism doubtless motivates many of these good deeds, so, too, does the need for an improved public image which is today so keenly felt by many unionists.

Functions and Problems of the Federation

For all that the AFL-CIO voluntarily abstains from doing or is restricted by its constitution from attempting, there can be no denying the aggressiveness with which the federation pursues the activities it does undertake. In the political arena, this is particularly true. As do most other major interest groups in the United States, the federation now employs a large corps of full-time lobbyists whose mission is to exert pressure upon members of Congress to support legislation favored by the AFL-CIO and to oppose those bills the federation regards as undesirable. Its principal officers themselves frequently testify before congressional committees and make public declarations of federation political policies. And, by its very dimensions, the federation provides a powerful sounding board for all of organized labor. Ostensibly, when the president of the AFL-CIO speaks, he represents some 14.3 million union members and their families, 89 national unions, 43,000 local unions, 51 state federations (including one in the Commonwealth of Puerto Rico), and over 700 citywide labor bodies. No other labor leader can claim as much attention and exert as much influence. He and other important federation officials are from time to time invited to the White House and are regularly invited by U.S. senators, members of Congress, and heads of major federal agencies dealing with labor matters to specify labor's position on vital issues of the day. It is doubtful that representatives of any other interest group make as many appearances at the nation's presidential residence as do members of the AFL-CIO high command.

At times of federal and state elections, the federation's role is equally important. The federation has created a Committee on Political Education (COPE) that coordinates the political action of organized labor during such periods. This political arm of the federation operates at the national, state, and local levels, where (since the Taft-Hartley law, as we know, forbids unions to contribute union dues to political candidates) it raises money on a voluntary basis from union members through so-called "political-action committees." Some of this money is given directly to political candidates who are regarded as friends of organized labor; the rest is expended for radio and TV programs of a political nature, the publication of voting records of candidates who have previously served in elective offices, the distribution of campaign literature, and kindred activities.

It is difficult to assess exactly how effective the federation has been in the political arena, since both successes and failures are amply in evidence. In 1980, for example, an estimated 44 percent of all union members voted for Ronald Reagan, whose candidacy was about as welcome to the bulk of the AFL-CIO leaders as Martin Luther King's would have been to the Ku Klux Klan,[3] and in 1984 some 46 percent did so. In 1988, well over 40 percent of unionized Americans continued the pattern by voting for Republican George Bush, another national politician whose AFL-CIO leadership support was conspicuous by its absence. On the other hand, between 60 and 70 percent of all COPE-endorsed congressional candidates (approximately 400 of them in most recent election years) have been victorious in each biennial election over the past decade, and for many of these candidates, labor's support was a critical factor. Certainly, the federation has been sufficiently encouraged by the results to continue to play an active political role.

COPE, under any conditions, has never thought small. It was responsible for most of the more than $50 million that labor as a whole pumped into both the 1984 and 1988 campaigns, through several hundred labor political-action committees, for example, and in election years it can regularly be counted on to recruit as many as 125,000 volunteers to work on community political activities. The federation estimates that such volunteers in each of these elections have placed over 10 million telephone calls from their more than 20,000 telephones (operating at COPE offices, local union and council offices, and the private homes of union members) during registration and get-out-the-vote campaigns, and have distributed hundreds of COPE films. COPE activity nowadays is, in short, something that neither its friends nor its foes can ignore.

The political objectives of organized labor and the federation are varied in character. The AFL-CIO supports legislation that strengthens the role of organized labor in collective bargaining, organizational drives, the strike, picketing, and boycotting. To these ends, the federation has, for example, consistently advocated such measures as the repeal of state "right-to-work" legislation and has lobbied for other changes in the federal and state laws that would strengthen the use of such union self-help methods as boycotts and picketing in labor's direct relationship with business. It has also, however, regularly supported such bills as those favoring national health insurance, low-cost public housing, liberalized minimum-wage laws, more comprehensive unemployment-compensation statutes, and more effective public education—all of which measures are intended to benefit all the workers of the nation and their families, rather than strictly those within the ranks of unionism. The AFL-CIO today fully recognizes that many of these less parochial objectives cannot be achieved through face-to-face union-management collective bargaining and has consequently supported such measures as the ones cited to gain additional leverage in its efforts to improve the status of the American wage earner.

Beyond the legislative and political function, the federation carries out a massive research program—the results of which are embodied in its regular publications, above all the weekly *AFL-CIO News,* as well as in special bulletins, briefs for the courts of the nation, and a series of pamphlets, monographs, and books. Through these varied publications, the federation tries to keep union members and others abreast of labor developments from the union point of view.

Another important function is that of promoting new organizations. Although the basic responsibility for such new organizations falls upon national unions, the federation also organizes on its own and helps affiliated unions in their organizational drives. When the AFL-CIO organizes a union by itself, it charters such a local union directly with the federation in much the same fashion that the old AFL did in the 1930s. There are 102 such directly affiliated labor unions now in existence, and through its field officers the AFL-CIO bargains contracts for these local unions and aids them in time of strikes and other difficulties with management. In return, members of such locals pay dues directly to the AFL-CIO. This collective bargaining function for directly affiliated local unions should not, however, be confused with the principle already established: The AFL-CIO does not bargain collectively for affiliated national unions or for locals that belong to such affiliated national unions. Moreover, most of these directly affiliated local unions are themselves ultimately assigned by the federation to a national union that has appropriate jurisdiction over the jobs and occupations of its members.

In recent years, the American labor movement has also demonstrated increasing concern with the labor movement in foreign nations. Two major factors lie behind this development. In the first place, the increasing tempo of international trade, now increasingly also tied into the rise of the "multinational," has threatened the job security and welfare of American workers. The impact in the United States of products produced by foreign labor under conditions of comparatively lower wages and poorer working conditions makes it more difficult for American unions to retain benefits already secured and to obtain improvements in them. American unions understand fully that benefits secured in their contracts are placed in jeopardy because of such competition from low-wage foreign nations. (Exhibits 4-2 and 4-3 typify one kind of union counterattack here. Generally, such efforts have not been very successful in influencing the union members at whom they have been directed.) Hence, by strengthening the foreign labor movement, American unions not only improve the status of workers within foreign nations but at the same time also protect the advances that have been gained through collective bargaining in this country.

The second reason concerns the threat of Communist domination of foreign labor movements and, through this tactic, the possible seizure of the governments of foreign nations by Communists. Even in the United States, as Chapter 2 has demonstrated, organized labor has been faced with such a threat, although in this country it has been successfully surmounted. The 1949–1950 expulsion from the CIO of the several Communist-con-

FIGURE 4–2

Toys Made Overseas

TOY	COMPANY	COUNTRY
Barbie™ Doll	Mattel	Hong Kong
Barbie™ Clothes	Mattel	China
Cabbage Patch™ Dolls	Coleco	Korea
Care Bears™	Kenner	Korea
GI Joe™	Hasbro-Bradley	Hong Kong
Gloworms™	Playskool	China
GoBots™	Tonka	Japan
Hotwheels™	Mattel	Malaysia
Masters of the Universe™	Mattel	China, Malaysia, Taiwan
Masters of the Universe™ (Vehicles)	Mattel	Mexico
My Little Pony™	Hasbro-Bradley	Korea
Pound Puppies™	Tonka	Korea
Princess of Power™	Mattel	Hong Kong
Rainbow Brite™	Mattel	Korea
Real Baby™	Hasbro-Bradley	China
Rough Riders™	Lnj	Macao
Smurf™ Dolls	Hasbro-Bradley	China
Snuggle Bums™	Playskool	China
Star Wars™ Figures	Kenner	Hong Kong
Teddy Ruxpin™	Worlds of Wonder	Hong Kong
Trucks	Tonka	Hong Kong
	Fisher Price	Hong Kong
Voltrons™	Matchbox	Taiwan

Source: *The International Teamster*, July 1989, back cover.

trolled unions, and the establishment of new unions to take over the membership of such unions, dealt a telling blow to Communism's influence on the American labor movement. The AFL, too, when it was the only federation in the nation, waged a continuous and bitter battle against the left and managed to maintain its basically conservative philosophy and objectives. There are today only a handful of American labor unions, all of them minor in strategic power (for example, the Furriers Union and, as noted earlier, the United Electrical Workers), that are even remotely believed to be dominated by Communists. But the problem is much more severe in foreign lands: In such nations as Italy and France, Communistic elements do have considerable influence on the affairs of the labor movements, the general recent weakening of Communism worldwide notwithstanding. And the important officers of America's labor movement, well schooled in the potential consequences of Communism, believe with considerable justification that should such totalitarianism spread to the governments of these countries, the first casualties would be the free labor movement, collective bargaining, and the right to strike. For such reasons,

FIGURE 4–3

Some Suggestions
for 'Made in the U.S.A.' Toys

(This list is not all-inclusive, so please, read the package labels.)

AGE GROUP	TOY	COMPANY
Toddlers	Building Blocks & Creative Toys Play Dinette Set Playtime Driver™ Many Pre-School Toys	Little Tike Most Made in U.S. Child Guidance Fisher-Price Johnson & Johnson Playskool
4–5 Years Old	Baby Dolls Crayon Sets Chutes & Ladders™ Educational Kits Lincoln Logs™ Playdough™ Rite-Hite™ Stove, Sink, Refrigerator Silly Putty™ Sweetheart Play Center™ Tea Sets Tinkertoys™	Horsman Crayola Milton Bradley Avalon Industries* Playskool Kenner* Wolverine Toy Co.* Binney & Smith Wolverine Toy Co.* Ohio Arts and Wolverine Toy Co.* Child Guidance
6–9 Years Old	Battery-Run Vehicles Battleship™ Checkers, Dominoes Cosmetics, Toiletries Etch-A-Sketch™ Junior Trivial Pursuit™ Steel Trucks Viewmaster™	Pines of America* Milton Bradley Pressman Corporation* Tinkerbell Ohio Arts Selchow & Righter* ERTL and Nylint GAF
10 Years +	Backgammon, Chess Collectable Dolls Doll Houses Erector Sets Frisbee™ Monopoly™ Nerf™ Products Ripley's Believe It or Not™ Scrabble, Parcheesi™	Pressman Toy Corporation* Madam Alexander* and Effenbee* Royal House of Dolls* Gabriel Wham-O Parker Brothers Parker Brothers Milton Bradley Selchow & Righter*
All Ages	Bikes	Columbia Huffy Murray Ross* Some Sears

(See Other "Buy American" Bike Consumer Tips Next Month.)

(Read labels for smaller U.S. companies, but do not buy Schwinn bikes. After the UAW won a strong first contract for the workers at the Chicago Schwinn plant, the company began shipping work to non-union sites in Taiwan, Japan and Tennessee. The Chicago plant closed permanently this spring, and the Schwinn employees have yet to receive their severance and vacation pay.)

*Indicates, to the best of our knowledge, companies which have union labor.

Source: Courtesy of *The International Teamster*, November 1985, p. 29.

the AFL-CIO works hard to help foreign trade unions remain free from Communist domination.

In the eyes of some of its member unions, in fact, the federation is working too hard in its foreign affairs efforts nowadays. In recent years almost half of all AFL-CIO expenditures have been geared to furthering the overseas goals. In a recent year, for example, the federation's International Affairs Department spent some $43 million on activities in eighty-three foreign countries—or a mere $2 million less than the $45 million that the AFL-CIO's domestic budget allowed it in the same time frame to spend in the United States.[4] And while few federation members begrudged the financing of such standard efforts as teaching foreign labor leaders how to recruit new members and better administer their unions, some of the AFL-CIO's more aggressively anti-Communistic activities had embroiled the federation in internal controversy.

The latter activities included aid to Nicaraguan rebels trying to overthrow that country's Sandanista government, the development of a moderate labor movement in the Philippines to prevent allegedly Communistic unions there from gaining strength, and attempts in El Salvador to strengthen the incumbent administration of middle-of-the-road José Napoléon Duarte. These and similar efforts, while quite consistent with official United States foreign policy, nonetheless were attacked by union critics for both their ambitiousness and their direction.

One unhappy federation union observer, for example, saw the AFL-CIO in such cases acting as "an extension of our government's foreign policy. That puts [it] outside the role labor should be playing."[5] And leaders of such prominent unions as the American Federation of State, County and Municipal Employees, and the UAW were beginning openly to challenge the projects themselves, frequently on the grounds that by being so conservative in their thrusts the latter simply didn't represent the desires of many federation members.

The federation efforts were, nonetheless, fully in keeping with longstanding AFL-CIO thinking—as the editors of *Business Week* could point out, "conservative foreign policies are nothing new for labor"[6]—and even the federation's severest critics could not accuse it of inconsistency.

Conflict between Craft and Industrial Unions

If the main benefit associated with federation membership is protection against raiding, one of the major problems of the AFL-CIO has been that of maintaining peace between affiliated unions in their jurisdictional disputes over jobs. Frequently, craft unions (formerly, for the most part, AFL affiliates) and industrial unions (CIO members when the two groups were separate) have battled each other avidly over such jurisdiction, particularly in establishments where an industrial union holds bargaining rights but where some jobs could be carried out more efficiently by members of a craft union. Such jobs as those involving the routine maintenance of machinery or other equipment, the major overhaul or installation of equipment, and the construction of new facilities often fall into this category.

What could spark a conflict is the desire of members of craft unions whose members are not employees of the industrial company to do the work that is being performed by the skilled tradesmen on the payroll of the factory. At times, employers find it cheaper to hire these outside craftsmen to perform the work and therefore seek out contractor-employers who control such skilled employees. On other occasions, a skilled-trade union, through a contractor-employer, makes overtures to the industrial employer. However, the problem could also arise from the other direction. That is, the industrial employer may have customarily subcontracted certain maintenance work to outside skilled tradesmen. To secure this work for its own membership, the industrial union that holds bargaining rights in the factory puts pressure upon the employer to cease this practice and to award the work to the employer's own employees who are, of course, members of the industrial union. It is not difficult to understand that when jobs are scarce, the conflict between craft and industrial unions can achieve major dimensions.

Indeed, the problem became so serious in the recession-marked first months of the 1960s that many observers predicted the imminent collapse of the entire federation through craft-industrial warfare. Remarkably, however, the leaders of the craft and industrial unions were able to arrive at a workable solution to the problem at the 1961 AFL-CIO convention and thereby rescue the federation from such a collapse. They adopted an "Internal Disputes Plan," often also referred to as the "Live and Let Live" plan, and incorporated it into the constitution of the AFL-CIO. The constitutional amendment officially preserved the integrity of past practices in work assignments. Henceforth a union's right to jobs would depend on what relevant customs or practices had been in force where it sought such jobs. If the members of an industrial union had held jurisdiction over new construction in the past, this customary work assignment would be respected by craft unions. If an employer had customarily subcontracted out maintenance work, this practice was to be respected by industrial unions, who were not to put pressure upon employers to change it.

An elaborate procedure has been adopted to implement this constitutional provision. In the event that a union charges that another union is violating the terms of the new policy, the AFL-CIO assigns a federation official to mediate the dispute. If this effort fails, an impartial umpire is appointed to make an award. Once the umpire hands down the decision, the rival union is expected to abide by the award. However, the losing union has the right to appeal to a three-person subcommittee of the AFL-CIO executive council. This subcommittee may disallow the appeal, in which event the umpire's decision is final and there is no other appeal procedure. But if the subcommittee is not fully satisfied with the umpire's award, it may refer the case to the entire executive council, which will decide the issue by majority vote. The council may uphold the award, reverse it, or modify it. In any event, however, the executive council's decision is final and binding on the unions involved.

If a union fails to comply with the decision rendered through this procedure, the amendment to the constitution provides that the federation may impose sanctions on the noncomplying union, and if the violation persists, the union can be expelled from the federation.

In the many years since the Internal Disputes Plan was implemented, noncompliance has been all but nonexistent. Of the first 2,200 complaints filed with the AFL-CIO president's office, in only twenty-six cases (involving fifteen unions) did affiliates even initially fail to heed the decisions of the umpire or directions of the subcommittee, and even in most of these instances compliance was later achieved. The threat of sanctions (preventing the penalized union from using all AFL-CIO services and facilities including the filing of charges to protest that *its* customary job jurisdiction is being violated by another union) appears to have been a potent weapon. No union has ever been expelled for a continuing violation.

And it is safe to say, accordingly, that the craft-industrial conflict, once one that threatened disaster for the labor movement, has now been satisfactorily resolved. The AFL-CIO, with this conflict basically behind it, will undoubtedly continue to exist as a permanent federation in the United States, and this can only be advantageous, since—from the viewpoint of stability in industrial relations—the preservation of the federation is a public necessity.

THE NATIONAL UNION

Relationship to Locals

If the national union is quite autonomous in the conduct of its affairs, the story is quite different when one examines the relationship between the national union and its local unions. Although there are many exceptions, most national unions exercise considerable power over their locals. Before a local union may strike, it must normally obtain the permission of the national union. And, should the local union strike in defiance of national union instructions, the national union can withhold strike benefits, refuse to give the local union any other form of aid during the strike, and in extreme cases even take over the local on a trusteeship basis. In addition, consistent with the regulations of many national unions, all local collective bargaining contracts must be reviewed by the national officers before they may be put into force. All national union constitutions today contain provisions that establish standards of conduct and procedures for the internal operation of their constituent locals—usually, the dues that the locals may charge, the method by which their officers may be elected and their tenures of office, the procedures for the discipline of local union members, the conduct of union meetings, and other rules of this kind.

Violation of these national union standards can result in sanctions placed upon the local union officers and on the local union itself. Recently, for example, many national unions have been at least as conscious of the problem of racial discrimination within the union movement as has the AFL-CIO, and almost all national constitutions now contain a nondiscriminatory clause, designed to guarantee minorities equal and fair treatment from the local unions. Several local unions have been seized by their nationals when they have failed to afford minorities equal protection in the negotiation of labor agreements or in the grievance procedure.

In addition, within the collective bargaining process, the national union is currently exercising considerably greater control and influence over the contracts that locals negotiate. This is particularly true when the members of the locals work for companies that sell their products in national product markets—an ever-increasing number. Nationals desire that companies over whose employees they have jurisdiction and that compete in national product markets operate under common labor-cost standards. They are less likely to exercise control over the unions whose members produce for local markets—for example, in the construction industry, because the labor costs involved in the construction of a building in one city do not directly compete with those affecting the construction of a building in another.

Service in Collective Bargaining

The national exercises much of its influence over the local in the direct collective bargaining process through the service that the national union provides its locals in the negotiation of labor agreements. To understand this national-local relationship, however, one should not regard the negotiation service of the national union as a function that is performed against the will of the local union. On the contrary, local unions not only generally desire and expect the help of the national union when they negotiate labor agreements with the employer, but should the national union either refuse to provide these services or perform them in an ineffective way, the local union members and their officers can be counted upon to be sharply critical of the national union. The officers of the national could safely assume, in fact, that such a disgruntled local union would attempt to take political reprisal against the officers of the national in the next election of national officers.

The chief reason for the local union's desire for help from the national union in collective bargaining involves the complexities of the contemporary collective bargaining process. As will be made more evident in future chapters, many of the issues of collective bargaining have become increasingly intricate. Most contracts focus upon such involved items as adjustment to technological change, pension plans, insurance programs, production standards, subcontracting, and complicated wage incentive programs. Beyond the complex character of the issues, moreover, the modern process is obviously made more difficult because of the character of the laws of labor relations. In short, it takes an expert to negotiate these days.

For effective representation, it is necessary to find people who are knowledgeable and experienced and have a professional understanding of the collective bargaining process; few local unions are fortunate enough to include such people in their membership. Each local union elects a negotiating committee, but the members of such committees typically work full time on their regular jobs. They simply do not have the opportunity to keep abreast of current developments in collective bargaining and to make a searching study of the problems involved in the negotiation of the difficult issues. On the employer side, moreover, there are normally management representatives who are well trained and equipped to handle the contemporary collective bargaining negotiation. Many of them have received special training in labor relations, and some devote full time to the problems of negotiation and administration of collective bargaining contracts.

Indeed, without the services of the national union, there would be a sharp disparity of negotiating talent at the bargaining table. In this light, it is easy to understand why the local union does not regard the intervention of the national union at the bargaining table as an invasion of the rights of the local, but rather views this service as indispensable.

Most national unions have well-qualified people to render this service: the so-called staff representatives, who devote full time to union affairs. They are hired by the national union, paid salaries and expenses for their work, and expected to provide services to the local unions of the national. All of them are union members, and they normally reach their position of staff representative by having demonstrated their ability as union members and local union officers. They are not, however, elected to their jobs but are hired because of their special talents.

Although the staff representatives perform a variety of duties, such as organizing new facilities, engaging in political-action work at times of federal and state elections, directing strikes, and representing the union and its members before the federal and state labor agencies, helping the local unions to negotiate labor agreements constitutes one of their primary functions.[7] Staff representatives gain much bargaining experience because they normally service several local unions, and in the course of one year they may be called upon to negotiate many different labor agreements, thus gaining on-the-job training that serves as an invaluable asset to them when they confront a specific management at the bargaining table. Many national unions also send their staff representatives to special schools, some of which are held on university campuses and are taught by specialists in the labor education field, for additional training. Moreover, the staff representative is invariably backed up by experts within the national union. Almost every national union has several departments that concentrate on the major issues involved in collective bargaining. For example, the United Automobile Workers not only has special departments that deal respectively with pensions, health insurance, and wage systems (among others), but—in 1989—created a department specifically mandated to coordinate the union's relationships with automakers owned entirely or in part by foreign companies. The specialists assigned to these national departments may be called upon freely by the staff representatives, should their services be needed.

The Regional or District Office

Staff representatives may work out of the headquarters of the national union, but more frequently they are assigned to a regional or district office. Almost every national union divides the nation into regions or districts, and locals of the national union that are located in the geographical area or the district obtain services from their respective district offices. For example, District 30 of the United Steelworkers of America, headquartered in Indianapolis, covers most of Indiana and Kentucky and is administered by a district director elected by the local unions of the district. About twenty staff representatives are assigned by the national union to District 30 and work under the immediate supervision of the district director.

Each staff representative services about seven local unions. The representative attends the local union meetings, works closely with the negotiating committees, hears the problems of the workers in the workplace in which the local holds control, and attempts to understand the values and objectives of the members. The representative is the liaison between the national and the local union, and in this capacity can do much to influence the local in the acceptance of national union collective bargaining policies. In such a role, moreover, the staff representative can serve as a mediator between local unions and the national when differences arise between them.

A good staff representative wins the confidence of local officers and members, and the local union will thus rely heavily upon this individual's counsel in collective bargaining matters. The representative can exert great influence upon the local to reject or accept the last offer of an employer. Indeed, frequently this person can provoke a strike or prevent one by the way in which he or she reports to the local union and makes recommendations to the members.

Multiemployer Bargaining

Although most multiemployer bargaining is in relatively small bargaining units in local-product markets, at times national unions bargain with employers on a multiemployer basis. That is, a group of managements band together as a unit to negotiate with the national union. Employers find this structure of collective bargaining valuable because it prevents a given union from "whipsawing" each employer: Usually, under a multiemployer bargaining structure, each employer is comparatively small in size and unimpressive in financial resources, and the companies compete fiercely; in the absence of multiemployer collective bargaining, the union could pick off one employer at a time. Such employer-association–national-union collective bargaining is found in industries such as clothing, coal, shipping, and trucking—all of which contain large measures of the unstabilizing factors noted.

When multiemployer collective bargaining exists and where the product market is not a local one, the national officers themselves typically bargain for the contract, and the local unions play a comparatively passive role—a situation that also holds at the other extreme, when unions bargain with industrial giants of the nation (such as General Motors and USX). The national unions negotiate the agreement in the latter instance, since no one local union could possibly measure up to the strength of these companies. Bargaining logic dictates that in both cases, the national union rather than the local union play the paramount labor relations role.

Additional National Union Services

Beyond providing considerable help in the negotiating of labor agreements, the national union renders other valuable services to its local unions. The national usually awards benefits to employees on strike, although the actual amount of money paid in strike benefits is invariably modest: Approximately $150 weekly (usually awarded to strikers with a minimum number of dependents, with other strikers getting less) constitutes the ultimate in union largess and even it, of course, is dispatched only until the strike fund is exhausted and assuming that beneficiaries take their turn on the picket line when and if asked to do so. More important, the national union intervenes with the strikers' creditors so that the automobiles, furniture, and other holdings of the union members will not be repossessed. And it ensures that no striking employee or his or her family goes hungry, even if this guarantee involves the actual distribution of food to the strikers. Management should be aware that unions in these days do not lose strikes because of hunger or unpaid bills. If there are insurance premiums to be paid, doctors to see, rent to be paid, or school tuition to be met, the national unions will see to it that the worker does not suffer. This is true despite the obvious fact that the national unions themselves have financial limitations, for virtually all nationals do under normal circumstances have the resources to assure that the minimum physiological needs of their member-workers are met, and many larger unions are quite amply financed. In addition, if a national union does run out of money, labor custom dictates that other national unions will lend it money to finance the strike.[8]

The national union also aids the locals in the grievance procedure and in arbitration, both of which subjects will be discussed in detail in Chapter 6. Normally, the staff representative represents the local in the last step of the grievance procedure. Along with the local union grievance committee, the staff representative attempts to settle the grievance to the satisfaction of the complaining worker, and if the case does ultimately go to arbitration, the staffer very often directly represents the grievant. In general, whether they win or lose their arbitration cases, staff representatives present the union's case very effectively. This fact is often offered by labor leaders as one reason why unions employ lawyers less frequently than do employers when cases go to arbitration. There is no need to incur the expense if the staff representative can do the job as competently as an attorney.

Of course, at times local unions *are* in need of an attorney, as when the local union has a case that requires testimony in the courts. For example, employers may sue a union for breach of contract, or workers may be indicted because of violence in picketing. When attorneys are needed, the local union can normally obtain the services of the national union's legal staff, whose members, although invariably paid less than comparable lawyers who work for corporations, are frequently highly competent and usually quite dedicated to the union movement.

The fact that the local does so readily receive such services from its national constitutes the reason why the vast majority of local unions belong to a national union. Indeed, less than 2 percent of all locals are not affiliated with a national, and all these "independents" (except for the relative handful of them belonging directly to the AFL-CIO and thus enabled to make use of the federation's services) must rely upon their own resources, whereas the many local unions that do belong to nationals can use the considerable resources of the latter.

Other Functions of the National Union

Although national union officers and staff representatives devote the major share of their time to providing services to the local unions, the range of the national union's activities includes many other important functions. Today, the major concern of all unions is, as we know, that of increasing membership. Responsible labor union officials understand that the unorganized must be organized, and the chief burden for this also falls to the national union staff representatives. Although the AFL-CIO does do some organizational work, it does not have the staff to perform this function effectively; nor can the responsibility for the organization of new places be undertaken by local officers or members. At times, local union people help in organizational drives, but because they are full-time employees, they do not have much opportunity to carry out this function.

Accordingly, the catalyst for new organization falls to the staff representatives of the national unions, upon whom constant pressure is exerted to organize nonunion operations. Indeed, in some national unions, not only the advancement but even the continued job tenure of the staff representative is determined by the latter's success in organizing such places.

The task is hardly an easy one. Most nonunion employers can be counted upon to wage a fierce fight against organization. Many employees who are not members of unions do not want a labor union, because management provides them with many of the benefits they would receive if organized. And the staff representative's organizing mission becomes even more difficult if attempts are made to organize in the South or in small communities regardless of sectional location. In any event, the representative must make contacts among the workers, convince them of the value of unions, and dispel notions that unions are corrupt, Communistic, or otherwise undesirable institutions. Many workers are ready to believe the worst about organized labor, and staff representatives often admit that these conceptions are difficult to erase. "Today," one veteran said a while ago, "the workers insult you, they spit at you, they throw [union membership] cards in your face."[9] And as a union leader could point out from his own unhappy experiences, even such institutions as church-administered hospitals can become formidable foes when faced with union organizers: "The Little Sisters of the Poor," as the president of the Hospital and Health Care Employees could observe, "can be hard as nails."[10]

Moreover, the potential union member "doesn't have the background in unionism his or her parents had; he doesn't view himself as a 'worker,' he probably doesn't even use the word 'worker,'" as the former organizing director of the Teamsters has said. "We have to do more to show him the relevance of the union situation."[11] Even otherwise friendly employees often equate unions, as was pointed out earlier in this volume, with manual workers, and while this is by definition no obstacle if the target work force is made up of construction workers or truck drivers, it can clearly handicap organizers who go after the growing body of office, professional, and other non-blue-collar types.

Staff representatives are thus forced to use their powers of imagination, and any understanding of law and psychology that they might have, to the fullest. The representative may initially attempt to organize "from inside," through the informal leaders in the enterprise. The next step may be to visit workers in their homes, distribute leaflets, and arrange organizational meetings (which frequently are poorly attended). Subsequently the representative must counteract whatever management does to block the organizational attempt; even in today's more enlightened atmosphere, some employers warn employees of dire consequences if they organize, tell their employees that unions exist only to collect dues for the personal benefit of the union "bosses," and—the organizing tactic laws cited in Chapter 3 notwithstanding—on occasion even threaten workers with loss of their jobs if a union is established, as well as promise them benefits if they reject the union. A while ago, the Farah Manufacturing Company was organized by the Amalgamated Clothing Workers (not yet merged with the Textile Workers) following a two-and-one-half-year struggle that included a boycott of Farah products. The victory, however, came only after a National Labor Relations Board administrative law judge had criticized Farah for carrying on "a broad-gauged antiunion campaign consisting of glaring and repeated violations" of the National Labor Relations Act and acting as if "there were no act, no board and no Ten Commandments."

There are other formidable obstacles for the organizer. If the plant is located in a comparatively small community, there may be a concerted attempt among the leaders of the community to keep the union out. The target employer may have good friends who run the newspaper, the radio and TV stations, the Chamber of Commerce, and the local stores, and these power centers may join forces to do what they can to keep the union from gaining a foothold. Indeed, it is not uncommon for the clergy in a town to be enlisted in the fight against the union.

The organizational mission of the staff representative is thus a highly challenging one and, in recent years, this person has probably experienced more failures than successful ventures. Often, in pondering the results of emotion-draining efforts, the staff representative doubtless feels like Marius contemplating the ruins of Carthage. But the staffer is typically persistent, and this tenaciousness occasionally reaps its reward: Illustratively, although clearly also an extreme, in late 1980, J. P. Stevens and Co. (the second largest textile manufacturer in the nation) signed an agreement with the Amalgamated Clothing and Textile Workers in the culmination of a seventeen-year concerted organizational campaign by the union. The company, the real-life backdrop for the 1979 film *Norma Rae,* had fought the union so aggressively that a New York court had branded it "the most notorious recidivist in the field of labor law" and the NLRB had cited it twenty-two times for violating the federal labor statutes.

Another major function of the national union concerns political action, although the nationals vary widely in the vigor that they display in this regard. The Teamsters raised an impressive $10.5 million in the 1990 election cycle, primarily through voluntary $1-per-week contributions to the union's political-action committee (known as DRIVE for Democratic Republican Independent Voter Education), and this total not only placed it first in that election among all of the nation's several thousand political-action committees but was almost double that of the second-place PAC, the American Medical Association. The money talked, too: Among other Teamster legislative victories in 1991, the Democratic campaign committees in both the Senate and the House agreed to stop using nonunion Federal Express for overnight deliveries and give the business instead to the Teamsters' largest single employer, United Parcel Service. Other politically active national unions are the State, County and Municipal Employees; the Automobile Workers; the Letter Carriers; the National Education Association; the Machinists; and the Communications Workers. In fact, the PACs of all six of these organizations in 1990 were, together with DRIVE, among the top fifteen PACs in the United States as ranked by total spending.

The Mine Workers, Air Line Pilots, and Teachers, impelled in each case by recent hard times, have also made intense political action a way of life. (Exhibits 4-4 and 4-5 show the sentiments of the Teamsters and Mine Workers, respectively, toward the 1992 White House hopefuls in that election year.)

At the other end of the spectrum, many of the building trades unions have rarely shown much interest in this area.

The trend, however, is definitely in the direction of more rather than less activity. As has already been noted, national leaders understand that the success of the union depends in large measure on the fashioning of a favorable legal climate for new organization and for the implementation of traditional trade union weapons when conflicts arise with employers. Moreover, a growing number of national unions share the belief of AFL-CIO leaders that the political programs of organized labor in the areas of social security, medicine, low-cost public housing, full employment, and the like are in the best interests of the nation as a whole.

But sometimes the political activity is more tailored to the specific membership. The Association of Flight Attendants, for example, not long ago began a campaign to persuade the Federal Aviation Administration to tighten its rules limiting carry-on luggage in the interest of flight safety. Exhibit 4-6 shows the questionnaire that was sent to all of the union's 33,000 members as a supplement to this effort. Members could return it, postage prepaid, to the office of the national president.

When the national union officers are politically motivated, they are normally aggressive in exerting pressure upon the local unions and their members to take an active role in political affairs. Their union newspapers are filled with political news, voting records of the candidates, and the union point of view when elections are impending. National unions also arrange political rallies, purchase radio and television time to get the national's story across to the members and the public, and issue a barrage

EXHIBIT 4–4

COMPARING THE CANDIDATES

The following is a comparison of the positions of the two apparent nominees of their parties, Republican George Bush and Democrat Bill Clinton.

	THE ECONOMY	HEALTH CARE	TRADE
George Bush	Under Bush and Reagan, taxes paid by the richest 1 percent of Americans went down by nearly $84 billion per year. That helped double their annual income. Bush's main answer to our economic problems is to cut taxes for the rich and big corporations even more. Bush proposes modest cuts in military spending. He does not support plans for creating jobs for those who will be displaced by his cuts.	Bush opposes major reforms to bring health care costs under control, saying they would interfere with the free market. Yet, he favors greater use of "managed care" programs which require working families to use certain doctors or hospitals. He also says he is considering cutting $40 billion per year from Medicare.	Bush has encouraged corporations to move operations to Mexico. He is negotiating a free trade agreement which will make it even easier to exploit Mexican workers and lay off U.S. and Canadian employees. He has ordered states to accept Mexican commercial drivers' licenses.
Bill Clinton	Clinton proposes to close tax loopholes for the rich, expand needed programs to rebuild our cities and towns, and make housing affordable for more Americans. He would make greater cuts in unnecessary military spending than Bush, freeing up more money to create American jobs. He says he would work to create jobs for former defense workers and military personnel.	Clinton proposes to make employers who don't provide health insurance pay into a fund to cover their workers. He says he would streamline insurance company procedures, control drug prices, and reduce the spread of unnecessary, expensive medical equipment. He does not support Teamster-backed proposals for a "single-payer" national health insurance plan.	Clinton told the Teamster Legislative conference that he favors "an agreement that will require that Mexicans in return for increasing trade to raise their environmental standards." He favored giving Bush the "fast track" authority to negotiate a free trade deal with Mexico and Canada, but says he would not sign an agreement if it does not include protections for workers and the environment.

STOPPING DEREGULATION

★ In the freight industry, 160,000 Teamsters have lost their jobs because of deregulation. Wages in the industry have dropped 20 percent. At least 122 companies have gone out of business.

★ In the airline industry, power has become concentrated in the hands of just a few companies. Thousands of workers are barely getting by on two-tier wage rates. Service has been cut to many communities.

★ All Teamsters will be paying higher taxes for many years to bail out the savings and loans after they were deregulated.

These are just some of the costs of the deregulation policy pursued by Bush and Reagan.

Deregulation means getting rid of public policies designed to assure Americans of safe workplaces, stable jobs, efficient transportation, safe food, safe banking, and clean air and water.

Regulations were needed in the first place because corporations and the wealthy often put profits before the rights of workers and consumers.

Many regulatory programs have not worked as well as they should. Companies have used their influence to water down enforcement. Many agencies have become too bureaucratic.

The solution is not to abolish regulatory programs but to make them work better.

We need to put government on the side of the people again.

WHO IS ROSS

Ross Perot's office could not provide us with his positions on any of the major issues that concern Teamster members.

But we do know this about the billionaire corporate dealer...

Opponent of Workers' Rights

★ **He fought Teamster efforts to organize.** When workers at one of Perot's companies in Los Angeles tried to organize to join the Teamsters Union in 1971, Perot's management team was instructed to strongly oppose their effort. The union lost.

★ **He fought other unions.** One of his executives wrote to workers at the Perot company, EDS, who were rying to organize to join the United Auto Workers: "Labor unions have no place in EDS . . . I want each of you to understand my firm commitment

EXHIBIT 4–4 (continued)

Gov. Clinton visited both management and United Auto Workers members during the Caterpillar strike in Illinois and urged a quick settlement.

DEREGULATION

Bush has pushed deregulation in many different industries.

He supports new proposals in Congress for further deregulation of the freight and small parcel industries.

He has also used the power of the federal government to remove state regulations which protected working people.

At the Teamsters Legislative Conference, Clinton said that "there have been some benefits and a lot of burdens from the deregulation movement of the '80s."

He cited the impact of deregulation in the trucking, airline, and savings and loan industries.

He said his positions on particular bills related to deregulation would depend on discussion with leaders of Congress and other interested groups, including the teamsters.

PEROT?

to oppose union efforts until total victory is ours."

Political Insider Who Bought Favors

★ Perot gave campaign contributions to members of a House of Representatives comittee which then voted for a special $15 million tax break that applied only to him!

The bill died after it became public and House members became too embarrassed.

★ He gave more than $200,000 in campaign contributions to Richard Nixon. He was given government contracts from the Nixon Administration in apparent violation of legal requirements that the jobs be given to the lowest bidder.

WORKERS' RIGHTS: Bush vs. Clinton

Bush and Clinton differ greatly on worker's rights.

At the Teamster Legislative Conference and in other public statements, Clinton has said that he favors many proposals which our union supports and which Bush opposes.

Gov. Clinton says that he . . .

★ Favors S.55, the Workplace Fairness Bill, which bans permanent replacement of striking workers.

★ Supports the Family and Medical Leave Act which Bush vetoed and which would have guaranteed the right to unpaid leave to care for a newborn child or a family member who is seriously ill.

★ Would guarantee every American the right to affordable loans for education.

★ Would appoint people to the National Labor Relations Board who would be more favorable to labor.

★ Would actively enforce the Occupational Safety and Health Act.

★ Supports an increase in the minimum wage.

★ Supports Davis-Bacon protections in the construction industry.

Bush opposes each of these positions.

Gov. Clinton has been accused by some Teamster leaders in Arkansas of siding with employers in labor disputes. In particular, he has been criticized for giving state money to a company that was trying to outlast a strike by United Auto Workers members.

Some other union officials in the state say they have had a good relationship with Clinton. The AFL-CIO and most of its affiliates, incluing the UAW, have endorsed Clinton.

Source: The New Teamster, June–July 1992, pp. 4–5.

EXHIBIT 4–5

Source: *United Mine Workers Journal*, February 1992, p. 19.

EXHIBIT 4–6

AFA Membership Survey on Carry-on Baggage Problems

Name of Carrier: _____

How well do you think the carry-on baggage program at your carrier is working?

Very well ❏   Well ❏   Poorly ❏   Very Poorly ❏

If you do not think it is working well, please rate the following problems by writing the appropriate number (1,2,3 as indicated) in the space provided:

① Major Problem   ② Minor Problem   ③ Not a Problem

a. __ Passengers bringing overly large bags on board.

b. __ Passengers bringing overly heavy bags on board.

c. __ Passengers bringing too many bags on board.

d. __ Lack of baggage screening before boarding.

e. __ Closing of door before baggage is stored.

f. __ Flight attendants not rejecting/removing bags.

g. __ Company resistance to removing bags from planes.

If you experienced a carry-on baggage problem in May or June, 1992, please describe the incident.

Date _____ From _____ To _____ Aircraft Type _____

Description: _____

_____

_____   Your name (optional) _____

of political leaflets and pamphlets. In some national unions, during the weeks before important elections, the staff representatives are ordered to suspend collective bargaining negotiations, grievance meetings, and arbitrations and devote their full time to political work. The fact that each national union employs many staff representatives—in such large unions as the Automobile Workers and Steelworkers, the numbers run into the hundreds—serves as an important advantage; and if the staff representatives are adroit and hardworking, the favored political candidate can benefit greatly from such support.

By some estimates, indeed, national unions spend many times as much on such noncash "in-kind" contributions to friendly political campaigns as they do on direct cash contributions to candidates of their choice through political-action committees. The *Wall Street Journal,* for example, has estimated that in 1988 unions gave $35.5 million to political candidates and about $200 million more in such in-kind help as free printing and voter registration drives.[12]

Depending on their size and leadership policies, national unions perform other functions. Some arrange educational programs for their staff representatives and local union officers. Most of the courses in these programs deal exclusively with the practical aspects of labor relations—how to bargain labor agreements, the best way to handle grievances, and the like. At times, however, the courses deal with foreign affairs, taxation, economics, government, and other subjects not directly related to the bread-and-butter issues of trade unionism. In addition, some national unions administer vacation resorts for their members, award university scholarships to children of members, organize tours to foreign nations, and sponsor a variety of social functions that are similar to those maintained by the state and city labor bodies but more tailored to the specific interests and aptitudes of the particular national union's members.

In recent years, there has also been a trend on the part of some nationals to engage in media campaigns to build a more favorable institutional image and often to attract members directly as well. Television, radio, billboard, and newspaper projects of some magnitude have been conducted by such unions as the Automobile Workers (who, among other approaches, have taken a page from the slogan of Honda, a UAW organizing target in Ohio, by advertising, "They make it simple. We make it fair."), Garment Workers (whose ads feature actual members of the union singing about looking for the union label), Communications Workers, Teachers, and an increasing number of others.

Sometimes, too, a desire to counteract damaging publicity has been the spur. In the wake of recent news that three former Northwest Airlines pilots were found guilty of drunken flying (leading to such widespread jokes as "How many Northwest pilots does it take to fly a plane? Three and one-fifth"), the Air Line Pilots created a 30-second television spot and a half-dozen 60-second radio commercials that depicted pilots as models of calm conscientiousness.

And no less well aware that sometimes the best defense is a solid offense, labor's public relations efforts have also not ignored occasional black marks on the record of the *employer* community. A few years ago the Teamsters announced with considerable fanfare that their (then) $6 billion Central States Pension Fund had stopped using E. F. Hutton & Co. as a stockbroker, because Hutton had pleaded guilty to a check overdrafting scheme, and under the terms of the fund's existing consent decree with the Labor Department it was banned from dealing with individuals or corporations guilty of a crime. For the union, itself the recipient of so much negative publicity for decades that in the eyes of many citizens the word "Teamster" was roughly equated to the word "hoodlum," even a little revenge was sweet.

Government of the National Union

When a national union is formed, a constitution is adopted that spells out the internal government and procedures of the union. Virtually every constitution provides that a convention should be held, and it designates this convention as the supreme authority of the union. Under the rules of most national unions, each local union sends delegates to the convention, with the number of delegates permitted to each local being dependent upon the local's paid-up membership totals. Hence, as in the AFL-CIO, the larger locals are more influential than the smaller units. Within most unions the locals range in size from several thousand to a literal handful of members in some locals that have contracts with small employers.

Ordinarily, the chief officers of the local unions are elected as delegates, although in the very large locals, which have the opportunity to send many delegates, rank-and-file members are chosen because the quota cannot be filled by the officers alone.

Many rank-and-filers consider being sent to a convention a definite plum, and not simply for the honor involved. Union conventions tend to be reasonably elaborate affairs, although few national get-togethers have remotely approached the level of tastelessly conspicuous consumption that the Teamsters reached at their 1986 convention in Las Vegas. There, following unlimited free drinks and the hospitality of a seemingly inexhaustible supply of top-quality caviar, shrimp, beef, and pastries, 300-pound IBT president Jackie Presser (who had been indicted the previous week for allegedly embezzling union funds) was wheeled into the Caesar's Palace ballroom on a golden sedan chair by four men dressed as Roman centurions. Like a Roman emperor in a Hollywood extravaganza, Presser reached out from a semi-reclining position to touch the many hands extending toward him as colored floodlights played upon the scene and a voice in the loudspeaker mellifluously declared, "Hail, Caesar." (Another party that was reputed to cost $600,000 was thrown at this same convention and was understandably viewed as an anticlimax.)

Even the Teamsters have, indeed, moved some distance from that ostentation. Their last convention, held in 1991, featured nothing much more expensive than run-of-the-mill chicken, cold soup, and cheesecake, had no side extravaganzas at all, and took place in the staid, family-oriented environment of Florida's Disney World.

But almost all national conventions, which are usually held in resort locations, do offer some luxuries and pageantry. When the delegates lose time from work, the local union normally pays their lost wages, and the convention often lasts a week or so, allowing a welcome change of pace from what is often a humdrum employment life. Many delegates, even at their own expense, take their families along and look on the entire experience as money well spent. (Las Vegas has been a particularly favored spot. Exhibit 4-7 refers to a recent convention of the Steelworkers, who, like the Teamsters, have often given convention business to America's western center of gambling.)

EXHIBIT 4–7

Source: Steelabor, July 1988, back cover.

Although under the terms of the Landrum-Griffin Act the delegates must be chosen by secret ballot, the officers of the nationals themselves may be selected in either of two ways: In about three fourths of the national unions, the constitution requires that the principal officers (president, vice president, and secretary-treasurer) be elected by the convention. In the others, the officers are elected by a direct referendum wherein each member of the union may cast a ballot. Some of the largest unions follow the latter procedure, including the Steelworkers, the Clothing and Textile Workers, and the Machinists, but, even among the larger unions, most utilize the convention election system.

Union business dealt with at national conventions, in addition to the election of chief officers, runs a wide gamut. At a recent convention of the UAW, for example, the 2,500 delegates were asked to consider avenues for improving job security of their members in upcoming negotiations with the Big Three automobile makers and ways of making the diminished UAW budget (diminished because the union had lost some 400,000 members in the previous five years) go further in the field of organizing. They also pondered the authorization of a major new lobbying effort designed to rebuild America's basic industries (including, needless to say, the automotive sector). Cutting membership contributions to the union's hefty $500 million strike fund, from 30 percent of each member's monthly dues to 15 percent, was another item on the agenda.

Special problems of the various locals are also aired, and this provides an excellent opportunity for an exchange of ideas and experiences and for otherwise breaking down the provincialism of the local unions; delegates from a large local union in, say, Chicago can learn of the problems of a small local in a small southern community, for example. The convention also permits local union officers to display themselves to their best advantage. Most of them would like to rise in the union hierarchy, and the convention offers a testing ground for their talents. A rousing speech by a local union president may attract the attention of the delegates, and this favorable showing may stand the local person in good stead later when an attempt at higher office is made.

The actual business of the convention may be initiated either by the national officers or by the delegates. Decision making takes the form of resolutions, proposals, and reports on which the delegates vote. As in any large convention, the officers have a distinct advantage in this respect, since the president appoints the committees that bring important issues before the delegates and is in a position to select members for these committees who the leadership knows are favorable to the national officers' point of view. On the other hand, a determined local union, or even individual delegates who feel strongly about their cause, can bring to the attention of the convention a resolution, a recommendation, or even an amendment to the constitution. There is a limit, in fact, to how far any national president can go in bottling up the resentment of determined delegates. And, particularly if a delegation from a local can enlist the support of delegates from other locals, there is an excellent chance that the entire convention will hear its point of view. For all the authority and control the nationals exert over the locals, if national officers gain the enmity of a sufficient number of local unions, the delegates of these locals can band together and cause an upheaval at the convention; and, if the issues are of extreme importance, the resentment of these locals could result in a change in national union leadership. Thus, the local unions do have a political check against their national officers. There is a line the latter can cross only at the risk of losing their jobs.

In short, as long as the national union holds regularly scheduled conventions, the democratic process has an opportunity of working. The convention provides the forum wherein the policies, behavior, and competency of the national union officers can be evaluated, and the key to the democratic operation of a national union therefore lies in the regularity with which conventions are held. More than half the national unions hold conventions either annually or biennially, and most of the rest hold them every three or four years. A small number of national unions, however, simply do not hold conventions at all, and this clearly eliminates almost entirely any practical opportunity for the local unions to participate in the government of their unions. Nothing in the Landrum-Griffin law, indeed, requires unions to hold regular and reasonably frequent conventions. The law does require that the union membership be afforded the opportunity to elect its national officers at least every five years, but a union managed by autocrats can legally avoid the holding of conventions indefinitely.

National Union Officers

The chief of the national union is, of course, its president. He or she administers the organization with the assistance of such other major officers as the vice president (or vice presidents), secretary-treasurer, and members of the executive board. The latter group is ordinarily composed of the district or regional directors (who, in some national unions, are also called vice presidents), and its members have a variety of official tasks: enforcing the constitution of the national, implementing its policies, filling a national officer's position when vacant, voting on important matters referred to them by the president, placing items on the agenda for deliberation and voting, and a host of related duties. Normally, the executive board of a national union meets regularly and frequently, according to the provisions of a constitution, and on occasion also meets at the call of the president to deal with some pressing problem. Since the members of the executive board are from all over the nation and have direct supervision of the locals in their particular districts, the board mechanism provides an excellent way for the national union officers to learn of the problems of all locals throughout the country. Likewise, it provides a channel for communicating policies of the national union to its locals and membership.

In some unions, however, executive boards merely rubber-stamp decisions of the national officers. This is true most often when a president, either by union custom or because of the person's particular personality, is allowed to exercise autocratic leadership. It is safe to say, however, that in most unions the executive board directs the affairs of the union and establishes the union's basic policies, which the president is then obliged to carry out. The exceptions in recent years have in fact generally been succeeded in office by leaders who appear to have taken extra efforts to alter the old images of power imbalance and to encourage the executive boards to participate more fully in policy-making decisions.

Ronald R. Carey, who became the reform candidate president of the Teamsters in 1992 following the first direct one-member, one-vote election in that union's history, and who is nothing if not responsive to his executive board, serves as a good illustration of this last situation.

For at least four decades, IBT chief executives had generally operated with complete disdain for their boards. Carey's immediate predecessor, William J. McCarthy, had gone so far as to rig the bidding on the contract to print the monthly Teamsters' magazine so that his son-in-law could get the $3.6 million business. All of the five other Teamster presidents who had served since 1952 (three were sent to prison for crimes of various kinds, partly explaining the high turnover) had at best been benevolent autocrats. Nepotism had been a way of life in these years and all that it had typically taken for these IBT leaders to remove any real or potential rivals from the post had been a command from the presidents to the board members. Nor had the boards given the presidents any trouble at all concerning the national political arena: In every one of the ten White House campaigns in these forty years, the Teamster boards had endorsed conservative Republicans without batting an eyelash simply because the various Teamster chief executives had informed the board members that this was their personal desire.

Carey, whose first announcement as president-elect was that he would cut the existing IBT presidential salary—at $225,000 the highest of any union leader—to $175,000, had campaigned on a platform of "returning the union to the members." Once in office, he sold not only the ostentatious limousine but also two jets that his predecessors had flaunted. Unlike them, he flew only by coach. With the consent of his executive board, he forced a strict budget on a union that had never known one. Indeed, by the previously described government-imposed anti-corruption machinery, at this writing, he had eased out most of the remaining mob-connected members of the bureaucracy that he had inherited. A *New York Times* headline accompanying a highly favorable profile of him could quite accurately assert: "New Image Promised for Teamsters: Honest Work by an Honest Leader."[13]

All responsible, devoted, and active national union presidents have a difficult job. One day they may be negotiating a contract with a major corporation, and the next day speaking at an important meeting of the union, or to the members of some other labor organization. They are also, typically, obligated to testify before congressional committees, preside over the union's executive board meetings, and travel to foreign nations as participants in international labor organization bodies. They are expected to take an active role in important national political elections, constantly put pressure upon the staff representatives to organize nonunion plants, mollify companies that are disgruntled because of wildcat strikes or other forms of unauthorized union behavior, and perform a variety of other duties that may be of major importance or strictly routine in character, but that also take up a great deal of time. Indeed, the management of even a small or medium-sized national union is a difficult one; the job becomes immensely more complicated and difficult in a large union.

The union president, moreover, is constantly torn between duties of a pressing character. In many cases, the leader must make the hard decision alone and hope it is the right one. As any chief executive, the president bears the ultimate responsibility for the organization's efficient, honest, and prudent management. Above all, the president must satisfy the membership, and at times this is a much more difficult job than dealing with management.

For all of this, union presidents hardly grow rich on the salaries of their offices. Even leaders of the largest unions rarely make more than $125,000. Indeed, while in a recent year the president of the Air Line Pilots Association (many of whose members themselves received six-figure incomes) earned some $192,000 and a handful of other union top officials approached that relatively affluent level (or in the previously cited case of the Teamsters, exceeded it until Carey's lowering of the amount), these numbers were easily balanced by the salaries of the presidents of such major unions as the Automobile Workers, Communications Workers, Clothing and Textile Workers, Mine Workers, Rubber Workers and Oil, Chemical and Atomic Workers: In these organizations, the salary range was between $55,000 and $90,000. It is clear that money was not the motivator, either, for the president of the United Electrical Workers: Limited in what he could get by the union's constitution to no more than the highest weekly wage in the industry, he earned a far from staggering $27,083 plus an equally unimpressive expense allowance. (The UE, nothing if not egalitarian, has a leaflet that asserts that "a boss-size salary can give you a boss-eye point of view. Champagne tastes can soon make you forget how important a 50 cent beer can be.") At the extreme of financial self-denial was Farm Worker president Cesar Chavez, the recipient at last report of a paltry $5,645.

It is certainly true that a few national leaders have taken things too far, financially speaking, while in office. Before the passage of the Landrum-Griffin Act, for example, Teamster president David Beck succumbed to an urge to buy items of a personal nature in copious amounts and charge them to his union. In more recent years, the authoritarian Mine Workers president W. A. "Tony" Boyle also flagrantly misused union money for his personal benefit. And although receiving pay from the holding of several union jobs simultaneously is not in itself illegal—in the Teamsters, it was almost a way of life for the top officials and even now at least ten IBT leaders currently get paychecks from at least three positions—some element of good judgment might be brought into question when the total derived incomes go well into the six-figure area. The same can be said of the practice in some unions (the Laborers, most conspicuously) of placing relatives in high-paying jobs with no seeming correlation of such placements to any merit on the part of the relatives.

Yet these latter situations are definitely the exceptions. No union leader remotely approximates the $2 million a year that the CEO of a large American corporation now typically earns (in 1991, the $1 million in salary and bonus that the top person at General Motors received placed him appreciably below the 100 highest-paid executives in the nation). And the most handsomely remunerated union official is many light-years in income away from such corporate chief executives as Anthony O'Reilly of H. J. Heinz, Martin J. Wygod of Medco Equipment, and Leon C. Hirsch of U.S. Surgical, who in a recent year got from their organizations $75.1 million, $33.7 million, and $23.3 million, respectively, while seven other industrial chieftains made at least $11.5 million.[14]

And who is to say that baseball pitcher Jack Morris, who at this writing was working under a four-year contract with the Toronto Blue Jays, which was paying him $10.85 million (or about $1,500 a pitch), was worth it—especially since his won-lost record for the previous four seasons had been a less than awesome 54-57? Or that Bobby Bonilla of the New York Mets deserved the $29 million that a five-year arrangement with his employer would ultimately give him? Or that boxing's Evander Holyfield warranted $20 million for a few minutes of what at least one sportswriter deemed his "waltzing" with George Foreman?[15] Or that another figure from the world of entertainment, Bill Cosby, was worth the $60 million that he reputedly earned during the last year of his hugely successful television show, in 1992?

Workers pay the salaries of their union officers, however. And the employee who earns $18,000 in a good year may still assess a $65,000 salary as being exorbitant. But an objective assessment must turn more toward a conclusion that the typical national union leader is, if anything, underpaid given his responsibilities. When measured by his own very formidable list of duties, even the president of the Air Line Pilots does not seem to be getting an unreasonable salary.

Although modestly paid, the national president wants to keep the job. Union leaders have power and prestige and play an important role in our society. Many presidents do indeed remain in office for considerable lengths of time, and some of them stay in the chief executive chair for so long that memory does not recall another president. Daniel J. Tobin was president of the Teamsters for forty-five years; William L. Hutcheson, of the Carpenters for forty-one years (immediately following which his son Maurice moved into that union's presidential office for a full additional two decades); and John L. Lewis, of the Mine Workers for forty years. James C. Petrillo, president of the Musicians, gave up his job, involuntarily at that, only when he grew so old and feeble that it is doubtful that he had the strength to play his instrument. Only a relative handful of unions—including the Automobile Workers, Steelworkers, and Machinists—have any provision for compulsory retirement of their national officers even now, and if national union board meetings can no longer be confused with "a collection of a wax museum," youth does not exactly hold sway in them, either. Richard L. Trumka, a lawyer and third-generation miner who was elected in 1982 at age 33 to head the 180,000-member United Mine Workers, is still the youngest leader of a major union in the United States, by some distance: Only a handful of other national presidents are even below the half-century mark and most are in their sixties or beyond. (Exhibit 4-8 illustrates the hard-fought election that took place for the presidency of the once fully

EXHIBIT 4–8

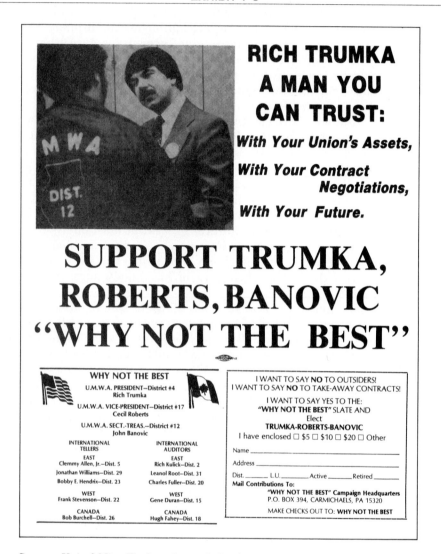

Source: United Mine Workers Journal, October 1–15, 1982, pp. 12–13.

autocratic Mine Workers. Neither candidate could find much good to say about the other, and after the incumbent, Church, was ultimately defeated he was conspicuously absent from the Trumka inauguration ceremonies.)

Most national union officers stay in power for years, in fact, and it is not difficult to explain why they do so. Once in office, they possess sufficient power to minimize centralized opposition and to make it extremely difficult for new candidates to present themselves to the membership in an effective manner. The point has been made that when conventions are not held regularly and frequently, it is difficult for a new face to get much backing.

EXHIBIT 4–8 (continued)

A Message From Sam

Dear Brothers and Sisters,

I trust the men and women of the United Mine Workers. I trust you to make intelligent and aware decisions based on facts. I trust you to be able to find the truth.

I believe you trust me, even those who disagree with me on some issues. One thing I have always done since I became president has been to be truthful, to be honest with you. You are the people who are the heart and soul of this Union. You deserve honest leadership.

A campaign should be based on ideas, achievements, records and plans. You know my record and achievements. You have seen my plans for the future (in the last UMWA Journal). You may not agree with all of them, b u t those things are out front for you to judge.

My opponent has suddenly found himself slipping from the solid ground of truth into quicksand of deception. Much of this you have probably already read about in your newspapers or have seen or heard on television and radio.

These stories have concerned his qualifications to be president of the UMWA. They are not what he has said they were.

The individual issues are not the main point.

The main point is the pattern of deliberate deception of every coal miner in the United Mine Workers of America.

I feel sorry for a young man who wants something so badly that he would go these lengths to get it. Ambition is a terrible master.

But you cannot lead a union by deception. When the membership begins to doubt your word, your honesty and your truthfulness, then there is no leadership, there is no progress, there is no future.

Let us continue to build our future together.

Fraternally,

Sam Church J

Sam Church Jr.

In addition, staff representatives are hired by the national union and can usually be removed at the pleasure of the national officers. It would take rare courage for a paid representative to oppose the incumbent president, and the tendency is, in fact, understandably in the other direction. In addition, most incumbent presidents get personal mileage out of their union newspapers. The editor of the national union newspaper is also a hired person, and subject to control of the national officers. Any upstart candidate could not expect much favorable publicity, if indeed the candidate received any publicity at all, in the union press. As Wilfrid Sheed once commented, "The [president] controls the newspaper and assorted promo

material, which is likely to feature pictures of himself peering knowingly
into a mine face or welding machine, like a bishop at a confirmation. (In
the Steelworkers, I'm told, a man could go mad staring at I. W. Abel. It's
worse than *Muhammed Speaks*.)"[16] (Exhibit 4-9 portrays Laborers International Union president Angelo Fosco in a light that only a disciple of the
Marquis de Sade could view with disapproval. Mr. Fosco's picture appeared
eight times in the twenty-two-page issue of *The Laborer* in which this
Dollars Against Diabetes message was published, and photographs of two
plaques expressing appreciation for his efforts also were offered readers of
that issue. The latter, shown as Exhibit 4-10, also presumably did not hurt
the Laborer leader's standing with his members.)

In short, the incumbent national officers have a political machine that
tends to perpetuate them in office. However, it would be incorrect to believe
that this is the only reason for long tenure of office. Sophisticated union
members understand that frequent changes of national union officers and
open displays of factionalism weaken the position of the union against
management in collective bargaining. Beyond this, a national union officer
may have genuinely earned reelection to office over the years because the
officer has been doing a good job for the membership. A national union
president who is devoted, honest, courageous, and competent does not need
a political machine to be reelected. Many national union officers fall within
this category, and representatives of management should not regard national union officers as incompetent people who hold office only because of
political machination.

THE LOCAL UNION

Where the People Are

Although we leave for the last an analysis of the local union, it does not
follow that the latter is the least important of the labor bodies in the union
movement. On the contrary, it could be argued successfully that for the
individual union member, the local union is the most important unit of all.
In a sense, the federation, the national union and its district organizations,
and the other labor bodies discussed previously are administrative and
service organizations. Although they are vitally important and carry out a
variety of significant activities, as we have seen, no union member really
"belongs" to such larger bodies. Unionists are members of these organizations only by reason of their membership in a local union, are geographically close only to the local, and largely condition their loyalty toward an
image of the total labor movement by what they perceive to transpire within
the confines of the local union. Many union members do not, indeed, even
know the names of their national and federation officers, but they do know
their local union president, business agent, and stewards. They know them
because they see them where they work and because these are the people
who handle the union members' day-to-day problems.

EXHIBIT 4–9

D.A.D.'s Day

This Father's Day weekend, we will observe the third annual Dad's Day. Dad stands for Dollars Against Diabetes. It is an event which takes place all across the United States, as laborers and other building tradesmen and their families collect money which helps fund research to find a cure for diabetes.

Father's Day offers us an opportunity to honor our fathers, or to be honored by our children. DAD's Day offers all of us an opportunity to fight a disease that affects many families throughout North America including some within our own union.

Diabetes respects no one. The disease attacks generation after generation—grandparent, parent, child. Not a day passes in the lives of most diabetics when an insulin injection does not have to be taken. In fact, some diabetics take 2–3 shots of insulin a day. Centuries have passed without a cure.

Yes, the disease has been around since biblical times. Even today, with our modern medical science, 100 people die each day of diabetes. That gives you some idea of how many lives have been lost over the years.

During the past three years, members of this International union and the entire building trades have volunteered their time and energies to DAD's Day

> "Diabetes respects no one. The disease attacks generation after generation— grandparents, parent, child."

and, each year, the event has raised more money than the year before. Most important to our efforts, the money raised through DAD's benefits the Diabetes Research Institute (DRI). DRI is responsible for the decade's most significant breakthrough in diabetes research—the discovery of a curative treatment in animals that, when applied to humans, has led to insulin production in human beings.

In addition, this year, our union also has its own special reason for encouraging maximum DAD's Day participation: her name is Katie Caruso, and she is 17 years old. As you will learn from our cover story,

Katie suffers from juvenile diabetes. To make up for her body's lack of insulin production, Katie must take 2–3 shots of insulin a day. She is forced to watch her diet closely and commit herself to the proper exercise.

One of the few "good things" about Katie's situation, according to her mother, is that Katie is a member of a very close-knit family. Her mother wrote to me that, in some strange way, she believes Katie and the family have actually drawn strength from their battle with diabetes. "We feel Katie truly is one of those young adults today who has gained from her experience," she said.

> "Let each of us pledge to show the Caruso family that LIUNA is also a close-knit family. . ."

The Caruso family, and Katie in particular, have faced this centuries-old disease with courage and determination. Our admiration pours out to them.

But that's not enough. This Father's Day weekend— June 16, 17 and 18—let each of us pledge to show the Caruso family that *LIUNA is also a close-knit family*, and that they are an important part of it. Let us pledge to do all that we can to make Katie's future years bright, full of opportunity and free from the shadow of diabetes.

I intend to be out raising money in my hometown of Chicago this DAD's Day; I hope all of you do the same in your area as well. Have a happy—and productive—DAD's Day!

Angelo Fosco
General President

MAY–JUNE, 1989

3

Source: The Laborer, May–June 1989, p. 3.

EXHIBIT 4–10

The Department of Labor recognized General President Fosco's efforts in the area of health safety with this plaque.

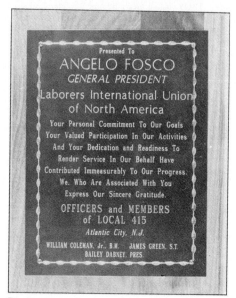

This plaque expresses Local 415's sincere appreciation of President Fosco's effort on their behalf.

Source: The Laborer, May–June 1989, p. 8.

Local Union Officers

Although some locals are formed before the employer is organized, a local union normally comes into existence when there is organization of an employer. After it has organized and secured bargaining rights, a local typically applies for and receives a national union charter. This document establishes the local's affiliation with the national union and entitles the local to its services, and by the same token it subjects the local to the rules and discipline of the national union. Depending upon the unit of organization, a local union may be confined to a single plant or several plants of a single company or may include workers of a single craft, such as electricians who perform their duties in a given geographic area.

There is absolutely no correlation between the size of a national union and its number of locals. The Teamsters, with 1.4 million members, have 745 locals, but the Steelworkers, considerably smaller with a membership of 500,000, have almost 5,000 of them. And while the Food and Commercial Workers have chartered 790 locals to support their 1 million constituents, the Barbers and Beauticians have almost as many locals (702) for their 41,000 members, allowing those who belong to the latter union the unusually small member-to-local ratio of about 59 to 1.

Once the local is established, the members, in accordance with their bylaws (which are usually specified in the national union constitution), elect their officers—typically a president, vice president, secretary-treasurer, and several lesser officials. Since such election procedures almost invariably allow direct participation by all union members, the local union officers are elected on a much more democratic basis than are those chosen to lead the national union. Moreover, the union member knows much more from firsthand experience about the local union candidates for office than he or she does about the national union officers. The vast majority of local union officers, in fact, work at regular jobs along with the other union members and are under constant and often highly critical observation by them. Both democracy and a far higher turnover rate for local officers than for the union's national officials also stem from the fact that the local union officer, unlike the national union president, has little if any patronage to dispense. Local leaders do not have a paid staff as does the national counterpart; nor, generally speaking, can the local officer make use of any other powers of patronage or the purse, since neither exist in any measure.

In general, the local union officers even work without pay. In only the large local unions are such officers reimbursed for their work, and, even then, their salaries tend to approximate the wages they would have earned from their employers. And in the relatively infrequent instances when the local union president and secretary-treasurer do receive some small compensation for their duties even when they are full-time employees in the plant, the amount of money is comparatively small when measured against the duties they perform. For example, in Bloomington, Indiana, one local's secretary-treasurer receives the far from awesome salary of $4,500 per year for taking care of the books, making financial reports, answering all correspondence, and assuming a volume of other miscellaneous duties. The size of his job is measured by the fact that the local has over 3,000 members and by the union's requirement that all his duties must be conducted on his own time.

A fair question, then, is why union members desire to acquire and retain local union officer jobs. Despite their nominal or totally nonexistent financial rewards, they must perform a variety of duties and assume considerable responsibility, and they are constantly being pressured by the membership under whose direct surveillance they labor. A leading reason is that the local union officers acquire prestige and status in the company and in the community. Virtually all people desire recognition once lower needs have been relatively well satisfied, and the attainment of a local officer's job accomplishes this objective for some workers.

Another reason may involve the local union officer's devotion and dedication to the union movement. "In general," Koziara, Bradley, and Pierson have concluded from their study of this topic, those who become union officers "are people who believe unions have a meaningful function to perform in our society."[17] If the local officer really believes in unions, he or she has the opportunity of making the movement work by carrying out the position's duties in an honest and effective manner.

Still other union members may genuinely court the competitive character associated with the office: The local union officers deal with the employer on a day-to-day basis, and many of the dealings regularly involve what some workers view as "the struggle" with management.

Finally, the reason may be a political one, involving the future of the local union officer in the national union. As stated, national union officers are elected officials, and staff representatives are union members who are hired by the national union. Thus, to go up the ladder, the union member must normally start at the local union level; a local union officer's job is commonly the first step in the long and hard pull toward the top. The large majority of all current national union officers and staff representatives have held a local union officer's job at some earlier period of their careers.

Functions of the Local Union: Relations with Management

The duties of local union officers are dependent, of course, upon the functions of the particular local union, but unless contracts are negotiated on a multiemployer basis or with a very large corporation, local union officers directly negotiate the labor agreement with the employer. If the national union staff representative often aids the local in carrying out this function and usually plays a highly visible role in the process, the fact remains that the local union officers who are also involved in negotiations are directly responsible to the members of the local union. The staff representative, a hired hand, does not face political defeat if he or she exercises poor judgment or fails to negotiate a contract that the membership feels is suitable. Should a contract, however, hurt the local union members, it is very likely that in the next election the local union officers will be changed. Because of its local character, factionalism in the local is, in fact, a constant problem. It is comparatively easy for a dynamic, aggressive, and ambitious newcomer to use a poor contract as a weapon to dislodge an incumbent officer.

Another important function of the local is that of negotiating grievances. Indeed, most of the union's time is devoted to this task; the labor agreement is negotiated only periodically, but, through the grievance procedure, it must be administered every day. To this end, each local union has a number of stewards—usually one steward to a department of the company, elected by the union members of that department—who serve as administrative personnel.

In most plants, the members also elect a chief steward to be chairperson of the grievance committee. At the lower steps of the grievance procedure, the worker's complaint is handled by the department steward, and, normally, the local union president or chief steward does not enter the picture until the grievance has reached the higher levels. But at the last step of the grievance procedure, the local union president and the union grievance committee (composed of the chief steward and several other stewards) will negotiate the grievance, typically with the staff representative of the national union also being present. Moreover, if a grievance goes to arbitration, the local union president and the union committee will attend the hearing, and although at this forum the national staff representative usually presents the union's case, the representative depends heavily upon the local union officers and the committee for the data that will be presented to the arbitrator.

It is difficult to overestimate the vital importance of the effective use of the grievance procedure as a function of the local union. Indeed, to the union member who has a grievance, the handling of that grievance means more to the individual than what the union secured in the collective bargaining agreement. This is particularly true when the grievant complains against a discharge or against an alleged employer violation of an important working condition.

In this capacity, however, the local union officers are also vulnerable. Take, for example, a grievance that, though important to the employee, does not have merit. If the local union president tells this to the union member, the president risks offending a constituent. And if this happens frequently and with many different workers, the union members can demonstrate their resentment in the next election. This appears completely unfair and senseless, but it is what the local union officers have to contend with, and explains why local union officers frequently take up grievances that do not have merit.

At times, too, the local officers are forced to deal with "borderline" grievances—complaints that may or may not have merit but that, for a variety of reasons, the local union officers cannot persuade the employer to grant. Often, the local does not want to risk losing the grievance in arbitration. It therefore refuses to handle the grievance, and the job now is to pacify the employee, who may have some justification for being resentful—not an easy mission when the grievance deals with an important issue and has some basis under the labor agreement. Consequently, the local officials may change their minds and take such grievances into arbitration, hoping for the best; if the arbitrator denies the grievance, the local union officers can always use the arbitrator as the scapegoat. However, in spite of an effective presentation at the arbitration hearing, the disgruntled union member may still blame union officers. It is said that victory has many fathers, but defeat is an orphan. Fortunately, unions win their share of grievances in the grievance procedure and in arbitration, and in the campaign before the next election, the local union officer can point with pride to successes and minimize or explain away defeats.

Judicial Procedures

Another function of the local union is that of disciplining union members who are alleged to have violated union rules. As does every organization, unions have standards with which members must comply. These standards are incorporated by the national union's constitution and are duplicated in the local union's bylaws. If a union member violates any of these rules, he or she may be disciplined by the local union membership in the form of a reprimand, a fine, suspension, or, in extreme cases, expulsion from the union.

Commonly proscribed standards of conduct that frequently merit expulsion include the promotion of dual unionism (when a union member seeks to take the local out of one national union and place it in another—true treason in unionism!), participating in an unauthorized or "wildcat" strike, misappropriating union funds, strikebreaking, refusing to picket, sending the union membership list to unauthorized persons, circulating false and malicious reports about union officers, and providing secret and confidential information to the employer. Under the official rules of some unions, a member may also be expelled because of membership in a Communistic, Fascistic, or other totalitarian group. We may quarrel with the justice or fairness of one or more of these rules, but the fact remains that they must be obeyed, since they have been adopted by the union at large. From the union point of view, each of them pertains to an important area of conduct.

The procedures used at the local level to enforce the rules of the union differ widely, but the following would probably reflect most local union procedures: Any union member may file charges against any other member, including the local union officers. When this occurs, the president has the authority to appoint a so-called "trial committee," composed of union members belonging to the local in question and normally including officers, stewards, and rank-and-file members who take an active role in the affairs of the union. The trial committee has the job of investigating the complaint, holding a hearing if it believes that the charge has substance, and reaching a decision that it will ultimately present to the entire local union body for final determination. To protect against a political situation within the local wherein favorites of the local union officers, or the officers themselves, may not be brought to account for a violation, the union members initiating the charge may appeal to the national union. Thus, a "not guilty" verdict, the dismissal of charges by the local union officers, or the pigeonholing of complaints does not necessarily end the disciplinary process.

After its investigation of the charges, the local union's trial committee holds a hearing at which the accused member is present. The accused may select another union member to act as his or her spokesperson. As in most other private or semiprivate organizations, the union member may not hire a defense lawyer while the case is being processed within the union, but witnesses are called, and cross-examination is permitted. And, although no oath is administered for the same reason (since the hearing is not in a court of law), union members who deliberately lie or who grossly misrepresent the facts may themselves be charged with a violation. After the hearing, the trial committee reports its decision and the reasons for the verdict to the local union membership. At this point, the membership may adopt, reject, or modify the committee's decision. At times, the trial is in effect reheld before the local membership, since some members might desire to review the evidence that the trial committee used to arrive at its decision.

If the decision is "not guilty," the member or members who filed the charge may appeal to the executive board of the national union. By the same token, when the decision of the local goes against the charged union member, that member may appeal to the national union and, under the provisions of virtually every constitution, the member can also ultimately appeal the decision of the national union officers to the national convention.

On the surface, this judicial procedure appears fair and calculated to protect the accused union member. It would seem that the accused receives a full and fair hearing and gains further protection through provisions for the right of appeal. In practice, however, there have been several instances of serious abuses of the local union judicial procedure, although, with some 50,000 locals to consider, it is absolutely impossible to make any kind of accurate judgment of the relative extent to which the abuse has existed, and any opinion is sheer speculation.

It was because of such union actions, however, that the Landrum-Griffin Act specified that no member could be disciplined, fined, or expelled without having first received a written list of charges, a reasonable time to prepare the defense, and a full and fair hearing. Today, if these legal standards are violated, a union member may bring suit in the federal courts for relief. Under the law, the union member may not go to court before he or she attempts to settle the case through union procedures, although to check dilatory union tactics the law also specifies that if the internal procedure consumes longer than four months the union member need not exhaust the internal remedies of the union before going to court.

In 1957, the same year that the Teamsters were expelled from the AFL-CIO for alleged domination by "corrupt influences," the Automobile Workers—who had led this expulsion action—dealt with the problem of abuse in the disciplinary procedure in a different manner. The UAW established a "Public Review Board, composed of seven citizens of respected reputation and impeccable integrity and having no other relationship with the union." Usually, such citizens have been nationally known members of the clergy, the judiciary, or academia, and in the years since the board's creation they have actively pursued their official charge of ensuring "a continuation of high moral and ethical standards" within the UAW. They have investigated all credible complaints, from allegations of individual member wrongdoing to charges by individual members that their union representatives have not adequately handled a grievance, and generally have done so to the full satisfaction of all concerned.

Experience has shown, indeed, that the board—which is empowered to reverse UAW executive board decisions that have upheld the discipline of union personnel—has been quite willing to make such reversals when it has believed that such a reversal has been justified. To date, however, only the Upholsterers International Union has followed the pattern of the UAW. If each national union were to establish such an agency, and if each agency were allowed the same freedom to act that has been granted the UAW Public Review Board, there clearly would be less need for legislation to protect the status of union members.

Political Activities

Although the AFL-CIO and national union officers and staff representatives play an effective role in lobbying and in supporting candidates in their campaigns for political office, it can be argued with much justification that the political efficiency of the union movement depends above all upon the vigor of the local. After all, the number of the federation and national officers and staff representatives is very small in comparison with the number of local union members. And much of the legwork during the national and state elections must necessarily be performed by local union members if it is to be performed at all on any large scale. Indeed, the success of the union movement in "rewarding its friends and punishing its enemies" depends in large measure on the willingness of local union officers and members to engage in politics.

Nonetheless, the degree to which local unions participate in politics is often determined by the basic philosophy of the national union. If the national union officers do not want their union to engage in politics, or if they merely go through the motions of indicating such a preference, the local unions of the nationals will reflect this kind of leadership. On the other hand, when the national union officers do take an active role in the political affairs of the nation, the local unions typically respond by placing a major emphasis on such political action of their own. However, even when the national unions do cajole their locals into taking this active role in politics, the members themselves may or may not follow the instructions of the national union officers, and the national's efforts must consequently be geared in two directions: toward the local leadership and toward the local membership.

If a constant problem of the national union that is politically inclined is thus to motivate the locals to follow its example, even within the ranks of such active unions as the UAW and the Machinists, there are many dozens of local unions that either refuse to participate or participate in a lackadaisical way. Locals of less politically conscious nationals often show even greater reluctance. Moreover, just because the AFL-CIO leadership or a national union president supports a candidate for elective office, this does not mean that every union member will vote that way. Some may not vote at all, of course, and postelection analyses of union member districts show that many others vote for the opposite candidate, as the millions of unionist votes for Ronald Reagan in 1980 and 1984 and for George Bush in 1988, noted earlier, vividly illustrate. There is no permanent "labor vote," as is sometimes claimed by people who view the political participation of the union movement as an evil.

Indeed, as long as we maintain secret elections, even the most homogeneous groups in the nation can never rest assured that their members or followers will vote as the organization urges them to. And if members of the most closely knit of unions do not lockstep to the polls and vote in accordance with the recommendations of their leadership, members of less cohesive labor groups are often significantly divided in their election choices.

Nonetheless, a local union that takes an active role in politics can be of great help to a favored candidate, and, in a close election, the support can tip the scales in the candidate's favor. The local union will encourage each member to register and to cast a ballot at election time. Prior to the election, it will do all in its power to "educate" the union member as to how to vote, through publications, meetings, house-to-house visits, and other forms of active political activity. In addition, the local union may legally make expenditures from union dues for such purposes as the holding of meetings of a political character and the publication and distribution of politically inspired newspapers and leaflets, although (as stated earlier) only money that is raised on a voluntary basis from the membership can be contributed directly to the people running for political office.

Other Functions and Problems

Beyond the major functions discussed above, local unions at times engage in a variety of social, educational, and community activities. Of late, as in the case of higher labor bodies, the last area has become increasingly important. Union leaders realize that the welfare of their members depends in part on a progressive and well-run community. How the schools are run, for example, is of vital interest to the local unionist who must pay taxes to operate the schools and who may have children attending the schools. As in the case of city labor bodies, representation of local union officials on United Way committees, Red Cross drives, and similar endeavors is also increasing in frequency. Moreover, unions recognize that the public image of organized labor, which has been tarnished in recent years, tends to improve to the extent that unions engage in such community services. Labor's various forms of participation in community service programs demonstrate that union members are not only collectively a socially oriented group but also individually responsible and interested citizens of the community. Likewise, the integration of unions in community work tends to lessen the tensions between management and organized labor. If a union leader can work effectively with the management representatives on the school board or in the United Way drive, there is a better chance for harmonious labor relations at the workplace.

Many local unions also conduct regularly sponsored and generally effective educational programs for the benefit of their officers and stewards. As noted previously, the need for these programs arises primarily from the complexity of the contemporary labor-management relationship, but it also stems to a great extent from the brisk turnover of the local union officers and stewards. Some of the programs are sponsored by the national unions, although in many cases the local itself arranges the educational program. Indeed, no union is considered modern today unless it has devised a well-planned educational program for its leadership. Such educational programs frequently bring to the surface workers of talent and high native intelligence. Through education, not only are they capable of doing a better job for their membership and acting more responsibly and rationally at the bargaining table, but education tends to make them more useful citizens. Of at least as much practical interest to many workers, union members who acquire such measures of education tend to rise more rapidly to important jobs at both the local and national levels.

One of the most important problems of the local is that of interesting the membership in attending regular monthly meetings of the union. Attendance at these meetings is frequently very poor, and the problem is not easy to solve. The vast majority of union leaders sincerely want their members to turn out at the meeting. They believe that the union has nothing to hide and that, by regular attendance and discussion at meetings, the members become more active, tend to be more devoted, and in general allow the local to deal with both employers and representatives of the public from a considerably stronger position than would otherwise be the case. The fact remains, however, that union members normally stay away from their meetings in droves; for the regular monthly meetings, only about 5 to 10 percent of the membership turns out (even a smaller percentage is common enough, especially in large locals); and one wonders why there has been so much said about union democracy when the union member does not seem sufficiently interested to participate in the affairs of his or her own union. When unions are poorly managed, when corruption exists, when leadership is second-rate, the fault is essentially that of the union member who does not care enough to attend the regular union meeting.

Thus, although from the days of the earliest unions labor organizations have undertaken a variety of measures (ranging from more convenient hours to the incorporation of social activities into the meeting schedule) to encourage attendance, in all these years unions have not found the solution to the problem of worker apathy toward attendance at meetings, and there is every likelihood that it will persist in the future. The only notable exception involves meetings at which a strike vote is scheduled to be taken. In general, the union members will turn out at this time because this issue of striking or working is, of course, of crucial importance.

On the other hand, management should not interpret poor attendance at the regular monthly meetings to mean that in crisis situations the members will not support their union. In a showdown, the typical union member will actively support the union; a management that makes a decision to chance a strike solely on the grounds of poor attendance at union meetings makes a very unwise choice. The members will invariably rally to the union's cause when there are issues involved that vitally affect their welfare, no matter how little interest they have demonstrated in the day-to-day operation of their local at more peaceful times.

UNION FINANCES

As do all other organizations, the union makes many expenditures and must meet its financial obligations. Chief expenditures of unions include the payment of salaries for their full-time officers and staff representatives, travel expenses, clerical expenses, office equipment and supplies, telephones, postage, arbitration fees, and rent or mortgage payments for office space and the union hall. Beyond this, the strike fund must be built up to pay strike benefits when needed.

At the international level, where the lion's share of the dollars is spent, most of the money paid out goes to staff members who provide direct and indirect services. It has been estimated that in the case of the United Automobile Workers, for example, about 85 percent of the spending is for this purpose. In a recent year, the UAW's research budget was approximately $700,000; its sixteen-member Washington staff spent about the same amount; the union's public relations expenditures were running at an annual rate of just over $1 million; and this fifth largest union in the country was even financing a six-member staff of safety experts who were flying around the country upon request from local unions to check for hazards.

The Teamsters, who have never been pressed for cash, spend it even more lavishly on services. Some 550 staff persons employed in fifteen different departments at the block-long union headquarters in Washington work in such fields of endeavor as lobbying, education (including the administration of a 30,000-volume library), communications (including the issuance of an impressively packaged monthly publication, *The International Teamster*), and a large legal department (itself supervising the activities of some 400 Teamster lawyers scattered throughout the country). They also staff a research wing (to compile information, above all, to back up contract bargaining demands), a steadily growing health and safety unit, an organizing department, and even an electronic data-processing department (supplying computer support nationwide to the several hundred Teamster locals).

At times, people are impressed by the relatively large amounts that unions collect in dues and initiation fees, forgetting that the union dispenses formidable amounts of money to meet its bills. By some estimates, the annual income of American unions from all sources—special assessments and earnings from investments, as well as the regular monthly dues paid by constituents, and initiation fees—amounts to about $3 billion. And there is little question that $3 billion looks like a lot of money, particularly when you don't have it. But when one considers the net worth of unions, a more accurate picture is gained. Such worth, for all unions in the United States, still remains under the $1 billion mark and in no way comes close to paralleling the wealth of corporations, at least two dozen of whom have net assets that *individually* exceed this billion-dollar figure. Income-wise, too, organized labor is a relative pygmy in relation to business: The ten most profitable U.S. corporations alone had profits of $24 billion in 1991, and the nation's top 500 industrial corporations in that same year racked up a staggering $2.3 trillion in sales.

In general, the dues paid by union members holding semiskilled and unskilled jobs in manufacturing are less than those paid by members who work in the skilled trades. The obvious reason for this is that electricians, plumbers, carpenters, and kindred skilled employees earn higher wages than do employees whose jobs require lesser skill levels. A substantial majority of union members now pay dues that come out to roughly two hours' wages per month, and two major unions—the Steelworkers and the Automobile Workers—have in fact officially set their monthly dues figures at exactly this two-hour level, thereby building automatic increases into the dues structure. Initiation fees—by definition, a one-shot affair—tend to be in the $50 to $100 range, with only a small handful of unionists (primarily in the building trades, airline pilot profession, and similarly highly remunerated groupings) being charged more than $200 in such fees by their labor organizations.

In the light of all that has been said about the functions of unions, the amount of money the typical member pays is thus comparatively small. Nonetheless, like everyone else, the union member desires maximum and ever-improving services for the least cost possible. Indeed, union leadership must be very careful when it seeks to raise the monthly dues. Even a modest increase of a dollar per month could cause an upheaval among the membership. With increasing expenses and sometimes declining memberships, unions *must* at times raise dues if they desire to maintain the same level of services for their membership, but this is a step normally taken only as an extreme last resort. Unions have often laid off staff representatives and otherwise tried to curb expenses drastically before requesting even a modest dues increase.

A CONCLUDING WORD

The American labor movement is vast and complicated, but its elements fit together in a systematic fashion and provide the framework for the carrying out of the basic functions and objectives.

In a day of increasing union dependence upon the sentiments of the general public, particularly as these sentiments are translated into legislative actions, these objectives have increasingly encompassed social and community activities that clearly extend well beyond labor's traditional campaigns for improved "property rights" on the job itself. These more broadly based endeavors can in no way be expected to diminish in the years ahead, for the advantages for the labor movement that can potentially be derived from them are certain to continue.

Yet this newer emphasis should not obscure either the pronounced strain of "bread-and-butter" unionism that has marked organized labor throughout its history or the internal union political considerations that continue to generate this more basic behavior. If unions are, by and large, not fully democratic, they are nonetheless highly political in nature. The union leader must above all be conscious of the general wishes of the constituents. And these wishes, particularly at the lower levels of the union structure where the collective bargaining process itself takes place, continue to be closely related to wages, hours, and conditions.

Just as internal political considerations have dictated national union autonomy within the AFL-CIO, so too have such considerations led to the complete responsibility of virtually all national union executives to at least the most pressing desires of local unionists, and to such commonly observed phenomena as the high turnover rates of local officers themselves.

It has often been said that a union "is a political animal operating in an economic framework." The story of a union that a while ago sent its hospitalized management adversary a basket of fruit with a card stating that the "members of Local 25 wish you a speedy recovery by a vote of 917 to 648" may or may not be fictitious: Corroboration is now impossible. But unions are by any standard highly "political." And no one who loses sight of this most fundamental labor relations factor can truly appreciate union behavior. Union members do have the ultimate control of their labor organizations—however much in practice union *leadership* has been the catalyst of the programs of the union—and the leadership can never ignore this fact of life.

DISCUSSION QUESTIONS

1. J. B. S. Hardman once described labor organizations as being "part army and part debating society." What considerations on his part might have led to this description?

2. It has been argued in many nonlabor quarters that it is socially undesirable for unions to take the initiative in organizational campaigns and that the public interest is served only when unorganized workers initially seek out the union. Is there anything to be said for this point of view? Against it?

3. "There are both advantages and disadvantages to AFL-CIO affiliation for national unions." Comment.

4. "The increasing sophistication and enlightenment of modern top business executives in dealing with their subordinates has led to a state of affairs wherein managements today are more democratic than unions." Do you agree? Why or why not?

5. "Unions are no less private institutions than country clubs or Masonic lodges, and as such should be no more subject to government regulation of their internal affairs than these other organizations." The present thrust of the laws notwithstanding, is there any validity to this argument?

6. Albert Rees has pointed out that it is "paradoxically true that the presence of strong unions may improve the operation of democratic processes in the general national or state government even if the internal political processes of the union are undemocratic." Explain this paradox.

7. Daniel Bell, the former labor editor of *Fortune* magazine, once commented that in taking over certain power from management, "the union also takes over the difficult function of specifying the priorities of demands—and in so doing, it not only relieves management of many political headaches but becomes a buffer between management and rank-and-file resentments." Is there any justification for such a comment?

MINICASES

#1 The Independent International

The Space Workers International Union withdrew voluntarily from the AFL-CIO in 1962, ostensibly because of a difference in organizing philosophy with the leadership of the federation at that time but actually because of personality differences between the Space Workers' president in those days and the then AFL-CIO president, the late George Meany. Its present officers have recently been assured, through informal overtures made to them by federation officials, that the international's return would be very much welcomed.

The Space Workers' current president, Homer T. Molloy, and a definite majority of the international's twenty-four-member executive board see no particular advantage in reaffiliating and are therefore inclined to let the union remain independent. But the board does vote unanimously to allow its popular First Vice President George C. Adams, who strongly favors a return to the federation, speak in defense of his position at its next meeting (scheduled for one month from now). In private conversation, however, Molloy warns Adams that "you don't stand a prayer, George, unless you can come up with some new arguments for reaffiliation: We've heard all the old ones."

What case, if you were Adams, would you build at the board meeting?

#2 Qualifications for Union Office

In a 1977 decision[*] involving the United Steelworkers of America, the U.S. Supreme Court by a split vote upset a union rule requiring candidates for local union office to have attended at least one-half of a local's regular meetings for the three years preceding the election. Under the union's rule, 96.5 percent of the members of the local were disqualified from union office. In its decision, the high court stressed that national labor legislation (and specifically the Landrum-Griffin Act of 1959) was designed to promote union democracy without interfering unduly with union internal affairs. It said:

> Applying these principles to this case, we conclude that...the anti-democratic effects of the meeting attendance rule outweighs the interests urged in its support.... An attendance requirement that results in the exclusion of 96.5 percent of the members from candidacy for union office hardly seems to be a "reasonable qualification" (as required by Landrum-Griffin) consistent with the goal of free and democratic elections. A requirement having that result obviously severely restricts the free choice of the membership in selecting their leaders.

The minority of the Court believed the attendance rule to be a reasonable qualification. It criticized the majority for using a statistical test. The rule was reasonable, it said, because it could encourage attendance at meetings, guarantee that candidates for office had a meaningful interest in the union, and assure that the candidates had a chance to become informed about union affairs.

[*]*Local 3489, United Steelworkers* v. *Usery*, 429 U.S. 305 (1977).

Do you agree with the majority or the minority here, and, in either case, why?

NOTES

[1]A number of such "independents" nonetheless belong to the AFL-CIO as federal locals.

[2]*Washington Post,* October 14, 1973, Sec. C, p. 1.

[3]A slight irony to this is the fact that Reagan was the first U.S. chief executive who was at one time a union president. He was head of the Screen Actors Guild from 1947 to 1952 and again in 1959.

[4]*Business Week,* November 4, 1985, p. 92.

[5]*Ibid.*

[6]*Ibid.*

[7]A major exception to all these remarks involves craft unions in local product market industries; here, local business agents are normally elected to perform such duties.

[8]In this regard, it should also be appreciated that striking workers usually have income sources beyond the aid that they might receive from their own union. Some get welfare payments. Some have working spouses, and/or they themselves can rather easily find full-time or part-time jobs. In two states—New York and Rhode Island—strikers are eligible for unemployment compensation. And while it can hardly be called an income source, the fact that this is, in addition, the age of widespread charge accounts must also be placed into the equation.

[9]*New York Times,* July 19, 1977, p. 22.

[10]*New York Times,* January 7, 1982, Sec. A, p. 18.

[11]*Wall Street Journal,* July 28, 1980, p. 13.

[12]*Wall Street Journal,* March 24, 1992, p. A16.

[13]*New York Times,* December 15, 1991, p. 46.

[14]*Business Week,* May 4, 1992, p. 142.

[15]*Time,* January 6, 1992, p. 86.

[16]Wilfrid Sheed, "What Ever Happened to the Labor Movement?" *Atlantic,* July 1973, p. 62. Abel was president of the union until June 1977, when he retired.

[17]Karen S. Koziara, Mary I. Bradley, and David A. Pierson, "Becoming a Union Leader: The Path to Local Office," *Monthly Labor Review,* February 1982, p. 46.

SELECTED REFERENCES

Brill, Steven, *The Teamsters.* New York: Simon & Schuster, 1978.

Bullush, Jewel, and Bernard Bullush, *Union Power in New York.* New York: Praeger, 1984.

Caddy, Douglas, *The Hundred Million Dollar Payoff: How Big Labor Buys Its Democrats.* New Rochelle, N.Y.: Arlington House, 1979.

Chitayat, Gideon, *Trade Union Mergers and Labor Conglomerates.* New York: Praeger, 1979.

Clark, Paul F., *The Miners' Fight for Democracy: Arnold Miller and the Reform of the United Mine Workers.* Ithaca, N.Y.: ILR Press, Cornell University, 1981.

Daniels, Gene, et al., *Labor Guide to Local Union Leadership.* Englewood Cliffs, N.J.: Prentice Hall, 1986.

Estey, Marten, *The Unions: Structure, Development, and Management* (3rd ed.). New York: Harcourt Brace Jovanovich, 1981.

Greenstone, J. David, *Labor in American Politics.* Chicago: University of Chicago Press, 1977.

Hall, Burton H., ed., *Autocracy and Insurgency in Organized Labor.* New Brunswick, N.J.: Transaction Books, 1972.

Herling, John, *The Right to Challenge: People and Power in the Steelworkers Union.* New York: Harper & Row, 1972.

Hutchinson, John, *The Imperfect Union: A History of Corruption in American Trade Unions.* New York: Dutton, 1972.

Matthiessen, Peter, *Sal Si Puedes: Cesar Chavez and the New American Revolution.* New York: Random House, 1969.

Nash, Allan, *The Union Steward: Duties, Rights and Status.* Ithaca, N.Y.: ILR Press, Cornell University, 1977.

Roth, Herrick, *Labor: America's Two-Faced Movement.* New York: Petrocelli/Charter, 1975.

Seidman, Joel, ed., *Trade Union Government and Collective Bargaining.* New York: Praeger, 1970.

Wallihan, Jim, *Union Government and Organization.* Washington, D.C.: Bureau of National Affairs, 1985.

At the Bargaining Table

■ Why collective bargaining is a two-way street

■ Why Boulwarism has both succeeded and failed as a bargaining technique, and why it's not necessarily now dead at all

■ Some further complexities: the current healths of both the economy and the industry, technology, the relative strengths of the parties, union politics, union rivalries, management heterogeneity, and the role of personality

However much specific unions may differ, virtually all of them share at least the same primary objective. Whatever in the way of concrete demands may be sought from the employer, the union's major goal is to negotiate with the latter a written agreement covering both employment conditions and the union-management relationship itself on terms that are acceptable to the union. But the employer, too, must be able to live with these terms, and it is because of this second requirement that bargaining sessions almost unavoidably contain stresses and strains; more for one party—not only in the economic areas of the contract but, as will be seen, in many of the so-called "institutional" and "administrative" areas—all but invariably means less for the other. Moreover, the labor-management tensions are *recurrent* in their nature, since contracts are regularly renegotiated—most commonly, today, every two or three years. No contractual issue can thus ever be said to have been permanently resolved.

There is always a certain glamour to any interorganizational bargaining situation, particularly when such conflicts as those above can be anticipated. Labor-management negotiations constitute no exception to this rule, and, indeed, the process of arriving at a labor relations agreement has been viewed in a number of colorful ways.

For example, Dunlop and Healy have pointed out that the labor contract negotiation process can be depicted as (1) a poker game, with the largest pots going to those who combine deception, bluff, and luck, or the ability to come up with a strong hand on the occasions on which they are challenged or "seen" by the other side; (2) an exercise in power politics, with the relative strengths of the parties being decisive; and (3) a debating society, marked by both rhetoric and name calling. They have also noted that what is done at the union-management bargaining table has, at other times, been caricatured in a somewhat less dramatic way—as (4) a "rational process," with both sides remaining completely flexible and willing to be persuaded only when all the facts have been dispassionately presented.[1]

In practice, it is likely that *all* these characteristics have marked most negotiations over a period of time. Occasionally, indeed, one such description seems to be extremely apt. Some bargaining sessions within the automobile industry have had all the attributes of the poker game except that the "losers" and "winners" have not been quite as easily identifiable. No one present at negotiations between the Teamsters and representatives of the over-the-road trucking companies, until recent years at least, could fail to be impressed by the far greater economic strength of the union. There are those who see a parallel between bargaining in the men's clothing industry and debating society activities. And the General Electric Company for years prided itself on its firm resolution to "let the facts govern," although its unions strongly disagreed that GE in fact adhered to this policy.[2]

Nor, since bargaining will always by its very nature pit the conflicting interests of the two parties against each other, is there any reason to expect any of these factors to die out. The increasing "maturity" of collective bargaining implies enlargement of the rational process, but it is doubtful that there can ever be such a thing as complete escape from the other elements.

Moreover, a number of additional factors will also, almost inevitably, have a bearing upon the conduct of the negotiations. Items such as the personalities and training of the negotiators, the history of labor relations between the union and management, and the economic environment operate to influence what happens at the bargaining table.

Some negotiators try to bluff or outsmart the other side; others would never even think of employing such tactics. Some employer or union representatives try to dictate a labor contract on a unilateral basis—"take it or else"—but most bargainers recognize that such an approach is ultimately self-defeating. In most instances, unions presenting their original proposals will demand much more than they actually intend to get, and managements' first counterproposals are usually much lower than the employers are actually prepared to offer. In other situations, however, managements and unions do not engage in these practices to any appreciable extent, and original proposals and counterproposals are relatively realistic. Representatives of employers and labor organizations differ in education, experience, and labor relations philosophy.

There are still other sources of variation. In some negotiations, the predominant feature might be union factionalism; in others, disagreement between management officials concerning objectives and policies. The history of labor relations in one situation might reveal that each side has had implicit faith in the other. In other negotiations, because of past experience, the bargaining might be conducted in a climate of mutual distrust, suspicion, and even hatred. Certainly, if the objective of the parties is to find a solution to their mutual problems on the basis of rationality and fairness, the negotiations will be conducted in an atmosphere quite different from one in which the fundamental objective of the union is to "put management in its place" or in which the chief objective of the employer is to weaken or even destroy the union. All these factors, as well as others, will have a profound influence upon the conduct of collective bargaining negotiations.

Two other preliminary remarks are in order. First, because so many variables do have a bearing upon the negotiations, a portion of the following discussion highlights some procedural practices that might help to reduce friction between employers and unions, to minimize the possibility of strikes, and to promote better labor relations. Nonetheless, if labor relations have been harmonious in the past, and if negotiations have been conducted with a minimum of discord, there is little reason to change procedures. "Let sleeping dogs lie" is a sound principle of collective bargaining negotiations. These observations should be kept in mind throughout the following discussion.

Second, there has been a marked change in the general atmosphere of negotiations in relatively recent years. Thirty-five years ago, the typical collective bargaining session involved a tussle between table-pounding, uninformed, and generally ill-equipped people. The side that came out better was often the one whose representatives shouted louder or that could use overt power threats more effectively. And each side's taking the adamant position of "take it or else" was frequently a foregone conclusion.

At present, however, collective bargaining is most commonly an orderly process in which employee, employer, and union problems are discussed relatively rationally and settled more or less on the basis of facts. There is less and less place in modern collective bargaining sessions for emotionalism, name calling, table pounding, and the like. Not many negotiators use trickery; distortion, misrepresentation, and deceit are not dominant characteristics. Advantages gained through such devices are temporary, and the side that sinks to such low levels of behavior can expect the same from the other party. Such tactics will merely serve to produce bad labor relations and to encourage the possibility of industrial strife. Certainly, one objective of collective bargaining sessions should be the promotion of rational and harmonious relations between employers and unions. To achieve this state of affairs, those to whom negotiations are entrusted should have the traits of patience, trustworthiness, friendliness, integrity, and fairness. If each party recognizes the possibility that it may be mistaken and the other side right, a long stride will be taken in the achievement of successful collective bargaining relations.

PREPARATION FOR NEGOTIATIONS

By far the major prerequisite for modern collective bargaining sessions is preparation for the negotiations. Both sides normally start to prepare for the bargaining table long before the current contract is scheduled to expire, and in recent years the time allotted for such planning has steadily lengthened. Six months or even a year for this purpose has become increasingly observable in both union and management quarters.

The now general recognition of the need for greater preparation time rests on the previously cited fact that contents of the "typical" labor agreement have undergone a major transformation in the comparatively recent past. In recognizing and attempting to accommodate new goals of the parties, contracts have steadily become more complex in the issues they treat. (Exhibit 5-1, the Table of Contents for the current bargaining agreement between United Food and Commercial Workers Local 56 and the Packaged Convenience Foods Division of the General Foods Corporation, indicates the wide range of topics now dealt with by the typical contract. Exhibit 5-2, the Index to the present contract between the National Association of Flight Standards Employees and the U.S. Department of Transportation, shows a few unique issues as well as a far larger number of now-standard ones.)

Take, for example, wage clauses—which have appeared in almost all contracts since the days of the earliest unions. Today, they make anything but easy reading. Where once such clauses noted the schedule of wages (generally the same for all workers within extremely broad occupational categories) and the hours to be worked for these wages, and usually little more than this, over the past few years they have become both far lengthier and considerably more complicated. Today, subsections relating to labor-

EXHIBIT 5–1 Table of Contents from Current Bargaining Agreement between the United Food and Commercial Workers Local 56 and the Packaged Convenience Food Division of the General Foods Corp.

TABLE OF CONTENTS

TABLE OF CONTENTS

EXHIBIT 5–2 Index to the Present Contract between the National Association of Flight Standards Employees and the U.S. Department of Transportation

grade job classifications, rate ranges, pay steps within labor grades, differentials for undesirable types of work, pay guarantees for employees who are asked to report to work when no work is available for them, and a host of other subjects are commonplace in contracts. Moreover, most of these subsections spell out their methods of operation in detail.

Nor can the question of hours any longer be cavalierly disposed of. The extension of premium pay for work on undesirable shifts, holidays, Saturdays, and Sundays has increased the room for further bargaining. In addition, the contract must resolve the question of remuneration for hours worked in excess of a "standard" day or week: All nonexempt workers in interstate commerce today receive, by law, time-and-one-half pay after forty hours in a single week, but an increasing number of contracts have more liberal arrangements from the worker's viewpoint. And having opened these issues to the bargaining process, the parties must now anticipate a whole Pandora's box of further related issues: Do workers qualify for the Sunday premium when they have not previously worked the full weekly schedule? Where employees are normally required for continuous operations or are otherwise regularly needed for weekend work (firefighters, maintenance workers, and watchmen in certain operations, for example), can they collect overtime for work beyond the standard week? The bargainers on both the labor and the management side must prepare their answers, and their defenses of these answers, to such questions and many similar ones; all may reasonably be expected to arise during the actual bargaining. And this necessity for anticipation is no less true merely because a previous contract has dealt with these matters, for each party can count on the other's lodging requests for modifications of the old terms in the negotiations.

The same can be said concerning the wide range of employee benefits, from paid vacations to pension plans, which have increased dramatically over the past two decades. This benefit list promises to become even lengthier. Job insecurity in an age of rampant competition and changing market demands should lead to increased income-security devices. Collectively bargained profit-sharing plans have received some recent impetus as either partial or total substitutes for wage increases at such companies as General Motors, Ford, Uniroyal, and Navistar and may now—after years of achieving only a foothold in industry—realistically be expected to spread. But it is even more likely that the continuous liberalization in the existing benefits, and the attendant costs and administrative complexities involved in all of them that have marked the history of each since its original negotiation, will continue. No one is more aware of this fact than the experienced labor relations negotiator.

Finally, increasingly thorny problems have arisen at the bargaining table regarding the so-called "administrative clauses" of the contract. These provisions deal with such issues as seniority rights, discipline, rest periods, work-crew and work-load sizes, and a host of similar subjects that vary in importance with the specific industry. All these topics involve, directly or indirectly, employment opportunities; and, therefore, treatment of them has become ever more complicated in a competitive industrial world that pits a management drive for greater efficiency and flexibility against a commensurately accelerated union search for increased job security.

Fuller discussion of all these areas is reserved for Chapters 7 through 10. Even the cursory treatment offered here, however, offers ample evidence that bargaining the "typical" contract necessitates far more sophistication than in an earlier, less technical age. Labor agreements can no longer be reduced to the backs of envelopes, and ever-more-specialized subjects confront labor negotiators. Accordingly, the need for thorough and professional preparation well in advance of the bargaining is no longer seriously questioned by any alert union or management.

In today's increasingly data-conscious society, much general information can aid the parties in their advance planning. The U.S. Department of Labor's Bureau of Labor Statistics is a prolific issuer of information relating to wage, employee benefit, and administrative clause practices—and not only on a national basis but for many specific regions, industries, and cities. Many employer groups stand ready to furnish managers with current and past labor contracts involving the same union with which they will be bargaining, as well as other relevant knowledge. International unions perform the same kind of function for their local unions and other subsidiary units where the bargaining will be on a subinternational basis. (Exhibits 5–3 and 5–4 from the Newspaper Guild's major publication, illustrate some of that union's handiwork in this regard, and Exhibit 5-5 shows the wide range of activities embraced by the Research Department of the Association of Flight Attendants.) And for both parties there is also no shortage of facts emanating from such other sources as the Federal Reserve Board, the U.S. Department of Commerce, private research groups, and various state and local public agencies.

Each bargaining party may also find it advisable to procure and analyze information that is more specifically tailored to its needs in the forthcoming negotiations. Most larger unions and almost all major corporations today enlist their own research departments in the cause of such special data gathering as the making of community wage surveys. On occasion, outside experts may also be recruited to make special studies for one of the parties; much of the bargaining stance taken by the Maintenance of Way Employees not long ago, for example, rested on a painstaking analysis of employment trends in that sector of railroading, conducted at union expense by a highly respected University of Michigan professor. Many managements have also made major use of the research services of academicians and other outsiders on an ad hoc basis. In multiemployer bargaining situations, whether or not an official employers' association actually handles the negotiations, the same premium on authoritative investigation has become increasingly visible.

The computer has now also become an invaluable assistant to both parties in these preparations. As one management organization a while ago informed its clients in this regard:

> With programmed information on wages, workers, and various economic scenarios, the computer has raised the calculation of contract costs to a fine art. Negotiators can approach the bargaining table with accurate knowledge of the cost of each of their proposals. Perhaps even more important...costs can be calculated in minutes instead of hours or even days. As a result, negotiators can consider many options in a short period of time, can work with reasonable assurance that hidden costs will not show up at a later date, and can avoid many of the delays which painstaking cost calculations created in the past.[3]

The list of uses to which such research can be put is literally endless. Depending upon its accuracy and stamp of authority, it can be used to support any stand, from a company's avowal that certain pension concessions would make it "noncompetitive" to a union's demand for increased cost-of-living adjustments. The management may find support for a desired subcontracting clause in the revelation that the union has been willing to grant the same clause to other employers. The union may gain points in its argument for a larger wage increase by mustering the bright outlook for

EXHIBIT 5–3

Library minimums for dailies, wire services

Top and flat minimum-pay rates for a variety of Guild-covered jobs in the libraries of daily newspapers and wire services in the United States, Canada and Puerto Rico as of March 1 ranged to as much as $1,259 a week ($65,468 a year), according to information from TNG's Collective Bargaining Dept.

The highest of the rates was for chief librarian at the New York Times. The lowest was $220.70 a week ($11,476.40 year) at the Terre Haute Tribune-Star.

Fifty-three percent (105) of the 196 rates were $500 a week or more ($26,000 a year). Forty-one percent (82) were $550 a week or more ($28,600 a year). Thirty percent (60) were $600 a week or more ($31,200); nearly a quarter of the rates (48, 24%) were $650 or more a week ($33,800); and 17% (35) were $700 a week or more ($36,400).

Top and flat minimum-pay rates are listed for employees at 113 daily newspapers and two wire services. Deferred increases and raises from settlements effective since March 1 are not reflected in the list. The listings are in the currencies of the country in which the affected employees and their employers are located, i.e. U.S. dollars for rates in the United States and Canadian dollars for Canadian rates.

Newspaper—Job Titles	Minimum—Exp.
New York Times	
Chief librarian	$1,259.00—6 mo.
Researcher/librarian	991.19—4 yrs.
Asst. reference librarian	797.69—3 yrs.
Morgue indexer, morgue picture indexer	753.49—3 yrs.
Morgue counter asst., program documentation library clerk	713.63—3 yrs.
Vancouver Sun and Province	
Librarian	1,055.35—flat
Library asst. I	722.03—flat
Library asst. II	661.64—1 yr.
Hamilton Spectator*	
Head Librarian	1,039.00—flat
Asst. librarian	614.00—2 yrs.
Library clerk	493.00—2 yrs.
Toronto Star*	
Librarian	$1,028.34—5 yrs.
Asst. librarian	851.20—3 yrs.
Library asst.	679.86—4 yrs.
Clerk I	632.17—3 yrs.
Clerk II	556.04—3 yrs.
Toronto Globe and Mail	
Asst. librarian	984.33—4 yrs.
Librarian asst.	701.09—4 yrs.
Clerk	561.91—3 yrs.
Ottawa Citizen	
Librarian	956.19—5 yrs.
Asst. librarian	663.64—2 yrs.
St. Paul Pioneer Press	
Head librarian	942.70—flat
Library asst.	543.91—4 yrs.
New York Daily News	
Head asst. librarian	913.17—3 yrs.
Library reader, library technician	664.77—3 yrs.
Asst. librarian	612.47—3 yrs.
Library file clerk	519.33—3 yrs.
St. Louis Post-Dispatch	
Head librarian reference dept.	897.85—5 yrs.
Asst. librarian reference dept.	670.77—5 yrs.
Reference dept. librarian .	519.63—4 yrs.
Montreal Gazette	
Librarian	889.00—4 yrs.
Asst. librarian	669.00—3 yrs.
Clerk library	564.00—3 yrs.
Buffalo News	
Librarian	872.40—flat
Library asst.	429.42—5 yrs.
Washington Post	
Librarian	860.70—3 yrs.
Asst. librarian, researcher	510.60—3 yrs.
Victoria Times-Colonist	
Asst. librarian	849.09—1 yr.
Library asst. II (indexing) .	658.60—flat
Library asst. I	581.22—2 yrs.
San Francisco Chronicle and Examiner	
Head librarian	846.51—flat
Asst. head librarian	706.56—2 yrs.
Librarian	632.43—4 yrs.
Librarian (marker) (Examiner)	558.32—2 yrs.
Boston Herald	
Librarian	831.11—1 yr.
Clerk	491.96—3 yrs.
Toledo Blade	
Head librarian	824.08—flat
Librarian I	571.98—3 yrs.
Librarian II	542.01—3 yrs.
Denver: Rocky Mountain News*	
Librarian	823.00—5 yrs.
Asst. librarian	461.00—4 yrs.
Long Beach Press-Telegram	
Head librarian	817.48—flat
Library clerk	534.79—3 yrs.
Providence Journal-Bulletin	
Asst. librarian	810.19—2 yrs.
Library asst.	494.40—3 yrs.
Santa Rosa (Calif.) Press Democrat	
Head librarian	780.37—6 yrs.
Asst. librarian	522.50—2 yrs.
Canadian Press	
Librarian	750.22—3 yrs.
Library assts.	490.83—2 yrs.
Denver Post	
Librarian	738.00—5 yrs.
Asst. librarian	579.00—3 yrs.
Research asst.	435.00—3 yrs.
Library tech. III	461.00—3 yrs.
Library tech. II	390.00—3 yrs.
Library tech. I	353.00—3 yrs.
Manchester Union Leader*	
Chief librarian	720.75—1 yr.
Librarian	525.62—2 yrs.
Philadelphia Inquirer and Daily News	
Classifier	718.74—4 yrs.
Library asst.	583.13—5 yrs.
Chicago Sun-Times	
Reference librarian	704.90—5 yrs.
Library classifier, library asst.	598.49—4 yrs.
San Jose Mercury-News	
Asst. chief librarian	704.37—3 yrs.
Librarian	632.16—4 yrs.
Minneapolis Star Tribune	
Library night supervisor	702.00—flat
Reference librarian	690.50—2 yrs.

Newspaper—Job Titles	Minimum—Exp.
Library classifier & researcher	502.25—3 yrs.
Library assistant	388.50—2 yrs.
Detroit News	
Degree librarian	695.29—4 yrs.
Reference clerk	463.91—3 yrs.
Detroit Free Press	
Librarian	670.29—4 yrs.
Library reference clerk	475.61—4 yrs.
Kitchener-Waterloo Record	
Librarian	662.00—2 yrs.
Library asst.	511.00—2 yrs.
Cleveland Plain Dealer	
Librarian	652.51—3 yrs.
Library clerk	482.46—3 yrs.

Newspaper—Job Titles	Minimum—Exp.
Knoxville News-Sentinel	
Librarian	575.00—4 yrs.
Oakland Tribune*	
Librarian	560.42—flat
Asst. librarian	474.50—2 yrs.
Library clerk	321.97—2 yrs.
Associated Press	
Head librarians/news librarians (New York & Washington)	558.71—flat
Head photo librarians (New York)	558.71—flat
Head asst. photo librarians	502.05—flat
Librarians (New York & Washington)	497.30—3 yrs.
Librarians	475.73—2 yrs.
Sudbury Star	
Librarian	557.12—4 yrs.
Monterey Herald	
Librarian	553.00—4 yrs.
Library clerk	515.00—3 yrs.
Seattle Times	
Indexer	532.63—4 yrs.
Library asst. & information clerk	505.64—4 yrs.
Allentown Call	
Librarian	527.03—2 yrs.
Library asst.	443.82—2 yrs.
Library clerk	332.86—1 yr.
San Mateo Times	
Head librarian	525.25—3 yrs.
Librarian	515.25—3 yrs.
North Bay Nugget	
Librarian	523.69—2 yrs.
Primos, Pa.: Delaware County Times*	
Librarian	508.52—4 yrs.
Waterbury Republican-American	
Librarian	500.90—2 yrs.
Asst. librarian	365.35—2 yrs.
Lexington Herald-Leader*	
Librarian	500.00—4 yrs.
Cincinnati and Kentucky Post	
Librarian	497.50—2 yrs.
Asst. librarian	430.00—3 yrs.
Waterville Sentinel	
Librarian	497.00—4 yrs.
Library asst.	317.00—3 yrs.

Newspaper—Job Titles	Minimum—Exp.
Los Angeles Daily News	
Librarian	650.00—6 yrs.
Library clerk	370.00—6 yrs.
Jr. librarian	475.00—6 yrs.
Albany Times-Union	
Librarian	639.29—4 yrs.
Asst. librarian	508.16—3 yrs.
Lowell Sun*	
Librarian	638.00—4 yrs.
Library aide	411.71—3 yrs.
Baltimore Sun and Evening Sun	
Asst. chief librarian	631.00—5 yrs.
Librarian I	554.00—5 yrs.
Librarian II	509.00—5 yrs.
Windsor Star	
Library asst.	626.38—3 yrs.
New York Post	
Librarian	604.44—3 yrs.
Asst. head librarian	601.80—3 yrs.
Library clerk	350.48—3 yrs.
Eugene Register Guard	
Librarian	602.80—5 yrs.
Pittsburgh Post-Gazette	
Librarian	600.00—2 yrs.
Asst. librarian	565.00—2 yrs.
Library clerk	466.00—3 yrs.
San Diego Union-Tribune	
Library asst.	594.03—4 yrs.
Seattle Post-Intelligencer	
Asst. librarian	583.50—3 yrs.
Library indexers	521.65—3 yrs.
Library clerk	494.57—3 yrs.
Lansing State Journal*	
Chief librarian	579.86—5 yrs.

Newspaper—Job Titles	Minimum—Exp.
Waukegan News-Sun*	
Librarian	491.42—3 yrs.
Asst. librarian	480.76—3 yrs.
Modesto Bee*	
Asst. librarian	486.00—4 yrs.
New Brunswick Home News*	
Chief librarian	480.00—1 yr.
London (Ont.) Free Press	
Library asst.	476.00—3 yrs.
Harrisburg Patriot and News*	
Librarian	471.68—2 yrs.
Library clerk	327.61—2 yrs.
Brantford (Ont.) Expositor*	
Librarian	470.46—3 yrs.
Akron Beacon Journal	
Chief librarian	470.00—2 yrs.
Asst. librarian	461.00—2 yrs.
Oshawa (Ont.) Times	
Librarian	461.27—2 yrs.
Sacramento Bee*	
Asst. librarian	455.49—flat
Clerk I	426.94—4 yrs.
Clerk II	364.17—3 yrs.
Sheboygan Press	
Head librarian	455.06—flat
Librarian	343.70—3 yrs.
Memphis Commercial Appeal	
Librarian	449.95—5 yrs.
Morgue asst.	433.25—5 yrs.
Woodbridge News Tribune*	
Librarian	443.18—3 yrs.
Milwaukee Journal and Sentinel*	
Group leader	443.00—3 yrs.
Classifier, photo group leader	365.00—3 yrs.
Filer	305.00—3 yrs.
Microfilmer, clipper	288.00—3 yrs.
Indianapolis Star	
Library asst.	435.00—4 yrs.
San Juan Star	
Librarian	430.00—4 yrs.
Asst. librarian	303.00—4 yrs.
Lynn (Mass.) Item*	
Librarian	426.79—3 yrs.
Fresno Bee*	
Library asst.	423.84—4 yrs.
Norristown (Pa.) Times Herald	
Librarian	423.60—4 yrs.
Mt. Clemens, Mich.: Macomb Daily and Royal Oak Tribune*	
Librarian	420.00—2 yrs.
Duluth News-Tribune	
Librarian	417.97—4 yrs.
Library clerk	266.20—2 yrs.
Great Falls Tribune*	
Librarian	413.88—5 yrs.
Erie News and Times	
Librarian	413.23—3 yrs.
Scranton Times and Tribune	
Asst. librarian	412.81—4 yrs.
Library clerk	349.30—4 yrs.
Salem (Mass.) News*	
Librarian	411.25—4 yrs.
Fall River Herald-News	
Librarian	409.70—2 yrs.
Portland (Me.) Press Herald*	
Library asst.	409.02—3 yrs.
Santa Barbara News-Press*	
Clerk	406.75—4 yrs.
Peoria Journal Star	
Head librarian	405.00—flat
Library clerk	345.00—2 yrs.
Wilkes-Barre Citizens' Voice*	
Clerk	397.00—2 yrs.
Woonsocket Call*	
Library	395.31—2 yrs.
Gary Post-Tribune	
Librarian	394.31—3 yrs.
Brockton Enterprise*	
Librarian	394.12—4 yrs.
San Antonio Light	
Librarian	391.50—2 yrs.
Pawtucket Times*	
Librarian	371.71—2 yrs.
Pueblo Chieftain	
Librarian	366.84—3 yrs.
Kenosha News	
Librarian	363.00—5 yrs.
Asst. librarian	330.00—5 yrs.
Canton Repository	
Library	333.94—3 yrs.
Yakima Herald-Republic	
Librarian	330.97—4 yrs.
York (Pa.) Dispatch*	
Librarian	316.37—4 yrs.
Youngstown (Ohio) Vindicator*	
Clerk	293.29—2 yrs.
Chattanooga Times*	
Librarian	291.00—3 yrs.
Sioux City (Iowa) Journal	
Librarian-clerk	280.35—2 yrs.
Bristol (Conn.) Press*	
Clerk	263.32—4 yrs.
Rochester Democrat & Chronicle and Times-Union	
Library asst.	245.00—3 yrs.
Terre Haute (Ind.) Tribune-Star	
Clerk	222.70—2 yrs.

* Rate(s) from previous/expired contract.

Source: The Guild Reporter, March 13, 1992, p. 7.

EXHIBIT 5–4

$1,001-a-week tops TNG list of top, flat minimum rates for variety of computer jobs

HIGHEST MINIMUM among 108 top and flat rates for a wide variety of computer-related jobs under Guild contracts with daily newspapers and wire services in the United States, Canada and Puerto Rico was $1,001.37 a week as of March 1, according to a compilation by TNG's Collective Bargaining Dept.

That rate is for senior programmers, systems analysts and senior systems programmers at the New York Times.

Overall, 42 percent, or 46, of the minimums on the list exceeded $600 a week, and 65 percent of them (71) were $500 a week or more. Twenty were $700 a week or more, and 13 of them topped $800 a week.

The minimum-pay rates listed here were those in effect March 1 under 40 contracts, the bargaining department reported. Results of settlements since or deferred increases effective since are not included.

	Minimum	After
New York Times		
Senior programmer, systems analyst, senior systems programmer	1,001.37	4 yrs.
Systems programmer, programmer	687.64	3 yrs.
Computer operator	867.16	4 yrs.
EDP control clerk	649.54	3 yrs.
EDP posting clerk	529.17	3 yrs.
EDP tape library clerk	497.91	2 yrs.
New York Daily News		
Systems analyst, senior programmer, computer operations supervisor	946.78	1 yr.
Programmer, senior computer operator, data control supervisor	799.95	6 yrs.
Computer operator	625.16	3 yrs.
Ass't computer operator, head data control clerk	582.34	3 yrs.
Data control clerk	454.94	2 yrs.
Systems and data processing clerk	392.49	3 yrs.
Vancouver Sun and Province		
System administration	926.32	flat
Programmer	911.53	5 yrs.
Programmer analyst/operations supervisor	911.53	flat
Computer operator	814.99	2½ yrs.
Toronto Star		
Senior programmer	858.21	1 yr.
Intermediate programmer	817.03	2 yrs.
Junior programmer	706.12	2 yrs.
Programmer trainee	557.10	1 yr.
Senior computer operator	686.91	2 yrs.
Computer operator	607.73	4 yrs.
Machine tender	526.01	3 yrs.

	Minimum	After
Ass't supervisor data processing	662.91	flat
Supervisor data processing	842.25	2 yrs.
Senior supervisor	850.54	flat
St. Louis Post-Dispatch		
Senior programmer, senior systems analyst	830.12	5 yrs.
Junior programmer, junior systems analyst	620.16	5 yrs.
Machine operator	576.70	4 yrs.
Ottawa Citizen		
Supervisor of operations	823.96	flat
Operator	674.83	5 yrs.
St. Paul Pioneer Press Dispatch		
Senior programmer-analyst	796.97	5 yrs.
Programmer-analyst	663.47	4 yrs.
Programmer	631.87	4 yrs.
Junior programmer	474.48	2 yrs.
Computer room shift supervisor	688.78	5 yrs.
Senior operator	602.62	4 yrs.
Operator	573.92	4 yrs.
Junior operator	391.19	1 yr.
San Francisco Chronicle and Examiner		
Computer programmer	787.34	6 yrs.
Senior computer operator	571.01	2 yrs.
Computer operator	517.38	2 yrs.
EDP machine room supervisor	642.32	2 yrs.
San Jose Mercury-News		
Computer programmer A	787.34	6 yrs.
Computer programmer B	655.14	3 yrs.
Senior computer operator	621.89	2 yrs.
Computer operator	517.38	2 yrs.
Detroit Free Press		
Systems Programmer	758.60	3 yrs.
Programmer-analyst	631.19	3 yrs.
Computer programmer trainee	432.75	2 yrs.
Computer operator	614.54	4 yrs.
Computer operator trainee	341.50	1 yr.
New York Post		
Ass't data processing supervisor	728.40	3 yrs.
Machine operator-data processing	[1]514.05	3 yrs.
Head machine operator-data processing	[1]583.60	3 yrs.
Associated Press		
Programmer	[2]695.00	5 yrs.
Computer maintenance controller	515.74	1 yr.
Toledo Blade		
Programmer	673.03	4 yrs.
Computer operator	572.78	3 yrs.
Washington Post		
T-5 data processing programmer analyst	664.35	4 yrs.
T-4 data processing programmer	463.35	3 yrs.
T-3 senior processing machine operator	401.10	1½ yrs.
T-2 data processing machine operator	351.75	3 yrs.
Honolulu Advertiser and Star-Bulletin and Hawaii Newspaper Agency		
Senior programmer	657.76	4 yrs.
Computer operator/junior programmer	574.83	3½ yrs.

	Minimum	After
Boston Herald		
Programmer	649.50	3 yrs.
Computer operator	532.87	3 yrs.
Memphis Commercial Appeal		
Senior programmer	638.10	5 yrs.
Computer programmer	528.95	5 yrs.
Computer operator	427.00	5 yrs.
Monterey Herald		
Computer operator	625.00	4 yrs.
Eugene Register-Guard		
Programmer/operator	590.00	5 yrs.
Programmer/operator on call	621.80	5 yrs.
Data processing B	388.70	5 yrs.
Data processing A	354.30	4 yrs.
Philadelphia Inquirer and Daily News		
Computer operator	582.08	4 yrs.
IBM programmer	499.58	4 yrs.
Providence Journal and Bulletin		
Computer operator	580.97	3 yrs.
Computer room supervisor	617.54	2 yrs.
Lowell Sun		
Computer operator-programmer	579.00	4 yrs.
Baltimore Sun and Evening Sun		
Programmer	575.00	5 yrs.
Computer operator/data control A	465.00	5 yrs.
Head computer operator	480.00	flat
Programmer librarian	382.00	5 yrs.
Victoria Times-Colonist		
Computer operator	573.86	flat
Portland Press Herald and Express		
Computer programmer	556.02	3 yrs.
Computer operator A	505.68	1 yr.
Computer operator B	415.07	1 yr.
Clerk-computer input	391.82	1 yr.
United Press International		
ADP programmer	515.00	5 yrs.
ADP operator	410.00	3 yrs.
Denver Post		
Computer operator	461.00	3½ yrs.
San Mateo Times		
Computer operator	458.05	4 yrs.
San Juan Star		
Programmer, EDP office operations supervisor	433.10	5 yrs.
Computer operator	306.00	4 yrs.
Salem News		
Computer applications specialist	428.72	flat
Computer operator	403.34	3 yrs.
Mt. Clemens: Macomb Daily, and Royal Oak Tribune		
Data processing operator	414.00	2 yrs.
Duluth News-Tribune		
Computer operator	375.17	4 yrs.
Brockton Enterprise		
Computer operator	371.81	4 yrs.
Allentown Call		
Computer operator	361.49	2½ yrs.
Albany Times-Union		
Computer operator	359.00	2 yrs.
Bristol Press		
Computer operator	333.97	5 yrs.
Pueblo Chieftain		
Computer operator	329.76	3 yrs.
Yakima Herald-Republic		
Computer operator	326.75	4 yrs.
Computer trainee	238.25	1 yr.
Great Falls Tribune		
IBM machine operator	324.93	4 yrs.
Glens Falls Post-Star		
Computer technician	260.00	1 yr.

[1] For those hired after March 30, 1982.
[2] Plus $15 to $65 geographic differential.

Source: *The Guild Reporter*, March 10, 1989, p. 7.

the industry that has been forecast by the Commerce Department. On the other hand, where poker, power, or debating traits mark the bargaining, and the "rational process" of appeal to facts counts for little, the whole effort may seem a fruitless one. And even amid the most elaborate fact-gathering efforts, very serious differences of opinion, naturally, can still be expected to emerge: In negotiations a few years ago, for example, the four U.S. Postal Service unions asserted with statistics that their wage and benefit demands would add $11 billion to that agency's $20 billion wage bill while the Postal Service management's figures showed a $14.6 billion increase (for a difference that exceeded the gross national products of many nations).[4]

Negotiators who approach the bargaining table without sufficient factual ammunition to handle the growing complexities of labor relations, however, operate at a distinct disadvantage: The burden of proof invariably lies with the party seeking contractual changes, and in the absence of facts, "proof" is hard to come by.

EXHIBIT 5–5

AFA's Research Department:

Behind-the-Scenes Support and Analysis

Surveys, bargaining, informational picketing, roadshows, media events, lobbying — these are some of the many activities that go into achieving Union contracts and legislation to benefit AFA members.

You may have participated in some of these activities, read about them in *Flightlog*, or even seen them on the news. Yet you may not know that behind the scenes, AFA's Research Department is providing vital information and analysis to bolster the Union's efforts.

"The Research staff's expertise in flight attendant contract issues, corporate financial analysis, and retirement and insurance issues makes them an invaluable resource for the basic functions of the Union," said AFA National President Dee Maki. "From bargaining and organizing to arbitrations and legislative efforts, the department provides the necessary facts and figures to help us reach our goals."

Negotiations: From Questionnaire to Contract

As AFA negotiating committees begin preparations for bargaining, the Research Department staff prepares to assist the committees and their National Bargaining Representatives (NBRs) with the arduous process of achieving a contract.

Before contract talks begin, the department helps the bargaining team write a questionnaire to determine which issues are most important to the members. The Research staff then tabulates and analyzes the responses to provide useful information on members' priorities. "We had no experience with surveys," said Jacki Pritchett, MEC president at newly-organized American Trans Air. "Research helped us go over the issues, develop the survey, and advised us on how to best utilize the results we got back."

The department also analyzes carriers' financial health, an important factor throughout contract talks. "Airline managements usually 'cry poverty' at the table, claim they can't afford any contract improvements, or ask for concessions to stay afloat," according to AFA Research Director Mary Converse. "By analyzing a carrier's financial reports filed with the Securities and Exchange Commission and the Department of Transportation, the department staff provides AFA bargaining committees with an objective assessment of the company's financial status."

In recent negotiations, spiraling healthcare costs have brought severe management pressure to slash benefits. Research staffers with expertise in retirement and insurance issues help negotiating committees evaluate their benefit plans, both to propose improvements and to design cost-effective ways of maintaining existing coverage. This is how flexible healthcare spending accounts, now in place at United

Photo by Earl Dotter

Research Department staff at work (l to r): Secretary Vicki Pratt, Benefits Research Analyst Antoinette Corbin-Taylor, Benefits Specialist Laurie Borman and Research Analyst Theresa McGlauflin. Not pictured: Director of Research Mary Converse.

EXHIBIT 5–5 (continued)

and Aloha, were established. If requested, department staff will also participate in bargaining for benefits.

Comprehensive Bargaining Support

There can be many twists and turns to negotiations, and the Research Department assists at every step. The department routinely develops comparisons of pay and workrules; provides graphs or charts for newsletters or roadshows; calculates the cost of wage or benefit proposals; and provides information about flight attendant contracts at other airlines. These are vital to effective negotiations.

Department staff "is always willing to help and has, therefore, been a tremendous asset to us in our current round of collective bargaining at USAir," said USAir Council 67 President and Negotiating Committee Chair David Alexander. "They have assisted in everything from the construction and processing of a topnotch negotiations survey, to the compilation of essential industry-wide comparisons covering a host of relevant negotiating topics."

In addition, the department undertakes unique, carrier-specific projects. For example, as members at United prepared for a possible strike last year, the department researched visa requirements for cabin crews who might be stranded at foreign layovers, and determined whether London-based flight attendants would be eligible for continuation of health insurance benefits like their U.S.-based counterparts.

Arbitration, Organizing and Legislative Affairs

The Research Department also provides support in areas beyond bargaining. • With contract violations by carriers occurring more frequently, the department provides increasing support to AFA attorneys in arbitrations. • Graphs, charts and comparisons prepared by the department are utilized by AFA's Organizing Department to show prospective members the superior pay, benefits and work rules provided by AFA contracts. Most recently, this vital information helped flight attendants at American Trans Air and Simmons Airlines make their decision to join AFA. • Legislatively, the department researches information for AFA testimony, and reviews contracts to determine the possible impact of proposed legislation. Recently, the department critically analyzed FAA and management estimates of the cost impact of the flight/duty time bill.

Training and Special Projects

Besides providing insurance and retirement expertise, the Research Department trains local committees in these areas. At an upcoming training this summer, AFA members will learn more about which healthcare cost-containment measures to anticipate in negotiations, comparisons of pension plans, and proposed legislation on benefits issues. Two similar trainings in 1990 met with enthusiastic member response.

In addition, the department carries out special, one-of-a-kind projects.

• The department calculated the back pay owed to each of 127 Aloha flight attendants in settlement of a 1983 concessions "snap-back" dispute involving lost wages and vacation since 1983, plus interest. (As a result, affected members received checks averaging approximately $1,000 per flight attendant, totalling more than $125,000.) • Prior to the Gulf war, the department researched the status of life, health, and accidental death insurance at each AFA carrier to see if any plans included waivers for acts of war that would put our members at risk of working without adequate insurance coverage. • The department undertook lengthy research to select the best company and to design the most useful plan for Long-Term Disability for AFA members and associate members. As a result, AFA was able to implement this benefit in 1990.

Maintaining the Vital Information Flow

Like a computer system in a busy airport control tower, AFA's Research Department keeps up the vital information flow which enables the Union to function at its best.

"I don't know how we would have gotten along without the Research Department," said United Strike Coordinator Susan Miller (UAL 09). "They helped our Bargaining Committee refine our proposals. So much of what we requested, comparisons and other information, was part of the step-by-step process leading to the final contract proposal. During the course of negotiations, they also provided information for various leaflets we passed out on the consumer price index and the impact of inflation after five years with no pay raise."

The Research Department's work is an important backdrop to the other work the Union does, and is an invaluable benefit of AFA membership.▲

Research Department Publications

The department keeps AFA leaders and members better informed through several specialized publications.

• **Sourcebooks for negotiations.** *The Summary of Flight Attendant Agreements, The Summary of Health & Welfare Plans,* and *The Summary of Retirement Plans* provide an instant reference on how contracts and benefits compare among flight attendant groups. Single-carrier flight attendant Unions which lack research departments also subscribe to these one-of-a-kind reference books.
• **Research Reports,** for bulletin board posting, briefly cover such topics as the male/female earnings gap, flight attendant productivity, the Union advantage for benefits and pay, and airline industry trends.
• **Retirement and Insurance Newsletter,** a new publication, informs R&I committees about benefits issues.
• **AFA Perspectives** informs AFA leaders about issues of concern to our Union. Recent articles have discussed weight policies and healthcare reform. The state of the airline industry and women's special problems in retirement programs will be covered in an upcoming issue.▲

Source: Flightlog, January–March 1992, pp. 6–7 (Association of Flight Attendants, AFL-CIO).

As painstaking a task as the fact-accumulation process may seem to be, far-sighted managements and labor leaders recognize that considerably more must be done to adequately prepare for bargaining.

Increasingly, the top echelons within both union and management circles have come to appreciate the necessity of carefully consulting with lower-level members of their respective operating organizations before framing specific bargaining table approaches. Supervisors, industrial engineers, union business agents, union stewards, and various other people may never become directly involved in the official negotiation sessions,[5] and the distance separating them from the top of the management or union hierarchy is usually a great one. But the growing maturity of labor relations has brought with it a stronger recognition by the higher levels of both organizations that the success or failure of whatever agreement is finally bargained will always rest considerably upon the acceptance of the contract by such people. In addition, unless the official negotiators are well informed on actual operating conditions in advance of the bargaining, there is every chance that highly desirable modifications in the expiring agreement will be completely overlooked.

On the management side, since the daily routines of the operating subordinates require their close contact with the union, such people are in a position to provide the bargainers with several kinds of valuable information. They can be expected to have knowledgeable opinions as to what areas of the expiring contract have been most troublesome; they can, for example, provide an analysis not only of grievance statistics within their departments but of employee morale problems that may lie behind the official grievances that have been lodged. They presumably have some awareness as to the existing pressures on the union leadership, and their knowledge of these political problems can help management to anticipate some of the forthcoming union demands. They may be able to assess how the union membership would react to various portions of the contemplated management demands.

Not to be dismissed lightly, either, is the fact that this process of consultation allows lower managers genuine grounds for feeling some sense of participation in at least establishing the framework for bargaining. The employer thus stands to gain in terms of morale, as well as in information.

For the union, the need for thorough internal communication may be even more vital. The trend to centralization of bargaining in the hands of international unions has in no way lessened the need of the union officialdom to be responsive to rank-and-file sentiments. It has, however, made the job of *discovering* these sentiments, and incorporating them into a cohesive bargaining strategy, considerably harder; and "middlemen" within the union hierarchy must be relied upon to perform this assignment. Thus, business agents, grievance committee members, and other lower union officials can play a key role even where the negotiations themselves have passed upward to a higher union body, for only they are in a position to take the pulse of the rank and file.

The long list of widely varying and frequently inconsistent rank-and-file demands cannot, however, be passed upward to the international level without some adjustment. Most internationals screen these workers' proposals—inevitably giving more weight to those of important political leaders at the lower levels than to those stemming from totally uninfluential constituents—through committees composed of the subordinate officials at successively higher levels within the union hierarchy. Ultimately, a "final" union contract proposal may be placed before the membership of each local, or at least before representatives of these locals, for their official stamps of approval. And here again, the support of lower union officialdom is vitally needed by the union negotiators—to rally rank-and-file support behind the finalized union demands and to gain membership willingness to strike, if need be, in support of these demands. Aside from the fact that the local unionists may be as well equipped to help the negotiators plan their strategy as are their management counterparts, local leaders who have been bypassed in the consultation process do not typically make loyal supporters of the union's membership-rallying effort.

Finally, both legal and (on many occasions) public relations considerations now clearly demand a major place in preparation for bargaining. Specialists in both these areas must be engaged and utilized by both sides to ensure that bargaining demands will be compatible with the labor statutes, and that public support (or, at the very least, public neutrality) will be forthcoming if this is needed. The legal ramifications of present-day trucking contract negotiations, for example, have necessitated for the involved union the employment of a huge corps of lawyers, who have become collectively known as the "Teamsters' Bar Association." Through their high levels of remuneration former Teamster president Hoffa could claim to have "doubled the average standard of living for all lawyers in the past few years," although the personal legal problems of Hoffa (who disappeared in 1975, a victim of gangland action) undoubtedly accounted for some of the high statistics. For the importance of public relations to both parties in the railroad industry, one need look no further than to the myriad of full-page newspaper advertisements placed separately over the past two decades by the railroad unions and managements to state their respective labor relations cases to the general citizenry in advance of the bargaining.

For both management and union, bargaining preparation also involves more mundane matters. Meeting places must be agreed upon and the times and lengths of the meetings must be decided. Ground rules regarding transcripts of sessions, publicity releases, and even "personal demeanor" (a designation that in labor relations can deal with a spectrum extending from the use of profanity to appropriate attire for the negotiators) are sometimes drawn up. Payment of union representatives at the bargaining table who must take time off from work as paid employees of the company must also be resolved. Only on rare occasions have the parties reached a major prebargaining impasse on such issues as these, but where relations are already strained between union and management such joint decision making can be a time-consuming and even an emotion-packed process.

The latter condition was certainly the case, to cite one relatively recent example, when in late 1991 the large earth-moving equipment producer Caterpillar Inc. and the United Automobile Workers were still deadlocked in a dispute over where to hold the negotiations for their new contract just forty-eight hours before these critical talks were supposed to begin. The company was holding out for its hometown of Peoria, Illinois. The union was arguing that such a site would give the employer an unfair advantage not only in ready access to its headquarters but in the prospect of home-cooked evening meals. It was proposing instead the "neutral" location of St. Louis. Objective observers suggested that both sides simply wanted to show who was boss from the outset. (The company won in this tense battle of wills, as it by any standard won in the negotiations themselves, although only after a bitter five-month strike and after Caterpillar's threat of permanently replacing the strikers.)

THE BARGAINING PROCESS: EARLY STAGES

No manager who is prone to both ulcers and accepting verbal statements at face value belongs at the labor relations bargaining table. Negotiations often begin with the union representatives presenting a long list of demands in both the economic and noneconomic (for example, administrative clause) areas. To naïve managements, many of these avowed labor goals seem at best unjustified, and at worst to show a complete union disregard for the continued solvency of the employer. Although extreme demands, such as a new golf course and free transportation in company cars to and from work for all employees, are rarely taken seriously, the management negotiators may be asked for economic concessions that are well beyond those granted by competitors, and noneconomic ones that exhibit a greater use of vivid imagination than that shown by Penn and Teller, Monty Python, and Woody Allen combined.

Recently, for example, the local police association in Rockville Centre, Long Island, demanded from its employer municipality eighty-five concessions, including a gymnasium and swimming pool; seventeen paid holidays, including Valentine's Day and Halloween; and free abortions. And these public servants hold no record for ambitiousness. The union leader Walter Reuther used to open automobile bargaining with so many holiday demands that on one occasion his management counterpart at General Motors is alleged to have asked, "Walter, wouldn't it be faster if you merely listed the days on which you would like to work?"

The experienced management bargainer, however, takes considerable comfort in the fact that the union is, above all, the *political* animal that the preceding chapter has depicted: There is no sense in the union leaders alienating constituents by throwing out untenable but "pet" demands of the rank and file (beyond what the various screening committees have been able to dislodge) when the employer representatives stand fully ready to do this themselves and thus to accept the blame. This is particularly true when the pet union demands originate from influential constituents or key locals within the international; alienation of such sources is a job for which the employer representatives, not being subject to the election procedure, are better suited.

There are other logical explanations for the union's apparent un-reasonableness. Excessive demands allow leverage for trading some of them off in return for management concessions. In addition, the union can camouflage its true objectives in the maze of requests and thereby conceal its real position until the proper time—a vital ploy for any successful bargaining.

Beyond this, labor leaders have frequently sought novel demands with the knowledge that these will be totally unacceptable to managements in a given bargaining year, but with the goal of providing an opening wedge in a long-range campaign to win management over to the union's point of view. Only in this light can, for example, Reuther's demand for supplementary unemployment benefits in the early 1950s be understood. Much more recently, "30 and out," or retirement after thirty years of service in the automotive industry regardless of age, had a similar genesis. Originally the managements in each case essentially accepted the initial union demands subject to only one condition: that implementation of what the union wanted had to be done over their dead bodies. After several years of pondering each request (and concluding that neither involved any important sacrifice of principle), however, the employers recognized both demands as desires for novel but completely acceptable kinds of employee benefits. They returned to the bargaining table fully prepared to grant them in return for union concessions in other economic areas.

Finally, since contract negotiations frequently extend over a period of weeks (on occasion, months), the union can gain a buffer against economic and other environmental changes that may occur in the interval. Technically, either party can introduce new demands at any time prior to total agreement on a contract, but the large initial demand obviates this necessity.

There is thus a method in the union's apparent madness. Demands that seem to managements to be totally unjustified and even disdainful of the enterprise's continued existence may, on occasion, be genuinely intended as union demands; far more often, however, they are meant only as ploys in a logical bargaining strategy. They are to be listened to carefully, but not taken literally.

In fact, if imitation is the sincerest form of flattery, there is ample evidence that some managements have increasingly come to appreciate the strategic value of the large demand. Many employer bargainers have, in recent years, engaged in such "blue-skying" in their counterproposals, and for many of the same reasons as unions have (although other employers have adamantly refused to engage in this process and have even, at least partially, accepted a GE-type approach).

As a result of the premium placed on exaggerated demands and equally unrealistic counterproposals, however, the positions of the parties throughout the early negotiation sessions are likely to remain far apart.

Standing in the way of early agreement, too, is the fact that these initial meetings are often attended by a wide variety of "invited guests" from the ranks of each organization. Given a large and interested audience of rank-and-file unionists, or a union negotiating committee that is so large as to be totally unable (and unexpected) to perform the bargaining function but is nonetheless highly advisable from a political point of view, the actual union bargainers sometimes find it hard to refrain from using creative but wholly extraneous showmanship. Management representatives, too, frequently succumb to a temptation to impress their visiting colleagues as to their negotiating "toughness." And when lawyers or other consultants are engaged by either party to participate in the bargaining sessions, the amount of acting is often significantly expanded.

Even amid the theatrics and exaggerated stances of these early meetings, however, there is often a considerable amount of educational value for the bargainers. The excessive factors still do not preclude each party from evaluating at least the general position of the other side and from establishing weaknesses in the opposing position or arguments. Frequently, indeed, if negotiators are patient and observing at this point, they will be able to evaluate the other side's proposals along fairly precise qualitative lines. Thus, during the first few sessions when each side should be expected to state its position, it can often be discerned which demands or proposals are being made seriously and which, if any, are merely injected for bargaining position. Such information will be of great help later on in the negotiations.

Actually, the principle of timing in negotiations is very important. There are times for listening, speaking, standing firm, and conceding; there are times for making counterproposals, compromising, suggesting. At some points, "horse-trading" is possible; at others, taking a final position is called for. There is a time for an illustration, a point, or a funny story to break ominous tension, and there is likewise a time for being deadly serious. Through experience and through awareness of the tactics of the other side, negotiators can make use of the time principle most effectively.

THE BARGAINING PROCESS: LATER STAGES

After the initial sessions are terminated, each side should have a fairly good idea of the overall climate of the negotiations. Management should now be in a position to determine what the union is fundamentally seeking, and the union should be able to recognize some basic objectives of management. In addition, by this time, each side should have fairly well in mind how far it is prepared to go in the negotiations. Each party to the negotiations in secret internal sessions should establish with some degree of certainty the maximum concessions it will be prepared to make, and the minimum levels it will be willing to accept. Negotiators will be in a better position to bargain intelligently if certain objectives are formulated before the negotiations enter into the "give-and-take" stage. However, even at this stage it is not wise to take extreme positions and to appear inflexible in the approach to the problems under discussion. Skilled negotiators who are striving to avoid a strike—and this is the attitude of the typical management and union—will remain flexible right down to the wire. It is not a good idea to climb too far out on a limb, since at times it may be difficult, or at least embarrassing, to crawl back to avoid a work stoppage.

Indeed, after the original positions of the parties are stated and explained, skilled negotiators seldom take a rigid position. Rather than take a definite stand on a particular issue, experienced negotiators (often, where negotiation units are large, through the use of subcommittees to focus upon the major bargaining issues individually before these are dealt with at the main bargaining table) "throw something on the table for discussion and consideration." The process of attempting to create a pattern of agreement is then begun. In this process, areas of clear disagreement are narrowed whenever they can be, mutual concessions are offered, and tentative agreements are effected. Counterproposals are frequently offered as "something to think about" rather than as the final words of the negotiators. In this manner, the parties are in a better position to feel one another out as to ultimate goals. By noting the reaction to a proposal thrown on the table for discussion and by evaluating the arguments and the attitudes in connection with it, a fairly accurate assessment can be made of the maximum and minimum levels of both sides.

Actually, flexibility is a sound principle to follow in negotiations, because the ultimate settlement between managements and unions is frequently in the terms of "packages." Thus, through the process of counterproposals, compromise, and the like, the parties usually terminate the negotiations by agreeing to one package selected from a series of alternative possibilities of settlement. The package selected will represent most closely the maximum and minimum levels acceptable to each of the parties. The content of the various packages will be somewhat different, because neither side in collective bargaining gets everything it wants out of a particular negotiation. By the maintenance of flexibility throughout the negotiation, certain patterns of settlement tend to be established over which the parties can deliberate.

The package approach to bargaining is particularly important in reference to economic issues. Once the parties obtain an agreement on a total cost-per-hour figure, it becomes a relatively uncomplicated task to allocate that figure in terms of basic wage rates, supplements to wages, wage inequities, and the like. The more difficult problem, of course, is to arrive at a total cost-per-hour figure. If, for example, through the process of bargaining, the parties established $1.80 per hour as the level of agreement, they might finalize the money agreement in terms of $1.22 per hour basic wage increase, $.20 per hour to correct any wage inequities, $.19 per hour to improve the insurance program, and $.19 per hour to increase pensions. Other subdivisions of the $1.80 would be possible depending upon the attitudes of the parties and their objectives in the negotiations.

Trading Points and Counterproposals

In establishing the content of the alternative packages, experienced negotiators employ a variety of bargaining techniques. Two of the most important are trading points and counterproposals. These procedures are best explained by illustrations.

Let us assume that management employs the *trading point* procedure. The first prerequisite in the use of this technique is to evaluate the demands of the union. Evaluation is necessary not only along quantitative lines but also along the line of the "intensity factor," which requires an assessment of the union demands to determine which of them the union is most anxious to secure. Management representatives should make mental notes of these strongly demanded issues as the negotiations proceed. For example, after a few sessions it may become apparent that the union feels very strongly about securing the union shop. At the same time, the labor organization also demands a $1.50-per-hour wage increase and three additional paid holidays. Use of the trading point technique in this situation may be as follows: Management agrees to the union shop but insists that, in return for this concession, the union accept a $.70-per-hour increase and just one more paid holiday.

Labor organizations also employ the trading point technique, as illustrated by the following example. Assume that, during the course of the negotiations, the union representatives sense that management will not concede to the union demand for a reduction of the basic workweek from forty hours to thirty-six. Assume further that the union feels that the issue is not worth a strike. Under these circumstances, the union may be able to employ the hours issue as a trading point. Let us say that, along with the hours demand, the union has insisted upon also securing a union shop and a $1.40-per-hour increase in pay. After the union presses the hours issue vigorously for some time (as part of the strategy, it may, of course, threaten a strike over the issue), the union negotiators agree to withdraw the hours demand in return for obtaining the union shop and the wage increase.

Counterproposals are somewhat different from trading points. They involve the compromise that takes place during the bargaining sessions. As a matter of fact, the use of counterproposals is one element that the National Labor Relations Board will consider to determine whether management and labor unions bargain in good faith. However, under the established rules of the board, employers and unions do not have to make *concessions* to satisfy the legal requirement of bargaining in good faith: The implementers of public policy are more interested in whether or not there have been *compromises*. The union may request four weeks' vacation with pay for all employees. Management might counter by agreeing to two weeks' vacation with pay for employees with five years of service and one week for the remainder. A union may demand a $1.44-per-hour increase, and management may agree to a $.70-per-hour increase. At times three or four counterproposals may be made before a final agreement is reached on an issue of collective bargaining.

Costing Out the Contractual Changes

It is suicidal, needless to say, for either party to proceed without a firm understanding of the costs of the contemplated changes. And these costs encompass more than just the additional direct payroll expenses. They also include changes in costs that directly stem from the added payroll costs—in the FICA contributions, for example. Nonpayroll costs such as the employer's annual payments for health insurance and life insurance and nonwork paid time such as any additional holidays, vacations, or sick leave allowances must also be taken into account.

Exhibit 5–6 illustrates all of this. For a more thorough discussion of costing, Granof's *How to Cost Your Labor Contract* and Morse's *How to Negotiate the Labor Agreement,* both of which are fully cited in the Selected References at the end of this chapter, are valuable.

THE BARGAINING PROCESS: FINAL STAGES

There is almost no limit to the ingenuity that skilled negotiators use in attempting to create an agreement pattern. At more sophisticated bargaining tables, even highly subtle modes of communication may do the trick while at the same time allowing the party making a concession to suffer no prejudice for having "given in." Stevens, for example, has pointed out that

> ...in some situations, silence may convey a concession. This may be the case, for example, if a negotiator who has frequently and firmly rejected a proposal simply maintains silence the next time the proposal is made. The degree of emphasis with which the negotiator expresses himself on various issues may be an important indication. The suggestion that the parties pass over a given item for the present, on the grounds that it probably will not be an important obstacle to eventual settlement, may be a covert way of setting up a trade on this item for some other.... The parties may quote statistics (fictitious if need be) as a...way of suggesting a position, or they may convey a position by discussing a settlement in an unrelated industry.[6]

Yet, however much the gap between the parties may be narrowed by such methods, even the most adroit bargainers frequently reach the late stages of negotiations with the complete contract far from being resolved. Given the potential thorniness of many of the individual issues involved, this should not be surprising; more than bargaining sophistication and flexibility is still generally required to bring about agreement on such delicate substantive topics as management rights, union security, the role of seniority, and economic benefits. And the fact that the bargainers seek an acceptable package that in some way deals with *all* these issues clearly makes the assignment a much more complicated one than it would otherwise be.

It is the *strike deadline* that is the great motivator of labor relations agreement. As the hands of the clock roll around, signaling the imminent termination of the old contract, each side is now forced to reexamine its "final" position and to balance its "rock bottom" demands against the consequences of a cessation of work. And, with the time element now so

EXHIBIT 5–6 Costing the Labor Contract

CHANGES IN COSTS

I. Direct Payroll—Annual

Straight-time earnings—36¢ per hour general increase
100 employees
100 × 2,080 hrs. × 36¢ =

Premium earnings, second-shift established differential—10¢ per hour
30 employees involved
30 × 2,080 hrs. × 10¢ =

Overtime: Overtime costs increased by increased straight-time rate, average
straight-time rate increase 36¢
36¢ × 12,000 overtime hrs. × .5 overtime rate =

Bonus—none

Other direct payroll cost increases

Total Increase in Direct Payroll Costs =

II. Added Costs Directly Resulting from Higher Payroll Costs—Annual

F.I.C.A.—5.85% times increase in average straight-time earnings below
$42,000 annually
100 employees
100 × 36¢ × 5.85% × 2,080 =

Federal and state unemployment insurance tax
Number of employees × 4,200 × tax rate (2.5%) =

Workmen's compensation
(Total cost or estimate)

Other

Total Additional Direct Payroll Costs =

III. Nonpayroll Costs—Annual

Insurance—company portion
Health insurance, no change
Dental insurance, none
Eye care, none
Life insurance—added employer contribution
$100 per year
$100 × 100 employees =

Pension Costs
Fully vested pension reduced from 25 years and age 65 to 20 years and age
62
Estimated additional cost per year =

Miscellaneous
Tuition reimbursements
Service rewards
Suggestion awards
Loss on employee cafeteria
Overtime meals
Cost of parking lots
Company parties
Personal tools
Personal safety equipment
Personal wearing apparel

EXHIBIT 5–6 (continued)

Profit sharing

Other

Total Additional Nonpayroll Costs, Annual =

IV. Changes in Nonwork Paid Time

Holidays—2 new holidays added to 6 already in contract

100 employees × 8 hrs. × 2 holidays × Average new wage ($3.96) =

Vacation, new category added—4 weeks (160 hours annual vacation) with 20 or more years service; former top was 3 weeks after 15; average number of employees affected annually, 15

15 × 40 × Average new wage ($3.96) =

Paid lunchtime—paid ½ lunchtime added to contract

100 employees × ½ hr. × days worked yearly (236) × Average new wage ($3.96) =

Paid washup time, none

Coffee breaks, no change

Paid time off for union activity—new, one hour per week per shop steward

10 shop stewards × Average new wage shop stewards ($4.20) × 1 hr. × 52 weeks =

Paid sick leave

Paid time off over and above workmen's compensation paid time, none

Jury-service time off, no change

Funeral-leave time off, no change

Paid time off for safety or training, no change

Other

Total Change in Hours Paid For but Not Worked, Annual =

V. Financial Data Derived from Costing Out

Total increase in contract costs

I + II + III

Average total increase in contract costs per employee payroll hour

I + II + III ÷ 2,080 hours

Average total increase in direct payroll costs per man-hour

I + II ÷ 2,080 hours ÷ 100 employees

Average total increase in nonpayroll costs per payroll-hour, per employee

III ÷ 2,080 hours ÷ 100 employees

Average total increase in nonwork paid time per payroll-hour per employee

IV ÷ 2,080 hours ÷ 100 employees

Average total increase in direct payroll costs per prod. (worked) hour (per employee)

I + II ÷ 1,888 hours ÷ 100 employees

Average total increase in nonpayroll costs per prod. (worked) hour (per employee)

III ÷ 1,888 hours ÷ 100 employees

Average total increase in nonwork paid time per prod. (worked) hour (per employee)

IV ÷ 1,888 hours ÷ 100 employees

important, each party can be counted upon to view its previous bargaining position in a somewhat different light.

For example, paid holiday demands, which once seemed of paramount importance to the union, may now appear less vital when pursuing them is likely to lead to the complete *loss* of paid holidays through a strike. The labor leaders may also conclude now that, although the union membership has authorized the strike should this prove necessary, a stoppage of any duration would be difficult to sustain—through either lack of membership *esprit de corps* or union resources that are insufficient to match those of management.

On its part, the management may also prove more willing to compromise as the strike deadline approaches. Up until now, it has sought to increase its net income by improving its labor-cost position. Now the outlook is for a *cessation* of income if operations stop.

These threats, in short, bring each party face to face with reality and can normally be expected to cause a marked reassessment of positions. The immediacy of such uncertainty generates a willingness to bridge differences that has not been in evidence at the bargaining table before.

The final hours before time runs out are, therefore, commonly marked by new developments. Frequent caucuses are held by each party, followed by the announcement from a caucus representative that his or her side is willing to offer a new and more generous "final" proposal. Leaders from each side frequently meet with their counterparts from the other side in informal sessions that are more private and have fewer participants than the official sessions themselves. These are also likely to result in new agreements. And issues that are still totally insoluble may be passed on to a newly established long-range joint study committee, with the hope that their resolution can be achieved at some later and less pressure-laden date.

Thus Stevens, in attempting to develop a systematic conceptual apparatus for the analysis of collective bargaining negotiation, has examined the implications of the deadline in the following terms:

> The approach of the deadline revises upward each party's estimate of the probability that a strike or lockout will be consequent upon adherence to his own position.... An approaching deadline does much more than simply squeeze elements of bluff and deception out of the negotiation process. It brings pressures to bear which actually change the least favorable terms upon which each party is willing to settle. Thus it operates as a force tending to bring about conditions necessary for agreement.[7]

Paradoxically, the imminence of the deadline can foster positive attitudes, as well as positive actions, between the parties: Its approach dramatically brings home to both groups that each will pay major costs, and thus emphasizes the existence of a common denominator. Walton and McKersie report an illustrative event occurring during the negotiations of a New Hampshire shoe company:

> The atmosphere was tense, and bargaining was definitely an adversary affair until the lights went out. Their common fate was dramatized by this incident, and the parties quickly reached settlement.[8]

Strikes do, however, occur. Sometimes the impasse leading to a work stoppage stems from a genuine inability of the parties to agree on economic or other terms; the maximum that the management feels it is able to offer in terms of dollars and cents, for example, is below the minimum that the union believes it must gain in order to retain the loyalty of its members. Or, where rank-and-file ratification is required to put the contract into effect, the negotiators may misjudge membership sentiments, bargain a contract that they feel will be fully acceptable to the membership, and then see their efforts overturned by the members' refusal to approve what they have negotiated.

On other occasions, inexperienced or incompetent negotiators fail to evaluate the importance of a specific concession to the other side and refuse to grant such a concession where they would gladly have exchanged it for a strike avoidance. At times, pride or overeagerness causes bargainers to adhere to initial positions long after these become completely untenable.

And, in rare instances, one or even both of the parties may actually *desire* a strike—to work off excessive inventories, to allow pent-up emotions a chance for an outlet, or for various other reasons. The highly respected Roger Angell has not disguised his feelings that desire for a strike on the part of the owners was indeed present in the 1981 major league baseball negotiations, for example:

> ...many of the owners privately acquiesced in the angry cries for action, for punishment, for any kind of enforced return to an older and simpler time.... I have heard the hard line for years now, in front offices and stadium club bars all around both leagues. "These players are getting too much money for their own damned good," it goes. "These salaries are insane—they're ruining the game.... Let's stick it to them just once and see what happens. Let the season go down the tubes, if that's what it takes."[9]

Management was also widely believed to have wanted the strike that deprived Philadelphians of their two daily newspapers during much of the fall of 1985. The theory here was that the publishers were trying to break a pattern that had led to eleven strikes against the papers in the previous thirteen years by forcing a long strike that would (in the words of the chief union negotiator) "teach the unions a lesson." The ranking management bargainer officially denied this but freely admitted that:

> ...If they're going to persist in strikes, there's going to be a lot of pain for everybody.[10]

And in 1989 the managements of three Bell Telephone companies—Bell Atlantic, Pacific Telesis, and Nynex—were anything but dismayed when 157,000 members of the Communications Workers struck them. There was little disruption of phone service as sophisticated computer switches and elaborate software systems routed billions of calls and the Bells could save the entire salaries of the striking employees: Based on an average union annual wage of $25,000, they had realized more than $75 million in savings after merely one week of the strike and presumably were something less than exhilarated after that as, in various locations, the strikers returned to their jobs.

Unions, too, have been known to favor a strike to a settlement without one, at least on occasion. When 57,000 members of the Machinists Union halted work on $80 billion worth of aircraft at Boeing in 1989, most of these workers welcomed the inactivity as allowing them a needed rest. They had been under pressure to turn out one new commercial jet every day, four times the pace of just two years earlier, and many had complained of exhaustion from seven-day workweeks and mandatory overtime. (In this situation, some analysts also believed that Boeing itself was happy to see the strike take place: It would ultimately fill the entire $80 billion in orders, anyhow, since these orders were firm ones, and the work stoppage allowed it, no less than the employees, to enjoy a bit of a "breather.")

And while on the surface the National Hockey League Players Association derived little tangible from its ten-day strike against the team owners in 1992 beyond some marginal gains in bonus money for playoff games and for individual awards, many of these unionists felt that the strike still was eminently justified. After a quarter-century of peaceful contract renegotiations, they believed, a work stoppage was imperative just to show the managements that it *could* happen.

The strike incidence has been almost steadily declining in the United States since the beginning of the 1960s, and strikes today, as noted earlier, idle only about one tenth of 1 percent of total available working time. As long as workers are free to engage in work stoppages, however, it is realistic to expect that they will occasionally do so.

CRISIS SITUATIONS

It would be strange, as a matter of fact, if there were not *some* crisis items involved in *any* particular negotiation. In the typical situation, some issues will be extremely troublesome, and they will severely tax the intelligence, resourcefulness, and good faith of the negotiators. Actually, if both sides sincerely desire to settle without a strike, a peaceful solution of any problem in labor relations can usually be worked out. As previously implied, the possibility of a work stoppage is increased when both sides are not sincere in their desire to avoid industrial warfare, or when one of the parties to the negotiation is not greatly concerned about a strike. If negotiators bargain on a rational basis, keep open minds, recognize facts and sound arguments, and understand the problems of the other side, crisis situations can be avoided or overcome without any interruption to production or any impairment of good labor relations.

One way to avoid a state of affairs where negotiations break down because of a few difficult issues is to bypass these issues in the early stages of the bargaining sessions. It is a good idea to settle the easy problems and delay consideration of the tough ones until later in the negotiations. In this way, the negotiation keeps moving, progress is made, and the area of disagreement tends to be isolated and diminished. Thus, at the early stages, the parties might agree to disagree on some of the items. If only a few items are standing in the way of a peaceful settlement toward the close of the negotiations, there is an excellent chance for full agreement on the contract. Moreover, what might appear to be a big issue at the beginning stages of the negotiations might, of course, appear comparatively insignificant when most of the contract has been agreed upon and when time is running out. (Nonetheless, contingency plans must inevitably be made just in case. Exhibit 5–7 shows the many variables that may well have to be dealt with.)

At times, crisis situations are created not as a result of the merits of certain issues, but because some negotiators make mistakes in human

EXHIBIT 5–7 One Major Corporation's Emergency Plan Checklist for Strike Situations

1. Fuel Oil
2. Food Services
3. Trash Removal
4. Janitorial Supplies
5. Mail Delivery
6. Maintenance Supplies
7. Security Equipment
    Cameras and Film and Tape Recorder
    Police and Guard Service
    Keys and Locks
    Passes and Parking Lots
    Portable Radios
    Flashlights/Binoculars
    Extension Cord
8. First Aid
9. Standby Facilities
10. Sleep-in Arrangments
11. Mechanical Maintenance
12. Electrical Maintenance
13. Emergency Transportation
14. Switchboard Operations
15. Supervisory Shift Coverage
16. Picket Line Instruction
17. Observer Teams and Forms
18. Salaried employee assignments—If/When permitted to enter facility
19. Communication Tree
20. Radio Stations to listen to
21. Vendor Notification
22. Payroll Distribution
23. Warehousing Requirements
24. Mailing Lists—labels/envelopes
25. Emergency Personnel Team
26. Hazardous Material Storage
27. Fire Brigade Team
28. Removal of necessary equipment/systems information
29. Return of all leased vehicles
30. Obtain all keys from union employees.
31. Contact local police.
32. Contact fire department.
33. Check all locks on buildings.
34. Check perimeter lighting of buildings.
35. Establish location for Company-owned vehicles.

relations. For example, it is good practice to personalize the things that are constructive, inherently sound, and defensible, and to depersonalize the items that are bad, destructive, or downright silly. Under the former situation, the union or the management, as the case may be, commends the other party, by saying "That is a good point," or "The committee certainly has an argument," or "Bill certainly has his facts straight." In the latter situation, it is sound policy to deal with the merits of a situation. Thus, in the face of a destructive or totally unrealistic proposal, the reaction of the other side might be something like this: "Let's see how this proposal will work out in practice if we put it into the labor agreement." It is elementary psychology that people like being commended and dislike being criticized. If this is recognized, rough spots and danger areas in the negotiations may be avoided.

Another way to avoid crisis situations is to be prepared in advance of negotiations to propose or accept alternative solutions to a problem. For example, suppose that the union desires to incorporate an arrangement into the labor agreement making membership in the union a condition of employment. In mapping its overall strategy for the negotiation, the union committee might decide first to propose a straight union shop but be prepared, in the face of strong management resistance, to propose a lesser form of union security. Suppose, for another illustration, that a company wants to eliminate all restrictions on the assignment of overtime. It plans first to suggest that the management should have the full authority to designate any workers for overtime without any limitation. At the same time, the company is prepared to suggest some alternative solution to the problem in the event that this proposal appears to create strong resistance. For example, it may propose that seniority be the basis for the rotation of overtime insofar as employees have the capacity to do the work in question. If both sides are prepared in advance to offer or to accept alternative solutions to particular problems, there will be less possibility for the negotiations to bog down. Instead, they will tend to keep moving to a peaceful climax. The momentum of progress is an important factor in reaching the deadline in full agreement on a new contract.

One additional procedure is available to minimize the chances of negotiation breakdowns. It has already been pointed out that many of the issues of contemporary collective bargaining are complicated and difficult. Issues such as working rules, pension plans, insurance systems, and production standards require study and sometimes are not suitable for determination in the normal collective bargaining process. As contract termination deadlines approach, a strike may result simply because not enough time has been allowed for *jointly* attacking these particularly complicated matters in a rational, sound, workable, and equitable manner. All the *unilateral* preparation in the world still does not dispose of the problem. The parties are, however, at liberty to consider such issues by the use of a joint study group, composed of management and union representatives *during the existing contractual period*. At times, managements and unions may see fit to invite disinterested and qualified third parties to aid them in such a project. The joint study group does not engage in collective bargaining as such; its function, rather, is to identify and consider alternative solutions.

But, by definition being freed from the pressure of contractual deadlines, such a group can gain sufficient time to study these necessarily difficult issues in a rational manner.

To work effectively, the joint study group should be established soon after a contract is negotiated; it should be composed of people who have the ability to carry out appropriate research and the necessary qualities to consider objectively and dispassionately the tough issues confronting labor and management. These are no small prerequisites, but such a procedure has worked successfully in industries such as basic steel, and modified versions of it are also currently being used with beneficial results in the automobile, glass, rubber, and aluminum industries. There is no reason to believe that other collective bargaining parties, including those bargaining on an individual plant basis, could not also profit from it in avoiding crisis situations.

Some parties have found the mediation process helpful when crisis situations are reached in negotiations. The Federal Mediation and Conciliation Service of the U.S. government, and state conciliation services, make mediators available to unions and employers. The Federal Service maintains regional offices in New York, Philadelphia, Atlanta, Cleveland, Chicago, St. Louis, and San Francisco, as well as field offices and field stations in many other large industrial centers. It employs some 300 mediators, whose services are available without charge to the participants in the collective bargaining process, and it currently mediates about 20,000 labor disputes a year.

Mediation is based on the principle of voluntary acceptance. Suggestions or recommendations made by the mediator may be accepted or rejected by both or either of the parties to a dispute. Unlike an arbitrator, the mediator has no conclusive powers in a dispute. This person's chief value is a capacity to review the dispute from an objective basis, to throw fresh ideas into the negotiations, to suggest areas of settlement, and at times to serve to extricate the parties from difficult and untenable positions. The profession constitutes, as one of the nation's more active mediators once observed,

> ...the public or private exercise of the last alternative. It is not repression. It is not dictation or decision-making for others. It is third-party participation in the bargaining process to minimize the external manifestations of conflict and to maximize the chances of agreement. It is intended to hasten agreement in the least offensive way. A mediator's lack of the customary forms of power is his greatest asset. The power of persuasion can be more potent than the powers of compulsion or suppression.[11]

This same observer also suggested, only partly in jest, that it would not hurt the mediator a bit were he to possess

1. the patience of Job
2. the sincerity and bulldog characteristics of the English
3. the wit of the Irish

   4. the physical endurance of the marathon runner
   5. the broken-field dodging abilities of a halfback
   6. the guile of Machiavelli
   7. the personality-probing skills of a good psychiatrist
   8. the confidence-retaining characteristic of a mute
   9. the hide of a rhinoceros
  10. the wisdom of Solomon[12]

But if the successful mediator must obviously be impartial, this does not by any means demand that he always be neutral. "He is," as Walter E. Baer has written, "not merely a badminton bird to be knocked back and forth between the parties. When he thinks a proposal is completely out of line, he tells the parties so. When the situation dictates, he offers positive leadership."[13] Under any conditions, the mediator is a potentially valuable appendage to the bargaining table process when the results of that process lead to crisis situations.

TESTING AND PROOFREADING

When all issues under consideration have been resolved, the contract should then be drafted in a formal document. Many unions and managements permit lawyers to draft the formal contract. No objection is raised against this practice provided that the lawyer writes the document so that it can be understood by all concerned. A lawyer does not perform this function effectively by including in the contract a preponderance of legal phraseology. Such a contract will serve to confuse the people affected by its terms.

Regardless of who writes the final document, the author or authors should draft the agreement in the simplest possible terms. No contract is adequately written until the simplest, clearest, and most concise way is found to express the agreement reached at the bargaining table. Whoever drafts the agreement should recognize the basic fact that unfamiliar words and lengthy sentences will cause confusion once the document is put into force and may lead to unnecessary grievances and arbitration. Hence, it is sound practice to use words that have special meaning in the plant or in the industry. Some contracts wisely include illustrations to clarify a particular point in the agreement. And it is of particular value to explain in detail the various steps of the grievance procedure. The contract is designed to stabilize labor relations for a given period. It is not drawn up for the purpose of creating confusion and uncertainty in the area of employer-employee relations.

Before signatures are affixed to the documents, the negotiators should have the contract test-read for meaning. No person who was associated with the negotiations should be used; each individual's interpretation will be colored by his or her participation in the negotiations. A better practice is to select someone who had no part in the conference. For this purpose, the union may utilize a shop steward or even a rank-and-file member. An office employee, such as a secretary, or a supervisor can serve the same purpose for management. If those who are to administer the contract were not parties to the negotiation, such people should also be used for testing purposes; this is an excellent opportunity for them to determine whether they understand the provisions before they attempt to administer the document. If the testing indicates confusion as to meaning, the author must rewrite the faulty clause or clauses until the provision is drafted in a manner that eliminates vagueness.

The final step before signing is the proofreading of the document by each negotiator. Particular attention should be given to figures. Misplacing a decimal point, for example, can change a sum from 1 percent to one tenth of 1 percent. Human errors and typographical mistakes are inevitable, and the proofreading of the contract should have as its objective the elimination of any such errors.

The signing of the contract is an important occasion. Newspapers and television stations may be notified of the event. Pictures may be taken to be inserted in union and company papers. The tensions of the negotiation terminated, the parties to the conference may well celebrate. They have concluded a job that will affect the welfare of many employees, the position of the labor union, the operation of the business, and, indeed, sometimes the functioning of the entire economy. They have discharged an important responsibility. Let us hope that they did it well!

COORDINATED BARGAINING AND MULTINATIONALS

An employer who must bargain with not just one but a number of different unions can frequently capitalize upon a built-in advantage to the situation. There often exists the possibility of dividing and conquering the various unions by initially concentrating upon the least formidable of them, gaining a favorable contract from it, and then using such a contract as a lever from which to extract similar concessions from the other unions. Recent corporate trends toward merger have increased such occurrences, not only by bringing together under one company umbrella a large number of unions but also, generally, by augmenting management bargaining strength as a consequence of the greater resources now provided the company. But even without mergers, many companies have—whether because of historical accident, union rivalry, or planned and successful management strategy— enjoyed this ability to play off one union against another, often even gaining widely divergent contract expiration dates (thus blunting the strike threat of any one union) in the process.

In recent years, many unions so affected have sought to offset their handicap by banding together for contract negotiation purposes in what has come to be known as "coordinated," or "coalition," bargaining. The concept, which is still so new as to lend itself to no rigorous definition but which universally denotes the presentation of a united union front at the bargaining table and often also involves common union demands, was first applied with any degree of formality in the 1966 General Electric and Westinghouse negotiations (and has been reapplied there in each triennial negotiation ever since). By the 1990s, it had also been used by organized labor as a weapon in bargaining with Union Carbide, Campbell Soup, the major companies in the copper industry, American Home Products, Olin, and General Telephone, among others.

Such union attempts to change the traditional bargaining structure had, understandably, been received with something less than enthusiasm by the managements involved. Why, as one scholar in the field had asked, "should a company whose employees have chosen different unions to represent them open [itself up] to more encompassing strikes by agreeing to widen the bargaining basis?"[14] Ironically, however, the management opposition *had* led to strikes, and some of these had been quite lengthy. Indeed, most of the endeavors had resulted in rather long stoppages. At Union Carbide, a dozen different plantwide strikes had occurred, with the shortest of them lasting 44 days and the longest going 246 days. The bulk of the copper industry was shut down for more than eight months. One set of General Electric negotiations was marked by a strike of more than three months' duration. Nor could it be said, at the time of this writing, that particularly impressive union victories had been recorded by the new labor strategy. Generally, unions that had not previously cooperated had found it hard to adjust to a policy requiring the sublimation of their own often intensely desired demands for the common good. In addition, the uncertain legal status of coordinated bargaining had remained a force to be reckoned with for organized labor.

At the moment, cooperation between unions is, at least in the opinion of the U.S. Court for the Second Circuit (New York), "not improper, up to a point."[15] But the absence of a clear-cut Supreme Court ruling to dispose of this issue once and for all has meant that the legally permissible boundaries of coordinated bargaining remain unclear.

Generally speaking, spokespersons for those unions that have thus far used the coordinated bargaining approach seem to be encouraged by its results for their specific situations and optimistic about its general growth prospects, but at the same time they appear to be realistic in assessing its general applicability. The view of one union observer is reasonably typical:

> Coordinated bargaining is no panacea for the bargaining process. It is a tool which adapts itself to the facts of modern industry and one which can be used wisely or poorly.... Certainly, the development of the skills to use the new tool is in its infancy. With the growing complexity of corporations, the diversity of the unions that deal with them, and the multiplicity of new problems, this instrument will continue to grow and will be perfected.[16]

On the other hand, the long-lasting failure of the United Steelworkers to form a genuinely strong multiunion coalition to bargain with the major copper companies because of internal schisms cannot be overlooked as a guide to the future, either. Many copper unionists, both leaders and rank and file, have vocally preferred their bargaining here to be at the local level and have been especially fearful that the Steelworkers would force "carbon copies" of its settlements elsewhere on them.

Whatever the future may bring, coordinated bargaining has grown relatively little lately. Although trying to advance it now consumes about 25 percent of the AFL-CIO Industrial Union Department's $4 million annual budget and such bargaining does currently affect a not inconsequential 750,000 employees, IUD officials freely admit that they had hoped for greater growth in the three decades since the concept was first applied. Company resistance and union parochialism are generally given most of the blame by the latter, who continue to view the recent corporate merger trend with much alarm.

Nor is organized labor happy about another growing phenomenon—that of the U.S.-based "multinational," or corporation operating plants in various countries. For many years, unions have watched fearfully as such firms—attracted by a combination of tax concessions, lower-cost labor abroad, and accessibility to vital materials—have expanded their employment well beyond not only the borders of the United States but also, quite probably, the reach of U.S. labor law. By any estimate, thousands of jobs each week are being exported in this fashion by U.S.-based multinationals, and it is of no consolation at all from the viewpoint of displaced workers (or those who because of the exporting have never been employed at all) that "multinationals" often make huge sense if corporate return on investment is the criterion applied.

The UAW was the first major union to be touched by this threat, long before other labor leaders noted any grounds for alarm, indeed, but UAW president Walter Reuther's resulting advocacy of "one big global union" was all but universally believed to be unrealistic. Given the continuing absence of international collective bargaining laws, the wide disparity in union strengths and ideologies throughout the world, the millions of totally unorganized workers, and interunion rivalries, it still is. American labor's counterattack to date has essentially been confined only to loose consultation with the unions and union federations abroad. And if the rationales for worldwide bargaining expiration dates, global strikes and boycotts, and international exchanges of information have all been intensively discussed, after many years no move toward genuine international collective bargaining at the global level can be even remotely detected.

It is not very conceivable that the American labor relations systems and its NLRB protection will prove to be of much help to unions even though their target employers are American-based themselves (in most cases). Actions taken by U.S. unions could well turn out to be illegal secondary boycotts, and most American laws could hardly be expected to bind Japanese, British, or German workers in any event. An "unbridled and immensely powerful adversary" for unionism, as Windmuller and Baderschneider have justifiably called it,[17] the multinational is something that to date has caused only frustration for the labor movement in the United States.

RECIPROCAL CHARACTER OF COLLECTIVE BARGAINING

The fact that collective bargaining is a two-way street is clearly evidenced in negotiation sessions. Some people hold the view that the give-and-take of the bargaining process involves only the management's giving and the union's taking. On the contrary, as earlier portions of this chapter have noted, the management will frequently resist and refuse to concede some issues. And when the employer believes that the stakes are extremely important, it will take a strike rather than concede a particular union demand. Thus, one function of management in collective bargaining is to review union demands in terms of the functions that management must perform in the operation of the organization. It will presumably resist when it believes that the union demands could impair its ability to operate on a dynamic and efficient basis. In addition, most managements play a positive role in the negotiations by making demands on the union. Skilled negotiators on both sides of the table recognize that employers do and should get something out of the negotiations.

Management demands, of course, will be dictated by the character of a particular collective bargaining relationship. In some cases, for example, management will have reason to demand that the labor agreement be negotiated for a longer period than twenty-four months; that the union be more responsible for the elimination of wildcat strikes; that the employer have more freedom in the assignment of workers to jobs; that skilled employees get a larger proportionate increase in wages than unskilled and semiskilled employees; that certain provisions of the labor contract that have served to interfere unnecessarily with efficient operations or have established "featherbedding" practices be eliminated; or that job descriptions be revised in the light of changing technology. Collective bargaining sessions are normally as productive in terms of protecting the basic interests of management as they are in protecting the legitimate job rights of employees. This result, however, cannot be accomplished when management remains constantly on the defensive.

Management demands need not be simulated. Over the course of a contractual period, events will arise that will provide the basis for legitimate management demands. Experienced union negotiators recognize their responsibility to agree to employer demands that are sound and fair, just as they expect such behavior on the part of the management representatives in reference to union demands. To the extent that management and unions recognize in good faith that collective bargaining is a reciprocal process, the negotiation sessions and the ensuing labor agreement will be conducive to serving the interests of all concerned. In this manner, the labor contract will be not a dictated peace treaty but a document that will establish a rational relationship between the employees, the union, and the employer.

BOULWARISM: A DIFFERENT WAY OF DOING THINGS

It can be argued with some justification that, for all its ultimate ability to effect a contract with which both parties can live for a fixed future period of time (even on the relatively infrequent occasions when a strike inter-rupts the negotiations), the conventional bargaining pattern is a highly inefficient one. With its exaggerated opening demands, equally inflated counterproposals, and particularly its seeming inability to motivate the parties into making satisfactory concessions until the fixed strike deadline is approached, it consumes the time and talents of many people for weeks, if not months, in a role-playing exercise that is often theatrical and almost always heavily laced with ritual. Could not the parties, it could well be asked, devise a system that comes to the point more quickly and deals with reality from the very beginning? The General Electric Company has had no doubts that such a system could be initiated. It sincerely believes, in fact, that its bargaining approach for almost three decades attempted to do exactly this.

From the 1940s until the 1970s GE religiously pursued a policy of (1) preparing for negotiations by effecting what company representatives de-scribed as "the steady accumulation of all facts available on matters likely to be discussed"; (2) modifying this information only on the basis of "any additional or different facts" it was made aware of, either by its unions or from other sources, during the negotiations (as well as before them); (3) offering at an "appropriate," but invariably a very early, point during the bargaining "what the facts from all sources seem to indicate that we should"; and (4) changing this offer only if confronted with "new facts." In short, the company attempted "to do right voluntarily," if one accepts its own description of the process. It alternatively engaged in a ruthless game of "take it or leave it" bargaining, if one prefers the union conclusion.

Aided by a highly favorable combination of circumstances—chief among them the presence of several competing unions, major internal friction within its most important single union (the International Union of Electri-cal Workers), a heavy dependence of many of its communities on the company as the primary employer, and an abundance of long-service (and thus less mobile) employees—GE was highly successful with this policy, known as Boulwarism after former GE Vice President of Public and Em-ployee Relations Lemuel R. Boulware, until the late 1960s. With essentially no exceptions, the company offer in its original form was transformed into the ultimate labor contract. Constantly communicating to both its employ-ees and the general citizenry of the various General Electric communities on the progress of the negotiations as these evolved—another major part of the Boulwaristic approach—the company could point with pride to the value of its policy.

For their part, GE's unions attacked Boulwarism not only as an unethical attempt to undermine and discredit organized labor but as an illegal endeavor in refusing to bargain. Triggered by charges lodged by the IUE following the 1960 negotiations, the NLRB did in fact (in 1964) find the company guilty of bad-faith bargaining in those negotiations. And almost five years later the U.S. Court of Appeals at New York upheld this NLRB ruling, as did the U.S. Supreme Court shortly thereafter by refusing to disturb that decision. But the facts on which these judicial actions were taken were, of course, those pertaining only to 1960, and it appeared that Boulwarism itself was far from dead.

By 1969, however, other changes had started to work against Boulwarism. The long-competitive GE unions had (as mentioned earlier) been able to coordinate their efforts. The IUE itself had been rescued from its intramural warfare by a new slate of officers. The GE communities had broadened their industrial bases and hence were no longer as dependent as they had been on the company's goodwill. And the high number of long-service employees on the GE payrolls had, by the normal processes of attrition, been greatly reduced. These factors all served to lessen the company's ability to transfer its offer in pristine form into the final contract. In 1969, indeed, a long and bitter strike did motivate GE to adjust its offer somewhat, with the strike itself being the only visible "new fact" in the picture. And in the 1973 negotiations, the original company offer was also modified in the course of the negotiations. Both the 1969 and 1973 changes were relatively minor and seemed to lie far more in the packaging than in the substance, but they presaged a new approach to the bargaining.

In the late 1970s, 1980s, and early 1990s, this new approach came to fruition. Triennial bargaining sessions were all conducted without one serious accusation of Boulwaristic practice being levied at the company. And while an Armed Truce philosophy could still be said to characterize the relationship, the old "doing right voluntarily"/"take it or leave it" strategy was completely supplanted by the far more typical pattern of proposals, counterproposals, and ultimate compromises in all of these contract negotiations.

Yet there remained at GE executives who believed that the old ways, having given the company so much success for so long, had been prematurely relinquished. They hoped that Boulwarism could still be drawn upon in GE labor relations. And it is of relevance, too, that more than a few other managements had at least partially utilized the Boulwaristic pattern in *their* bargaining in the more recent past. Employers at AMF, Timken, Allis-Chalmers, J. P. Stevens—and those in the worlds of both professional baseball and professional football—had acknowledged some indebtedness to the approach even in the 1990s. Many smaller and less visible organizations had also embraced Boulwarism in these years, without any fanfare at all.

Whether or not such efforts as the latter represented anachronisms or—with the tougher recent stance of management in general—the shape of things to come, Boulwarism even at the time of this writing thus could not be entirely disregarded. Whatever its deficiencies, it was at least a different concept that, certainly in the case of one major corporation, for a time operated with enormous efficiency. Such successes, however temporary, are never totally forgotten.

SOME FURTHER COMPLEXITIES

Generalizations such as those offered in the bulk of this chapter cannot, of course, do justice in accounting for a *specific* contract settlement or strike. To appreciate adequately the complexities and variations involved in the negotiation process, one must turn to the interdependent variables that are apt to be influential in determining bargaining outcomes.

The *current healths of both the economy and the industry,* for example, have been of major effect in determining the relative settlements of the United Automobile Workers and major car manufacturers for years. In 1967, when automobile-company production and profitability set new all-time records and the general economy was booming, the management quest for uninterrupted production led the companies to grant terms that dwarfed all earlier times. In 1970, company costs were way up and sales (owing primarily to foreign car inroads) were way down at the same time that union members felt themselves badly hurt by inflation. A strike (at General Motors, the target employer of the UAW) was probably inevitable as a result, and the union, even after sixty-seven days of striking, achieved a settlement that was so relatively unexciting to its members that for a while its ratification was in definite doubt. In 1973, a rather intermediate year for both the economy and the industry, union gains were moderate. In 1976, the economy and the industry had rebounded nicely from a lean period a year earlier, and the union fared well indeed, particularly with the negotiation of an additional twelve days off with pay annually to counter any future threats of unemployment. In 1979, an average economy produced average gains. And in the bargaining of the 1980s and early 1990s, hard times unknown to the industry since the 1930s generated mammoth economic concessions (to be described in Chapter 7) from the union in its desperate quest for maximum job retention. A Rip Van Winkle awakening after many years could without much difficulty discover how the overall economy had fared in the interval (assuming that he cared to, of course) simply by learning the extent of union successes while he was asleep.

Paradoxically, in 1983, when most unions were relatively pleased to come away with wage increases of 6 percent per year, Eastern Airlines granted the Machinists a whopping 32 percent over three years—not because it was rolling in wealth, however, but because it was so relatively poverty-stricken that it simply could not afford a strike: By its own admission, a strike would have caused severe cash problems for it within two weeks.

On the other hand, the shoe industry has been plagued by consistently poor economic conditions for many of its individual employers for years, and, in the face of this variable and its persuasive logic, the Shoe Workers have shown considerable bargaining self-restraint for over two decades. And when the Brewery Workers struck several breweries in 1981, they undoubtedly regretted the actions (forced on the leadership by militant memberships) far more than did the employers: The industry had been hard hit by too great a beer-making capacity and slumping sales—particularly, indeed, involving several of the struck facilities—and, not urgently needing the plants in operation, the managements basically felt no great pressures to settle.

Even the entertainment industry, for decades seemingly immune from the consequences of national economic slumps, is at least these days very much affected, as Exhibit 5-8, drawn from the quarterly journal of the Screen Actors Guild, demonstrates.

GUILD AFFAIRS

Riding Out the Recession

BY ROBERT CAIN
SAG HOLLYWOOD DIRECTOR OF RESEARCH

By now it has become distressingly apparent that the entertainment industry is not, as many of us had hoped, recession-proof. Until the current recession began early last year, the conventional wisdom held that in times of economic distress Americans turn more often to filmed entertainment for relief from their troubles.

The statistics do not, unfortunately, support this comforting but questionable theory. Movie theater admissions in 1991 fell to their lowest level in almost two decades. Television advertising revenue, the engine that drives the network business, suffered a dramatic decline of 6.7 percent, the first drop since 1971. And more than 20 entertainment companies were forced into bankruptcy by withering business conditions. Screen Actors Guild members, for their part, faced the triple whammy of a shrinking employment base, falling salaries, and an expansion in membership which heightened the competition for work. All in all, it was a pretty tough year.

Total income under the four basic SAG contracts fell by 2.2 percent to $1.08 billion, the biggest year-to-year drop since the disastrous box-office year of 1971. Television, theatrical, and industrial earnings all declined, by 6.8%, 4.4%, and 12.6% respectively (*see chart below*). The one bright spot was commercial earnings, which rose 3.7% last year; although the number of job opportunities in commercials diminished, this trend was more than offset by the significant increases in session and use fees implemented with the new SAG contract in February 1991.

Fewer Jobs, Smaller Checks

Actors had to get by with fewer jobs, smaller residuals checks, and reduced salaries at every level. But the tough earnings climate did little to dissuade new members from joining the ranks, and the roster of dues-paying SAG members swelled by 3.2%. When coupled with the 2.2% contraction of the total income pie, this resulted in a 5.3% decline in the average member's earnings, from $12,596 in 1990 to an estimated $11,920 last year.

Actors at the top of the earnings scale were hit just as hard as those at the bottom — the number who earned over $100,000 fell last year by 5.2%, from 2,261 to 2,144. New York actors suffered perhaps the most, since the studios' production boycott of the Big Apple halted all television and film production until May. Female performers also experienced a tougher time than their male counterparts, particularly in commercials, as advertisers tend to revert to more conservative, male-dominated ad campaigns during times of economic uncertainty. All told, almost two-thirds of all SAG actors earned less in 1991 than they did in the previous year.

Fortunately, history has shown that the entertainment industry, and SAG in particular, are remarkably resilient. In the past decade SAG earnings have experienced two major setbacks: the 1982 recession, and the 1988 writers' strike. In the year following each slowdown, earnings vigorously rebounded, by 22.6 percent in 1983, and 17.7 percent in 1989. Several encouraging indicators point to the likelihood of a similar rebound in the next 12 to 18 months: the broadcast networks' combined ratings and shares are up substantially over last year; home video continues to boom; and the global appetite for American entertainment product shows no sign of diminishing.

(continued ⟶)

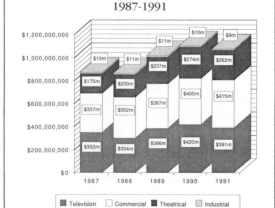

★ **SAG EARNINGS BY CONTRACT** ★
1987-1991

	1987	1988	1989	1990	1991
Television (top)	$10m	$11m	$11m	$10m	$9m
Commercial	$175m	$200m	$237m	$274m	$262m
Theatrical	$337m	$352m	$387m	$400m	$415m
Industrial (bottom)	$352m	$304m	$386m	$420m	$391m

■ Television □ Commercial ■ Theatrical □ Industrial

Source: Screen Actor, Spring 1992, p. 12.

A Chill In Film & TV Residuals

A winter's worth of reruns barely keeps us warm

A year-end report reveals that SAG residuals from theatrical films, television films and television series totalled $190.4 million in 1991, a modest 5.5% increase from 1990 (data on commercial and industrial residuals were not yet available at press time). This represents a dramatic slowdown from the double-digit increases of recent years. Reruns of television series — on network, syndicated, cable, and foreign TV — accounted for half of the residuals earned; ancillary markets for theatrical films generated 40%; and reuse of TV movies provided the remaining 10% (*see chart below*). The share of residuals generated by foreign sales continues to grow, now accounting for an estimated 20 to 25 percent of all film and TV residuals.

Residuals have become an increasingly essential component of SAG members' income. The $190 million in film and TV residuals accounted for almost one-third (29.2%) of all film and TV earnings in 1991, up from 26% just two years ago. The residual check, which was once merely a welcome supplement to acting pay, is now the only means for many actors to keep food on their tables. That is why the SAG contract negotiating committee rejected the broadcast networks' demands for an 80 percent roll-back of network rerun residuals.

There is no question that the networks had a tough year in 1991, but it is equally evident that SAG members suffered right along with them. A substantial cut in residual pay at this point would be excessively punitive, and would hurt actors far more than it would help the networks. SAG's Board and staff have always considered these residuals to be sacrosanct in the past, and will continue to do so in the future. ■

— **Robert Cain**

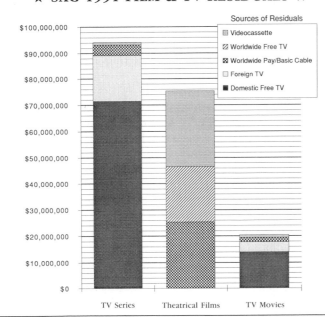

★ SAG 1991 FILM & TV RESIDUALS ★

Sources of Residuals
- ▨ Videocassette
- ▧ Worldwide Free TV
- ▩ Worldwide Pay/Basic Cable
- ☐ Foreign TV
- ■ Domestic Free TV

(Bar chart with y-axis from $0 to $100,000,000; categories: TV Series, Theatrical Films, TV Movies)

Source: Screen Actor, Spring 1992, p. 14.

Technological innovations—running a wide gamut from turbojet aircraft to computerized newspaper typesetting—have been the primary cause of many recent major bargaining stalemates and subsequent strikes, as even the cursory follower of current events is well aware. (In turn, job insecurity, resulting partly from improved technology in such competitive industries as trucking and the airlines, has made railroad workers a particularly touchy group to deal with in the past several years.) Recently, the Screen Actors Guild and the American Federation of Television and Radio Artists struck for a share of the industry's profits on videocassettes and videodiscs, something that they could hardly have done a few years earlier when these new forms of technology were barely visible and anything but lucrative.

And a 1992 announcement by American Telephone & Telegraph that by the end of 1994 it would replace as many as one-third of its unionized operators with a computerized voice-recognition technology recently developed by AT&T's Bell Laboratories for a while made relations between that giant organization and its two largest unions especially unpleasant. (In this case, as Chapter 1 has indicated, cooler heads ultimately prevailed, however, and the unions agreed in their new contract that the real enemy was the competition and that the technological changes that had already resulted in job losses of some 100,000 since the breaking up of the Bell System in 1984[18] were the price to be paid if the employer was to remain competitive in a global market.)

The influence of other major variables, all of them noted earlier in this book, can be illustrated. The *relative strengths of the two sides* can be decisive in particular negotiations as in the case of the management of New York City's Jacob K. Javits Convention Center and the several enormously powerful unions representing its employees: By the 1990s, exhibitors at the center were used to being charged some $50 (by the Teamsters) to retrieve a packing crate, $70 (by the Electrical Workers) to plug in a lamp, and a formidable $200 (by the Carpenters) to install a prefabricated booth that, absent union work rules, could have been assembled by the exhibitors themselves without tools. From its opening in 1986, the center had taken to union strike threats like a fish to land and its philosophy of peace at any cost had caused these and scores of other aberrations.

Conversely, Xerox has held virtually all the power in *its* labor negotiations, above all because it has convinced its union—the Amalgamated Clothing and Textile Workers—of its sincerity in threatening to move significant copier production overseas because of 20 percent lower wage rates abroad. In 1991, the union agreed to let the company use large numbers of part-time and temporary employees at a modest $8 per hour (well below scale) in an effort to keep the work in Rochester, N.Y., and the future will presumably see more such concessions.

Some negotiations have not been easily resolved because of *political problems within the union:* The very public rancor between the State, County and Municipal Employees' national president Wurf and the powerful New York district leader of AFSCME, Victor Gotbaum, throughout the 1970s is still a major topic of conversation when AFSCME members get together: New York area public officials with whom the union bargained were frequently caught in the cross fire between the two men. And in the 1980s, the rank and file of an increasing number of unions—the Steelworkers and Mine Workers conspicuously among them—supported the charges of their local leaders that the bargainers were ignoring local problems, by temporarily refusing to ratify their negotiated settlements. On occasion, they engaged in protest work stoppages as well.

Hostility between different unions may, of course, also cause problems, as in much of the past decade when the three biggest postal unions (the Postal Workers, the Letter Carriers, and the Mail Handlers) were for a while barely on speaking terms. (By the 1990s, the Postal Workers and the Letter Carriers had gotten together to agree on something: the irresponsibility of the Mail Handlers in their 1991 negotiations for accepting a U.S. Postal Service offer providing lump-sum bonuses in lieu of wage increases and authorizing lower wages for new workers.) This situation has made the achievement of labor peace quite elusive for the Postal Service as it has sought to negotiate contracts that would be fair to all parties.

Heterogeneity among managements in an industrywide bargaining situation may also play a large role in complicating negotiations. The team owners in major league baseball, for example, have widely varying degrees of financial strengths. By and large, they are strong-willed property holders and personal animosities abound. Some of this friction, indeed, cannot be divorced from the financial factors (for example, many American League owners harbor a suspicion that their National League counterparts—on the whole, a wealthier class—are selfishly resistant to needed changes in the game). Other rifts are not as clearly rooted to money: The owner of the Atlanta Braves, for example, is unpopular in the inner circles because of his "unpredictability." Either way, negotiating a contract that will be acceptable to a majority of these mutually suspicious owners has been anything but easy for the owners' chief negotiator, in enormous contrast to the union side where Players Association Executive Director Marvin J. Miller enjoyed all but total confidence from his more than 600 constituents until his retirement in the 1980s.

The *personalities* of labor and management representatives often have a major bearing on the outcome. The 111-day coal mining strike in 1977–1978 was surely lengthened and possibly triggered in the first place by the sheer weakness of United Mine Workers leadership. Totally unprepared in any way for the union presidency when he was elected to it in 1972 at the head of a reformist ticket, Arnold Miller by all accounts trusted almost no one, delegated almost nothing, forced many able young staff assistants whom he deemed to be "insubordinate" to resign, and generally thwarted any agreement with the coal operators because nothing could be done without his approval and his near-paranoia prevented him from bestowing this.

The painful concessions that nine striking unions granted the late British press baron Robert Maxwell in 1991 to end a five-month strike at the *New York Daily News* stemmed from a consensus among these unions that Maxwell's proffered purchase of the sick paper was the *News*'s only alternative to extinction. But the concessions could also be in good measure explained by the sheer force of personality of the swaggering, egocentric Maxwell: "He can charm the birds out of the trees," one of Maxwell's labor antagonists later said (although the labor leader added "and then shoot them").

And what was believed to be the longest strike in U.S. history was settled in 1992, when Park-Ohio Industries, Inc., announced its intentions of naming Edward Crawford—a man very much respected by the striking United Automobile Workers for his integrity and industrial relations competencies—as its new chairman and chief executive officer. (The announcement ended a labor dispute that had, rather amazingly, lasted nine years and the union shortly thereafter told the media that the *Guinness Book of World Records* was in fact looking into the situation as a precondition of awarding the parties' inclusion in that publication.)

In professional football, on the other hand, the eight-week 1982 strike clearly had many causes—not the least of them a deep desire on the players' part to move away from being the least well paid of all major league athletes—but a widespread belief by the owners that the chief negotiator for the 1,500 players was nothing if not power-hungry undoubtedly prolonged it. The owners, not exactly shrinking violets themselves as individuals, strongly resented Edward R. Garvey's aggressiveness and adamancy. They ultimately took their last offer directly to the players, undercutting Garvey's base, and were successful in this tactic.

Personalities of management negotiators have been known to trigger strikes, too. A short-lived but highly disruptive 1985 Transport Workers strike against Pan American World Airways was not exclusively due to the style of Pan Am's major bargainer—the airline's economic problems also played a role—but it owed a heavy indebtedness to the abrasive, acerbic approach of this vice president for industrial relations, C. Raymond Grebey. "He can anger twenty-eight people by just walking into the room," one observer of these negotiations told the press.[19] And one ranking unionist would say only, "You can't print what I would call Grebey."[20] (Mr. Grebey was the chief negotiator for the major league baseball team owners from 1978 to 1983 and as such is to this day also held responsible by some for helping to bring about the previously discussed 1981 stoppage in that industry.)

And while a bitter, long-lasting 1989 strike against Eastern Airlines that was waged by all three of its major unions (the Pilots, the Machinists, and the Flight Attendants) had many causes, the enmity that the strikers had for Francisco A. Lorenzo, the intense and demanding chairman of Eastern's parent Texas Air Corporation, was a dominant factor. Lorenzo, who had been able to slash his air fares considerably only by draining resources from the airline and taking a hard line on labor costs had, in the opinion of the Pilots Union president "a mind that would make Machiavelli look like Gomer Pyle."[21] The leader of Eastern's Machinists went so far as to call the entire strike "a Frank Lorenzo strike" and to term Lorenzo's battle with his union "the purest case of evil vs. good." And picket lines across the country vilified the chief executive as a "corporate buccaneer," carried placards with a bull's-eye over Lorenzo's face, and chanted, "Eastern, yes! Lorenzo, no!" Lorenzo retaliated by blaming the union leaders for all of Eastern's considerable financial problems and the personal feuding for months made meaningful negotiations impossible.

The preceding examples are only a few of the many that could have been chosen to illustrate each category of variable. In any given contract negotiation, one factor might be of major importance—or of no significance at all. The degree of importance of each also, of course, changes over time. And, clearly, many (or none) of these variables can be at play at one time on the bargainers. Contract negotiation is, in short, no more susceptible to sweeping statements than are the unions and managements that participate in the process.

The foregoing *has* indicated, however, that the negotiation of the labor contract in the contemporary economy is a complex and difficult job. The negotiators are required to possess a working knowledge of trade union principles, operations, economics, psychology, statistics, and labor law. They must have the research ability to gather the data necessary for effective negotiations. Negotiators must be shrewd judges of human nature. Often, effective speaking ability is an additional prerequisite. Indeed, the position of the negotiator of the modern contract demands the best efforts of people possessing superior ability. Today's collective bargaining sessions have no place for the uninformed, the inept, or the unskilled.

DISCUSSION QUESTIONS

1. Assume that a large, nationwide company is negotiating a contract at the present time. What economic, political, legal, and social factors might be likely to exert some influence upon these negotiations?

2. It has been argued by a union research director that "a fact is as welcome at a collective bargaining table as a skunk at a cocktail party." Do you agree?

3. Evaluate the statement that "in the absence of a strike deadline, there can be no true collective bargaining."

4. What might explain the frequently heard management observation that "highly democratic unions are extremely difficult to negotiate with"?

5. How do you account for the fact that the joint study approach still remains confined to a relative handful of industries?

6. From the viewpoint of society, is there anything to be said in favor of strikes?

7. Of all the personal attributes that this chapter has indicated are important for labor relations negotiators to have, which single one do you consider to be the most important, and why?

8. "Successful labor contract bargaining should no longer be viewed as an 'art.' It is far more appropriate today to refer to it as a 'science.'" Discuss.

MINICASES

#1 Trying to Strike a Balance

In order to bargain for the health and safety of employees, the Oil, Chemical and Atomic Workers Union demanded that several employers disclose the generic names of chemical substances used or produced, as well as the medical records of employees. The employers refused, claiming that disclosure would both invade the privacy of employees and compromise trade secrets. With some limitations, the NLRB in 1982 held that the employers did not bargain in good faith when they refused to divulge such information.[*] While upholding the union's request, the board asserted that few matters could be of greater concern to employees "than exposure to working conditions potentially threatening their health, well-being or their very lives."

However, the board also ruled here that the employers could conceal individual employee identities before turning over the medical records and also that the managements did not have to disclose the generic names of chemicals that constituted proprietary trade secrets. Thus, the NLRB attempted to strike a balance between conflicting interests: the employer's desire to protect both worker privacy and trade secrets, and the union's need for material information about potentially life-threatening work conditions.

How do you feel about this NLRB decision?

*Minnesota Mining & Manufacturing Co., 261 NLRB 27 (1982).

#2 An Advocate of Boulwarism

"I don't care a bit that Boulwarism is long gone at General Electric," says Susan B. ("Ralph") Grishaver, labor relations vice president at the Grand Junction Light Company ("Let There Be Light"). "It's a terrific way of dealing with the union.

"It's not only honest, since the employer literally lets everything hang out, but efficient—because it eliminates all of the wasteful ritual of hyperbolic opening demands and far-out counterproposals. The ridiculous unwritten rule that no agreement will be reached until the strike deadline two months or more down the road is, of course, done away with, too. And it remains completely legal.

"You tell me one thing wrong with it as a strategy for us to use in our 1994 negotiations, in fact. I think that we should seriously consider trying it."

As Grishaver's colleague, how would you advise her?

NOTES

[1]John T. Dunlop and James J. Healy, *Collective Bargaining,* rev. ed. (Homewood, Ill.: Richard D. Irwin, 1955), p. 53.

[2]General Electric's unique and controversial bargaining approach, known as "Boulwarism," will be discussed later in this chapter.

[3]Drawn from "The Impact of the Computer on Employee Relations," a paper issued by Organization Resources Counselors, Inc., in 1983.

[4]These union demands, needless to say, constituted only the opening union position. As the next section of this chapter will show, there are reasons for such hyperbole. The parties ultimately settled for an estimated $3.5 billion increase.

[5]This depends on the scope of the negotiations, however. Where the bargaining is on the local level (as opposed to areawide, industrywide, or nationwide bargaining), the business agent (for example) will very likely be an active union participant in the formal sessions. The same can be said for many management superintendents.

[6]Carl M. Stevens, *Strategy and Collective Bargaining Negotiation* (New York: McGraw-Hill, 1963), pp. 105–6.

[7]*Ibid.,* p. 100.

[8]Richard E. Walton and Robert B. McKersie, *A Behavioral Theory of Labor Negotiations* (New York: McGraw-Hill, 1965), p. 232.

[9]Roger Angell, "Asterisks," *New Yorker,* November 30, 1981, p. 61.

[10]*New York Times,* October 13, 1985, p. 60.

[11]William E. Simkin, *Mediation and the Dynamics of Collective Bargaining* (Washington, D.C.: Bureau of National Affairs, 1971), p. 357.

[12]*Ibid.,* p. 53.

[13]Walter E. Baer, *Labor Arbitration Guide* (Homewood, Ill.: Dow Jones-Irwin, 1974), p. 94.

[14]Herbert R. Northrup, "Boulwarism v. Coalitionism—The 1966 G.E. Negotiations," *Management of Personnel Quarterly,* 5, No. 2 (Summer 1966), 8.

[15]*General Electric Co.,* 173 NLRB 46 (1968).

[16]Industrial Relations Research Association, *Proceedings of the 1968 Annual Spring Meeting*, p. 517.

[17]John P. Windmuller and Jean A. Baderschneider, "International Guidelines for Industrial Relations: Outlook and Impact," in *Proceedings of the Thirtieth Annual Winter Meeting, Industrial Relations Research Association,* December 28–30, 1977, p. 81.

[18]*Wall Street Journal,* March 4, 1992, p. A4.

[19]*Business Week,* January 21, 1985, p. 40.

[20]*Wall Street Journal,* March 6, 1985.

[21]*Newsweek,* March 20, 1989, p. 20.

SELECTED REFERENCES

Banks, R. F., and Jack Stieber, *Multinationals, Unions and Labor Relations in Industrial Countries.* Ithaca, N.Y.: New York State School of Industrial and Labor Relations, 1977.

Brecher, Jeremy, *Strike!* San Francisco: Straight Arrow, 1972.

Cohen, Herb, *You Can Negotiate Anything.* Secaucus, N.J.: Lyle Stuart, 1980.

Granof, Michael H., *How to Cost Your Labor Contract.* Washington, D.C.: Bureau of National Affairs, 1973.

Hershfield, D. C., *The Multinational Union Challenges the Multinational Company.* New York: Conference Board, 1975.

Holoviak, Stephen J., *Costing Labor Contracts and Judging Their Financial Impact.* New York: Praeger, 1984.

Kagel, Sam, and Kathy Kelly, *The Anatomy of Mediation: What Makes It Work.* Washington, D.C.: Bureau of National Affairs, 1989.

Kolb, Deborah M., *The Mediators.* Cambridge, Mass.: MIT Press, 1983.

Loughran, Charles S., *Negotiating a Labor Contract: A Management Handbook.* Washington, D.C.: Bureau of National Affairs, 1984.

Morse, Bruce, *How to Negotiate the Labor Agreement.* Southfield, Mich.: Trends, 1984.

Raiffa, Howard, *The Art and Science of Negotiations.* Cambridge, Mass.: Harvard University Press, 1982.

Simkin, William E., and Nicholas A. Fidandis, *Mediation and the Dynamics of Collective Bargaining* (2nd ed.). Washington, D.C.: Bureau of National Affairs, 1986.

Ury, William, *Getting Past No.* New York: Bantam, 1991.

Zack, Arnold M., *Public Sector Mediation.* Washington, D.C.: Bureau of National Affairs, 1985.

———, and Richard I. Bloch, *Labor Agreement in Negotiation and Arbitration.* Washington, D.C.: Bureau of National Affairs, 1983.

Zartman, I. William, and Maureen R. Berman, *The Practical Negotiator.* New Haven, Conn.: Yale University Press, 1982.

*A*dministration
of the Agreement

OUTLINE OF KEY CONTENTS

- What a grievance is and why a union rather than a management generally files it

- A concrete illustration of a grievance procedure

- The flexibility of the grievance procedure and why it can lead to harmonious labor relations

- What arbitration is and why it has grown significantly as a method of resolving collective bargaining disputes

- How public policy has treated arbitration in recent times

- Some other relevant arbitration topics: limitations to the process, key characteristics of arbitration hearings, major responsibilities of the arbitrator, how arbitrators are chosen, and arbitration costs and time lag

When agreement is finally reached in contract negotiations, the bargainers frequently call in news reporters and photographers, smilingly congratulate each other (as the cameras snap), and announce their satisfaction with the new contract. The exact performance, of course, varies from situation to situation. In general, however, such enthusiastic phrases as "great new era" and "going forward together for our mutual benefit" are often heard.

There is a minimum of sham in these actions. Public relations are, as has been stressed at several earlier stages in this book, important to both sides; and both management-stockholder and union leader—union member relationships are also not overlooked by the management and union participants, respectively, as they register their happiness with their joint handiwork. But typically the negotiators are genuinely optimistic about what they have negotiated: Compromise and statesmanship have once again triumphed.

It will be some time, however, before one can tell whether this optimism is justified. The formal signing of the collective bargaining agreement does not mean that union-management relations are terminated until the next negotiation over contract terms. No contract—whether it involves marriage, insurance on an automobile, or terms and conditions of employment—is any better than its administration. And it is a safe prediction that problems—many of them, in fact—will arise involving the *application* and the *interpretation* of the various clauses in the labor agreement.

The application of the contract is, in fact, a daily problem. Representatives of the two parties normally devote a considerably larger share of their time to the administration of the labor agreement than to its negotiation. Moreover, the climate of labor relations in the workplace will be determined to a large extent by the manner in which management and union representatives discharge their obligations in the day-to-day application of the labor contract.

The source of many administrative problems is in the language of the agreement. Owing to the conditions under which bargaining takes place, many contractual clauses are themselves written in rather broad terms. The day-to-day job in labor relations is to apply the *principles* of the contract.

Many problems can arise under a single clause. A contract may limit the right of management to discharge for "just cause," for example, and an employee is discharged for talking back to a supervisor in harsh terms. Is this just cause within the meaning of the agreement? In another case, a seniority arrangement may provide that the employee with the longer service in the plant will get the better job, provided that he or she has ability to perform the job equal to that of any other employee who desires the position. Whether or not the employee with longer service *is* awarded the job is an administrative problem. Or the parties may have agreed that employees will be expected to perform jobs falling within their job description. An emergency arises, and the company directs some employees to work outside their job description. Did the company violate the agreement? Or, as a final example, the labor agreement provides that wage rates of new jobs are to be established in a manner that is equitable in terms of comparable jobs. Does a rate established for such a job in fact compare fairly with that for kindred jobs?

These illustrations suggest the multitude of problems that can arise on a day-by-day basis. Practically every provision in a collective bargaining contract can be the basis for problems that must be resolved.

GRIEVANCE PROCEDURE

Problems such as those posed above are handled and settled through the grievance procedure of the labor contract. The grievance procedure provides an orderly system whereby the employer and the union can determine whether or not the contract has in fact been violated. Only a comparatively small number of violations involve willful disregard of the terms of the collective bargaining agreement. More frequently, employers or unions pursue a course of conduct, alleged to be a violation of the collective bargaining agreement, that they honestly believe to conform with its terms. Through the grievance procedure, the parties have an opportunity to determine whether or not the contract has actually been violated. Such a peaceful procedure, of course, is infinitely superior to a system that would permit the enforcement of the contract through the harsh vehicle of the strike or lockout. Each year, literally hundreds of thousands of grievances are filed alleging contract violations. Industry would be in a chaotic state if the strike or the lockout were utilized to effect compliance with the contract every time non-compliance is alleged.

A grievance is an official complaint that the contract has been violated. What makes it official depends on the further understanding of the parties (e.g., it must be reduced to writing on Form 117), and the exact specifics of this can vary widely from relationship to relationship.

What does not vary significantly any place is that the vast majority of all grievances are filed by unions on behalf of themselves or on behalf of one or more bargaining unit members. This one-sidedness of grievance activity has nothing to do with any greater combativeness or militancy on the part of unions as compared to the behavior of management. It can be explained exclusively by the definition of "grievance" itself. Unions do not administer employee benefits, make promotion decisions, subcontract work, or discharge employees. Only managements take these and similar actions and thus only managements are most often in a position to be seen as violating the labor agreement. Managements, as a labor relations maxim has it, act and unions react—except on the relatively rare occasions when employers charge unions with such contractual violations as encouraging a slowdown or causing damage to property during a work stoppage. In the latter situations, the grievance rules are understandably reversed.

Here is a concrete example of a grievance.

Monadnock Swift, a rank-and-file member of Local 1000, had been employed by the Ecumenical Bagel Company for a period of five years. His production record was excellent, he caused management no trouble, and during his fourth year of employment he received a promotion. One day, Swift began preparations to leave the plant twenty minutes before quitting time. He put away his tools, washed up, got out of his overalls, and put on his street clothes. O. Leo Leahy, an assistant foreman in his department, observed Swift's actions. He immediately informed Swift that he was going to the front office to recommend his discharge. The next morning, Swift reported for work, but Leahy handed him a pay envelope that, in addition to wages, included a discharge notice. The notice declared that the company discharged Swift because he made ready to leave the plant twenty minutes before quitting time.

Swift immediately contacted his union steward, Harold F. Thomas. The steward worked alongside Swift in the plant and, of course, personally knew the assistant foreman and foreman of his department. After Swift told Thomas the circumstances, the steward believed that the discharge constituted a violation of the collective bargaining contract. A clause in the agreement provided that an employee could be discharged only for "just cause." Disagreeing with the assistant foreman and the front office, Thomas felt that the discharge was not for just cause.

The contract covering the employees of Ecumenical contained a carefully worded grievance procedure which provided that all charges of contract violation must be reduced to writing. Consequently, the steward and the discharged worker filled out a "grievance form," describing in detail the character of the alleged violation.

The steps in processing the complaint through the grievance procedure were also clearly outlined in the collective bargaining agreement. First, it was necessary to present the grievance to the foreman of the department in which Swift worked. Both Thomas and Swift approached the foreman, and the written grievance was presented to him. The foreman was required to give his answer on the grievance within forty-eight hours after receiving it. He complied with the time requirement, but his answer did not please Swift or Thomas. The foreman supported the action of the assistant foreman and refused to recommend the reinstatement of Swift.

Not satisfied with the action of the foreman, the labor union, through Thomas, the steward, resorted to the second step of the grievance procedure. This step required the appeal of the complaint to the superintendent of the department in which Swift worked. Again the disposition of the grievance by management's representative brought no relief to the discharged employee. Despite the efforts of the steward, who vigorously argued the merits of Swift's case, the department superintendent refused to reinstate the worker. Hence the second step of the grievance procedure was exhausted, and the union and the employee were still not satisfied with the results.

Actually the vast majority of grievances are settled in the first two steps of the grievance procedure. This is a remarkable record, indicating the fairness of employers and labor unions. The employer or the union charged with a contract violation may simply admit the transgression and take remedial action. Or the party charged with violating the collective bargaining agreement may be able to persuade the other party that, in fact, no violation exists. Frequently, both parties work out a compromise solution satisfactory to all concerned.

In the Swift case, however, the union refused to drop the case after the complaint was processed through the second level of the grievance procedure. Grievance personnel for the third step included, from the company, the general superintendent and his representatives; and for the labor union, the organization's plantwide grievance committee. The results of the negotiations at the third step proved satisfactory to Swift, the union, and the company. After forty-five minutes of spirited discussion, the management group agreed with the union that discharge was not warranted in this particular case. Management's committee was persuaded by the following set of circumstances: Everyone conceded that Swift had an outstanding record before the dismissal occurred. In addition, the discussion revealed that Swift had inquired of the department foreman whether there was any more work to be done before he left his bench to prepare to leave for home. The foreman had replied in the negative. Finally, it was brought out that Swift had had a pressing problem at home that he claimed was the motivating factor for his desire to leave the plant immediately after quitting time.

The grievance personnel reached a mutually satisfactory solution of the case after all the factors were carefully weighed. Management repeatedly stressed the serious consequences to production efficiency if a large number of workers prepared to leave the plant twenty minutes before quitting time. Recognizing the soundness of this observation, the union committee agreed that some sort of disciplinary action should be taken. As a result, it was concluded that Swift would be reinstated in his job but would be penalized by a three-day suspension without pay. In addition, the union committee agreed with management's representatives that better labor relations would be promoted if a notice were posted on the company bulletin boards stating that all workers would be expected to remain at their jobs until quitting time. Union and company grievance personnel were in agreement that the notice should also declare that violations would be subject to penalty. Thus the grievance procedure resulted in the amicable solution of a contract violation case.

What would have occurred, however, if the company and the labor union had not reached a satisfactory agreement at the third step of the grievance procedure? In this particular contract, the grievance procedure provided for a fourth step. Grievance procedure personnel at the fourth step included, for the company, the vice president in charge of industrial relations or a representative, and, for the union, an officer of the international union or a representative. It is noteworthy that this particular contract provided four chances to effect a mutually satisfactory disposition of a complaint alleging a contract violation.

All collective bargaining contracts do not provide for the same structural arrangements as the one described in the Swift case. Some contain only three steps while others may have as many as five; in still others, the time limits may be different; or the particular management and union personnel participating at the various steps of the grievance procedure may be somewhat different, as in Exhibit 6-1, illustrating a different but still quite common third-step situation. If their structural arrangements vary slightly from contract to contract, however, the fact remains that the essential

EXHIBIT 6–1

Local 117
Record of Grievance

Date: _____ June 8, 1992

Name _____ Raymond R. Mellish _____   Home Phone _____

Address _____   Status: Regular____Seasonal____

Date of Hire _____   Pay Rate _____ Job Class _____

Department _____   Supervisor _____

NATURE OF COMPLAINT (Give dates) ___I was discharged for fighting on company property. I feel that this is unfair and unjustified because the company does not fire everyone for fighting. I ask to be reinstated with back pay and seniority. _____

_____

_____

_____

_____

Steward or Business Representative ___Rupert P. Smith_____

COMPANY RESPONSE: ___Grievance denied. Rule #39 in the "Employee Handbook" outlines the amount of discipline to be administered for violation of this rule. This grievance is untimely. Incident occurred on 5/4/92.

Date _6/9/92_ **Plant Manager** _J. Wyner_____

characteristics of grievance procedures are similar. All have as their basic objective the settling of alleged contract violation cases in a friendly and orderly manner. In each there is provided a series of definite steps to follow in the processing of grievances. A certain time limit is placed on each step, and an answer to a grievance must be given within the allotted time. Failure to comply with the time limits could result in the forfeiture of the grievance by the errant party. For example, where a union fails to appeal a grievance within the stipulated time limit, the employer may deny the grievance on that basis. Where such cases go to arbitration, the arbitrator may under appropriate circumstances hold that, since the union did not comply with the time limit, the grievance is not arbitrable. That is, the arbitrator may deny the grievance on these grounds and without inquiry into the merits of the employee's complaint. (*Case 1, found at the end of this chapter, deals with the time limit problem. It is the first of twelve cases offered by this volume to illustrate specific problems in labor relations.*)

GRIEVANCE PROCEDURE: ITS FLEXIBILITY

Since management officials and union officers make up grievance procedure personnel, people intimately connected with the work will decide whether or not a particular pattern of conduct violates the terms of the collective bargaining agreement. Obviously, these people are in a favored position to make such a determination. Frequently, some of them helped negotiate the collective bargaining contract itself. Such participation in the contract-making negotiations should result in a clear understanding of the meaning of particular contract terms. Not only do grievance procedure personnel normally possess a thorough and firsthand knowledge of the meaning of the contract, but they are well aware of the character of the conduct alleged to be a violation. Grievance cases are at times complex in nature. The line dividing "lawful" from "unlawful" conduct under a collective bargaining contract is not always sharply drawn.

The local people are also well aware of the environmental context in which the alleged violation occurred. Weight can be given to human or economic factors involved in alleged violations. This does not mean that an "explainable" violation will go unchallenged. However, the grievance procedure personnel might resolve an "explainable" violation in a different manner from one in which no extenuating circumstances were involved.

Since grievance procedure personnel are closely associated with the circumstances, they are in an excellent position to anticipate the effects of the disposition of a grievance on employers, on the union, on union leadership, and on plant operations. To promote sound industrial relations, management and union grievance procedure personnel, as noted, frequently compromise on the solution of grievance cases. It is not unknown for management to allow the union to "win" a grievance case to bolster the prestige of union leadership in the eyes of union membership; the state of industrial relations may be improved when union leaders have the confidence of the membership. On the other hand, a labor union may refuse to challenge a management violation of a contract when the employer engages in conduct absolutely essential to operations.

Contrary to the seniority provisions of an existing collective bargaining contract, for example, a company recently laid off longer-service employees and retained shorter-service employees. Such action constituted a direct violation of the particular contract. However, the union representatives agreed with the company, when the case was resolved through the grievance procedure, that the retention of the shorter-service workers was vital to the continued operation of a crucial department. Union and management grievance procedure personnel concluded that had the longer-service workers been retained and the shorter-service employees been laid off, the plant, the union, and all employees of the company would have suffered irreparable damage.

It is not intended here to create a false impression of the operation of the grievance procedure. Certainly, the mechanism does not function to condone employer, employee, or union violations of collective bargaining contracts. In the overwhelming number of cases disposed of through the grievance procedure, practices inconsistent with the terms of the agreement are terminated. At times, retroactive action must be taken to implement rights and obligations provided for in the contract. Thus, the employer may be required to reinstate with back pay a worker who had previously been discharged in violation of the discharge clause of the labor agreement. Or perhaps a union caused damage to the company's property while on strike; to comply with a particular contract provision, this union might be required to pay the company a certain sum of money.

But it is still true that the grievance procedure is singularly adaptable for the settlement of contract disputes to the maximum satisfaction of all concerned. Interests of all parties can be considered. The procedure's flexible and personalized character permits compromise when this is deemed the best way to settle a particular grievance. Extenuating circumstances can be given weight. Precedent can be utilized or disregarded, depending on the particular situation. Solutions to problems can be reached that will serve the basic interests of sound industrial relations. These observations lead to one conclusion: Resort to the grievance procedure provides management and unions with the most useful and efficient means of contract enforcement.

Grievance Procedure and Harmonious Labor Relations

The grievance procedure may be regarded as supplying the "psychotherapy" of industrial relations. Small problems can be discussed and settled promptly before they become major and troublesome issues. Serious problems can be analyzed in a rational manner and resolved speedily, peacefully, and in keeping with the terms of the contract. The rights of employees, employers, and unions guaranteed in the contract can be protected and implemented in an orderly fashion. Not only does the grievance procedure serve as a means for the enforcement of the labor agreement, but it also provides the parties with the opportunity of establishing the *reasons* for complaints and problems.

Indeed, depending upon the attitudes of the management and the union, the grievance procedure can also be used for functions other than the settlement of complaints arising under the labor agreement. Many parties, for example, use the grievance machinery to prevent grievances from arising as well as to dispose of employee, union, and employer complaints. Major grievances are viewed here as symptomatic of underlying problems, and attempts are jointly made to dispose of these problems to prevent their future recurrence. In other cases, the parties may utilize the scheduled grievance meeting time, after the grievance itself has been dealt with, to explore ways of improving their general relationship and also as an avenue of bilateral communication on matters of interest to both institutions (such as new employer plans, the economic prospects for the industry, or the upcoming union election).

In the last analysis, in fact, the grievance procedure should be regarded as a device whereby managements or unions can "win" a grievance only in the most narrow of senses. It should also be viewed as a means of obtaining a better climate of labor relations, rather than as the machinery whereby either the employer or the union can exercise authority over the other. This does not mean that rights guaranteed in the labor contract should be waived or compromised, but that in discharging obligations under the grievance procedure, the parties should understand the broader implications involved. Employer and union representatives who regard the grievance procedure in this light gear their behavior, arguments, and general approach toward the objective of the improvement of labor relations.

This objective is not realized when representatives of management look upon their obligations under the grievance procedure as burdensome chores, as wastes of time, or as necessary evils. Likewise, it is not attainable to the extent that unions stuff the grievance procedure with complaints that have no merit whatsoever under the collective bargaining contract.[1] It cannot be achieved when the parties regard the grievance procedure as a method to embarrass the other side or to demonstrate authority or power. Nor can opportunities for more harmonious labor relations through the use of the grievance procedure be realized to the extent that the system is used to resolve internal political conflicts within the union or the management. If the grievance procedure does not contribute to a better labor relations climate, the fault lies not with the system, but with the representatives of unions and management who either misunderstand or distort the functions that the procedure plays in the industrial relations complex.

ARBITRATION

The vast majority of problems that arise as the result of the interpretation and application of collective bargaining contracts are resolved bilaterally by the representatives of management and the labor organization. Through the process of negotiation, the parties to a contract manage to find a solution to grievances at some step in the grievance procedure. Such a record testifies to the utility of the grievance procedure as a device for the speedy, fair, and peaceful solution of disputes growing out of the application of the collective bargaining contract. It also shows rather clearly that the great majority of management and union representatives understand fully the purpose of the grievance procedure and discharge their responsibilities on the basis of good faith.

Indeed, in healthy union-management relationships, the great bulk of grievances is disposed of at the lower levels of the procedure. This is as it should be; were most such complaints merely bucked up the union and management hierarchical ladders, the time and efforts of the more broadly based officials would be hopelessly drained. Lower-step settlement also helps maintain the status of lower supervision and assures that the grievance is allowed treatment by the people who are apt to be most familiar with the circumstances under which it arose.

Under even the most enviable of labor relationships, however, there will undoubtedly be some grievances that prove themselves completely incapable of being solved by *any* level within the bilateral grievance procedure. Each party genuinely believes that its interpretation of the contract is the right one, or the parties remain in disagreement as to the facts of the case.

There may also, on occasion, be less commendable reasons for a stalemate. The union leadership may feel that it cannot afford to "give in" on an untenable grievance because of the political ramifications of doing so. Management may at times prove quite unwilling to admit that the original employer action giving rise to the grievance was in violation of the contract, even though in its heart it realizes that the union's allegation is right. The union may, the remarks previously offered in this connection notwithstanding, seek to "flood" the grievance procedure with a potpourri of unsettled grievances, with the hope of using the situation to gain extracontractual concessions from the employer. The employer may, in turn, seek to embarrass the union leadership by making it fight to the limit for any favorable settlement. And grievances involving such thorny issues as discipline, work assignment, and management rights are sometimes accompanied by emotional undercurrents that make them all the more difficult to resolve by the joint conference method of the grievance procedure.

Given all these possibilities, it is, in fact, a tribute to the maturity of labor-management relations that the great majority of all grievances are settled by the joint process.

Nonetheless, some contractual provision must be made by the parties to handle the relatively few issues for which the grievance procedure proves unsuccessful—those occasions upon which the parties to the labor contract are still in disagreement over a problem arising under the contractual terms after all bilateral steps in the grievance procedure have been exhausted. To break such deadlocks, the parties have the opportunity to resort to the arbitration process. An impartial outsider is selected by the parties to decide the controversy. This person's decision is invariably stipulated in the contract as being "final and binding upon both parties."

As a method of dispute settlement, arbitration is anything but new. King Solomon was an arbitrator—and, from all accounts, a first-rate one—some three thousand years ago. Arbitration (sometimes with more than one arbitrator) was also used to settle disputes between towns in ancient Greece and was an accepted avenue for resolving controversy in ancient Babylon, the early Islamic civilization, and under Roman law. Not to be outdone, the Confucian Chinese used it, too, and so did the medieval Germans. In the United States, George Washington showed his high regard for the concept by providing for binding arbitration in his will (should any disputes arise concerning the intent of the latter).

As American unionism grew, the advantages of arbitration became visible in this sector, also. Above all, it was seen that the arbitrator could resolve the labor dispute in a peaceful manner. In the absence of arbitration, the parties might use the strike or lockout to settle such problems, a process that not only could be costly to the management, the union, and the employees but would tend to foster embittered labor relations. Impressed by these arbitral facts of life, some 97 percent of all U.S. labor agreements provide for arbitration as the final step in the grievance procedure. This national percentage is significantly greater than it was in the early 1930s, when fewer than 8 to 10 percent of all agreements contained such a clause. And even by 1944, arbitration provisions had been included in only 73 percent of all contracts.

What with the advantages of arbitration and the growth of the labor movement, the volume of arbitration increased sharply. A major Supreme Court decision in 1957 added to the trend. It ruled that an employer may not refuse to arbitrate unresolved grievances when the labor agreement contains an arbitration clause.[2] In 1980, arbitrators serving under the auspices of the Federal Mediation and Conciliation Service (FMCS) issued 7,539 awards compared to 2,849 in 1970. In more recent years, however, the volume has been decreasing, attributable largely to the decline in union membership. In 1987, the number of awards reported by the FMCS dropped to 4,145, and in 1989 a modest total of 3,769 was registered. In 1991, the last year for which the official statistic is available, an upswing that might prove to have been temporary resulted in 5,451 awards being issued.

The "Trilogy" Cases

In 1960, the U.S. Supreme Court handed down three other decisions that provide even greater backing for the arbitration process.[3] These decisions are commonly referred to as the "Trilogy" cases. Each of them involved the United Steelworkers of America, and each demonstrates that the system of private arbitration in the United States has now received the full support of the highest court in the land.

In the *Warrior & Gulf Navigation* case, the Court held that in the absence of an express agreement excluding arbitration, the Court would direct the parties to arbitrate a grievance. The Court stated that a legal order to arbitrate would thenceforth not be denied "unless it may be said with positive assurance that the arbitration clause is not susceptible to an interpretation that covers the asserted dispute. Doubts should be resolved in favor of coverage."

More precisely, the courts will not decide that a dispute is *not* arbitrable unless the parties have taken care to *expressly remove* an area of labor relations from the arbitration process. This could be accomplished by providing, for example, that "disputes involving determination of the qualifications of employees for promotion will be determined exclusively by the company and such decision will not be subject to arbitration." But, needless to say, not many unions would agree to such a clause, since management would then have the unilateral right to make determinations on this vital phase of the promotion process.

In so ruling, the *Warrior & Gulf Navigation* decision eliminated a course of action that some managements had followed. When faced with a demand by a union for arbitration, some employers had frequently gone to court and asked the judge to decide that the issue involved in the case was not arbitrable. On many occasions, the courts had agreed with the management, with the effect of sustaining the employer position in the grievance, and denying the union an opportunity to get a decision based on the merits of the case.

In the instant case, the Warrior & Gulf Navigation Company employed forty-two workers at its dock terminal for maintenance and repair work. After the company had subcontracted out some of the work, the number was reduced to twenty-three. The union argued in the grievance procedure that this action of the company violated certain areas of the labor agreement—the integrity of the bargaining unit, seniority rights, and other clauses of the contract that provided benefits to workers. On its part, the company claimed that the issue of subcontracting was strictly a management function and relied on the management rights clause in the contract, which stated that "matters which are strictly a function of management should not be subject to arbitration." When the Supreme Court handled the case, it ordered arbitration because the contract did not *specifically* exclude such activity from the arbitration process. It stated:

> A specific collective bargaining agreement may exclude contracting-out from the grievance procedure. Or a written collateral agreement may make clear that contracting-out was not a matter for arbitration. In such a case a grievance based solely on contracting-out would not be arbitrable. Here, however, there is no such provision. Nor is there any showing that the parties designed the phrase "strictly as a function of management" to encompass any and all forms of contracting-out. In the absence of any express provision excluding a particular grievance from arbitration, we think only the most forceful evidence of a purpose to exclude the claim from arbitration can prevail, particularly where, as here, the exclusion clause is vague and the arbitration clause quite broad.

One additional important point must be emphasized to understand the significance of this decision. Though the court may direct arbitration, it will not determine the merits of the dispute. A federal court decides only whether the grievance is arbitrable, but the private arbitrator has full authority to rule on its merits. As the Supreme Court stated in *Warrior &*

Gulf Navigation, "Whether contracting out in the present case violated the agreement is the question. It is a question for the arbiter, not for the courts." This principle was reaffirmed in 1986 by the Supreme Court in *AT&T Technologies* v. *Communications Workers.*[4]

In the second case, *American Manufacturing,* the issue of arbitrability was also involved, but in a different way. The American Manufacturing Company argued before a lower federal court that an issue was not arbitrable because it did not believe that the grievance had merit. Involved was a dispute concerning the reinstatement of an employee on his job after it was determined that the employee was 25 percent disabled and was drawing workmen's compensation. The lower federal court sustained the employer's position and characterized the employee's grievance as "a frivolous, patently baseless one, not subject to arbitration." When the U.S. Supreme Court reversed the lower federal court, it held that federal courts are limited in determining whether the dispute is covered by the labor agreement and that they have no power to evaluate the merits of a dispute. It stated:

> The function of the court is very limited when the parties have agreed to submit all questions of contract interpretation to the arbitrator. It is then confined to ascertaining whether the party seeking arbitration is making a claim which on its face is governed by the contract. Whether the moving party is right or wrong is a question of contract construction for the arbitrator. In these circumstances the moving party should not be deprived of the arbitrator's judgment, when it was his judgment and all that it connotes that was bargained for.

Essentially, this means that the courts may not hold a grievance to be nonarbitrable even if a judge believes that a grievance is completely worthless. It is up to the private arbitrator to make the decision on the merits of a case. The arbitrator may dismiss the grievance as being without merit, but this duty rests exclusively with the individual arbitrator, and not with the courts.

In the third case, *Enterprise Wheel & Car Corporation,* a lower federal court reversed the decision of an arbitrator on the grounds that the judge did not believe that his decision was sound under the labor agreement. The arbitrator's award directed the employer to reinstate certain discharged workers and to pay them back wages for periods both before and after the expiration of the collective bargaining contract. The company refused to comply with the award, and the union petitioned for the enforcement of the award. The lower court held that the arbitrator's award was unenforceable because the contract had expired. The Supreme Court reversed the lower court and ordered full enforcement. In upholding the arbitrator's award, the Court stated:

> Interpretation of the collective bargaining agreement is a question for the arbitrator. It is the arbitrator's construction which was bargained for; and so far as the arbitration decision concerns construction of the contract, the courts

have no business overruling him because their interpretation of the contract is different from his.

The significance of this last decision is clear. It shows that a union or a management may not use the courts to set aside an arbitrator's award. The decision, of course, cuts both ways: It applies to both employers and labor organizations. Whereas the other two decisions definitely favor labor organizations, this one merely serves to preserve the integrity of the arbitrator's award. Thus, even if a judge believes that an arbitrator's award is unfair, unwise, and not even consistent with the contract, that judge has no alternative except to enforce the award.

With the Trilogy decisions, private arbitration had come very much of age, its integrity fully established by the judiciary. The most fanatic devotee of the process really could have asked for nothing more.

Post-Trilogy Developments

In 1974, however, the pendulum started to swing slightly in the other direction, with the Supreme Court's decision in *Alexander* v. *Gardner-Denver*,[5] and other decisions from the bench over the next decade also detracted to some extent from the Trilogy.

In *Gardner-Denver*, the high court held that an arbitrator's decision is not final and binding when Title VII of the Civil Rights Act is involved. An arbitrator had sustained the discharge of a black employee on the grounds that he was terminated for just cause. The employee had claimed, however, that he had been discharged for racial reasons, in violation of Title VII. Lower federal courts upheld the decision of the arbitrator, in line with the Trilogy doctrine. However, the Supreme Court remanded the case to the federal district court to determine whether or not the employee's rights under Title VII were violated. What *Gardner-Denver* means, therefore, is that if an employee loses a case in arbitration, the employee may still seek relief from the courts, provided that Title VII rights are involved.

In 1976, the Supreme Court decided *Anchor Motor Freight*,[6] which also represents a departure from the finality of an arbitrator's award. In this case, the Court held that an arbitrator's decision is subject to reversal by a federal court when a union does not provide fair representation to employees involved in the arbitration. An employer discharged eight truck drivers for allegedly submitting inflated motel receipts for reimbursement. Their union took the discharges to arbitration, but the union failed to heed the drivers' request to investigate the motel employees. After the arbitration, in which the discharges were sustained, evidence turned up that a motel clerk was the guilty party. He had been making false entries in the motel register and pocketing the difference.

Thereupon, the drivers sued the employer and the union. A lower federal court upheld the arbitrator's award on the basis of *Enterprise Wheel*. However, the U.S. Supreme Court ruled that when a union fails to provide fair representation to employees involved in arbitration, they are entitled to an appropriate remedy. Obviously, the truck drivers were not discharged for just cause, and elementary fairness should dictate their reinstatement to their jobs with full back pay. The arbitrator's award should not stand in the way of providing justice to the discharged employees. *Anchor Motor Freight* put the union on notice. In effect, the Court has said that the courts have the authority to upset an arbitration award when a union commits a gross error in the representation of employees in arbitration or otherwise fails to live up to its arbitration responsibilities.

Then, in 1981, the Supreme Court ruled that an arbitrator's decision involving rights established by the Fair Labor Standards Act may be reviewed and reversed by the federal courts,[7] and thereby, when taken in conjunction with *Gardner-Denver,* implicitly gave a clear signal that arbitration decisions are not final and binding when the issue falls within any labor law.

And in 1984, the high court once again determined that an employee's claim, based on statutory rights, is not foreclosed by an arbitration award. In *McDonald* v. *City of West Branch, Michigan,*[8] a police officer—a union steward—was discharged for allegedly participating in a sexual assault on a minor. An arbitrator sustained the discharge, finding that McDonald was discharged for just cause. Asserting that his discharge was in reprisal for his activities as a union steward, the police officer sued in federal district court requesting that damages be assessed against the chief of police and other city officials. His suit alleged a violation of Section 1983 of the Civil Rights Act of 1871, claiming that his discharge violated his First Amendment rights of freedom of speech and association, and freedom to petition the government for redress of grievances. A federal district court permitted McDonald to proceed with his suit and a jury eventually awarded him an $8,000 judgment against the police chief. On appeal by the city, however, a federal appeals court reversed the lower court's decision, finding that the First Amendment claim was an unwarranted attempt to litigate a matter already decided by the arbitrator.

In a unanimous decision, the U.S. Supreme Court reversed the federal appeals court, finding that arbitration was not the proper forum to address issues involving statutory and constitutional rights. Following its earlier decisions, the high court stated:

> ...although arbitration is well suited to resolving contractual disputes, our [earlier decisions] compel the conclusion that it cannot provide an adequate substitute for a judicial proceeding in protecting the federal statutory and constitutional rights that Sec. 1983 is designed to safeguard.

One should not believe, however, that the high court intends to undermine the arbitration process just because of these decisions. It would not be correct to conclude that they demonstrate the Court's intent to upset arbitration decisions on a wholesale basis. In fact, the courts have sustained an NLRB policy that makes private arbitration an even more important feature in labor relations.[9] In 1971, the NLRB held, in *Collyer*

Insulated Wire,[10] that it would defer some cases to arbitration even though they contained elements of unfair labor practices. In these cases, contractual provisions were arguably involved, and the NLRB believed that private arbitrators could not only decide whether or not the contract was violated but also determine the unfair labor practice issue. Though this *Collyer* decision has been criticized on the grounds that the NLRB should not abandon its statutory duty to enforce the Taft-Hartley Act, the fact remains that the doctrine makes arbitration an even more viable instrument for the settlement of labor-management disputes.

And in *Misco,* a 1987 case, the Supreme Court further underscored the integrity of arbitration awards.[11] An employee was discharged for possessing marijuana on plant premises. An arbitrator reinstated him with full back pay on the basis that the company had insufficient evidence to prove that he violated the rule against drug use and/or possession. After the employer moved to vacate the award as contrary to public policy, lower federal courts upset the arbitrator's decision. A federal appeals court held that reinstatement would violate the public policy "against the operation of dangerous machinery by persons under the influence of drugs or alcohol."

Reversing the lower courts and upholding the arbitrator's decision, the Supreme Court ruled that "absent fraud by the parties or the arbitrator's dishonesty, reviewing courts in such cases are not authorized to reconsider the merits of the award, since this would undermine the federal policy of privately settling labor disputes by arbitration without governmental intervention." As for reversal on the basis of public policy, the Court significantly limited the federal courts by saying that such action is only justified when policy is well defined, dominant, and ascertained by reference to laws and legal precedents, rather than general consideration of supposed policy. In other words, a court may not use its subjective judgment of what constitutes public policy, or what the policy ought to be. Surprising even the arbitration fraternity, the high court's decision in *Misco* was *unanimous.* It remains to be seen, however, whether the lower federal courts will abide by the Supreme Court's resolve to maintain the integrity of arbitration awards.

For the arbitrator, the Trilogy, *Collyer,* and *Misco* decisions are equally important. Private arbitrators bear an even greater degree of responsibility as they decide their cases. Not only is the post one of honor, in which the parties have confidence in the arbitrator's professional competency and integrity, but the arbitrator must recognize that for all intents and purposes his or her decision is completely "final and binding" upon the parties. Indeed, if the system of private arbitration is to remain a permanent feature of the American system of industrial relations, arbitrators must measure up to their responsibilities. Should they fail in this respect, managements and unions would simply delete the arbitration clause from the contract and resolve their disputes by strikes or by going directly to court. These are not pleasant alternatives, but the parties may choose these routes if they believe that arbitrators are not discharging their responsibilities in an honorable, judicious, and professional manner. Arbitrators should not feel so smug as to believe that their services are indispensable to labor unions and employers. They are as expendable as last year's calendar.

Limitations to Arbitration

If employers and unions support the arbitration process as an accepted method of disposing of disagreements relating to problems arising under the terms of a labor contract already in existence, there is almost no approval on the part of industry and organized labor for using arbitration as the means of breaking deadlocks in the negotiations of *new* agreements. Most employers and unions would rather have a work stoppage than refer such disputes to arbitration. Many reasons are advanced in support of this position, but the chief consideration lies in the parties' extreme aversion to having an outsider determine the conditions of employment, the rights and obligations of management, and the responsibilities and rights of the union. Employers and unions almost invariably believe that, since the labor agreement will establish their fundamental relationship, they should have the full authority to negotiate its terms. For these reasons, the use of arbitration during the negotiation stage of a labor contract is rare.

It is also important to note that in the United States the system is one of *private and voluntary arbitration.* That is, the government does not force the parties to include arbitration clauses in their labor agreements. They do so voluntarily as they negotiate the latter. Either party can refuse to incorporate any arbitration provisions at all, as has been the case in the building construction industry, where the duration of the job is deemed too brief to make use of a neutral feasible, and in much of the trucking industry, where the Teamster hierarchy has traditionally insisted that neutrals "attempt to please both sides and actually please nobody."

Equally significant is the fact that arbitrators are private rather than government officials. Most of them are lawyers and college professors. As a matter of fact, the Federal Mediation and Conciliation Service and some state agencies that provide mediation services will not permit their mediators to serve as arbitrators.

Characteristics of Arbitration Hearings

Since the decision of the arbitrator *is* final and binding, arbitration is quite different from mediation, a process wherein the parties are completely free to accept or reject the recommendations or suggestions of the mediator. Whether the arbitrator rules for or against a party to the arbitration, that decision must be accepted. This is true even when the losing side believes that the decision is not warranted by the labor agreement, by the evidence submitted in the hearing, or on the basis of fairness or justice. Frequently, an arbitrator's decision will establish an important precedent that must be followed by the employer, the union, and the employees. At times the party that suffers an adverse ruling in an arbitration case will attempt to change, during the next labor contract negotiations, those sections of the labor agreement that proved to be the basis of the decision. Obviously, the side that is benefited by the decision will be reluctant to alter those features of the labor agreement that were interpreted and applied by the arbitrator.

These considerations tend to show the seriousness of arbitration as a tool of labor relations. When the decision to arbitrate is made, the employer and union representatives are undertaking a deep responsibility. To discharge this responsibility in a competent and intelligent manner, it is necessary to put the arbitrator in such a position that the latter can make a decision in the light of evidence and of the relevant contractual clauses. Consequently, the parties have the obligation of preparing fully before coming to the hearing. This means the accumulation of all evidence, facts, documents, and arguments that may have a bearing on the dispute. Careful preparation also means the selection of witnesses who can give relevant testimony in the case. Management and union representatives should leave no stone unturned in preparing for the arbitration.

At the arbitration hearing, each side will have full opportunity to present the fruits of its preparation. Normally, although arbitration hearings are much more formal than grievance procedure negotiations, they are considerably less formal than court proceedings. In addition, the rules of evidence that apply in the courts of the land do not bind the conduct of the arbitration. This means that the hearing can be conducted not only more informally but much faster than a case in court. However, the parties should not be deluded into believing that the arbitrator's decision will not be based on evidence and facts. Even though the arbitration proceedings might be regarded as semiformal, arbitration cases are not won on the basis of emotional appeals, theatrical gestures, or speechmaking. The arbitrator is interested in the facts, the evidence, and the parties' arguments as they apply to the issues of the dispute. Such material should be developed in the hearing through careful questioning of witnesses and the presentation of relevant documents.

The parties cannot, moreover, take too much care to make sure that they have presented *all* evidence that might support their case. Representatives of unions and managements who have dealt with a problem in the grievance procedure, and who therefore are fully aware of all the facets of a case, will at times not fully present their case because they believe that the arbitrator is likewise familiar with the facts and issues. Unless prehearing briefs are filed by the parties, it should be recognized that the arbitrator knows absolutely nothing about the case at the time of the hearing. It is the responsibility of the parties to educate the arbitrator about the issues, the facts, the evidence, the arguments, and the relevant contractual clauses. Clearly, if the arbitration process is to have a significant positive value, the parties to the arbitration must discharge their obligations fully and conscientiously. They must be indefatigable in their efforts to prepare for the arbitration and absolutely thorough in the presentation of their case to the arbitrator.

Responsibilities of the Arbitrator

The arbitrator, of course, is the key person in the arbitration process, possessing the cold responsibility for the decision in the case. The arbitrator decides, for example, whether a discharged employee remains discharged or returns to work, which of two workers gets the better job or whether the employer placed a correct rate on a new job. Few members of the profession have ever rendered a decision that even remotely approximates a 1982 one of Sidney A. Wolff in its direct financial ramifications: In a case involving the Pabst Brewing Company and the Teamsters, he ordered Pabst to negotiate a new plant-closing settlement that cost it some $18 million in back pay. But arbitration is always of critical importance to everyone who is a party to it—or at least those who are asked to arbitrate must operate under that assumption—and it is beyond argument that one of the most important jobs that a person can receive is the assignment by an employer and a union to an arbitration case.

In discharging their responsibilities, arbitrators are expected to adhere to a strict code of ethics. The decision must be based squarely on the evidence and the facts presented. The arbitrator must give full faith and credit to the language of the labor contract at the time of the case. It should be recognized by all concerned that the language of the labor agreement binds the employer, the union, the employees, *and the arbitrator*. It is not within the scope of the arbitrator's authority to decide whether or not a particular contractual clause is wise or unwise, desirable or undesirable. The arbitrator's job is to apply the language of a labor contract as he or she finds it in a particular case. To follow any other course of action not only would be a breach of faith to the parties but would create mischief with the labor agreement. The arbitrator must regard the collective bargaining contract as a final authority and give it full respect. If a case goes against a party because of the language of the contract, the responsibility for this state of affairs lies not with the arbitrator but with the parties who negotiated the agreement.

If the language of the contract is clear-cut and unequivocal, the arbitrator's job is not too difficult. Under these circumstances, the award will favor the party whose position is sustained by the precise contractual language. Of course, there are not many cases of this type, since, if the language is clear-cut and precise, the dispute should not have gone to arbitration. It should have been resolved in the grievance procedure on the basis of the contractual language.

What complicates the problem is contractual language that is subject to different shades of meaning. That is, impartial people could find that the language involved may be reasonably interpreted in different ways. Under these circumstances, what is called "past practice"—the way in which the language has been applied in the past—serves as the guide for construction of the ambiguous contractual language. (*Case 2 deals with this topic.*)

The idea behind past practice is that both parties have knowledge of the practice and both expect that the practice will be honored as the basis of administration of the relevant language. Thus, when the arbitrator is confronted with language that is ambiguous, the decision will normally be based on the evidence demonstrating practice. However, if the language is unambiguous and unequivocal, and the practice conflicts with the clear-cut contractual language, the arbitrator will normally base the decision on the language rather than on the practice. Unequivocal contractual language supersedes practice when the two conflict.

Also, arbitrators generally recognize that past practice should not be used to restrict management in the changing of work methods required by changing conditions. Thus, past practice is normally not used to prevent management from changing work schedules, work assignments, workloads, job assignments, and the number of workers needed on the job. The key to such an arbitration principle is that changing conditions have made the practice obsolete. Of course, there may be written contractual language that would forbid the management's making such changes in work methods. Under these circumstances, the arbitrator's decision would be based on the written contractual language; but past practice would not normally be used to block management action when conditions change. Despite these limitations, past practice is frequently used as the basis for arbitrator decisions, particularly, as stated, when contractual language is subject to different shades of meaning.

Much has been said and written about the necessity of the arbitrator's being "fair" in making a decision. A decision is fair only when it is based on the evidence of a case and the accurate assessment of the relevant provisions of the labor agreement. Furthermore, fairness does not mean charity, compromise, or an attempt to please both sides. At times, a management and a union arbitrate a number of different grievances in one hearing. An arbitrator who deliberately decides to compromise or "split" the grievances is not worthy of the confidence of the parties. An arbitrator who is a "splitter" not only violates the ethics of the office but causes untold confusion and damage to the parties. What managements and unions desire in arbitration is a clear-cut decision on each grievance, based on the merits of each dispute; they do not want splitting. They are invariably unhappy with an award that appears to have been shaped from the formula $AA = (E + U)/2$, where AA = arbitrator's award, E = employer's position, and U = union's position. The parties can divide by 2 themselves and presumably have no desire to go to the trauma, expense, and uncertainty of the arbitration process for this kind of result (even while recognizing that on occasion—rare occasion—it is nonetheless inevitable).

Compromise or "horse trading" of grievances may be accomplished in the grievance procedure. However, once grievances are referred to arbitration, every one of them must be decided on its own merits. Clearly, a "split-the-difference" approach to arbitration can do irreparable harm to the parties, the collective bargaining contract, and the arbitration process. Managements and unions would quickly lose confidence in arbitration if cases were decided not upon their merits but upon the determination of the arbitrator to "even up" his or her awards.

In fact, before hearing a case, each arbitrator normally takes a solemn oath of office to decide the dispute on the evidence, free from any bias. Any arbitrator who transgresses this oath by striving to decide a case on a split-the-difference formula has absolutely no business serving as an arbitrator. A famous and respected baseball umpire once said he called them as he saw them. Even though umpiring a baseball game is quite different from arbitrating a labor dispute, and although the qualifications for baseball umpires are quite different from those for arbitrators in labor relations, the homely statement "call them as you see them" has real significance for arbitration of any kind of dispute.

Additional responsibilities and personal qualities are required in the person serving as an arbitrator. The latter not only must be incorruptible, free from any bias, and aware of the principles of arbitration but must also have a deep and well-rounded understanding of labor relations. It takes more than honesty and integrity to serve effectively as an arbitrator. Arbitrators who are not trained in labor relations matters, even though they may be paragons of virtue, can cause irreparable damage to the parties by decisions that do violence to the collective bargaining contract.

At the hearing, the arbitrator should treat both sides with the dignity and the respect that is characteristic of the judicial process. The arbitrator should be patient, sympathetic, and understanding. Experienced arbitrators do not take advantage of their office by being arrogant or domineering. Arbitrators who have a tendency to exaggerate their own importance should be aware of the fact that arbitration, although important, plays a distinctly minor role in the overall union-management relationship. The arbitrator should permit each side to the dispute the fullest opportunity to present all the evidence, witnesses, documents, and arguments that it desires. While a desire for relevancy is, as Justice Oliver Wendell Holmes once wrote, a "concession to the shortness of life," experienced arbitrators frequently lean over backward to permit the introduction of evidence that may or may not be relevant to the dispute. This procedure is better than a policy that could result in the suppression of vital information.

The arbitrator also has the responsibility for keeping the hearing moving. When there is a deliberate or unconscious waste of time by either or both of the parties, the arbitrator is obligated to take remedial action. This does not mean that the arbitrator should not permit recesses, coffee breaks, or the occasional telling of a humorous story; what it means is that part of the arbitrator's fee is earned by conducting a fair, orderly, thorough, and speedy hearing. To this end, the arbitrator, while at all times demonstrating the qualities of patience and understanding, must remain in full *control* of the hearing.

Perhaps J. Paul Getty was overdoing it a bit in declaring that "the meek shall inherit the earth but not its mineral rights," yet there is at least some relevancy in that observation to arbitral obligations. Anyone who unwittingly or by design attempts to take over the hearing must be dealt with courteously but firmly. Of course, if the arbitrator is not experienced, is unsure, or for some reason cannot or will not make definite decisions, the hearing can get out of hand.

The arbitrator also has an obligation to the witnesses called upon to give testimony in the hearing. Even though they should be subject to searching examination, the arbitrator should make sure that they are treated in a courteous manner by the examining party, or by the arbitrator if it is necessary to ask questions of witnesses to clarify a point. The arbitrator should not permit witnesses to be "badgered" or insulted. Even in cross-examination, where the examining party has more leeway with witnesses than it does in direct examination, they should be treated with decorum.

Finally the arbitrator has a responsibility to the parties relative to the award. One significant advantage of arbitration is the comparatively fast disposition of disputes. Thus the arbitrator has an obligation to get the decision in the hands of the parties in a prompt manner after the end of the hearing. Unless unusual conditions are involved, the American Arbitration Association requires awards to be submitted not more than thirty days from the date of the hearing. The Federal Mediation and Conciliation Service is less demanding on arbitrators appointed under its jurisdiction and allows sixty days.

Of course, when the parties elect to file post-hearing briefs, as they do in about 75 percent of all cases, the arbitrator's time tolls from the receipt of such briefs. Either way, however, the deadline should scrupulously be observed by the arbitrator. In fact, in discharge cases the interest of the parties and the employees would be best served by decisions rendered even more promptly than in other types of cases, perhaps in about fifteen days. Arbitrators who are constantly late in their awards do a disservice to the arbitration process. As a matter of fact, under the FMCS rules, the failure of an arbitrator to render timely awards may lead to removal from the FMCS Roster.

The award should be clear and to the point. There should be no question in the minds of the parties as to the exact character of the decision in the case. If the grievance is denied, the award should simply state that fact. Under these circumstances, some arbitrators in the decision also mention the contract provision or provisions that the employer did not violate. For example, in a work-assignment case, the award might read as follows:

> The grievance of Mr. Elmer Beamish, Grievance No. 594, is denied on the basis that the company, under job description for Tool- and Die-makers, Class A, Code 286, and for Maintenance Men, Class A, Code 263, and without violating Article XVI of the Labor Agreement, may properly assign either category of employees to repair the classes of machinery in question in this case.

When a case is decided in favor of the union, the award should clearly and specifically direct the employer to take action to bring it into compliance with the contract. In addition, to avoid any misunderstanding, the decision should require the action within a certain number of working days after the receipt of the award. For example, in a "bumping" case, the award might read as follows:

> Within three working days after the receipt of this award, the Company is directed to place the grievant, Reva Snodgrass, into the job of Spray Painter, Class "B," Labor Grade No. 7, and to make her whole for any financial loss that she suffered because of the refusal of the Company to permit her to roll into the aforementioned job on the grounds that the Company violated Article IX, Section 7, Paragraphs A and B of the Labor Agreement.

In addition to the incorporation of a clear award, arbitrators are charged with the responsibility of writing an opinion to support their decision. Although technically opinions are not required to explain a decision, the fact is that arbitrators almost universally write an opinion. What is more important in this connection, the parties expect their arbitrators to write them, and so do agencies such as the Federal Mediation and Conciliation Service and the American Arbitration Association, which submit to managements and unions the names of arbitrators.

In the opinion, the arbitrator sets forth the basic issues of the case, the facts, the position and arguments of the parties, and the reasons for the decision. The arbitrator deals with the evidence presented in the case as it relates to each decision. Arbitrators are frequently extraordinarily careful to deal in an exhaustive manner with each major argument and piece of evidence offered by the losing side. Patently, the arbitrator has an obligation to tell the losing side just why it lost the case. Since normally the losing side will be very disappointed with the decision, the arbitrator should at least indicate in a careful manner the reasons for the adverse ruling. This will probably not make the losing side feel any better, but at least an opinion that is carefully written and covers thoroughly the major arguments and areas of evidence will demonstrate that the character of an arbitration opinion is a guide to the amount of time, energy, and thought the arbitrator puts into the case.

In the middle and late 1990s, it is safe to predict, the caseloads of labor-management arbitrators will still contain many of the traditional issues. It is, however, an equally safe bet that such emerging topics as alcohol and drug use by employees and AIDS will increasingly find their way into arbitration. In the public sector, privatization—the transfer of governmental functions to the private sector—will raise subcontracting controversies between public employers and labor organizations to a dimension and complexity not encountered in the past. Modern workplace surveillance technology such as video cameras, closed circuit television, and video display terminals make employer monitoring easier and more efficient: In increasing frequency, arbitrators will be called upon to decide disputes pitting the right of employers to use such devices against an employee insistence on a right to privacy, too. Arbitrators will tread new and challenging paths as they explore problems that were thought about either scarcely or not at all in past years.

Selection of the Arbitrator

After the parties decide to arbitrate a dispute, the problem of the selection of the arbitrator arises. To solve this problem, most labor agreements provide that the parties will select the arbitrator from a panel of names submitted by the Federal Mediation and Conciliation Service or the American Arbitration Association. When called upon by the parties to an arbitration, these agencies will supply the management and the union with a list of names, and the parties, in accordance with a mutually acceptable formula, will select the arbitrator from the list. Under some labor agreements, the Federal Mediation and Conciliation Service and the American Arbitration Association have the authority to select the arbitrator on a direct-appointment basis in the event that none of the names on the panel is acceptable.

The Federal Mediation and Conciliation Service is administered independently from the U.S. Department of Labor. It maintains a roster of
arbitrators totaling about 1,700. About 60 percent are lawyers or law
professors. Thirty percent are college professors not in law schools. The
remainder are a mixed bag, mainly members of the clergy and former
management and union officials who have shed their partisan roles. Upon
the selection of the arbitrator, the service withdraws from active participation in the case, and the relationship thereafter is between the parties and
the arbitrator, although (as Exhibit 6-2 shows) the latter must ultimately
file a report with the service.

Unlike the FMCS, the American Arbitration Association is a private
organization. In its formative years, it devoted itself almost exclusively to
the promotion of commercial arbitration, but since 1937 its Industrial
Arbitration Tribunal has become increasingly active in labor disputes. In
addition to furnishing the parties with arbitrator-selection aid similar to
that of the Mediation Service, it administers arbitration hearings in accordance with a number of formalized rules. The association's panel of available arbitrators currently contains about 1,500 names, although most of
the work is actually done by fewer than 500 active arbitrators, and the
heavy majority of these are the same people who are listed on the FMCS
roster. It, too, keeps reasonably close tabs on its arbitrators, as Exhibits
6-3 and 6-4 indicate.

There is no obligation on the parties to use either the FMCS or the AAA,
of course, and some relationships avoid both organizations in their selection of arbitrators. They contact directly someone of their own choosing,
draw upon the names on arbitration panels of individual states (although
not all states have such panels), or even designate a person of unimpeachable integrity to select an arbitrator for them. What satisfies one relationship may not satisfy another, and in this activity as in so many others in
our system of private collective bargaining, it is a case of different strokes
for different folks.

Regardless of the method, the majority of labor contracts provide some
definite procedure for the appointment of the arbitrator. At times, managements and unions find that in practice they cannot agree on any arbitrator
when the contract merely states that an arbitrator "mutually acceptable" to
the parties will decide the dispute. It is sound procedure to incorporate some
method for the selection of arbitrators by an outside agency when the parties
are unable or unwilling to agree on a neutral on a mutual-acceptance basis.

Some employers and unions solve the problem of selection by appointing
a permanent arbitrator under the terms of a labor agreement. Under this
arrangement, one person will decide each dispute that is arbitrated. However, managements and unions are not in agreement on the use of a
permanent arbitrator as against the ad hoc method of selection, in which
a different arbitrator may be chosen for each case. Some employers and
unions, as a matter of policy, will use a different arbitrator for each dispute;
others find it a better practice to use the same arbitrator. The permanent
arbitrator is used most frequently when a management has a number of
different locations. Such a procedure makes for uniformity of labor policy
within the different operating units of the enterprise.

EXHIBIT 6–2

FMCS FORM R-19
(Revised June 1984)

FEDERAL MEDIATION AND CONCILIATION SERVICE
WASHINGTON, D.C. 20427

ARBITRATOR'S REPORT AND FEE STATEMENT

Form Approved
OMB No. 23-R0004

FILE NO. _____   **ARBITRATOR** _____   **DATE OF AWARD** _____
                                    (Name)

1. COMPANY _____
                        (Name)   *(City)*   *(State)*   *(Zip Code)*

2. UNION _____
                        (Name)   *(Local No.)*   *(Affiliation)*

3. ISSUES: *(Please check either a or b, and complete c and d)*

a. ☐ New or reopened contract terms

b. ☐ Contract interpretation or application

c. Issue or Issues *(Please check only one issue per grievance)*

1. ☐ Discharge and disciplinary actions
2. ☐ Incentive rates or standards
3. ☐ Job evaluation
4. ☐ Work assignment
5. ☐ Job classification
6. ☐ Seniority:
   a. ☐ Promotion and upgrading
   b. ☐ Layoff, bumping and recall
   c. ☐ Transfer
   d. ☐ Other
7. ☐ Overtime:
   a. ☐ Overtime pay
   b. ☐ Overtime distribution
   c. ☐ Compulsory overtime
   d. ☐ Other
8. ☐ Union officers—superseniority and union business
9. ☐ Strike or lockout issues *(excluding disciplinary actions)*

10. ☐ Vacations and vacation pay
11. ☐ Holidays and holiday pay
12. ☐ Scheduling of work
13. ☐ Reporting, call-in and call-back pay
14. ☐ Health and welfare
15. ☐ Pensions
16. ☐ Other fringe benefits
17. Scope of agreement:
   a. ☐ Subcontracting
   b. ☐ Jurisdictional disputes
   c. ☐ Foreman, supervision, etc.
   d. ☐ Mergers, consolidations, accretion, other plants
18. ☐ Working conditions, including safety
19. ☐ Severance pay
20. ☐ Rate of pay
21. ☐ Discrimination
22. ☐ Management rights
23. ☐ Job posting & bidding
24. ☐ Wage issues
25. ☐ Arbitrability of grievances
26. ☐ Miscellaneous

d. Was arbitrability of grievance involved?   ☐ Yes   ☐ No   If yes, check one or both   ☐ Procedural   ☐ Substantive

283

EXHIBIT 6–2 (cont.)

4. HEARING:

a. Were briefs filed? ☐ Yes ☐ No   If yes, give date _____

b. Was transcript taken? ☐ Yes ☐ No

c. Number of grievances _____

d. Dates of Hearing: _____

e. Date of grievance _____

f. Was there any waiver by parties on date the award was due?
   ☐ Yes ☐ No

5. FEES AND DAYS: For services as Arbitrator

No. of Days: _____ + _____ + _____ = _____ × $ _____ = $ _____
           Hearing   Travel   Study   Total   Per Diem Rate   Total Fee

Expenses: Transportation $ _____ + Other $ _____ = $ _____
                                       Total Expense

TOTAL $ _____

Amount payable by Company $ _____

Amount payable by Union $ _____

6. PANEL: If tripartite panel or more than one arbitrator made the award, check here _____

7. Date of this report _____   Signature _____

(Please attach to this report copies of the submission agreement and the award)

Please do not write below this line

REVIEWED BY: _____

DATE CLOSED: _____

U.S. GOVERNMENT PRINTING OFFICE 1974—O—538-235

EXHIBIT 6–3

American Arbitration Association

VOLUNTARY LABOR ARBITRATION TRIBUNAL

In the Matter of the Arbitration between

CASE NUMBER:

AWARD OF ARBITRATOR

THE UNDERSIGNED ARBITRATOR(S), having been designated in accordance with the arbitration agreement entered into by the above-named Parties, and dated and having been duly sworn and having duly heard the proofs and allegations of the Parties, AWARDS as follows:

Arbitrator's signature (dated)

STATE OF
COUNTY OF   } SS.:

On this   day of   , 19   , before me personally came and appeared

to me known and known to me to be the individual(s) described in and who executed the foregoing instrument and   he   acknowledged to me that   he   executed the same.

EXHIBIT 6—4

ARBITRATOR'S BILL
This bill is submitted on behalf of the Arbitrator

Make check payable to, and mail directly to, the Arbitrator

ARBITRATOR_____ Case No._____

ADDRESS_____ No. of Grievances_____

_____

Appointed from List ☐   Administrative Appointment ☐

UNION

EMPLOYER

To be filled out by the Arbitrator

ARBITRATOR'S COMPENSATION

Number of hearing days_____ @ $_____ $_____

Study and preparation days___ @ $_____ $_____

Other (specify)_____ @ $_____ $_____

FEE TOTAL $_____

ARBITRATOR'S EXPENSES

Transportation $_____

Hotel $_____

Meals $_____

Other (specify) $_____ $_____

TOTAL $_____

Payable by Employer $_____

Payable by Union $_____   Arbitrator's Soc. Sec. No._____

Date _____   Signature_____

AAA Signature_____

AAA-116

DO NOT PAY UNLESS AAA SIGNATURE IS AFFIXED

Actually, there are advantages and disadvantages to each method. Perhaps the chief argument in favor of the ad hoc method is that the parties will not be "stuck" with an arbitrator whom they do not want. The parties can simply dispense with an arbitrator who proves incompetent or otherwise unqualified, even though it appears unlikely that a management and a union would have selected such a person to arbitrate on a permanent basis in the first place. Balancing the chief advantage of the ad hoc system are several disadvantages. The time and effort required to select an arbitrator for each case delays the rapid disposition of the grievance, sometimes to the detriment of employee morale. At times, out of desperation, a person who has little or no experience or real qualifications is selected to serve as an arbitrator. Such a choice may be made because he or she is the only person available who has not handed down an award somewhere at some time that the employer or the union did not like. Moreover, because each new arbitrator must be educated in the local conditions, a comparatively long period may sometimes be required to conduct the hearing.

Perhaps the chief disadvantage of ad hoc arbitration, however, is the fact that this method does not assure consistency in decisions or the application of uniform principles to contract construction. No arbitrator is bound by any other arbitrator's decisions or principles of contractual construction. Consequently, disputes involving fundamentally the same issues could be resolved in as many different ways as there are arbitrators chosen to decide cases. Thus, there is no assurance that a particular decision will bring stability to labor relations. It may have precedent value only until the next time the issues involved in the case are tested before another arbitrator.

The latter consideration indicates the greatest advantage of the selection of permanent arbitrators. The parties have the assurance of consistency and uniformity of decisions and consistent contractual interpretation. As a result, precedent will be established, the parties will know what to expect, and cases dealing with essentially the same issues as contained in a grievance previously decided in arbitration can be settled in the earlier stages of the grievance procedure. In addition, the permanent arbitrator becomes familiar with the labor agreement, the technology, and the "shop language." This means that cases can frequently be expedited much more effectively than under circumstances of ad hoc arbitration.

Perhaps the chief disadvantage of the permanent selection method is that the parties involved may tend to arbitrate more disputes than are absolutely necessary, rather than first exhausting the possibilities of settling them in the grievance procedure. This is particularly true when arbitrators are paid a set fee for a year and are obligated to arbitrate any and all cases submitted to them.

This possibility, of course, is a serious charge against the permanent selection method. As stated before, arbitration should be employed only after the parties have honestly exhausted every possibility of settling disputes in the grievance procedure. One method that might be effective in obtaining the advantages of the permanent method without incurring the possible disadvantages of excessive arbitration would be to compensate the permanent arbitrator on a per diem or a per case basis, rather than on an annual fee basis. In the last analysis, however, the amount of arbitration needed by a management and a union depends upon the attitudes of the parties rather than on the method of selection or the procedure of payment.

ARBITRATION COSTS AND TIME LAG

In recent years, arbitration has been criticized as being unduly expensive and involving too much time, but beyond these two criticisms the process has always been criticized for other reasons. Parties complain when they lose a case that they believe should have been decided in their favor. The criticism may not have much validity, but justified censure involves an arbitrator who ignores unambiguous contractual language and thereby rewrites the labor agreement. At times, opinions are confusing, leading to unnecessary discord between the parties; and, indeed, there are instances where the opinion does not even reflect the award. As one dissatisfied party has said, "We won everything except the decision." Sometimes arbitrators include so-called "dicta" (gratuitous remarks not required for a decision in a case) in their opinions, which could lead to serious problems the next time a labor agreement is negotiated. And, obviously, it is understandable why the losing side believes it has been treated unjustly when the arbitrator does not conduct a fair and impartial hearing, or fails to deal with major arguments, or ignores material evidence.

However, the most vocal criticism recently has pertained to the costs and the delays associated with arbitration. Even though alternatives to arbitration—a strike or court enforcement of a labor agreement—would be far more expensive, arbitration costs, at least on the surface, appear to be quite high.

For 1991, the Federal Mediation and Conciliation Service reported that the arbitrators who served under its jurisdiction charged an average of about $471 per day. The average cost per case for that year amounted to $1,976, normally shared equally between the parties. This figure included not only the charge for the hearing day and the arbitrator's expenses (travel, hotel, meals) but also payment for the time devoted to the analysis of the evidence and the writing of the arbitrator's opinion. Beyond the fee and expenses of the arbitrator, there are other costs. Some parties use lawyers and also may have a stenographic transcript of the proceedings prepared, and there is the payment of personnel on both sides who take part in the arbitration hearing. It is presently estimated that employers use attorneys in over three quarters of all of their cases, that unions do so in over half of theirs, and that one or both sides desire a transcript in just under one quarter of all arbitrations.

There are ways to cut arbitration costs. Grievances that are of minimal importance to the parties, particularly those that go to arbitration for political and tactical purposes, should be eliminated from the process. Other suggestions include the use of local arbitrators to save on expenses, elimination of the transcript and attorneys when they are not necessary, and the consolidation of grievances of the same type to be determined in one hearing. To reduce costs, the parties may instruct their arbitrators not to write an opinion but merely to issue an award. The writing of an opinion takes considerable time, even after the arbitrator has carefully reviewed the evidence and has reached a decision. Of course, there is genuine value in a carefully written opinion, as pointed out earlier, but there are cases where the merit of cost saving outweighs the advantages of an opinion.

One delay is not attributable to arbitrators or the process but to dilatory tactics of the parties. This involves the time before arbitration is requested on a grievance. For example, recently one of the present authors handled a case in which three years had elapsed before the parties invoked the arbitration process. Such an incredible delay is not usual, but grievances commonly vegetate for many months before the parties decide to take them into arbitration. The time-lag criticism properly starts from the point at which the parties request arbitration. For 1991, the Federal Mediation and Conciliation Service reported that, on the average, 253 days elapsed from the time the parties requested a panel of arbitrators until the award was issued. This is much too long, and the parties understandably wonder in such circumstances if the process really constitutes a viable forum for the disposition of grievances in arbitration. One consequence of the delay is the lowering of the morale in the workplace, in the same way that the morale of students suffers when their teachers take much too long in returning examination papers. Employees become impatient waiting for the award; their resentment could have an adverse impact on the quantity and quality of their work, and, frequently, they badger their union representatives about the problem. Employers could also suffer a large financial loss (should they lose their case) if the arbitrator directs a monetary remedy for a contractual violation.

One way to deal with the time problem is for the parties to use comparatively new arbitrators rather than requesting the services of so-called "mainline," or veteran, arbitrators. Since the latter group receives the lion's share of the cases, its members may be unable to provide prompt hearing dates. Indeed, in fiscal 1991, the FMCS reported that 107 days elapsed between the time an arbitrator was appointed and the day of the hearing. It follows that arbitrators with small case loads might be able to offer more prompt hearing dates. The problem, of course, is to convince the parties to use new arbitrators rather than those with considerable experience. It is true that there is no substitute for experience, but it is equally true that new arbitrators could be just as qualified as those who have been in the profession for many years and who have handled a great number of cases. Many veteran arbitrators would agree with this and would encourage employers and unions to provide opportunities for the comparatively newer arbitrators.

To avoid the delay associated with the use of arbitrators from the FMCS or the AAA, a growing number of employers and unions are making use of a *permanent panel* of arbitrators. That is, they choose a number (seven is modal) of arbitrators when they negotiate the labor agreement; when grievances are ready to be arbitrated, one of the members of the panel is selected through some agreed-upon procedure. This could save considerable time, since the use of the traditional agencies for the selection of arbitrators necessitates some delay: A letter goes from the parties to the Federal Mediation and Conciliation Service or the American Arbitration Association; the agency then sends a panel of arbitrators to the parties; additional time elapses while the parties decide which one of the arbitrators on the panel is to be used; then they write the appointing agency of the choice; the agency notifies the arbitrator; and then the arbitrator must write the parties to arrange a hearing date. For 1991, the FMCS reported that 85 days elapsed between the time a request for arbitration was made to the agency and the appointment of the arbitrator. By the use of the permanent panel, most of this delay is avoided. A telephone call or a single letter sent directly to the selected arbitrator is all that is needed.

Not only could costs be reduced by relieving the arbitrator of the responsibility of writing an opinion, but the same practice is a time saver. To reduce the time lag, stenographic transcripts of the proceedings and posthearing briefs could be eliminated. (Indeed, one of the authors is currently serving on a permanent panel of arbitrators of a major airline and a labor organization, and by contractual agreement transcripts and posthearing briefs are expressly prohibited.) Transcripts and posthearing briefs delay the process; it is not unusual to wait a month or longer for a transcript, and then another month for the briefs. In the "normal" case, these are not really needed. The arbitrator simply takes his or her own notes at the hearing and provides the opportunity to the parties to offer an oral argument at the close of the hearing. To be fair about it, however, there are some cases where a transcript is valuable, and a posthearing brief could be helpful to the arbitrator in reaching a decision.

Finally, there is the matter of the dilatory arbitrator. As stated before, it is customary, and indeed directed by the FMCS and the AAA, that an arbitrator's decision is due within a specified number of days after the close of the hearing or the filing of posthearing briefs. Unfortunately, there are arbitrators who take much longer than this allowed time—chiefly because they are handling so many cases that they cannot meet this deadline.

Mini-Arbitration

First applied in the basic steel industry in 1971, "mini-" or expedited arbitration has been adopted by other employers and unions, including the U.S. Postal Service and the postal labor organizations, the League of New York Theatres and Actors' Equity, and the UAW and the automobile manufacturers. The chief value of the mini-arbitration process is the sharp reduction of the time element and costs. Under the steel plan, the hearing must be held within ten days after the appeal to arbitration is made, and the arbitrator's decision must be made within forty-eight hours after the close of the hearing. No transcripts or briefs are permitted, and the arbitrator is expected to provide the parties with a short but precise award. Costs are also much lower than in regular arbitration. A fee is paid only for the hearing day, and this fee is only about $200 for each party per case.

To provide for such rapid service at an economical charge, the steel corporations and the United Steelworkers of America use a battery of about 200 inexperienced arbitrators, including a significant number of minorities and women. The panel includes relatively young lawyers or a local university's faculty. One advantage of the new process, therefore, is to train new arbitrators.

Indeed, this spinoff from the mini process is of significant value to arbitration. Arbitrators may not as yet, to paraphrase the UAW secretary-treasurer's previously cited remark regarding labor leaders, look like a wax museum collection when they hold a meeting, but the bulk of the profession is hardly made up of youngsters nowadays. Many still-active arbitrators entered the field on the strength of their experiences in the War Labor Board days of World War II and are now nearing the end of their careers. Unless newcomers can rather quickly be developed at this point, the field will be in some trouble.

Not all cases, however, are disposed of in the mini process—only, in general, those of the more simple and routine type—with the regular arbitration process still being used for those cases of difficult nature and representing substantial interest to the parties. Normally, cases suited for the expedited procedure are those involving individual and not contractual disputes. In addition, either the employer or the union may demand that a case go through the regular arbitration process. Indeed, even during an expedited hearing, the parties may transfer the case to regular arbitration should it be discovered that the issue is more complex than originally believed.

In any event, the mini procedure has generally worked successfully in the several sectors where it has been tried. Undoubtedly, there is a place for it within our system of labor relations. It provides a swift and economical forum for the determination of grievances that are well within the capability of inexperienced arbitrators. It is likely that the process will spread. The most difficult problem is to determine which grievances should go the mini- and which the regular arbitration route; but this problem is not insoluble, since skilled and mature labor relations representatives on both sides can easily spot those grievances that can best be handled through the expedited procedure.

Finally, the parties and expedited arbitrators must take due care that the desire for speed should not sacrifice the judicial nature of the arbitration process. Whether expedited or regular, arbitration is a judicial process where thoughtful consideration of the evidence controls the outcome of the case. To purchase speed at the price of quality undermines the integrity of arbitration.

Grievance Mediation

Another alternative is available to employers and unions who desire to reduce costs and time delay associated with regular arbitration. This is called *grievance mediation,* a procedure which combines elements of both mediation and arbitration. After the final step of the internal grievance procedure, the parties have the option of resorting to this procedure rather than regular arbitration. An experienced arbitrator is used, but one who possesses the skills and temperament of a mediator. After hearing the circumstances of a dispute, he or she first seeks to assist the parties in reaching a mutually satisfactory settlement. At this stage of the proceedings, the focus is on the problem which caused the grievance and not necessarily on the labor agreement. To be sure, the labor agreement establishes the limits within which a settlement can be reached. Nonetheless, by this approach there is ample room for innovative problem solving. The procedure is very informal. Witnesses relate their versions in narrative fashion and cross-examination normally does not take place. No briefs are submitted, and no record of the proceedings is made. So brief is the procedure that several grievances may be handled in one day.

If a settlement is not achieved through this initial step, the mediator-arbitrator issues an advisory opinion as to how the grievance would likely be decided if it were to go to conventional arbitration. This opinion is immediate, oral, and nonbinding. Should the parties accept the opinion, the grievance is resolved on that basis. If they do not, the parties are free to proceed to regular arbitration. Of course, in such an arbitration, the person who handled the grievance may not serve as arbitrator. Nothing that was said by the parties at the previous step, including the advisory opinion, may be used in the regular arbitration.

Though not used extensively, grievance mediation has apparently proved successful where employed. The procedure works well in the coal industry, not only substantially reducing costs and time, but otherwise serving the needs of the parties. Grievance mediation will presumably never replace arbitration, but it should be considered by employers and unions who have extensive arbitration.

DISCUSSION QUESTIONS

1. "The handling of workers' grievances on the job is perhaps the single most important function of modern unionism." How accurate is this statement?

2. It is generally agreed that a low grievance rate does not necessarily prove the existence of good union-management relations and that a high grievance rate does not necessarily prove the existence of poor relations between the parties. Why might the grievance statistics be misleading as a guide to the quality of the relationship?

3. From the employer's viewpoint, what advantages and disadvantages might there be in reducing a grievance to writing?

4. Harold W. Davey has argued that "a genuine grievance requires an airing, even if it is not strictly in order under the existing contract." What considerations, again from the employer's point of view, might justify this opinion?

5. Why might (a) a management or (b) a union prefer *not* to have an arbitration provision in the contract?

6. Dunlop and Healy have pointed out that although it is often said that "arbitration is an extension of collective bargaining," it is also frequently held that "arbitration is a judicial process." What are your own feelings regarding these two apparently inconsistent descriptions?

7. Given the fact that arbitrators have no compulsion to follow any other arbitrator's award or line of reasoning, how do you account for the fact that there are available at least three widely distributed publications that feature arbitration awards from all over the country? On the surface, would it not appear that such publications are a waste of time and money, since each arbitrator is in effect a law unto himself?

8. How could the present system of labor contract administration, as described in general terms in this chapter, be improved?

9. Beyond the authors' ideas to reduce arbitration delays and costs, can you offer additional suggestions to accomplish this goal?

10. Do you believe that arbitrators, like doctors and lawyers, should be certified by government before they could be permitted to arbitrate labor cases? Defend your position.

MINICASES

#1 A Dissenting View Regarding Arbitration

Years ago, the colorful and controversial leader of the International Brotherhood of Teamsters, Jimmy Hoffa, explained his adamant opposition to arbitration as follows:

> Even if it takes one or two hours or longer [for the management and the union] to work out a [grievance] settlement among ourselves we are better off, knowing the business as we do from both sides, than to submit a grievance to some third party who attempts to please both sides and who actually pleases nobody. In my opinion, the best method of settling grievances is to leave open the end for final settlement and, if we cannot mutually agree, either for the employer to lock out the union or for the union to strike the employer. If we don't come out with a completely satisfactory settlement we come out with a settlement both sides can live with and one which doesn't change the terms of the contract.

What do you think of this argument?

#2 An Embarrassing Incident for the Arbitrator

Professor Grover Harrison has been jointly selected as impartial ad hoc arbitrator by a union and management, none of whose principals he has ever met. Eating his breakfast alone in a booth in the dining room of the hotel in which the hearing will shortly be held, he overhears the following words emanating from the next booth:

> Well, of course, it's not the truth, but if we're to have any chance of winning this thing, we'd damned well better consistently stick to our claim that the supervisor on at least one occasion made lewd and suggestive remarks to Mary. She can be counted on to testify this way at the hearing, and she's a good enough liar so that there's no chance of her being shaken in the cross-examination.

If you were Harrison, what (if anything) would you now do?

NOTES

[1] Many unions specifically instruct their stewards and grievance committee members not to process grievances that have no merit under a labor agreement. Thus, in one union manual, "After you have thoroughly investigated the case, if you decide that no grievance exists, it is your duty to the worker and the union to state this, and to take time to explain why."

[2] *Textile Workers* v. *Lincoln Mills,* 353 U.S. 488 (1957).

[3] *United Steelworkers of America* v. *Warrior & Gulf Navigation Co.,* 363 U.S. 574 (1960); *United Steelworkers of America* v. *American Manufacturing Co.,* 363 U.S. 564 (1960); *United Steelworkers of America* v. *Enterprise Wheel & Car Corp.,* 363 U.S. 593 (1960).

[4] 475 U.S. 643 (1986).

[5] 415 U.S. 36 (1974).

[6] *Hines* v. *Anchor Motor Freight,* 424 U.S. 554 (1976).

[7] *Barrentine* v. *Arkansas-Best Freight System, Inc.,* 450 U.S. 728 (1981).

[8] 104 Sup. Ct. 1794 (1984).

[9] *Nabisco, Inc.* v. *NLRB,* 479 F (2d) 770 (CA 2, 1973).

[10] 192 NLRB 837 (1971).

[11] *United Paperworkers International Union* v. *Misco,* 108 S. Ct. 364 (1987).

SELECTED REFERENCES

Bureau of National Affairs, Inc., *Grievance Guide* (8th ed.). Washington, D.C.: Bureau of National Affairs, 1992.

Elkin, Randyl D., and Thomas L. Hewitt, *Successful Arbitration.* Reston, Va.: Reston, 1980.

Elkouri, Frank, and Edna Elkouri, *How Arbitration Works* (4th ed.). Washington, D.C.: Bureau of National Affairs, 1985.

Fairweather, Owen, *Practice and Procedure in Labor Arbitration* (2nd ed.). Washington, D.C.: Bureau of National Affairs, 1983.

Grossman, Mark M., *The Question of Arbitrability: Challenges to the Arbitrator's Jurisdiction and Authority.* Ithaca, N.Y.: ILR Press, Cornell University, 1984.

Hill, Marvin, Jr., and Anthony V. Sinicropi, *Evidence in Arbitration* (2nd ed.). Washington, D.C.: Bureau of National Affairs, 1987.

_____, *Remedies in Arbitration.* Washington, D.C.: Bureau of National Affairs, 1981.

Levin, Edward, and Donald Grody, *Witnesses in Arbitration.* Washington, D.C.: Bureau of National Affairs, 1987.

McKelvey, Jean T., ed., *The Changing Laws of Fair Representation.* Ithaca, N.Y.: ILR Press, Cornell University, 1985.

McPherson, Donald S., *Resolving Grievances: A Practical Approach.* Reston, Va.: Reston, 1983.

Pops, Gerald M., *Emergence of the Public Sector Arbitrator.* Lexington, Mass.: Lexington Books, 1976.

Repas, Bob, *Contract Administration: A Guide for Stewards and Local Officers.* Washington, D.C.: Bureau of National Affairs, 1984.

Zack, Arnold M., ed., *Arbitration in Practice,* Ithaca, N.Y.: ILR Press, Cornell University, 1984.

Zimny, Max, William F. Dolson, and Christopher A. Barreca, eds. *Labor Arbitration: A Practical Guide for Advocates.* Washington, D.C.: Bureau of National Affairs, 1990.

ARBITRATION CASES

As in the ten other arbitration cases that follow in later chapters, the two arbitration cases presented here are drawn from the authors' own experiences. They are actual cases; but since arbitration is a confidential process, the names of the employers and unions have been deleted. Also, to maintain confidentiality, fictitious names have been used for the witnesses.

In six of the cases, you will play the role of arbitrator. To reach a proper decision, be sure that you fully understand the basic facts and contractual provisions. Clearly establish the reasons for your decision in each case. In the discussion of these cases, at the instructor's discretion, the actual arbitrators' decisions may be disclosed to the class. These decisions can be found in the *Instructor's Manual.*

In six cases, the complete case is presented, not only the factual background and material contractual language but also the arbitrator's entire decision. Students are urged to read the cases. A great deal can be learned about the practical day-to-day problems of labor relations by faithful study of them. They show how a professional arbitrator handles cases submitted by the parties. Whether you agree with a decision is not really important. Rather, the value is to learn how arbitrators apply and interpret contractual language, evaluate evidence, apply commonly accepted principles of contractual construction and arbitration practices, and defend their decisions with what they would like to believe is logical and unassailable reasoning.

If you desire to read additional arbitration cases, thousands have been published by the Bureau of National Affairs, *Labor Arbitration Reports,* and Commerce Clearing House, *Labor Arbitration Awards.* These services have been available for many years. (In keeping with the confidentiality of the arbitration process, the employer and the union involved must agree to publication.) However, the published cases represent only a small percentage of the cases decided by arbitrators; the vast majority are found only in the private files of the arbitrators and the parties.

Each of the twelve cases has been placed at the end of the chapter in which reference to the case is made. As a result of the interest that they generated and their unusual nature, three cases from previous editions have been repeated. They are Case 5, "The Case of the Life-Support System"; Case 11, "The Case of the Employee Who Was Paid and Not Required to Work"; and Case 12, "Plant Closing: The Case of the Silent Sale."

Carefully selected questions follow the six cases appearing in their entirety. If you can answer the questions adequately, you should have a good understanding of the case. In the other six cases, your problem is this: If you had been the actual arbitrator, what would have been your decision and why?

Time Limits: The Case of the New Union President

CAST OF CHARACTERS

Bilbo	Grievant
Gill	Press Supervisor
Calls	Production Manager
Foote	General Manager
Bratt	Shop Steward
Battle	Supervisor of Quality Control and Safety
Mills	Steward
Galt	Employee
Hall	International Union Representative
	(Union Advocate at Arbitration)
Wills	Inpatient Counselor
Tilly	Local Union President
Brans	Regional Vice President
Sands	Company Attorney

(A "cast of characters" in this form is not contained in actual arbitration cases. It appears here and in the other cases in this volume to aid in the reading of the cases.)

Should a union fail to comply with the time limits stipulated in the grievance procedure, it could lose a grievance that might have merit. Equally, depending on the contractual language involved, an employer who ignores time limits could be required to grant a grievance that otherwise might not have merit. Time limits are incorporated into the grievance procedure to ensure that a grievance will be processed properly. To accomplish this purpose, both sides are under a time pressure to keep the grievance moving expeditiously through the various steps of the grievance procedure.

In the following case, the employer denied the grievance, protesting the discharge of an employee on the basis of time limits and its merits. Since the grievance was denied on the basis of time limits, the arbitrator did not determine whether or not the grievant was discharged for just cause. Pay particular attention to why the arbitrator did not accept the union's excuse for its failure to conform to the time limits.

Of course, the unfortunate employee had no responsibility for the failure of the union to meet the contractually stipulated time limits. Nonetheless, the employee did not have his day in court, and the arbitrator never reached the issue of determining whether he was discharged for just cause. Although the arbitrator did not learn what happened after he issued his decision (arbitrators seldom do), it is possible that the employee sued the union in federal court for failure to represent him fairly because it allowed time limits to expire. A prediction of whether such a lawsuit would have merit would be hazardous, to say the least. Federal courts, however, have held unions derelict in their legal requirement to represent all members in the bargaining unit in a fair manner. In those cases, under proper circumstances, the courts have directed unions to make a monetary award to compensate workers for the wages they lost. On the other hand, the U.S. Supreme Court held in the lead case, *Vaca* v. *Sipes* (386 U.S. 171, 1967), that the employee must prove that the union was "arbitrary" or engaged in "bad-faith conduct" in the processing of the grievance. Mere negligence does not normally add up to arbitrary and bad-faith conduct.

Note that the arbitrator used published arbitration cases to support his decision. Though other arbitration decisions are not binding on an arbitrator, case precedents are cited at times to show that the decision is consistent with accepted arbitration principles and practices.

GRIEVANCE

Effective March 13, 1990, Richard Bilbo was discharged by the Company. In protest, the Union filed Grievance No. 3-90 which stated:

> On March 13, 1990, Richard Bilbo was terminated. The Union feels this action was unjust.

Having failed to settle the dispute in the Grievance Procedure, the Parties convened this arbitration for its determination.

LABOR AGREEMENT

Article 3—Rights of Management

3.1 Subject to the provisions of this Agreement and the Collective Bargaining Rights of the Union, the right to hire, lay off, promote, demote, transfer, discharge for just cause, maintain discipline, require observance of reasonable Company rules and regulations and maintain efficiency of employees is the sole responsibility of the Company.

Article 10—Grievance Procedure

10.1 Definition of Grievance

a. Any difference between the Employee or the Union and the Company involving wages, hours of work, or conditions of employment shall constitute a grievance.

10.2 Steps and Time Limits of Grievance Procedure

e. Fifth Step: If the grievance is not settled in Step 4, the Union may appeal the written answer of the Manager of Industrial Relations, or his representative, to arbitration in accordance with the procedure and conditions set forth in the Arbitration Clause, Article 11. However, the Union shall give the Company notice of its intent to arbitrate within fifteen (15) days of receipt of the Company's answer.

10.3 Right of Appeal to Next Step

a. The parties agree to follow each of the foregoing steps in the processing of the Grievance.

b. If at any step the Company's representative fails to give his written answer within the time limits set forth therein, the Union may appeal the grievance to the next step at the expiration of such time limit.

c. If at any step in the Grievance Procedure the Union fails to indicate in writing its desire to proceed to the next step within the time limits specified in this Article, the grievance will be considered settled.

Article 11—Arbitration

11.1 Arbitration Procedure

a. If a grievance is not satisfactorily settled after having been fully processed in accordance with the Grievance Procedure, Article 10, it will be submitted to arbitration by the party desiring arbitration.

b. In such case, the party desiring arbitration shall notify the other party in writing within fifteen (15) days after the termination of the proceedings set forth in the Grievance Procedure.

General Plant Rules

An employee who fails to maintain at all times proper standards of conduct or who violates any of the following rules shall subject himself to disciplinary action including discharge.

6. Bringing...intoxicating liquors onto company property, drinking or possessing alcoholic beverages on company property or reporting to work intoxicated is strictly prohibited.

17. Insubordinate conduct or refusal to follow foreman's orders.

30. An employee must report for and remain at work at all times in a fit physical condition.

ISSUES

1. Is the grievance arbitrable on its merits under Articles 10 and 11 of the Labor Agreement?

2. If the preceding issue is resolved in the affirmative, the issue then is whether Grievant Bilbo was discharged for just cause. If not, what should the remedy be?

BACKGROUND

Events of March 9

When the circumstances of this case arose, Richard Bilbo, hired October 1972, No. 86 Press Operator, worked the first shift starting 7 A.M. Paul Gill, Press Supervisor, was his direct supervisor. Dennis Calls served as Production Manager, and George Foote was General Manager. Allen Bratt, currently Union Vice President, was the Shop Steward when the events of the case occurred.

Bilbo was a Union officer intermittently during his eighteen years of employment with the Company. However, he did not hold Union office at the time of his discharge.

On March 9, the Grievant reported at 7 A.M., but no work was available for him to run on the 86 Press. As a result, Gill assigned him to the 37 Flexo for training. When daylight occurred, the supervisor assigned him to clean up the yard. At 11 A.M., Gill instructed him to report to the 86 Press since work was available.

When Gill met Bilbo at the Press, the supervisor said:

...he was hollering, throwing up his hands, and acting real irate, causing a disturbance; that he could not find his dies.

And

> ...he was causing a commotion where everybody else was looking, and I just wanted to get him off the floor, sit him down, talk to him.

Gill told the Grievant that he wanted to talk to him in the office. He [Gill] located Shop Steward Bratt. In the office, the supervisor told Bilbo that he would not tolerate the way the Grievant spoke to him and disrupted the department. The Grievant said that he could not find the dies for the Press. Bratt and the supervisor told him that they would find the dies for him.

When they returned to the Press, the dies had been located. Gill instructed Bilbo to install the dies and start operations. At this point, the supervisor left to find Calls. Gill said that he wanted the Production Manager because he felt that the Grievant

> ...was drunk or on drugs or whatever. I figured he was either drunk or under the—drunk or something like that.

Unable to locate Calls, Gill returned and observed Bratt and Bilbo walking down the aisle. The Grievant told the supervisor that he was sick and going home. At the request of Gill, Jim Battle, Supervisor of Quality Control and Safety, arrived at the scene.

Gill told the Grievant that he could not leave, and wanted him to see the Company doctor. Bratt said Bilbo did not have to see the Company doctor, testifying:

> I said, "Paul [Gill], you cannot send him to the company doctor. He's got a right to go to his own doctor, if he's sick. If a man is sick, you cannot postpone him leaving."

In any event, the Grievant left the plant after clocking out.

By this time, Calls arrived, and Gill informed him what had occurred. For some reason, Bilbo returned to the plant. When the Grievant spoke to the Production Manager, Calls testified, he smelled alcohol on his breath. When the Grievant told him he was leaving, Calls warned him:

> Richard, you can't leave. If you do, you're going to be involuntarily or voluntarily—either way—terminating your employment here.

Calls scheduled a meeting in the Plant Superintendent's office located in the center of the plant and elevated. He said he did this intentionally so he could observe Bilbo while he walked there. Calls testified that the Grievant had difficulty walking, was very unsteady, and had trouble climbing the stairs.

March 9 Meeting

In attendance at the meeting were Bilbo, Battle, and Steward Terry Mills of the Union, and the Company was represented by Calls, Gill, and Battle. Calls believed that the Grievant was intoxicated, and asked him several times what he had been drinking, testifying he said:

...."You know, it's apparent you're intoxicated. It's obvious you've been drinking on company property. And what have you been drinking?" He never gave me a response.

Calls requested the Union representatives to go to the Grievant to verify that he smelled of alcohol. Bratt, sitting about 8 to 12 feet from the Grievant, said he did not have to do that because he could smell the alcohol from where he was.

When Calls asked the Grievant where he had been drinking, he replied: "Out by the fence," located on Company property. At this point, Bilbo said it was "no big deal" that Calls accused him of being intoxicated on Company property. Calls retorted:

Richard, yes it is a big deal, because we're talking about your job.

Calls suspended Bilbo until further notice. At this point, Bilbo pleaded for his job, asking for a second chance. Calls testified:

In this meeting [March 9], after I told Richard that he was suspended until further notice, he broke down and started to cry. And he said, "I need my job." And I said, "Well, Richard, you should have considered that before you committed the offenses that you did today." And he said, "Well, I need my job. And I can't afford to lose my job."

We sat for a few minutes, and gave him a chance to gather himself together. And just before the close of the meeting, he said, "What if I get help?" And I said, "The Company will consider that in our decision; give it consideration."

About this matter, Bratt testified:

I recall Mr. Bilbo saying, "I've got problems. I'm messed up. Would you give me a chance to get straightened up; give me a break?"

Mr. Calls then said, "I'll take it into consideration."

Company Policy and Alcohol Abuse

Testimony was supplied dealing with Company policy concerning employees who abuse alcohol. General Manager Foote supplied information about the Company's policy. Employees have requested help when they have a problem with alcohol and/or drugs. No employee has been discharged when bringing that problem to the attention of the Company.

Testifying on this matter, the General Manager added:

A: Well, we've assisted some employees—an employee who needed to go out of town to a clinic for rehabilitation. We helped make arrangements at the center, plus was able to give him some financial help, and plane tickets and so forth.

On occasion have had—have met with the doctor or the counselor in a rehabilitation center, to try to, I guess collectively work with that employee, and understand what was going on.

Also at the end of one employee's stay in a center, we met with the counselor there, just to get an up-to-date report on progress.

There have been employees that have gone to institutions, where we
have requested, and an employee has granted, that particular institution
to send us an up-to-date report on a weekly basis.

Q: Would we provide leaves of absence for people who approached us about
problems they were having?

A: Yes.

In connection with this matter, the record contains information about
Donnie Galt, Triplex Operator, still an employee. Foote testified that
Galt has had an alcohol problem, and that the Company has helped him.
Union Steward Bratt said that Galt has participated in alcohol rehabil-
itation programs three or four times. At least one time, said Foote and
Bratt, Galt was incarcerated because of the problem, and the Steward
testified that the Company had him released from jail.

In regard to Galt, the General Manager testified:

Q: Did Donnie Galt ever do anything on company time or company property
that had to do with possession of alcohol, use of alcohol, being under the
influence of alcohol, being drunk on the job, drinking on the job, or anything else to do with his work and alcohol?

A: No.

   Mr. Hall: He don't know that.

Q: Well, to your knowledge?

A: To my knowledge.

Along the same line:

Q: In fact, Mr. Bratt, wouldn't it be true to say that you have no knowledge
whatsoever that Mr. Galt has ever done anything on the job on company
time or on company property, that has anything to do with drinking alcohol, being under the influence of alcohol, being drunk, or anything like
that?

A: No.

According to the Company, it offered to help employees for alcohol abuse
before being disciplined for a Plant Rule infraction. Thus, Foote testified:

Q: Now on the other side of the coin, have we also had people who did
not approach us about a problem until after they did something
wrong?

A: Yes.

Q: In fact, within the last year, haven't we discharged an employee who came to us for help and received it, and then later committed violations of the rules because of the same problems, and was discharged?

A: Yes.

Q: Was that discharge upheld?

A: Yes.

The Parties disagree on whether the Company discriminated against the Grievant when it discharged him without offering him rehabilitation. The Company denies such a charge, arguing:

> The Employer respectfully submits that the Union has failed to establish that Grievant was the victim of disparate treatment. Only employees who have approached the Employer *before* violating the contract or work rules have been given an opportunity for rehabilitation without disciplinary penalty. Employees who have sought help *after* such rule violations have been disciplined appropriately without regard to such claims of "rehabilitation." [Emphasis in original]

On its part, the Union asserted:

> The other employees who have drinking problems, Mr. Foote himself has said—and will tell you—that he's helped people that's had drinking problems. He's taken them to these dry-out centers. And he's went to the hospital with them, and all these kinds of things. Very considerate to some employees.

> But yet Mr. Bilbo has the same kind of problem, but won't give him the consideration that's been given to other employees, for one reason and one reason only; he plain just wants to get rid of him. That's all.

> We feel that he deserves the same consideration that other employees have been given, whether you like him or whether you don't like him.

> You have employees working today who have the same kind of problems as Mr. Bilbo had, that the Company has gone along with, and has helped those employees and tried to rehabilitate them.

> But in Mr. Bilbo's case, they won't give him the same consideration. We just simply ask that he be given the same consideration that the other employees are given.

In the event that the grievance is held arbitrable, the discrimination issue will be resolved when the merits of the grievance are discussed.

Grievant's Rehabilitation Program

On March 9, after being suspended, Bilbo entered the alcoholic treatment program at Jefferson Alcohol and Drug Abuse Center (JADAC). He spent twenty-eight days as a resident patient at the Center.

On April 18, Mariana Wills, Inpatient Counselor, prepared a letter concerning the Grievant's period of residence. It stated:

To Whom It May Concern:

This letter is to inform you that Richard Bilbo entered treatment on 3-9-90 to address his presenting problem of chemical dependency. He was discharged from treatment on 4-3-90. He demonstrated a basic understanding of chemical dependency and the disease concept and the motivation to stay sober.

We recommend that he attend AA/NA maintain daily (sic) contact with his sponsor and attend aftercare counselling at JADAC.

If you have any further questions or need additional information, please feel free to contact me at 716-583-3951.

After his release, the Grievant said he participated in the aftercare program established by JADAC. He attended meetings for nine days following his release. After that he attended three meetings per week, absent only when his part-time job conflicted with the nighttime meetings.

Bilbo testified that he has not consumed alcohol since he participated in the JADAC program, having received a six-month token from his group "for not having a drop of alcohol."

Grievant Discharged: Grievance

Effective March 13, the Company discharged the Grievant. The discharge letter said:

As stated in the General Plant Rules, an employee who fails to maintain at all times proper standards of conduct or who violates any of the following rules shall subject himself to disciplinary action including discharge.

On March 9, 1990 you violated the following plant rules:

#6 Bringing firearms, weapons of any kind, illegal drugs or intoxicating liquors onto company property, drinking or possessing alcoholic beverages on company property or reporting to work intoxicated is strictly prohibited.

#17 Insubordinate conduct or refusal to follow foreman's orders.

#30 An employee must report for and remain at work at all times in a fit physical condition.

The violation of these rules on this occasion alone is enough to warrant discharge, however, these violations combined with your work history of repeated reprimands and suspensions for poor quality, poor performance, misconduct and violation of plant rules, leave me no alternative but to terminate your employment with the Company. Effective March 13, 1990.

Fourth Step Meeting

On April 24, the Fourth Step meeting was held concerning the grievance. Aside from Bilbo, the Union was represented by Kenneth Hall, International Union Representative, and Leonard Tilly, Local Union President. Representatives for the Company included Howard Brans, Regional Vice President, and General Manager Foote.

In that session, the Grievant advised the Company that he had participated in the JADAC program, asking it to take that into consideration.

Foote testified that the Grievant said he had an alcohol problem, and he and the Union requested the Company for help. Bilbo testified:

Q: ...Now, during this fourth-step meeting, Bilbo, do you recall making an appeal to the Company to give you a second chance?

A: Yes, sir. Not only that, I made an appeal the day the incident happened.

On April 30, the Company denied the grievance at the Fourth Step.

Executive Board Action: Unfair Labor Practice Charge

On May 1, 1990, Tilly wrote Foote that the grievance would be "submitted to the Union Executive Board for arbitration." Six days later, May 7, the Union President advised Foote that the Union "will not arbitrate Grievance N3-90 Richard Bilbo."

Advised of the Executive Board's action, the Grievant filed an unfair labor practice charge against the Union. Submitted to the National Labor Relations Board on May 22, alleging a violation of the National Labor Relations Act, it stated:

> Since on or about May 11, 1990, the above-named labor organization has failed to fairly represent the interests of Richard Bilbo by refusing to process his discharge grievance to arbitration for reasons which are arbitrary, capricious and invidious.

> Additional the Union has failed to process another grievance on his behalf concerning health insurance premiums for reasons which are arbitrary, capricious and invidious.

Responding to the charge on May 25, the Company advised the National Labor Relations Board:[*]

Charge No. 1

> See attached letter to Richard Bilbo terminating his employment with this Company.

*Though filed against the Union, the NLRB requested the Company to reply to the charges.

The Union filed a grievance on his behalf. The grievance followed the Grievance Procedure as outlined in the current labor contract (Page 13, Article 10.2). This meant that it was heard at steps 1 thru 4. The fifth step is presentation for arbitration. The Union did not wish to arbitrate this grievance.

Charge No. 2

This grievance was filed by Richard Bilbo regarding payment of insurance premiums by the Company.

This grievance went thru steps 1, 2 & 3. The Company's answer was "Company portion of insurance," "it has always been the practice that the company pay up to 13 weeks if the employee is receiving S & A benefits."

Richard Bilbo was not denied any benefits based on this grievance.

Comment: The Union did state after the Company answer (step 3) that they would discuss the "13 weeks" at the next contract negotiations, June 1990.

Reversal of Executive Board's Decision

On June 10, the Local Union convened a membership meeting for the purpose of ratifying the Labor Agreement negotiated by the Parties. At this meeting, appealing to the membership, Bilbo requested it to reverse the decision of the Executive Board refusing to arbitrate his discharge grievance. The membership voted to override the Executive Board.

Subsequently, Union President Tilly wrote the International Union Vice President and International Union President concerning the matter. Both advised Tilly that under the Local Union's bylaws the membership had the authority to override the Executive Board.

On June 26, the NLRB approved the Grievant's request to withdraw the unfair labor practice charge previously filed against the Union.

Request for Panel of Arbitrators

On July 15, International Union Representative Hall requested a panel of arbitrators from the American Arbitration Association. The Union supplied the Company with a copy of the letter. Complying with the Union's request, AAA furnished a panel to the Company and Union.

While making his selection, David Sands, Company Attorney, advised the Tribunal Administrator (Cincinnati Region) on July 24 that the

> Union did not request arbitration of the subject grievance in a timely manner under the collective bargaining agreement, and, therefore, the matter is not arbitrable.

In any event, said Sands, the Company was prepared to put the issue of procedural arbitrability to the arbitrator, and indeed would strongly propose the arbitrator decide that issue, and only that issue, before the Employer is forced to argue about the merits of the case.

At the arbitration, both Parties eventually agreed with the Arbitrator's recommendation that the evidence pertaining to arbitrability and the merits be presented at the same hearing. He advised the Parties he would not inquire into the merits of the discharge unless he held the grievance arbitrable. Thus:

> What I would do is I take the evidence on arbitrability, if it can be divorced from the merits, and then take the evidence of the merits. And then, when I work on the case, of course, I decide the issue of arbitrability.
> If I find it's not arbitratable, that's it. I don't [inquire into] the merits. But if I find it arbitratable, then I go into the merits.

POSITIONS OF THE PARTIES

Whereas the Company requests that the grievance be denied, the Union asserts that it should be granted. In the Company's view, the grievance is not arbitrable because the Union did not comply with the time limits for appeal to arbitration. In the event that the grievance is held arbitrable, the Company claims that Bilbo was discharged for just cause.

According to the Union, not only is the grievance arbitrable on its merits, but also Bilbo was not discharged for just cause.

EVALUATION OF THE EVIDENCE

Timeliness of Appeal to Arbitration

Sequence of Events

Should it be held that the Union did not comply with the time limits governing appeal to arbitration, the grievance shall be denied on that basis without inquiry into the merits of Bilbo's discharge. On the other hand, should it be held the Union complied with such time limits, a determination shall be made as to whether the Company discharged him for just cause.

Undisputed is the sequence of the events involved in the time limits issue. Effective March 13, the Company informed Bilbo of his discharge. On the same day, he filed the grievance protesting the discharge. On April 30, the Company denied the grievance in the Fourth Step of the Grievance Procedure.

On May 1, Union President Tilly notified the Company that the grievance would be submitted to the Executive Board to determine whether to proceed to arbitration. On May 7, he notified the Company that the Union would not arbitrate the grievance.

In a membership meeting held on June 10, the Local Union overrode the Executive Board, voting to arbitrate Bilbo's grievance. In a letter dated July 15, the Union requested a panel of arbitrators from the American Arbitration Association. A copy of the letter was supplied to the Company. When the Company made its selection, it advised the AAA that the Union had not requested arbitration in a timely manner.

Applicable Contractual Provisions

Based on the material language contained in Article 10, Grievance Procedure, the Union did not comply with the time limits for its appeal to arbitration. Section 10.2, Fifth Step, states that if the grievance is not settled in the Fourth Step the Union may appeal the grievance to arbitration. Such appeal, however, requires the Union to give "notice of its intent to arbitrate within fifteen (15) days" of the receipt of the Company's Fourth Step answer. Given this language, the Union should have advised the Company of its intent to arbitrate not later than May 15.

Section 11.1 of Article 11, Arbitration, states that if a grievance is not settled in the Grievance Procedure, it shall be submitted to arbitration by the party desiring arbitration. In such case, the party desiring arbitration shall notify the other party "within fifteen (15) days after the termination of the proceedings set forth in the Grievance Procedure." When the Union received notice from the Company on April 30 of its denial of the grievance in the Fourth Step, the Grievance Procedure proceedings were terminated. Once again the Union had until May 15 to notify the Company of its desire to arbitrate.

Section 10.3 of Article 10 states that if at any step of the Grievance Procedure the Union fails to indicate in writing its desire to proceed to the next step within the time limits specified in the Article, "the grievance will be considered settled." Under this language, the Union had until May 15 to notify the Company in writing to proceed to arbitration as established by the language contained in the Fifth Step of the Grievance Procedure.

But such written notice was *not* supplied until the Company received a copy of the Union's letter, dated July 15, to the American Arbitration Association requesting a panel of arbitrators.

True, rumors floated in the plant about arbitrating the grievance before the Company received a copy of the Union's letter addressed to the AAA. About this, General Manager Foote testified:

Q: George, when did you first learn that the Union was going to arbitrate this case?

A: Ken, when I got your letter requesting the list of Arbitrators.

***

...there was rumors that you were considering taking this to arbitration, but I had no facts to that.

***

Q: Are you saying, George, you had no conversation with anyone in regard to this; you had no knowledge until you got that letter?

A: Right. All I had was, Ken, what I would say rumor. They were by your people.

Nonetheless, no evidence demonstrates that even those rumors circulated prior to May 15. In short, the Company was not advised orally or in writing that the Union intended to arbitrate Bilbo's grievance by May 15.

Burden of Union

In the light of the foregoing, the Union bears an extremely heavy burden in this dispute. Its burden is to persuade the Arbitrator to ignore the time limits provision written in clear, unambiguous, and unequivocal terms. No possible confusion or conjecture exists regarding the Parties' agreement concerning the time limits:

> The Union shall give the Company notice of its intent to arbitrate *within fifteen (15) days of receipt of the Company's* [Fourth Step] answer. [Emphasis added]

> If at any step in the Grievance Procedure the Union fails to indicate in writing its desire to proceed to the next step within the time limit specified in this article, *the grievance will be considered settled.* [Emphasis added]

> In such case, the party desiring arbitration shall notify the other party *in writing within fifteen (15) days after the termination of the proceedings set forth in the Grievance Procedure.* [Emphasis added]

The language contains no ambiguity whatsoever. Not only is the language clear-cut, but the Company invoked time limits immediately after being informed in writing by the Union of its intention to arbitrate the grievance.

The Union's burden becomes even greater because of the time period involved. It missed the contractually mandated time limits by two months. Whereas the Union's appeal to arbitration should have been made by May 15, it was not until July 15 that it notified the Company in writing of its intention to arbitrate. This is not a situation where an employer or union is one or two days late which might reasonably be overlooked.

Finally, the burden of the Union becomes even more difficult because of the language contained in Section 11.3 of Article 11 of the Labor Agreement. It states:

> The Arbitrator shall have no power to add to, subtract from, or modify the terms of this Agreement.

Given the strict limitation on his authority, would not the Arbitrator add to, subtract from, or modify the language in question should he ignore the fifteen (15) day limit for appeal to arbitration? Just to raise this question is to provide the obvious answer.

Union's Excuse

To meet its burden, the Union asserts that the time limit in question should not prevail because Tilly was a relatively new Union President. At the time of the circumstances of the dispute, he had held office for nine months. Tilly testified that he did not know that the Local Union membership could override the Executive Board concerning the appeal of a grievance to arbitration. Had he known about the power of the Local Union, the Union President testified, he and/or the Executive Board would not have informed the Company that the Union would not arbitrate the grievance.

On these grounds, the Union asserts:

Now, as far as the arbitrability issue that the Company is going to raise, here was a new Local president who's been president of the Local for nine months, who was not familiar with the procedures; who on one other occasion—I won't bring it out—that the Company has taken advantage of him, wrote a mistakenly—was under the assumption that the Local Union Executive Board's decision was final.

To deny the person the right to go to arbitration because some Local president screwed up, because the Company took advantage of their inexperience, is what happened. The Company has plain taken advantage of inexperience. To deny that person the right to go to arbitration would be wrong.

While addressing this problem, it is recognized that under proper circumstances arbitrators have held that time limits do not prevail. In *Associated Grocers of Colorado* (74 LA 14), a case cited by the Company, Arbitrator Finston stated:

The underlying purpose of a grievance and arbitration clause in a collective bargaining agreement is to promote the quick and final settlement of disputes arising under the contract. In the interest of fostering constructive day-to-day relations between the parties, arbitrators have tended to resolve disputes involving procedural arbitrability in favor of proceeding with the case on its merits, where procedural violations are deemed relatively minor or where mitigating circumstances are involved.

In this regard, the Elkouris have observed:

If the agreement does contain clear time limits for filing and prosecuting grievances, failure to observe them generally will result in dismissal of the grievance if the failure is protested. Thus, the practical effect of late filing in many instances is that the merits of the dispute are never decided.

It has been held that doubts as to the interpretation of contractual time limits or as to whether they have been met should be resolved against forfeiture of the right to process the grievance. Moreover, even if time limits are clear, late filing will not result in dismissal of the grievance if the circumstances are such that it would be unreasonable to require strict compliance with the time limits specified by the agreement.[*]

[*]Elkouri and Elkouri, *How Arbitration Works,* 4th ed. (1985), pp. 193, 194 (citations omitted).

In this light, the fundamental issue here is whether the excuse offered by the Union constitutes a minor or mitigating circumstance so as to make it unreasonable to require strict compliance with the time limit in question as mandated by the Labor Agreement. Certainly, the Union's action does not amount to a minor procedural violation. Not when two (2) months elapsed between the time the Union should have appealed to arbitration and when it finally notified the Company of its intention to arbitrate.

With full deference to the Union and its Advocate, the excuse does not stand as a mitigating circumstance to justify ignoring the unambiguous time limit in question. A party does not take advantage of the other party when it insists that unambiguous contractual terms be applied as written. What would be the attitude of the Union if in another case the Arbitrator denied a grievance, ignoring crystal-clear contractual language supporting its position? It would be incensed and rightfully so!

Either Tilly and/or the Executive Board knew or should have known the authority of the Executive Board and the Local Union membership in matters of arbitration. In all candor, it is very difficult to believe that a person holding the highest office of a local union would not be aware of its bylaws. It was Tilly's responsibility to be aware of the responsibilities of his office and that of the Executive Board.

In no way may the Union shift the responsibility to the Company concerning the fate of the Bilbo grievance. It accepted the Union's decision not to arbitrate the grievance. In error or not, the Union was two months late in its appeal to arbitration. That was the Union's doing and not that of the Company. Nor is arbitration the proper forum to rescue a party from an error of its own making.

At stake here are not the bylaws of the Local Union or the constitution of the International Union. Instead, the crux of this dispute is the integrity of crystal-clear contractual language.

Processing of Grievance No. 9-89

Nor may Bilbo's discharge grievance be held arbitrable based on the processing of Grievance No. 9-89. On or about May 2, 1989, the Union filed that grievance dealing with Bilbo's insurance benefits. It stated:

> On May 14th, 1989 Richard showed me a letter he received May 2nd from the Co. It states that after 13 wks. off work for S.A. he is responsible for the total amount of his insurance premiums.
>
> Richard believes this action is unjust.

For settlement, the Union requested that Bilbo be made whole. Production Manager Calls denied the grievance in Step 2 of the Grievance Procedure on January 15.

Given the hiatus, the Union asserts:

> ...Now there have been—The Union will put on evidence to show the same Mr. Bilbo had a grievance on insurance, that the Company kept dragging their feet, dragging their feet.

It took over a year to get the Company to give us an answer on that grievance. And finally, in my step of the grievance procedure, I said, "Look, damn it, give us an answer. Give us an answer in writing."

The Company thinks it's okay. They want to sit on their can and let the time limits roll on and on and on. That's all right. But when we screw up or the Local screws up, then they want to holler foul.

Under the terms of Section 10.3 of the Labor Agreement, the Union argument has no merit. It states:

If at any step the Company's representative fails to give his written answer within the time limits set forth therein, the Union may appeal the grievance to the next step of the expiration of such time limit.

When the Company failed to respond to the insurance grievance in a timely manner, the Union had the contractual right to appeal the grievance to the next step. At Step 2, the Production Manager had five (5) working days to provide an answer after the discussion of the grievance at that level. Accordingly, the Union had the contractual right to appeal the grievance to Step 3 and to Step 4 and arbitration should the Company have failed to meet its time limits obligations. With regard to Grievance 9-89, the Union did not exercise its contractual right to advance the grievance when the Company failed to meet the mandated time limits.

It is understood, however, that the Union believes an inequity exists concerning the penalty for violations of the time limits. Should the Union fail to meet its time limits, Section 10 C states "the grievance will be considered settled." When it is late, the Union forfeits the grievance as in the case at hand. However, when the Company is late, the grievance may only be appealed to the next step. The Company does not forfeit the grievance if it fails to comply with the time limits.

Nonetheless, if the Union believes the unequal penalties constitute an inequity, the remedy must be achieved at the bargaining table and not in arbitration. Given the limited authority provided arbitrators in labor agreements (as in the instant contract), they do not have the authority to erase language from a labor agreement that they may feel is unfair, inequitable, or unwise.

Conclusion and Award

The Arbitrator would have much preferred to deal with the grievance on its merits. Whatever may have been its outcome on that basis, at least Bilbo would have had his day in court.

As stated, the burden of the Union is extremely heavy in this dispute. Unambiguous contractual language establishes the time limits. Two months elapsed before the Union appealed the grievance to arbitration. At no time did the Company waive its right to invoke time limits. To ignore the time limits, the Arbitrator would have added to, subtracted from, or modified the Labor Agreement—action that is strictly forbidden by the provision establishing the parameters of his allowable authority.

The Union's excuse is simply not sufficient to override these observations. It did not meet its burden because its excuse does not justify ignoring the clear and unambiguous contractual language establishing the mandated time limits. For this reason, the grievance shall be denied as procedurally defective, ruling out a determination of whether Bilbo was discharged for just cause.

QUESTIONS

1. Was it fair for the arbitrator to deny the grievance on the basis of time limits, sustaining grievant Bilbo's discharge without a determination of whether he was discharged for just cause?

2. Why did the arbitrator hold that Bilbo's previous insurance grievance was not material to the issue of time limits in the discharge proceeding?

3. What did the arbitrator mean when he said "...the Union bears an extremely heavy burden in this dispute"?

4. Why did the arbitrator rule that the company did not waive its right to invoke time limits?

5. Explain why the arbitrator refused to accept the union's excuse for its failure to meet time limits. Would you have accepted the excuse?

Past Practice: The Case of Unambiguous Contract Language

Past practice is an extremely important standard for the application of vague or ambiguous contractual language. When the language of the material provisions is unambiguous, however, the language normally prevails over an inconsistent practice.

In the following case, the union contends that past practice should be used to grant the grievance. Although Article VII, Section 6, the seniority provision, does not address curtailments or layoffs for less than two weeks, the union claims that past practice authorized a senior qualified employee to "bump" or displace a junior service employee from a layoff of even one day. That is what happened in this case: Because of lack of work, assemblers, the classification of the grievant, did not work on Friday, May 13, 1988. However, the cutting machine did operate, and the grievant had the qualifications to do the work assigned to two junior service employees. When the company refused to permit her to bump either junior service employee, she filed her grievance.

As you read the case, pay particular attention to the fundamental arbitration principle that the arbitrator used to deny the grievance, ruling that past practice did not prevail.

GRIEVANCE

On May 13, 1988, Mildred Hunt filed Grievance No. MH51308B which stated:

> The company curtailed the operation Friday, May 13, 1988 except for the Die Cutter and other miscellaneous work. This curtailment and/or layoff was without regard to seniority. This curtailment and/or layoff procedure is in violation of Article VII and any other provisions of the labor agreement that may apply.

For its settlement she requested that "the appropriate number of senior employees be made whole for all wages lost due to the improper curtailment and/or layoff."

Failing to settle the dispute, the Parties convened this arbitration for its determination.

LABOR AGREEMENT

Article VII—Seniority

Section 6—Curtailment, Layoff and Recall Procedure

> In the event the Company's operations are curtailed for more than one (1) week (five [5] days), and some of the employees receive less than a forty (40) hour work week because of the curtailment, the Company shall discuss the operations outlook with the Local Union Committee.
> If the curtailed operations is expected to continue for more than two (2) weeks, then the Company will lay off the least senior employee(s) by plant seniority and maintain as near as possible a forty (40) hour work week schedule for the remaining employees.
> When laying off help, the least senior employee in plant seniority will be the first to be laid off. When calling help back, the senior employee in plant seniority on layoff shall be the first to be called back, providing he is qualified to perform the work available.
> ***

To the extent necessary, other provisions will be cited.

ISSUE

Under the circumstances of this case, did the Employer violate Article VII of the Labor Agreement? If so, what should be the remedy?

BACKGROUND

Employer Operations

Located in Monroe County, Ohio, the Employer manufactures corrugated cardboard partitions used by its customers to separate bottles within boxes. To produce the product, a band saw machine or a rotary die cutter is used. More expensive to operate, the rotary die produces a cleaner and more precise cut compared to partitions made on the band saw. At the minimum, the band saw produces 15,000 pieces per manhour and the rotary die produces 1,800 pieces per manhour. The plant operates on a three-shift basis.

Assigned to the band saw are Saw Operator, Slitter Operator, and Take-Off Person. The latter checks the quality of the product and stacks the finished partitions on carts. Assigned to the rotary die are a Die Cutter Operator, an Assistant Operator, and at least two Take-Off Persons. Under the line of the progression system of seniority established in the Labor Agreement, the Saw Operator, Die Cutter Operator, and Assistant Die Cutter Operator are not subject to plantwide bumping in the event of a curtailment, layoff, or reduction in the work force.

Theresa Fritz, Operations Manager, explained:

> The operators in the cutting equipment are in what we call a line of progression job. They are protected under the contract. They do not fall into plantwide seniority status. They fall into plantwide seniority status within the line of progression. There is a very distinct advantage to being in a line of progression job, because you are protected under the contract in case of a layoff. The operator and the assistant operator are protected. Within the line of progression the seniority prevails. And the intent of that is always to have on the two machines that control the flow of materials through our plant, to always have a ready, producing at capacity operator. If the saw operator or the die cutter operator is not there you have an assistant operator who can step right in and produce at capacity in order to keep the assemblers running. And that's why they are not within plantwide seniority status.

After the material is cut by either the band saw or rotary die, Assemblers put the partitions together by operating fully automatic or semi-automatic assembly machines. Within the plant are three fully automatic and two semi-automatic machines. Whereas the cutting machines operate on all three shifts, normally assembly work is performed on the first and second shifts. Assemblers are expected to average 1,000 assembled sets per hour per machine where the partition contains the normal five piece set.

Week of May 9, 1988

Events of this week generated the grievance subject of this proceeding. At that time the Employer was filling a Clorox order for about 130,000 sets. They were produced on the rotary die machine, using white two-sided paper. This resulted in double the cost compared with kraft paper, which is normally used to make partitions. Fritz testified it was the first order of that kind ever produced in the plant.

Production difficulties involved the brittle nature of the paper and the requirement to strip out by hand excess material from each slot. A sufficient number of employees was not available for the stripping process. As a result, said the Operations Manager, the die cutter operated at a "snail's pace," production dropping from the normal 1,800 pieces per manhour to 300–400 pieces per hour.

Given the reduction of parts from the die cutter, sufficient work was not available for the Assemblers. On Monday, they were kept busy with the parts left over from the previous week. By Tuesday, Fritz testified, they worked "hand-to-mouth." Though the saws were operating, the product did not make up for the lack of output from the die cutter. Between Tuesday and Thursday, the Assemblers were assigned to a variety of clean-up work.

Character of Grievance: Events of Friday, May 13, 1988

On Thursday, May 12, the Employer scheduled only the die cutting crews for the Friday, May 13 shift. A notice to that effect was posted, listing the cutting crews, saying:

> Due to production requirements we find it necessary to work the die cutting crews only tomorrow, May 13, 1988.

As a result, the Assemblers were not scheduled for Friday. One of the Assemblers not scheduled was Grievant Hunt. Employed at the plant since September 10, 1976, her classification was Automatic Assembler assigned to the first shift.

For the first shift May 13, Robby Rett was the Die Cutter Operator and Lee Toulon served as Assistant Operator. Also assigned to the machine were Nombe and Evans, classified at that time as Utility, the entry-level classification. On that day they served as Take-Off Persons. Stipulated by the Parties was that Hunt is senior to Nombe and Evans. Also stipulated was that the Grievant was qualified to work as Assistant Die Cutter Operator and Die Cutter Take-Off.

Hunt said she filed the grievance because she was senior to Evans and Nombe and qualified as Assistant Die Cutter Operator and Take-Off.

EVALUATION OF THE EVIDENCE

Curtailment or Schedule Change

Certain propositions are not in question in this dispute. No question exists that the Grievant had the qualifications and seniority to be assigned to the die cutter on May 13, 1988. The Parties stipulated that she is qualified as an Assistant Die Cutter and Take-Off Person for the machine. They also agreed she had seniority over Nombe and Evans, who were assigned to the take-off operation on the day in question. Finally, despite the line of progression system of seniority, Hunt could have displaced either Nombe or Evans as Take-Off Person on the die cutter, as Fritz testified.

The Arbitrator: So the takeoff person is not a line of progression job.
The Witness: No. On the die cutter it is not.
                              ***
The Arbitrator: ...But in any event the job in question in this case is
    subject to bumping.
The Witness: Right.

In contrast, disagreement exists as to the term to be used to describe the event which occurred on May 13. According to the Union, a curtailment and/or layoff took place on that date. Thus:

> ...Ms. Hunt's permanent classification is Automatic Assembler Operator, which was the position affected by the partial curtailment.

In the Employer's view, the event was not a curtailment of operations or layoff:

> The schedule change of May 13 did not constitute a layoff and therefore was not in violation of the collective bargaining agreement. Labor arbitrators have consistently held that merely decreasing work hours due to legitimate business necessity does not constitute a layoff or curtailment.

The proper term to be used relates to the application of Article VII, Section 6, of the Labor Agreement. Under its terms, should the Employer's operations be curtailed for more than five days, and some employees receive less than a forty hour work week, the Employer and Local Union Committee shall discuss the operations outlook. If the curtailment is expected to continue for more than two weeks, the Employer is mandated to lay off the least senior employees by plant seniority.

In other words, if the May 13 event is called a schedule change, the grievance would have no standing under the provision. Layoffs by seniority are permitted only when there is a curtailment of Company operations. Consistent with its position, the Employer argues that under Article III, Management Rights, it has the unilateral right to change schedules:

However, the Union's position is without merit as the contract language is clear with respect to management's right to alter an employee's work schedule without regard to seniority. The Contract unequivocally states that management has the exclusive right to "*establish work schedules* and to make changes therein essential to the efficient operation of the plant." [Emphasis in original]

On the other hand, if the event is called a curtailment of operations, the grievance has standing under Section 6 of Article VII. Under these circumstances, the proper application of the provision is material for the decision in this proceeding.

Past Practice: Hunt's Testimony

According to Hunt, the provision does not address a curtailment of less than two weeks. It says layoffs by seniority are mandated when the curtailment is expected to exceed two weeks. In the Union's view, however, past practice supports its position requiring layoff by seniority even if the curtailment, as here, was only for one day. Thus:

> It was the testimony of Ms. Hunt that though the Labor Agreement did not expressly address curtailments of operation of less than a fourteen day duration that under those circumstances, the senior qualified employees were afforded the opportunity to work before the less senior employees.

Certainly, this practice is the "common sense" approach to such a situation.

To demonstrate the practice, the Grievant testified:

Q: Have senior employees, if qualified, since your employment at the Company been asked before junior employees in these circumstances?

A: Yes, we have.

Q: And you have been employed at the Company how long?

A: Twelve and a half years.

In the past, said Hunt, Jim Sparks, Plant Manager, would ask her to work under circumstances like those of May 13. She said May 13 was the first time a qualified senior employee did not displace a junior service employee during a curtailment of less than two weeks. Stressing the practice, the Union stated:

> Ms. Hunt testified Ms. Fritz was the first manager not to follow the practice of affording the opportunity to the senior employees to work before less senior in situations such as the one that transpired on May 13, 1988. This testimony went unrebutted.

Hunt also related an instance that occurred during the 1984 contract negotiations. For nine years, Hunt served as Union Steward and also participated in contract negotiations. Paul Root, former Manufacturing Manager, informed the Grievant she would be laid off for three days because only the saw crew would work and the Assemblers were to be laid off. When she protested, telling him she was senior to the employee on the Saw Take-Off, Root instructed her to work the three days as Saw Take-Off and Slitter.

In short, the Union claims that the grievance should prevail on the basis of past practice. Commenting on the absence of Plant Manager Sparks at the arbitration, the Union asserted:

> The Company, for reasons known only to them, did not produce Mr. Jim Sparks, the Plant Manager, to testify even though he is still employed by the Company. The plant, as stated by counsel for the Company, is located approximately an eighth of a mile from the hearing site, thus Mr. Sparks was certainly [accessible].

> There was unrebutted testimony by the grievant, that Paul Root, former Manufacturing Manager, and Mr. Sparks, Plant Manager, had always asked the senior employees to work before junior employees under circumstances such as those that existed on May 13, 1988.

> One would question why Mr. Sparks was not called to rebut the testimony of the grievant.

Past Practice: Fritz's Testimony

In contrast, Operations Manager Fritz testified to instances when due to production difficulties and delay employees were sent home regardless of seniority, and not offered the opportunity to displace junior service employees. She said:

Q: ...you say, we have many, many times run out of anything to saw cut and have sent the saw crews home.

A: Yes.

Q: Can you elaborate on that at all?

A: Yes. Due to our previous discussion that we just went through, there are times when there is nothing for the saw to run and we send them home. I think there were three or four days in one week that we sent the saw crew home, without a grievance, because they ran out of anything to do. They came in and did their job and went home when it was finished.

Q: When you send the saw crew home do you offer the members of the saw crew the opportunity to bump or displace other workers?

A: No. There are times whenever there might be work, you know, miscellaneous type work that needs to be done. And if there is anything for them to do we will ask them if they want to do it before they go home sometimes. There are times when there is nothing to do and we just say go home.

When Fritz denied the grievance she stated:

On May 13, only one machine, the die cutter, and maintenance was scheduled to work. There were no parts for the assemblers to run, due to very low productivity on the die cutter. We have run out of parts many, many times in the past and have sent the assembler operators home. We have many, many times run out of anything to saw cut, and have sent the saw crews home. We have had many times when the cutting dept. machinery has broken down and we have sent people home and/or called people to tell them not to come in because we don't need them on the machine etc. We do not lay-off and bump down by plantwide seniority to accomplish this. We simply tell the people that we don't need to go home.

To support its position on practice, the Employer refers to a letter denying a grievance, December 16, 1982, addressed to the Union. It stated:

Re: Grievance CG111882

As stated by the aggrieved, the second shift assembly operators were called prior to the start of their shift and told not to report for work November 16, 1982, as there was a lack of cut parts. The second shift saw operation was to report as normal, for their regular shift operation.

Prior to the start of second shift, one member of the saw crew called and reported "Off sick."

The Plant Manager started calling, by seniority, all second shift qualified saw take-off employees looking for a replacement to fill the saw take off vacancy. Those employees reached declined the opportunity to report for work and some employees, the aggrieved being one, were not home to receive our call.

The aggrieved was called more than once, November 16, 1982. The Plant Manager, Mr. Sparks, and the shift supervisor, Mr. Ambos, in Mr. Sparks's presence, also tried to reach her by phone.

Because the Company followed the call-in procedure as outlined in our Labor contract, two members of management tried to reach the aggrieved by phone, without success. We must deny Grievance CG111882.

The circumstances that prevailed on November 16, 1982 were not the same as those of May 13, 1988. The issue in the former grievance was the use of seniority to fill a vacancy. The issue in this dispute is whether Hunt had the contractual right to displace or bump a junior service employee. In regard to the aforecited letter, the Employer argues:

...As in the instant case, on November 16, 1982 the Company, due to a lack of cut parts, told the assemblers to stay home for one day. The Union did *not* grieve that rescheduling, but only claimed that a vacancy caused by an illness on the saw crew should be filled by a senior worker.

Obviously, the Union acquiesced in the Company's decision to schedule only the saw crews and it cannot now claim a contrary past practice. [Emphasis in original]

Nonetheless, the Union claims that the grievance should be granted on the basis of practice. It believes Fritz is not qualified in contract administration compared to Hunt, who has served as Union Steward for nine years and participated in contract negotiations. Fritz became Operations Manager in the middle of 1987.

About this matter the Union says:

> The Union questions Ms. Fritz's knowledge of the Labor Agreement and its past application, as well as the operation of the plant in general.

Practice and Controlling Language

To place the Union's position in its most favorable light, we shall assume that the events of May 13 constituted a curtailment within the meaning of Article VII, Section 6, and further assume past practice supports its position. Needless to say, the Arbitrator fully understands the critical importance of past practice in labor relations. Over the years he has denied and granted grievances based on this principle of the arbitration process. Early in his career, for example, he stated:

> Such an assessment of the place of past practice in labor relations conflicts with a cardinal principle of arbitration. *Thus, a longstanding past practice mutually engaged in by a company and union is as binding on both sides as a written clause in a collective bargaining contract.* If the Company's position were to be sustained on this basis, it would be the same in principle as an affirmation of the right of the Company to break with impunity a written clause of the Labor Agreement which proves to be burdensome to its operation. *Witco Chemical Co.*, 30 LA 901, 907. [Emphasis in original]

With full deference to the Union and its Advocate, however, its reliance on past practice is misplaced in this dispute. Past practice becomes the determining factor when contractual language is vague, uncertain, or ambiguous. Under such circumstances, practice normally controls the meaning of that kind of language. When contractual language is unambiguous and crystal-clear, language prevails over practice. Perhaps Arbitrators Justin and Wyckoff put it best when they said

> Plain and unambiguous words are undisputed facts. The conduct of Parties may be used to fix a meaning to words and phrases of uncertain meaning. Prior acts cannot be used to change the explicit terms of a contract. An arbitrator's function is not to rewrite the Parties' contract. His function is limited to finding out what the Parties intended under a particular clause. The intent of the Parties is to be found in the words which they, themselves, employed to express their intent. When the language used is clear and explicit, the arbitrator is constrained to give effect to the thought expressed by the words used. *Phelps Dodge Copper Prods. Corp.*, 16 LA 229, 233 (Jules Justin)

And

[Established practice] is a useful means of ascertaining intention in case of ambiguity or indefiniteness; but no matter how well established a practice may be, it is unavailing to modify a clear promise. *Tide Water Oil Co.* 17 LA 829, 833 (Hubert Wyckoff)

Analysis of Section 6, Article VII

In the case at hand, the material contractual language is not ambiguous calling for construction on the basis of practice. To the contrary, it is clear and unambiguous, making a decision based on practice wholly unacceptable. Consider the language contained in Section 6 of Article VII:

If the curtailed operation is expected to continue *for more than two (2) weeks,* then the Company will *lay off the least senior employee(s)* by plant seniority. [Emphasis supplied]

In other words, the Parties agreed that seniority will be used to reduce the labor force when a layoff is expected to last for more than two weeks. What construction may be placed on its terms other than seniority does not prevail for layoffs of less than two weeks. Two weeks is the critical and governing period for the application of seniority. A layoff of more than two weeks mandates the displacement of the least senior employees. A layoff of less than two weeks does not require the layoff of junior service employees. This is the plain and only possible construction of the provision.

Grievant Hunt testified:

Q: The one day and three days are both less than two weeks, correct?
A: Yes.
Q: Are layoffs of that nature addressed in the labor agreement?
A: No.

Since Section 6 of Article VII does not address layoffs of less than two weeks, says the Grievant, past practice should govern its application calling for the exercise of seniority in the reduction of the labor force. On the contrary, the provision does address the layoff situation of less than two weeks. By clearly stating that seniority shall be applied in layoffs of more than two weeks, shorter term layoffs, here one day, are certainly addressed. True, the provision does not say something like this: "Layoffs of less than two weeks shall not be based on seniority." But language like this is not needed because Section 6 expressly tells us that the least senior employees shall be laid off when layoffs are expected to last for more than two weeks. Given such language, it is redundant to say that seniority shall not govern for shorter term layoffs.

True, the provision is quite unusual in collective bargaining. Normally contracts provide that seniority shall govern when layoffs exceed three days. Though rare, the two week criterion is what the Parties agreed to at the negotiating table. The Arbitrator must honor this bargain given the restrictions on his authority. Article XVI, Section 2, Fourth Step, provides that arbitrators "shall have no authority to add to, subtract from, or in any way modify the terms of this Agreement." To require the Employer to lay off the least senior employees in the reduction of the labor force for layoffs of two weeks or less would certainly constitute a flagrant abuse of the Arbitrator's legitimate scope of his authority.

CONCLUSION AND AWARD

Even though we have assumed that the May 13 event constituted a curtailment of operations, and further assumed that past practice supports the Union's position, the grievance has no merit and must be denied. It must be denied because crystal-clear contractual language establishes that layoff by seniority prevails for reduction of the labor force for layoffs of more than two weeks. A cardinal principle of the arbitration process is that when clear and unambiguous contractual language and practice clash, the language must prevail.

Probably the Union will be disappointed with this decision. So be it. Given the material contractual language, this decision is the only one that the Arbitrator can support in his conscience as based on the evidence.

QUESTIONS

1. Explain carefully the fundamental arbitration principle that the arbitrator used to deny the grievance.

2. What contractual provision did the arbitrator use to justify his decision? Be specific in your answer. Just to say "Article VII, Section 6" would not be satisfactory.

3. What concessions did the arbitrator make "to place the union's position in its most favorable light"?

4. Do you agree with the following? The arbitrator denied the grievance because he held that the event of Friday, May 13, was a schedule change and not a curtailment or layoff. Why or why not?

5. What impact might the decision have the next time the parties negotiate their contract?

Wage Issues under Collective Bargaining

Almost all contract negotiations pivot upon, and most grievances and arbitrations thus ultimately deal with, four major areas: (1) wages and issues that can be directly related to wages; (2) employee benefits or economic "fringe" supplements to the basic wage rate; (3) "institutional" issues that deal with the rights and duties of employers and unions; and (4) "administrative" clauses that treat such subjects as work rules and job tenure. In this chapter and the three that follow it, each of these areas will be discussed in turn. As in the preceding chapter, arbitration cases will also be used, where appropriate, to illustrate particular problems.

Job security considerations are currently running a close second to wage issues as the most vexatious bargaining table problem, but wage and wage-related considerations historically have been the leading overt cause of strikes. During the past decade, for example, controversies over wages have been either the exclusive or the primary cause of almost 40 percent of the nation's work stoppages.[1]

This record highlights the vital character of wage negotiations in collective bargaining and also suggests that in the area of wages much can be done to decrease management-labor conflict substantially.

In fact, as is the case perhaps with no other area of collective bargaining to that extent, wage problems test the skill, understanding, and attitudes of negotiators. The latter are, as we know, now confronted with a legion of wage issues, including the establishment of the basic wage rate, wage differentials, overtime rates, and wage adjustments during contractual periods, as well as with the thorny problems involved in the negotiation of the so-called fringe, or supplemental, wage payments, which will be discussed in the next chapter. It is hoped that the following discussion of some of the principles, practices, and trends concerning these several wage and wage-related areas will contribute to a better understanding of them.

DETERMINATION OF THE BASIC WAGE RATE

If union and management representatives are exhibiting an ever-greater willingness to deal with factual information at the bargaining table, there is still no single standard for wage rate determination that has anything approaching a "scientific" base. Both the bargaining parties, indeed, commonly utilize at least *three different* such standards, each of which has definite advantages from the viewpoint of achieving an "equitable" settlement but also significant limitations: the "comparative-norm," ability-to-pay, and standard-of-living criteria.

Comparative Norm

The basic idea behind the "comparative-norm" concept is the presumption that the economics of a particular collective bargaining relationship should neither fall substantially behind nor be greatly superior to that of other employer-union relationships; that in short it is generally a good practice to keep up with the crowd, but not necessarily to lead it.

The outside observer would very probably agree with this principle, at least on the surface. When a firm is operating with a highly competitive product or in highly competitive labor markets, there is safety for employee relations in keeping labor costs and wage rates consistent with the local and industrial pattern, but not necessarily any need to exceed this pattern. Unions tend to maintain harmony and contentment among the rank and file as long as wage conditions are competitive; on the other hand, it is at times quite difficult and embarrassing for union leaders to explain to the membership why their economic terms of employment are not at least equivalent to those of other unionists (particularly where one local of an international union falls substantially behind another local of the same international). In short, the comparative-norm principle is often valid for economic, sociological, and psychological reasons.

Thus, the parties frequently make a careful and comprehensive study of the community and industry wage structure before negotiations begin and then compare these rates with the rates in existence at the location involved in the negotiations. The strategic implications of such comparisons, already cited in Chapter 5, are quite obvious. If the plant rates are below the community or industry pattern, the union can be expected to argue for a wage increase on this basis. When the plant rates are in excess of the community or industry pattern, the employer has an argument *against* a wage increase.

Notwithstanding these considerations, there are limitations to this approach to the bargaining process. Not all firms have the same capacity to meet economic demands. This is the case not only for firms in different industries but also for companies operating within the same industry. Even though economic forces are at work that tend to place firms operating within the same industrial grouping on the same economic footing, many other factors—such as imperfections in the product market, technological differences, location, stage of economic development, and financial resources—may place such firms on different economic levels. From this it follows that at any one time firms may be quite different in their individual capacities to meet economic demands and that the optimum wage level for one firm of a particular industry could be quite low (or quite high) in comparison with that of the industry in general.

In the troubled U.S. basic steel industry, for example, it would not take much of a wage increase at the present time to put such financially ill smaller producers as Wheeling-Pittsburgh and McLouth entirely out of business. And Bethlehem, Armco, and LTV, among the larger companies, are not rolling in wealth now, either. The wolf is much farther from the door, on the other hand, at USX, Inland, and National. The United Steelworkers, representing employees at all of these producers, has increasingly recognized these realities and to preserve jobs has necessarily granted various forms of economic relief to the harder-pressed producers in separate company-by-company negotiations.

Only in recent years has the union been forced to grant such individual treatment: The steel producers, in their generally healthy state before the rise of the competition from low-wage foreign steel and nonunion domestic minimills, wanted to remove wages from competition. Consequently, starting in the 1950s, they bargained jointly with the union for a single industry-wide basic steel manufacturer contract. But the nation's steel *fabricating* firms, with very different financial and market circumstances historically not only from the producers but (often) from each other, have *always* tried to strike their own wage bargains with the union in company-by-company negotiation. The inevitable result, even before the breakup of the industry-wide bargaining and obviously all the more so now, has been a wide variety of wage levels in what is nonetheless still referred to as the "steel industry."

The major rubber companies—Uniroyal-Goodrich, Goodyear, and Firestone—have more or less identical contracts with the United Rubber Workers, although they bargain these separately with a pattern developing after one company settles. None of them in recent times has been in significant financial trouble and therefore none has felt a pressing need to strike its own bargain with the union. But General Tire, hard pressed to pay its bills, broke away from this pattern in the early 1980s and today pays lower wages. And nontire members of the rubber industry—the highly competitive footwear manufacturers (although some tire companies also manufacture footwear)—have historically settled with the union for considerably less than the pattern established with the Big Four.

Other examples would include the larger meatpackers who, even amid the ill health of their industry, have generally been better equipped to support higher wage levels than have their smaller competitors. However, even within the ranks of the major packers, wage-paying capacities differ and in the late 1980s Hormel workers were averaging $9 per hour while Armour employees—represented by the same union, the United Food and Commercial Workers—averaged a rather niggardly $6. In the automobile industry, there are obviously significant economic differences between General Motors and Checker Motors. These considerations must be recognized before one accepts the proposition that the comparative-norm principle of wage determination should be used as the exclusive, or the most desirable, standard for wage settlements in collective bargaining.[2]

There are at least four other factors to be considered in regard to the comparative-norm principle. *First,* not only do firms within a given industry at any given time have unequal capabilities to meet economic demands, but frequently it is quite difficult to classify a firm in a particular industrial grouping for wage comparison purposes. Some firms may logically be classified in two or more industries, because of the products they manufacture or the services they provide. Likewise, even if a firm is classified within a particular industry, there are frequently significant subgroupings in each major industrial classification. Within the oil industry, for example, there are large, medium, and small producers of oil, and producers can be classified considerably further in terms of exact product and nature of operations. Such complicating circumstances illustrate the difficulty of classifying a particular firm in a particular industry or in a segment of an industry for purposes of wage determination.

A *second* limitation involved in the use of the comparative-norm wage principle for collective bargaining is the fact that it is at times misleading to compare employees within a particular job classification, because the content of jobs may be substantially different among plants within the same labor market. The duties of an employee classified as a "subassembler, B" in one plant may be quite different from those of an employee classified identically in another plant. The fact is that job classifications within industry have not been standardized, and therefore, the usefulness of the comparative-norm wage principle is proportionately reduced.

This wage criterion is limited in its applicability by still a *third* complication. It is difficult to use the principle when comparing workers who are within the same job classification but who are paid by different systems of wage payments. Some workers are paid on a straight hourly rate basis, others on an individual incentive system, and still others on a group incentive plan. The kind of wage system in operation can in itself have a significant impact upon wage rates.

Briefly described, incentive wages constitute a method of wage payment by which earnings are geared more or less directly to actual output instead of to time spent on the job. Employees are thus granted a relatively clear-cut financial motivation to increase their outputs, essentially by increasing the effort on which such outputs depend.

On the other hand, determination of the actual rate of pay for each "piece" or unit of output is, of course, open to union-management controversy; the management's conception of an appropriate rate is typically somewhat less liberal than is the union's. And the problem is compounded when the original job on which the rate has been set is in any way "modified" (as virtually all jobs ultimately are, because of a host of factors ranging from worker-implemented shortcuts to management job reengineering) and each party seeks a new rate that is beneficial to its own interests.

Some unions have historically opposed such plans from their inception, through fear of management rate cutting (for example, artificial reconstruction of the job in order to pay it a lower rate) and because of a deeply harbored suspicion that there is nothing "scientific" to *any* established rates. But managements that have yielded too readily to union requests for higher rates have also suffered, in inequities between earnings and effort, and in consequent problems involving not only finances but also employee morale. Increased automation of industry to the point where many workers cannot control their output rates has caused some further deemphasis of incentive plans in recent years. However, about one quarter of all production plant workers in the United States continue to be paid under such plans, and it is obvious that the presence of such workers can make the comparative-norm principle severely misleading.

Fourth, and finally, consideration must be given to the existence of the wide variety of fringe benefits previously cited. These benefits are not distributed equally throughout industry. Thus, it could be wrong to conclude that workers in different organizations are not equal in terms of net economic advantage where one group earns a lower basic wage rate but surpasses another group in terms of paid holidays and vacations, pensions, health coverage, and other benefits.

These considerations do not mean that the comparative-norm principle is of no value in collective bargaining. Its utility is demonstrated by its widespread use. But bargainers who utilize this avenue of wage comparisons without recognition of the several problems and limitations involved in its implementation do so only at their peril.

Ability to Pay

A second leading criterion involved in wage determination under collective bargaining is the ability of the employer (or industry, where negotiations are on an industrywide basis) to pay a wage increase. The outcome of wage negotiations is frequently shaped by this factor, and many strikes occur where there is disagreement between management and union negotiators relative to the wage-paying capacity of the enterprise. Careful consideration and better understanding of this factor of wage determination is no less imperative for reducing the area of disagreement between industry and organized labor than is familiarity with the comparative-norm factor.

The level of profits is one indicator of the wage-paying ability of the firm involved in the negotiations. If a firm is earning a "high" rate of profit, union representatives will frequently claim that it can afford all or most of the union wage demand. If the firm is earning a "low" rate of profit, management negotiators will frequently argue that the firm does not have the financial capacity to meet the union's wage demands. But the heart of this controversy is, clearly, the determination of what constitutes a rate of profits sufficient to meet a given union wage demand. Unfortunately, no economic formula can answer this question with precision and exactness.

As in the case of the preceding criterion, the problem is complicated by further considerations. In the *first* place, it is not certain whether a given rate of profits earned by a company over a given time in the past will hold for the future. Further profits may fall or rise depending upon the behavior of a number of economic variables that are themselves uncertain: Changes in sales, output, productivity, price, managerial efficiency, and even the state of international relations will all bear upon the future profit experience of a particular firm or industry. Thus, a wage rate negotiated in the light of a given historical profit experience may not be appropriate in the future. Moreover, if profits are to be used as an indicator of the firm's ability to meet a given wage demand, consideration must be given to anticipated government tax structures. The wage-paying ability of the firm may be quite different before and after the payment of the federal income tax, as many business administrators can testify. There are additional elements of the never-static national and state tax programs that tend to have an impact on the wage-paying ability of industry.

Second, the use to which a company intends to put its profits also has a vital bearing upon this problem. Since profits are frequently used to promote capital growth and improvement, the future plans of the enterprise itself must receive consideration by the negotiators. The problem of whether profits should be used for growth and improvement, for lower commodity price, or for higher wages is one of the most troublesome issues in industrial relations. Concepts of "fair treatment"—always subjective—

are inevitably involved. And so are a host of fundamental business decisions whose optimal resolution is vital to the very survival of the organization. Dealing with this determinant of wages alone is, in short, anything but child's play.

Third, although the level of profits is an important factor in the determination of a firm's ability to pay wages, it is not the only factor. Other considerations that have an important bearing on the problem are the ratio of labor costs to total costs, the amount of money expended for the financing of fringe benefits, and the degree of elasticity of demand for the firm's product or service.

The ratio of labor costs to total costs particularly conditions the ability of a firm to afford increased wage rates. An employer is in a better position to grant higher wages when the firm's labor costs represent a comparatively small part of the total costs. For example, a 10 percent increase in wage rates will result in a 1 percent increase in total costs when wage costs are 10 percent of total costs (as they are, for example, in portions of the petroleum industry). Where, however, wage costs are 50 percent of total costs (as in segments of the leather industry), a 10 percent increase in wage rates will result in a 5 percent increase in total costs. This illustration, of course, is based on the assumption that there is no increase or decrease in labor productivity after the wage rates are negotiated. If output increases faster than the wage rise, labor cost per unit of production tends to decrease. The reverse is true when labor productivity does not increase with higher wages.

Moreover, the ratio of labor cost to total cost cannot by itself be taken as conclusive evidence of the wage-paying ability of a particular firm. Firms with a low labor cost do not necessarily have the capacity to pay higher wages. By the same token, it would not be accurate to conclude that firms with a high labor cost can never afford wage increases. All that can be said with some degree of accuracy is that if all economic variables were held constant, a firm with a low labor-cost ratio could afford to pay higher wages more easily than a firm with a high labor-cost ratio.

As in the case of the comparative-norm principle, it should also be emphasized that an employer's total wage bill includes not only direct wage costs but costs incurred in providing employees with nonwage economic benefits.

Employer payments for such benefits have been rising rapidly, as Chapter 8 will relate with documentation. Today, after a rise of about 1 percent of payroll per year in terms of national average over the past two decades, benefits consume almost 40 percent of the typical employer's labor payout—although hardly uniformly, with some organizations being far more tight-fisted in this area than are others.

The ease with which a company can pass on the costs of a wage increase in the form of higher prices to other firms or to the consuming public is still another determinant of its wage-paying ability. Some firms (in the brewing and cigarette industries, for example) operate in a highly competitive selling market. Under these circumstances it is very difficult, if not impossible, for an employer to shift the burden of a wage increase to the consumer. Even a slight increase in price could result in a significant decrease in sales, since consumers would simply buy from other sellers. To the degree that a firm sells its products in a highly competitive market, it will find strong consumer resistance to price increases. In contrast, some companies (for example, major league baseball teams in virtually all cities and newspaper publishers in single-newspaper cities) operate in monopolistic markets. Under these circumstances, companies have a greater degree of freedom to raise prices without experiencing a sharp decrease in sales. This would be particularly true where the product in question is sold under conditions of inelastic demand. Such a demand characteristic would apply to goods that are necessities or to those for which there are few satisfactory substitutes. Thus, if a company is operating in a monopolistic market and is selling a product for which the demand is relatively inelastic, it has an excellent opportunity to shift the costs of wage increases to other firms or to the general public in the form of higher prices.

Negotiators at times take advantage of such an economic environment. Wage increases are agreed upon and the result is higher prices. From the public's point of view, it would be much more desirable if unions and employers could work out an arrangement whereby wages could be increased without price increases. Certainly, a wage agreement that increases the prices of basic economic commodities and thereby generates a general inflation of the price level cannot be regarded as socially sound.

Wage and Price Controls

Throughout history, governments confronted with major inflationary movements have imposed some kind of limit on wage and price increases. Almost four thousand years ago, King Hammurabi of Babylonia set the annual wages of field workers at eight gur (75 bu.) of corn and those of herdsmen, whose job was presumably less valuable to society, at six gur (56.25 bu.). The Roman Emperor Diocletian in A.D. 301 established price maximums for transportation by camel and for artichokes and he meant business: Anyone caught charging more was put to death. In the United States, a wage and price controls program during World War II was itself a major industry: It needed 60,000 full-time officials and almost five times that many volunteer checkers for its implementation.[3]

In more recent decades, on more than one occasion, the executive branch of the federal government has also turned to labor-related controls in an effort to thwart large rises in the general level of prices. Three recent Presidents have promulgated so-called "voluntary wage-price guidelines," and in a 1971–1973 program of the Nixon administration, mandatory wage and price controls were imposed.

In most of these experiences, single figures were announced as the maximum allowable annual increase in pay: 3.2 percent in the noninflationary early 1960s under Presidents Kennedy and Johnson; 5.5 percent in base pay plus another 0.7 percent for certain fringe benefits in 1971–1973;

and 7.0 percent in President Carter's program of the late 1970s (in 1980, a range of 7.5 to 9.5 percent was substituted by Carter). In all of these, exceptions were permitted for "special circumstances," a term that to most observers appeared to mean roughly the same as "political pressures." None of these programs achieved anything approaching complete success in holding down inflation, and in retrospect most of them can be judged to have been definite failures insofar as any beneficial long-run effect on the economy is concerned. Most scholars agree that while mandatory controls can restrain wages for a short while, they also cause shortages, bureaucratic complexities, inequities, and—sooner or later—inflationary explosions. Most agree, too, that guidelines alone are not much more than cosmetic attempts, conveying the impression of governmental concern but frequently doing little else.

Organized labor opposed all of the attempts in one way or another. The 3.2 percent Kennedy-Johnson guidelines (called "guideposts" by the government in those years) were attacked as inequitably "freezing" worker shares in the income-distribution pie at their existing levels, in the absence of a convincing reason why such wage income shares should not be *increased*. And unionists also viewed with some alarm the increased governmental intervention presented by the guideposts, as did their counterparts on the management side. One labor leader said that the 3.2 percent figure was "as welcome to organized labor as 3.2 beer."

Nixon's mandatory arrangement was not, at least as the majority of union leaders saw it, at all fair, either. AFL-CIO president Meany described it as "window dressing for the benefit of business profits" and labor generally argued with some justification that the program was enforced neither fairly nor effectively.

And the AFL-CIO felt so strongly that President Carter's officially "voluntary" program could not legally withhold federal government contracts from firms not in compliance with Carter's guidelines, as the government was in 1979 threatening to do, that it filed suit in federal court requesting that such a practice be enjoined as violating the Procurement Act of 1949. Unsuccessful in this activity (a federal district court agreed with the federation but a few weeks later the U.S. Circuit Court of Appeals for the District of Columbia reversed the lower court), labor subsequently confined its attack to public pronouncements, once again arguing that the controls inequitably favored profits over wages (a charge that, with prices escalating at about 13 percent annually in 1979 and 1980, gained considerable nonlabor support). The AFL-CIO announced that it *would* support a mandatory wage and price controls program (although "for the duration of the emergency only") because if truly mandatory, the latter would impose "equal sacrifices" on all citizens.

With inflation very much under control after the early 1980s, no further governmental programs of this kind were in the immediate offing. History having a way of repeating itself, however, any predictions that such federal controls would not sooner or later—amid rapidly rising prices—be tried again would be rash. And so very likely, too, would be any bets either that labor would support such controls or that the controls would be very successful in dampening inflation in any long-term way.

Standard of Living

Orientation of the plant wage structure to community and industry levels and ability to pay are not the only criteria utilized for wage determination in contemporary industry. Many management and, particularly, labor representatives are concerned with the problem of the adequacy of wages to guarantee workers "a decent standard of living." Disagreements arise, however, as to what constitutes such a standard.

The problem is most often resolved by personal judgment and opinions of the negotiators. More objective information is, however, at the disposal of the parties, and it has frequently been used to support demands and counterdemands at the bargaining table.

The most widely publicized source of standard-of-living data was that published by the U.S. Department of Labor's Bureau of Labor Statistics. Unfortunately, after 1982, because of budget constraints, the Department of Labor ceased publishing this information.[4] However, when adjustments are made for the rate of inflation since 1983, it is still useful as a general guide to establish the standard of living. First developed in 1946–1947 at the request of Congress, and revised periodically since that time, the BLS's "City Worker's Family Budget" attempted to describe and measure a "modest but adequate standard of living." It was necessarily selective, restricting itself to a measurement of the income needed by a family of four (a 38-year-old employed husband, a wife not employed outside the home, and two children of school age—a 13-year-old boy and an 8-year-old girl), living in a rented dwelling in a large city or its suburbs. By studying the prices of a "representative list of goods and services" presumably purchased by such families, for about forty representative cities (weighted according to their population), the BLS showed the cost of "a level of adequate living standards prevailing in large cities of the United States in recent years."

To make the "City Worker's Family Budget" more relevant, the Bureau of Labor Statistics provided levels for three standards of living—"low," "intermediate," and "high." Naturally, employees who earn sufficient wages to live at the high level enjoy more of the good things of life as compared with those whose wages can claim only the goods and services at the low level.

The low budget recently required an annual outlay of $18,483, while the intermediate one demanded $30,547 and the high budget called for a rather formidable $45,909. Food costs had increased about 4 percent in each of the budgets over the past few years. But since they absorbed a larger percentage of total living costs at the lower-budget level, these food costs clearly had a greater influence there, making it less likely that the lower-budget families would eat much in the way of quality foods on any sustained basis.

Not unexpectedly, the amount required varies considerably depending on the city involved. The most expensive city to live in is Honolulu, followed by Anchorage, New York, Boston, and Washington. Dallas is the cheapest major city in which to live; slightly more expensive are Atlanta and Houston. In all cases, however, the overall weighted averages at the time of this writing were sufficiently beyond those earned by most workers to make the budget an attractive bargaining weapon for union negotiators.

For example, with the low budget mandating its annual outlay of more than $18,000, the average employee within private industry earned $16,796. Of course, averages can be deceptive, and employees lucky enough to be in high wage industries earned considerably more, as in manufacturing, $21,684; construction, $25,532; and mining, $27,872. Labor spokespersons had not been hesitant about arguing the "need" for substantial wage increases to reach the budgeted levels while also pointing out that the overall weighted average was required to meet the necessities of life, pay taxes, and enjoy a few amenities—but that it contained no allowance for luxuries or savings.

Employers, equally logically, had taken bitter exception to the "City Worker's Family Budget." They had argued that the items used in computing the budget were far too generous to warrant the description "modest but adequate"; frequently cited in this regard were the budget's annual allowance for gifts and contributions, and certain of its provisions for furniture, appliances, automobiles, and recreation. In addition, they pointed out that wage earners do not have uniform responsibilities in terms of dependents (with many, of course, having no dependents), and that many families have more than one wage earner.

The arguments and counterarguments can be expected to continue indefinitely, without mutual agreement as to their validity; the line of demarcation between "luxury" and "necessity" has never been susceptible to exact location, and the concept of "decency" allows much room for emotion. Moreover, despite the use of the standard-of-living criterion at the bargaining table, it does not carry as much weight as the other wage factors analyzed in the previous sections of this chapter. After all, an employer who truthfully cannot pay wages that will realize the "modest but adequate standard of living" may be entirely sympathetic to the worker's needs, but the cold realism of economic life will not persuade it to grant the additional wages. Likewise, a union will not stop at the level of wages required of the budget if it can get more from the employer because of the operation of the other wage criteria; indeed, under these circumstances, the union will probably argue that the items of the budget are too meager.

But use of such standard of living information is still to be preferred to total recourse to personal opinion on the subject. The data may not be accepted, but even in rejecting them the recalcitrant party is forced to deal with information that is more objective than mere individual sentiment.

COST OF LIVING: ESCALATOR AND WAGE-REOPENER ARRANGEMENTS

In addition to the comparative-norm, ability-to-pay, and standard-of-living principles, experienced negotiators pay close attention in wage negotiations to the status of the *cost of living*. This economic phenomenon is important because trends in the cost of living have an important bearing upon the real income of workers. Increases in the cost of living at a given level of earnings result in decreased capacity of workers to buy goods and services. By the same token, real income tends to increase with decreases in the cost of living at a given wage level. Real income for a particular group of workers also increases for a time when money wages increase faster than the cost of living.

As a matter of fact, during the soaring inflation in the 1978–1981 period, the cost of living was the major determinant for wage negotiations, as union leaders raced to keep up with higher and higher prices to protect the real income of their members. Of course, to the extent that wage rates exceeded productivity, negotiated wages aggravated the inflation problem. If the lessons of inflation teach us anything, it is that a stable price level is the way to achieve the negotiation of noninflationary wage rates.

It is beyond the scope of this volume to analyze the multitude of factors that influence the cost of living in the American economy. This cost is affected by a variety of forces, including the general climate of business activity, productivity, the financial and monetary policies followed by financial institutions, the rate of new investment, and the propensity of consumers to spend money, as well as by the wage policies that are followed under collective bargaining itself. Government policies relating to interest rates, tariffs, the lending capacity of national banks, taxation and agriculture also have an impact upon the cost of living. And, of course, as we have come to realize in recent years, energy costs can constitute another important factor. When the OPEC nations increased the cost of oil from about $5 per barrel at the beginning of the 1970s to more than seven times that figure by the end of the decade, the effect was felt not only in increasing gasoline prices but in other goods manufactured by petroleum-chemical industries, in transportation and heating costs of all users, and ultimately in the prices of almost all goods and services. By the same token, the rapid deterioration of oil prices in the later 1980s significantly dampened the level of price increases.

The uncertain character of the forces determining the cost of living makes it very difficult to predict with certainty its future trends. The difficulty inherent in using the cost of living as a determinant in wage negotiations is simply this: Wages are negotiated for a *future* period, whereas the cost-of-living data are *historical* in character. It is a comparatively simple task to adjust wages for historical trends in the cost of living if this is the desire of the negotiators. The criterion is of limited usefulness, however, in the attempt to orient wage rates to future trends in the Consumer Price Index. The capricious character of the index makes forecasting extremely hazardous. In any event, for intelligent utilization of this wage determinant, it becomes necessary not only to have accurate information on historical trends but also to make an assessment of the future trends of the factors that determine the Consumer Price Index.[5] It cannot be emphasized too much that such predictions are fraught with difficulties and uncertainties.

Some parties in labor relations have, however, adopted one or both of two procedures—escalator clauses and wage reopeners—that take into account the fickleness of cost of living and likewise recognize the importance of trends in the Consumer Price Index as they relate to the real income of employees and to the financial position of employers.

Escalator Clauses

The philosophy behind the incorporation of so-called "escalator clauses," also known as cost-of-living adjustment (COLA) provisions, in labor agreements is that wages of workers should rise and fall automatically with fluctuations in the cost of living. The escalator arrangement first attained national prominence in the 1948 General Motors–United Automobile Workers collective bargaining agreement. As a result of the anticipated price inflation growing out of the Korean War, many other companies and unions soon negotiated similar arrangements, and by 1952 such arrangements covered about 3.5 million workers.

Since 1952, use of the wage-escalator clause appears to have depended to great extent on the upward movement of the cost-of-living index. By 1955, for example, three years of comparatively steady prices had elapsed, and the number of workers covered by such escalator clauses had dropped considerably, to about 1.7 million.[6] In 1956, on the other hand, the Consumer Price Index moved strongly forward, and a study conducted late in that year estimated that approximately 3.5 million workers were once again covered by escalator arrangements.[7] The incorporation of an escalator formula in the 1956 basic steel contract—at that time covering 600,000 workers—alone accounted for almost one third of this increase.

With relatively modest annual price movements from 1956 through mid-1965, interest in the escalator temporarily waned once more and only about 2 million workers were covered by escalator clauses in the latter year.[8] On the other hand, the significant surge in the price level after mid-1965 brought another half-million employees under coverage by 1969. And the enormous surge of prices in the 1970s and first two years of the 1980s again stimulated the growth of cost-of-living escalator clauses. Where in 1970 only about one quarter of all workers under major labor agreements (those covering at least 1,000 employees) had COLAs, this figure rose to a high of 61.2 percent in 1976 and remained at approximately that level until prices stabilized in the mid-1980s, at which point it rapidly declined once more.[9] As inflation picked up in 1988 and early 1989, unions were again reaching for more COLA and by June 1989 the percentage increased to about 40 percent.[10] With union fears of inflation abating in the early 1990s, the statistic again went down: By 1992, somewhat less than one-third of the 5.7 million workers subject to major union contracts were covered.

Historically, managements have been anything but enthusiastic about the escalator concept. They have voiced fears that prices could not be commensurately raised without undesirable effects on profits. They have also argued what they view as the inequities of a system that allows workers to benefit without effort of any kind on their part: One mid-1960s increase in the cost-of-living index, for example, was attributed by government spokespersons primarily to increases in sugar and cigarette prices—a situation that even the most sugar-consuming and chain-smoking work force could not noticeably influence. Still other managers have stressed the potential inflationary ramifications of the escalator in opposing its use. Above all, however, employers have attacked the constant "freezing" of cost-of-living allowances into basic wage rates: Most labor contracts ultimately make such allowances a permanent part of rates when the agreements are renegotiated and to many workers the allowances are, consequently, really additional wage increases temporarily couched in other terms. Not only do cost-of-living allowances realistically become a part of basic wage rates, but frequently they are also "rolled" into pay for vacations, holidays, and other employee benefits tied to basic wage rates. Thus, not only are employers' direct wage costs increased, but also costs associated with a variety of fringe benefits. As Hendricks and Kahn have pointed out, one need look only to where COLAs exist today to see this absence of pro-COLA sentiment on the part of managements: "[The] fact that COLAs are generally confined to the union sector in the U.S. suggests that companies in general would prefer not to have them."[11]

On the other hand, unions have favored the COLA concept through the years and indeed, even when forced to give back compensation previously won at the bargaining table in distressed industries in recent years (a topic which is treated later in this chapter), have chosen to give up COLA only as a very last resort.

Inflation has not been the only generator of COLA clauses. A second, if lesser impetus over the past four decades has been the gradual lengthening of the durations of labor contracts. In 1948 about 75 percent of collective bargaining agreements were for one year or less; by 1963 the proportion of contracts running for longer than one year had increased sharply—to as much as 86 percent, by some estimates, and by 1989 as many as 90 percent of all contracts may have been for more than one year. Longer-term contracts lend greater stability to labor relationships, and by definition they reduce the problems of negotiation and the traumas of frequent strike threats. However, as contracts are negotiated for longer periods of time, negotiators must recognize the necessity of providing some method for the adjustment of wages during the contractual period. Some authorities believe that increasing awareness of this situation, together with the continuation of the trend to contracts of longer duration, will lend greater allure to the escalator formula, even in the face of continuing managerial opposition to the whole idea.

How Escalators Work

Although there is a wide variety of escalator arrangements, all contain a number of common principles. The most significant characteristic of the escalator formula is its automaticity. For the duration of the labor agreement, wage changes as related to cost of living are precisely determined by the behavior of a statistical index—almost always the Consumer Price Index. Wages are increased or decreased in accordance with comparatively small changes in this index. For example, the labor agreement might provide, as many recent ones have, for a $.01-per-hour adjustment of wages for every 0.26-point change in the CPI.

Each escalator arrangement specifies the time at which the CPI is reviewed. At the time of the review, a determination is made as to whether the index increased sufficiently to trigger a wage increase. Of the workers covered by escalators in 1992 quarterly reviews were by far the most common, covering about 50 percent compared with about 25 percent each for annual or semiannual reviews. Though only a matter of academic interest in a period of inflation, escalator provisions normally specify the floor to which wages can fall in response to a decline in the cost-of-living index. On the other hand, the escalator formula does not normally contain a *ceiling* on wage increases occasioned by increasing prices. Only about 20 percent of the workers covered by the arrangement are currently subject to a ceiling, also called a "cap," on their cost-of-living wage increases.[12] When the labor agreement provides for a cap, it means that wages can only increase by a certain specified amount during the contractual period regardless of the size of the increase in the Consumer Price Index. Needless to say, when a cap appears, the employer and not the union insisted on it at the bargaining table. When an escalator arrangement contains a cap, the employer is in a better position to estimate the firm's labor costs for the contractual period. Employer resistance, of course, increases during periods of economic recession. This occurred during the economic recession of the early 1980s. Faced with declining sales, employers demanded caps on the operation of COLAs.

Finally, the escalator method of wage adjustment is often accompanied by a definite and guaranteed increase in wages for each year of a multiyear labor agreement. Such an increase is popularly called the *annual improvement factor*. These increases are not offset by any increase generated by an escalator clause. By the same token, any increase triggered by an escalator clause is not reduced by the payment of the annual improvement factor. For example, a recent three-year contract negotiated by one union states:

> Effective as of April 24, 1990 and April 23, 1992, each employee covered by this Agreement shall receive an annual improvement factor of ten cents ($.10) per hour added to his or her hourly rate.

Those employees are guaranteed the 10-cent increase on each anniversary date of the agreement regardless of the results of the escalator provision. As expected, when a labor agreement does not contain an escalator clause, the annual improvement factor normally calls for a higher increase as compared with a contract that includes a cost-of-living adjustment provision. In the former situation, it is understandable that union leaders press for a much higher annual increase, recognizing that inflation affects adversely the real income of the members. When an escalator clause is contained in the contract, the union's leaders need not be so aggressive in the matter of the annual improvement factor.

However, it should be noted that the operation of escalator arrangements *does not* provide employees with 100 percent protection against inflation. For 1968–1977, the average escalator yield met only 57 percent of the inflation occurring during those years. In not one year did the yield match the CPI increase.[13] This will come as a genuine surprise to many who believe, in error, that escalator provisions provide the employee full protection against the ravages of inflation.

Moreover, in recent years COLAs have actually *cut* wage rates in some industries. In giving economic relief to such financially ailing sectors as steel, aluminum, and (for a while) automobiles and trucking, unions often surrendered fixed wage increases and agreed to make pay increases fully dependent on COLAs. But the "engines of inflation," as COLAs were called in the years of high inflation prior to 1982, were reduced to what the editors of *Business Week* could accurately call "little more than sputtering outboards"[14] in the minimal annual inflations after that time. In fact, in some cases—the automobile, aluminum, and can industries most notably—the price index on which the quarterly adjustment was contractually made actually dropped once or twice and employees had to surrender past wage gains on these occasions.

Such occurrences as the last, however, were complete anomalies. Prices have virtually always risen—even in quarterly periods and except for only two years, both during the Great Depression—invariably from year to year throughout the century. Sporadic periods of high inflation have been regular problems in the United States, as elsewhere, for many decades. Only the most naive of employees could possibly believe that inflation is now permanently under control. And, given these circumstances, it seems a safe prediction that, despite management opposition to COLAs and the present minimal levels of price increases, COLAs—and generally ones without caps, at that—will continue their common appearances in labor-management contracts.

Wage Reopeners

A second method for wage adjustments during the life of a labor agreement involves a provision that permits either the employer or the union to *reopen* labor agreements *for wage issues* at stated intervals. Where such a procedure is employed, labor agreements normally provide that contracts negotiated for one year may be reopened for wage issues after six months. Contracts written for two-year periods or longer are customarily open for wage negotiations once each year.

Two major characteristics of the wage-reopening clause arrangement distinguish it from the escalator principle as a method of wage adjustment. The most important involves the fact that whereas the escalator arrangement provides for an *automatic* change in wages based on a definite formula, under wage reopeners the parties must *negotiate* wage changes. This could be an advantage or a disadvantage, depending upon the particular circumstances of a given collective bargaining relationship. In addition, the wage-reopener arrangement can be utilized to take into account determinants of wages other than the cost of living. The fact that both the escalator and the reopener arrangements are frequently used in industry indicates that both procedures apparently fill the needs of employers, employees, and unions. What may be suitable for one collective bargaining relationship, however, clearly might be unsuitable for another management and union.

To invoke a wage-reopening clause, collective bargaining contracts require that the party that desires to change wages give a written notice to the other party within a specified period. Under the terms of the Taft-Hartley law, as we know, a party to a collective bargaining agreement desiring to modify or terminate the agreement must give sixty days' notice of its intention to do so. Following such notice, the law declares that there may be no lockout or strike "for a period of sixty days...or until the expiration date of such contract, whichever occurs later." Employees who engage in a strike during this period lose their status as employees under Taft-Hartley and have no legal right to be reinstated.

These provisions of the Taft-Hartley law are important in connection with this discussion because wage-reopening arrangements invariably provide that a union may call a strike over wage issues if a settlement is not reached during the negotiation period. Such a strike takes place after the negotiation period as provided for in the wage-reopening clause but before the termination date of the entire contract.

The National Labor Relations Board has held that such a strike is lawful even though it occurs before the termination date of the entire labor contract, provided that the sixty-day notice requirement of the Taft-Hartley law is met.

But a wage-reopener provision is to be used only to negotiate a new wage structure. Some employers and unions use the opportunity to gain changes in other areas of the labor agreement, using the wage issue as the pretext. For example, a union might strike ostensibly for wages but send a message to the employer that the strike would terminate were the employer to grant certain concessions to the union, say in the matter of the application of the seniority provisions. Such tactics are not necessarily very subtle. They can, however, be potent.

WAGE DIFFERENTIALS

Under certain circumstances, collective bargaining contracts provide for different rates of wages for different employees performing the same kind of work and holding down the same types of jobs. Such differentials are completely lawful except when used by the parties to discriminate on the basis of race, color, religion, sex, or national origin; the latter practices were forbidden under the terms of Title VII of the Civil Rights Act of 1964.[15] To many employers (as well as to unions), moreover, utilization of the "nondiscriminatory" differentials appears mandatory to ensure an adequate supply of willing employees for work under arduous or otherwise unpleasant conditions.

The most common of these differentials involves premium payment for work on relatively undesirable shifts—in the late afternoon, evening, night, and early morning hours. Practically all workers scheduled on late shifts receive extra pay.

In addition, under most contracts there is now a graduated increase in compensation for working the second and third shifts. All but a tiny fraction of workers in establishments where there is a third, or "graveyard," work schedule now receive a rate for it that is higher than that received by second-shift workers. But second-shift workers themselves have received relatively significant premiums for their acceptance of these working hours: Premium rates for second-shift work are now often as high as 10 percent above first-shift rates. Premiums often up to 10 percent of second-shift rates are the general rewards for the graveyard-shift workers.

The rationale for the shift differential is quite easy to understand. When an employee works a less common shift, there is obvious interference with family life and with full participation in the affairs of society. In Western society, the school system, recreational activities, cultural pursuits, and the like assume that employees work during the day. Since working the odd hours tends to interfere with the employee's family and societal affairs, the premium is designed to compensate the employee for this sacrifice. And although it is a fact of industrial life that some employees because of certain conditions may actually prefer to work the afternoon or midnight tour (under these circumstances, the employee reaps a net benefit for the shift differential premium), the overwhelming number of employees prefers the day shift, and thus the shift differential will undoubtedly always be a common feature in the collectively bargained wage package.

Under many collective bargaining contracts, special premiums are also provided for workers who handle certain supervisory or instructional duties, especially demanding tasks, or particularly hazardous, dirty, or otherwise undesirable work. For these jobs, extra pay is again granted as a premium to the basic wage rate of the worker concerned. For example, under one current agreement in the Midwest, a $1.50-per-hour premium is paid to employees who are engaged in "dirty work." Such work is spelled out in the labor agreement and includes, among other possibilities for premium-rate reimbursement, "work in oil tanks where not cleaned out." Another labor agreement provides for the regular overtime rate for employees engaged in hazardous work. This provision covers employees working at elevations "where there is danger of a fall of fifty feet or more."

In addition to these *premium*-rate practices, many collective bargaining contracts allow *lower* differentials for other situations. A number of agreements provide lower rates for workers who are handicapped, superannuated, temporary, or learners. Such differentials are rooted in the belief that these qualities make workers comparatively less productive, and even the federal government, recognizing the persuasive economic logic involved, has gone along with this employer argument to the extent of exempting such workers from the minimum wage laws. Abuses have occasionally been in evidence, however: Some "temporary" employees turn out, upon closer inspection, to be deserving of twenty-five-year pins; and some "handicapped" employees appear to have nothing more than a proneness to getting hay fever. Such situations notwithstanding, employer good faith in regard to these workers is far more the rule than the exception, and the differential can be defended on the grounds that the alternative to a lower rate of remuneration for such employees is, most often, unemployment.

Until passage and implementation of the Civil Rights Act, some contracts also contained lower wage rates for women than for men and for minorities than for white employees. For women, the practice was traditionally defended on such presumed grounds as a lesser productivity of women than men, a female inability to do all the tasks performed by men in accomplishing a job, and the argument that the employment of women at times involves extra costs not incurred when men are employed. Racial discrimination per se appears to have motivated the minority differential, although some of the lower-productivity claims used to defend lower women's wages were also heard. Neither type of differential is, understandably, promulgated by labor contracts governed by the act, although whether or not the practices involved will continue is subject to employer and union compliance, which goes well beyond the official wording of their agreements.

OVERTIME AND FLEXTIME

Overtime

Collective bargaining agreements invariably establish a standard number of hours per day and per week during which employees are paid their regular rate of pay. For hours worked in excess of the standard, however, employers are required to pay employees overtime rates. By far the most common standards found in labor agreements are eight hours per day and forty hours per week, with only a fraction of labor agreements establishing standards differing from this formula. In the wearing apparel, printing, and publishing industries, a number of agreements do provide for a basic seven- to seven-and-one-half-hour day and thirty-five-hour workweek; and in the food-processing, retail, and service industries some contracts establish a standard forty-four-hour week; but these remain the exceptions.

The fact that the Fair Labor Standards Act of 1938 provides a basic forty-hour week has undoubtedly caused the adoption of a forty-hour standard workweek under collective bargaining. Labor agreements that provide for a basic workweek in excess of forty hours without premium overtime pay presumably do not fall within the scope of this legislation, or within the reach of the many state wage and hour laws that regulate this activity within certain states for their intrastate commerce. On the other hand, nothing in the federal wage and hour law prohibits employers and unions from negotiating a workweek of *fewer* than forty hours, and (although thus far with more potential than actuality) the shorter workweek as a partial answer to the unemployment threats of the era loomed as a new labor relations issue in the 1990s, after years of relative quiescence. In addition, the Fair Labor Standards Act places no restriction on employers who desire their employees to work *more* than forty hours in a workweek, other than that the employees who work more than forty hours must be paid at least one and one-half times their regular rate of pay for all hours in excess of forty.

The vast majority of labor agreements provide overtime rates of exactly one and one-half times the regular rate of pay for employees who work in excess of forty hours per week, thus offering a not surprising conformity to the provisions of the Fair Labor Standards Act, but a relatively small number of labor agreements do call for overtime rates of greater than time-and-one-half pay, most frequently double-time. With respect to hours worked in excess of the *daily* standard, most labor agreements also provide for time-and-one-half, although some labor agreements provide for double-time after a certain number of hours are worked or after a stipulated hour of the day or night. For example, some employers and unions have agreed that double-time rates should be paid if employees work more than four hours' overtime on any one workday. In this connection it should be noted that—since the Fair Labor Standards Act does not establish a basic work-day—if employees are to be paid for working hours in excess of a certain number per day, the parties to the collective bargaining contract must negotiate this objective.

In addition to establishing standard workdays and workweeks and providing the rate for hours worked in excess of these standards, collective bargaining contracts deal with other phases of the hours and overtime problem. Most labor agreements prohibit the *pyramiding* of overtime. This means that weekly overtime premiums are not required for hours for which daily overtime premiums have already been paid; moreover, many contracts provide that only one type of overtime premium can be paid for any one day. Also, in many relationships the employer also has the right to force employees to work overtime.

However, labor agreements and arbitration decisions establish certain standards that employers must follow before discipline can be assessed against employees who refuse to work overtime. For example, in the absence of some dire emergency—a flood in the plant, perhaps—the employer must give proper notice and not grab an employee for overtime just as the person is about to clock out. Also, the employer must accept a "reasonable" excuse from an employee who refuses to work overtime. Of course, what is "reasonable" is subject to controversy, and arbitrators are often called upon to apply the concept in the light of the particular facts of a case. Should an employee be excused from overtime because he was scheduled to be the best man at a wedding? This was the basic issue involved in a case handled by one of the authors. When the employee refused, he was suspended for three days. How would you decide this issue if you were the arbitrator?

As in the case of the shorter-hour workweek, the issue of compulsory overtime invariably pops up during periods of excessive unemployment. Because unemployment was so high during the recession of 1975—a post–Great Depression high of 9.2 percent was reached during the summer of that year—some unions pressed for a flat prohibition against any overtime in an attempt to preserve job opportunities. Not many unions succeeded in this goal. They were more successful in negotiating voluntary overtime provisions; that is, the employee could refuse the assignment without facing discipline. This development was dramatically highlighted in the 1973 basic automobile industry labor agreement. For the first time in that industry, production employees under certain circumstances gained the right to turn down overtime without penalty. Compulsory overtime was a major strike issue, and only by compromise on it did the automobile corporations and the UAW avoid open conflict. During the severe recession in the early 1980s—unemployment reaching 10.8 percent in December 1982—some unions attempted to forbid all overtime, without notable success. However, a step in this direction occurred when at General Motors and Ford, the UAW negotiated a fifty-cents-an-hour penalty charged to the company for every hour of overtime beyond 5 percent of straight-time hours worked. This penalty discourages scheduling of overtime, and all penalty money goes into a fund for retraining.

Nonetheless, it seems a reasonable speculation that both the mounting union drive for outright overtime prohibition and sanction for the independent employee's refusal to work overtime will grow—despite often fierce employer antagonism to both developments—should the numbers of unemployed not decrease to a more generally tolerable level. Nor, indeed, can one discount the possibility of new governmental action in the overtime arena—perhaps along the lines of an abortive 1964 proposal of the Johnson administration that minimum overtime pay rates in selected industries be increased to double-time (with the goal of lessening the national unemployment figures of that time by encouraging new hiring). Such proposals, however, were not made during the recessions of either the early 1980s or the early 1990s.

Even without government limitations, moreover, the employer's overtime authority has rarely been an unrestricted one. In addition to the above standards, contracts frequently provide that overtime work must be shared equally within given classifications of employees, or at least that overtime is to be rotated equally "as far as is practicable." Some agreements limit overtime to regular employees as against seasonal, temporary, part-time, or probationary employees.

By the same token, however, under many agreements, penalties may be assessed against employees who refuse to work overtime. Such penalties range from discharge to ineligibility to work overtime at the next opportunity. For all that has been said regarding union pressures for overtime discouragement, the premium earnings even of overtime at time-and-one-half remain sufficiently attractive to individual employees on most occasions to make the ineligibility penalty a significant one.

Indeed, a prolific source of grievances and even arbitration is the employee complaint that the employer has improperly, under the labor agreement, failed to offer employees the opportunity to work overtime. Where the grievance is found to have merit, the employer typically has the obligation of paying the employee the amount of money he or she would have earned on the overtime tour of duty. (*Case 3 deals with this problem.*)

The employee, of course, has nothing to lose by filing such grievances, even if the worker would have refused the assignment if offered the opportunity to work overtime. If the opportunity has *not* been offered, the employee can file a grievance and possibly get paid for work the grievant never intended to do in the first place. For these reasons, employer representatives are very careful to assure that eligible employees are afforded the opportunity to work the overtime. Where a supervisor, for example, makes an error in this regard, the company may be faced with the situation of paying for the same work twice and at premium rates. To say the least, the organization's controller would take a dim view of this state of affairs! (Exhibit 7-1 illustrates a reasonably typical overtime provision.)

EXHIBIT 7-1

ARTICLE 34. OVERTIME

Section 1

Employees who are required to work overtime will be compensated in accordance with applicable laws and regulations.

Section 2

The Employer agrees to make a reasonable effort to distribute overtime equitably among qualified and available employees, consistent with the specialized skills and abilities necessary for the work to be performed. Adequate records of overtime will be maintained by the Employer and will be available to the Union upon request.

Section 3

In the assignment of overtime, the Employer agrees to provide an employee with as much advance notice as the situation permits. Consideration will be given, in light of the workload involved and the ready availability of other qualified employees willing to accept the assignment, to an employee's request to be excused from an overtime assignment.

Section 4

Callback overtime shall be a minimum of 2 hours.

Section 5

The Employer agrees to make a reasonable effort consistent with operational needs to avoid situations involving callback overtime or from requiring employees to work overtime on their regularly scheduled days off.

Section 6

An employee performing overtime work on his/her regularly scheduled day off shall be guaranteed 4 hours of work.

Flextime

A relatively recent innovation in collective bargaining involves letting employees select within limits their daily work schedules. Daily shift hours are normally spelled out in labor contracts, and all employees are required to work the hours of the stipulated shift. These newer schedules are popularly called "flextime." Under this innovation, all employees still must work eight hours per day. However, they have more flexibility in selecting their starting and quitting times. Typically, there is a daily fixed schedule during which all employees are expected to work. This period, called "core time," may range between four and six hours per day. Surrounding the core time, employees may select the starting and quitting times. For instance, core time may be established between 10 A.M. and 3 P.M. During those five hours all employees must work. Then within certain limits the employee may select starting and quitting time. For example, the schedule may require that all hours be worked between 6 A.M. and 6 P.M. An employee may elect to start at 10 A.M. and work until 6 P.M. or may elect to start at 7 A.M. and work until 3 P.M. to complete the eight-hour day. Thus employees may adjust their starting and quitting times in accordance with their personal needs and preferences. Of firms surveyed by a management association not long ago, nearly one third permitted workers to help determine their own schedules, double the percentage of a decade ago.

Some employers, indeed, have eliminated even core time. U.S. West, with continuous operations, lets its payroll members set any hours that they want subject only to the approval of their supervisors. Equifax, Inc., allows its employees to come to and leave their work anytime between 7:30 A.M. and 9:30 P.M. as long as they are on the job for 7.5 hours each workday. At NCNB Corporation, a bank holding company headquartered in Charlotte, North Carolina, workers can leave on both Thursdays and Fridays at noon and can make up the hours on evenings of the same or other weekdays.

Unions have not been overly enthusiastic about flextime schedules, though this attitude is changing to make organizations more attractive to women. Married women, particularly those with children, may find that such a schedule fits their personal needs. In any event, in general, unions look at flextime as a managerial tool to reduce the need for overtime payment and to increase the intensity of the work pace. For example, unions charge that supervisors may encourage employees to "volunteer" for a schedule to avoid the need for overtime. If flextime is to spread in the United States, objections raised by organized labor will have to be resolved. And of course, even if employees and their unions are willing, some employers may find flextime scheduling an impossibility under certain kinds of operations. To produce effectively under certain types of technology and operations, all employees must be present at the same time.

JOB EVALUATION AND JOB COMPARISON

Thus far we have been dealing with *general* changes in the level of wages under collective bargaining. The comparative-norm, ability-to-pay, standard-of-living, and cost-of-living principles—as well as the principles relating to wage differentials and overtime rates—rather than affecting any particular jobs apply either to all jobs within the plant or to all jobs that fall within certain widely delineated areas (for example, night work, "dirty work," and overtime work).

Another important problem, however, involves the establishment of *relative* wage rates (or rate ranges) for each particular job, so that wage differentials are rationalized (jobs of greater "worth" to the management are rewarded by greater pay), and the overall wage structure is stabilized on a relatively permanent basis.

Essentially, employers adopt one of two methods to achieve this goal: (1) job evaluation and (2) what, for lack of a universally accepted descriptive designation, might be best described as "job comparison."

Job evaluation in its broadest sense is actually used by all employers. It occurs whenever the management decides that one job should be paid more than another, and this is *invariably* done by organizations in the sense that some jobs obviously do deserve more pay than do others.

In the more technical sense in which it is used here, however, job evaluation requires a more systematic approach. Briefly, job evaluation—through the use of thorough job descriptions and equally detailed analyses of these descriptions—attempts to rank jobs in terms of their (1) skill, (2) effort, (3) responsibility, and (4) working requirement demands on the jobholder. Each job is awarded a certain number of points, according to the degree to which each of these four factors (or refinements of them) is present in it, and the total number of points consequently assigned to each job (usually on a weighted-average basis, depending on the importance of each factor) determines the place at which the particular job falls in the job hierarchy of the employer. Wage rates or ranges are then established for all jobs falling within a single total point spread (usually called a "labor grade") of this hierarchy. All jobs awarded between 250 and 275 points, for example, might constitute labor grade 4 and be paid whatever wages are called for by this labor grade.

Many managements have found the appeal of such a system to be irresistible. In addition to simplifying the wage structure through the substitution of a relatively few labor grades for individual job listings, it allows the employer a basis for defending particular wage rates to the union and provides a rational means for determining rates for new and changed jobs (through using the same process for these jobs, and then slotting their point totals into the hierarchy of labor grades). At least three quarters of all American managements probably make use of such a system today.

This growth of job evaluation, at least for unionized companies, has nonetheless been accomplished only in the face of rather adamant union opposition. Only a few unions—most notably the Steelworkers—have done anything but strongly attack the system. Virtually all others have voiced deep suspicion of the technique itself and have decried the reduced possibilities for union bargaining on individual wage rates allowed by job evaluation.

Why, then, has this method of evaluation spread so pervasively to industry? Livernash years ago conveyed an authoritative opinion that remains valid:

> In part, unions have been bought off. Objection was not strong enough to turn down evaluation if an increase in the rate structure was also involved.... In part, unions became willing to accept less bargaining over individual job rates.... Unions found that job evaluation did not freeze them out of a reasonable voice in influencing the wage structure and continuous wage grievances became a union problem. Particularly when accompanied by formal or informal joint participation in the evaluation process, the technique became acceptable.[16]

Unions on these grounds have been far more receptive to the concept than a mere reading of their official statements would lead one to believe.

Job comparison is, in many cases, the manager's answer to intransigent union opposition to job evaluation where this remains a force. It has also been utilized by many employers whose job structures do not appear complex enough to warrant job evaluation, or (in some cases) where the management itself is divided on the worth of the evaluation technique. Although it has certain refinements, it most frequently involves (1) the establishment of an appropriate number of labor grades with accompanying wage rates or ranges, and (2) the classification of each job into a particular labor grade by deciding which already classified jobs the particular job most closely resembles. The systematic approach of the evaluation method is, in short, dispensed with—and so are the many subsidiary advantages of such an approach. By the same token, however, whatever deficiencies the management or union sees in evaluation are also bypassed. The procedure, a not too satisfactory compromise between evaluations and individual rates for each job, is not now common in industry and, for the reasons indicated in the discussion of evaluation, can probably be expected to become increasingly less so in the years ahead.

CONCESSIONARY BARGAINING

Organized labor officially marked its one-hundredth anniversary in 1981, but it was hardly a time for rejoicing. Starting in the summer of that year, the nation slid into the worst recession since the Great Depression. Unemployment soared from 7.2 percent in July 1981 to the previously noted 10.8 percent in December 1982, the highest level since 1940, and remained in double digits until well into 1983. And these were just the overall figures. Statistics for much of the blue collar world, labor's strongest base of operations by far, were generally far more gloomy.

Not since the 1930s, indeed, had labor-management contracts been negotiated under such adverse conditions. In a few individual industries— shoe manufacturing, in the 1950s when foreign competition began to flood the United States marketplace; and meatpacking, in the 1950s and 1960s when nonunion packing in the South endangered many unionized northern packers—the unions involved had been forced by economic adversity to give back some of their previously gotten wages and benefits. And in previous post–World War II recessions, the pace of wage increases and benefit gains had, of course, slowed. Wholesale concessions granted employers at the bargaining table, however, had not been given in any significant way. Now, they were.

In an effort to save jobs, unions made concessions on wages as they never had before and forfeited benefits that had been enjoyed for as long as forty years. At times, union leaders were put in the awkward position of urging members to accept the lower standards of employment and frequently these concessions were negotiated before the expiration date of contracts. As a UAW spokesperson put it, "All of the things we win at the bargaining table don't mean a thing to someone without a job."[17]

The overall statistics indicate just how widespread the assault on wages alone was. Where, according to the Bureau of Labor Statistics, first-year wage increases in multiyear contracts negotiated in 1981 had been 8.3 percent, the corresponding figure for 1982 was a paltry 3.8 percent, the lowest in the seventeen-year period during which the BLS had been publishing such data, and in 1986 it was an even more minuscule 1.2 percent.[18] But even these figures concealed the major wage and benefit concessions made by several million unionists. And in 1988, when unemployment dropped to 5.5 percent and the economy was generally regarded as robust, the first year increase of multiyear contracts was only 2.5 percent, and 2.4 percent for the life of the contract.[19] This, despite the increase of the rate of inflation in 1988 to 4.1 percent, reducing workers' real income.[20]

Concessions in automobiles and steel got the most publicity, but several thousand other negotiations resulted in either a pay freeze or a reduction. The mighty Teamsters agreed to freeze the hourly pay of their more than 200,000 over-the-road truck drivers at $13.30 for thirty-eight months and to use all cost-of-living adjustments scheduled to be made during this period to finance health care. They later granted further economic concessions to particularly marginal employers. In the hard-pressed meat packing industry, the United Food and Commercial Workers allowed weaker companies to reduce pay and benefits by up to $4 per hour—in some cases thereby chopping compensation levels by 40 percent. At Eastern Airlines, three major unions agreed to wage decreases of up to 22 percent and work-rule changes valued at an estimated $350 million. In return, workers got company stock and the right to designate candidates for two seats on the airline's board (later increased, amid further union concessions, to four seats). At Continental Air Lines, pilots and flight attendants accepted wages that were a whopping 45 percent below previous levels, although only after the carrier had filed for bankruptcy and dismissed 12,000 of its workers (prior to rehiring 4,200 of them) and after the unions had gone out on an unsuccessful strike.

To a degree, *lump sum* payments offset the low wage settlements, and many employees did receive a fixed one-time payment, often in the neighborhood of $500, at the time the new contract went into effect. These payments were not included in the basic wage rate, and did not increase costs affected by the basic wage rate, such as overtime, holiday and vacation pay, and pensions. This is why employers, refusing to increase wages, consent to lump sum payments.

Lump sum payments were included in contracts covering 28 percent of the workers under 1988 settlements.[21] For 1991, the BLS reported the figure increased to 37 percent of the 5.6 million workers covered by major contracts in private industry.[22] Nonetheless, their impact on employee living standards should not be magnified. For 1987, the AFL-CIO reported that lump sum payments for that year amounted to the equivalent of only about a 0.5 percent wage increase.[23]

With the ending of the recession in late 1983, many observers felt that this remarkable period of labor concessions was also over. Employers who were once again making money (in cases such as the automobile industry, quite sizable amounts of it) could no longer credibly ask further sacrifices of their workers. (If they did so, at least in the eyes of one labor leader, "it would be about as brazen as the guy who killed his mother and his father and then threw himself on the mercy of the courts on the grounds that he was an orphan.") Most experts also could agree with Harvard economist James J. Medoff's observation that "As the economy is picking up, the threat of bankruptcy and shutdown has no credibility for the senior workers. If the cost of wage increases is that some junior people are laid off or others are not hired, the senior members will say 'That's too bad, but we'll take the wage increases.'"[24] Most union leaders, in fact, reflecting the opinion of Mine Worker president Trumka that concessions were "a form of suicide by degree," took strong stands against making more of them, and the members of some unions (notably the UAW at Caterpillar Tractor and the Machinists at Brown and Sharpe) put their monies where their leaders' mouths were by engaging in long and costly strikes in attempts to make the point.

Some employers—not all of them by any means running in the red—still felt the need for concessions from their unions to survive amid accelerating foreign imports and nonunion competition, however. And, with the threat of job losses still a very meaningful one here, they continued to negotiate concessions—sometimes, as at Eastern Airlines, with contingent compensation such as stock ownership plans and/or some guaranteed union input into corporate business decisions (both of which topics will be dealt with in Chapter 9). Pay freezes and reductions went on in the food, trucking, airlines, and electrical products industries, in particular. Years after the general recession, some employers were still demanding concessions and at times unions capitulated. In 1988, at its Indianapolis engine plant, Navistar negotiated the equivalent of a $3-per-hour wage cut with the UAW. In 1989, the independent union of flight attendants agreed to a $33 million wage cut with Pan American World Airways. (Worker concessions were not sufficient to keep this venerable and proud carrier flying. It closed in December 1991.)

But not all workers and their unions submitted meekly to concessions. Strikes, some bitter and prolonged, were touched off by employer demands for concessions. For 165 days—the longest work stoppage in basic steel history—the United Steelworkers of America struck USX (formerly United States Steel) because of further demands for concessions (after the strike ended in 1987, the steelworkers did accept a wage and benefit cut of $2.25 per hour and the loss of about a thousand jobs by a combination of craft-worker classifications). In 1989, as noted earlier, the Machinists struck Eastern Airlines, rejecting Eastern CEO Frank Lorenzo's demands for sizable wage concessions. Also in 1989, Pittston Coal's demand for concessions touched off widespread wildcat strikes within the coal industry. When Pittston operated its mine with supervisors and strikebreakers, violence occurred, requiring the presence of law enforcement officers.

These labor disputes were a harbinger of a new attitude on labor's part, as it turned out. By the 1990s, despite the appearance of a new and long-lasting recession, Trumka's equation of concessions with "suicide by degree" seemed to have fully taken hold, as Exhibits 7-2 and 7-3 (both typical labor publication cartoons published in 1992) illustrate. Labor would henceforth insist, as a general rule, on some kind of wage improvement to bring back to the bargaining unit members even at the risk of job loss. What one union leader had called the "era of masochism" seemed to be over.

EXHIBIT 7–2

Source: Carol/Simpson Productions

EXHIBIT 7–3

Source: AFL-CIO News.

TWO-TIER WAGE SYSTEMS

Concessionary bargaining obviously (unless everyone in the industry has made concessions) violates the deeply rooted union principle of "equal pay for equal work." Employees who perform the same jobs as others working elsewhere now get less (or more) pay than these others. But at least the violation of the principle is an indirect and relatively subtle one. Being out of sight, the better-paid workers of competitors in other places are generally out of mind—if, indeed, the latter's now-favored position is even recognized by those who have made concessions. Under any conditions, there can be no direct jealousies on the part of the have-nots: Their own immediate colleagues are paid no more than they are.

In the case of another development of the past decade, "equal pay for equal work" is frontally assaulted. Under the two-tier wage system, workers hired after the labor agreement is signed get pay rates that are below, and sometimes well below, those in the same work force whose dates of hire took place under a previous contract. Thus, newly hired pilots at American Airlines, which in the mid-1980s had a two-tier system in place and estimated that it was saving a rather handsome $100 million annually from it, could in those days expect to be paid at a rate 50 percent less than pilots whose hiring predated 1983, when two-tiering was sanctioned by a new contract. And, under the language of that contract, they would never have an opportunity to catch up with the more favored pilots. They had been penalized as unborn employees to protect those who were already present (and who were, not coincidentally, voting union members) when the negotiations were carried on.

American Airlines hardly stood alone then, either. By the mid-1980s, the two-tier system had become increasingly important in wage negotiations. And where such arrangements were included in less than 4 percent of all new contracts in 1980, the number soared to 9 percent by 1987 and probably covered over one million workers.[25] Nor was two-tiering engineered by only employers who were relatively poverty-stricken. Such comparatively well-off organizations as Boeing, United Parcel Service, Giant Food, Safeway Stores, Dow Chemical, the U.S. Postal Service, Alcoa, and General Dynamics also implemented it in this period.

But if the two-tier system can strengthen an employer's competitive situation and income statement, it can also cause problems in the form of employee unhappiness and, ultimately, worker retention and recruitment. The system has an obvious unfairness to it that only a candidate for sainthood among the newly hired workers could be expected to ignore. And as employees came aboard at the lower rate, they almost inevitably, and rather quickly, became discontented. The package sorter for UPS who could expect $9.18 an hour when the person working next to him got $14.01 could be excused for studying the help-wanted ads at his first lunch hour. And many new hires would undoubtedly empathize with the supermarket clerk whose $7.01 wage rate allowed her barely 60 percent of the earnings of many of her colleagues and who asserted with some finality, "Sure, I knew what this work paid when I accepted it. What I didn't realize was just how inequitable it was. Just as soon as I find something else, I'm gone."

Nor has the system necessarily pleased members of the upper-wage tier. They have often worried that because of their higher rates their employers now have a logical reason to get rid of them—or, at the least, to allow them fewer hours of work per week than the newer hires.

By the close of the decade, not a few employers had also become disenchanted with the system, primarily because of lower employee morale, increased labor turnover, reduced labor productivity, and poor quality of workmanship. When the U.S. Navy complained about sloppy work done by its employees, Hughes Aircraft abolished its two-tier scale. So did General Dynamics, LTV Corporation, and the U.S. Postal Service. In 1987, American Airlines agreed with its pilots union to merge by stages the pay scales of those newly hired with the scales of senior pilots and in 1988 it completed the cycle by merging the pay scales for its flight attendants. There were still a few conspicuous exceptions here—Northwest Airlines pilots and Lockheed machinists, for example, accepted two-tier arrangements in widely publicized new agreements relatively recently. But by 1992, two-tier wage plans appeared in only 5 percent of newly bargained labor-management agreements, and it was clear that a trend that had so recently developed was now being reversed. Two-tiering will probably remain a feature of labor relations, since its advantages to hard-pressed employers remain quite visible. But it will presumably have a somewhat more minor role than was, even a very few years ago, predicted for it.

A FINAL WORD

As this chapter has tried to show, wage issues pose very difficult collective bargaining problems. But if the resultant complications do make wage controversies a major cause of strikes, the fact remains that such strikes take place in only a comparatively few instances. Although the stakes can be very high and the problems formidable, employers and unions in the vast majority of cases ultimately find a peaceful solution in the wage area as in other areas of bargaining.

Some of the settlements, admittedly, may not be the kind that would be advocated by economists, and some clearly fail to adjust the issues in a way that reflects equity and fairness. But the parties most often do resolve their wage disputes in a manner that proves generally satisfactory to all concerned.

It should be remembered that these wage problems are not resolved in an antiseptic economic laboratory where wage models may be constructed. If the settlements do, at times, offend the economic purist, it must be appreciated that these issues are dealt with in the practical day-to-day world, where pressures, motives, and attitudes cannot be isolated from negotiations. Given such realities, it is to the credit of both parties that mutual accommodation has become increasingly visible.

DISCUSSION QUESTIONS

1. Both industry A and industry B are extensively organized by conscientious and honestly run labor unions. Still, since 1968, the wages within industry A have risen at about three times the rate of those in industry B. How might you account for the difference in the wage situation between these two industries?

2. "Even though the actual wage rate that will be negotiated in a particular negotiation is not determinable, it is certain that the set of arguments that union and management representatives will use to support their respective positions will not change from negotiation to negotiation." To what extent, if any, do you agree with this statement?

3. Compare the methods available for the adjustment of wages during the effective period of a labor agreement, and defend what you would judge to be the most desirable arrangement.

4. "From the employer's point of view, it is inherently inequitable—the laws notwithstanding—to require the payment of equal wages to women and to men for performing the same job." Construct the strongest case that you can in support of this statement, and then balance your case with the most convincing opposing arguments that you can muster.

5. Recognizing the present-day circumstances in which you reply to this question, what do you believe to be the most important wage determinant in collective bargaining? Why?

6. What possible problems might confront management and unions in the negotiation and administration of contractual language dealing with overtime?

MINICASES

#1 Dispensation

The Marsh Company, a 90-year-old Akron clothing maker best known for its golf shirts and men's underwear, is genuinely convinced that unless it can cut its labor costs appreciably, it will soon be on the brink of extinction. Although the union with which it has dealt for many years has prided itself on enforcing uniform industrywide contractual terms (in separate contracts for each company), relations between the parties have been good in recent years. Accordingly, Personnel Vice-President Lillian Rosenblatt believes that "if the cards are played right" (as she puts it) the union could be amenable to some holding of the line on employee benefits for the first two years of the new three-year contract for which bargaining is scheduled to begin in four weeks, and perhaps even a temporary wage freeze.

If such dispensation is not achieved in the bargaining, Rosenblatt personally has no doubts but that Marsh will have to close its doors within a year, thereby terminating the employment of its 295 workers. All but 44 of these employees are union members and most of them are relative old-timers since the work force has an average age of 43. She also recognizes, however, that if the union grants concessions to Marsh, other companies in this currently depressed industry would immediately pursue the labor organization for similar downward revisions in their own contracts. The latter consequence is something that the union clearly would not welcome and might not be politically able to sustain in any event.

If you were Vice-President Rosenblatt, how would you deal with this subject of contractual dispensation?

#2 An Employee Refusal to Work Overtime

The labor agreement stipulates that "changes in the work schedule" must be "mutually agreeable to both the company and the union." Gryzmisk, who has refused to work six hours of overtime as he was requested to do by his supervisor, is given a one-day suspension for his action.

The union supports Gryzmisk all the way to arbitration on the grounds that the relevant overtime constituted a "change in the work schedule" that it had not approved. The management argues before the arbitrator that the six hours in no way could be considered a change that needed union acceptance since it was for a "limited and specified" duration.

As the arbitrator in this case, what would you have decided?

NOTES

[1] Data furnished by the Bureau of Labor Statistics, U.S. Department of Labor.

[2] Recognition of the difference between firms and industries should also be taken into account when the *nonmoney* items of collective bargaining are negotiated. A seniority system, for example, that is suitable for one employer-union relationship may not fit the needs of the employer and employees of another plant. Union security formulas, checkoff arrangements, managerial prerogative systems, grievance procedures, discharge and disciplinary arrangements, and the character of the union obligations should be geared fundamentally to the particular collective bargaining relationship. Management and union representatives are at times astonished to learn of the contractual arrangement of another employer-union relationship. The fact is, however, that such a formula can frequently be explained logically in terms of the environment of that firm.

[3] *Time,* February, 25, 1980, p. 77.

[4] Ben Burdetsky, "The U.S. Bureau of Labor Statistics: 100 Years of Service and Support to the Industrial Relations Community," in *Proceedings of the Thirty-Seventh Annual Meeting, Industrial Relations Research Association,* December 28–30, 1984, p. 39.

[5] The Consumer Price Index (CPI) is the index that is almost universally utilized in collective bargaining by employers and unions. It is prepared and published by the Bureau of Labor Statistics and appears each month in the Bureau's *Monthly Labor Review.*

[6] "Wage Escalation—Recent Developments," *Monthly Labor Review,* 77, No. 3 (March 1955), 315.

[7] Bureau of National Affairs, ed., "What's New in Collective Bargaining Negotiations and Contracts," No. 300 (November 30, 1956), p. 4.

[8] "Deferred Increases Due in 1965 and Wage Escalation," *Monthly Labor Review,* 87, No. 12 (December 1964), 1384.

[9] Wallace E. Hendricks and Lawrence M. Kahn, "Wage Indexation in the United States: Prospects for the 1980s," in *Proceedings of the Thirty-Seventh Annual Meeting, Industrial Relations Research Association,* December 28–30, 1984, p. 413.

[10] *New York Times,* March 7, 1989.

[11] Hendricks and Kahn, *op. cit.*

[12] Figures furnished by Bureau of Labor Statistics.

[13]Victor J. Sheifer, "Cost of Living Adjustment: Keeping Up with Inflation," *Monthly Labor Review,* 102, No. 6 (June 1979), 15. Reasons offered to explain this state of affairs are these: The formula of a 1 cent increase for each 0.3- or 0.4-point CPI rise is not sufficient for total compensation; "caps" or ceilings on escalator increases; escalation adjustments lag behind price changes; escalator yields are at times diverted to finance other employee benefits; and some escalators do not operate until a significant increase in the CPI occurs, as in some clothing contracts that yield gains only when the CPI increases by 7.5 percent and 6 percent in the second and third contract years.

[14]*Business Week,* April 11, 1983, p. 28.

[15]Title VII did, however, grant exemptions to work forces of fewer than twenty-five persons.

[16]Summer H. Slichter, James J. Healy, and E. Robert Livernash, *The Impact of Collective Bargaining on Management* (Washington, D.C.: Brookings Institution, 1960), pp. 563–64.

[17]*U.S. News & World Report,* February 2, 1982, p. 65.

[18]William Davis, "Major Collective Bargaining Settlements in Private Industry in 1988," *Monthly Labor Review,* May 1989, p. 34.

[19]*Ibid.,* p. 35.

[20]*Monthly Labor Review,* April 1989, p. 83.

[21]Davis, *op. cit.,* p. 35.

[22]Commerce Clearing House, *Labor Law Reports,* No. 280, February 7, 1992.

[23]*AFL-CIO News,* May 2, 1987.

[24]*Business Week,* January 16, 1984, p. 23.

[25]*Wall Street Journal,* April 18, 1989, p. 1.

SELECTED REFERENCES

Gold, Michael Evan, *A Dialogue on Comparable Worth.* Ithaca, N.Y.: ILR Press, Cornell University, 1983.

Hill, M. Anne, and Mark R. Killingsworth, eds., *Comparable Worth: Analyses and Evidence.* Ithaca, N.Y.: ILR Press, Cornell University, 1989.

Milkovich, George T., and Jerry M. Newman, *Compensation.* Plano, Tex.: Business Publications, 1984.

Mitchell, Daniel J. B., *Unions, Wages and Inflation.* Washington, D.C.: Brookings Institution, 1980.

Okun, Arthur M., and George L. Perry, eds., *Curing Chronic Inflation.* Washington, D.C.: Brookings Institution, 1978.

Owen, John D., *Working Hours.* Lexington, Mass.: Lexington Books, 1979.

Patten, Thomas H., Jr., *Pay: Employee Compensation and Incentive Plans.* New York: Free Press, 1977.

Rees, Albert, *The Economics of Trade Unions* (2nd rev. ed.). Chicago: University of Chicago Press, 1977.

Reynolds, Lloyd G., Stanley H. Masters, and Colletta H. Moser, *Economics of Labor.* Englewood Cliffs, N.J.: Prentice Hall, 1987.

Silverstein, Pam, and Jozetta H. Srb, *Flextime: Where, When, and How?* Ithaca, N.Y.: ILR Press, Cornell University, 1979.

Stigler, George J., *The Theory of Price.* New York: Macmillan, 1966.

Weber, Arnold R., and Daniel J. B. Mitchell, *The Pay Board's Progress.* Washington, D.C.: Brookings Institution, 1978.

Overtime: The Case of the Material Handler

CAST OF CHARACTERS

Stark	Grievant
Harrel	Union Committeeman
Basley	Plant Superintendent
Mills	Supervisor
Black	Chairman, Union Bargaining Committee
Griff	Plant Manager

You are the arbitrator in this case, which deals with overtime. Understand that an employee has nothing to lose and much to gain by filing an overtime grievance. If the grievance is denied, the employee is not penalized because the Union pays the costs of the arbitration. However, should the grievance be granted, the employee receives pay at the overtime rate of pay. In this case, the employee, if the grievance is granted, would receive twelve hours of pay without working even a minute—a costly matter for the employer, which has already paid the employee who actually worked twelve hours of pay. If required to pay an additional twelve hours, the employer would have paid twenty-four hours for eight hours of work!

In the case at hand, the employee, Material Handler, filed a grievance when he learned that a Machine Operator performed work in his classification on Saturday. He requested eight hours of pay at the overtime rate, since Saturday is an overtime day, even though the work in question took the Machine Operator only about two or three minutes (and even though supervision had not instructed the Machine Operator to perform the work).

In the past, two grievances were filed that had the identical set of circumstances. In both instances, the Company granted the grievances and paid the employees. In fact, one of the former grievants was the same employee complaining in the instant case. One of the problems you will have, therefore, is to determine what weight to give to the previous grievance settlements. Understandably, the Union with vigor asserts that the settlement of the prior two grievances constitutes past practice and that the instant grievance should be granted on that basis. Just as vehemently, the Company contends that those settlements should not be used for the purpose of precedent in the case at hand.

Depending on how you resolve that issue, another one will command your attention. To what extent is an employer responsible for an employee's violation of classification lines when the employee on his own decides to perform work falling in another classification?

Your job is to apply Article VII, Section 7.3, the Overtime provision, to the circumstances of this case. Make sure that you have a firm understanding of the facts before deciding the case. Although arbitrations fall within "pigeonholes," such as overtime, discipline, management rights, seniority, and holidays, each case has its particular factual setting.

In the final analysis, therefore, your task is to apply Article VII, Section 7.3, under the circumstances of this case. Whatever decision you make, be prepared to defend it with clear and logical reasoning, rooted to the facts and contractual language.

GRIEVANCE AND LABOR AGREEMENT

Involved in this case is a claim for compensation for an overtime day because the employee was not scheduled. In protest, Marvin Stark filed Grievance No. Y-92-90, dated October 24, 1990. It states:

> On Sat. Oct. 20, 1990 the Co. worked the Case Besley & the Cross line to the Sputnik. The Co. failed to work a Material Handler on this overtime day. The operator of the Case Besley made moves with a jack stacker which are normally made by the Material Handling class.

As a settlement for his complaint, the Union requests:

> 8 hrs. pay at time and one-half for Marvin Stark, and when Machining works, work a material handler to perform work that belongs to material handlers on a normal work day.

Having failed to resolve the dispute in the Grievance Procedure, the Parties convened this arbitration for its determination.

Material to the dispute are the following provisions of the Labor Agreement:

ARTICLE VII—Hours of Work and Wages

Section 7.3—Overtime

B. Time and One-Half Pay

3. All hours worked on Saturday.

E. Distribution, Selection, Records and Equalization

2. If it is necessary to fill a job assignment on Saturday, Sunday, or holidays by overtime, the following procedure will be used.

(a) Employees assigned to the affected classification on the affected shift...

APPENDIX A

Classifications and Rate of Pay

	Hourly Rate
Material Handler	$9.39

Also pertinent to the dispute is the settlement by the Parties of Grievance No. Y-214-84, dated October 4, 1984. The settlement was in effect at the time of arbitration. It applies to regular workdays and overtime days. Of significance to this dispute, the document states:

> Employees other than Material Handlers can still move material within their department as long as it consists of production in process. However, effort will be made to utilize Material Handlers assigned to Dept. 31 to as great an extent as is possible.

BASIC QUESTION

The basic question to be determined in this case is framed as follows:

Under the circumstances of this case, did the Company violate the overtime rights of Grievant Stark? If so, what should the remedy be?

BACKGROUND

Duties of Material Handler: Servicing the Case Besley Machine

When the circumstances of this dispute arose, Stark was classified as a Material Handler assigned to the third shift. The problem arose in the

Machine Department, Department 31. Primary machines are located in this department, including the Case Besley, the machine directly involved in this dispute.

By the use of a forklift truck, a Material Handler brings pallets or skids of parts to the machine in question. On each pallet there are about 320 parts weighing 1,300 pounds. Located adjacent to the machine is a conveyor. The Material Handler loads the conveyor, the capability of which is four pallets, including the one contained in a turntable or "scissors." This apparatus lifts a pallet so the parts are readily accessible to the Machine Operator.

At times, the Material Handler removes a pallet from the conveyor and replaces it with another pallet. This could occur when for some reason the parts on one pallet are different from those parts contained on the other pallets. This switch of parts is known as a "cavity" or "vendor" change.

The Company purchases its parts from two vendors, Lester and Doller-Jarvis. Parts are designated by a number; in this case Parts No. 19 and No. 20 are involved. Should a Machine Operator change his run of parts from one vendor to the other vendor, the Case Besley must be reset. According to Dave Harrel, Union Committeeman, the reset of the machine under these circumstances could take from 4 to 8 hours. Joseph Basley, Plant Superintendent, said that the machine downtime for such a purpose would be about an hour.

Machine downtime also occurs when the Machine Operator changes his run from one part number to another part made by the same vendor. To adjust the machine for this purpose, Basley said, downtime would be about 5 to 10 minutes. Harrel testified that machine downtime could range between

5 minutes to 4 to 8 hours depending upon the problem involved.

In order to minimize downtime, Machine Operators are instructed to process the same parts to the extent possible. Thus, should a Machine Operator notice that a pallet has parts of a different number, or from a different vendor, from those he is running, he will take action to remedy this situation. For this purpose, he or the Supervisor contacts the Material Handler to make the proper switch of parts. Normally the Material Handler will use a forklift truck to make the change. At times, however, not too frequently, he will use a jackstacker, a manual battery operated lifting device.

Stark testified that he makes such a change about three or four times per week. Harrel, who previously operated the Case Besley, said that it is a

common occurrence for the wrong parts to be on the conveyor.

Under these circumstances, he told the Material Handler to correct the situation, or to contact his Supervisor, who in turn would instruct the Material Handler to make the needed change of parts.

The Company Plan

The Company scheduled the Case Besley for the third shift, Saturday, October 20, 1990. That is, it was to be operated between 11 P.M. Friday, October 19, until 7 A.M. Saturday, October 20.

The Company made a plan to operate the machine without scheduling a Material Handler for that shift. To carry out this plan, Basley gave the following instructions to the second shift Supervisor at 4 P.M. on Friday, October 19.

At 11 P.M., a pallet of parts was to be placed on the scissors. This pallet was to provide a supply of parts for the third shift Machine Operator when he reported at that time. (The second shift Machine Operator leaves the plant at 11 P.M.) By having the pallet on the scissors, the third shift Machine Operator would be able to start processing parts immediately upon his report to work.

At 11:40 P.M., the pallet would be removed from the scissors and another one placed on that apparatus. Also at that time three additional pallets would be placed on the conveyor back to back. In addition, one pallet was to be placed on the floor adjacent to the scissors. Three feet separate that location and the work station of the Machine Operator. Another pallet was to be placed on the floor at the end of the conveyor.[*] From that location and the Machine Operator's work station there are about 20 feet. Movement of the pallets would be completed by the second shift Material Handler whose regular shift ended at midnight on October 19.

It was expected that the third shift Machine Operator would process between 1,600 and 1,800 parts. This amount constitutes the normal production of the Case Besley for an eight-hour shift. As stated, there are about 320 parts to a pallet. To achieve this goal, the Machine Operator would process parts in this way: Between 11 P.M. and 11:40 P.M. he would run the parts from the pallet located on the scissors. Then he would process the parts from the new pallet placed on the scissors at 11:40 P.M. After that supply was exhausted, he would use the parts contained on the other three pallets located on the conveyor.

After that supply was exhausted, the Machine Operator would obtain parts from the pallet located on the floor next to the scissors. To get those parts the Machine Operator would walk three feet to the pallet, reach down to get a part, walk back to the machine, and process the part. He would repeat this process until all the parts contained on that floor-situated pallet had been run.

In this way, had the plan been executed as established by Basley, there would be no need for the services of a Material Handler. The expected production would be achieved without the movement of pallets. As it turned out, between 1,705 and 1,720 parts were produced on the machine during the shift in question.

---

[*]Basley said this pallet was for use by the Machine Operator who was scheduled to report at 7 A.M. Saturday, October 20. Under this plan, the parts on that pallet were not to be processed by the third shift Machine Operator. To meet the production goal, as explained below, the third shift Machine Operator would not need those parts.

Events of Saturday, October 20

An event occurred, however, that interfered with the proper execution of the plan. During the shift in question, Doller-Jarvis parts were to be processed. All parts contained on the six pallets in question were those of that vendor. However, one pallet contained parts of a different number. The first three pallets on the conveyor and the two pallets located on the floor contained No. 20 parts. In contrast, the end pallet on the conveyor contained No. 19 parts.

When the Machine Operator became aware of the No. 19 parts, instead of adjusting the machine to run those parts, he moved the pallet located on the floor at the end of the conveyor to his machine. To make the move, he used the jackstacker. It took him about two or three minutes.

Later on, Basley interviewed the third shift Machine Operator in the presence of a Union Committeeman. As to this interview, Basley testified:

> I asked the Machine Operator what he did that night. He told me that he moved the pallet from the back to the front of his machine because he did not want to adjust his machine to run the No. 19 parts. He also told me that no one told him to make that move. He said he did it on his own.

When Stark learned that the third shift Machine Operator moved the pallet in question, he filed his grievance which generated this arbitration. In this respect, Stark testified:

> I asked Doug Mills, my Supervisor, why I was not scheduled that night. It would have been an overtime day for me. I asked him why I was getting the shaft. He told me there was no need for me on that shift, and whether I worked that night was not up to him, but up to the "higher-ups" in the Company. Then I wrote my grievance.

Settlement of Grievance No. Y-58-86 and No. Y-124-86

On May 10, 1986, Grievance No. Y-58-86 was filed. It stated:

> On Sat. May 10, 1986 in Dept. 31. Machine operators were moving skids of cases, normally moved by a material handler Monday thru Friday. This is in violation of a settled grievance. We feel this was done to avoid paying a material handler overtime pay for 8 hours.
>
> 8 hours pay at 1-1/2 times for low man on overtime in material handler classification.

Investigation of the grievance established that the Machine Operator moved three pallets of rough stock within the Machine Department. The Parties also agreed that

> the time spent to move the three skids could only be nominal.

With regard to this grievance, Nelson Black, Chairman, Union Bargaining Committee, testified:

> The Machine Operator moved the material by herself. No one told her to do it. No supervisor told her to make the move.

In settlement of this grievance, the Company paid three hours of pay at the overtime rate. The settlement stated:

> In order to resolve this grievance, the Company will pay three (3) hours at 1 1/2 times to the low person on overtime in the material handling classification. The payment will be made without precedent or prejudice to the Company or the Union.

On October 30, 1986, Stark (the grievant also in this case) filed Grievance No. Y-124-86.

> Incident: Saturday, Oct. 25, 3rd shift, the piston head ran 5,000 parts. There are approx. 2,500 pistons in a tub, so some time through the night parts were moved.
>
> A setup man moved them.
>
> The grievant wants 8 hrs. pay at time and a half.

Investigation of this grievance reveals that the Set Up Man was not told by supervision to perform the move as he did. It was also established that the move in question took him not more than two minutes.

In settlement of this grievance, the Company paid Stark three hours pay at the overtime rate. While settling the grievance, the Company stated:

> The Company acknowledges an error may have occurred and will pay three (3) hours at time and one-half to the third shift Material Handler, without precedent or prejudice to other cases, in a good faith effort to resolve this grievance.

Skilled Trades' Assignment on Overtime Days

During the Step 3 Grievance Procedure meeting on the current Stark grievance, the Union pointed out that skilled tradesmen are automatically scheduled on an overtime day (Saturday, Sunday, holiday) even though they do not typically perform any work in their trade because nothing occurs to require their services.

In the session, according to the minutes kept by the Union, the Union said the following to the Company:

> The Company had worked trade skilled employees [on an overtime day] when there was no work for them, but just the possibility of a breakdown was enough to let them work.

Then the following exchange occurred between Black, Chairman of the Union Bargaining Committee, and Jim Griff, Plant Manager:

Black said that if an Inspector lets some bad parts get by him during the week he gets an A.V.O., but on Sat. or Sun. the parts don't even get inspected. Black pointed out that service dept. employees have a right to do their work on Sat. just the same as trade skill employees have a right to their work. Jim Griff said that they do without a material handler and inspector because of economics, you would do the same if you were in my shoes. Black said, you are telling that there is one world for trade skills and another world for the unskilled. Jim said yes that is right. Black said that in the union, the unskilled have the same right as a trade skill, they have to feed their families too...

POSITIONS OF THE PARTIES

Union

In the Union's judgment, the Company violated Article VII, Section 7.3, Overtime, under the circumstances of this case. It contends that the provision requires that an assignment made to a classification during regular hours must be made to the same classification during an overtime day. During regular hours, Material Handlers move parts by the use of material handling equipment. During the Saturday overtime day in question, the Machine Operator moved a pallet of parts by use of the jackstacker. This violated Stark's overtime rights, and he is entitled to proper compensation for the violation.

In addition, grievance settlements of October 4, 1984, Grievance No. Y-214-84; May 10, 1986, Grievance No. Y-58-86; and October 30, 1986, Grievance No. Y-124-86, support the Union's cause. The parts the Machine Operator moved on the Saturday in question did not constitute "production in process" within the meaning of the October 4, 1984 settlement. Instead, they were rough stock, to be moved only by a Material Handler.

The settlement of the May and October 1986 grievances constitutes in the eyes of the Union a past practice requiring the granting of Stark's complaint. As on Saturday, October 20, 1990, those two grievances involved only a few minutes to move the parts, and in all three grievances, the Machine Operators moved the material on their own. No supervisor told them to move the parts.

Finally, the Union claims that the grievance should be granted on the basis of fairness and equity. This contention is based on the Company policy of automatically assigning skilled tradesmen to overtime days. They are assigned to use their skill to correct or repair any equipment which may break down during the shift. According to the Union, Material Handlers should also be assigned automatically on overtime days to move parts to machines when necessary. Just as an Electrician is assigned to an overtime day on a stand-by basis ready to use his/her skills, so should a Material

Handler be assigned on a stand-by basis ready to move material in the event that becomes necessary. As the Union said, "What is fair for one, should be fair for the other."

Company

With respect to the settlement of Grievances No. Y-58-86, May 10, and No. Y-124-86, October 30, 1986, the Company claims that they should not be used as precedent for purposes of this case. It asserts that the Parties agreed that such settlements were made "without precedent or prejudice to the Company or Union." Therefore, it would not be appropriate for the Arbitrator to use either of them as a controlling precedent in this proceeding.

The Company also argues that it was not responsible for the Machine Operator's action at the time in question. No supervisor told him to move the pallet containing No. 20 parts to the conveyor to replace the one containing No. 19 parts. No one from Management instructed him to use the jackstacker to move the pallet. In addition, the Machine Operator did not ask his supervisor whether to move the pallet to the conveyor or adjust the machine to run the No. 19 parts. "We should not be held responsible," said the Company, "for what the Machine Operator did entirely on his own."

Economic Supplements under Collective Bargaining

- What supplementary unemployment benefit plans can and can't do

- Six problem areas related to the huge growth of the benefit package

The incorporation of employee supplementary economic benefits—from paid vacations to pension plans—in collective bargaining contracts is widespread throughout American industry. Such benefits have increased dramatically in recent years, both in their value to the employee and in their variety. And, since these supplements to the basic wage rate are now commonly equivalent to almost 40 percent of payroll, it is understandable that some managers express hostility when the once accepted designation "fringe benefits" is used to describe this area. Nor does the adjective seem particularly applicable when it is realized that such benefits now cost employers close to $500 billion annually. Habits are not easily broken, however, and "fringe" will probably still be utilized even when the benefits approach one half of payroll, as—since they have been steadily rising at the rate of about 1 percent of payroll per year for some time—they most likely will do within a relatively few years.[1]

Many of these benefits are not new to personnel administration, and indeed, some of them were introduced by employers on a unilateral basis before the advent of unionism. However, unions have by all accounts been a major force behind the mushrooming of this form of compensation—and, due in no small measure to pressure from labor, many benefits have found their way into the world of work with increasing regularity: pension plans; paid vacations and holidays; various health insurance arrangements, including life insurance and hospital and other medical benefits; accidental death and dismemberment payments; and dismissal and reporting pay, among many others. Supplementary unemployment benefit plans also may properly be regarded as a supplement to the basic wage rate.

Beyond all this, many labor agreements contain special benefits, ones that are either absolutely unique or at least not widely prevailing as guaranteed benefits in the working world. Resort hotels in Hawaii grant free use of their golf courses to their International Longshoremen's and Warehousemen's Union members. Clerks at a West Coast supermarket chain can receive almost unlimited use of free psychiatric services and so, too, under certain conditions, can every member of their families. Some employers provide workers with help in filling out their income tax returns; others emphasize tuition subsidization for college-attending children of employees. Some unionists—Steelworkers conspicuously among them—are eligible for comprehensive alcohol- and drug-addiction rehabilitation, going well beyond the token benefits offered in many other employment settings. Day care for employee children has become more common as a contractually granted benefit: By 1993, about 10 percent of all unionized workers were entitled to some variation of it. Family leave for fathers is now growing, although such a benefit remains a relative rarity for unionists and non-unionists alike: An estimated 20 percent of both populations presently receives it, almost always on an unpaid basis. Many teachers can receive additional compensation for helping out in extra-curricular activities.

Prepaid group legal plans, too, have taken root in recent years. An estimated 10,000 such arrangements now offer free routine services such as uncontested divorces, wills, title transfers, and help with landlord-tenant problems, and some even provide free counsel for (limited) criminal offenses. It is possible that such a benefit will burgeon in the years ahead: In the recent past, the UAW has implemented legal services plans with the automobile manufacturers, and UAW activities have, of course, often proven influential in generating trends. Not long ago another potential shot in the arm was provided when the American Telephone and Telegraph Company, in new contracts with its 175,000 Communication Workers and Electrical Workers, agreed to provide generous legal services at reduced rates at qualified law firms. Many benefit trend watchers predict that such plans, which generally cost employers only several cents an hour per worker, will become as commonplace as health insurance and pensions before many more years have elapsed. On the other hand, even a free will and a bargain rate criminal defense may prove to have limited appeal as compared with, for example, more money in the pay envelope. And, in any event, this chapter focuses on the more currently widespread and thus presently costly economic supplements.

PENSION PLANS

Private pensions began to be a labor relations issue of some consequence in the late 1940s. A definite boost was given such plans by the U.S. Supreme Court's 1949 *Inland Steel* decision that employers could not refuse to bargain with their unions over this issue.[2] Managers still did not have to grant such employee benefits, but they could no longer legally dismiss union demands for them out of hand.

Other factors, particularly in more recent years, have also contributed to the growth of the pension plans. One of them is the modest level of benefits provided by the Social Security System. Another is the population's increased longevity and a commensurate lengthening of the number of postretirement years. Still a third, it is generally agreed, is the spread of union-spawned seniority and related provisions in labor contracts, making it all but impossible to terminate employment for older bargaining unit members *except* by pension.

In addition, there has been a growing managerial awareness—on the part of nonunion employers as well as unionized ones—of an organizational obligation to employees after their retirement. The typical present-day employer is willing to consider pensions a part of normal business costs, something to be charged against revenues in much the same way that insurance of plant and machinery is so charged.

Not that there is unanimity on details. Some managers insist that employees help pay for their pensions by making regular contributions to the pension fund during their working years. There are, understandably, wide differences of opinion among executives as to appropriate payment levels for pension plans. Some employers argue that their lack of financial resources rules out the establishment of any pension plan even though they would otherwise be happy to have one. Many smaller employers (in particular) have also cited the long-term character and unknown aspects of pension costs as justification for strengthening other fringe benefits in lieu of pensions. And most, but not quite all, managements have never even remotely thought of extending pension privileges to the part-time work force.

All of these facts notwithstanding, the moral imperative of providing some kind of private pension to the retired full-time employee if at all possible is no longer seriously questioned by any responsible management at the labor relations bargaining table.

From a modest beginning in 1946, pension plans in American industry have grown phenomenally. Roughly 10 million employees were covered by the end of the 1940s, but this figure had doubled to 20 million by 1960, and the most recent Bureau of Labor Statistics information shows some 32 million wage and salary workers, about half of them in the ranks of unions, currently encompassed by private pensions.

Other growth-related figures are at least as impressive. In 1970, only 30 percent of couples aged 65 to 69 received a private pension, but by 2004, 88 percent will.[3] By 1990, pension funds were holding a staggering $2.5 trillion in assets—26 percent of the equity and 15 percent of the taxable bonds in the United States—and on a per capita basis this equated to some $8,000 for every person in the nation.[4] By the beginning of the 1990s, retirees were annually receiving from these private plans $220 billion, or half again as much as the $148 billion that the Social Security program was then paying out each year.[5]

On the other hand, some of these pension figures can be somewhat misleading. The considerable inflation of some relatively recent years has at times made gains more apparent than real: Average pensions increased 20.6 percent between 1974 and 1978, for example, but the Consumer Price Index rose 23 percent in this period and the real benefits therefore actually dipped a bit.[6]

Retirees did not fare quite as badly in the 1980s and early 1990s, since inflation was relatively modest in these years. But even now the typical private pension recipient is hardly being overwhelmed with riches. In 1992, the average retiree received just under $6,000 per year from his or her pension, and even considering that most but far from all pensioners also receive a Social Security benefit this still does not add up to an opulent standard of living.

Many pension fund students—including most union pension negotiators—have urged that the payout amounts at least be indexed to changes in the Consumer Price Index (as Social Security benefits have been since 1975), but their urgings have largely gone unheeded. Only about 3 percent of all private pension plans currently have any indexation at all, and even there limits usually exist.[7]

Major Pension Features

Until national legislation banning mandatory retirement before age 70 went into effect in 1979, to be followed by later legislation making mandatory retirement at any age (except for law enforcement officers and airline pilots) illegal, most plans set the required age for retirement at 65. The changes were not expected to make much practical difference, however, since as a general statement the heavy preponderance of employees have not chosen to work beyond their early sixties if allowed even minimally acceptable pensions prior to that. Certainly, this is the present belief of the U.S. Department of Labor, which has estimated that only about 200,000 more people annually will continue working as a result of the legal change.

The Labor Department was aware, in making this estimate, that of the 41,631 workers who retired from federal positions in a recent year for reasons other than disability, only 1,773 had to be terminated at the (existing) federal age limit of 70.[8] Possibly, it also knew of such other relevant situations as that at the Northrop Corporation, where each year only about one in fifty employees has chosen to stay on beyond age 65, and that at Chicago's Bankers Life and Casualty Company, which has had voluntary retirement for over four decades but where only 3.5 percent of the 3,900 home-office employees are over 65.

Nor have many unions—particularly in manufacturing (where the size of recent-year unemployment figures has been of significant influence) done anything to discourage voluntary early retirement. In fact, labor organizations have increasingly sought to open up further job opportunities in the face of automation and changing market demands even before age 65, and some provision for this benefit is now made under the pension stipulation of many contracts.

The UAW, for example, has for some years now prided itself on a "30 and out" policy in the automobile industry, whereby workers can retire as early as age 47, with relatively generous monthly pensions. In a typical year, approximately 70 percent of these UAW members do choose retirement as soon as they can gain it, and the average retirement age at General Motors is a not very ancient 59.[9]

Under the steel industry arrangement, there is a variant of "30 and out," but the Steelworker approach has been to encourage at least skilled workers in that sector (always at a premium) to stay on at a minimum until age 62, and those who choose to retire prior to that age receive reduced benefits in return for their decision. The steel industry benefit reduction system for voluntary early retirement is more common than the automobile situation of having identical benefits for all workers, regardless of age, subject to their meeting minimum service requirements. But contracts in the clothing, maritime, and mining industries—to name only three of a fast-growing number—have adopted the latter arrangement. If workers in these industries meet most often thirty years of service (and invariably at least twenty), they have nothing to gain in the way of pension size by staying on (although, again, soaring prices could always be a greater dissuader to those otherwise tempted to leave the payroll).

Under plans that provide for pension benefits to workers who have been permanently disabled and who have not reached the normal retirement age, it is also usually required that such workers have a specified number of years of service with the employer to be eligible for such benefits. Under many of these contracts, ten to fifteen years of service is required before an employee may expect to draw pension benefits because of permanent disability.

The question of who is to finance the pension plans—the employer alone or the employer and the employee jointly—has been an important issue ever since collectively bargained pensions attained prominence, and it continues to pose problems at the bargaining table. At the present time, in about three out of four plans, employers finance the entire cost of retirement benefits (and the plans involved are therefore called "noncontributory," in recognition of the lack of expense to the employee); the remainder are financed jointly (and thus on a "contributory" basis). Jointly financed plans remain common in some manufacturing industries (notably textiles, petroleum, and chemicals), as well as in finance and teaching.

Arguments can be, and are, erected in favor of either position. In favor of noncontributory plans, it is frequently contended that (1) the average employee cannot afford to contribute; (2) the employee is already making a contribution to another retirement program, that of Social Security, and enough is enough; (3) the employer should exclusively bear the costs of pensions because these are no less important than depreciation expenses for machinery and plant; (4) the return to the management from the plan in terms of lower labor turnover rates (the pension acting as an inducement to stay) and increased efficiency justifies the cost; and (5) employers can charge their pension plan contributions against taxes, whereas employees cannot.

On the other, or procontributory plan, side of the ledger, proponents claim that (1) since there is a definite limit to the economic obligations that employers can assume at a given time, employee contributions ensure better pensions; (2) employees will appreciate plans to which they contribute, as they might not appreciate the noncontributory arrangement, and hence the contributory plan is psychologically better for the organization in terms of heightened morale and loyalty; and (3) when workers contribute, they have a stronger claim to their pensions as a matter of right.

Most employees and their unions, having heard both sets of arguments, have preferred the first one.

Whether the plan is contributory or noncontributory, of course, it must be financed so that the benefits that have been promised upon retirement are indeed available at that point. If the money is simply not there, or if the employer is unwilling for whatever reason to make the counted-upon disbursement, it is of small consolation to the retiree that the plan was a noncontributory one. The same statement, needless to say, applies if the employer vanishes from the scene by virtue of going out of business.

Funded pension plans—those in which pensions are paid from separated funds, isolated from the general assets of the firm and earmarked specifically for retirees—ensure that the benefits are in fact guaranteed. *Unfunded* plans depend strictly upon employer ability and willingness to comply with the pension plan provisions by making pension payments out of current funds. As such, the latter can offer no assurances at all.

Vesting refers to the right of workers to take their credited pension entitlements with them should their employment terminate before they reach the stipulated retirement age. The member of the organization's labor force who is permanently laid off or who quits without possessing a nonforfeitable vesting right is obviously no better off than the employee who has stayed all the way to stipulated retirement only to find that lack of appropriate funding has made the pension a cruel hoax.

As pensions spread in the 1950s and 1960s, improvements in both of these areas took place. Only 7 percent of all workers covered by private pension systems belonged to unfunded plans even as early as 1960,[10] and even fewer did a decade later. As for vesting, where only 25 percent of the plans studied by the Department of Labor in 1952 allowed it, 67 percent of those surveyed eleven years later did so, however much the vesting privilege remained qualified,[11] and by common estimate the figure greatly exceeded 80 percent by the 1970s.

Yet a blatant amount of abuse with respect to private pension plans had nonetheless also developed by the 1970s. Many employees who had counted on a pension simply, if tragically, did not receive the benefit. Hearings held by the Senate Labor Committee at this time disclosed that in some cases funded pension plans had been plundered or misused by their administrators. Another abuse involved the discharge or permanent layoff of employees just before they would (having qualified under age and service requirements) have been entitled to vesting. Situations such as these were unfortunately widespread.

Even more often, however, neither plunder nor specific immorality was involved, but rather the simple inability of the employer to pay. Such a case was that of the Studebaker Corporation, which permanently stopped its operations in the United States in 1964 and because it had never had a funded plan was unable to offer its many terminated employees the pension benefits established in the Studebaker collective bargaining contracts. As one source could quite justifiably say about the general situation, "In all too many cases, the pension promise shrinks to this: 'If you remain in good health and stay with the same company until you are sixty-five years old, and if the company is still in business, and if your department has not been abolished, and if you haven't been laid off for too long a period, and if there is enough money in the [pension] fund, and if that money has been prudently managed, you will get a pension.'"[12]

There were too many contingencies in all of this for Congress to ignore, given the importance of the subject to so many, and in late 1974 it enacted a major piece of legislation, the Employee Retirement Income Security Act [ERISA], that was designed to deal with the obstacles to pension payment.

To deal with the abuse involving the age and service requirements, ERISA provides for vesting of pension benefits. The employer has two options to protect its employees: either 100 percent vesting after five years of service or 100 percent vesting after seven years of service. Under the latter, 20 percent is vested after three years and 20 percent additional in each of the next four years.

So that funds will be available upon employees' retirement, the law requires that all newly adopted pension plans be fully funded to pay the benefits due retired employees. For those plans in existence before the law became effective, employers have the obligation to fund for past service obligations over a period of specified time. To ensure further that employees receive the pension benefits upon retirement, the 1974 law established a Pension Benefit Guaranty Corporation, a government agency that in 1992 guaranteed pensions up to a maximum of $2,352 per month should an employer go out of business and/or terminate the plan. To raise the necessary funds to provide the guarantee, employers were initially required to pay annually $1 per worker for single-employer plans. Other safeguards, involving the placing of a fiduciary responsibility on the administrators of pension plans, the reporting and disclosure annually to the Secretary of Labor of financial information showing the operation of the plan, and the right of each employee each year to receive information concerning his or her vesting and accumulated benefit status, are included in the law.

In 1992, however, the PBGC was operating at a gigantic deficit. The bankruptcy of firms in the basic steel industry had left it holding the bag for more than $2.5 billion by the end of the 1980s, and it had had to assume an additional $1.2 billion burden in 1992 just from the bankruptcy of Pan Am and Eastern Airlines alone. At the time of this writing, the PBGC had taken over almost 1,700 plans and was obligated to pay the up to $2,352 per month to 325,000 retirees.

In 1987, Congress had allowed the agency to increase its employer premiums to a range of between $16 and $50, and by 1992 these limits were further raised, to from $19 to $72 per participant. But even these moves could not reverse the bailout and PBGC deficit trends and the future did not look promising, either: PBGC officials themselves now think that roughly one-quarter of the approximately 85,000 plans that the agency insures are underfunded to the magnitude of some $40 billion and that this latter total will grow appreciably in the 1990s: With fewer than 600 people, the PBGC simply does not have the human resources to oversee the system.[13]

Of course, it is unthinkable that Congress would break faith with the retired citizens of the nation. In the final analysis, as it did with the savings and loan industry, the federal government would have to make good on the pensions.

ERISA may not have deserved the description given it by one of its sponsors, the late Senator Jacob K. Javits of New York, when it was enacted. He called it "the greatest development in the life of the American worker since Social Security," and other developments, including many of the ones directly involving labor-management relations and thus outlined in earlier portions of this book, might strike the student as having been even "greater." It is difficult to arbitrate in these matters of taste.

It is safe to say, however, that the law has already gone a long way toward protecting employee interests. A staggering $250 billion in assets are now covered by ERISA. The scandal-ridden $8.2 billion Central States Pension Fund of the International Brotherhood of Teamsters has essentially been cleaned up and more improvements—inspired by the Labor

Department—will undoubtedly come. The federal standards have certainly given pension fund trustees a better sense of what their responsibilities are, and the vesting and guarantee features of ERISA have also worked in no small measure in favor of workers.

The impact of the law has, it is true, increased the cost of pension programs and thus in some cases led to smaller benefits. A smaller but guaranteed pension, however, is better than no pension at all for an employee who has devoted all or most of a working life to an employer.

VACATIONS WITH PAY

Vacations with pay for wage earners also constitute, as was noted earlier, a comparatively new development in American history. A scant six decades ago, very few workers covered by collective bargaining contracts received pay during vacation periods, and, at that time, other employees were permitted time off only if they were willing to sacrifice pay. But vacations with pay are now a standard practice in practically every collective bargaining contract, and this has been true for some time. As far back as 1957, in fact, a Department of Labor study of 1,813 agreements, each covering more than 1,000 workers, found that only 8 percent of these contracts did not provide some form of paid vacation;[14] today, the employer not furnishing this type of pay for time not worked is a true individualist.

In addition to the influence of World War II and Korean War wage controls (which generally did not deal with fringes and implicitly allowed such benefits to be given in lieu of wage hikes) in spearheading the spread of paid vacations and also of paid holidays, a growing recognition by employers, employees, and unions of the benefits of such a policy (in terms of worker health, personal development, and productivity) has contributed to the growth. And as job security considerations have become more important in the recent past, employee representatives have also seen in vacations (as they have in holidays) a way to preserve existing jobs. This has been especially true in such troubled industries as automobiles, steel, and rubber, and it has in fact been in these sectors that vacations, the most expensive of all payments for time not worked, have received particular priority in the bargaining. Once liberalized there, they have gone on to exert pressures (by their very visibility in these major industries) on other unions, and on nonunion employers who would be just as happy remaining nonunion, to expand them where *they* operate.

One eye-catching vacation experiment, however, has not spread very far. In 1962, the Steelworkers and metal can manufacturers negotiated a "sabbatical" paid vacation of thirteen weeks' duration, allowed all employees with fifteen or more years of service every five years, and the following year the basic steel industry incorporated essentially the same agreement for the senior half of its work force. After over three decades, the concept had had no other takers, perhaps because its lavishness in terms of both leisure time and cost to the employer had made it too much of a good thing (and it is now no more—a victim of the bargaining concessions of the 1980s—even in steel). Its very creation, however, says something about vacation appeal.

Paid vacations have also undergone steady liberalization as a worker benefit. In recent years, an annual five-week vacation (normally requiring twenty years of service or more) has been bargained by the parties in some situations, and while this length of paid leisure time is still enjoyed by less than one half of all unionists, it is relevant that such a vacation was all but nonexistent until the late 1960s. Six-week vacations for employees with high seniority are, in fact, now beginning to emerge as a vacation entitlement of some visibility, and there are even seven-week vacations at American Metal Climax, Rockwell International, and Boise Cascade and in the rubber industry (among other places). Four-week vacations (usually after at least fifteen years) are today included in 90 percent of all agreements, or more than triple the 1960 frequency. Of more significance to shorter-term workers is the three-week vacation, provided for in over 95 percent of contracts (as against 78 percent in 1960) and most frequently requiring ten years of service (where fifteen years was the modal prerequisite a very few years ago). Virtually all employees, moreover, can count on a two-week vacation after building up five years of seniority, and contracts increasingly allow this length of time off after only one or two years of service. The only stagnation that has occurred is, in fact, in the one-week vacation area: One year of service has entitled most employees to a single week of vacation with pay for well over a decade now, and the next frontier relating to the one-week vacation will probably be its total abolition in favor of the two-week vacation after one year—an arrangement that is even now granted by perhaps as many as one quarter of all agreements.[15]

In qualifying for vacations, most labor agreements require that an employee must have worked a certain number of hours, days, or months prior to the vacation period, and failure of the employee to comply with such stipulations results in the forfeiture of the vacation benefits. The rate of pay to which the employee is entitled during a vacation is ordinarily computed on the basis of the regular hourly rate, although in a comparatively small number of agreements vacation benefits are calculated on the basis of average hourly earnings over a certain period of time preceding the vacation, and, in some agreements, vacation pay is calculated as a specified percentage of annual earnings; usually this latter figure amounts to between 2.0 and 2.5 percent of the annual earnings.

A problem arises involving the payment of workers who work during their vacation periods. In some contracts the employees have the option of taking the vacation to which they are entitled or of working during this period. Other labor agreements allow the employer the option of giving pay *instead* of vacations if production requirements make it necessary to schedule the worker during the vacation period. No less than in the case of the sabbaticals, when employees work during their vacation periods either upon their own or the employer's option, the principles upon which paid vacations are based (health, productivity, and so on) are, of course, violated. In any event, in most labor agreements, employees under these circumstances are given their vacation pay plus the regular wages they earn in the place. In a few cases, particularly when the employer schedules work during a vacation period, the wage earned by the employee working during a vacation period is calculated at either time-and-one-half or double the regular rate. Such earnings are in addition to the employee's vacation pay.

In a majority of contracts, management has the ultimate authority to schedule the vacation period. Under an increasingly large number of agreements, however, the employer is required to take into consideration seniority and employee desires. A fairly sizable number of labor agreements permit management to schedule vacations during plant shutdowns.

An additional vacation problem involves the status of employees who are separated from the payroll before their vacation period. In some collective bargaining agreements, these employees are entitled to accumulated vacation benefits when they leave employment under certain specified circumstances, such as permanent layoff, resignation, and military duty. In a comparatively small number of contracts, workers discharged for cause may also claim vacation benefits. (Exhibit 8-1 is drawn from one current, not atypical, contract.)

HOLIDAYS WITH PAY

Similar to paid vacations, paid holidays for production workers were not a common practice before the middle of this century. At present nearly all labor agreements incorporate some formula for paid holidays, with some construction contracts being the only conspicuous exceptions at this point.

The modal number of such holidays granted in 1993 was ten and almost no unionized employee could expect fewer than six (although workers in a class with the Bath Iron Works's 4,500 shipbuilders, who received thirty-five holidays, or almost three for each month, were not in great supply). There was almost universal agreement among the contracts on at least four of these specific holidays: More than 98 percent allowed paid time off for Independence Day, Labor Day, Thanksgiving, and Christmas. And well over 96 percent of all contracts paid for holidays on New Year's Day and Memorial Day. Wider variation takes place where more than six holidays are sanctioned, but half-days before Thanksgiving, Christmas, and New Year's Day are frequently specified, and in an increasing number of cases some holidays are oriented on an individual basis, such as the employee's birthday, the date on which the employee joined the union (in some Transport Worker contracts, among others), and "personal" days off. Under this latter agreement, the employer by definition is not penalized with whatever inefficiencies may result from a complete shutdown, and this is probably the major reason why it has become increasingly popular: Almost 50 percent of all contracts now sanction such an arrangement, up from just under 40 percent as recently as 1980. Many agreements also recognize any of a variety of state and local holidays, ranging from Patriot's Day in Massachusetts to Mardi Gras in parts of the South. Company—and even union—picnics are declared occasions for paid holidays in a somewhat

EXHIBIT 8–1

ARTICLE 7. VACATIONS

Section 1. Eligibility

1. After one (1) year of continuous service, an employee shall be eligible for vacation benefits as follows:

Service	Time	Vacation Pay at Rates According to Section 2
1 year	2 weeks	80 hours
7 years	3 weeks	120 hours
15 years	4 weeks	160 hours
20 years	5 weeks	200 hours

2. The employee with the greatest seniority in the vacation scheduling group shall have first preference in selection of his vacation. Vacation quotas will be applied by classification, unit or division, and across shifts.

Section 2. Vacation Year

1. The vacation year begins on the anniversary date of employment. Each employee becomes eligible for the revised vacation schedule in his next anniversary date. Vacations must be taken during the year. They are not cumulative.

2. If an employee is ill during his scheduled vacation period and the illness extends beyond his anniversary date, the employee has the option—upon notification to his supervisor, of either being paid for unused vacation or taking this unused vacation prior to returning to work.

Section 3. Emergency Cancellations

1. In case of an emergency the Company may, at its option, require any or all employees to work in lieu of receiving a vacation from work, and in such event an employee shall receive two (2) times his normal base rate for time actually worked. Wherever possible, reasonable advance notice of an emergency will be given to the employee and a Union officer. It is clearly understood any employee who worked the emergency time shall not be required to work any other emergency work that may occur within their anniversary period and shall have the right to vacation selection by seniority preference or elect to take vacation pay in lieu of time off.

2. In the event an employee must work due to the emergency, the Company shall reimburse the employee for provable losses of deposits, license fees, and reservations.

3. In the event a cancellation exceeds the anniversary date, an employee will have an additional sixty (60) days in which to take vacation. In any case an employee must take all vacations or forfeit the remainder.

EXHIBIT 8–1 (continued)

Section 4. Vacations during Planned Shutdowns

1. It is the Company intent to schedule planned maintenance shutdowns during the summer months whenever feasible in order to provide employees an opportunity to schedule summer vacations. The company shall post its intended shutdown schedule on or before March 1.

2. Employees, in affected units, who do not schedule vacations for the shutdowns shall be assigned according to the temporary transfer language.

3. These provisions shall not be construed to limit the Company's right to schedule planned maintenance shutdowns at any other time.

Section 5. Approval

1. All vacations must be scheduled in increments of one full week except that employees with at least three weeks' vacation eligibility may schedule up to one week of their vacation in one-, two-, or three-day increments with advance approval.

2. A vacation scheduling list will be posted on or about January 15 of each year. Final vacations will be awarded according to plantwide seniority within the vacation selection group on March 31. The vacation scheduling period shall cover the full payroll weeks beginning in April through year end. The Company will schedule vacations in the first quarter on a first-come, first-served basis. The vacation quota shall not be less than 10 percent.

3. All requests for one-day vacations must be made in writing to the immediate supervisor at least 48 hours in advance and not more than thirty (30) days in advance. The request will be honored providing that the operation in any work area is not seriously affected.

4. If an employee is absent due to an emergency beyond his control, he may request on his first day back, vacation time for the absence using only those single day vacation days allotted to him. All answers to emergency vacation requests will be made by the end of the Division Manager's second scheduled shift following the day the request is made. (Failure to comply on a timely basis will result in automatic approval.)

Section 6. Vacation Pay upon Retirement or Termination

Upon retirement or termination, employees will be paid for vacation earned during the period worked beyond their anniversary date in accordance with the following formula—calendar days between anniversary and retirement date divided by 365 days multiplied by normal vacation benefits and defined in Article 7 of the present Agreement.

Section 7. Vacation Pay upon Death

The estate of a deceased employee will be paid for all vacation earned during the period worked beyond his anniversary date in accordance with the following formula—calendar days between anniversary and date of death divided by 365 days multiplied by normal vacation benefits as defined in Article 7 of the present Agreement.

smaller number of contracts.[16] (The Electrical Workers [IUE] at the Newport, Tennessee, plant of Electro-Voice, Inc., may be absolutely unique, however; a few years ago they won as a new paid holiday February 2, Groundhog Day.)

In addition to the trend toward the "personal" holiday, there has been a steady movement toward three-day weekends. The latter owes its genesis to Congress, which in 1968 enacted a Monday Holidays Law, shifting the observance of four holidays (President's Day, the third Monday in February; Memorial Day; Columbus Day; and Veterans Day) to Mondays for employees of the federal government. Not binding on any other employers, there has nonetheless been a decided tendency for the latter to follow suit, frequently in accommodation of union demands, in the years since the congressional action. Martin Luther King, Jr. Day, observed always on a January Monday, has in recent years, allowed yet one more long weekend for many.

A definite shot in the arm to the spread of paid holidays was also effected in 1976, by the so-often-influential UAW. Alarmed by declining employment for automobile workers and buoyed on by its own estimate that production in 1990 would be almost 50 percent higher than in 1976 but that only 5 percent more workers would be needed to yield this higher output ("How long," asked the UAW president, "can we go on providing higher and higher benefits for fewer and fewer workers?"),[17] the union negotiated seven "personal paid holidays" in addition to thirteen existing regular holidays. By this action, which was obviously geared fully to job security and not directed a whit toward increased leisure time per se, the UAW claimed to have created 11,000 new jobs just at General Motors alone. It expected that in future bargaining (not only its own but, by a process of coercive comparison, the bargaining of other unions) such acts of creation would be expanded, and to some extent this has been true.

Most labor agreements place certain obligations upon employees who desire to qualify for paid holidays, with the common objective in this respect being that of minimizing absenteeism. The most frequently mentioned such requirement is that an employee must work the last scheduled day before and the first scheduled day after a holiday. The obligation is waived when the employee does not work on the day before or after the holiday because of illness, authorized leave of absence, jury duty, death in the family, or some other justifiable reason. Under some collective bargaining relationships, illness must be proved by a doctor's certificate, by nurse visitation, or by some other device. (*Case 4 deals with an employee's eligibility for holiday pay.*)

Production requirements and emergency situations at times require that employees work on holidays, and such circumstances raise the problem of rates of pay for work on these days. About three quarters of all labor agreements provide for double-time for work on holidays, and a small number of contracts now call for triple-time. In the continuous operation industries, such as hotel, restaurant, and transportation sectors, labor agreements frequently substitute another full day off with pay for a holiday on which an employee worked.

An additional problem involves payment for holiday time when the holiday falls on a day on which the employee would not ordinarily work.

For example, if an organization's work force does not normally work on Saturdays and if in a particular year July 4 (a paid holiday under the collective bargaining agreement) falls on a Saturday, the question arises as to whether employees are entitled to holiday pay. Another aspect of the same general problem involves a paid holiday falling during an employee's vacation period. Some unions claim that pay for holidays constitutes a kind of vested benefit to employees, regardless of the calendar week on which the holiday occurs. Thus, if the holiday falls on a regular nonworkday, some unions ask that another day be designated as the holiday or that the employee be given a day's wages; or if the holiday falls during an employee's vacation period, that the employee receive another day's paid vacation or wages for the holiday. The opposing view holds that payment for holidays falling on a day on which employees do not regularly work violates the basic principle underlying paid holidays, which is protection of employees from loss of wages. Many labor agreements reflect the thinking of the labor unions on this issue and designate, for example, another day off with pay if a holiday falls on a nonworkday, but a large number of labor agreements do not treat the problem one way or the other, and frequently because of the nature of the language establishing holidays with pay, controversies in this respect are settled in arbitration. Public-sector contracts generally reflect those in the private sector except that the issue may be complicated by legislation.

NEGOTIATED HEALTH INSURANCE PLANS

Private employers now provide health coverage to two out of every three Americans, and it doesn't come cheaply. In 1991, the average cost for employers per employee (both union and nonunion) was a whopping $3,573 and this figure had shown a dramatic jump from 1984, when it was only $1,453 and indeed from just three years earlier, when the statistic was $2,555.[18] Health plans have, in fact, now passed pensions as the most expensive single employee benefit: They cost an estimated 10.9 percent of total payroll in 1991, considerably more than the approximately 6.5 percent of payroll consumed by pensions.[19]

In collective bargaining agreements, all of the following are generally covered: life insurance or death benefits; accidental death and dismemberment benefits; accident and sickness expense defrayal; and either cash or services to cover hospital, surgical, maternity, and medical care. Recently the boundaries of the package have been extended to such areas as major medical insurance (often defraying all such expenses up to 80 percent of their total), dental insurance, and psychiatric benefits.

These economic supplements gradually spread for a variety of reasons. Insurance programs were also a major fringe issue in the period of wage control during World War II and the Korean War, although to a far smaller extent than were vacations and holidays. Increasingly, both employers and unions have recognized that few of their workers are remotely prepared to handle the rapidly rising health costs on their own. The Internal Revenue Service has also provided some spur by permitting employers to deduct most such payments as business expenses for tax purposes. Group insurance allows purchasing economies not available to individuals. And the fact that the Social Security program has not provided protection for most risks covered by these insurance plans has made the private insurance system a widely sought one.

Today's typical bargained health and welfare package is of no small dimensions. There is a strong likelihood that it includes life insurance for an amount approximating twice the employee's annual salary; disability and sickness benefits of at least $300 weekly for at least six months; semiprivate hospital room and hospital board for as long as ninety days, together with such add-ons as drugs and medicines, X-ray examinations, and operating-room expenses (under either Blue Cross or a private insurance company plan); surgical expenses up to a $5,000 maximum for contingencies not covered by workmen's compensation legislation; and coverage for the employee's dependents as well as himself or herself for all or most of these benefits. And, as in the cases of pensions, vacations, and holidays, these emoluments are continuing their own process of liberalization, with discernible trends in recent years involving an increase in the amount and duration of the benefits; the extension of the benefits to retired workers, as well as to those dependents not yet covered; defrayal of the expenses of at least some medically related drugs; and the added protection for catastrophic illnesses and accidents, and addition of dental and mental health benefits cited previously. They have come a long way since the 1950s and 1960s, when only catastrophic illnesses were covered (assuming, of course, that there was health-care expense defrayal at all) and even then only a small portion of the total cost—$30 to $40 per day was a common payment—was picked up by the employee plan.

Until the mid-1980s, there was a commensurately strong trend toward exclusive employer financing of the health benefit package. Twenty-one percent of all unionized employers footed the entire bill in 1949; roughly 40 percent did so in 1956;[20] an estimated 53 percent paid the full cost in 1984.[21] (*Case 5 involves an unusual problem relating to a group life insurance program.*)

But as these health-care costs for managements skyrocketed in the 1980s—by 1983 they added up to some $77 billion on an annual basis and were rising at twice the rate of inflation—employers, for the first time, were pressing unions to help them contain such major expenses through collective bargaining.

Two particularly significant milestones in this regard were implemented in 1985. At General Motors, whose health-benefit expenditures had almost quadrupled in the past decade (and in whose health plan roughly 1 percent of the U.S. population, counting retirees and dependents, was enrolled), the UAW agreed to help pare $220 million annually from GM's $2.2 billion health-care bill without penalizing employees at all. Under an "Informed Choice Plan," employees can now select one of three options, each of them less costly to General Motors (which continues to foot essentially all of the health bill) than the pre-1985 programs. They can opt to use a health maintenance organization, or HMO, providing specified services—hospitalization included—for a predetermined amount. They can choose, instead, to deal with a "preferred provider" organization, which charges for each service provided but at a discount or otherwise favorable rate to GM. Or they can elect to continue receiving their traditional insurance coverage but now with the requirement of preauthorization from an independent review group before certain specified treatments.

And in another widely publicized action, the joint labor-management Teamsters Central States Welfare Fund contracted with Voluntary Hospitals of America, Inc. for discounts through a "preferred provider" relationship geared to slicing a similar 10 percent from the fund's $350 million medical bill. As the fund's executive director quite justifiably commented as these negotiations were concluded, "These dollars will be available for wages and other things if we don't utilize them for health."[22]

A decade later, labor's bargaining table support for such measures as these and related health-cost containment ones (mandatory second surgical opinions, for example) is anything but a rarity. In addition to the Automobile Workers and the Teamsters, whose original actions have now been duplicated in many other negotiations of these two unions, the Communications Workers, Mine Workers, and Rubber Workers have been particularly receptive to accepting such cost-containment measures. Numerous other labor organizations have also moved in this direction, recognizing that in these actions the burden falls fully on the health-care providers and not on bargaining unit members themselves (whose actual benefits are rarely reduced in the process and often, indeed, even expand). As the *New York Times* observed in analyzing this new development not long ago, "Health care provides ample room for labor-management infighting, but many unions seem to be discovering a self-interest in joint approaches to the broader question of bringing the system under control."[23]

Where the burden *does* fall on the bargaining unit members, however, health-cost containment efforts of employers have been met not nearly as positively by the unions involved. And, the cooperative efforts and joint approaches noted above notwithstanding, this more conflict-ridden side of labor-management relations has also increasingly been seen.

Perhaps, given the mushrooming of general health-care costs, this grimmer consequence was also inevitable. The joint efforts could, after all, only do so much in thwarting the price hikes if based on the premise that the benefits themselves would not be cut. And while the "preferred provider" and similar approaches have clearly kept costs less than they would otherwise have been, they simply haven't been enough. General Motors' health bill, for example, has still risen annually by over 30 percent, its new system notwithstanding.

By the late 1980s, many nonunion employers—unfettered by a labor contract—had shifted some of the new costs to their workers. Employees there typically were now asked to pay a deductible of $150 and 20 percent of their medical bills up to at least $1,000 annually. Unionized workers, on the other hand, were not nearly as amenable to such requests, and a variety of bitter strikes in these years—most notably in the telephone industry against three regional Baby Bell telephone companies (where picket signs declared, "Cutting Our Health Benefits Is Sick") and in the bituminous coal industry against the Pittston Coal Group—stemmed almost exclusively from this emotional issue. The strikes were being closely watched by other unions and their managements, for much was at stake for both sides.

Far worse than such new health-cost shifting, of course, would be the total unavailability of medical insurance benefits, which unionized workers had thought were guaranteed them as a matter of contractual right. Yet that threat was a very real one for some 118,000 United Mine Worker retirees and their families by the early 1990s. Over the previous decade, annual medical claims had doubled while the number of unionized coal mines contributing to the UMW retiree benefit fund that was negotiated years earlier by union leader John L. Lewis had plummeted (from about 2,000 in 1950 to 300 in 1992). By 1992, annual fund expenses were exceeding employer contributions by a whopping $137 million.

Much of the decline in employer numbers had stemmed from companies that had been under the UMW health-care agreement. By insisting on negotiating separately with the union, they had moved out from under obligations, despite not only strong UMW opposition to such actions but also the companies' own apparently binding original agreements, to pay into the fund indefinitely. Nor did the growing percentage of nonunion companies (the figure is now 70 percent of the industry, as contrasted with 20 percent in 1950) understandably show any desire to help bail out the fund. The U.S. Senate, after bitter debate, passed a tax bill providing for an industrywide mandatory financial levy on all employers to restore the fund to health. But President Bush vetoed the bill in the spring of 1992, and what Senator John D. Rockefeller IV of West Virginia (the bill's most avid supporter) had called an "extraordinary moral issue" was far from resolved at this writing. (The union vowed 1992 vengeance on Bush, as Exhibit 8-2, published in the UMW's monthly magazine, indicates.)

DISMISSAL PAY

Unlike all the wage supplements discussed above, dismissal, or "severance," pay is still not a common product of collective bargaining. According to Bureau of Labor Statistics information, only about 30 percent of all contracts provide such a benefit at the present time and this figure portrays a standstill in the growth of dismissal pay, since two decades ago some 30 percent of the agreements studied by the bureau also did so. And on an industrywide basis, the practice remains largely confined to contracts negotiated by the Steelworkers, Auto Workers, Communications Workers, Ladies' Garment Workers, and Electrical Workers—although many sectors of the newspaper and railroad industries also have such plans.

Dismissal pay provisions normally limit payments to workers displaced because of technological change, plant merger, permanent curtailment of the company's operations, permanent disability, or retirement before the employee is entitled to a pension. Workers discharged for cause and em-

Exhibit 8–2

"George Bush Vetoed My Health Care..."

Pennsylvania retiree Frank Daniels Sr. of L.U. 6310 worked nearly 43 years in the mines for the promise—sealed in a 1946 agreement between the union, the coal industry and the federal government—of a secure pension and guaranteed comprehensive health care for life.

Now that those health benefits are threatened because a large part of the coal industry has reneged on its obligation, it's up to the government to step in and make good on its promise.

But when Frank Daniels and thousands of other UMWA members succeeded in getting legislation passed that would do just that, George Bush vetoed it.

That's why Frank Daniels says,

"On Nov. 3, I'm Going To Help Veto George Bush."

Source: United Mine Workers Journal, June 1992, back cover.

ployees who refuse another job with the employer usually forfeit dismissal pay rights, as do workers who voluntarily quit a job.

The amount of payment provided for in dismissal pay arrangements varies directly with the length of service of the employee. The longer the service, the greater the amount of money. Ordinarily, a top limit is placed upon the amount that an employee can receive. Although labor agreements vary in respect to the payment formula, as a general rule low-service workers receive one week's wages for each year of service prior to dismissal, with higher than proportional allowances for high-service employees (up to 60 weeks' pay, for example, for fifteen or more years of service and as high as 105 weeks' pay for workers with twenty-five or more years).

A problem involving dismissal pay occurs when an employee is subsequently rehired by the employer. There is little uniformity in collective bargaining contracts relative to the handling of this problem. Actually, a large number of labor agreements that provide for dismissal pay are silent on whether employees must make restitution to the employer upon being rehired or whether they may keep the money paid to them when their employment was originally terminated. Some agreements, however, specifically provide that such employees must return the money; for example, one telephone industry collective bargaining contract stipulates that such employees must repay to the company any termination payment, either in a lump sum or through payroll deduction at a rate of not less than 10 percent each payroll period until the full amount is paid.

Since the dismissal provision is designed to cushion the effects of employment termination through technological change, merger, and cessation of business (as well as through involuntary retirement due to personal health misfortunes), it is logical to conclude that this benefit, too, will spread in the years ahead despite its plateau in recent years.

REPORTING PAY

Under the provisions of over 90 percent of the collective bargaining contracts currently in force, employees who are scheduled to work, and who do not have instructions from the employer *not* to report to their jobs, are guaranteed a certain amount of work for that day or compensation instead of work. Issues involved in the negotiation of reporting pay arrangements are the amount of the guarantee and the rate of compensation, the amount of notice required for the employer to avoid guaranteed payment, the conditions relieving the employer of the obligation to award reporting pay, and the conditions under which such pay must be forfeited by employees.

Labor agreements establish a variety of formulas for the calculation of the amount of the guarantee. Reporting pay ranges from a one-hour guarantee to a full day. About 60 percent of labor contracts dealing with this issue provide for four hours' pay; approximately 10 percent call for eight hours' pay. These rates are calculated on a straight-time basis. However, under circumstances where workers are called back to work by management outside of regularly scheduled hours, such employees are frequently compensated at premium rates, ordinarily at time-and-one-half the regular rate. Such reimbursement, popularly styled "call-in" pay, might be awarded a worker, if, for example, the worker is called back to work before having been off for sixteen hours. Thus, if the employee regularly works the first shift and is called back under some emergency condition to work the third shift, the labor agreement might require that there be payment at premium rates. In the event that the employee reports for such work only to find that the company no longer has need for his services, the employee will still be entitled to a certain number of guaranteed hours of pay calculated at premium rates.

In most agreements providing for reporting pay, the employer is relieved of the obligation to guarantee work or to make a cash payment to employees when the employer notifies employees not to report to work. Contracts frequently provide that such notice must be given employees before the end of the workers' previous shift, although in some cases the employer may be relieved of the obligation by giving notice a certain number of hours before employees are scheduled to work. Eight hours' notice is provided in many labor contracts. In addition, employers are relieved of the obligation to award reporting pay when failure to provide work is due to causes beyond the control of the management. Thus, when work is not available because of floods, fires, strikes, power failures, or "acts of God," in most contracts either employers are fully relieved of the obligation to award reporting pay or the amount of the pay is substantially reduced. Of course, there are many questions of interpretation involved in this situation. For example, does power failure resulting from faulty maintenance relieve the employer of the obligation to award reporting pay? As in so many previous cases, such questions are resolved through the grievance procedure and at times through arbitration. (In Case 6, the issue is whether a strike relieves the employer from giving reporting pay.)

Under certain circumstances, employees forfeit reporting pay. If employees, for example, fail to keep management notified of change of address, reporting pay is forfeited under many labor agreements. Other forfeitures might result if employees refuse to accept work other than their own jobs, leave the plant before notice is given to other employees not to report to work, or fail to report to work even though no work is available.

SUPPLEMENTARY UNEMPLOYMENT BENEFIT PLANS

The supplementary unemployment benefit (SUB) plan attracted national attention in 1955 when such a plan was negotiated by the Automobile Workers and the basic automobile manufacturers, and in 1956 when the basic steel corporations and the Steelworkers included another in their new labor agreement.

Essentially, SUB plans constitute a compromise between the "guaranteed annual wage" demanded by many unions in the late 1940s and early 1950s, and a continuing management unwillingness to grant such relatively complete job security as the "guaranteed wage" designation would indicate. The plans are geared primarily to two goals: (1) supplementing the unemployment benefits of the various state unemployment insurance systems and (2) allowing further income to still-unemployed workers after state payments have been exhausted. And they implicitly recognize at least one weakness in the state systems: Since the states started paying benefits in the late 1930s, the average ratio of these benefits to average wage levels of employees when working has steadily dropped from approximately 40 percent then to somewhat less than 35 percent today. At present, Hawaii has the most liberal ratio, 46 percent, while Louisiana, with a meager 27 percent, comes in at the bottom of the states.[24]

Half of all manufacturing workers in the United States now have some kind of SUB plan. Almost total coverage has been achieved in the rubber and plastics industries, where 95 percent of the workers have such a benefit. In second place are automobile and aerospace employees, some 82 percent of whom are covered. Other industries now granting significant SUB protection are "primary metals" (steel and aluminum, in particular), where the coverage statistic is 70 percent, and apparel, 61 percent of whose employees have an SUB arrangement. In all of these heavily unionized sectors—as well as in the glass, farm equipment, electrical, can, printing and publishing, petroleum, and maritime industries, where significant but lesser proportions are covered—there are some major elements of similarity.

All SUB plans, for example, require that employees have a certain amount of service with the company before they are eligible to draw benefits; the seniority period varies among the different plans—with a one-year requirement in the basic auto and can contracts contrasting with a five-year prerequisite (the most extreme) in a few contracts negotiated by the Oil, Chemical, and Atomic Workers Union. In addition to seniority stipulations, virtually all plans require that the unemployed worker be willing and able to work. The test in this latter connection is, most often, the registration for work by the unemployed worker with a state unemployment service office. Beyond this, the plans invariably limit benefits to workers who are unemployed because of layoff resulting from a reduction in the work force by the company. Workers who are out of work because of discipline, strikes, or "acts of God" cannot draw benefits. Nor can workers do so whose curtailment of employment is attributable to government regulation, or to public controls over the amount or nature of materials or products that the company uses or sells.

Under the most prevalent type of SUB agreement, all employees start to acquire credit units at the rate of one-half unit for each week in which they work. When they complete enough service to qualify for the benefits (the one to five years cited in the preceding paragraph), they are officially credited with these units, which they can then trade off for SUB pay when unemployed up to a maximum unemployment duration. Most plans now have set this maximum at fifty-two weeks, and consequently, an automobile or steel industry worker with two years of continuous employment has achieved the maximum amount of SUB coverage. Under about half the current plans, however, the ratio of credit units to weeks of benefit can be increased when the SUB fund falls below a certain level, thereby shortening the duration of benefits. Another common variation is to adjust the ratio in such a way that laid-off workers with long service are protected for a proportionately longer length of time than are shorter-service employees.

Almost universally, employees are entitled to draw benefits only up to the amount of credits that they have established and can receive no benefits—no matter how large the amount of their credits—during the first week of unemployment, a stipulation that is consistent with the one-week waiting period under most state unemployment insurance plans. In addition, credit units are canceled in the event of a willful misrepresentation of facts in connection with the employee's application for either state or SUB income.

Benefit formulas under most layoffs currently set a normal level of payments at 60 to 65 percent of take-home pay (gross pay minus taxes) for all eligible employees. This level comprises payments from both the negotiated benefit plan and the state system. If, for example, a worker whose normal take-home amount is $480 is laid off, a plan calling for 65 percent of his take-home pay allows him $312. And if the worker's state unemployment compensation totals $160 weekly, the SUB plan would then pay him the weekly sum of $152 to make up the difference. There is some debate even among the most rabid advocates of SUB plans as to whether the level should be pushed much beyond this 65 percent figure, for even at this percentage several plans have experienced the ironic situation of workers' preferring total layoff to work. Under UAW contracts in the automobile industry, workers with the minimal years of seniority now actually receive 95 percent of their after-tax wages while on layoff (minus $12.50 for such work-related expenses as transportation, work clothing, and lunches) for up to fifty-two weeks—and almost invariably prefer such a well-remunerated enforced leisure period to their normal work assignments! The same preference for layoff has been amply in evidence in steel, where in recent years senior workers have been guaranteed SUB payments of up to $400 per week for two full years—and after that either a job at another plant or a pension.

To establish the fund for the payment of supplementary unemployment benefits, most plans require that the employer—who invariably exclusively finances all SUB plans—contribute a certain amount of money per work hour. Many agreements call for a cash contribution of 20 cents per hour, although several go as low as 5 cents and about the same number require 30 or more cents. The payment into this fund most often represents the *maximum* liability of the company, however. Typically, a maximum size of the fund is defined, and company contributions for any one contractual period stop completely when this limit is reached and maintained; the objectives, aside from relieving the companies of too rigorous payments, are to prevent too large an accumulation of fund money and to encourage the companies to stabilize their employment levels. On the other hand, when fund finances fall below the stipulated amount, because of SUB-financed payments the employer must resume payments at the rate required by the plan. In addition, many SUB plans—including most of those negotiated by the Steelworkers—require a further company liability: When the SUB fund reaches the "maximum" level, companies continue to make contributions—first to a Savings and Vacation Plan (to keep its benefits fully current) and then once again to the SUB fund—until approximately $400 per employee is accumulated. Only at this point do company contributions cease.

There seems to be little question that SUB plans not only warded off individual hardship but also maintained a good deal of consumer purchasing power in the United States during the several general recessions of the past quarter-century. Without them, the bleak economies of countless cities and states with a heavy dependence on automobile, steel, rubber, and other mass-production factory employment would undoubtedly have been even bleaker.

But it is also true that such plans are quite vulnerable to long-term plant closings and mass layoffs and that in several SUB industries marked by such circumstances in the 1974–1975, 1981–1983, and 1991–1992 recessions, the SUB money simply ran out. Hundreds of thousands of automobile and steel workers in particular found themselves receiving only state unemployment compensation when their employers' funds were depleted amid mammoth and long-lasting unemployment. And many of these workers, ultimately exhausting their state entitlements as well, wound up on welfare rolls.

This outcome should have come as no surprise. SUB was never designed to cope with anything but normal, short-term plant closings and recessions that were relatively mild in their impact. And if the monies had been a major consolation both in lesser post-1955 recessions and in the early stages of the more major ones, it was inevitable that sooner or later the horrendous layoff statistics of the latter would cause the SUB wells to run dry. Although constantly liberalized and always replenished when good times returned, there was no way that such benefits by themselves could offer sufficient protection against large-scale and enduring unemployment, even when incurred by such historically opulent organizations as General Motors and USX (to say nothing of their less-affluent competitors). As a valuable (and expensive) segment of the overall employee benefit package, SUB would undoubtedly be of help to the *short-term unemployed* in at least the cyclical industries where it—had not by accident—been established, and perhaps in others where it might be implemented in the years ahead. To make claims that it could do anything more than this, however, would be both unfair to the parties who had negotiated it and cruelly misleading to the employees covered by it.

At any rate, outside of the manufacturing sector, the growth of SUB plans has been far from impressive. Most craft unions continue to greet such a device with total apathy, preferring to substitute other economic improvements for its introduction. And seniority protection appears to have thus far satisfied workers in many noncraft industries sufficiently so that SUB has not become a major union demand there. But the continuing hold of SUB upon the several major industries in which it was originally negotiated, and the constant improvement of SUB allowances there, remain facts that cannot be ignored, either in assessing the creativity of the collective bargaining process or in judging the potential impact of this "guaranteed annual wage" compromise should the employment instabilities that have always characterized most industries in which SUB has now been implemented spread to other parts of the economy. If SUB extensions have not been impressive in total, SUB today does exist in sectors where it is needed—namely, those where job insecurity is the greatest.

SOME FINAL THOUGHTS

If whether or not SUB will ultimately achieve the universality of pension plans, health insurance, paid vacations, and paid holidays (and such various other widespread but considerably lesser benefits as paid time off for obligations stemming from death in the family, jury duty, and voting) thus remains an open question, even in the case of SUB, a broader issue does not. It appears to be all but axiomatic to collective bargaining that *any* benefit, once implemented by the parties, becomes subject through the years to a process of continuous liberalization from the workers' viewpoint. Even supplementary unemployment benefits have undergone this process in the years since 1955, when the automobile industry's maximum of $30 weekly for no more than twenty-six weeks was considered generous.

Many of these benefits continue to allow the same cost advantages to the parties, in terms of both "group insurance" savings and tax minimization, that they did at the time of their various inceptions. Generally tight labor markets have further led employers to amass attractive benefit packages, to be placed in the front window as recruitment devices. And considerations of worker retention, productivity, and pure pride have also undoubtedly stirred both managers and union leaders in their bargaining on these economic supplements. As the new worker needs and wants in the benefit area have become active, the collective bargaining parties have clearly responded to the challenge.

However, neither for the bargaining parties nor for the nation as a whole is this situation an unmixed blessing. Increasing caution from both managements and unions will, in fact, be required as the liberalization process continues, and at least six caveats appear warranted.

In the first place, many improvements in the benefit portfolio automatically present potentially troublesome sources of union grievances that would otherwise be absent. Increasing latitude for employee choice of vacation time, by the incorporation of a "seniority shall govern, so far as possible, in the selection of the vacation period" contractual clause, for example, carries far more potential for controversy than a clear-cut statement reserving vacation scheduling strictly for management discretion. As a second example in this area, with two weeks the maximum vacation allowance, there is usually no question of carry-over credit from year to year; workers are not confronted with "too much of a good thing" and normally do not seek to bank unwanted vacation time until it may be worth more to them. Under a more liberal allowance, however, the question does arise, as many employers and unions can testify, and policies must be both established and consistently adhered to if problems on this score are to be averted.

The list of such newly created grievance possibilities could be extended considerably, to virtually all the benefit sectors. Who qualifies as a dependent under an expanded health insurance plan that now accommodates such individuals? What religious credentials must be established to authorize paid time off "as conscience may dictate" on Good Friday or Yom Kippur? Is a suddenly decreed national day of mourning an "act of God," relieving the management of an obligation to grant reporting pay, or do its circumstances compel the employer to pay such amounts? How many hours or weeks of work—and under what conditions—constitute a year, for purposes of calculating pension entitlement within a system granting a flat monthly payment "per year of service?" In a less generous age, these and obviously a myriad of similar questions were automatically excluded.

Second, even on the now rare occasions upon which the benefits are not formally liberalized, many of them automatically become more costly simply because wages have been increased. All wage-related benefits fall into this category, and a 50-cent-per-hour wage increase will thus inevitably elevate total employment costs by considerably more than this face amount because of the simultaneous rise in the worth of each holiday, vacation period, and any other allowance pegged to the basic wage rate. This industrial relations truism would hardly be worth citing were it not so often ignored in union-management bargaining rooms, in favor of accommodating only wage increases to increases in productivity (for example) rather than wage increases plus wage-related benefit increases. The degree of danger in overlooking these inflationary ramifications, moreover, obviously rises with the increasing value of the benefit itself.

In the third place, one suspects that managements have—at least at times—generated *negative* employee motivation by implementing benefits without either participation or approval of work force representatives in the process. The day of company paternalism, fortunately, now lies far in the past for the large mainstream of American industry. But the arousal of employee ego-involvement is all the more imperative in today's sophisticated industrial world. Describing a deep and enthusiastic interest in unionization on the part of employees at a large Pittsburgh plant "that was well known as having excellent wages and working conditions, and supposedly had almost perfect employee relationships," Leland Hazard once memorably quoted the following remarks of "one attractive girl" to explain the general sentiment:

> It's about time something like this happened. We have got to stand on our own feet. They do everything for you but provide a husband, and I even know girls who they got a husband for. And them what ain't got time to get pregnant, they get foster kids for.[25]

Related to this question of negative motivation, but isolable as a fourth potential problem, must stand the very real alternative possibility of *no* employee motivation whatsoever. Not being masochistic as a class, employers logically expect some benefits from their expenditures in the wage supplement area—particularly more satisfactory worker retention figures, an improved recruitment performance, and, above all, generally increased employee productivity. Without such returns on the benefit investment, managements would be engaging in clear-cut wastage.

One can readily locate situations in which employee benefits have obviously achieved at least some of the desired results. Particularly in those areas where benefit entitlement expands with increasing seniority (pensions and vacations, for example), greater worker retention has undoubtedly often been fostered. Yet there is to this moment no convincing proof that benefits have significantly affected employee motivation on any large-scale basis in American industry. There is a critical need for much more research into this subject by employers and other interested parties than has thus far been conducted, for the possibility that industry may be undergoing an ever-increasing expense that may be returning very little in the way of concrete worker performance cannot as yet be safely dismissed.

Fifth, it is possible that overall employment has suffered—and conceivably will continue to suffer—from the continuation of benefit expansion of the type described in this chapter. As in the preceding case, the evidence thus far is not fully conclusive. But the increasing cost pressures and personnel administration complexities involved appear to have combined with related factors to push in this direction. New employees must receive the full panoply of benefits that present employees already have: It is a lot cheaper, many employers believe, to work existing employees harder by tightening up on managerial controls and even by asking for (and paying for) overtime than to add new members to the payroll.

Finally, unlike wage increases (which can often be at least partially negated by such mechanisms as job reevaluation and incentive rate implementation or modification), the benefit package has a strong tendency to remain a permanent part of the landscape. Except in extreme cases of corporate financial crisis, it is quite immune from disintegration. And if any significant positive effect of benefits on employee motivation thus far remains to be proven, the annals of industrial history are replete with examples of managements that have encountered surprisingly intense worker resistance in attempting to dismantle even such relatively minor portions of their benefit packages as physical fitness programs or banking facilities. Downward revisions of the leisure time, health, and pension offerings remain several miles beyond the realm of the conceivable. In short, once the parties introduce a benefit, they can expect to be wedded to it for life, with the only important questions focusing on the timing and degrees of the subsequent benefit liberalizations.

For all the reservations expressed in the paragraphs above, employee benefits hardly warrant an evaluation similar to that given by the old railroad baron James Hill to the passenger train ("like the male teat, neither useful nor ornamental"). They do provide considerable security at minimal cost to the covered employees (whether or not the latter explicitly desire such protection in lieu of other forms of compensation), at least at times abet the employer's recruitment and retention efforts in a tight labor market, and minimize the tax burdens of both company and worker. If there is room for doubt that they also allow the employer any significant return in the form of worker morale and productivity, these other reasons alone are probably sufficient to justify their dramatic spread since the 1940s.

And because the benefit package has become so relatively standardized among employers in this time interval, too, the wage supplements probably also perform a further (if less constructive) function for managers and the unions with which they deal. Their presence in anything approaching the typical dimensions prevents invidious comparisons by both current and potential employees in evaluating the desirability of the organization as an employer. The extent of worker knowledge of specific benefits may fall far short of perfection, but at the present time, because corporate pattern-following has been so prevalent in this area, the absence of nine or ten paid holidays, a three-week paid vacation after no more than ten years of service, significant medical coverage for all members of the family, satisfactory pensions, and any of the various parts of the generally conspicuous benefit portfolio are often grounds for workers' dissatisfaction.

Thus it can be predicted quite fearlessly that the years ahead will see a continuation of the benefit growth. As indicated, it appears to be all but axiomatic to industrial relations that any benefit, once implemented, through the years becomes subject to a process of continuous liberalization from the worker's viewpoint. And, while variety in these economic supplements has now become increasingly difficult to achieve, there is little doubt that new ones (perhaps more emphatically in the areas of income stabilization and employment relief) will join the already crowded ranks.

Possibly, however, increasing awareness on the part of fringe benefits implementors as to the various problem areas outlined here will result in some slowing down of the continuous liberalization process and restrain the introduction of new types of benefits until thorough investigation—tailored to the needs of individual managements and unions—has taken place. At the very least, the future demands considerably more research into these areas than has thus far been carried out. And such an omission seems particularly blatant when one realizes that there remain few other aspects of industrial relations that have not been subjected to searching scrutiny. But one must be a pessimist on these scores: Thus far, both the research and the benefit deceleration have been notably absent.

DISCUSSION QUESTIONS

1. "If there had been no labor unions in this country in the past thirty years or so, the growth of employee benefits would perhaps have been only a small fraction of what it has actually been." Discuss.

2. "It is not the business of the government to protect employee pension interests. ERISA is a classic example of unjustified governmental intervention in private employer-employee matters." Comment fully.

3. "Vacations and holidays are far more important for what they do in the way of job security than for what they do in the area of leisure time." Does this statement seem valid to you? Why or why not?

4. Which set of arguments as expressed in this chapter's section on pensions carries more weight with you: the case *for* contributory plans or the case *against* them?

5. "SUB plans of the type negotiated in the automobile and steel sectors are wholly undesirable. They discourage employees in the incentive to work, replace state unemployment compensation systems, discriminate against the worker not represented by a union, place an undetermined but intolerable burden on management, are financially unsound, and can actually cause permanent unemployment among some workers." In the light of your understanding of the character of these SUB plans, evaluate this statement.

6. Paul Pigors and Charles A. Myers have argued that "management should offer employee benefits and services, not because [it has] to, not only within legal limits, and not as a camouflaged form of bribery, but because such benefits and services are in line with the whole personnel program." Do you agree? Why or why not?

MINICASES

#1 The Case of Henry Jennings

After Henry R. Jennings, a stockroom employee who only last week celebrated the tenth anniversary of his coming to the Kruger Corporation, hits his supervisor, he is discharged and, having spent his fury in the single blow, he accepts this consequence with understanding.

"I don't know what got into me, Mr. Reilly," he tells the divisional labor relations manager. "But I deserve to be fired and I accept my punishment like a man. Just tell me where I should go to collect my four weeks' vacation pay, though. I'm due it because the collective bargaining agreement here says that 'the standard annual vacation allowance for ten years and more of continuous active employment is four weeks (twenty business days) of vacation.' I don't deserve a recommendation from the company after what I've done, but I am entitled to my vacation money."

Assuming that his reading of the relevant language is accurate and that there is nothing else in writing concerning vacation pay, is he entitled to what he is requesting, or is he not?

#2 The Case of Timmy Aldrich

Exactly one year ago this week, Timothy ("Timmy") Aldrich was hired by the Smedley Bottled Gas Company to come in each Friday afternoon at 2 P.M., following his day of classes as a senior at Andover High School, and spend two hours sweeping out the back rooms of the employer's warehouse.

He now asks Human Resources Vice President Louise Perlmutter where he should go to get his two weeks' vacation pay, for he has decided—he says—to take his paid vacation over the next fortnight. Informed that he is entitled to no vacation at all, much less a paid one, he becomes irate, and produces a copy of the labor agreement. From the latter, he reads aloud a provision that says, "All employees shall be entitled to two weeks of paid vacation after one year of employment." Informed that the language is not applicable to him, he replies, "It says all employees. What do you think I am: the company mascot?"

Would you give Timmy the two weeks' pay?

NOTES

[1]The percentage of payroll figures is, it is true, generally a bit less impressive for smaller firms. The figures here pertain to large and medium-sized firms, the only ones studied intensively thus far.

[2]*Inland Steel Co.* v. *United Steelworkers of America,* 336 U.S. 960 (1949).

[3]*Denver Post,* May 31, 1982, pp. 1C, 8C.

[4]*Wall Street Journal,* May 15, 1990, p. A1.

[5]*Ibid.,* January 16, 1990, p. A1.

[6]*Monthly Labor Review,* April 1979, p. 32.

[7]*Wall Street Journal,* April 3, 1990, p. A1.

[8]*Business Week,* June 19, 1978, p. 75.

[9]*Ibid.,* p. 74. In recent years of rampant inflation, however, the percentage of voluntary retirements is understandably lower: Working still yields a good deal more income than any pensions for UAW members.

[10]*Monthly Labor Review,* December 1963, p. 1414.

[11]*Monthly Labor Review,* September 1964, p. 1014.

[12]James H. Schulz and Guy Carrin, *Pension Aspects of the Economics of Aging: Present and Future Roles of Private Pensions* (Washington, D.C.: U.S. Senate Special Committee on Aging, 1970), p. 39.

[13]Statistics in this and the previous paragraph are from *Wall Street Journal,* June 10, 1992, p. A14.

[14]U.S. Bureau of Labor Statistics, *Paid Vacation Provisions in Major Union Contracts, 1957,* Bulletin No. 1233, June 1958.

[15]All the information cited in this paragraph is based on data furnished by the Bureau of Labor Statistics, U.S. Department of Labor.

[16]Data from the Bureau of Labor Statistics, U.S. Department of Labor.

[17]*Business Week,* October 25, 1976, p. 116.

[18]*Wall Street Journal,* August 11, 1989, p. B1.

[19]*Trade Union Advisor,* May 5, 1992, p. 4.

[20]U.S. Department of Labor, Office of Welfare and Pension Plans, Welfare and Pension Plan Statistics, 1960 (Washington, D.C.: Government Printing Office, 1963), pp. 3–4.

[21]*Time,* September 11, 1989, p. 54.

[22]*New York Times,* July 9, 1985, Sec. D, p. 2.

[23]*Ibid.*

[24]*Wall Street Journal,* February 25, 1991, p. A1.

[25]Leland Hazard, "Unionism: Past and Future," *Harvard Business Review,* March–April 1958.

SELECTED REFERENCES

Allen, Everett T., Jr., et al., *Pension Planning.* Homewood, Ill.: Richard D. Irwin, 1984.

Coffin, Richard M., and Michael S. Shaw, *Effective Communication of Employee Benefits.* New York: American Management Association, 1971.

Crane, F. G., *Insurance Principles and Practice* (2nd ed.). New York: John Wiley, 1984.

DeCenzo, David A., and Stephen J. Holoviak, *Employee Benefits.* Englewood Cliffs, N.J.: Prentice Hall, 1989.

Drucker, Peter, *The Unseen Revolution: How Pension Fund Socialism Came to America.* New York: Harper & Row, 1976.

Griffes, Ernest J. E., *Employee Benefits Programs* (2nd ed.). Homewood, Ill.: Dow Jones–Irwin, 1990.

McCaffery, Robert M., *Employee Benefit Programs: A Total Compensation Perspective.* Boston: PWS-Kent, 1988.

Prentice Hall Editorial Staff, *Employee Benefit Plans under ERISA: Federal Regulations.* Englewood Cliffs, N.J.: Prentice Hall, 1985.

Rifkin, Jeremy, and Randy Barber, *The North Will Rise Again: Pensions, Politics and Power in the 1980s.* Boston: Beacon Press, 1980.

Root, Lawrence S., *Fringe Benefits.* Beverly Hills, Calif.: Sage, 1982.

Rosenbloom, Jerry S., ed., *The Handbook of Employee Benefits: Design, Funding, and Administration* (2nd ed.). Homewood, Ill.: Dow Jones–Irwin, 1988.

Weeks, David A., ed., *Rethinking Employee Benefits Assumptions.* New York: Conference Board, 1978.

Holiday Pay: The Case of the Striking Teachers

CAST OF CHARACTERS

Gallo   *School Superintendent*
Andrew   *Union President*
Owens   *School Board Attorney*

You are the arbitrator in this case, a public-sector one involving schoolteachers. Your fundamental problem is a determination of whether the School Board violated Article XIV, Section 1, of the Master Contract by refusing to pay teachers for Labor Day. The dispute was generated by a teacher strike that was not settled until after the semester started. Because of the violation of the no-strike clause contained in the Master Contract, the School Board denied the holiday pay to the striking teachers.

Pay particular attention to the events that took place during the contract reopening negotiations. As you will see, the Parties differed on the impact of the negotiations for the proper outcome of this dispute.

When the School Board refused to pay for the Labor Day holiday to striking teachers, Grievance No. 77, dated October 19, 1990, was filed,stating that the

School Board violated the Master Contract because of its failure to meet contractual agreement providing payment for Labor Day as a paid holiday.

Material to the dispute are the following provisions of the Labor Agreement:

Master Contract

Article XIV

Section 1—Length of the School Year

The length of the school year shall be on the basis of 182 days including the following days with pay, namely, two (2) organizational days, President's Day, Memorial Day, and Labor Day. Teachers shall have the following days off without pay: two (2) days at Thanksgiving, election day (s), Veteran's Day, and two (2) professional days. In addition, teachers shall have five (5) school days off at Spring vacation and ten (10) days off at Christmas.

Article XXII

The American Federation of Teachers (AFT) agrees not to engage in a strike during the length of this contract.

Article XXIII

This agreement shall be effective on August 25, 1989, and shall continue in effect until 12 o'clock midnight, prior to the first day all teachers report for the 1991–92 school year except the following items, which shall be in effect until August 24, 1990:

1. Salary
2. Salary-related fringe benefits
3. Pro rata payments of bargaining expenses by all unit members
4. Collection of lunch monies in the elementary schools
5. Intercom
6. 1991–92 Calendar
7. Any other mutually agreed upon items

Supplement to Master Contract
No Reprisal Clause

No reprisal or punitive action of any kind shall be taken against any teacher who participated in the strike action starting August 27, 1990, and continuing until resolution of the dispute.
Punitive actions prohibited by this clause shall include, but not necessarily be limited to, dismissal, transfer, schedule change, reassignment, administrative harassment and cessation of dues withholding.
The AFT and the striking teachers agree not to take reprisals against administrators, non-striking employees, substitutes, and students.

However, it is understood that this does not imply that striking teachers will receive pay for days they failed to report to work. Additionally, any actions taken by the school employer prior to the settlement of the strike are not covered by this clause.

Basic Question

The basic question to be determined in this arbitration is framed as follows:

Under the circumstances of this case, did the School Board violate Article XIV, Section 1, of the Master Contract?

CIRCUMSTANCES OF DISPUTE

The two-year Master Contract was scheduled to expire on August 23, 1991. Pursuant to Article XXIII, the reopener provision, the Parties started to engage in serious collective bargaining in July 1990, over the items permitted by its terms. School started for the 1990–91 academic year on August 27. As a result of the Parties' failure to agree on matters being negotiated under the reopener provision, 450 teachers struck. The bargaining unit includes about 1,000 teachers. The strike started on August 27 and ended on September 5. Teacher strikes are illegal in this state, Indiana.

Since Labor Day, Monday, September 3, a paid holiday, fell during the period of the strike, the School Board refused to pay the striking teachers for that holiday. Labor Day pay was awarded to teachers who did not strike. The dispute arose because the Union believes that the teachers on strike were entitled to Labor Day pay.

On August 30, School Superintendent B. Gallo sent the following letter to the striking teachers:

The Board of School Trustees and I understand that you are participating in a work stoppage in violation of your individual contract. We are extremely disappointed that you have chosen to take this step. In addition to the detrimental effects upon the education of students enrolled in our schools, which should be the first concern of all of us, there can be serious adverse effects upon each individual teacher who participates in a strike.

The law clearly states that such a strike is illegal so that those who participate are breaking the law. A teacher who goes out on strike breaches his contract with the school corporation. The implications of such a breach are many and should be of utmost concern, not the least of which would be grounds for dismissal. Loss of salary and fringe benefits are also matters to be carefully considered.

We wish to make clear that you will not be paid for any day you are on strike. The Federation and each participating teacher could possibly be liable for damages for breach of contract and participation in an illegal strike.

> The Board of School Trustees and I are respectfully requesting and directing all employees to perform their duties under their agreements with the Community School Corporation without further interruption.

Subsequently, on Sunday, September 2, Gallo told each school principal to notify the striking teachers that they would not be paid for Labor Day unless they returned to their jobs on Tuesday, September 4, and did not strike after that date.

On Monday, September 3, the Parties were in negotiations and exchanged proposals and counterproposals concerning the matters in dispute. About fifteen (15) items were involved in the negotiation. Specific references to Labor Day pay were made at that time. The School Board proposed that it would pay for this holiday provided the teachers returned to work the next day. The Union refused the School Board package that contained its Labor Day proposal and substituted a counterproposal including Item I (c), which said "holiday pay excluded." Steve Andrew, Union President, testified that this item meant that

> all teachers had the right to pay for Labor Day, and there was no need to negotiate about Labor Day pay.

William Owens, School Board Attorney, testified that "no statement was made by the Union concerning item I (c)."

In any event, the School Board made a second proposal, including item 3, which stated:

> Holiday pay for Monday (Labor Day) provided that the strike is settled prior to the opening of school Tuesday.

The Union again refused the package offered by the School Board and the strike continued until a settlement was reached on September 5. Teachers returned to work on September 6. In the agreement that settled the strike, there is no mention of pay for Labor Day. As part of the September 5 settlement, the Parties also adopted the "no reprisal" provision.

During the negotiations, Andrew testified, the Union would not sign any contract that did not include Labor Day pay for the striking teachers. That is, the strike would have continued until Labor Day pay was assured.

POSITIONS OF THE PARTIES

Union

In the Union's view, the grievance should be granted based on the events that occurred during the negotiations. It points out that the Union rejected the School Board's proposal of September 3, conditioning Labor Day pay on the teachers' return to work the next day. That proposal was not included in the agreement reached on September 5. Moreover, the Union claims that the School Board violated the no reprisal clause by denying Labor Day pay. It also asserts that the strike would not have ended had there been any indication from the School Board that it would withhold Labor Day pay.

Finally, the Union stresses that the Master Contract does not require teachers to work the day before and after the holiday as is found commonly in labor agreements. Since the contract does not require work on the days immediately prior to and after a holiday, the teachers are entitled to holiday pay. Thus:

> No contractual provision exists with respect to requiring employees to work a given number of days *before* and *after* any paid holiday in order to qualify for compensation for the holiday in the contracts between the parties. Yet, the arbitrator is well aware that in many labor agreements such requirements exist and it is reasonable to conclude that the failure to include such a pre- and post-holiday work requirement is supportive of the view that the parties never intended for such requirements to be associated with pay for scheduled holidays. [Emphasis in original]

School Board

Contrary to the Union, the School Board argues that the events of the negotiations are not material to this issue. They are not material because the Union and teachers promised in the Master Contract that there would be no strikes on any day during the contract period, including Labor Day.

The Board's unsuccessful attempt to include its proposal of September 3 should not be interpreted to mean the teachers would receive Labor Day pay even if they did not return to the classroom on September 4. It was proposed only to make it more clear to the Union and teachers that holiday pay would be forfeited unless the teachers returned to work the next day. Failure to include the proposal should not prejudice the Board's position in this proceeding, in the Board's opinion.

Teachers should not be paid for Labor Day, asserts the School Board, because they violated the no-strike clause contained in the Master Contract. Article XXII constitutes the Union's and teachers' promise that no strike would take place for any reason during the effective period of the contract. Since the promise was broken, the School Board with justification under the Contract refused to pay for Labor Day. The teachers forfeited such pay because they engaged in a strike that violated the Master Contract and state law.

Reasonably viewed, argues the School Board, Labor Day pay is not covered by the no reprisal clause. Denial of such pay was not reprisal or punitive action against the teachers because they forfeited their pay by the strike.

The Case of the Life-Support System

Coincidentally, this case arose in the midst of a heated public debate concerning the use of a life-support system to prevent death. Although the arbitrator did not deal directly with that problem, as you will see, the use of a life-support system was a feature of the dispute. The employee, who subsequently died as a result of injuries sustained in an automobile accident, was kept alive for a time by the use of a life-support system. Under the company's insurance policy, double indemnity (twice the amount for natural death) for loss of life resulting from an accident is paid provided that the employee dies within ninety days following the accident.

In this case, the employee died after the ninety-day period, and the employer refused to award the widow of the employee the double indemnity benefit. On behalf of the widow, the union carried the case to arbitration requesting that the arbitrator direct double indemnity despite the ninety-day rule.

GRIEVANCE AND LABOR AGREEMENT

Involved in this case is the determination of when an employee's loss of life occurred resulting from an accident for purposes of insurance. On the grounds that his loss of life occurred after the allowable time limits expired for double indemnity under its insurance program, the Company refused to pay the beneficiary of Dills the sum of $9,000. In protest, Dills's widow and the Union filed Grievance Number 27046, dated June 27, 1975, which states:

Art. XIX, Par. 98

Every employee upon acquiring seniority with the Company will receive a life insurance policy of $9,000 plus A D and D,* provided that the employee remains in active employment. The full premium will be paid by the Company.
On 6/2/75 Dills died from injuries received in an accident. Company refuses to pay accidental death benefit.

As a remedy, the Union requests that the Company pay "Mrs. Dills all monies due."

BASIC QUESTION

The basic question to be determined in this dispute is framed as follows:

Under the circumstances of this case, did the Company violate Article XIX, Paragraph 98 of the Labor Agreement? If so, what should the remedy be?

BACKGROUND

Death of Dills

Dills was hired by the Company on December 4, 1956. He was assigned as an Inspector in Plant 2 on the second shift. He also served as a Union Steward.
On February 5, 1975, Dills was involved in an automobile accident. He was taken to a hospital, and he eventually died 117 days after the accident. In his death certificate, the cause of death resulted from:

Internal injuries with fractured left ribs, left hemathorax, and ruptured spleen—2-vehicle accident.

*"A D and D" means accidental death and dismemberment.

While in the hospital, Dills underwent four (4) operations, the last of which took place on April 25, 1975. After the second operation, Dills was placed on a life-support system. This system consisted of a respirator to facilitate breathing and to keep his lungs free from fluid; a heart monitor; intravenous feeding, and blood transfusions. For one (1) week, the life-supporting system was removed, but after this week his condition dictated the resumption of the life-support system.

On April 28, 1975, three (3) days following his last operation, Mrs. Dills testified, the attending doctor told her:

> He will die. He is a terminal case. Only the life-support system is keeping him alive.

Dills became progressively worse, and despite the life-support system, he died on June 2, 1975.

Ninety (90)-Day Limit

Hoosier Life and Casualty carries the insurance for the Company. Under the accidental death and dismemberment (A D and D) feature of the insurance program, it is stated:

> If an employee suffers a nonoccupational bodily injury caused by an accident and as a direct result of such injury and, to the exclusion of all other causes, *sustains within no more than ninety days* after the date of the accident which causes such injury *any of the losses listed* in the Table of Benefits in this section, then, provided:
>
> **A.** the injury occurs while insurance is in force for the employee under this Title: and
>
> **B.** the loss resulting from the injury is not excluded from coverage in accordance with Section 2 of this Title:
>
> the Insurance Company shall, subject to the terms of this policy, pay a benefit in the amount provided for such loss in said Table of Benefits but in no case shall more than the Principal Sum be paid for all losses sustained by an employee through any one accident.

Along with the entire insurance program, the A D and D feature, including the 90-day limit, was made known to the employees in a booklet distributed to them. As indicated below, the Union was also aware of the 90-day feature governing A D and D benefits.

Following Dills's death, Mrs. Dills was paid the $9,000 life insurance death benefit. Through the Union, the widow also claimed that she was entitled to an additional $9,000 because her husband's death resulted from an accident. White, Manager of Insurance Benefits, submitted the claim,

Table of Benefits

In the Event of Loss of	The Benefit Will Be
Life	The Principal Sum
A Hand	One-Half the Principal Sum
A Foot	One-Half the Principal Sum
An Eye	One-Half the Principal Sum
A Hand and a Foot	The Principal Sum
A Hand and an Eye	The Principal Sum
A Foot and an Eye	The Principal Sum
Both Hands	The Principal Sum
Both Feet	The Principal Sum
Both Eyes	The Principal Sum

but it was denied by the Insurance Carrier. Mrs. Dills testified that the carrier denied the claim because Dills's death occurred more than 90 days following the automobile accident.

This arbitration was convened because the Union contends that an additional $9,000 should be paid to Dills's beneficiary on the grounds that his death resulted from an accident. Its chief argument is that the 90-day limitation contained in the insurance policy has no standing under the Labor Agreement since the Labor Agreement, including Paragraph 98, was negotiated between the Union and the Company and not between the Union and the Insurance Carrier. In other words, the Union argument is that the 90-day stricture, relied upon by the Company to deny the accidental death benefit, does not control this dispute because there is no such limitation in Paragraph 98.

NEGOTIATIONS OF 1974 LABOR AGREEMENT

In January 1974, the Parties were in the negotiations that eventually resulted in the adoption of the current Labor Agreement. On January 9, the Union presented the following proposal to the Company:

Under A D & D it is proposed that if medical treatment begins prior to the ninety (90)-day period for the injury incurred, that it would not waive the right of collection of the principal sums listed, if loss occurs after the ninety (90)-day period. Also refer to proposal #29. (Anywhere 90-day appears—rewrite.)

On April 24, 1974, while discussing the 90-day limitation in question, the following exchange took place between Paul, Director of Industrial Relations; Johns, Union President; and Sykes, Union Committeeman:

Paul: ...All through here, Charlie, I have forgotten how many references you people made to—90 days. I would say there was something like 8 to 10 places. Just guessing off the top of my head. Talking about the 90 days on A D & D and that type of thing. I went over this in quite some detail with the guys in Insurance. This is pretty much standard language. In almost all your insurance policies.

Johns: It might be standard language. But it looks like if somebody was to die and they need 90 days afterward or the fact they was to have to take an arm off, or something like that. It all has to be done within 90 days or they don't get it.

Paul: That's right—that's exactly true. If you had 120 days, it would be the same damn problem.

Sykes: No, Marv. You take now—say a man has got his arm all messed up and hell, they're operating on it and operating on it, trying to save that arm. Now you're putting a burden on that man there, saying it gets up to 89 days and say, "Hell, hack it off." If he's got any chance at all you know they're gonna keep working on that arm. It may be...

Paul: I think you're going for outside choices. I can't recall, in my brief tenure here, that we've had that happen.

Sykes: We had it on a guy's eye. It came up and he thought they were going to take it out. I don't know right now how he stands. But it was going over 90 days and they were talking about taking it out after 90 days.

Paul: But, really, this thing...

Johns: We've got two of them. Page is about to lose his eye—about 120 days after—from a nail. Then also Goodwine, he got carbide in his eye and they had several operations on it and there's a chance he might lose it.

Paul: This is pretty much standard. This 90-day thing is all the way through your entire program.

Johns: Well, what we're saying here is, if treatment starts before the 90 days period ...

Paul: I know what you're saying. But we've talked about it quite a lot and the consensus is that you got to stay with something so you might as well stay with the standard clause, which we've got and which is preferable among everybody else.

In any event, the Company did not agree to the union's proposal as cited above. It rejected the Union demand that the 90-day limitation would not count if the loss of life, sight, or limbs occured after that time period provided that medical treatment started within the 90-day period. On June 19, 1974, the current Labor Agreement became effective, and contained Paragraph 98 as cited earlier. This provision appeared in the previous Labor Agreement in its current form except that the life insurance benefit was raised to $9,000 from $7,500. In addition, the Company continued to use the same Insurance Carrier, and the policy contained the 90-day limitation for loss of life, sight, or limbs resulting from an accident.

ANALYSIS OF THE EVIDENCE

Union Position: Paragraph 98 Controls Dispute

According to the Union, Paragraph 98 establishes the merits of the claim in an unambiguous manner. It urges further that the 90-day limitation contained in the insurance policy is solely between the Company and the Insurance Carrier and may not be used to apply Paragraph 98. It argues:

> We contend that the insurance contract is not incorporated in Paragraph 98. Any provision of the insurance policy is not binding upon the Union. It may not be used to undermine the unambiguous language of Paragraph 98. The Labor Agreement is determinative and not the insurance policy which is a contract between the Company and the Insurance Carrier. Paragraph 98 says the Company shall pay the benefit. There is no ambiguity in Paragraph 98. It is clear. It says the Company will pay the benefit. It does not say the Insurance Carrier will pay the benefit.

As a matter of fact, the Union, with vigor, argues that the Arbitrator should base his decision strictly on the language of Paragraph 98. It says that evidence submitted by the Company is not material and should not be given any weight. Included in this category are the 1974 negotiations that resulted in the instant Labor Agreement, previous administration of the A D and D program,[*] and the booklet distributed to employees explaining the insurance program. To buttress its position, the Union refers to an arbitration decision, dated December 15, 1972, involving the Parties, rendered by Arbitrator Kess. In that case, the issue involved the application of that portion of the Labor Agreement (not Paragraph 98) that deals with weekly benefits for employees who are absent from work because of accident or illness. While granting the grievance, Arbitrator Kess observed that the controlling contractual language was "clear and unambiguous." In addition, he relied on the Union argument that the insurance policy between the Company and the Insurance Carrier was not incorporated in that area of the Labor Agreement involved in this case.

Character of Paragraph 98

It is self-evident, of course, that Paragraph 98 is an agreement reached solely by the Parties. As the Union says, the Insurance Carrier and the policy under which benefits are paid are not expressly mentioned in the provision. To this extent, the Union agreement has merit—the Company and the Union reached the agreement contained in Paragraph 98, and this

---

[*]The Company submitted two instances demonstrating that 50 percent of the principal sum was paid to two (2) employees who each lost the sight of one eye. It points out that this benefit was paid under the insurance policy, and stresses further that Paragraph 98 does not provide for a specific amount of benefit for accidental death, dismemberment, or loss of sight. Hence, the Company argues that the insurance policy is incorporated into Paragraph 98.

agreement is solely between them and not between the Union and the Insurance Carrier. Thus, the Union is on sound ground when it argues that Paragraph 98 should govern the dispute. If there is a conflict between the language of the provision and the contract executed by the Company and the Insurance Carrier, any such conflict should be resolved in favor of the language contained in Paragraph 98.

On the other hand, the Union argument breaks down because Paragraph 98 is not written in unambiguous terms as it relates to the dispute at hand. The provision is clear to the extent that each employee acquiring seniority will be covered by a $9,000 life insurance policy. It also is clear that the Company will pay the premium. However, what about benefits for accidental death and dismemberment? Paragraph 98 says that each employee will be covered by a life insurance policy "plus A D and D." It does not specify the amount of any such benefit, and it does not spell out the circumstances under which such a benefit will be paid. In addition, the provision is silent as to when loss of life, limbs or sight must occur following an accident for the benefit to be paid.

Union Counsel argues that Paragraph 98 does not say that loss of life must occur within 90 days of an accident for the accident death benefit (double indemnity) to be paid. This is true. However, it is equally true that Paragraph 98 does not specify that such a benefit will be paid regardless of when loss of life occurs following an accident.

In short, for purposes of this case, Paragraph 98 is ambiguous and unclear. Indeed, for the Union position to prevail solely on the basis of contractual language, Paragraph 98 would have to say unambiguously and unequivocally that the accidental death benefit shall be paid "regardless of when death occurs following an accident." It obviously does not say this, and Paragraph 98 by reasonable inference simply cannot be held to mean what the Union would like it to mean. Thus, the position of the Union may not prevail solely on the basis of the language of Paragraph 98. As to the material issue involved in this dispute—when loss of life must occur following an accident for accidental death benefit eligibility—the provision is obviously not clear at all. For this reason, the Kess decision does not stand as a valid precedent. Not only did the dispute arbitrated by Kess arise under a different provision of the Labor Agreement, but what is equally important, Kess held that the controlling language in his case was clear and unambiguous. In this case, it is incontrovertible that Paragraph 98 is not written in unambiguous terms as it relates to the instant dispute. To hold that the language is clear beyond reasonable doubt as to the material issue would be a masterpiece of error.

Union Recognition of 90-Day Limit

It would likewise be a most grievous error for the Arbitrator to find that the Union and the employees are not bound by the 90-day limit contained in the policy in effect between the Company and the Insurance Carrier. True, the Insurance Carrier is not a party to Paragraph 98. As mentioned earlier, Paragraph 98 is a contractual provision negotiated by the Parties. It was not negotiated between the Union and the Insurance Carrier.

Despite these considerations, *the evidence is incontrovertible that the Union recognized that the 90-day limit contained in the insurance policy is incorporated into Paragraph 98.* The best evidence for this conclusion is the fact that the Union attempted unsuccessfully to broaden the 90-day limit. In his argument, Union Counsel says that the negotiations do not count and should not be given any weight. He argues that under the *parol-evidence* rule what was proposed, discussed, and rejected in negotiations should not prejudice the Union's position. Such an argument would have merit if Paragraph 98 were written in clean-cut and unambiguous terms as it relates to the material issue in this case. Under these circumstances, the events of the 1974 negotiations would not count and would not prejudice the Union's case. Under the parol-evidence rule, what was proposed, discussed, and rejected may not properly be held to vary *unambiguous* contractual language. As abundantly demonstrated, however, Paragraph 98 is ambiguous as it related to the circumstances of this dispute.

Since it is ambiguous and uncertain, the events of the 1974 negotiations are squarely material to the application of Paragraph 98. In those negotiations the Union endeavored to change the 90-day limit. It demanded that the 90-day limit not apply if medical treatment were obtained within the 90-day period. That is, if medical treatment were administered to an employee within the 90-day period, the employee would be eligible for A D and D benefits regardless of when loss of life, limbs, or sight would occur. Indeed, if the Union really believed that the 90-day limit did not apply to Paragraph 98, why in the world did it make such a proposal? Common sense alone tells us that the Union made this proposal because it recognized that A D and D benefits are not paid when loss of life, limbs, or sight occurs after 90 days following an accident. In short, the Union was fully aware of the limit. The Company rejected the Union's demand, and Paragraph 98 remains in the current Labor Agreement as it appeared in previous contracts except for the increase of the principal benefit.

That the Union knew what the 90-day limit was all about is made crystal-clear in the exchange between the Company and Union representatives in the 1974 negotiations. This entire exchange was cited earlier in this Opinion. In any event recall the following:

Johns: (Union President) But it looks like if somebody was to die and they need 90 days afterward or the fact that if they was to have to take an arm off, or something like that. It all has to be done within 90 days or they don't get it.

Paul: (Director of Labor Relations) *That's right—that's exactly true.* [Emphasis added]

In other words, the 90-day limit is a part of Paragraph 98. The Union knew it and tried without success to change it. Union Counsel cautions the Arbitrator that he would commit the cardinal sin of arbitrators if he were to read the 90-day limit into the provision. To the contrary, the conduct of the Union in the 1974 negotiations proves conclusively that it recognized the 90-day limit. *That is why it tried to remove the stricture in the 1974 negotiations.* The Arbitrator does not inject into Paragraph 98 the 90-day limit. It was there before the Arbitrator was called upon to decide this dispute. He does not read into the provision a restriction that was not previously recognized by the Union.

In the light of these observations, the Arbitrator finds that Paragraph 98 contains the 90-day limit, which is in the insurance policy. Though not expressly mentioned in the provision, one would have to shut one's eyes to the most clear and incontrovertible evidence that the Union was fully aware that the 90-day limit is incorporated into the provision.

In short, the Arbitrator regards Paragraph 98 as if it expressly contained the stricture found in the insurance policy. The limitation on the payment of accidental death benefits is this: *Loss of life caused by accident must occur within 90 days after the date of accident.*

Meaning of "Loss of Life" under Paragraph 98

It should logically follow, therefore, that the grievance should be denied. Dills's accident occurred on February 5, 1975, and he did not die until 117 days later. His death certificate was executed on June 2, 1975. Though his loss of life was caused by an accident, he died beyond the 90-day limit. Understandably, the Company argues:

> The Union has failed to prove that the Company violated the contract by not paying an additional $9,000 to the widow of employee Dills.

> The Union acknowledged, by virtue of their proposal submitted to the Company during the negotiations that they recognized the 90-day limitation in A D & D and wished to broaden this limitation...

> It is very evident and clear that the Union is attempting to obtain in this arbitration proceeding what it could not obtain at the bargaining table of negotiations in the formulation of this labor agreement.

In other words, since the Union failed to broaden the 90-day limit, and since Dills died after the 90-day limit, the Company requests that the grievance should be denied.

Without question, Dills died on June 2, 1975. The death certificate was executed on this date. It was not, of course, executed within the 90-day limit. On these grounds, the grievance should have no standing under Paragraph 98. The fact that the Insurance Carrier denied the claim is additional proof that for purposes of Paragraph 98 Dills died after the 90-day limit.

What is involved here, however, is the construction of the term "loss of life" as contained in the A D and D feature of the insurance program. It says that in the "event of loss of life" the benefit will be the principal sum of the life insurance policy. At the risk of inviting understandable censure by the Company, the Arbitrator construes Dills's "loss of life" for purposes of Paragraph 98 as of April 28, 1975, which was within the 90-day period. On this date, the uncontested evidence demonstrates that the medical authorities said that Dills had no chance to live. Uncontested evidence demonstrates that "life" was prolonged beyond that date by a life-support system. For all practical purposes, Dills's life expired as a human being on April 28. If the life-support system of Dills had been taken away, he would have officially died before the 90-day period expired. Only by the use of the life-support system did he linger until June 2, 1975.

For purposes of Paragraph 98, "life" means more than being maintained as a vegetable by a life-support system. "Life" means that the person can function as a human being and has a reasonable chance for recovery. We should not believe in miracles, and no miracle occurred in this case. Medical authority said that Dills had absolutely no chance to recover, and he did die as predicted. Only by the use of a life-support system did he technically "live" until after the 90 days had expired. In other words, the Company places an unrealistic construction on the term "life" under the circumstances of this case. For all realistic purposes, Dills for purposes of Paragraph 98 lost his life as of April 28, 1975. For these reasons, the Arbitrator shall grant the grievance.

CONCLUSIONS

Having reached this conclusion under the circumstances of this case, the Arbitrator cautions all concerned not to read too much into his decision. He does not write into Paragraph 98 the proposal that the Union unsuccessfully attempted to advance in the 1974 contract negotiations. The 90-day limit still applies for purposes of Paragraph 98. That is, loss of life, sight, or limbs must occur within 90 days following an accident. Nothing in this decision is intended to undermine the integrity of the 90-day limit.

Put succinctly, the Arbitrator grants this grievance solely and exclusively because of the particular circumstances of this case: Dills effectively and realistically lost his life within the 90-day period. He was maintained beyond this time by a life-support system. Beyond this, the Arbitrator establishes no precedent and makes no exception to the 90-day limit. As a result of the narrow set of facts under which the Arbitrator has applied Paragraph 98 in this particular case, the Union, of course, does not gain in arbitration what it failed to achieve in contract negotiations. What is at stake in this case is exclusively the Arbitrator's construction of "loss of life" under its particular facts and circumstances. This is the full and only extent of the Arbitrator's decision to grant the grievance.

If the Union believes that the 90-day limit is unfair and unrealistic, it must change it in collective bargaining and not in arbitration. Nothing the Arbitrator has said in this case removes the 90-day limit for the purpose of the application of Paragraph 98. All that the Arbitrator has said in this case is that for purposes of Paragraph 98 Dills lost his life effective on April 28, 1975. On that date, the 90-day limit had not expired.

QUESTIONS

1. Why did the arbitrator find that the ninety-day rule is incorporated into Paragraph 98 though it does not appear in the express language of the provision?

2. Was the arbitrator's decision to award the widow double indemnity consistent with his finding that the ninety-day rule was incorporated into Paragraph 98? Defend your position with cogent arguments.

3. Assume that an employee injures his hand and after ninety days the hand is amputated. To what extent would the arbitrator's decision in this case stand as a valid precedent for the employee's claim that he should be indemnified for the loss of the hand?

4. Why did the arbitrator hold that the employee lost his life within ninety days for insurance purposes following the accident even though he died on the 117th day?

Reporting Pay: The Case of the Strike

CAST OF CHARACTERS

Yost	General Manager
Viss	Production Manager
Walt	Union President
Mills	International Union Representative
Gost	Union Vice President
Strong	Western Region Employee Relations Manager

In this case, you are again the arbitrator. Before unionism and collective bargaining, reporting pay was not normally part of employees' conditions of employment. If no work was available when they reported, the employer simply sent them home. No compensation was paid for the inconvenience and expenses required to report to work. Employees were not even paid when they were required to hang around the premises only to be told to leave after staying there for perhaps several hours.

To protect employees from such treatment, practically every labor agreement contains a reporting pay provision. In the case at hand, Article V is fairly typical. When employees are required to report, and work is not available in their classification or area, the employer must offer substitute work, including production or clean-up work. If no work at all is offered, employees are guaranteed four hours of pay at the base rate.

Though not involved in this case, Article V does not contain a condition that relieves the employer from reporting pay obligation by giving employees due notice not to report to work. On the other hand, as is virtually universal, Article V relieves the employer when the reason for not providing work is beyond its control.

Among other reasons, employees are not entitled to reporting pay when failure to offer work is due to a strike situation. That is the setting of your problem in this case. A strike did take place, and when it was over the employees reported to work. Claiming that its failure to provide work was attributable to the strike, the Company refused to award reporting pay. Not so, argued the Union, asserting that the employer should have been aware that the labor force would report the morning immediately following the end of the strike.

So your job is to apply Article V under the circumstances of this case.

GRIEVANCE

This dispute involves the Company's refusal to pay reporting pay to employees who reported to work on November 25, 1991. In protest, the Union filed Grievance No. 85-77, dated December 6, 1991, which stated:

> Company refusing to pay 4 hrs. call in pay to employees who reported to work on 11/25/91.

For settlement of the grievance the Union requested that the Company pay reporting pay "to all employees that reported for work."

Failing to settle the dispute in the Grievance Procedure, the Parties convened this arbitration for its determination.

LABOR AGREEMENT

Article V—Reporting Time

When an employee is directed to report to work and the anticipated work does not materialize, they shall be offered substitute work at their base rate to the extent of at least four hours' time; such substitute work means any work within the reasonable capacity of the individual to perform, whether in actual production or in sweeping, cleaning or otherwise assisting in plant maintenance. If no work is offered, then such employee shall receive four hours' pay as aforesaid. This stipulation will not apply where stoppages of work are due to strike, power failure, flood, riot or other major causes beyond the Employer's control. It is understood that such substitute work shall not be offered if it displaces another employee already assigned to that work.

ISSUE

Under the circumstances of this case did the Company violate Article V of the Labor Agreement? If so, what should be the remedy?

BACKGROUND

Events During Strike

In the plant, located in Columbus, Ohio, the Company manufactures corrugated containers, employing approximately eighty bargaining unit people. About fifty work the day shift and thirty are assigned to the night shift. The Company also operates plants in Martinsville, Indiana, Canton, Ohio, Champaign, Illinois, and Lexington, Kentucky. Failing to reach an agreement for a new contract, a strike at the Columbus plant started at midnight October 29, 1991.

When the strike appeared imminent, Management made plans to use the Company's four sister plants to fill customer orders. It shipped cutting dies, printing dies, and rolling stock to those plants.

Except for the exchange of letters, no negotiations were conducted during the strike.

On November 4, James Yost, General Manager, sent a letter to all striking employees. It stated:

> On October 28, 1991, negotiations ended when the Union requested, and was given, the Company's final contract offer. In a meeting in our cafeteria on October 29, 1991, I detailed the rationale behind our offer and confirmed that it was indeed our final offer. That offer was rejected by the Union membership and the plant was struck at midnight on October 29.

> As you know, we are involved in a highly competitive business. As each day of the strike goes by, our future as a supplier to our customers (and the ultimate job security of all of us) is jeopardized, especially if we are unable to properly service our accounts. Our competitors are more than willing to use any excuse to take accounts away from us. We have therefore resumed our manufacturing operation, keeping the job security of this plant, and all of us, in mind.

> In returning to production, we hope to preserve the business that has taken a great deal of effort to obtain. The plant is open for business and we urge you to reconsider your prior decision and return to work. Should you choose not to return, we have little choice other than to take appropriate measures that will preserve both our business and our jobs.

During the strike, the Company operated the plant, using approximately twenty office employees and supervisors. Some of the supervisors came from the Company's four sister plants. Eight bargaining unit employees returned to work during the strike. Five were production workers and three were truck drivers. According to Ernie Viss, Production Manager, the office employees and supervisors performed simple jobs that could have been carried out by bargaining unit employees.

On Saturday, November 16, the Company by letter informed all strikers that it intended to replace them if they did not return to their jobs by November 25. This letter, signed by Yost, stated:

> We are now going into the third week of the strike against the Company. From our perspective, the Union appears to be taking no steps to end this work stoppage.
>
> As you know, we have resumed operations with the help of our salaried employees and other employees. Even though we have resumed production, the use of our salaried work force is not a permanent solution to running the plant in a cost-efficient manner.
>
> While we would prefer to have each of you return to your jobs, it does not appear that will occur soon; consequently, we are examining the options available to us that will provide us with a reliable and steady work force. One of these options is the replacement of those employees who wish to remain on strike.
>
> The decision to continue the strike is up to you; however, you should each know that if you elect to make that decision, the Company will have to decide whether, in the best interests of the future of this plant and the Corporate Shareholders, those employees not returning to work should be replaced. The law gives you the right to strike, and the law also gives you the absolute right to return to work if you decide that is in your own best interest and in the interests of your family.
>
> While we hope that replacement will not be necessary, you need to know we are prepared to do so and will have no other choice than to begin that process for those employees who have not returned to their jobs by November 25.

David Walt, President of the Union, and Jack Mills, International Union Representative, Region IX, responded to the Company's November 16 letter on November 19. The response, addressed to Yost, stated:

> When you were notified of the outcome of the ratification meeting, you were also notified that the Union was ready and willing to sit down with the Company to further try to negotiate an acceptable agreement between the parties.
>
> With your two letters to the employees, it seems that you are trying to convince the employees that the Union is unwilling to negotiate.
>
> To restate our position, the Union is willing to sit down at any time and try to reach a settlement acceptable to both parties. The employees will return to work when and if we get an acceptable agreement.

According to Walt, the Union letter was not only in response to the Company's letter, but also to inform Union members it was prepared to negotiate with Management. For this purpose copies were sent to Union members.

On November 22, the Union sent another letter to Yost. This one, signed by Mills, Walt, and Glenn Gost, Vice President, Region IX, stated:

> The Union has completely reviewed their position as it relates to the negotiations for a new Collective Bargaining Agreement with the Company.
>
> At this time, we feel it would be useful to resume negotiations and make some modifications. Accordingly, we are requesting the resumption of contract negotiations with you at your earliest possible date.
>
> Looking forward to a successful conclusion of these negotiations, we are sincerely yours.

Union Meeting: Sunday, November 24

The letter was mailed presumably on Saturday, November 16, and Walt said he received the Company letter of that date on Monday, November 18 or Tuesday, November 19. After receiving the letter, the Union President testified that he discussed it with Gost and the International Union attorneys located in Nashville, Tennessee. The outcome of the discussion was recognition that the Company intended to replace permanently the striking employees unless they returned to work by November 25.

As a result, the Union scheduled a special meeting for Sunday, November 24. Under its constitution, explained Walt, the meeting could not have been scheduled before that time because Union members must receive 72 hours' notice prior to a special meeting.

Starting at 2 P.M. on the Sunday in question, a meeting was held concerning the Company's letter of November 16. Union officials explained to the membership that the Company intended to replace them permanently should they fail to report to work the following day, November 25. Walt recommended they report to work the next day. No one objected to his recommendation. Had a member objected, the issue would have gone to a vote.

Between 6 and 7 P.M. on that Sunday, the picket line was removed. Picketing employees were told to go home and report to work the next morning, and picket signs were removed. Company guards, stationed at the plant area during the strike, according to Walt, saw the removal of the picket line. Walt said the guards did not ask whether the strike was over, and the Union President did not volunteer the information to the guards. Walt said, however, he expected the guards to call Management to tell them the strike had ended.

Events of November 25

At 6:50 A.M. about fifty employees reported for work at the plant gates. Guards did not permit them to enter the plant. Viss, the Production Manager, came out and told the employees no work was available, telling them to go home and they would be called when needed. However, five truck drivers were permitted to enter the plant and work.

Viss testified that he did not know exactly how many people were at the plant site, saying it was dark, and it looked like a "hell of a lot" of people there. The Production Manager told Walt that the Company did not have work available for that many people. He also testified that he told the Union President that he would like to meet with the Union Committee to recall employees to work in an orderly fashion. Such a meeting did not take place because the Union wanted to negotiate the contract.

On November 25, the Union sent Yost a Mailgram. It was dispatched from Nashville, Tennessee at 11:22 A.M. EST, stating:

> On behalf of all striking employees of the Company, please be advised that all employees unconditionally offer to return to work, effective immediately. If you have any questions please contact me.

Recall to Work

On Tuesday, November 26, the Company recalled twenty-five employees for work. Three could not be contacted, so twenty-two employees actually worked. On that date, November 26, the equipment previously shipped to the sister plants had not yet been returned to Columbus. Viss testified that the employees worked on orders already in the plant and orders immediately pulled back from the four sister plants. On November 25, said Viss, he contacted the sister plants to determine which orders could be processed in Columbus.

On Wednesday, November 27, the Company recalled thirty-eight employees. Thursday, November 28, and Friday, November 29, were holidays. On the following Monday, December 2, the remaining employees were recalled to work.

POSITIONS OF THE PARTIES

Company

The Company asserts that it has no liability under the Reporting Time provision because the failure to provide work for the employees who reported on November 25 was attributable to the strike. Under this provision, strikes are specifically stated as an exception to entitlement for reporting pay. The language found in the article is very clear and unambiguous.

In addition, the Company argues that it had no reason to believe that employees would report to work on November 25. Even the Union's letter of November 22, the last one before the deadline, only said that the Union desired to resume negotiations on the basis of the modification of its position. But this letter did not assure that the employees would show up for work on November 25.

A Union position is that Viss should have visited the plant during the evening of November 24. If he had done that, he would have known that the strike was over. On this point, the Company asserts that Viss's visit would not have made work available for the fifty employees who reported the next morning, when the production equipment was scattered to its sister plants in Illinois, Indiana, Kentucky, and Ohio. That equipment could not have been returned and put into production between the night of November 24 and the morning of November 25.

Other arguments advanced by the Company include its desire to recall workers in an orderly and efficient manner, respecting the seniority rights of the employees; and an opinion that the employees who reported on November 25 did so not because they really wanted to work but to protect their jobs, fearing that they would be replaced.

Union

The fundamental position of the Union is that the Company should have anticipated that the employees would return to work on November 25. It stresses that the Company's letter of November 16 warned the employees that they would be replaced if they did not report for work on November 25. Under these circumstances, the Company should have recognized that they would stop striking and work on November 25, and it should have made arrangements for their return to work, including the recall of the equipment from its sister plants. Therefore, since work was not available, and the employees reported, they were entitled to reporting pay.

Although the Union asserts that the fifty employees who reported November 25 are entitled to reporting pay, it takes an alternative position. That is, at least the Company should have permitted the regular employees who were replaced by "strike-breakers" to work. To support this position, it stresses that the Production Manager testified that the work performed by the twenty office employees and supervisors was simple and could have been performed by the bargaining unit employees. In addition, the replacements did not use the equipment that was farmed out to the sister plants. In the Company's view, to remove the replacements from the jobs and to try to determine which returning employees had the right to these jobs would have been inefficient, throwing the plant into "disarray and confusion."

Institutional Issues under Collective Bargaining

■ Why, although common in some other countries, codetermination has been very rare in the United States, and why this latter situation may finally be changing

■ Why unions have historically resisted both employee stock ownership plans and quality of work life programs and why these stances, too, may at last be changing

Labor contracts encompass many issues that do not fall into the general category of wages or economic supplements. Such subjects deal with the rights and duties of the employer, the union, and the employees themselves. Some of them—such as seniority and discharge—most directly serve to protect the job rights of workers and might be most appropriately thought of as "administrative" concerns. They will be treated in such a manner in Chapter 10.

Other subjects, however, tend to supply the institutional needs of either the labor organization or the particular management—through "compulsory union membership" clauses, for example, or by provisions explicitly allowing the management the right to make decisions for the direction of the labor force and the operation of the plant. These matters will be dealt with in the paragraphs that follow in this chapter.

In considering this institutional dimension of collective bargaining, it must be recognized that the topics it encompasses can on occasion give the negotiators considerably more trouble than do the wage or benefit issues. It is, for example, at times infinitely easier to compromise and settle a wage controversy than to resolve a heated difference of opinion as to whether or not a worker should be compelled to join a union as a condition of employment. For all the thorniness of many wage-related issues, some of the longest and most bitter individual strikes have had as their source conflicts dealing with the institutional issues of collective bargaining.

UNION MEMBERSHIP AS A CONDITION OF EMPLOYMENT

Prior to the passage of the Wagner Act in 1935, there was essentially only one way in which a union could get itself recognized by an unsympathetic management: through the use of raw economic strength. If the labor organization succeeded in pulling all or a significant part of the employees out on strike, or in having its membership boycott the production or services of the employer in the marketplace, it stood a good chance of forcing the employer to come to terms. Lacking such economic strength, however, the union had no recourse—even if all the organization's workers wanted to join it—in the face of management opposition to its presence.

The 1935 legislation, as we know, greatly improved the lot of the union in this regard. It provided for a secret-ballot election by the employees, should the employer express doubt as to the union's majority status. It also gave the union the exclusive right to bargain for all workers in the designated bargaining unit, should the election prove that it did indeed have majority support. As Chapter 3 has indicated, these new ground rules for union recognition continue to this day.

Legally fostered recognition has not been synonymous with any assured status for the union as an institution, however. Indeed, in the many years since the Wagner Act, unions have still been able to find three grounds for insecurity. For one, the law has given the recognized labor organization no guarantee that it could not be dislodged by a rival union at some later date. For a second, there have still been many communication avenues open to antagonistic employers who choose to make known to their employees their antiunion feelings in an attempt to rid themselves of certified unions after a designated interval following the signing of the initial contract. And for a third, the government has not granted recognized unions protection against "free riders"—employees who choose to remain outside the union and thus gain the benefits of unionism without in any way helping to pay for those benefits. Under the law, the union clearly has not only the right but also the obligation to represent all employees in the bargaining unit, regardless of their membership or nonmembership in the union. Unions have particularly feared that the "free-rider" attitude could become contagious, resulting in the loss through a subsequent election (in which nonmembers as well as members can vote) of their majority status and thus of their representation rights.

Consequently, organized labor has turned to its own bargaining table efforts in an attempt to gain a further measure of institutional security. By and large, such attempts have been successful. Today, possibly as many as 83 percent of all contracts contain some kind of "union security" provision.[1]

Such provisions, which are frequently also referred to as "compulsory union membership" devices, essentially are three in number: the closed shop, the union shop, and the maintenance-of-membership arrangement. Brief reference has already been made to each of these mechanisms. A common denominator to all is that in one way or another membership in the union is made a condition of employment for at least some workers. They differ, however, in the timing for the requirement of union membership and in the degree of freedom of choice allowed the worker in the decision about joining the labor organization.

The closed shop and union shop are dissimilar in that under the former the worker must belong to the union *before* obtaining a job, whereas the latter requires union membership within a certain time period *after* the worker is hired. Under a maintenance-of-membership arrangement, the worker is free to elect whether or not to join the union. The worker who does join, however, must maintain membership in the union for the duration of the contract period or else forfeit the job.

These forms of compulsory union membership can also be viewed as differing with respect to the freedom of the employer to hire workers. Under the closed shop, the employer must hire only union members. This allows the union in effect to serve as the employment agency in most situations and to refer workers to the employer upon request. Under union shop and maintenance-of-membership arrangements, the employer has free access to the labor market. The employer may hire whomever it wants, and the union security provision becomes operative only after the worker is employed.

A final significant feature of union security is that it has received considerable attention from both Congress and the state legislatures. The laws these bodies have enacted must be taken into account at the bargaining table, and union security provisions that disregard these relevant public fiats do so only at a definite risk.

The *closed shop,* obviously the most advantageous arrangement from labor's point of view, appeared in 33 percent of the nation's agreements in 1946. Prohibited for interstate commerce by the Taft-Hartley Act of 1947, it visibly decreased in its frequency in the years thereafter, and less than 5 percent of all contracts today contain such a provision. Many of these are in intrastate commerce, of course, but some are in the construction industry on an interstate basis. Much of the latter sector refused, rather bluntly, to abide by the Taft-Hartley stricture and in fact openly flaunted it until 1959, when the Landrum-Griffin Act recognized the special characteristics of that sector and officially allowed it a stronger form of union security that approximates the closed shop.

With the decrease in usage of the closed shop, the *union shop* became the most widespread form of union membership employment condition. After being part of only 17 percent of all contracts in 1946, it appeared in about 64 percent of all labor agreements in 1959, and the figure is at about the 72 percent level today.

The *maintenance-of-membership* arrangement, originating in the abnormal labor market days of World War II, is still fully legal but is utilized relatively infrequently. After appearing in about one quarter of all contracts in 1946, it steadily lost ground thereafter, and only about 2 percent of all contracts now make provision for it. Much of the loss has undoubtedly been absorbed by the gains of the union shop, which maintenance-of-membership employers, having already taken this step toward accommodating the union, have rarely resisted very adamantly. (But some of *this* loss, in turn, is not entirely real: Some arrangements have adopted the name of "union shop" but been modified in practice to equate or nearly equate to maintenance-of-membership. There is sometimes a danger in taking things at face value.)

Two other brands of union security, neither at all common, constitute compromises between the union's goal of greatest possible security and the management's reluctance to grant such institutional status. Under the *agency shop,* nonunion members of the bargaining unit must make a regular financial contribution—usually the equivalent of the union dues—to the labor organization, but no one is compelled to join the union. The money is, in fact, at times donated to recognized charitable organizations. Nonetheless, the incentive for a worker to remain in the "free-rider" class is clearly reduced in this situation, and the union thus gains some measure of protection. The *preferential shop* gives union members preference in hiring but allows the employment of nonunionists, and its value seems to depend on how the parties construe the word *preference*.

Although the straight union shop thus appears to be the most popular form of union security, some employers and unions have negotiated variations of this species of compulsory union membership. Under some contracts, employees who are not union members when the union shop agreement becomes effective are not required to join the union. Some agreements exempt employees with comparatively long service with the organization. Under other contracts, old employees (only) are permitted to withdraw from the union at the expiration of the agreement without forfeiting their jobs. Under this arrangement, a so-called "escape period" of about fifteen days is included in the labor contract. If an employee does not terminate union membership within the escape period, he or she must maintain membership under the new arrangement. Newly hired workers, however, are required to join the union.

Whether the straight union shop or modifications of it are negotiated, Taft-Hartley forbids an arrangement that compels a worker to join a union as a condition of employment unless thirty days have elapsed from the effective date of the contract or the beginning of employment, whichever is later. In administering this section of the law, the National Labor Relations Board has held that the thirty-day grace period does not apply to employees who are already members of the union. However, it interprets the provision literally for workers who are not union members on the effective date of the contract or who are subsequently employed. Thus, in one case, a union shop arrangement was declared unlawful because it required workers to join the union twenty-nine days following the beginning of employment. Another union security arrangement was held to be illegal because it compelled employees to join the union if they had been on the company's payroll thirty or more days; in invalidating this agreement, the board ruled that it violated the law because it did not accord employees subject to its coverage the legal thirty-day grace period for becoming union members *after the effective date* of the contract.

Whereas some negotiators have adopted variations of the straight union shop, others have devised a number of alternatives to the maintenance-of-membership arrangement. Only at the termination of the agreement are employees under most maintenance-of-membership arrangements permitted to withdraw from the union without forfeiting their jobs, and usually only a fifteen-day period is provided at the end of the contract period during which time the employee may terminate union membership. But many agreements have a considerably less liberal period of withdrawal, from the worker's viewpoint, and some contracts allow more than the modal fifteen days. If an employee fails to withdraw during this "escape" time, the worker must almost invariably remain in the union for the duration of the new collective bargaining agreement.

Under some labor agreements, maintenance-of-membership arrangements also provide for an escape period after the *signing* of the agreement, to permit withdrawals of existing members from the union. Other agreements do not afford this opportunity to current members of the union but restrict the principle of voluntary withdrawal to newly hired workers.

These modifications are fully consistent with the law in all but the twenty-one "right-to-work" states, which ban any form of compulsory union membership, but certain other arrangements are not. Reference has already been made to the terms of Taft-Hartley under which an employee cannot lawfully be discharged from a job because of loss of union membership unless the employee loses the membership because of nonpayment of dues or initiation fees. In spite of the existence of an arrangement requiring union membership as a condition of employment, expulsion from a union for any reason other than nonpayment of dues or initiation fees *cannot* result in loss of employment. The National Labor Relations Board will order the reinstatement of an employee to his former job with back pay where this feature of the law is violated. Depending upon the circumstances of a particular case, the board will require the employer or the union, or both, to pay back wages to such an employee.

The board has, in fact, applied a literal interpretation to this feature of Taft-Hartley. In one case the board has held that a worker actually does not have to join a union even though a union shop arrangement may be in existence.[2] The employee's only obligation under the law is the willingness to tender the dues and initiation fees required by the union. In this case, three workers were willing to pay their union dues and initiation fees but they refused to assume any other union-related obligations, or even to attend the union meeting at which they would be voted upon and accepted. As a result, the union had secured the discharge of these workers under the terms of the union security arrangement included in the labor agreement. The board held that the discharge of workers under such circumstances violated the Taft-Hartley law, ruled that both the union and the company engaged in unfair labor practices, and ordered the workers reinstated in their jobs with full back pay.

The right-to-work laws themselves, of course, serve as formidable obstacles to union security arrangements in the primarily southern and southwestern states in which they remain on the books. The labor movement in these states does not have much political muscle because union membership there is very low. On the other hand, not only has their effect on labor relations been highly debatable, but in its 1965–1966 session, Congress came close to repealing the relevant Taft-Hartley Act passage permitting the enactment of such state laws (Section 14b),[3] and while there was at the time of this writing little likelihood that the repeal efforts would soon be resumed on Capitol Hill, it was a safe bet that ultimately they would be.

Were Congress to remove Section 14b, this action would nullify all right-to-work laws as far as these laws apply to interstate commerce, because of the *federal preemption* doctrine, which forbids states to pass laws in conflict with a federal statute. And in that event the right-to-work laws existing in Alabama, Arizona, Arkansas, Florida, Georgia, Idaho, Iowa, Kansas, Louisiana, Mississippi, Nebraska, Nevada, North Carolina, North Dakota, South Carolina, South Dakota, Tennessee, Texas, Utah, Virginia, and Wyoming would have application only in the area of intrastate commerce. They would cease to have any effect upon firms engaged in interstate dealings.

In the other direction, there was also a strong chance as this edition approached publication that several states would be battlegrounds for new right-to-work laws. Until 1985, when Idaho became the twenty-first right-to-work state, no state had passed such a law since 1976, when Louisiana did so (and the voters in Arkansas overwhelmingly voted to *keep* their longstanding right-to-work laws). But many right-to-work advocates were optimistic about near-term prospects for antiunion shop legislation in New Mexico, Colorado, Maine, and Vermont. And there was even an outside chance as this was being written that Pennsylvania, Illinois, and Delaware—states whose unionized percentages of the work force were greater than the national average—would have right-to-work laws on *their* books within a matter of an election year or so. If any of them in fact did, new ground would be broken in the sense of a northern industrial state joining the right-to-work states' roster: Indiana, which can fairly also be called a "northern industrial state," did have such legislation between 1957 and 1965 but repealed it in the latter year, the only state ever to throw out a right-to-work law after installing it. New Hampshire, certainly northern and increasingly industrial, was viewed by many observers in 1992 as another potential ground-breaker, but right-to-work advocates in the Granite State suffered defeat in that year when their legislative effort fell short of passage in the New Hampshire House of Representatives by a 211–134 margin. They also, nonetheless, remained optimistic about the future.

Nor were the forces seeking these new right-to-work laws exactly poverty stricken. The National Right to Work Committee, based in Fairfax, Virginia, by some estimates now receives $10 million in annual contributions (and sends out approximately 25 million letters to and on behalf of its 1.7 million individual and institutional members). Some of the money goes to such relatively broader projects as attacks on public-sector unionism and investigations into what the organization sees as the spread of prounion materials into public schools, and the committee recently pushed hard if unsuccessfully for a congressional bill that would make the committing of violence on picket lines punishable by up to twenty years in prison and a $10,000 fine. But most of the group's money is directed to the key item on the committee's agenda, the advance of the right-to-work movement itself.

Regardless of the fate of right-to-work legislation, however, it seems very likely that the question of whether union security provisions should be negotiated in labor agreements will remain a controversial one for some time to come—among the general public and some direct parties to collective bargaining if not among the large segment of unionized industry that has already granted such union security.

This controversy actually contains three major elements: morality, labor relations stability, and power.

Whether or not it is *morally* right to force an employee to join a union in order to be able to work is not an easy issue to resolve. Unions and supporters of unionism often argue that it is not "fair" to permit an employee to benefit from collective bargaining without paying dues, given the fact that the union must under the law represent all workers in the bargaining unit. And the argument is not without logic. Improvements obtained in collective bargaining *do* benefit nonunion members as well as union-member employees, and the union *is* compelled by law to represent nonunion bargaining unit employees, even in the grievance procedure, in the same fashion that it represents union members. Against this argument stands the equally plausible one that employees should not be forced to join a union in order to work. Such compulsion seems to many people to be undemocratic, immoral, and unjust. Almost everyone, however, has different ideas on what is "morally" correct in this controversy. Indeed, even the clergy has been drawn into the fight, and its members have exhibited the same lack of unanimity in their opinions as have other people. And if these stewards of God are not certain what is morally correct, how can two college professors make a judgment that will once and for all resolve the moral issue?

Congress itself, however, has now made a judgment as to what employees should appropriately do when they have bona fide religious beliefs against joining labor organizations or financially supporting them. In a 1980 amendment to Taft-Hartley, it decreed that such workers need not violate these beliefs. Instead, in something of a variation of the agency shop, they must make a contribution equal to the amount of the dues to a nonlabor, nonreligious charity. The amendment also provides that if the religious objector requests a labor organization to handle a grievance on his or her behalf, the union may charge the employee a "reasonable" amount for such servicing.

Some observers claim that union security is the key to *stability in labor relations*. They argue that a union that operates under a union-shop arrangement will be more responsible and judicious in the handling of grievances and in other day-to-day relations with its employers because of its guaranteed status. And, again, there is some strength to this argument. At times, conflict between union members and nonunion employees does hamper the effective organizational operation, and on this basis some employers may welcome an arrangement that forces all employees to join the union, as a way of precluding such conflicts. Moreover, unions can also claim that in the absence of a union security provision, the union officers must spend considerable time in organizing the unorganized and keeping the organized content so that they will not drop out of the union. Proponents of this position justifiably declare that if union officers are relieved from this organizational chore, they can spend their time in more constructive ways, which will be beneficial not only to the employees but also to the employer.

On the other hand, other debaters point out with equal justification that unions that do enjoy a union security arrangement sometimes use this extra time to find new ways to harass the employer. The solution to this particular controversy appears to an outsider to depend upon the character of the union involved and upon its relationship with the employer. Clearly, no one would blame an employer for resisting the granting of the union shop to a union that had traditionally engaged in frequent wildcat strikes, continually pressed grievances that had no merit, and, in short, sought to harass management at every turn.

At times, finally, employers and unions themselves argue along morality and labor relations lines to conceal a different purpose—their respective desires for *power* in the bargaining relationship. It is self-evident that the union does have more comparative influence in the negotiation of labor agreements and in its day-to-day relationship with the employer when it operates under a union shop. And, by the same token, the employer has more comparative influence when employees need not join the union to work and may terminate their membership at any time. Or, in short, the parties may speak in terms of morality merely as a smoke screen to conceal an equally logical but less euphemistic power issue.

But "power" still remains a rather nebulous term. The old saying that in poker a Smith and Wesson beats four aces is certainly true and lucidly pinpoints exactly where the power lies, and why. However, as a general statement, depending upon the assumptions one makes, a union could have infinitely more power than a management, and the reverse would be true under a different set of assumptions and circumstances. Given this elusiveness, as well as the unhappy connotations often placed on the word, it is perhaps not surprising that the verbal controversy over union security continues to be waged along the other lines described as well as those of power.

THE CHECKOFF

Checkoff arrangements are included in the large majority of collective bargaining contracts. This dues-collection method, whereby the employer agrees to deduct from the employee's pay monthly union dues (and in some cases also initiation fees, fines, and special assessments) for transmittal to the union, has obvious advantages for labor organizations, not only in terms of time and money savings but also because it further strengthens the union's institutional status. For the same reasons, many managers are not enthusiastic about the checkoff, although some have preferred it to the constant visits of union dues-collectors to the workplace. Once willing to grant the union shop, however, employers have rarely made a major bargaining issue of the checkoff per se. And the growth of this mechanism has been remarkably consistent with that of the union security measure: Where in 1946 about 40 percent of all labor agreements provided for the checkoff system of dues collection, this figure is, as we know, somewhat over 80 percent today.

Taft-Hartley, as was also pointed out earlier, regulates the checkoff as well as union security; under the law, the checkoff is lawful only on written authorization of the individual employee. It is further provided that an employee's written authorization may be irrevocable for only one year or for the duration of the contract, whichever is shorter.

Checkoff provisions frequently deal with matters other than the specification of items that the management agrees to deduct. Some arrangements specify a maximum deduction that the employer will check off in any one month, require each employee to sign a new authorization card in the event that dues are increased, indemnify the management against any liability for action taken in reliance upon authorization cards submitted by the union, require the union to reimburse the employer for any illegal deductions, and provide that the union share in the expense of collecting dues through the checkoff method. Not all these items, of course, appear in each and every checkoff arrangement; many labor agreements, however, contain one or more of them.

From the foregoing, it appears rather clear that although the checkoff is an important issue of collective bargaining, it does not normally constitute a crucial point of controversy between employers and unions. It does not contain the features of conflicting philosophy that are involved in the union security problem, falls far short of other problems of collective bargaining as a vexatious issue, and has rarely by itself become a major strike issue, since the stakes are not that high. As a matter of fact, even though the checkoff serves the institutional needs of the union, employers often find some gain from the incorporation of the device in the agreement. This would be particularly true where the labor contract contains a union security arrangement. Not only does the checkoff obviate the previously noted need of dues collection on the employer's premises, with the attendant impact upon orderly operations, but it avoids the need of starting the discharge process for employees who are negligent in the payment of dues. Frequently, without a checkoff, an employee who must belong to a union as a condition of employment will delay paying dues, and the employer and union are both faced with the task of instituting the discharge process, which is most commonly suspended when the employee, faced with loss of employment, pays the owed dues at the last possible minute. The checkoff eliminates the need for this wasted and time-consuming effort on the part of busy employer and union representatives.

Even when the union shop is not in effect, moreover, the checkoff need not necessarily be given permanent status. The employee is obligated to pay dues for one year only, and if he or she desires to stop the checkoff it is possible to do so during the "escape period." But under any circumstances, if the management believes that the union with which it deals is so irresponsible as not to deserve the checkoff, it need not agree to it as part of the renegotiated contract, and the mechanism is consequently also revocable from the employer's point of view.

UNION OBLIGATIONS

The typical collective bargaining contract contains one or more provisions such as those listed in Exhibit 9-1 (drawn from a current contract between the Oil, Chemical and Atomic Workers and a medium-sized chemical company) that establish certain obligations on the part of the labor organization. By far the most important of these obligations involves the pledge of a union that it will not strike during the life of the labor agreement. Most employers will, in fact, refuse to sign a collective bargaining contract unless the union agrees that it will not interrupt production during the effective contractual period.

EXHIBIT 9–1

ARTICLE 2

Section 3. No Strike—No Lockout

1. During the life of this Agreement there shall be no strike, work stoppage, slowdown, nor any other interruption of work by the Union or its members, and there shall be no lockout by the Company. In the event of a violation of this provision, either party to the Agreement may seek relief under the Grievance and Arbitration provisions of the Agreement or may pursue his remedy before the court or the Labor Board, as the case may be.

2. As an alternative, either party, in the event of an alleged or asserted breach of the no strike–no lockout clause, may institute expedited arbitration by telegram to the Federal Mediation and Conciliation Service and request that the FMCS designate an Arbitrator as quickly as possible. The Arbitrator shall hold the hearing as promptly as possible, notice to be served on any officer of the Company and on the President, Vice President or Secretary-Treasurer of the Union (any one of the three officers of the Union). The Arbitrator shall set the date, time and place of hearing and shall issue his award orally as soon after the completion of the hearing as possible.

3. Individual employees or groups of employees who adopt methods other than those provided in the grievance procedure for the settlement of their grievances shall be subject to disciplinary action, including discharge. Any disciplinary action taken by the Company under this clause shall be subject to review under the grievance procedure.

4. Should any dispute arise between the Company and the Union, or between the Company and any employee or employees, the Union will cooperate to prevent and/or terminate a work stoppage or suspension of work or a slowdown on the part of the employees on account of such dispute. A violation of this paragraph by any employee or group of employees will give the Company the right to administer discipline, including discharge. In administering discipline, including discharge, the Company shall have the right to distinguish between those instigating or leading the work stoppage or suspension of work or slowdown and those who simply participate therein. Any disciplinary action taken by the Company under this clause shall be subject to review under the grievance procedure.

The incorporation of a no-strike clause in a labor agreement means that all disputes relating to the interpretation and the application of a labor agreement are to be resolved through the grievance and arbitration procedure in an orderly and peaceful manner, and not through the harsh arbiter of industrial warfare. The pledge of the union not to strike during the contract period stabilizes industrial relations and thereby protects the interests of the employer, the union, and the employees. Indeed, a chief advantage that employers obtain from the collective bargaining process is the assurance that the organization will operate free from strikes or other forms of interruption to production (slowdowns, for example) during the period of the agreement.

Managements and unions have negotiated two major forms of no-strike provisions. Under one category, there is an *absolute and unconditional* surrender on the part of the union of its right to strike or otherwise to interfere with production during the life of the labor agreement. The union agrees that it will not strike for any purpose or under any circumstances for the duration of the contract period. Employers, of course, obtain maximum security against strikes from this provision.

Under the second major form, the union can use the strike only under certain *limited* circumstances. For example, in the automobile industry the union may strike against company-imposed production standards. Such strikes may not take place, however, before all attempts are made in the grievance procedure to negotiate production standard complaints. Other collective bargaining contracts provide that unions can strike for any purpose during the contract period but only after the entire grievance procedure has been exhausted, when the employer refuses to abide by an arbitrator's decision, or when a deadlock occurs during a wage-reopening negotiation. The union cannot strike under any other conditions for the length of the contract.

In the vast majority of cases, labor organizations fulfill their no-strike obligations just as most unionized employers fulfill all their contractually delineated responsibilities. However, in the event that violations do take place, employers have available to them a series of remedies. In the first place, under the terms of Taft-Hartley, they can sue unions for violations of collective bargaining contracts in the U.S. district courts. And, although judgments obtained in such court proceedings may be assessed only against the labor organization and not against individual union members, additional remedies are provided for in many collective bargaining contracts. Under some of them, strikes called by a labor union in violation of a no-strike pledge terminate the entire collective bargaining contract. In others, the checkoff and any agreement requiring membership as a condition of employment are suspended.

In addition, the employer may elect to seek penalties against the instigators and the active participants, or either group, in such a strike. Many contracts clearly provide that employees actively participating in a strike during the life of a collective bargaining contract are subject to discharge, suspension, loss of seniority rights, or termination of other benefits under the contract, including vacation and holiday pay. The right of an employer to discharge workers participating in such strikes has been upheld by the Supreme Court.

Finally, arbitrators will usually sustain the right of employers to discharge or otherwise discipline workers who instigate or actively participate in an unlawful strike or slowdown. Such decisions are based on the principle that the inclusion of a no-strike clause in a labor agreement serves as the device to stabilize labor relations during the contract period and as a pledge to resolve all disputes arising under the collective bargaining contract through the orderly and peaceful channels of the grievance procedure.

In 1970, the Supreme Court provided employers with a powerful legal weapon to deal with strikes that violate a no-strike clause. The high court, in *Boys Markets v. Retail Clerks*,[4] held that when a contract incorporates a no-strike agreement and an arbitration procedure, a federal court may issue an injunction to terminate the strike. This decision permits employers to go into court to force employees back to work when a labor agreement contains these features. The idea behind the decision is that the grievance procedure and arbitration should be used to settle disputes that arise during the course of a collective bargaining contract.

At times, strikes and other interruptions to production that are not authorized by the labor organization occur. These work stoppages, commonly known as "wildcat strikes," are instigated by a group of workers, sometimes including union officers, without the sanction of the labor union. Under many labor agreements, the employer has the right to discharge such employees or to penalize them otherwise for such activities. At times employers impose a stiffer penalty on local union officers, including stewards and grievance committee persons, compared with rank-and-file employees who commit the same offense. Disparate discipline is justified because union officials have a greater obligation to comply and enforce the no strike clause. In a 1983 case, however, the U.S. Supreme Court held that employers may not impose more severe discipline on union officials who commit the same offense as rank-and-file employees.[5] If both, for example, instigate a wildcat strike, engage in picketing, or encourage other employees to join the strike, an employer may not discharge the union officials while only suspending the rank-and-file employees. Should a management desire to penalize union officials more severely, it must negotiate a contract provision that specifically authorizes disparate treatment by placing special obligations on the officials. It is not likely, however, that many unions would agree to such a contractual provision.

A special problem has been created by Taft-Hartley in reference to wildcat strikes. Under this law, a labor union is responsible for the action of agents even though the union does not authorize or ratify such conduct.[6] Thus, an employer may sue a union because of a wildcat strike even though the union does not in any way condone the stoppage. As a result of this state of affairs, unions and employers have negotiated the so-called "nonsuability clauses," which were mentioned in Chapter 3. Under these arrangements, the management agrees that it will not sue a labor union because of wildcat strikes, provided that the union fulfills its obligation to terminate the work stoppage. Frequently, the labor contract specifies exactly what the union must do in order to free itself from the possibility of damage suits. Thus, in some contracts containing nonsuability clauses, the union agrees to announce orally and in writing that it disavows the strike, to order the workers back to their jobs, and to refuse any form of strike relief to the participants in such work stoppages.

Other features of some contracts also deal with strike situations. Under many labor agreements, the union agrees that it will protect the employer's property during strikes. To accomplish this objective, the union typically pledges itself to cooperate with the management in the orderly cessation of production and the shutting down of machinery. In addition, some unions agree to facilitate the proper maintenance of machinery during strikes even if achieving this objective requires the employment of certain bargaining unit maintenance personnel during the strike. Finally, it is not uncommon for unions to agree in the labor contract that management and supervisory personnel entering and leaving the plant in a strike situation will not be interfered with by the labor organization.

Many collective bargaining contracts place other obligations upon unions, extending well beyond the area of strikes and slowdowns. Under many agreements, for example, the union obligates itself not to conduct on the employer's time or property any union activities that will interfere with efficient operations. The outstanding exception to this rule, however, involves the handling of grievances: Meetings of union and employer representatives that deal directly with grievance administration are usually conducted on employer time. Some agreements also permit union officials to collect dues on employer property where the checkoff is not in existence. Another exception found in many contracts involves the permission given to employees and union officers to discuss union business or to solicit union membership during lunch and rest periods.

Another frequently encountered limitation of union activity on plant property involves restrictions of visits by representatives of the international union with which the local is affiliated. Still another denies unions permission to post notices in the plant or to use company bulletin boards without the permission of the employer. Where the union is allowed to use bulletin boards, many labor contracts specify the character of notices that the union may post; notices are permitted, for example, only when they pertain to union meetings and social affairs, union appointments and elections, reports of union committees, and rulings of the international union. Specifically prohibited on many occasions are notices that are controversial, propagandist, or political in nature.

MANAGERIAL PREROGATIVES

Once upon a time, a vice president for industrial relations of a large corporation was bargaining against a strike deadline with only hours to spare and making no progress whatsoever. The parties remained poles apart and the executive—not an especially calm person to start with—was approaching the condition of a nervous wreck.

Suddenly, a messenger informed him that his wife, nine months pregnant, had been taken to the hospital and the union (which had not to that point shown itself to be particularly accommodating) in no way argued with his suggestion that he make a quick trip to see her. At his wife's bedside, however, a strange contrast could be seen: The baby had not yet arrived, and she, though in considerable pain, was nonetheless amazingly calm and composed; he, without child at all, was more of a nervous wreck than ever.

The industrial relations man asked the nurse to explain his wife's commendable placidity and was told, "It must be that wonderful new tranquilizer that she's been given: Twilight Zone." The executive said, "Great! Great! Give me some, too! Give me some, too!" The nurse responded, "I'm sorry, sir, but that's only for labor." And the executive replied, "My God! Is there nothing left for management?"

That collective bargaining is in many ways synonymous with limitations on managerial authority is an observation that was offered on the earliest pages of this book. A fundamental characteristic of the process is restriction on the power of the management to make decisions in the area of employer-employee relations, and much of the controversy about collective bargaining grows out of this factor. On the one hand, the labor union seeks to limit the authority of management to make decisions when it believes that such restrictions will serve the interests of its members or will tend to satisfy the institutional needs of the union itself. On the other hand, the responsibility for efficiency in operation of the enterprise rests with management. The reason for the existence of management, in fact, is the overall administration of the business, and executives attempt to retain free from limitations those functions that they believe are indispensable to this end.

The problem is, moreover, hardly disposed of simply because most union leaders assert—and normally, in good faith—that they have no intention of interfering with the "proper functions of management." Years of witnessing official union interest expand from the historical wages and hours context into such newer areas as those outlined in this portion of the book have understandably led managers to conclude that what is "proper" for the union depends on the situation and the values of the union membership.

Nor do employers find much consolation in the fact that the managerial decision-making process is already limited and modified by such economic forces as labor market conditions, by such laws as those pertaining to minimum wages and discrimination, and by the employee-oriented spirit of our society. If unionism is not by any means the only restriction on employer freedom of action in the personnel sphere, it is nonetheless a highly important one for managements whose employees live under a union contract.

Beyond this, finally, the controversy is hardly confined to the personnel area, for managers can point to numerous (although proportionately infrequent) instances of strong union interest in such relatively removed fields as finance, plant location, pricing, and other "proper" management functions. In recent years, for example, some railroad unions have constantly blamed their employers' high degree of bonded indebtedness for depriving railroad workers of "adequate" wage increases; legal representatives of the Ladies' Garment Workers as well as those of several other unions have become familiar faces in courtrooms, to protest plant relocations of their union's employers; and the United Automobile Workers' interest in the pricing of cars is now all but taken for granted in automobile industry bargaining rooms (although the UAW's freely offered advice on this subject has yet to be accepted by the automobile manufacturers). Given the present state of the government's "legal duty to bargain" provisions, as Chapter 3 has indicated, no one can assert with complete confidence that such examples will not multiply in the years ahead.

In many ways, in fact, ramifications of the subject extend far beyond the two parties to collective bargaining. There is justification, indeed, for arguing that the "managerial rights" issue really pivots upon the broader question of what the appropriate function of labor unions in the life of our nation should be.

Managements have frequently translated their own thoughts on the subject into concrete action. Approximately 60 percent of all labor agreements today contain clauses that explicitly recognize certain stipulated types of decisions as being "vested exclusively in the management." Such clauses are commonly called "management prerogative," "management rights," or (more appropriately, to many managers) "management security" clauses.

Fairly typical of management prerogative provisions is the following, culled from the current agreement of a large midwestern durable goods manufacturer:

> Subject to the provisions of this agreement, the management of the business and of the plants and the direction of the working forces, including but not limited to the right to direct, plan, and control plant operations and to establish and to change work schedules, to hire, promote, demote, transfer, suspend, discipline, or discharge employees for cause or to relieve from duty employees because of lack of work or for other legitimate reasons, to introduce new and improved methods or facilities, to determine the products to be handled, produced, or manufactured, to determine the schedules of production and the methods, processes, and the means of production, to make shop rules and regulations not inconsistent with this agreement and to manage the plants in the traditional manner, is vested exclusively in the Company. Nothing in this agreement shall be deemed to limit the Company in any way in the exercise of the regular and customary functions of management.

Some rights clauses, by way of contrast, limit themselves to short, general statements. These are much more readable than the one above, but considerably less specific—for example, "the right to manage the plant and to direct the work forces and operations of the plant, subject to the limitations of this Agreement, is exclusively vested in, and retained by, the Company." On the other hand, the management rights clause cited is itself a model of brevity when compared with that of at least one of its counterparts: The current agreement between the Kuhlman Electric Company of Detroit and the UAW contains one that consumes over a dozen pages; it is, as one observer commented when it was originally inserted in a prior contract, a "likely candidate for the *Guinness Book of Records*."[7]

No matter which way management injects such clauses into the contract, however, two industrial relations truisms must also be appreciated: (1) The power of the rights clause is always subject to qualification by the wording of every other clause in the labor agreement; and (2) consistent administrative practices on the part of the management must implement the rights clause if it is to stand up before an arbitrator.

According to one point of view, moreover, the inclusion of such a clause in a labor agreement is unnecessary, and, of course, many agreements do not make any reference to managerial rights. This practice of omission is often based on the belief that the employer retains all rights of management that are not relinquished, modified, or eliminated by the contract. Thus, in the absence of collective bargaining, according to this view, the employer has the power to make any decision in the area of labor relations that he desires (subject to considerations of law, the marketplace, and so on). This right is based on the simple fact that the employer is the owner of the business. For example, the employer's right to promote, demote, lay off, make overtime assignments, and rehire may be limited by the seniority provisions of the collective bargaining contract. Or the contract may stipulate that layoffs be based on a certain formula. However, to the extent that such a formula does not limit the right of the employer to lay off, it follows that management may exercise this function on a unilateral basis. (*Cases 7 and 8 deal with management rights.*)

This concept of management prerogatives is sometimes called the "residual theory" of management rights. That is, all rights reside in management except those that are limited by the labor agreement or conditioned by a past practice. Where a management embraces the residual theory, it most commonly takes a stiff attitude at the bargaining table relative to union demands that would tend to further limit rights of management. With more elements of an "Armed Truce" than an "Accommodation" philosophy, it views the collective bargaining process as a tug of war between the management and the union—management resisting further invasions by the union into the citadel of management rights, which are to be protected at all costs as a matter of principle.

Such employers are not particularly concerned with the merits of a union demand; *any* demand that would impose additional limitations on management must be resisted. For example, such a management, regardless of the merits of a particular claim, would typically resist the incorporation of working rules into the labor agreement—rules dealing with such topics as payment to employees for work not actually performed, limitations on technological change or other innovations in the operation of the business, the amount of production an employee must turn out to hold a job, and how many workers are required to perform a job. One can also safely predict that a residualist management would strongly resist any demand that would limit its right to move an operation from one plant to another, shut down one plant of a multiple-plant operation, subcontract work, or compel employees to work overtime. In addition, such a management would quite probably try aggressively, when the occasion seemed appropriate, to regain "rights" that it had previously relinquished.

Indeed, today many employers are striving to reclaim the right to make unilateral determinations of working rules. Many recent strikes in a host of industries as diverse as the airlines, petroleum, and printing and publishing have been waged because managements desired to erase from the bargaining relationship working rules to which they had agreed in previous years. It is understandable why labor organizations resist these attempts of management: With the elimination of working rules, employees could more easily be laid off, for example. Since new technology and changing market demands constitute in many relationships constant threats to job security, it is no mystery why some unions would rather strike than concede on this point.

The opposing view of the theory of residual rights is based on the idea that management has responsibilities other than to the maximization of managerial authority. It proceeds from the proposition that management is the "trustee" of the interest of employees, the union, and the society, as well as of the interests of the business, the stockholders, and the management hierarchy. Under the "trusteeship theory," a management would invariably be willing to discuss and negotiate a union demand on the merits of the case rather than reject it out of hand because it would impose additional limitations on organizational operations. Such an employer would not necessarily agree to additional limitations but would be completely amenable to discussing, consulting, and ultimately negotiating with the union on any demand that the latter might bring up at a collective bargaining session. Exhibiting an attitude of "Cooperation," the trusteeship management does not take the position that the line separating management rights from that of negotiable issues is fixed and not subject to change. Rather, it attempts to balance the rights of all concerned with the goal of arriving at a solution that would be most mutually satisfactory. As such, the "trusteeship" and "residual" theories are poles apart in terms of management's attitude at the bargaining table and even in the day-to-day relationship between the employer and the union.

There is no "divine right" concept of management in the trusteeship theory, a statement that cannot be made for the residualist camp. No better summary of the differences between the two theories on this score has ever been made than that offered many years ago by the then–general counsel of the United Steelworkers of America:

> Too many spokesmen for management assume that labor's rights are not steeped in past practice or tradition but are limited strictly to those specified in a contract; while management's rights are all-inclusive except as specifically taken away by a specific clause in a labor agreement. Labor always had many inherent rights, such as the right to strike; the right to organize despite interference from management, police powers, and even courts; the right to a fair share of the company's income even though this right was often denied; the right to safe, healthful working conditions with adequate opportunity for rest. Collective bargaining does not establish some hitherto nonexisting rights; it provides the power to enforce rights of labor which the labor movement was dedicated to long before the institution of arbitration had become so widely practiced in labor relations.[8]

It is impossible to determine how many employers follow the residual theory of management rights and how many follow the trusteeship theory.

Cross-currents are clearly at work: the previously mentioned management attempt to regain work-rule flexibility, and the equally visible trend to more employee-centered management that was described in Chapter 1. The relative infrequency of "Cooperation" philosophies would, however, indicate that trusteeship managements remain in the distinct minority. Moreover, there is no universal truth as to which would be a better policy for management to follow, or whether some compromise between the two might form the optimum arrangement. The answer to this problem must be determined by each employer in the light of the particular labor relations environment.

"CODETERMINATION" AND UNIONS IN THE BOARD ROOM

The concept of workers *directly* playing a major role in corporate decision making by means of board of director membership, or "codetermination" as it is generally called, has never taken root in the United States. At least to date, American labor leadership has preferred to oppose rather than to join in any kind of partnership with management, and the official AFL-CIO position has been one of not desiring "to blur in any way the distinctions between the respective roles of management and labor in the plant."[9] Managers act; unions react.

Yet in other countries codetermination has become a reality, most notably in Germany where in 1946 the occupying British administrators in the Ruhr Valley introduced the idea to the West German steel industry as something of a compromise between nationalization and free enterprise. It was extended to the coal industry in that country in 1951 and—in the face of concerted union pressure magnified by the threat of a general strike—to larger companies in all German industries one year later.

Even in Germany employees have not received literal codetermination powers in the typical situation. Only in steel and coal, the original frontiers, have stockholders and workers controlled an identical number of directors; in all other sectors workers were legally allowed only a one-third representation on corporate boards until 1976, and they still, under a complicated formula, lack fully equal representation in practice. But after almost five decades even executives in Germany seem to be wholly adjusted to the concept. They are, indeed, cooperating—as are their unions—in helping other European countries (Sweden and Denmark most notably) experiment with it, being in the main convinced that Germany's economic prosperity and generally peaceful labor relations owe something to the idea.

Why codetermination has nonetheless been as welcome to United States business managers as a drunkard at an Alcoholics Anonymous meeting, and not of much interest to American unionists either, can undoubtedly be explained along several lines. As Koch and Fox have written, "In Western Europe..., community attachments have traditionally been much stronger, and upward mobility has been more constrained than in the U.S. Together, these forces have increased the impetus for workers to pursue more actively (as compared to the U.S. situation) a better lot in their present work-place."[10] As earlier chapters in this book have outlined, the values of private enterprise, property rights, and individualism have been developed here to a degree absolutely unknown in other lands: Against this backdrop, codetermination seems dangerously socialistic. Nor can the aforemen-tioned general resistance of U.S. employers throughout labor history to unionizing efforts be completely overlooked as an explanation, either: "In a real sense," Kassalow has declared, "a conflict situation is the midwife of almost all new American unions."[11] On such adversary initial relationships are adversary later relationships often built.

Yet even in the United States the situation may finally be changing. In May 1980, the Chrysler Corporation gave the then–UAW president Douglas A. Fraser one of the eighteen seats on its board of directors. And the impressive performance that he registered in the several years following this milestone, the first instance of a major American corporation electing a union leader to such a position, had led at least some observers to predict that the future would see more such union directors.

Chrysler had not offered Fraser, despite his universal reputation as a man of considerable intellect and unimpeachable character, this seat with any notable enthusiasm. It had done so quite reluctantly, in fact, as part of the price that it had to pay to win economic concessions vital to its survival from the UAW. And even within Chrysler's managerial hierarchy itself, many people had undoubtedly shared the sentiments of General Motors Chairman Thomas A. Murphy that the move would make "as much sense as having a member of GM's management sitting on the board of an international union."[12] Nor did Fraser's acceptance of the directorship, his considerable popularity within the union notwithstanding, occur without a good deal of negative comment from his own constituents: The word "sell-out" received particularly frequent mention from the UAW rank and file. Some other critics—among them, law professors—feared that a conflict of interest on Fraser's part was unavoidable, since the interests of the share-holders and those of the union would inevitably operate, at times, in opposing directions.

Within months of the UAW leader's advent to the board, however, all of these sentiments appeared to have been groundless. Chrysler itself could muster nothing but praise for Fraser's contributions, especially his ability to ask pointed, well-informed questions: "He has," corporation Chairman Lee Iacocca could assert, "stimulated our board to think."[13] Another com-pany insider declared that "Doug [can] speak with credibility to the workers because, as a director, he [has] seen the detailed financial data."[14] And there was general agreement among all who saw Fraser in action that the UAW leader, who temporarily suspended his participation in the board meetings when UAW members in Canada struck Chrysler in late 1982, had been flawless in avoiding not only any conflict of interest but even the appearance of such conflict.

By his own admission, Fraser's chief objective in accepting the board seat had been to incorporate worker thinking into managerial decision making. ("I can't represent my members if I'm always reacting to management decisions," he had said, "...we can bring an important resource to the board. People in the plants will tell me things they won't tell management").[15] When he retired four years later, to be succeeded on the board by his successor as UAW president—Owen W. Bieber—his board tenure as judged by this standard had clearly been a successful one. Iacocca had in fact come to have so much respect for Fraser that despite the latter's retirement from the union, the Chrysler chief executive reportedly tried, without success, to keep him on as a director instead of Bieber.

And to some extent, the favorable precedent set by Fraser had generated interest in duplicating such union participation elsewhere. By the time of this writing the now-defunct Pan American World Airways and Eastern Airlines (where, as noted earlier, not one but four board of director seats were filled by union nominees), Western Airlines, Weirton Steel, Rath Packing, and Hyatt Clark had followed Chrysler's lead in electing union-proposed directors. So, too, had a variety of smaller trucking, steel, and food industry employers. Companies in other industries—rubber and communications, most notably—were seriously studying the board membership idea and appeared on the verge of implementing it. Most of these companies had, moreover, also accompanied their bestowal of board membership with a transfer of stock ownership into bargaining unit member hands (discussed in the next section).

But most American companies, nonetheless, remain adamantly opposed to such union activities. "The pure and simple notion of opening the books and being a member of the board is a cure for which there is no known illness," one not atypical company negotiator has said.[16] And many managers also continue to advance the argument, presumably in all sincerity, that having a unionist on the board would expose the corporation to lawsuits for conflict of interest, Fraser's performance notwithstanding. Moreover, it is not irrelevant that virtually every employer that has granted unions the greater privileges has been, as Chrysler, confronted with significant financial problems at the time of the offering and has sought some kind of union pay concession in return. Nor does any reputable authority in the field see anything that remotely resembles full German-style codetermination in the United States as being closer than several million light-years away.

Nor, ironically, does a union leader now sit on Chrysler's board. In 1991, the automobile company cut its number of directors from eighteen to thirteen by not renominating Bieber and four others. The company defended its move as part of its then–current $3 billion cost-cutting campaign, although detached observers (who realized that the most that would be saved in annual directors' fees and expenses was a relatively modest $150,000) thought that the action was an unnecessarily gratuitous insult to a unionist who simply hadn't measured up to the high Fraser standard.

But for the first time, some thoughtful students of the subject were starting to believe that the concept of unionists in the board room would spread. Past Industrial Relations Research Association president Douglas A. Soutar, a managerial industrial relations careerist, had declared that it is likely to be the "in" thing for the future. Under union pressure, some companies might think it is a forward-looking thing to do in terms of broadening corporate accountability and responsibility in the same way they did when they put women and blacks on boards. I myself can see some situations where it could be a good thing, particularly for corporations that are in trouble. I do not have a knee-jerk reaction against it, though if I advocated it now in my own company I'd get thrown out the 37th floor window.[17]

And former Federal Reserve Board chairman Arthur F. Burns, a conservative economist and a man never accused of harboring prounion sentiments, went even further. He applauded the trend and both felt and hoped that it would continue to spread. "We want to educate some of these labor leaders," he said. "I work on the theory that, by sitting in on board meetings and studying the company's affairs, they will learn something about the company's needs and problems and especially its need for profits."[18]

It seems safe to say, under any conditions, that whether or not the Fraser precedent ever becomes a normal part of American corporate governance, the topic can never again really be ignored.

EMPLOYEE STOCK OWNERSHIP PLANS

Employee Stock Ownership Plans, or ESOPs, have, as Exhibits 9-2 and 9-3 illustrate, their share of enthusiastic supporters. Such supporters did not, however, until very recent years, include union leaders. Up until the mid-1970s, organized labor was generally against the concept; but by the 1990s many unions were actively participating in ESOPs.

Labor's historical antagonism to employee ownership tended to be based on two considerations.

First, many past plans—most notably in the paternalistic era of the 1920s—had a definitely antilabor purpose. If the worker could be given more reason to identify with the management, it was reasoned by plan advocates, there would be less need to identify with management's bargaining table adversary.

Second, labor was—and is—well aware that a major decline in the price of the company stock would carry with it obvious penalties for the participating employee. Such major declines did, of course, occur on a wholesale basis in the 1930s (as did, even worse, bankruptcies) and presumably could be expected to occur again. Post-Depression employee stock ownership plans were therefore in union eyes something like lexicographer Samuel Johnson's description of a second marriage, the triumph of hope over experience.

Such misgivings continue to be nursed by unions. But increasingly since the mid-1970s they have been outweighed, at least for many labor leaders, by another consideration: Many hard-pressed employers have simply been unwilling to allow further increases in fixed payroll expenses and have

EXHIBIT 9–2

E·S·O·P

Buyout secures workers' jobs

CANTON, OHIO

When USWA members formed an ESOP to buy Republic Storage Systems Co., they weren't trying to stave off a threatened shutdown. Republic Storage, which had been acquired by LTV in its 1984 merger with Republic Steel, was a steady money-maker and one of the nation's leading manufacturers of lockers and steel shelving.

But when LTV put the unit up for sale, its 400 USWA workers, led by Local 2345 President Lou Chastain, decided to seize the opportunity to buy the plant themselves. The attempt succeeded, and on June 18, Republic Storage workers and managers celebrated their second anniversary as owners of their company.

It wasn't easy. Republic Storage was a hot property, and seven other companies wanted to buy it. Chastain knew what might happen if somebody else took over; possible transfers of the plant's work, layoffs and eventually, shutdowns.

"Our jobs were on the line," Chastain says. "If somebody else was going to buy the plant, why not us?"

Walt Conley, president of Local 5537, representing office and technical workers, agreed.

Chastain consulted with USWA members at Republic Container Corp. in Nitro, W. Va., who were mounting an ESOP buyout of their plant from LTV, and was encouraged by what

he heard. District 27 Director Joe Coyle backed the project. The City of Canton put up $55,000 for a feasibility study and $10,000 for legal fees.

To fund the buyout, PruCapital of Cincinnati, a subsidiary of Prudential Insurance Co., offered a $17 million loan, plus a revolving credit line to make up the balance of the purchase price, estimated at $22-24 million.

As is customary in such ESOP buyouts, the employees took wage cuts in exchange for company stock, to be distributed to the ESOP as the $17 million loan is paid off. In a three-year contract that took effect the same date as the ESOP—June 17, 1986—the workers gave up $1.75 per hour and now take home about $10.23 per hour.

In its first two years, Republic Storage has been breaking even, while paying off its debts on schedule. So far more than $3.8 million of the $17 million loan has been repaid, and more than 22 percent of the company's stock has been released to the ESOP. If all goes well, the seven-year loan will be paid off in another five years, and all of the company's 500,000 shares will be held by the ESOP in trust for each employee, both union and non-union.

Meanwhile, the company is guided by a seven-member board of directors: two from the union—including

Union presidents Lou Chastain (LU 2345) and Walt Conley (LU 5537) like ESOP's prospects.

Chastain—two from management, and three outside directors representing PruCapital.

The board has handled some sticky issues, such as the decision whether to grant performance bonuses to top managers. Chastain, although leery of such a deal, voted for it to be sure of keeping the managers from leaving. Now, he says, he is working to get similar bonuses for all workers.

The key manager is President and CEO Lowell Marshall, formerly senior vice president of LTV's manufacturing group.

Marshall says that as the ESOP was being put together, he had to fire several managers who wouldn't join the labor-management team. "They were against any participatory group in which labor had any input. That's the way the old steel industry operated.

"As we grow as an ESOP, people will see this all revolves around trust," Marshall adds. "If we don't trust each other it won't work."

Chastain also concedes the ESOP has not wiped out all problems or disputes between the union and management. But, he says, "we've got more say now than we ever did."

"We'd do it over and over," Chastain says. "Our future is in our hands. We wouldn't want it in anybody else's."

ESOP members Larry Gabrys (left) and Kelly Snyder inspect locker doors.

Donald Hiddleson, a Local 2345 steward, checks shelving units.

Source: Steelabor, October 1985, back cover.

EXHIBIT 9–3

Raymond Fields: He is an "owner-worker," along with 55 others.

Cletus Price: Local 5712 member now has an ownership in the company.

Gayla Tincher: "This can be an investment in the future."

Oran Booth: He sees "a bright future" for the worker-owned plant.

In Nitro, USWA members are owners

NITRO, W. VA.

Six months ago, Local 5712 President Mike Cable was worried about his job and the jobs of 55 co-workers at Republic Container Co. Today, he is a member of the company's Board of Directors, and the steel drum-producing plant appears to have a bright future.

That's because he and his local union members own the company along with 10 salary and supervisory employes. What is significant is that they are purchasing the plant without investing a dime of their own money or mortgaging personal assets. Also significant is that the USWA is retained as the bargaining agent.

When Cable learned that the plant, profitable during its 27 years of existence, was up for sale by LTV Corp., he moved quickly to head a Buy-Out Association which successfully purchased the plant by forming an ESOP—Employe Stock Ownership Plan.

"It was hard work but we made it with the cooperation of many," Cable says proudly. "We're elated and relieved for our people. Our jobs and status as union members are secure." Cooperation came from all levels of government: West Virginia Senators Robert Byrd and Jay Rockefeller, from the state and community, especially the banking community. "And we feel that, had it not been for the international, we wouldn't have been in a position to buy the plant," Cable said.

A chain of letters and phone calls resulted in then-Governor Rockefeller obtaining an initial grant of $30,000 to hire a consultant and do a feasibility study. The grant does not have to be repaid.

Similarly, a $61,000 grant to pay lawyers' fees came from Kanawha County. "The study was favorable," Mike Cable reports. "We held a series of membership meetings because our bid had to include wage adjustments of about $1.25 per hour and some minor benefits cuts which totaled $1.89 per hour. The decision to go ahead was unanimous."

Next came the funding. Loans were secured from the Bank of Nitro ($600,000) and National Bank of Commerce ($900,000) at 90 percent of prime, and the State Economic Development Agency ($500,000) at four percent interest. "This plant has always been profitable," Cable emphasizes. "It's clean, modern and staffed by efficient workers and supervisors who care."

A five-year agreement was signed on Sept. 1 which provides for wage increases during each of the years. Ironically, Mike Cable and Local 5712 Vice President Larry Hill, who is also on the Board of Directors, wore two hats—as union negotiators and managers who did the negotiating. All holidays, vacations, SUB benefits and the pension plan remain intact. In addition, the board can review benefits and wages, grant bonuses and increase benefits. The real bonus is that the ESOP gives each member (employe) a trust fund which can pay as much as 25 percent of total wages for that year. This trust is collectible upon retirement or termination of employment, and payable to heirs in case of death. Hourly wages currently range from $9.20 to $11.60.

Did Larry Hill change upon becoming a member of the Board of Directors? "Hell no," he responded quickly. "I don't feel any different. We're the same workers, the same crew, only with more responsibility." Repairman Ray Fields, who was there when the plant started, proclaims, "The ESOP is the best thing that could happen. We were going to be sold and probably offered half our wages and might have lost the union. Now we own the plant and offer a union-made, American-made, quality product." □

Board of Directors meets to review financial status. From left are Local 5712 Vice President Larry Hill, Local President Mike Cable and Plant Manager Wayne Grimm.

Source: Steelabor, July 1988, p. 11.

refused to consider anything but compensation that is tied to the firm's economic performance. Labor has, in short, embraced ESOPs because it has had little choice.

Board representation—costless to the employer economically, if not philosophically—has usually been accompanied by such stock ownership. And, in fact, most companies cited in the previous section have, as noted, granted both. Employees currently own 15 percent of the stock at Chrysler, 32 percent at Western, and 50 percent at Rath. At Weirton Steel, they own literally all of the company, the 8,000 workers there having been forced in 1984 by Weirton's then-parent National Steel either to buy it or let it die a natural death. ("We had to buy the mill. It was either that or nothing," in the words of one mill worker.)[19] Employees also own all of Avis, having bought that company in late 1987 for $1.75 billion, and if the 12,500 Avis payroll members act as though they own the place, it is because there, too, they do and, through their representatives, have a significant say in how the firm is run.

But board representation is hardly an inseparable part of an ESOP, and many more unionized employers—in steel, autos, rubber, glass, trucking, the airlines, and food—have granted only the latter than have given both kinds of concession to their unions. As of 1991, overall, some 27 percent or the Fortune 500 companies had at least 4 percent of their shares in the hands of their employees.[20]

Actually, many employers have seen a variety of advantages for themselves in the ESOP beyond the reduction of wage pressures and often have needed very little if any prodding before installing it. Under the Employee Retirement Income Security Act (ERISA) of 1974 and the 1975 enactment of a further congressional sweetener, significant tax benefits are allowed employers who implement ESOPs. And the plans can help capital-intensive companies raise vast amounts of money cheaply: Even if the provisions of the ESOP let workers buy their shares at some kind of discount, a not uncommon situation, the monies involved are still usually far less than managements would have to pay a bank or, in the case of floating debt issues, less than the underwriting costs. Moreover, as the median age of employees rises markedly, the cost of pension plans is bound to climb and ESOPs become a relatively more desirable way for organizations to help their employees develop some kind of supplemental savings plan.

In an era of corporate takeovers, ESOPs can also both finance takeover attempts and frustrate them, depending upon which goal is embraced: Investors trying to take over can decrease their costs of borrowing if part of the stock is reserved for employees; but raiders can also be thwarted by using the ESOP device to put a portion of the company into presumably friendly hands. Nor can management's long-held belief that when workers have an ownership interest they may well have an incentive to put forth extra effort be ignored in explaining why companies have warmed to the ESOP concept. Unionized employees—as well as nonunion workers—have not necessarily had their stock forced upon them, but unions that have indicated a willingness to accept an ESOP in lieu of a wage improvement have generally found a ready audience on the other side of the bargaining table. A good deal of the notable growth in ESOPs since 1975—from a

mere 200 plans then to over 10,000 now, with the over 10 million participating workers typically owning from 15 to 35 percent of the company's
stock—has been due to the concessionary bargaining of unions in this area
and management's favorable response as far as employee stock ownership
has been concerned.

As in the case of union board membership, fears of a potential conflict of
interest have accompanied the growth of labor-management ESOPs. "Some
observers and many international labor officials worry," as one expert has
pointed out, "that worker [representatives] may be co-opted, getting caught
up in the predominant interest to make company profits rather than fight
for individual worker rights."[21] He sees, with or without board representation, "a dangerous potential for stock ownership...to lead to a type of
in-house unionism, in which there is the appearance of a...battle, when in
reality, labor representatives are simply going through the motions of
conflict for political reasons."[22]

Against this consideration, however, can be stacked the very real fact
that the new arrangement has already shown that it can improve the
level of corporate efficiency. At one leading airline, for example, within
a year of the ESOP's implementation, the productivity of that carrier's
mechanics was increasing at an annual rate of 5 percent. ("There is a
tremendous dynamic for employees to run a better company and provide
the best service," the union president involved here commented with
obvious pride, "because they're owners now.")[23] Similar performances
have been registered in parts of the steel, trucking, and food industries.
And among the companies fully owned by workers, Weirton Steel is today
amidst a highly cooperative labor-management relationship one of the
nation's most profitable steelmakers, while Avis seems to be trying even
harder with its ESOP to overtake first-place Hertz in market share and
lately has recorded considerably higher profit-sales ratios than its arch-
competitor.

On the other hand, major worker ownership has yet to rescue Rath,
which continues to have as many financial problems as ever, or a host
of other poverty-stricken ESOP workplaces. New Jersey's Hyatt Clark
Industries, a ball-bearing maker that *its* workers bought from General
Motors in 1981 in another example of buy-or-die, died six years later, its
widely heralded ESOP notwithstanding. Nor at the time of this writing
did workers at the large brokerage firm Thomson McKinnon (where 77
percent of the shares are owned through ESOPs), retailer Carter Hawley
Hale (about 45 percent employee-owned), or Burlington Industries (49
percent until a controversial public offering by the North Carolina company diluted this employee portion to 3 percent in 1992) have much
optimism that their barely solvent firms would ultimately return to them
any of the nonfunded, uninsured ESOP monies on which they had once
counted for their retirements.

Again, as in the case of unions-in-the-boardroom, it could be said with
certainty only that the ESOP even in its infancy as a labor relations topic
was something that the parties could never again entirely overlook.

QUALITY OF WORK LIFE PROGRAMS

Still something else that may be changing in labor-management relationships is the historic unwillingness of both parties to allow joint worker and management problem solving of workplace problems. An increasing number of unions, either on their own initiative or on the employer's, have become involved in so-called "quality of work life" activities, denoting a movement whose title has no fully acceptable simple definition but basically connotes direct participation by workers in day-to-day decision making on the job.[24] Most often, employees get a voice in work scheduling, quality control, compensation, a determination of the job environment itself, and/or other significant working factors, and the goal is a twofold one: increased productivity and improved union-management relations.

It is impossible to know how many organizations currently have such programs, since not only is there no formalized record keeping but many "QWL" programs go by some other name—"employee involvement," "jointness," or "worker participation," for example. The list of unionized users even now, a mere fifteen years after the first major implementation, is nonetheless impressive. All of the nation's automobile manufacturers have a QWL program, most notably General Motors, which has one in each of sixty-six plants, and Ford, where thousands of worker-management teams at eighty-six of that company's ninety-one locations meet every week to attack production and quality problems; Westinghouse has worker-management "quality circles," small groups that meet regularly to discuss product quality improvement, in fifty facilities (sixty-three such groups are in its Baltimore defense complex alone); the major steelmakers have a variety of "labor-management participation committees"; and the entire Bell System is experimenting with QWL principles. Programs have also been installed in coal mining and retail food.

General Electric, which for years resisted the concept, rapidly implemented it in the last years of the 1980s and an estimated 35 percent of the unionized GE workforce was included in QWL arrangements by 1993. The list of unionized employers with QWL efforts very much in place now also includes, among literally hundreds of others, Boeing, Caterpillar, the U.S. Postal Service, the Philadelphia Zoo, and the New York City Sanitation Department.

Many nonunion organizations have had such worker involvement efforts for years, often with the thought that such projects might help preserve nonunion status by improving employee morale. But unions have almost unanimously opposed the idea, partly because of fear that membership loyalty to the labor organization might be weakened by closer exposure to management and partly because of a suspicion (often fully justified) that the concept (as in the case of ESOPs) constituted a direct effort on the employer's part to pave the way for ultimate nonunion status. ("You've got to put up or shut up," one union chief executive told a group of major industrial leaders a while ago on this subject. "You can't ask unions to walk hand in hand into the unknown land of worker participation while going

EXHIBIT 9–4

'COOPERATE OR ELSE'
How To Avoid Management Traps

It goes by many names—"worker participation," "labor-management cooperation," "quality of work life circles"—but no matter what it's called, UMWA members should proceed with caution if your employer tries to implement one of these programs.

If your company tries to implement, or approaches your local union about negotiating, a so-called cooperative agreement you should *immediately* contact your UMWA regional director. The four UMWA regional directors have been trained to distinguish legitimate efforts to improve labor-management relations from attempts to circumvent the union structure.

✔ **Watch out** if management attempts to impose a "cooperative" program without first negotiating with the union. It's not cooperation when when one side has no say-so in the formulation or implementation of the program.

✔ **Watch out** if management attempts to cut the union out of the process by using a cooperative program to subvert or go around contractual provisions. "Cooperative" efforts which require workers to go without things like job classifications and seniority rights undercut the reason our union fights for a contract in the first place.

✔ **Watch out** if the company attempts to get the union leadership to endorse questionable business decisions. If those decisions later turn out to be bad, management can then blame the union.

✔ **Watch out** if management's only goal seems to be to increase production. A truly cooperative effort means that *both* sides get something they want: if the union helps management increase production or meet other company goals, then the company should give the workers, through the union, more control over the day-to-day conditions that affect the quality of workers' time on the job.

No two cooperative programs are alike, but those that are in the best interest of the union and the company, such as the union's EESP agreement with Island Creek Coal Co.*, share several characteristics:

● Top-level management must be involved. Otherwise, middle and lower management, down to the mine level, may make agreements with the union that the ultimate decision makers in upper management can later abandon, claiming "miscommunication" with lower-level managers.

● The company must recognize the union leadership as the representative of the workers. "Cooperative" efforts that minimize the role of local

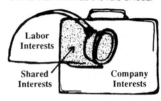

union leadership are usually nothing more than elaborate union-busting techniques designed to get workers to believe they don't need a union to solve problems on the job.

● The union leadership must have a co-equal role in formulating and implementing the program. Cooperation is a two-way street, and any program that allows management to independently decide and change the rules is not about cooperation.

● Both parties must be committed to making the program work. Efforts continually plagued by "miscommunications" and "misunderstandings" between upper management (the policy makers) and middle and lower management (the implementers) or by agreements between upper-level management and the union that somehow never get implemented may be signals that the company is not serious about making the program work.

● There should be regular progress meetings to evaluate the program and a mechanism to deter management from ignoring the parts of the program that benefit workers or from unilaterally ending the program.

* **Note:** A future issue of the *Journal* will examine the Employment and Economic Security Pact (EESP) begun by the UMWA and the Island Creek Coal Co. in 1987

Source: United Mine Workers Journal, July 1990, p. 6.

EXHIBIT 9–5

Source: United Mine Workers Journal, July 1990, p. 7.

full speed ahead with union-bashing antilabor programs. There has to be a greater acceptance of unions in this country. I want very much to cooperate in consensus-building and problem-solving, but management can't expect cooperation when the hand it puts around my shoulder has a knife in it.")[25] Many unions still take a dim view of worker participation. (Exhibits 9-4 and 9-5, illustratively, constitute something less than a resounding endorsement on the part of the United Mine Workers.)

Why, then, the new collaboration? One reason has certainly been the same factor that has generated offers of board membership and ESOPs to unionists: economic adversity. Most, if not all, of the unionized organizations have suffered financial hardship and jobs have definitely been at stake. According to one scholar in the field, employees recognize that if they can improve quality and productivity, "they'll be more competitive, they'll increase their company's share of the market, and, in the final analysis, they'll keep their jobs."[26] Another reason for the collaboration seems to be an increasing awareness on the part of unions (and managements) of a trend toward a dehumanization of work in many situations: Kahil Gibran may have called work "love made visible" and the Benedictines may say that "to work is to pray," but most people have always been less than enthusiastic about their own jobs and in recent years the level of discontent amid new technology and an ever-lessened worker control over the working environment appear to have grown appreciably. Many unions have been willing to explore new solutions in the face of this development.

A QWL landmark of sorts was reached in late 1990 when the world's largest industrial company, General Motors, opened a new $5 billion automobile plant 35 miles south of Nashville in the town of Spring Hill, Tennessee. Designed to produce an entirely new small car, Saturn, in GM's first new car-making division since the company acquired Chevrolet in 1918, the facility was conceived with the idea of enlisting the United Automobile Workers as a virtually equal partner with management and in so doing to narrow the existing $2,000-per-car cost advantage enjoyed by the Japanese on their smaller cars. Over the previous decade, this advantage had been a major factor in decreasing GM's share of the U.S. market from 46 percent to a frightening 32 percent.

Spring Hill opened with UAW representatives on all planning and operating committees from the shop floor to the top management of this wholly owned GM subsidiary. The unionists have been granted a major role in these committees, which make decisions on such matters as deciding on the suppliers of parts and equipment as well as on more orthodox labor-management issues. And the workers can in fact block a potential decision, although not indefinitely ("In the event an alternative solution is not found," in the words of the GM-UAW agreement at Saturn, "the blocking party must reevaluate [its] position in the context of the philosophy and mission").

In addition, all 4,500 Saturn production employees have been assigned to work teams of six to fifteen UAW members and permitted to make all of their decisions—including work and vacation scheduling and the controlling of variable costs—without the presence of any supervisor in an attempt to substitute peer pressure and work pride for the traditional management methods that in recent years have seemed not to serve GM so well. Teams of workers are even charged with doing the hiring in an attempt to ensure that only those who can accept the new autonomy on a day-to-day basis will be included in the new arrangement. All workers get virtually total protection against layoffs and annual salaries instead of hourly pay.

As the dean of MIT's Sloan School of Management said in examining all of this,

> If Saturn is successful it will prove that it's possible to junk the old bureaucracies, change the corporate culture, change the adversarial relationship between union and management, and put it all back together right. If they succeed, it will be a big positive for America. If not, it will be a huge downer.[27]

The Saturn venture got off to a slow start. Bugs in the form of faulty seat backs that could flip over without warning and bad engine coolants forced the management to back off from its initial daily production goal of 900 cars to a more realistic 700. And another key innovation at Spring Hill—the tying of 20 percent of pay to the achievement of the original productivity and quality goals and the payment of a bonus if these objectives were exceeded—was accordingly, at the union's request, delayed. But even amid the inauspicious beginning, great expectations on the part of both labor and management continued, and the parties indeed pointed to the mutually agreed-upon pay basis adjustment as an example of teamwork and good-will.

Such ambitious QWL programs as Saturn's notwithstanding, the possibility that the growth of QWL may also reflect—even primarily—nothing more than a fad cannot be dismissed, however. As the respected president emeritus of the Communications Workers has pointed out, "packaged, narrowed participation programs [have been] the hottest selling item in the management consulting field"[28] over the past few years, and it is reasonable to expect that if no satisfactory rewards for both managements and unions can be attributed to QWL, the latter's tenure on the collective bargaining landscape may be short-lived. To date, even amid economic hard times that cannot be expected to continue indefinitely, the returns in many workplaces have not been particularly impressive, indeed, in terms of documented major improvements in either morale or productivity. And it must be recognized again (as it was in Chapter 1) that the United States has never been a particularly fruitful territory for the genuine union-management cooperation that QWL obviously requires if it hopes to survive.

John F. Kennedy frequently declared to proud parents who presented him with their new baby for what was at least for them a memorable moment, "It looks like a nice baby. We'll know more later." The same statement can perhaps be made on behalf of quality of work life programs.

CONCLUSIONS

If unions and management are viewed as institutions, as distinct from the individuals whom they represent, the issues considered in this chapter take on special meaning. Institutions can survive long after individuals have perished, and in a real sense the problems of union security, union obligations, and management rights are related to the *survival* of the bargaining institutions. Union security measures preserve the union per se (although in so doing they may also allow it to do a better job for the members of the organization). Similarly, to survive and function as an effective institution, management must be concerned with its prerogatives to operate the business efficiently. It must also be concerned with union obligations as these might affect its continued effectiveness.

In principle, therefore, the devices of collective bargaining that feed the institutional needs of the union and the firm are cut from the same cloth. They are designed to assure the long-run interests of the two organizations. The objectives of labor unions and companies are quite different, but to carry out their respective functions both need security of operation. Business operates to make a profit and thus must be defended against encroachments of organized labor that might unreasonably interfere with its efficiency as a dynamic organization in the society. Its insistence upon management prerogatives stands as a bulwark of defense in this objective.

But unions also justify themselves as institutions on the American scene in their attempting to protect and advance the welfare of their members, and union security arrangements are an important avenue toward the realization of this objective. Although there may be philosophical objections to compulsory union membership, there cannot be any question that union security arrangements serve the long-run survival needs of organized labor.

If we view in retrospect the labor relations environment over the years, the conclusion appears irrefutable that business and unions have been relatively successful in reconciling these fundamental objectives, however much the verbal controversies continue to rage (and however foreign to both of their philosophies the idea of full "codetermination" may be). Businesses that have engaged in collective bargaining relationships have by and large not only been able to survive but have often flourished. Many of the most influential and prosperous firms in this country (the automobile companies and the airlines, at least in normal years, come immediately to mind) have, as we know, been highly unionized for years. Likewise, organized labor not only has survived but has grown appreciably in strength over time, the contemporary unexciting performance of union membership totals being accountable chiefly by causes other than management destruction. Although the objectives of the two institutions are quite different, and although occasional major impasses are reached by unions and managements in their bargaining on these issues, sufficient protection for both organizations has been provided in the vast majority of unionized industry.

DISCUSSION QUESTIONS

1. Arguing in favor of right-to-work laws, a publication of the National Association of Manufacturers has expressed the view that "no argument for compulsory unionism—however persuasive—can possibly justify invasion of the right of individual choice." Do you agree or disagree? Why?

2. "From the viewpoint of providing maximum justice to all concerned, the agency shop constitutes the optimum union security arrangement." To what extent, if any, do you agree with this statement?

3. "Good unions don't need compulsory unionism. Bad unions don't deserve compulsory unionism." Comment.

4. Evaluate the opinion of a former Steelworker Union president that "nothing could be worse than to have...management appease the union, and nothing could be worse than to have the union appease management," relating these remarks to the areas of management rights and union security.

MINICASES

#1 A Question of Freedom

"I can see arguments both for and against right-to-work laws," says a fellow student in your class. "But there is one overriding reason why I'm on balance against these laws. And it involves the question of freedom".

"Specifically, it relates to freedom of contract, a basic and critical right in this land of free enterprise and individualism in which we live. A union shop can only come about in one way: The union—for whatever reason—has asked for such an arrangement in its collective bargaining with the management, and the management—again, on whatever it considers to be good grounds—has agreed to grant the union shop. This being the case, what right does the government have to intrude and tell the two parties, 'That's too bad—you still can't have it'"?

How would you respond?

#2 An Original Proposal

MEMORANDUM TO: John T. Kelly, Chairman of the Board, Fenwick Chemical Corporation

FROM: Joyce M. Walters, Senior Vice President for Labor Relations

SUBJECT: Proposed Appointment of Four Union Leaders to Fenwick Board of Directors

I'm not saying that it would solve all our problems, but I'd like to know what we'd lose by giving four of the twenty seats on our board of directors to officer nominees of the Chemical Workers Union.

By my calculations, we're talking about only one-fifth of the board membership, so there's no way that board decisions could actually result even if all four union people were united on something. And since the union has been yelling for years for just one seat, imagine how pleased it would be with four. We'd save a bundle in the wages and benefits that the Chemical Workers wouldn't demand in the face of our magnanimity. Maybe one or two of the union people would make real contributions to board deliberations at least once in a while. And can you imagine a union voting to strike under these conditions?

I know that almost no U.S. company has even one such director, but with our currently depressed earnings and gloomy near-term financial outlook, we've got to do something. The race these days is won by those who are imaginative.

How much of a point, if any, does Ms. Walters have?

NOTES

[1]All statistics in this section are based on information furnished by the Bureau of Labor Statistics, U.S. Department of Labor.

[2]*Union Starch & Refining Co.,* 87 NLRB 779 (1949).

[3]The repeal measure passed the House by a twenty-vote margin, but a filibuster led by the late Sen. Everett M. Dirksen of Illinois prevented the bill from being formally considered by the Senate. AFL-CIO officials, nonetheless, claimed that as many as fifty-six Senate votes, or more than the majority needed, would have been forthcoming in favor of repeal had the measure been brought to a vote. In 1977, too, the AFL-CIO was optimistic (in the face of a newly-elected liberal Democratic Congress) that it could get repeal enacted; this time labor's efforts were tabled by both Houses.

[4]398 U.S. 235 (1970).

[5]*Metropolitan Edison Co.* v. *NLRB,* Case No. 81-1664, April 4, 1983.

[6]Section 301(e) states: "...For purposes of this section, in determining whether any person is acting as an 'agent' of another person as to make such other person responsible for his acts, the question of whether the specific acts performed were actually authorized or subsequently ratified shall not be controlling."

[7]*New York Times,* December 12, 1976, Sec. F, p. 13.

[8]"Management's Reserved Rights under Collective Bargaining," *Monthly Labor Review,* 79, No. 10 (October 1956), 1172.

[9]Thomas R. Donahue, "Collective Bargaining, Codetermination, and the Quality of Work," *World of Work Report,* 1 (August 1976), pp. 1–7.

[10]James L. Koch and Colin L. Fox, Jr., "A Proposed Model of Factors Influencing Worker Participation," in *Proceedings of the Thirtieth Annual Winter Meeting, Industrial Relations Research Association,* December 28–30, 1977, p. 389.

[11]Everett M. Kassalow, "Industrial Conflict and Consensus in the United States and Western Europe: A Comparative Analysis," *Proceedings of the Thirtieth Annual Winter Meeting,* p. 120.

[12]*Time,* May 19, 1980, p. 78.

[13]*Wall Street Journal,* March 12, 1981, p. 33.

[14]*Ibid.*

[15]*Business Week,* November 22, 1982, p. 30.

[16]*Ibid.,* February 1, 1982, p. 17.

[17]*New York Times,* April 27, 1980, Sec. 3, p. 14.

[18]*Ibid.*

[19]*Wall Street Journal,* September 17, 1985, p. 1.

[20]*Wall Street Journal,* January 25, 1991, p. C1.

[21]Warner Woodworth, "Promethean Industrial Relations: Labor, ESOPs, and the Boardroom," *Proceedings of the 1985 Spring Meeting, Industrial Relations Research Association,* April 18–19, 1985, p. 623.

[22]*Ibid.*

[23]*Business Week,* May 7, 1984, p. 151.

[24]Glenn Watts, former president of the Communications Workers of America, is one of many involved leaders who uses exactly this definition. See his thoughtful article, "QWL: CWA's Position," *QWL Review,* March 1983, pp. 12–14.

[25]A. H. Raskin, "Frustrated and Wary, Labor Marks Its Day," *New York Times,* September 5, 1982, Sec. F, p. 6.

[26]*Business Week,* June 30, 1980, p. 101.

[27]*Time,* October 29, 1990, p. 74.

[28]Watts, *op. cit.,* p. 12.

SELECTED REFERENCES

Barra, Ralph, *Putting Quality Circles to Work.* New York: McGraw-Hill, 1983.

Foulkes, Fred K., *Personnel Policies in Large Nonunion Companies.* Englewood Cliffs, N.J.: Prentice-Hall, 1980.

Gold, Charlotte, *Labor-Management Committees: Confrontation, Cooptation, or Cooperation.* Ithaca, N.Y.: ILR Press, Cornell University, 1986.

Haggard, Thomas R., *Compulsory Unionism, the NLRB, and the Courts.* Philadelphia: University of Pennsylvania Press, 1977.

Harris, Howell John, *The Right to Manage.* Madison: University of Wisconsin Press, 1982.

Hill, Marvin F., Jr. and Anthony V. Sinicropi, *Management Rights: A Legal and Arbitral Analysis.* Washington, D.C.: Bureau of National Affairs, 1986.

Kilgour, James, *Preventive Labor Relations.* New York: Amacon, 1981.

Klingel, Sally, and Ann Martin, eds., *A Fighting Chance: New Strategies to Save Jobs and Reduce Costs.* Ithaca, N.Y.: ILR Press, Cornell University, 1988.

Meyers, Scott, *Managing Without Unions.* Reading, Mass.: Addison-Wesley, 1976.

Rosen, Corey, and Karen M. Young, eds., *Understanding Employee Ownership.* Ithaca, N.Y.: ILR Press, Cornell University, 1991.

Whyte, William Foote, et al., *Worker Participation and Ownership.* Ithaca, N.Y.: ILR Press, Cornell University, 1983.

Management Rights

Critical in arbitration are cases in which a union challenges the right of an employer to manage the plant. To promote efficiency, employers constantly introduce new methods, adopt technological improvements, and make more effective use of the labor force. In the typical labor agreement, a management prerogative clause guarantees the employer the sole right to adopt measures calculated to ensure efficient operation. Disputes arise, however, when a union claims that the exercise of such a management right violates terms and conditions of employment specified in the labor agreement. In general, the rule is that an employer may make any decision in the operation of the plant or in the direction of the labor force unless such decision violates provisions of the collective bargaining contract. In such cases, the arbitrator's responsibility is to determine whether or not a violation has occurred. The arbitrator reviews the material provisions of the labor agreement and the relevant evidence in the light of the employer's action. In the event that a violation is found, the arbitrator will restore the status quo and award back pay if that issue is involved in the dispute. On the other hand, should it be determined that no violation has occurred, a grievance protesting the right of the employer to manage the plant and direct the labor force will be denied.

On the surface, Case 7 appears complicated and highly technical. Actually it is not, instead presenting a simple but extremely important and controversial issue for employers, unions, and employees. In an effort to promote plant efficiency, the Company consolidated nine different material handling classifications into one material handling classification. It did this in order to reduce the number of "bumps" allowed in the previous multiple classification system. Bumping causes employee displacement, which places a burden on the efficient operation of a plant. For example, it may require additional training as employees bump from job to job. This is the case even if the employee previously worked in the classification. As explained in this case, the layoff of one material handler under the previous system could result in the displacement of several employees.

Nonetheless, the Union asserted that the Company violated a provision of the labor agreement. It grieved even though material handlers did not lose any wages under the new system. As a matter of fact, some had their wages increased, but the Union still claimed that the consolidation adversely impacted on their conditions of employment.

As you read the case, you will discover that the Arbitrator fully agreed that the Employer's purpose was worthwhile—to promote plant efficiency to enhance its capability to meet domestic and global competition. From that point of view, the consolidation would advance employee job security. Nonetheless, the Arbitrator granted the grievance, directing the Company to abolish the consolidation and restore the employees to their former classifications. Find out why the Arbitrator reached that decision, even though he agreed that the consolidation was undertaken for a legitimate business reason.

This case demonstrates a fundamental arbitration lesson that should be understood by all participants and observers of the collective bargaining process. Arbitrators do not permit employers to change conditions of employment to promote plant efficiency when the action violates an express provision of a labor agreement.

Another interesting feature is the NLRB deferral of the case to private arbitration. Recall the discussion of the *Collyer* doctrine in Chapter 6. The Union filed an unfair labor practice charge against the Employer, but the NLRB deferred to arbitration to determine whether the Company violated Taft-Hartley. As you read that portion of the case, establish why the Arbitrator held that the Company not only violated the labor agreement but also the statute.

You are the arbitrator in Case 8. It involves public-sector labor relations in a small community located outside of Chicago. The dispute was generated when the Village hired a new employee from the outside for a vacant job instead of giving the position to a qualified bargaining unit employee. Needless to say, the Union and its members were very upset by this action, and the grievance filed was inevitably destined for arbitration.

According to the Employer, it had the right to hire from the outside as a matter of Management rights. It asserted that no express provision in the labor agreement invalidated such a right. Your job is to determine whether any express provision of the contract required the Village to award jobs to qualified current employees ahead of new hires.

Another feature of the case involves the negotiation of the first labor agreement between the Village and Union. The material provisions of the contract at the time of the arbitration were in the same form as originally adopted. Each Party argued that the history of the negotiations supported its position. Proposals dealing with the issue in this case were raised in the negotiations. Some were withdrawn and/or deleted. On the basis of the negotiations, the Employer and Union both claimed that the intent of the Parties supported its position. Since both could not be correct, your job is to determine on the evidence which version to accept for your decision.

Management Rights: The Case of the Consolidated Classifications

CAST OF CHARACTERS

Allford	Union President
Stern	Manager Labor Relations
Pato	Personnel Manager
Lest	International Union Representative
Shelly	Union Vice President

BACKGROUND

Consolidation of Material Handler Classifications

This case concerns the consolidation of nine (9) Material Handlers into a new classification called Material Handler A, Occupational Code MHA-6. For wage purposes the new classification was placed in Labor Grade 6. Effective August 15, 1988, the maximum rate of Labor Grade 6 was $9.94 per hour. Under the wage system, the lower the labor grade, the higher the rate of pay.

Involved in the consolidation were five (5) Labor Grade 6 classifications and four (4) Labor Grade 7 classifications. Effective August 15, 1988, the maximum rate for Labor Grade 7 was $9.65 per hour. Classifications consolidated were:

Classification	Occupational Code
Utility Heavy Equipment Operator	TRU-6
Warehouseman	SKM-6
Material Selector	MS-6
Loader	LD-6
Equipment Operator Heavy	TRB-6
Receiver	RE-7
Stockman	SKB-7
Stockman, Departmental	SKL-7
Material Handler, Storerooms/Receiving	MH-7

Out of the approximately 600–700 employees in the bargaining unit, approximately 70–80 were assigned to the nine (9) classifications when the consolidation occurred.

Duties of the Classifications

In synopsis form, Joe Allford, Union President, described the duties of the consolidated classifications. The Utility Heavy Equipment Operator picked up trash in the plant, driving a "mole," and emptied the trash barrels into a large receptacle. The employee also operated the street sweeper and cleaned the aisles.

Assigned to a storeroom, the Warehouseman receipted finished goods, which were packaged ready for transfer to the Shipping Department. Assigned to another storeroom, the Material Selector received material from the Receiving Department and partially finished work from production departments. Allford said that the Warehouseman and Material Selector classifications were similar.

Employees working in the Loader classification, assigned to the Shipping Department, assembled parts in cardboard boxes and loaded the material into trucks.

At the time of the consolidation, the Equipment Operator, Heavy classification was not occupied. When it was used, employees moved escalator frames outside the plant. In the early 1980s, the plant ceased producing escalators.

In the Receiver classification, employees unloaded trucks, moving material to the Inspection Department and at times to production departments.

The Stockman unloaded raw steel from trucks, placing the material in the storage system.

Stockman, Departmental classification employees made lifts for Assemblers and Machine Operators. In addition, they provided production employees with flat skids or empty boxes for the parts. Employees in this classification also delivered parts to production departments or to a storeroom.

Driving a "mule," employees working in the Material Handler, Store-rooms/Receiving classification transported parts from the main plant to the warehouse or from the warehouse to the main plant.

Meetings Between the Parties

On September 11, 1987, Teresa Stern, Manager Labor Relations, handed a letter to Allford notifying the Union of the consolidation. It stated:

> Please find attached new job rating substantiating data sheets to be imple-mented at the Plant beginning on 9/14/87.
>
> New products and rearrangements have necessitated the classifications of Machine Operator and Assembler (MOA-5) and Carousel Operator (COR-5), be created.
>
> Rearrangements and other developments have necessitated the classifications of Material Handler "A" (MHA-6) and Material Handler "B" (MHB-7) be created to reflect changes in job content.
>
> Current job duties and responsibilities of TRU-6, SKM-6, MS-6, LD-6, TRB-6, and SKV-6 incumbents have been incorporated into the MHA-6 job classification.
>
> Current job duties and responsibilities of RE-7, COC-7, SKB-7, SKL-7, and MH-7 incumbents have been incorporated into the MHB-7 job classification.

Objecting to the consolidation, Allford said that the consolidation had to be negotiated; Material Handlers were paid below the local labor market average; and the Overhead Crane Operator classification should be kept separate from the consolidation for safety reasons.

On October 22, 1987, Michael Pato, Personnel Manager, informed the Union of the Company's intention to implement the consolidation. Allford objected. The next meeting occurred on October 23, 1987, attended by Stern, Allford, and three other Union representatives. By the time of this session, Stern decided to place the new classification in Labor Grade 6 based on her survey of Material Handler rates paid by other local firms. She also eliminated the Overhead Crane Operator from the consolidation. When Allford inquired whether the Company was going to bargain about the consolidation, Stern replied, said Allford, that the Union already had some input into it, and this would be an informational meeting.

In the session, Stern advised the Union that the Company intended to establish a training program for all employees assigned to the consolidated classification. When the Union objected, the Labor Relations Manager abandoned the training program. To justify the consolidation, Allford testified, the Management representative said it was designed to provide the Company with more flexibility by reducing the number of "bumps" by employees involved in layoff situations. Stern allayed a Union fear by informing its representatives that the new program would not include a general job pool for all Material Handlers. The Union had feared that such a pool would jeopardize job security.

In the meeting, Stern distributed Job-Rating-Substantiating Data sheets for the new classification.

Grievance Filed

Stern sent a notice to General Supervisors to implement the new classification effective October 26, 1987. It stated:

Effective October 26, 1987 the Material Handling classifications of TRU-6, SKM-6, MS-6, LD-6, TRB-6, RE-7, SKB-7, SKL-7, and MH-7 will be consolidated into a new Material Handler "A," MHA-6 job classification. All departments will remain the same for affected employees.

Employees currently in labor grade 6 classification will remain at existing rate of pay.

Employees currently in the labor grade 7 classifications outlined above will be paid at the qualifying rate of a labor grade 6 unless:

1) Employee is in probationary period in which case he/she will be paid at the hiring rate of a labor grade 6.
or

2) Employee previously held and qualified on the TRU-6, SKM-6, MS-6, LD-6, or TRB-6 classification, in which case he/she will be paid at the labor grade 6 step previously held.

All employees must rank their current classification as their first preference on the job preference sheets. Therefore, employees in the MHA-6 classification will have this ranked first on their job preference sheet automatically.

Employees not currently in a material handling classification, who have previously qualified on one of the affected classes will be given the opportunity to re-rank their job preferences at a later date.

On October 28, 1987, the Union filed Grievance No. H87-68 protesting the consolidation, stating:

Nature of Grievance: Violation of Contract including but not limited to Preamble and Letter 6, Section 1. The Company has unilaterally transferred job classifications into and out of the B/U in the material handling areas. Violation also of Article IV, Section 12.

Settlement Requested: Request Company follow Contract and transfer classifications in B/U only with mutual agreement between the parties.

Unsuccessful attempts were made to settle the dispute in the Grievance Procedure. Denying the grievance in Step 3, the Company stated:

...The Company has the right and the responsibility to create new job rating substantiating data sheets and furnish copies to the Union. The Union has the right to challenge any discrepancies or omissions found in new sheets. No violation of contract. Grievance denied.

Failing to settle, the Union notified the Company on January 14, 1988, of its intention to arbitrate the dispute.

Unfair Labor Practice Charges Filed: Deferral to Arbitration

On January 18, 1988, the Union filed unfair labor charges against the Company alleging a violation of Section 8(a)(5), Labor Management Relations Act. The charge stated:

> On October 26, 1987, the Company did unilaterally change nine (9) job classifications into one (1) job classification. This change was not negotiated with the union and affects the entire bargaining unit (hourly).

On February 19, 1988, William T. Little, Director, National Labor Relations Board, Region 25, deferred the case to arbitration, under the *Collyer* doctrine.

In the arbitration, the Parties addressed the unfair labor practice charge:

Mr. Arbitrator: This is a *Collyer* Case, the Unfair Labor Practice should be addressed. Why do you think the company violated the Taft-Hartley Law?

Mr. Lest: We believe that they violated the act by unilaterally changing conditions of employment without first bargaining.

***

Mr. Arbitrator: ...Why do you think the employer did not violate the National Labor Relations Act?

Mr. Pato: Our position is that the negotiated contract that we're operating under clearly and unequivocally gives us the right underneath Article 11, Section 5, which appears on page 34 I believe.

LABOR AGREEMENT

Article IV—Seniority

Section 11—Layoff Procedure
Sub-Section 1. Policy

(a) In the event of a surplus, the least senior employee in the classification, department and shift where the surplus occurs shall be determined to be surplus.

(b) An employee shall pre-select his job classification and shift preference according to the process outlined in Sub-Section 2. The employee shall rank his job preference in labor grades one (1) through six (6) from his previously held classifications in which he has qualified. The employee will indicate his preferences within each labor grade.

The employee also shall rank job preferences in the Common Block (labor grades 7–10) regardless of whether he previously has held such classifications. The employee need not indicate his preferences within the Common Block by labor grades.

For purposes of this Article only, the Common Block shall be treated as one labor grade.

***

Sub-Section 2. Guidelines

(a) The pre-selection process is:

    (1) The Company will provide a list by grade of all previously held jobs for which the employee is qualified.

    (2) The employee will indicate his job preference within labor grade(s) and within the Common Block.

***

(d) If an employee fails to submit a Job Preference form for jobs in the Common Block, he shall bump the least senior person in the Common Block.

***

Section 12—Additional Layoff Procedure

(c) Definitions.

The term "occupation" as used in this procedure and the chart attached hereto ("Exhibit B") refers to the various job classifications with their corresponding job symbols. The term "block" as used in this procedure and the chart attached hereto ("Exhibit B") refers to the various groups of occupations enclosed on a single rectangle on the chart.

(d) The "Family of Occupations" chart (Exhibit B) is the chart referred to in this section and is contained in the back of this Agreement.

"Exhibit B," attached hereto, refers to the various groups of "occupations" or classifications and is for reference only. The Employee may "bump" any job in a classification in the chart subject to the provisions of this Article. Revisions in the "Exhibit B" will be made by mutual consent.

Article IX—General Provisions

***

Section 3—Management Clause

The Management and the operation of the Plant and the direction of the working forces, including but not limited to the right to hire, transfer, promote, suspend or discharge employees for just cause and the right to lay off employees because of lack of work is vested in the Company, subject to the expressed terms of this Agreement.

Article XI—Wages

***

Section 5—Job Evaluation

The classifications presently included in this Bargaining Unit, copies of which have been supplied to the Union, have been defined and rated in accordance with the agreed to Job Rating Plan. If new products, rearrangements or other developments indicate that other classifications should be created, or present classifications modified to reflect changes in job content, these classifications shall be rated by the Company and copies of the new Job Rating Substantiating Data Sheets will be promptly furnished to the Union. Only discrepancies or omissions found by the Union in these new sheets may be the subject of a job classification grievance. If such discrepancy, omission or change is called to the attention of the Company within ninety (90) days after the new job classification was put into effect, any corrections shall be effective as of the date of such new job classification. If such discrepancies or omissions in the Job Rating Substantiating Data Sheets are found by the Union on these new sheets and are not called to the attention of the Company until after ninety (90) days from the date said job classification was put into effect, the correction shall be effective as of the Monday following the date of the grievance.

Changes or modifications in job content of previously established Job Rating Substantiating Data Sheets which may result in changes in the degree scoring of either the education factor, experience factor, or initiative and ingenuity factor, may be the subject of a job classification grievance. Any correction shall be effective as of the Monday following the date of the grievance.

ISSUES

1. Under the circumstances of this case, did the Employer violate the Labor Agreement? If so, what should the remedy be?
2. Under the circumstances of this case, did the Employer violate Section 8(a)(5) of the Labor Management Relations Act?

POSITIONS OF THE PARTIES

In the Employer's view, the Company had the contractual authority for its action. In its brief, it stated:

The Company has the contractual right under the current Collective Bargaining agreement to create and consolidate job classifications. *Only* discrepancies or omissions found by the Union in the job rating substantiating data sheets may be a subject of a job classification grievance. The jobs consolidated had similar duties and responsibilities. Past practice supports the Company's right to combine job classifications. The job consolidation was neither arbitrary nor capricious. Finally, the Company demonstrated good faith by attempting to discuss this issue with the Union prior to implementation. [Emphasis in original]

In particular, the Company relies on Article IX, Section 3, Management Clause, and Article XI, Section 5, Job Evaluation.

On its part, the Union asserts that the Company violated the Labor Agreement under the circumstances. In its brief, it asserts:

The Employer's contention, through the cross-examination of Employer witness Teresa Stern, that the consolidation of the nine (9) classifications into a single classification did not constitute a revision in Exhibit B of the current Agreement is completely without foundation. Joint Exhibit #3, the MHA-6 Job Rating-Substantiating Data sheet and Union Exhibit #5, the Internal Correspondence memo dated October 26, 1987, both clearly indicated the Employer's intention to eliminate, through consolidation, any future bumping opportunities into the affected classifications.

The Union relies upon the Seniority provisions of the Labor Agreement, including Article IV, Section 12(d).

EVALUATION OF THE EVIDENCE

Purpose of Consolidation

If the sole issue in this dispute were whether the elimination of the nine (9) Material Handler classifications and the creation of the new classification advanced the more efficient operation of the plant, the Company's position would clearly prevail. Before the consolidation, at time of layoffs, the classifications were subject to multiple or chain bumping. This was particularly true for those classifications in Labor Grade 7. Under the terms of Article IV, Section 11, Sub-Section 1, those classifications in Labor Grades 7–10 are known as the "Common Block." To exercise seniority in the Common Block an employee need not have previously held the classifications. As Labor Relations Manager Stern explained:

...The difference is I guess that common block is called the common block because you can bump into those jobs without previously having held those positions.

Assume that a Stockman is displaced by a more senior employee. The Stockman would have the choice of four classifications to exercise seniority. If he bumped a Receiver, the Receiver could displace a junior service employee in Stockman, Departmental (SKL-7) or a Material Handler, Storeroom/Receiving. Such displaced employee could then bump in the remaining classification. In other words, the displacement of one employee could result in four bumps.

To exercise seniority in Labor Grade 6 or lower, the employee must have held the classification. Nonetheless, before consolidation, multiple bumping could occur within the five (5) Labor Grade 6 classifications. Assuming employees held the classifications, displacement of one employee could result in five (5) bumps.

Clearly, the consolidation drastically reduces the bumping process.

Fundamental Issue: Management Rights Provision

But whether the consolidation advances efficient plant operations is not the fundamental issue in this dispute. The critical question is not the inherent value of the consolidation, but whether the Company had the contractual authority to abolish the nine (9) Material Handler classifications and consolidate them into the new classification.

In this respect, Section 3 of Article IX, Management Clause, states that the operation of the Plant and the direction of the working forces "is vested in the Company subject to the expressed terms of this Agreement."

As such, the provision reflects a cardinal principle of labor relations conducted under collective bargaining. All rights are vested in the employer except as limited by expressed provisions of a labor agreement. This doctrine is called by some the "residual rights of management."

Arbitrators, though recognizing the residual rights principle, naturally expect employers to use their authority in a reasonable manner devoid of arbitrary, capricious, or bad-faith action. But here, assuming contractual authority to implement the consolidation, the Company met the reasonableness standard. It informed the Union of the action, accepted some of its recommendations, and consolidated the classifications for a legitimate business purpose.

In short, the basic issue is whether an expressed contractual provision exists forbidding the Company action that is the subject of this proceeding.

Application of Job Evaluation Provision

Not only does the Company argue that it had the right to create the new classification as a matter of residual Management rights, but it also asserts that such action is expressly authorized by Section 5 of Article XI, Job Evaluation. Referring to this provision, the Company says:

> The Contract between the Company and the Union specifically allows the Company to create new job classifications. The Contract establishes the right of management to create and modify jobs or job classifications and makes provisions for the Union to challenge discrepancies or omissions in the job rating sheets.

***

The Union has not obtained any contract provisions limiting the Company's right in this respect, and there is no contract language forbidding job consolidations.

And:

The Company has the contractual right under the current Collective Bargaining agreement to create and consolidate job classifications. *Only* discrepancies or omissions found by the Union in the job rating substantiating data sheets may be a subject of a job classification grievance. [Emphasis in original]

The provision contemplates the Company's right to create new classifications and modify existing classifications, but this right is limited by the express language contained in the provision:

...If *new products, rearrangements or other developments* indicate that other classifications should be created, *or present classifications modified to reflect changes in job content,* these classifications shall be rated by the Company and copies of the new Job Rating Substantiating Data Sheets will be promptly furnished to the Union. Only discrepancies or omissions found by the Union in these new sheets may be the subject of a job classification grievance. [Emphasis added]

In other words, the Company has the right to create new classifications because of the manufacture of new products, or rearrangements or developments, and modify present classifications to reflect changes in job content. To explain the application of the provision to this dispute, Stern testified:

Q: Why did the Company go ahead with this consolidation after the Union made it clear that they were opposed to it on the basis of bad faith bargaining?

A: Because the contract clearly states in my mind that the Company has an obligation and responsibility to correctly evaluate jobs and reevaluate jobs for the purpose of reflecting changes in job content, new products or rearrangements or other developments. The necessity of rearranging this classification into one to provide the flexibility I felt clearly fell under the rearrangement and other development section of this contract.

Nothing in the record demonstrates that the Company introduced new products at the time of the consolidation. Nor does the record demonstrate a change in the job content of the classifications abolished by the Company. Stern said: "...The same work, the work hasn't changed."

This raises the question of whether the Company action was justified by the language that authorizes the creation of new classifications based on "rearrangements or other developments." This language could reasonably be related to change in technology or methods of production, commonly recognized as the basis for employer unilateral establishment, elimination, or combination of classifications. In the case at hand, the Company does not argue that its action was related to change in technology or methods of production. Its purpose was solely to promote plant efficiency by reducing the number of bumps during a layoff process.

In any event, though the language in question could reasonably be related to change in technology or methods of production, the phrase "rearrangements or other developments" otherwise is inherently vague and uncertain. It is not subject to any kind of objective determination. It could mean anything and everything. No evidence was supplied to establish the Parties' intent when the language was negotiated.

Below we shall consider specific contractual language that bears upon the Company's action that generated this dispute. At that time, we shall determine when the Company action was authorized on the basis of "rearrangements or other developments."

Impact on Bargaining Unit

The Company's action did adversely affect employees' layoff rights.

In the first place, the elimination of four (4) Labor Grade classifications restricted the scope of the Common Block. As said, an employee need not have held classifications within the Common Block to exercise seniority during a layoff situation. To this extent, the opportunity of employees to select jobs within the Common Block on the basis of seniority was constricted.

Previously, a laid-off employee had the opportunity to select between nine (9) Material Handler classifications, four (4) Labor Grade 7 and five (5) in Labor Grade 6. Without refutation, Allford testified that the Material Handler jobs are different with respect to desirability. Thus:

Q: Why was the Union so opposed to this consolidation?

A: Well, there were a number of reasons. The jobs were greatly dissimilar. Some jobs are very unpleasant compared to other jobs. The storeroom jobs were typically cleaner jobs and were more thinking jobs, as opposed to like a SKB-7, which you have to climb up and down steel racks, handle heavy steel bars. An SKL-7 job in certain departments was a wide variety in those assignments...

With the advent of the consolidation, a qualified employee only had the right to bump the least senior employee within the new classification regardless of the desirability or attractiveness of the job. To this extent, seniority rights were diluted for purposes of job selection. Limited to the displacement of the least senior employee in the new classification, the laid-off employee could wind up in the least desirable job. Without refutation, the Union President testified:

I was just going to say, including the job such as the old SKL-7, SKB-7, MH-7, and RE-7, including those jobs into the MHA-6 classification someone involved in a surplus who had qualified as a storeroom person before is going to have to take out the least senior person in MHA-6 classification. That may land them in the steel room department climbing steel racks or being a stockman in a department as opposed to they used to be able to potentially go into one of the storerooms or a shipping department.

In sum, the consolidation adversely impacted upon the bargaining unit. It limited bumping in the Common Block, and reduced the use of seniority in the choice of jobs within the new classification.

Application of Exhibit B: Mutual Consent

If the choice presented to the Arbitrator were solely between bargaining unit impact and plant efficiency, he probably would come down on the side of efficiency. Though there were disadvantages to employees, the consolidation advanced plant efficiency, which could serve the interests of employees as well as those of the Company.

Specific contractual language, however, nullified the option presented to the Arbitrator. Consider the character of Article IV, Section 12(d):

> The "Family of Occupations" chart ("Exhibit B") is the chart referred to in this section and is contained in the back of this Agreement.

> "Exhibit B," attached hereto, refers to the various groups of "occupations" or classifications and is for reference only. The employee may "bump" any job in a classification in the chart subject to the provisions of this Article. Revisions in the "Exhibit B" will be made by *mutual consent*. [Emphasis added]

From what was said previously, the consolidation clearly revised Exhibit B. No longer could employees bump in the four (4) eliminated Labor Grade 7 classifications, restricting their right to the Common Block. No longer did a laid-off employee have the right to select among the nine (9) eliminated Material Handler classifications. Now the laid-off employee had one and only one option—bump the least senior employee in the newly created Material Handler classification. Unless we totally ignore the clear and undisputed evidence, the consolidation revised Exhibit B by limiting the seniority rights of laid-off employees.

With regard to this matter, the Company argues:

> ...However, the listing of occupations currently included in the contract as the family of occupations chart Exhibit B, does not freeze such occupations, and the contract does not otherwise limit the Company's right to combine jobs.

In support of this view, Arbitrator Wayne Quinlan determined that the mere listing of jobs currently included in a contract does not restrict management's right to reevaluate and combine existing jobs:

> "The Company would be in an almost impossible position competitively speaking, if the only new jobs that they might be able to create were jobs involving duties which had never been or were not at the time being performed within

the Company. Jobs are not frozen by the act of classifying them." (*Phillips Petroleum Co.*, 33 LA 379, (1959))

We agree that the mere listing of classifications in a collective bargaining contract does not freeze them, making them immune from elimination and consolidation.

Indeed, in *Alton Box Board Co.* (54 LA 197), this Arbitrator affirmed this principle (contractual listing of classifications do not freeze them in the contract) when he denied a grievance protesting the Employer's elimination of a classification. With full deference to the Company and its Advocate, however, this principle does not apply in this case. It does not apply for a very simple reason: Before the Company may revise Exhibit B there must be MUTUAL CONSENT between the Parties. *Here is specific and express contractual language limiting the right of the Company to eliminate and combine classifications.* In its brief, the Company does not even mention the mutual consent precondition.

Purely and simply, the Company completely ignores the specific and expressed limitation on its authority. The Company does not instruct this Arbitrator as to why he should ignore what the Parties bargained for when they adopted the language. It does not instruct him as to why he should ignore the limitation on his authority as contained in Article VI, Arbitration:

> ...the arbitrator shall not have the power to add to, *subtract from,* or modify the terms of this agreement. [Emphasis added]

In the final analysis, the Company requests the Arbitrator to shut his eyes to "*mutual consent*" and/or to find mutual consent is not required when the Employer revised Exhibit B to promote plant efficiency. In either case, to affirm such a position would be a clear and wanton disregard of his authority and professional responsibilities. Clearly, what the Company seeks in this arbitration must be achieved in collective bargaining. Neither an employer nor a labor organization may secure in arbitration what must be gained at the bargaining table.

Job Evaluation: "Rearrangements or Other Developments"

We are now prepared to deal with the language contained in the Job Evaluation provision (Article XI, Section 5) authorizing the Company to create new classifications because of "rearrangements or other developments." As mentioned earlier, this language is inherently vague, uncertain, devoid of any kind of objective determination. It contains general language, failing to articulate its meaning.

On the other hand, the specific and expressed language contained in Article IV, Section 12(d), places a clear limitation on the Company's authority to revise Exhibit B by abolishing and creating classifications—it must obtain the consent of the Union as a precondition. Here the language is clear, unambiguous, specific, and unequivocal. Even if a conflict exists between the provisions in question, it is well settled in arbitration that specific language will govern.

For this reason, we reject the Company's position that it had the authority to establish the new classification based on the aforesaid language contained in the Job Evaluation provision.

Past Practice

Nor may the Company's position prevail based on past practice. In this respect, the Company states:

> Past practice further substantiates this basic management right. During the 22 year history of Collective Bargaining between the Company and the Union, the Company was consistently and solely responsible for the evaluation of new jobs and the re-evaluation of existing jobs.

And:

> The Company has taken similar action in the past without objection from the Union.

But what the Employer's evidence amounts to is a single instance occurring in the late 1960s when the Company consolidated two classifications—103 Paint Line and 105 Assembly Area. In no way does a single instance occurring in twenty-two years amount to a binding past practice as the concept is used in labor arbitration. To constitute a binding past practice, the event must occur frequently and regularly. In addition, the Union did not object to the consolidation because it felt

> it was the best interest of the people to combine that work with assembly work because it was too much of a physical stress for line loaders to stand there eight hours a day physically handling big bulky doors and heavy structural steel.

To say the Union forfeited its rights in this case based upon that single instance would be a masterpiece of error. Indeed, if past practice constitutes a legitimate basis to determine this dispute, it would appear to be on the side of the Union. Consider the unrefuted testimony offered by Union President Allford:

Q: During this growth that the plant has enjoyed the last year, has there been new work, new classifications introduced into the facility?

A: Yes.

Q: Have those been by mutual agreement?

A: Yes.

Q: They've been established by the employer, is that true?

A: The jobs were put in place by the employer with our help in several situations.

And:

Q: Your approximate little over ten years' service with the company, during that period of time have you known of the Company to ever prior to this case consolidate classifications?

A: Never.

Consider also the testimony offered by Virgil Shelly, Union Vice President:

Q: ...In your twenty-three years at the Company and numerous years experience as a Union representative, has the Company ever in the past consolidated classifications?

A: No way.

When he testified that way, he was not aware of the single instance related above when the Company consolidated two classifications *without protest from the Union.*

In other words, a fair evaluation of the record demonstrates that the Company *never* in the past consolidated classifications save for the single exception noted above. It also shows that new classifications were established with the help of the Union. It would appear, therefore, that, if anything, past practice supports the Union's position. In any event, the evidence overwhelmingly demonstrates that past practice does not support the Company's position. One instance without Union protest does not make a past practice.

Application of Labor Management Relations Act

As indicated earlier, the Union filed an unfair labor practice charge against the Company alleging a violation of the Labor Management Relations Act. On January 18, 1980, the National Labor Relations Board, Region 25, deferred the case to arbitration. Section 8(5) makes it an unfair labor practice for an employer "to refuse to bargain collectively with the representatives of his employees."

Under *Fibreboard*[*] and its progeny, the federal courts and the NLRB held that an employer violates national labor policy when it refuses to bargain with a labor organization prior to changing terms and conditions of employment during the effective period of a labor agreement. Applying this doctrine to the case at hand, we find the Company changed conditions of employment when it combined the previous Material Handler classifications consolidating them into a single classification. As noted earlier, the consolidation affected the seniority rights of employees during layoff situations. Their opportunity to exercise seniority in the Common Block was circumscribed because four (4) Labor Grade 7 classifications were eliminated. By eliminating the Material Handler classifications, qualified laid-

---

Fibreboard Paper Products Corporation v. *NLRB,* 379 U.S. 203 (1964).

off employees no longer had the right to select jobs on the basis of seniority, which they believed most desirable and attractive. Under the consolidation such an employee could bump only the least senior employee within the newly created Material Handler A classification. Before the consolidation such employees had the opportunity to exercise seniority in nine (9) different Material Handler classifications.

Not even the Employer argued that it met its statutory obligation to bargain with the Union before it implemented the consolidation. True, it notified the Union of the consolidation, accepted some of its recommendations, and made the change in working conditions to promote plant efficiency. Nonetheless, consider the testimony offered by Labor Relations Manager Stern:

Mr. Arbitrator: On that point while I think about it, in the chronology here you did meet with the Union several times about this problem?

Witness: Yes.

Mr. Arbitrator: Do you consider that a negotiating session? Or an information session?

Witness: I changed my actions based on what information I was getting from the Union.

Mr. Arbitrator: Like the crane operator?

Witness: Like the crane operator, changing it to the labor grade 6.

Mr. Arbitrator: Can you put a label on it? Would you say those sessions were negotiating sessions as we understand the term in labor relations or were they informational sessions?

Witness: I would probably call it an effects bargaining.... We bargained what the effects were going to be on the employees.

***

For purposes of the Labor Management Relations Act, employer discussion or bargaining on the effects of a change in the terms and conditions of employment is not the same as bargaining about the change itself. In other words, the Company unilaterally made the consolidation without prior bargaining with the Union. It was willing to discuss or bargain about the effects of the consolidation but did not bargain on the consolidation. For these reasons, under the circumstances of this case we find that the Company violated Section 8(a)(5) of the National Labor Relations Act. As this decision demonstrates, the Company did not have the contractual authority for its action. Given the material contractual provisions and the previous discussion, the Company did not have the unilateral right to abolish the nine (9) Material Handler classifications consolidating them into one (1) classification.

We find further that this arbitration complied with the standards in *Spielberg Mfg. Co.,* 112 NLRB 1080. The arbitral proceedings were fair and regular; the unfair labor practices were addressed in the arbitration; the unfair labor practice issues were considered and decided; and the

Award is consistent with the purposes and policies of the Labor Management Relations Act.

Conclusion and Award

The Arbitrator fully understands the purpose of the Company's action. It consolidated the classifications to improve plant efficiency. Indeed, as a professional economist, the Arbitrator is sympathetic to the Company's quest for more efficiency. It could be reasonably argued that the Company's action could be in the interest of the employee's job security. By improving efficiency, the Company would be in a better position to meet domestic and international competition.

But the Company did not have the contractual authority to eliminate the nine (9) Material Handler classifications consolidating them into one (1) classification. For this reason, the grievance must be sustained on the grounds that the Company violated the Labor Agreement.

As the remedy, the Arbitrator shall direct the Company to rescind the consolidated classification, Material Handler A, Occupational Code MHA-6, and reestablish the nine (9) Material Handler classifications that it abolished. In addition, the Company shall be directed to reinstate employees affected by consolidation to the Material Handler classification that they held prior to consolidation.

QUESTIONS

1. Why did the Arbitrator reject the Company's argument that it had the managerial authority to consolidate the material handling classifications into one classification?

2. Although it was obvious that the Union never consented to the Company action as required by Article IV, Section 12(d), the Mutual Consent provision, the Arbitrator might have granted the grievance solely on that basis. Explain why he considered other aspects of the case, including the purpose of the consolidation, Job Evaluation provision, Management Rights, and past practice.

3. Even though no employee lost wages in the consolidation—indeed, some received an increase—why did the Arbitrator find that the consolidation impacted adversely on the Material Handlers?

4. Explain why the Arbitrator held that the Company violated the National Labor Relations Act (Taft-Hartley).

Management Rights: The Case of Hiring an Outside Employee

CAST OF CHARACTERS

Snyder	Grievant
Hall	Director of Public Works
Mann	Former Employee
Creel	Supervisor Street Division
Gash	Supervisor Wastewater Division
Carr	Hired for Position
Short	Village Attorney
Loos	Union Representative

GRIEVANCE

This dispute arose when a community in Illinois refused to transfer an employee to a job vacancy. Instead, it filled the job with a person hired from the street. In protest, Glenn Snyder filed his grievance dated May 23, 1989. It alleges a violation of Article VI, Sections 6.2 and 6.6, of the Labor Agreement and any other pertinent provisions. For adjustment, Snyder requests he be awarded the position.

Having failed to settle the dispute in the Grievance Procedure, the Parties convened this arbitration for its determination.

LABOR AGREEMENT

Article III—Management Rights

Except as specifically limited by the express provisions of this Agreement, the Village retains traditional rights to manage and direct the affairs of the Village in all of its various aspects and to manage and direct its employees, including but not limited to the following:...to employ employees and to determine the conditions for their continued employment; to schedule and assign work; to assign or to transfer employees within the Village;...

Article VI—Seniority

Section 6.1—Definition. Unless stated otherwise, seniority shall, for the purpose of this Agreement, be defined as an employee's length of continuous service with the Village since the employee's last date of hire.

Section 6.2—Application of Seniority. In the application of seniority to promotions from one bargaining unit position to another, filling of permanent openings in classifications within the bargaining unit, layoff and recall of bargaining unit employees, seniority shall be the determining factor when, among employees involved, the qualifications, skill, ability, experience, knowledge and physical fitness to perform the work without further training is relatively equal between two or more employees. When determining the application of seniority, the Village's decision concerning qualifications, skill, ability, experience, knowledge and physical fitness shall be made in good faith and its actions shall not be arbitrary or capricious.

Section 6.6—Transfers and New Job Openings. Employees desiring to transfer to other jobs within the bargaining unit shall submit an application in writing to their immediate supervisor. The application shall state the reason for the requested transfer. Normally, all new bargaining unit jobs will be posted for a period of five (5) working days before being filled, except in an emergency.

STIPULATED ISSUE

The Parties stipulated the issue to be determined in this proceeding:

Did the Employer violate Article 6 of the contract when it denied the grievant's request for a transfer to the Wastewater Department and instead placed a newly hired employee in that position? If so, what should the remedy be?

BACKGROUND

Posting of Vacancy

On May 5, 1989, Mike Hall, Director of Public Works, posted a notice informing employees of a vacancy for Public Works Technician I in the Wastewater Division of the Public Works Department. It stated:

> We are about to have a position open in our Wastewater Division which we are moving rapidly to fill. Before we do, you have the opportunity again to request a transfer of any kind between divisions, subject to approval of any supervisors affected and myself. If you are interested in a transfer please advise me of this in writing no later than end of the workday, Friday, May 12th.

The vacancy was created by the resignation of Michael Mann, effective May 9. On May 11, Grievant Snyder, Mechanic Technician 2, Street Division, Public Works Department, asked to fill the vacancy. At that time, he had served as Mechanic Technician for seven and one-half years. His bid, submitted to Hall, stated:

> I would like to be considered for transfer to the opening in the Treatment Plant.

When Snyder submitted his bid, he spoke to Hall concerning his application. According to the Grievant, Hall told him that if both Division supervisors agreed, the Director of Public Works would approve the transfer. Dan Creel was Snyder's direct supervisor in the Street Division, and Larry Gash was the supervisor in the Wastewater Division. Both supervisors, said the Grievant, approved the transfer.

When Snyder informed Hall about that, Hall told the Grievant that he would speak to the supervisors and report back to him. A few days later, Hall advised the Grievant that Gash dissented to the transfer. Hall instructed Snyder to contact Gash "immediately." Gash told the Grievant he had not dissented, but felt Snyder was "not serious about requesting the transfer." After a conversation, the Grievant testified, the supervisor was satisfied he was serious and "would be more than happy to have me."

When the Grievant reported the results of that conversation to Hall, the Director of Public Works, testified Snyder, said:

> ...and at that point, Mike [Hall] said that was fine. He would be more than willing to let me go, but he's already hired somebody.

Hall, Creel, and Gash did not appear at the arbitration. However, the Parties stipulated that had Hall testified he would have said:

> After considering Snyder's request to be considered for transfer, including speaking with the supervisors involved, I decided not to transfer him. Instead, I decided to place Carr in the position.

Carr Hired for Position

In January 1989, the Village had another opening for the job in question. Hall received 101 applications, narrowing them down to four candidates for personal interviews. One of the four interviewed by Hall was Pat Carr. Another person was selected to fill the vacancy, but the Director of Public Works wrote Carr on February 17:

> I urge you not to be discouraged by not being chosen at this time. I fully intend on keeping your application in my file and if another opening occurs in the Public Works Department in the next 6 months or so you may well be called to see if you are still interested. I don't know this is going to happen but in a department this size it might. Obviously, I do not want to go thru so many applications again so soon.

Instead of transferring the Grievant, Hall hired Carr to fill the vacancy. At that time, Carr was neither a member of the bargaining unit nor a Village employee. Hired from the outside, he started to work on May 24.

Lateral Transfer

Should the grievance prevail, back pay will not be awarded because the job in question pays the same rate as Snyder's current position. Thus, the Parties stipulated:

> Grievant's transfer from Mechanic to Public Works Technician would have been a lateral move. Thus, there would have been no increase in grievant's pay rate.

Negotiation of Labor Agreement

Effective April 18, 1986, the Parties negotiated their first Labor Agreement, which was scheduled to expire on April 30, 1987. (The Parties later negotiated the subsequent contract, effective May 1, 1987, through April 30, 1989, and stipulated that the material provisions of both Labor Agreements, Article III and Article VI, Sections 2 and 6, are identical.) The following relates to the negotiations of the first Labor Agreement.

Attorney Robert Short served as Chair for the Village and Representative Ted Loos was Chair of the Union committee. Negotiations started in the summer of 1985 and were completed in April 1986. More than twenty-three sessions were held by the Parties.

In the third session, held on September 9, 1985, the Union submitted a proposal that included the following:

Section 1. Filling of Vacancies

Whenever a job vacancy occurs in any existing job classification or as a result of the development or establishment of new job classifications, a notice of such vacancy shall be posted on all bulletin boards for 10 working days.

During this period, employees who wish to apply for the vacant job may do so.

Section 2. Selection

The Village shall fill the vacancy by promoting from among qualified applications the employee with the longest continuous service.

An outside applicant will not be hired unless no current employees who are qualified for the position have submitted applications.

On September 25, 1985, at the fourth meeting, the Village proposed a contract that contained the following:

Section 6.2. Application of Seniority. In the application of seniority to promotions from one bargaining unit position to another, filling of permanent openings in classifications within the bargaining unit, layoff and recall of bargaining unit employees, seniority shall be the determining factor when, among employees involved, the qualifications, skill and ability to perform the work without further training is equal between two or more employees. When determining the application of seniority, the Village's decision concerning skill and ability shall be made in good faith and its actions shall not be arbitrary or capricious. Nothing herein shall be construed to preclude the Village's ability to hire new employees to fill vacancies.

Negotiations of February 28, 1986

On this day, the Parties met in their twenty-third session. Apparently nothing of significance for purposes of the case occurred between September 25, 1985, and February 28, 1986. At that time, the Union submitted the following seniority proposal:

Section 6.2. Application of Seniority. In the application of seniority to promotions from one bargaining unit position to another, filling of permanent openings in classifications within the bargaining unit, layoff and recall of bargaining unit employees, seniority shall be the determining factor when, among employees involved, the qualifications, skill, ability, experience, knowledge and physical fitness to perform the work without further training is equal between two or more employees. When determining the application of seniority, the Village's decision concerning qualifications, skill, ability, experience, knowledge and physical fitness shall be made in good faith and its action shall not be arbitrary or capricious.[*]

Also on the table was the Union proposal of September 9, 1985, concerning the posting of job vacancies. On February 28, 1986, the Village proposed to amend it to read:

---

[*]At the suggestion of the Union, the Parties inserted the word "relatively" before the word "equal." So modified, it appears in Article VI, Section 6.2, in both Labor Agreements.

Section 6.6. Transfers and New Job Openings. Employees desiring to transfer to other jobs within the bargaining unit shall submit an application in writing to their Immediate Supervisor. The application shall state the reason for the requested transfer. Normally, all new bargaining unit jobs will be posted for a period of five (5) working days before being filled, except in an emergency.

So modified, the provision appears as Article VI, Section 6.6, of the Parties' collective bargaining agreement.

As indicated in the Village's initial proposal (September 25, 1985), the last sentence stated:

Nothing herein shall be construed to preclude the Village's ability to hire new employees to fill vacancies. (For convenience, hereinafter it shall be called the Last Sentence.)

With regard to the Last Sentence, authorizing the Village to hire outside people to fill job vacancies, Loos testified:

...As I said, the Village had had a practice of doing—you know—in terms of filling job openings any way they wished; and we wanted to make some changes in that.

And one of the things that was important, we told them that what we had to do was people—that people from the inside, when a job opening of any kind occurred, needed to be given the—need to be given the jobs.

And

Arbitrator: Was this proposal [Last Sentence] submitted initially by the Employer or by the Union?

The Witness: The initial proposal was by the Employer, and it included this final line which we couldn't live with, and we told them that. And in order to get an agreement, this is what we had, this is what we needed, and told them that at the table.

Loos also said the Union wanted the Last Sentence struck, testifying:

A: And that is what we did, have to limit it to the extent that people that wanted jobs from the inside would be given the jobs. We wanted that sentence struck.

Q: And both parties agreed to that?

A: Right.

With regard to this matter, Short testified:

Q: Mr. Short, let me show you Union Exhibit 1 which has been previously marked. The last sentence has been struck.

Why did the Village agree to strike the last sentence of 6.2?

A: Well, Union Exhibit 1 and Village Exhibit 4, in other words 6.2 and 6.6 for purposes of our discussion here, were signed off simultaneously as part of a package.

And the last sentence of Section 6.2, the statement that "nothing herein shall be construed to limit the Village's ability to hire new employees to fill vacancies," really was no longer true once we agreed to Section 6.6, because what the Village was agreeing to in Section 6.6 was a procedural obligation, a requirement, that it post and make known to bargaining employees job openings before the Village filled them. So it really no longer was precisely true.

In any event, the Last Sentence does not appear in Article VI, Section 6.2, of the Labor Agreement.

POSITIONS OF THE PARTIES

Employer

The Employer asserts that it has the authority under the Management Rights provision to fill jobs by hiring from the outside. It is not required to fill jobs from qualified employees in the bargaining unit. In this regard, the Employer says it has the right to manage and direct the affairs of the Village, including the right "to employ employees," except "as specifically limited by the express provisions of this Agreement."

It claims "nothing in the Labor Agreement (except the posting requirement) has express provisions limiting our right to hire from the outside in preference to filling job vacancies with bargaining unit employees."

According to the Village, nothing occurred in the Parties' negotiation of the first contract that impairs its right to hire from the outside. True, it agrees that it ultimately dropped the Last Sentence of its proposal, which said "nothing herein shall be construed to preclude the Village's ability to hire new employees." It was dropped, asserts the Employer, not because the latter relinquished the Management right to hire from the outside, but because it agreed in Section 6.6 to post all new bargaining unit jobs for five (5) working days before being filled. Once the Village agreed to post all jobs, it was no longer true that nothing in the Labor Agreement limits its right to hire from the outside. Once posted for five (5) days, the Village has the right to fill the vacancy with an outside employee.

In fact, claims the Employer, the Union in effect agreed that the Village has the right to fill posted jobs from the street because it dropped that portion of its proposal of September 9, 1985, which stated:

An outside applicant will not be hired unless no current employees who are qualified for the position have submitted applications.

In sum, the Employer contends:

The Union has failed to prove a violation of the Contract. By the express and implied terms of the Contract, as supported by relevant bargaining history, the Village retains the right to hire outside applicants rather than transfer employees, subject only to the posting requirements of Article VI, Section 6.6. The grievance, therefore, must be denied in its entirety.

Union

In the Union's judgment, the grievance should be granted. It contends that Article VI, Section 6.2, Application of Seniority, constitutes contractual language that gives preference to bargaining unit employees ahead of new employees in the filling of job vacancies. In addition, the Union contends that the initial contract negotiations between the Parties demonstrate their intent that the Employer may not hire from the outside when qualified bargaining unit employees desire to fill the job.
Thus, the Union asserts:

Based on the literal wording of the collective bargaining agreement, and even by extrinsic evidence, the instant collective bargaining agreement should be construed so as to include both current bargaining unit employees and newly-hired employees in the contract's seniority/ability measurement. Such an interpretation gives effect to the literal wording of all contract clauses, and is consistent with the written record of negotiations.

*A*dministrative Issues under Collective Bargaining

■ The importance of production standards and staffing

■ How unions have responded to the unparalleled challenges of recent technological change

■ Plant closings and the Worker Adjustment and Retraining Notification Act of 1988

Provisions relating to seniority, discipline, health and safety, subcontracting, and the various other "administrative" areas of the labor relationship have, as in the case of institutional provisions, the common characteristic of falling into the noneconomic classification of collective bargaining. They nonetheless have a profound influence upon the economic welfare of the employer and the economic status of the employees.

The character of a seniority clause, for example, can have a vital impact upon the efficient operation of the productive process. And the protection afforded an employee as a result of a discharge clause can be of much greater importance than any of the rights enjoyed as a result of the negotiation of wage rates or fringe benefits. It matters little to the worker who has been discharged for an obviously unfair reason that the wages called for by the labor contract are very generous.

Moreover, nowadays, technological change is of overriding importance in many labor relationships, dwarfing even the subject of wage issues in such instances. Literally thousands of jobs are being eliminated by such change each week in the economy, and it is a rare union that does not see the development, now an accelerating one indeed, as a formidable one from the viewpoint of job security. This volume has already dealt with union economic demands that are rooted at least partially in this problem: early retirement, severance pay, and SUB plans, among others. As we shall see, many administrative issues also flow from workers' fears that amid rampant technological innovation their jobs are very vulnerable.

In short, as important as the negotiation of economic issues may be, one cannot ignore these nonwage administrative issues of collective bargaining. Both are interwoven and to ignore or slight either—or, clearly, the institutional area of the contract as well—would represent a distortion of present-day labor relations in the United States.

SENIORITY

The principle of seniority, under which the employee with the greater length of organizational or organizational subunit service receives increased job security and improved working conditions (and, commonly, greater entitlement to employee benefits), is not new either to the world of work in general or to American industry. Over a thousand years ago promotion in the Chinese civil service was governed by time in grade, and two centuries ago it was rigorously applied in the Prussian bureaucracy to determine personnel advancement as the only alternative to the corruption that was almost a national pastime of the period. And while in the British civil service in the mid-nineteenth century promotion was theoretically to be based on "merit," in practice seniority was the dominant factor—again, as an antidote to favoritism by decision makers.[1]

In the United States, the armed forces have emphasized it from the days of Andrew Jackson, and the railroads and printing trades have stressed it for almost a century.

For at least three reasons, however, seniority has received increasing stress in labor contracts over the past few decades. In the first place, both management and employee representatives have become convinced that there is a certain amount of justice to the arrangement, especially in times of work contraction or recall opportunities after layoffs. Second, the application of seniority is an objective one, calculated to avoid arbitrariness in the selection of personnel for particular jobs and consequently less irksome for the labor negotiators to deal with than alternative devices. Third, the employee benefit programs that have mushroomed in these years have been geared almost exclusively to seniority—often, to make them more acceptable to the managements by restricting the number of employees entitled to the benefits.

Almost every labor agreement now includes some seniority formula, and this practice has become a deeply imbedded feature of the collective bargaining process. It is a chief method whereby employees obtain a measure of security in their jobs. It also limits the freedom of management to direct the labor force and influences considerations of plant efficiency. A seniority structure that approaches the ideal would be one that affords protection to employees in their job rights and at the same time does not place unreasonable restrictions on the right of management to make job assignments without sacrificing productivity and efficiency in the plant. This objective can best be realized to the extent that a seniority system is constructed to fit a particular plant environment. It must be tailored to fill the requirements of the technology, the kinds of jobs, the skills and occupations of the employees, and the character of labor relations of a specific employer. A seniority formula that might be desirable in one industrial situation might not be suitable to another.

Many problems are inherent in the formulation and application of a seniority structure. Among these, beyond the crucial determination of the phases of the employment relationship that are to be affected by the length-of-service principle, are establishment of the unit in which employees acquire and apply seniority credits; identification of circumstances under which employees may lose seniority; determination of the seniority status of employees who transfer from one part of the bargaining unit to another, or who leave the bargaining unit altogether; and the fixing of certain exceptions to the seniority system. As can be expected, these problems are handled in a multitude of fashions in collective bargaining relationships. Some labor agreements, moreover, attempt to cover all these issues, and some deal with only some of them.

The heavy majority of all labor agreements, for example, provide that seniority play a part in the determination of layoffs, in rehiring, and in promotions. But, as discussed below, the same labor agreement might use one seniority system to govern layoffs and rehiring and a different one in connection with promotions (where considerations of ability and physical fitness are often as important as, and in many cases more important than, length of service). Where a fixed-shift system exists, labor agreements may permit workers their choice of shifts on the basis of seniority, and factors such as personal convenience, wage or hour differentials, and the kind of job itself may dictate the senior worker's choice in this respect. Under other contracts, however, seniority plays no role in shift assignments.

Units for Seniority

There are three major systems relating to the unit in which an employee acquires and applies seniority credits: company- or plantwide, departmental or occupational, and a combined plant and departmental seniority system.

Under a *company- or plantwide seniority system*, the seniority status of each employee equals that person's total service with the firm. Thus, transfers from job to job within the establishment or transfers from one department to another have no effect on an employee's seniority standing. Subject to other features of the seniority structure, an employee under the company- or plantwide system will apply his or her seniority for purposes covered by the seniority system on a strictly company- or plantwide basis. In actual practice, this system is not used in companies in which it would be necessary for an employee to undergo a considerable training period when the employee takes a new job to replace a worker with less seniority. It is practicable only for companies in which the jobs are more or less interchangeable. A companywide system obviously gives the greatest protection to employees with the longest length of service. On the other hand, depending upon the other features of the seniority structure, it could serve as a deterrent to the efficiency and productivity of the organization.

Under *departmental* or *occupational seniority systems*, separate seniority lists are established for each department or occupational grouping in the plant. If such a system does not have any qualifications or limitations, employees can apply seniority credits only within their own department or occupation. Such a system facilitates administration in large companies employing a considerable number of workers. It minimizes the opportunity for large-scale displacement of workers from their jobs in the event of layoffs or discontinuation of particular jobs because of technological innovations, or because of permanent changes in the market for the products of the company. On the other hand, additional problems arise as the result of the use of this kind of seniority system. If layoffs in one department become necessary, or if certain jobs in such a department are permanently discontinued while other departments are not affected, a state of affairs could develop wherein employees with long service in a company would find themselves out of a job while employees with less seniority were working full time. In addition, under a strict departmental seniority structure, transfers between departments tend to be discouraged because a transfer could result in complete loss of accumulated seniority.

As a result of the problems arising from a strict company or departmental seniority system, many managements and unions have negotiated a number of plans combining these two types of seniority structures. Under a combination system, seniority may be applied in one unit for certain purposes and in another unit for other purposes. Thus, seniority may be applied on a plantwide basis for purposes of layoffs, whereas department-wide seniority is used as the basis of promotion. A variation of this system is to permit employees to *apply* their seniority only within the department in which they are working but to *compute* such seniority on the basis of total service with the employer. In addition, although the general application of seniority is limited to a departmental basis, employees laid off in a particular department may claim work in a general labor pool in which the jobs are relatively unskilled and in which newly hired employees start out before being promoted to other departments. At times, a distinction is drawn between temporary layoffs resulting from lack of business or material shortages, and permanent layoffs resulting from changes in technology or permanent changes in the products manufactured by the company. Under the former situation, seniority may be applied only on a departmental basis, or seniority might not govern at all (as in the automobile industry), whereas under the latter circumstances, employees have the opportunity to apply their seniority on a plantwide basis. Other variations of the combination system are utilized within industry as determined by the circumstances of a particular plant.

Limitations upon Seniority

Regardless of the type of system under which seniority credits are accumulated and applied, many collective bargaining agreements—possibly as many as one third of them—place certain limitations and qualifications upon length of service as a factor in connection with layoffs. In some cases, seniority systems provide for the retention of more senior employees only when they are qualified to perform the jobs that are available. In considerably fewer labor agreements, a senior employee will be retained in the event of layoffs in the plant only when the employee is able to perform an available job "as well as" other employees eligible for layoff.

Although a large number of labor agreements permit employees scheduled for layoff to displace less-senior employees, limitations on the chain displacement or "bumping" process are also included in many labor agreements. Employers, unions, employees, and students of labor relations recognize the inherent disadvantages of seniority structures that permit unlimited bumping. Bumping could result in serious obstacles to efficiency and productivity to the detriment of all concerned, could cause extreme uncertainty and confusion to workers who might be required to take a number of different jobs as a result of a single layoff, and could result in serious internal political problems for the labor organization.

For these reasons, limitations are usually placed on the bumping process. Many labor agreements allow an employee to displace a less-senior worker in the event of a layoff only when the former employee has a minimum amount of service with the employer. Other contracts circumscribe the bumping process by limiting the opportunity of a senior employee to displacement of a junior worker from a job that the employee with longer service has already held. Under this system, the worker comes down in the same fashion that he went up the job ladder. Under other seniority systems, the area into which the employee may bump is itself limited: It may be stipulated that employees can bump only on a departmental or divisional basis, or can displace workers only with equal or lower labor grades. In addition, the objective of limiting the displacement process is achieved by permitting the displacement of only the *least*-senior employee in the bumping area and not of any other less-senior employees.

Most labor agreements provide for rehiring in reverse order of layoffs—the last employee laid off is the first rehired. In addition, laid-off employees are given preference over new workers for vacancies that arise anywhere in the plant. However, such preferences given employees with longer service are frequently limited to the extent that the employee in question is competent to perform the available work. In this connection, the problem of the reemployment of laid-off workers becomes somewhat complicated when a straight departmental seniority system is used. In such a case, although a labor agreement might provide for the rehiring of workers in the reverse order of layoffs, production might not be revived in reverse order to the slack in production, and thus employees with shorter service might be recalled to work before employees with greater seniority. To avoid such a state of affairs, some labor contracts provide the older employee in terms of service with the opportunity of returning to work first, provided that the person has the ability to carry out the duties of the available job.

Length of service as a factor in promotion is of less importance than it is in layoffs and rehiring, and in only a relative handful of labor agreements is length of service the sole factor in making promotions. The incidence is low because all parties to collective bargaining realize that a janitor, for example, in spite of many years of service in this position, is not qualified to be promoted to, say, a tool-and-die-maker's job. But if such a criterion is rarely the sole factor in the assignment of workers to higher-rated jobs, the vast majority of labor agreements now require that seniority along with other factors be given *consideration*. In many contracts, seniority governs promotions when the senior employee is "qualified" to fill the position in question. Under others, seniority becomes the determining criterion in promotions when the senior employee has the ability and physical fitness for the job in question "equal to that" of all other employees who may desire the better job. Under the latter seniority structure, length of service is of secondary importance to the ability and physical fitness factors, however. (*Case 9 deals with seniority and relative qualifications.*)

In practice, management makes the decision about which worker among those bidding for the job gets the promotion; and in the heavy majority of cases, this decision of the employer is satisfactory to all concerned, usually because the senior employee *is* best qualified for the job in question or because the employer is completely willing to give preference to the senior employee when ability differences among employees are not readily discernible. At times, however, when the management passes over a senior employee in favor of an employee with shorter service in making a promotion, the union may protest the action through the grievance procedure. For example, the union may argue that the senior employee bidding for the better job has equal ability to that of the worker whom the management tapped for the promotion. The problem in such cases is to evaluate the comparative abilities of the two workers. Such a determination involves the study and appraisal of the entire work record of both workers. Consideration here is usually given to such items as the previous experience of the workers on the actual job in question or on closely related jobs; the education and training qualifications of the workers for performing the job in question; production records of the employees; and absenteeism, tardiness, and accident records, when relevant. Ordinarily, such disputes are resolved on the basis of these considerations. At times, however, the parties are still in disagreement, and the matter is then most often referred to an impartial arbitrator, who will make the decision in the case.

Seniority in Transfers

Another seniority problem involves the seniority status of employees who transfer from one department to another. As stated above, interdepartmental transfers do not create a seniority issue under a straight plantwide seniority system. To the extent that seniority is acquired or applied on a departmentwide basis, however, the problem of transfers becomes important to employers, unions, and employees; reference has been made to the fact that interdepartmental transfers are discouraged when employees lose all accumulated seniority upon entering a new department. Some contracts deal with this problem by allowing a transferred employee to retain seniority in the old department while starting at the bottom of the seniority scale in the new department; under these circumstances, such an employee would exercise seniority rights in the old department in the event that the employee were laid off from the new department. Some contracts even permit such an employee to further accumulate seniority for application in the old department in the event that he or she is laid off from the new department. Another approach to the problem permits the transferred employee to carry seniority acquired in the old department to the new department. This is a common practice where the job itself is transferred to a new department, where the job or the department itself is permanently abolished, or when two or more departments are merged.

Still another seniority problem arises under the circumstances of an employee's transferring entirely out of the bargaining unit. This issue is particularly related to the seniority status of workers who are selected by management to fill supervisory jobs. There are three major approaches to this problem. Under some contracts, a rank-and-file employee who takes a supervisory job simply loses accumulated seniority. If for some reason the supervisory job is terminated and the employee desires to return to a job covered by the collective bargaining contract, he or she is treated as a new employee for purposes of seniority. Another method is to permit such an employee when serving as a supervisor to retain all seniority credits earned earlier. Under this approach, if the employee transfers back to the bargaining unit, the employee returns with the same number of seniority credits as before the transfer. Finally, under some contracts, an employee taking a supervisor's job accumulates seniority in the bargaining unit while serving as a supervisor. If the employee returns to the bargaining unit, that worker comes back not only with the seniority credits acquired before taking the supervisory job but with seniority credits accumulated while serving as a member of management. Rank, at times, does have its privileges.

Obviously, seniority status is not a problem when management fills its supervisory posts by hiring outside the plant. On the other hand, the problem is a real one when the employer elects to fill such jobs from the rank and file. It is apparent that a worker with long seniority in the bargaining unit would hesitate to take a first-line supervisory job if doing so would forfeit accumulated seniority. In recognition of this situation, many employers and unions have agreed that workers promoted from the bargaining unit to supervisors' jobs may at least retain the seniority they accumulated while covered by the labor agreement. Whatever approach unions and managements take to this problem, it would generally be desirable to spell out the method in the labor agreement. Confusion, uncertainty, and controversy could arise when the contract is silent on this issue.

At times seniority may be used as the basis of a transfer to a job within the same wage classification. Such an opportunity may be used by an employee who desires to move to a different shift, for instance from the night to the day shift. Or if the employee and the supervisor cannot get along, the employee may exercise transfer rights to a job in another area of the plant or to a different shift. Under these circumstances, the transfer would be beneficial to the management and the employee. Normally, however, there are restrictions on employee transfer rights. When the transfer is within the same wage classification but to another job, the employee must have qualifications to perform the work. It is common for different jobs to be grouped within the same wage classifications. Transfer provisions also do not ordinarily permit bumping. Before a transfer may occur, there must be a job vacancy. Recognizing that promiscuous transfers could be harmful to plant efficiency, employers insist that the employees' right to transfer be limited. For example, some contracts require that an employee be within a job classification, often for six months or a year, before the employee may exercise transfer rights. In addition, when two or more employees desire to transfer to the same job, normally labor agreements will give preference to the senior employee provided that the senior bidder has qualifications relatively equal to those of a junior service employee.

Exceptions to the Seniority System

Under many collective bargaining contracts there is provision for some exemptions from the normal operation of the seniority structure. One of these involves the issue of "superseniority" for union officers. Some managements and unions have agreed that designated union officers may have a preferred status in the event of layoffs. Such employees are protected in employment regardless of their length of service. They are entitled to such consideration strictly by virtue of the union office they hold, however, and lose their superseniority status when their term of office is terminated.

Preference is afforded union officers because their presence in the plant is necessary for the effective operation of the grievance procedure. On this basis, the National Labor Relations Board held in 1983 that only those union officers, such as stewards, who participate directly in the processing of grievances are entitled to superseniority status.[2] Such a benefit for officers who do not perform on-the-job contract administration functions is not lawful, said the NLRB, because to grant them superseniority unjustifiably discriminates against employees for union-related reasons.

The test is whether a particular officer is involved in grievance processing and not status in the union. As a result, the board has held unlawful superseniority granted to a union treasurer, a recording secretary, and a sergeant-at-arms because their presence in the plant was not required for the day-to-day operation of the grievance procedure.

Beyond specifying the precise union officers who are entitled to protection against layoff, another problem concerns the bumping rights of employees protected under such an arrangement. Contracts are usually clear as to just what job or jobs such employees are entitled when they are scheduled for layoff. In addition, it is common practice to make clear the rate of pay that the employee will earn in the new job. Thus, if a worker protected by superseniority takes another job that pays a lower rate than his or her regular job to avoid layoff, the contract specifies whether or not that employee will get the rate of the job filled or the rate of the regular job. Obviously, when these problems are resolved in the labor agreement, there is less chance for controversy during the hectic atmosphere of a layoff itself.

Some labor agreements also permit management to retain in employment during periods of layoff a certain number of nonunion-officer employees regardless of their seniority status. Such employees are designated as "exceptional," "specially skilled," "indispensable," or "meritorious" in collective bargaining contracts. As in the case of superseniority, problems growing out of this exception to the seniority rule are normally resolved in the collective bargaining contract. Problems in this connection involve the number of employees falling into this category, the kind of jobs they must be holding to receive such preferential status, their bumping rights (if any), and the rate of pay they shall earn in the event that they are retained in employment in jobs other than their regular ones.

Another general exception to the normal operation of a seniority system involves newly hired workers. Under most labor agreements, such workers must first serve a probationary period before they are protected by the labor agreement. Such probationary periods are frequently specified as being from about thirty to ninety days, and during this period of time the new worker can be laid off, demoted, transferred, or otherwise assigned work without reference to the seniority structure at all. However, once such an employee serves out this probationary period, seniority under most labor agreements is calculated from the first day of hire by the employer.

Under the terms of many collective bargaining contracts, employers may lay off workers on a *temporary* basis without reference to the seniority structure. Such layoffs are for short periods of time and result from purely temporary factors, such as shortages of material and power failures. It is, of course, vital in this connection that the labor agreement define the temporary layoff. At times, contracts incorporate the principle that employers may lay off without reference to seniority on a temporary basis but fail to specify what is meant by the term *temporary layoff.* Some agreements define the term as any layoff for fewer than five or even ten working days. Other contracts, however, specify that the seniority structure must be followed for any layoff in excess of twenty-four hours. Whatever time limit is placed on the term, the labor agreement should specify the duration of a temporary layoff. By this means, a considerable amount of future argument will be avoided.

Finally, virtually all seniority structures specify circumstances under which an employee loses seniority credits. All employees should fully understand the exact nature of these circumstances and the significance of losing seniority credits. Under the terms of most collective bargaining contracts, employees lose seniority if they are discharged, voluntarily quit, fail to notify the management within a certain time period (usually five working days) of an intention to return to work after the employer recalls employees following a layoff, or fail to return to work after an authorized leave of absence. They also generally are separated from their seniority if they neglect to report to work within a certain period of time (usually ninety working days) after discharge from military service, or are laid off continuously for a long period of time, usually from about twenty-four to forty-eight months.

An Overall Evaluation

However qualified it may be in particular situations, there can be no denying the current acceptability of the seniority criterion in regulating potential competition among employees for jobs and job status. The traditional arguments that seniority fosters laziness, rewards mediocrity, and crimps individual initiative are no longer automatically brought into play by managers to oppose this length-of-service criterion. And the on-balance benefits of seniority, both in improving employee morale and in minimizing administrative problems, are no longer seriously questioned by progressive managements, *if* length of service is limited by such other factors as ability when these are relevant. Although it is probably true that in general a seniority system tends to reduce the efficiency of operations to some extent, if care is taken to design a system to the needs of the particular organization, and if length of service is appropriately limited in its application, the net loss to efficiency is normally not very noticeable.

Beyond this, many would argue that efficiency, despite its obvious importance, should not be the only goal of American industry. The advantages of providing a measure of job security to employees, and thereby relieving them of the frustrations of discrimination and unfair treatment, cannot be easily quantified. But human values have become the increasing concern of modern management, and the judicious use of seniority clearly serves the human equation.

Seniority versus Affirmative Action

Because seniority is such a major factor in layoffs—almost 50 percent of all contracts now use it as the exclusive criterion in such circumstances, indeed, with another 30 percent commanding that it be a determining layoff factor—it has generated considerable tension between white male workers and minority and female ones. Generally having been more recently hired, both of the latter groups of employees have also been, in accordance with seniority, the first to go when work forces are pared to accommodate hard times. Thus, amid declining economic conditions of both the mid-1970s and the early 1980s, for example, many workplaces within months became once again as white and as male as they had been years earlier.

Equal opportunity had, of course, finally come to minorities and females in the 1960s and 1970s. It had had many causes—among them, certainly, more progressive mores of society and more enlightened attitudes on the part of the new breed of industrial leader. But, patently, one factor had been paramount: Title VII of the Civil Rights Act of 1964, with its ban on job discrimination by race, sex, color, religion, or national origin and its application to all corporations, state and local governments, labor organizations, and employment agencies having more than fifteen employees. Following this landmark legislation, blacks and other minority group members, as well as women, had been hired and promoted, often in some abundance, into jobs for which even in an expanding economy they had generally been treated like wallflowers at an orgy.

To the Equal Employment Opportunity Commission, charged (together with the Justice Department) with enforcing Title VII and empowered to sue the title's violators, what employers should do in the face of the need for layoffs was clear: give special protection to the newly recruited groups to compensate them for past discrimination. At least as clear, however, was the fact that union contracts commanded respect for the seniority principle and its "last in, first out" principle. And, all but universally, the second of these Hobson's choices was embraced by the management community as the economy sank to its lowest levels since the Great Depression of the 1930s in a 1975 tailspin that would be exceeded in its enormity only by the impact of the 1981–1983 recession.

As court dockets became clogged with consequent affirmative action vs. seniority suits (with the EEOC lending its full weight to minorities and women, and the U.S. Department of Justice generally supporting seniority), most experts felt that seniority would ultimately triumph—at the U.S. Supreme Court level, where the issue would inevitably wind up. For one thing, the 1964 Civil Rights Act itself specifically approved "bona fide" seniority systems in layoffs (although it omitted any helpful interpretations as to what was "bona fide"). For another, the lower courts had already consistently upheld the seniority system, most notably in the case of *Jersey Central Power and Light Co.*, where a U.S. appeals court judge ruled that Congress had not mandated such a sweeping remedy as that proposed by the EEOC and that only Congress could do so. And for a third, layoff by seniority was specifically sanctioned even on the occasion of the EEOC's most conspicuous victory: In 1973, when, by a consent decree, the American Telephone and Telegraph Company agreed to pay $51 million in back wages and raises.

In two complex 1977 decisions involving United Air Lines flight attendants and truck drivers employed by T.I.M.E.–D.C. Inc., the Supreme Court ruled that although it might perpetuate the effects of past discrimination against women and minorities, an otherwise "neutral" seniority system did not violate the Civil Rights Act. The Court drew upon the act's own approval of bona fide seniority systems to assert that Congress had allowed no recourse for those who claimed that the discrimination occurred before the law took effect on July 2, 1965. And it added that even charges of discrimination since 1965 might themselves be moot unless they were made in a "timely" way.

But this was not to be the last judicial word on the subject. In 1979 the Court ruled on a major new "reverse discrimination" suit, brought by a white worker at a Kaiser Aluminum plant in Louisiana on the grounds that he had been discriminated against by being turned down for a company training program designed to increase the number of blacks in skilled craft jobs. The worker, Brian F. Weber, pointed out that he had been rejected even though two black workers who were accepted had less seniority. The case stemmed from a 1974 company-union agreement to establish a new skilled job program, open to blacks and whites on a 50–50 basis until blacks had achieved a 39 percent representation in such skilled jobs (39 percent because this equaled their current representation in the area work force).

The Court decided against Weber. By a 5 to 2 majority, it declared that an employer could give preference to minorities (and women) in hiring and promoting for "traditionally segregated job categories" and that it didn't matter that the employer had never practiced discrimination. In so doing it greatly relieved Kaiser Aluminum (and, obviously, many other employers) of an understandable worry: Up until this decision the Civil Rights Act had appeared to allow remedial discrimination only where past discrimination had been proven, and if Kaiser, amid this circumstance, had admitted any such past discrimination it would have opened itself to all sorts of lawsuits from injured employees. The Court's *Weber* ruling extricated Kaiser, which perhaps for a while was starting to believe the old adage that no good deed goes unpunished, from this unenviable dilemma.

Yet the decision was decided on rather narrow grounds. As Justice William Brennan pointed out in writing the majority opinion, the only key was whether the Civil Rights Act forbade *voluntary* endeavors of the Kaiser variety. The decision that it did not was hardly tantamount to *requiring* employers to establish affirmative action programs.

More Recent Supreme Court Decisions

In a series of decisions issued between 1984 and 1989, the U.S. Supreme Court continued to address the problem of affirmative action. In *Fire-fighters* v. *Stotts,* the high court held that an affirmative action program may not be used to lay off senior white employees and retain junior service black workers. Under a federal court decree, the City of Memphis was required to increase the number of black firefighters from 4 to 11 percent. Subsequently, the city laid off senior white employees ahead of junior service black employees to maintain the balance between white and black firefighters. Reversing a federal appeals court that sustained the layoff procedure, the U.S. Supreme Court held that Title VII was violated by such preferential treatment afforded black employees. As in *T.I.M.E.–D.C.,* the high court held that the seniority system as it applies to layoffs was bona fide and not intended for discrimination against black employees.

In 1986, the high court again held that junior service black employees could not be retained and senior white employees laid off in *Wygant* v. *Jackson Board of Education.* In Jackson, Michigan, the board of education had negotiated a labor agreement with the teachers' union stipulating that junior service black teachers would be kept on while senior white teachers would be laid off. Such a system was negotiated to keep black teachers as "role models." By a 5-to-4 majority, the high court held that the white teachers were denied equal protection of the law, and that the affirmative action program to maintain black teachers as role models could not alone justify laying off the senior white teachers. That the Court found the issue to be perplexing and highly controversial is demonstrated by the fact that five separate opinions were written, none of them joined in by more than three justices.

The Court did not slam the door on all aspects of affirmative action. Even in the matter of layoffs, it hinted in *Wygant,* such special circumstances as a showing of blatant historical discrimination by the employer against minorities might even now justify the layoffs of white employees who were senior to minority employees and the retention of the minority group members. And in two later 1986 decisions—respectively involving black firefighters in Cleveland and sheet metal workers in New York—the judges continued this latter theme. The judiciary could, as Justice Brennan wrote for the majority in the latter case, properly order "race-conscious affirma-tive action [as] relief to dissipate the lingering effects of pervasive discrim-ination."

For women, moreover, the Court had even better news. In 1987, the justices ruled in *Johnson* v. *Transportation Agency,* that the public transportation agency of Santa Clara County, California, had properly awarded a road dispatcher's job to Diane Joyce, even though she had scored two points less than a man (the plaintiff, Paul Johnson) on a performance test and Johnson had had more seniority than Joyce. Joyce had been found to be fully qualified in all respects by a supervisory panel. And the Court decreed that because there had been a "manifest [sexual] imbalance" in the work force and such affirmative action would not by itself "unnecessarily trammel" the rights of other workers, the employer could voluntarily implement the affirmative action.

But a variety of 1989 decisions dispelled any real doubt as to where the Ronald Reagan appointees who now firmly fashioned the high court decisions stood on such matters. In *Lorance* v. *A.T. & T. Technologies,* the Court severely restricted the time period during which certain discriminatory practices involving a seniority system could be challenged. In *Price Waterhouse,* while declaring that employers must prove that their refusal to promote employees is based on legitimate business reasons, it lowered the burden of proof required in these situations to the weakest possible standard.

Warming to their work, the judges then reversed in *Wards Cove* v. *Atonio* an 18-year-old precedent and ruled that plaintiffs, not employers, have the burden of proving whether a job requirement that is shown statistically to screen out minorities or women is a "business necessity." In further votes, the members of the highest judiciary decided that court-approved affirmative action settlements can be reopened to let white male employees file reverse discrimination lawsuits (*Martin* v. *Wilks*) and that an 1866 civil rights law is inapplicable to cases of racial harassment or other discrimination by an employer after a person is hired (in *Patterson* v. *McLean Credit Union*).

The Court, even before two additional conservative justices replaced liberal ones on it during George Bush's White House years, had drifted very much to the right. Without some kind of legislative intervention, it was obvious that both women and minorities would find it much harder to prevail in their attacks on alleged job discrimination than they had prior to the new wave of rulings.

The Civil Rights Act of 1991

Legislative intervention did, however, come about—during, in fact, an economic recession that was even more severe than the tailspins of the 1970s and 1980s. Strong actions by any of our three branches of government can generally be counted upon to produce reactions from others of them. And while the Civil Rights Act of 1991 is hardly in a class with the 1964 Civil Rights Act in its ambitiousness, it is notable for two major thrusts: (1) the effective countering of the several 1989 Supreme Court decisions; and (2) the extension for the first time of punitive damages to victims of employment discrimination based on sex, race, or (under an amendment to the 1990 Americans with Disabilities Act) disability.

Now a plaintiff claiming that a seniority system is discriminatory may rely on the date that the system was adopted, the date that he or she became subject to the system, or the date that the person was allegedly injured by the system (reversing *Lorance*). The *Price Waterhouse* required burden of proof has been raised appreciably; *Wards Cove* has been negated by the actual shifting of the "business necessity" proof burden back to the employer; and the tenets of both *Martin* and *Patterson* have vanished as though they had never been.

Nor can employers found guilty of intentional discrimination henceforth get off with the mere payments of compensatory damages (future economic losses, pain and suffering, mental anguish, inconvenience, and other non-pecuniary losses), as onerous as these may be. If the plaintiff can prove that the management acted in a discriminatory practice "with malice or with reckless indifference to the federally protected rights of an aggrieved individual," an additional price must be paid by the employer—up to $300,000 in punitive damages depending on the size of the organization. Employers with 15 to 100 employees can expect to pay up to $50,000; those with 101 to 200 employees, up to $100,000; those with 201 to 500 employees, up to $200,000; and those with over 500 employees, up to the $300,000 maximum (the law exempts businesses with 14 or fewer people on the payroll).

Perhaps the ideal mix of seniority and affirmative action will never be found, but it will surely not be for lack of governmental trying.

DISCHARGE AND DISCIPLINE

To the naked eye, in the absence of a collective bargaining agreement, the employer is relatively unfettered in applying discipline. Actions cannot be taken, to be sure, that conflict with federal, state, or local labor laws. The government has also, as we know, been anything but bashful in dealing with the subject of discrimination against individuals on a variety of grounds, and clearly the disciplinary efforts cannot run afoul of these constraints either. Except only for such considerations, however, the management is as free to deal disciplinarily with its payroll members as it chooses—even if it chooses to act quite arbitrarily, inconsistently, autocratically, and harshly. The employer can discipline for any reason or, indeed, for no reason at all.

The advent of the union changes all of this, in the sense that *specific standards* are now established for the discipline. Generally, labor-management contracts state that employers may discipline only for "just cause" (or "just and proper cause" or "proper cause"); and even where they do not, such a stricture is assumed to be implied if there is no concrete language to the contrary. And the critical interpretation of just cause is accomplished through industrial practice and common sense, as well as (if need be) the grievance procedure and the arbitration process.

A large percentage of arbitration cases involve discipline, most frequently discharge situations, and this is entirely understandable. The right of the employer to discipline is essential to operating a successful enterprise, but—as one arbitrator phrased it in ruling against a company in a discharge case:

> If the Company can discharge without cause, it can lay off without cause. It can recall, transfer or promote in violation of the seniority provisions simply by invoking its claimed right to discharge. Thus, to interpret the Agreement in accord with the claim of the Company would reduce to a nullity the fundamental provision of a labor-management agreement—the security of a worker in his job.[3]

In addition, the stigma of discharge would hardly make it easier for the former employee to find another job. Thus, discharges have even more serious consequences for workers than do permanent layoffs.

Although the majority of contracts contain only the previously noted general and simple statement that discharge can be made only for just cause, many labor agreements list one or more specific grounds for discharge: violation of company rules, failure to meet work standards, incompetence, violation of the collective bargaining contract (including in this category the instigation of or participation in a strike or a slowdown in violation of the agreement), excessive absenteeism or tardiness, intoxication, dishonesty, insubordination, and fighting on company property. Labor agreements that list specific causes for discharge normally also include a general statement that discharge may be made for "any other just or proper reason."

In addition, many contracts distinguish between causes for immediate discharge and offenses that require one or more warnings. For example, sabotage or willful destruction of property may result in immediate discharge, whereas a discharge for absenteeism may occur only after a certain number of warnings. In recognition of the fact that not all employee infractions are grave enough to warrant discharge, lesser forms of discipline are imposed at times under collective bargaining relationships. Into this category fall oral and written reprimand, suspension without pay for varying lengths of time, demotion, and denial of vacation pay. Frequently, union and management representatives in the grievance procedure will agree upon a lesser measure of discipline even though the employer presumably has the grounds to discharge an employee for a particular offense. At times, the union and the employee in question will be willing to settle a case on these terms rather than risk taking the case to arbitration.

A very large number of collective bargaining contracts specify a distinct procedure for discharge cases (and many also do so for disciplinary layoffs, as Exhibit 10-1, culled from the current General Motors-UAW agreement, demonstrates). Many of them require notice to the employee and the union before the discharge takes place. Such notification is generally required to contain the specific reasons for the discharge. A hearing on the case is also provided for in many labor agreements, typically requiring the presence of not only the worker in question and an appropriate management official but also a representative of the labor organization. Frequently, collective bargaining agreements provide for a suspension period before the discharge becomes effective. The alleged advantage of this procedure is that it provides for an opportunity to cool tempers and offers a period of time

EXHIBIT 10–1

Disciplinary Layoffs and Discharges

(76) Any employee who has been disciplined by a suspension, layoff or discharge will be furnished a brief written statement advising him of his right to representation and describing the misconduct for which he has been suspended, laid off or discharged and, in the case of a layoff or discharge, the extent of the discipline. Thereafter, he may request the presence of the committeeman for his district to discuss the case privately with him in a suitable office designated by the Local Management, or other location by mutual agreement, before he is required to leave the plant. The committeeman will be called promptly without regard to the restrictions on his time as provided in Paragraphs (18) and (19a) of the Representation Section. Whether called or not, the committeeman will be advised in writing within one working day of 24 hours of the fact of written reprimand, suspension, layoff or discharge and will be given a copy of the statement given to the employee. After a suspension has been converted to a layoff or discharge, the committeeman will be notified in writing of the fact of layoff or discharge. The written statement furnished to the employee pursuant to the first sentence of this paragraph shall not limit Management's rights, including the right to rely on additional or supplemental information not contained in the statement to the employee.

(76a) When a suspension, layoff or discharge of an employee is contemplated, the employee, where circumstances permit, will be offered an interview to allow him to answer the charges involved in the situation for which such discipline is being considered before he is required to leave the plant. An employee who, for the purpose of being interviewed concerning discipline, is called to the plant, or removed from his work to the foreman's desk or to an office, or called to an office, may, if he so desires, request the presence of his District Committeeman to represent him during such interview.

(76b) The employee will be tendered a copy of any warning, reprimand, suspension or disciplinary layoff entered on his personnel record, within three days of the action taken. In imposing discipline on a current charge, Management will not take into account any prior infractions which occurred more than three years previously nor impose discipline on an employee for falsification of his employment application after a period of eighteen (18) months from his date of hire.

(77) It is important that complaints regarding unjust or discriminatory layoffs or discharges be handled promptly according to the Grievance Procedure. Grievances must be filed within three working days of the layoff or discharge. Within two working days after a grievance has been answered by higher supervision, pursuant to Paragraph 30 above, the specific charge will be discussed with designated representatives of local Plant Management, the Chairman of the Shop Committee, or his designated representative, and another member of the Shop Committee or the district committeeman who filed the grievance. If the grievance is not resolved, local Plant Management will review and render a decision on the case within three working days thereafter. In any event, local Plant Management will render a decision on the case within 10 working days from the date the grievance is filed. If a Notice of Unadjusted Grievance is not submitted by the Shop Committee within five (5) working days of a decision of the local Plant Management, the matter will be considered closed.

for all parties to make a careful investigation and evaluation of the facts of the case.

In 1975, the U.S. Supreme Court decided a case that has an important bearing on the right of employees to union representation when discipline is an issue. In *Weingarten,* the Court held that an employee has a right to the presence of a union representative at employer-conducted investigatory interviews that the employee may reasonably believe could lead to disciplinary action. At times, employers conduct a "fact-finding" interview with an employee to determine whether or not such action should be imposed. In such a session, the employer does not impose a penalty but obtains information to decide whether the employee should be disciplined. Since it is an investigation session, some employers have refused requests by employees for union representation. However, under the Court's rule, the employer must grant an employee's request for union representation in such a session. Failure of an employer to obey this obligation violates the employee's right as protected by Taft-Hartley.

Originally the NLRB enforced the employer's right by directing the reinstatement of employees with back pay when they were discharged for the subject of the unlawful interview. In 1984, however, the Reagan board reversed this policy.[4] As long as an employee is discharged for good cause, it held, the board will not direct reinstatement even though the employer unlawfully denied him representation during an investigatory interview. In these cases, the agency will issue only a cease and desist order instructing the employer to grant union representation at such interview. To the employee, of course, the current remedy is worthless because the discharge stands. Clearly, under this construction, the *Weingarten* decision of the U.S. Supreme Court has no practical value. It will encourage employers to deny employees union representation at the investigatory interview. To change the current policy, the high court would be compelled to direct reinstatement of employees who are discharged over the matter covered in the unlawful interview. In another reversal of policy, the Reagan board held in *Sears, Roebuck and Co.* that employees within nonunion plants are not entitled to representation. Previously the board held an employee could select a co-worker for representation within a nonunion plant.

Part of the procedure for discharge cases is provided for in the general grievance procedure of the contract. As suggested, almost every labor agreement provides for appeal of discharge cases, and this appeal is taken through the regular grievance procedure, since the appeal is looked upon as a grievance. If, for example, the labor agreement provides that the employee or the union must appeal a discharge within a certain number of days, such appeal must be made during this period or the discharge may become permanent regardless of the merits of the case. Likewise, a management that neglects its obligation to give an answer to the appeal within the stipulated number of days may find that it has lost its right to discharge the worker regardless of the justice of the situation.

Frequently, labor agreements also provide that a discharge case has a priority over all other cases in the grievance procedure. Some of them even waive the first few steps of the grievance procedure and start a discharge case at the top levels of the procedure. In these arrangements, employers and unions recognize the fact that it is to the mutual advantage of all concerned to expedite discharge cases. Workers want to know as quickly as possible whether or not they still have a job. The management also has an interest in the prompt settlement of a discharge case, because of the disciplinary implications involved and because labor agreements normally require that the employer award the employee loss of earnings where a discharge is withdrawn.

From the foregoing, it should be clear that under a collective bargaining relationship, the employer does not lose the right to discipline or discharge; it is, however, more difficult for management to exercise this function. There must be just cause, a specific procedure must be followed, and, of course, management must have the proof that an employee committed the offensive act.

If a case does go to arbitration, in fact, the arbitrator will be particularly concerned with the quality of *proof* that management offers in the hearing. On many occasions, employers have lost discharge cases in arbitration because the evidence they have presented is not sufficient to prove the case for discharge. At times, the management's case against the employee has simply been poorly prepared; at other times, the management has not been able to assemble the proof despite the most conscientious of employer efforts. (One difficulty in this latter regard, as all arbitrators are well aware, is that employees dislike testifying against other employees who are charged with some offense.)

If the arbitrator did not demand convincing proof before sustaining discipline, however, the protection afforded employees by the labor agreement would be worthless. The same situation prevails in our civil life, wherein juries have freed criminals because the state has not proved its case. Such courses of action reflect one of the most cardinal features of our system of justice, the presumption that people are innocent until proven guilty, and this hallmark of our civil life plays no less a role in the American system of industrial relations. This situation has undoubtedly resulted in the reinstatement to their jobs with full back pay for employees who are in fact "guilty," but it is beyond argument that an employer bears the obligation to prove charges against employees it has displaced. In the absence of such an obligation, this most important benefit allowed employees under a collective bargaining contract, protection against arbitrary management treatment, is obviously negated. (*Cases 10 and 11 involve the discharge of employees. Case 11 is particularly called to your attention because of its strange circumstances.*)

Fully as important, the rules must be *clear* and *specifically communicated* or employees simply cannot be held responsible for violating them. It is generally agreed that this stricture need not apply where the conduct involved is so obviously wrong on both moral and legal grounds that a specific rule is not needed: There is certainly no need, for example, to have an explicit rule banning employees from threatening supervision with a knife, and falsification of one's work records is—again—so clearly reprehensible that workers need not be given advance notice that this constitutes unacceptable behavior. On the other hand, it cannot be taken for granted by the employer that employees will always know what is expected of them and most often specific communication is essential to sound discipline. It is better to saturate the landscape with such information than not to give enough.

Machinery for conveying behavioral expectations abounds in organizations. Employee handbooks, bulletin board postings, house organs, special memorandums from the management, and incorporation of the rules into the union contract are common avenues of communication. So, too, is oral publicity, by the personnel office (during orientation, for example) and also by supervision (perhaps simply as reinforcement of the original exposition). Consistent enforcement of the rules, let it not be forgotten, lends another kind of visibility to them.

What is important, however, is obviously not the exact methodology by which the rules are made known, but rather the fact that they *are* made known. No employee, when confronted with discipline, should be able to argue credibly that he or she did not realize that the conduct involved was forbidden, or—for that matter—that *changes* in the rules or a managerial intention to apply an existing rule more strictly had not been brought to the attention of the work force.

Finally, in assessing penalties, the arbitrator will fully weigh *extenuating* or *mitigating circumstances*. Is it appropriate, for example, to discipline an employee, who, at the company Christmas party, gets drunk, throws the contents of a can of beer in the face of the industrial relations manager, and makes the air purple with obscene remarks in the process? One would certainly think so, but a case involving exactly this set of circumstances reached the arbitration stage a while ago, and the arbitrator overturned the thirty-day suspension that the employee had been given for his behavior by the company and ordered that he be given full back pay as well. The decision was based primarily on the following considerations: (1) the man had worked for the company thirty-three years without a prior incident of insubordination; (2) the offense had been committed neither during working hours nor under plant disciplinary conditions, and the employee's conduct appeared to stem from his consuming too much alcohol rather than being connected with the employment relationship; and (3) although there had been prior incidents of drunken fights at the Christmas party, the company had continued to give out free and unlimited liquor and it consequently ran the risk of "predictable consequences."[5]

Mitigating circumstances—here, of course, three of them—completely changed the outcome from what might have been expected. Whether or not there is a labor arbitrator in the picture, a sound disciplinary policy commands nothing less than that these circumstances be carefully scrutinized where they exist.

Particularly when it is notably superior or glaringly inferior, a *past record,* for example, can make a large difference in evaluating the severity of a given offense. Even incidents that by themselves may hardly warrant much of a penalty at all, much less discharge, may generate a termination of employment under the most enlightened of disciplinary policies if they form a "last straw" in a long history of similar incidents. The alcoholic employee who has been warned on many occasions about his bad attendance record (as well as counseled about his underlying problem) and then is suspended for five days with the understanding that one more similar absence will cause his discharge and who then absents himself for the same drink-related reason may be said to illustrate this category. On the other side of the scales, a worker who might otherwise be terminated for a very serious offense—using abusive language in talking to a supervisor, let us say—could conceivably be given a lesser penalty in view of the worker's eleven years of superior performance (and absence of disciplinary infractions within it) in the service of the company.

In fact, *length of service,* in its own right, irrespective of its quality, can serve as a mitigating circumstance. Arbitrators have regularly accepted long service as something working in the disciplined employee's favor and so, too, in general have nonunion employers. Longevity itself presumably deserves some reward, but there are other considerations as well: As Elkouri and Elkouri assert, "[it is] recognized that the loss of seniority may work great hardship on the employee, and that it is not conducive to the improvement of relations between other workers and management."[6]

Still another kind of extenuating circumstance at times lies in the *behavior of management personnel* themselves. The employer is on very thin ice in attempting to enforce a rule against solicitation by employees on company premises if it is known that supervisors regularly peddle merchandise within the building, and the employer deserves no better fate in administering an antiobesity rule if members of management tip the scales at significantly more than their allotted poundage. Employees can hardly be expected to observe rules that are so obviously ignored by their superiors.

SAFETY AND HEALTH OF EMPLOYEES

Despite significant progress over the decades, working for a living remains something less than the safest of all human endeavors.

The statistics, understandably, vary widely industry by industry—with the mining of coal, for example, being potentially more dangerous to worker safety and health than, say, the practicing of dermatology, by several light-years. But it is a common estimate on the part of experts that as many as 100,000 deaths (or more than twice as many as are caused by automobile accidents) occur every year as a result of occupational disease and that some 400,000 people annually develop a debilitating occupational illness. Another 10,000 deaths are caused each year by workplace accidents—about 30 each day.

Other figures relating to employee safety and health are similarly discomforting. In the opinion of many informed observers, roughly 25 percent of all workers are regularly exposed to major health and safety hazards. A job-related illness or injury is annually incurred by one out of every eleven workers in the United States, costing the nation an estimated $23 billion each year in the form of lost wages, medical expenses, insurance claims, and decreased productivity.[7] And it has been predicted that one out of every six working men presently 35 years of age will be disabled for at least six months before they reach age 65 and that one tenth of these men will be permanently disabled.[8] (There are no comparable statistics available for working women.)

Given all of this, few people would argue that employees do not have a real interest in the area of industrial safety and health. After all, it is the worker and the worker's family who suffer the most devastating consequences of neglect in this area. And although most employers can sincerely claim that they, too, are deeply interested in safe and healthy working environments, such concern cannot restore to life a person killed on the job, or restore an employee's limbs, or succor an employee's family when an employment-caused accident or illness leads to a long-term disability. Indeed, this consideration is at the root of a longstanding policy of the National Labor Relations Board that safety and health demands of unions are mandatory subjects of collective bargaining. Employers must bargain on these issues even though working conditions are also subject to the many safety regulations imposed by federal and state statutes.

Not surprisingly, then, most collective bargaining contracts contain explicit provisions relating to the safety and health area, although such provisions take one of two routes, depending upon the particular contract.

On the one hand, many contracts merely state in general terms that the management is required to take measures to protect the safety and health of employees. At times, the term *measures* is qualified by the word *reasonable*. When a contract contains such a broad and general statement, the problem of application and interpretation is obviously involved, and disagreements between the management and union in this regard are commonly resolved through the regular grievance procedure, or by the operation of a special safety committee.

The second category of contracts provides a detailed and specific listing of safety and health measures that obligate the employer. Thus, many agreements stipulate that the latter must provide adequate heat, light, and ventilation; control drafts, noise, toxic fumes, dust, dirt, and grease; provide certain safety equipment, such as hoods, goggles, special shoes and boots, and other items of special clothing; and place guards and other safety devices on machines. In addition, under many contracts, the management must provide first-aid stations and keep a nurse on duty. Of course, whether or not a collective bargaining contract contains safety rules, an employer must comply with the federal and state safety and health laws applicable to its operations.

Many labor agreements impose obligations on employees and unions as well as on employers in the matter of safety. Such provisions recognize the fact that safety, despite the individual employee's crucial stake in it, is a joint problem requiring the cooperation of the management, employees, and union. Under many labor agreements, employees must obey safety rules and wear appropriate safety equipment, and employees who violate such rules are subject to discipline. In some labor agreements, the union assumes the obligation of educating its members in complying with safety rules and procedures of the plant. And some agreements, in the interest of safety, also establish a joint union-management safety committee. Many of these committees serve as advisory bodies on the general problem of safety and health; others, however, have the authority to establish and enforce safety and health rules, allowing the union a considerably more active role.

The Occupational Safety and Health Act and Its Consequences to Date

A high point in the area of employment safety and health was reached in the last days of 1970 with the enactment of the Occupational Safety and Health Act, generally referred to (as is the federal agency primarily charged with administering it) as OSHA. Under it, the federal government assumed a significant role in this area for the first time in history, and individual states were allowed to share jurisdiction if their plans for doing so could meet with the approval of Washington. OSHA inspectors were granted authority to inspect for violations (without prior notice to the employer) at the nation's 5 million workplaces and to issue citations leading to possibly heavy fines and even, as a last resort, jail sentences.

AFL-CIO president Meany applauded OSHA's enactment as "a long step down the road toward a safe and healthy workplace"; Richard M. Nixon, in signing it as President, referred to the act as "a landmark piece of legislation"; and the normally unemotional *Monthly Labor Review* passionately proclaimed it a "revolutionary program." Great expectations, in short, accompanied passage.

Yet disillusionment was quick to set in and, within a very few years, OSHA appeared to be all but friendless, its critics coming in almost equal numbers from the ranks of labor and management. By the end of the 1970s, the administrator of OSHA could sadly point out that the legislation had succeeded in alienating both sides. "Business and labor," she declared, "have criticized OSHA for nit-picking and the stringent enforcement of so-called nuisance standards.... Organized labor has complained that OSHA has been excruciatingly slow in adopting major health standards to protect large numbers of workers from widespread threats to their health."[9]

The complaints were justified. With fewer than 3,000 inspectors available to visit the 5 million places of work, the average employer could expect to see an OSHA agent roughly every seventy-five years. Yet when they did show up, these civil servants, as the administrator also pointed out, "were citing violations of regulations on everything from coat hooks to split toilet seats."[10] Moreover, OSHA's 325 pages of safety and health standards were so technical as to be unintelligible to the vast majority of employers without professional (and thus costly) help: In its first months alone, the agency had adopted almost 5,000 "consensus" safety standards. And the standards themselves were under any conditions expensive to satisfy, OSHA's noise-control demands alone potentially costing management anywhere from $13 billion to $31 billion (depending upon the final severity of these rules). OSHA, as one by no means atypical employer said of it at the end of its first decade, "is to a management what a knife is to a throat."

On the other hand, the agency's penalties for violations had averaged a not very punitive $25 each, with companies convicted of criminal violations being so rare as to be essentially invisible. And for all the "safety" standards, only three major "health" standards and a fourth one covering fourteen carcinogenic substances had been promulgated by the 1980s.

And it was the latter trend—only—that continued after the inauguration of Ronald Reagan as the nation's chief executive in 1981. Budgetary cuts reduced the meager inspection staff by more than half, to a far more meager 1,100 within a year. Under a presidential executive order, health and safety standards and regulations were weakened by a requirement that benefits be weighed against costs (although a subsequent Supreme Court ruling, in a dispute involving worker exposure to cotton dust, commanded that worker health must remain the overriding consideration even in such circumstances). Three of every four manufacturing firms were exempted from routine safety inspections (in the interests of more governmental concentration on high-hazard manufacturing industries). And much emphasis was generally placed on voluntary employer compliance.

By 1985, the AFL-CIO was charging the Reagan administration with having "undertaken a systematic assault" upon OSHA and pointing out that since Mr. Reagan had taken office, OSHA inspections had dropped by 45 percent, citations for serious violations had decreased by 47 percent, citations for willful violations had declined by 92 percent, and penalties imposed for overall violations had been reduced by almost 80 percent.[11] With minimal restraint, the federation's magazine commented, "Students of public administration may well rate the Reagan administration's emasculation of the Occupational Safety and Health Administration as its greatest bureaucratic coup."[12]

Stung by the criticism, the Reagan appointees at OSHA began to take a much harder line toward health and safety after 1985. In the next three years, the agency issued twenty new protective regulations, compared with twenty-seven such rules in the previous fourteen years, and by 1988 it was regularly making headlines by hitting some of the nation's largest employers with significant fines. In one week alone, the Chrysler Corporation was fined $1.57 million for violating OSHA rules and the country's biggest meatpacker (IBP Inc.) was docked a hefty $2.59 million, in both cases subject to appeal. Ford, General Dynamics, and Caterpillar were also the recipients of major financial penalties for failing to monitor the safety of their workplaces adequately.

After it took office in January 1989, the Bush administration continued the trend, vehemently denying that even amid its own budgetary constraints it would ever remotely retreat from safety and promising to finance OSHA better in the years ahead. It encouraged the agency to seek financing from Congress for another 179 inspectors, the first increase in the inspector contingent in a decade. In these early months of the Bush era, too, a more aggressive OSHA was busy promulgating the agency's first standard to protect on-the-job motor vehicle drivers, trying to raise the size of criminal fines for the most blatant job-site violations, and greatly expanding efforts to reduce carpal tunnel syndrome (involving arm, hand, and wrist injuries caused by repetitive motions).

Congress responded to the Bush desire for a more activist OSHA by authorizing even more inspectors than the White House had sought and greatly raising the level of fines. In the early 1990s, a record $10 million was levied against IMC Fertilizer after an explosion at a Louisiana nitro-paraffin plant killed eight IMC workers and injured 120 more, and Citgo Petroleum had to pay $6 million in the aftermath of a six-worker-fatality explosion. Phillips Petroleum was socked with a $4 million fine and Arco Chemical with a $3.5 million one for their roles in similar tragedies. No one expected this trend to be reversed.

And a highly regarded Bush-appointed OSHA chief, Gerard G. Scannell, broke new ground in restricting workplace smoking, developing new "ergo-nomics" requirements to cut down on the repetitive employee motions (particularly in the meatpacking and automobile industries), upgrading rules in the chemical processing sector, and working closely with such outside advocacy groups as the National Safe Workplace Institute. His personal concern for the families of workplace accident victims seemed to symbolize Scannell's generally sensitive yet professional approach to his high-profile job. To many union leaders he was, as the health and safety director of the United Food and Commercial Workers said of him, "the best that you could hope for in this administration."[13]

Presumably, OSHA will continue to have money problems in this era of government penny-pinching. For all of the agency's new aggressiveness, the Reagan era budgetary cuts have never been fully restored, and there is still much truth to the bitter charge of one observer, made in the wake of a 1991 North Carolina poultry plant fire that killed an awesome total of twenty-five employees, that "there's a USDA inspector in every poultry plant to protect consumers from getting a stomachache, but there's nobody protecting people from getting killed."[14] (Exhibit 10-2 explains this in somewhat more detail.) This situation continued even as Bill Clinton began his White House tenure.

But OSHA has continued to have a significant and positive impact on employee health and safety. Despite the cutbacks, most of OSHA's formidable standards still govern, and their very presence has generated enormous expenditures on capital investments linked to this area. By some estimates, as much as $6 billion annually is being spent by managements for health and safety, representing a doubling of the annual rate of a decade ago, and there is no question that the employer community's willingness to correct hazards and improve such vital environmental ingredients as ventilation, noise levels, and machine safety is much greater now than it was before OSHA's passage.

Essentially all experts also agree that because of OSHA employers know far more about such dangerous substances as asbestos, vinyl chloride, cotton dust, and many other actual or probable carcinogens than they formerly did and that appropriate actions to protect workers from these have been taken. It is also a widely held belief among OSHA watchers that simply by pressing the issue of employee safety and health, OSHA has made employers much more aware of workplace dangers than they would otherwise have been.

From organized labor, the activity has been even more pronounced. Ironically, the dissatisfaction with OSHA's enforcement has added impetus to labor's efforts, and literally hundreds of recent major contract innova-tions can be traced to this impetus.

EXHIBIT 10–2

Source: AFL-CIO.

Such innovations include the establishment in Oil, Chemical, and Atomic Worker-employer agreements of local joint health and safety committees with not only access to company data but the right to arbitrate unresolved safety controversies. They encompass also the training of local

UAW officials as full-time paid health and safety monitors in the automobile industry and a requirement won by the Steelworkers that when steel and aluminum industry workers are transferred out of dangerous jobs to lower-paying ones because of the hazards of continued exposure to toxic substances they must be paid at the higher rate.

The Rubber Workers have now won access to the lists of chemicals used by most rubber companies; the union also now has a program whereby rubber companies are required to contribute one-cent-per-hour worked for research (conducted by both Harvard and North Carolina) into potential health hazards. (Exhibit 10-3 illustrates typical language negotiated by the Oil, Chemical, and Atomic Workers in the chemical and petroleum industries, and Exhibit 10-4 attests to the emphasis placed on truck driver safety and health protection by the Teamsters in recent national negotiations with trucking companies. The Flight Attendants have taken a particular interest in AIDS, explained in Exhibit 10-5 and resulting in such activities as a confidential questionnaire sent to all members and included here as Exhibit 10-6.)

And an ever-growing number of unions now makes ambitious use of the national Freedom of Information Act to obtain companies' health and safety records, and in some cases thereupon to file complaints of their own with OSHA charging the management with violations of the law.

Many unions, possibly most, are still not much more active than they have been historically in the area of safety and health. Others do no more than the minimum required to prevent membership outbursts. But the momentum set in motion, first by the high hopes for OSHA and then by the fears of the act's inadequacies, shows no sign of abating. Most probably then, the years ahead should see even more activity and expenditure both at the bargaining table and (from all concerned groups) in lobbying efforts toward a goal that all but the most selfish segments of society can applaud: the minimization of occupational hazards in the American workplace.

PRODUCTION STANDARDS AND STAFFING

Certainly one of the most important functions of management is that of determining the amount of output that an employee must turn out in a given period. So important is this area to management's objective of operating an efficient plant that employers at times suffer long strikes to maintain this right as a unilateral one.

It is easy to understand why employers have such a vital interest in production standards. To the degree that employees increase output, unit labor costs decline. With declining labor costs, employers make a larger profit, or else they can translate lower labor costs into lower prices for their products or services with the expectation of thereby increasing the total volume of sales and strengthening the financial position of the company.

There is still another way to look at production standards in the operation of the firm. If employees produce more, the employer will have to hire commensurately fewer additional employees, or may even be in a position

EXHIBIT 10–3

ARTICLE 18. SAFETY AND HEALTH

1. The Company shall institute and maintain all reasonable and necessary precautions for safeguarding the health and safety of its employees, and all employees are expected to cooperate in the implementation thereof. Both the Company and the Union recognize their mutual obligations to assist in the prevention, correction and elimination of all unhealthy and unsafe working conditions and practices.

2. A Safety Committee, composed of three (3) Union members and the Union President and four (4) members of Management, one (1) of whom shall be chairman, shall be established. The Union shall have the right of selection of its members. The Committee shall meet at least once each month on a regularly scheduled basis for the purpose of jointly reviewing and discussing plant safety conditions and investigating accidents. In addition to Company established safety rules and procedures, the Safety Committee may develop and recommend the adoption of appropriate safety rules and procedures to improve and correct unsafe conditions. The Company further agrees to examine any recommendation with respect to safety and health, and to take such action as may be appropriate on recommendations which are submitted by a majority of the Safety Committee.

3. Written minutes shall be made at each Safety Committee meeting. These minutes shall be posted on the plant safety bulletin board. Union members shall be paid at the rate of their assigned jobs for time spent at Safety Committee meetings and other appropriate Safety Committee functions as approved by the Division Manager.

4. Representatives of the International Union may request a meeting or inspection with Company officials to review safety problems and procedures. Such requests shall be made to the Plant Manager or his designee who shall arrange for such meeting or inspection at a mutually agreeable time. No request for such meeting or inspection will be unjustifiably denied.

5. The Company will continue to furnish employees with gas masks, gloves, and goggles, and where needed, raincoats, coveralls, rubber pacs or shoes for sandblasting, and slush boots, and lenses and frames for prescription safety glasses. Maintenance employees shall be furnished necessary tools by the Company.

6. The Company agrees to provide medical examinations or health tests when the necessity, nature of and/or frequency of such medical examination or health test is appropriate for exposures and/or working conditions. The results of such examinations or tests will be made available to the employee and his personal physician. These tests will be provided at no cost to the employee.

For the purposes of applying the above provisions, the Company will provide annual physical examinations of all hourly employees. The following shall be the basic contents of the annual examinations. The contents of the examinations may be modified by addition or deletion in compliance with federal (OSHA) standards promulgated by the Secretary of Labor and/or recommended testing from an accredited medical group or association. The tests performed and the procedure used shall be determined solely by the company medical department. Special examinations or tests on a more frequent basis than annually will be made as required by specific exposures and industrial hygiene standards.

EXHIBIT 10–3 (continued)

Annual Physical Exams

1. Chest X-Ray
2. Pulmonary Function
3. Audiometric Testing
4. Ortho-Rater Eye Test
5. Electro Cardiogram
6. Urinalysis
7. Blood Tests
8. Blood Pressure
9. Breast Exam (Females Only)
10. Hands-on Test by Doctor (Eyes-Ears-Nose-Throat-Reflexes-Skeletal-Muscle)
11. Follow-Up Discussion between Doctor and Employee

Blood Tests—Annual on All People Tested

Chen-Zyme Panel includes twenty-two (22) separate tests plus complete blood count (CBC) with differential for base line data.

Special Blood Tests for Benzene Exposure People
CBC with differential
Reticulocyte count
Serum bilirubin (included in chen-zyme panel on annual exams)

Special blood tests for exposure to lead, asbestos and pesticides (research) will also be provided.

7. The Company will pay all costs of employee's eye examination when the examination results in a prescription for eyeglasses or a change in the employee's existing prescription.

8. The Medical Program and physical examination shall not be used as a basis for shifting of personnel between jobs and classifications except for valid medical reasons. Upon request of the employee, the employee's physician shall be provided with a duplicate report in writing of the plant physician's examination. The employee will be given a report of the conclusions of the findings of the physical examination except in special cases.

Any dispute arising out of the results of a physical examination shall be limited to the question of whether the physical condition constitutes a hazard to the health and safety of the employee and his fellow employees or to the Company assets and whether the employee is physically capable of performing the job.

9. The Union may designate one representative from among the active employees to accompany Federal or State safety inspectors while they conduct walk-around safety inspections within the plant. The designated employee shall be compensated at his regular straight time rate for the time lost from the job while accompanying the inspector in the walk-around inspection.

EXHIBIT 10–4

New Brochure Shows Safety and Health Advantages of National Master Freight Agreement

The new Teamster brochure shown here illustrates the many safety and health benefits enjoyed by Teamster truck drivers under the National Master Freight Agreement, which are not provided by laws.

Teamster Safety and Health Director R.V. Durham cited this often unnoticed benefit of Teamster representation in a letter introducing the brochure to local unions with members covered by this Agreement: "For many years now, the IBT and our local unions have actively pursued safety and health issues at the bargaining table. We have often won safety and health protections for our members

"The Employer shall not require employees to take out on the streets or highways any vehicle that is not in safe operating condition, including, but not limited to equipment which is acknowledged as overweight or not equipped with the safety appliances prescribed by law."

—From Article 16, Section 1
National Master
Freight Agreement

through collective bargaining which go well beyond the minimum requirements imposed on employers by government agencies such as DOT and OSHA."

The brochure is aimed primarily at truck drivers, but Durham pointed out that the current agreement also contains important new safety and health gains for Teamster mechanics and dock workers. Numerous other Teamster contracts also contain safety and health provisions which are stronger than government standards.

Several IBT local unions have been requesting copies of the new brochure for use in organizing campaigns, as well as for distribution to their own stewards.

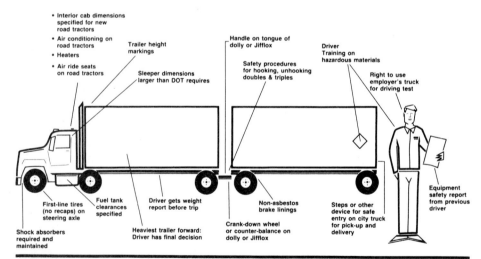

The National Master Freight Agreement offers drivers more safety and health protection than government regulations, and gives drivers stronger rights to see that safety regulations are followed.

DECEMBER 1988   13

Source: *The International Teamster,* December 1988, p. 13

EXHIBIT 10–5

AIDS, Critical and Terminal Illnesses:

ASSOCIATION OF
FLIGHT ATTENDANTS, AFL-CIO

AIDS, CRITICAL AND TERMINAL
ILLNESS AWARENESS MONTH

Support From Flying Partners Can Make a Difference

Ironically, some of the key health and interpersonal problems confronting flight attendants today are an unexpected byproduct of past victories. Flight attendants successfully struggled to make the profession a career that could last until retirement. No longer do we have to quit by age 32, or leave the job if we marry or become pregnant. These gains have raised our stature as seasoned, mature professionals in the eyes of the public and management. That's the good news.

The bad news is that growing older is not easy. The flight attendant population is now affected by the illnesses that go with age, like hypertension and heart disease. We are also more likely to have flying partners who are fighting cancer or who are HIV-positive than we were when the average career length was two years.

We're a maturing work force, a diverse work force, and sensitivity toward those among us with serious illnesses has become vital to our unity and solidarity. In recognition of this, AFA's Board of Directors has established March, 1992 as time for us to begin increasing our awareness about AIDS, and Critical and Terminal illnesses (ACT); how they impact our flying partners who are living with them; and how to interact caringly and tactfully with ill co-workers.

Living With Life-Threatening Illness

Imagine this: You've been a flight attendant for a number of years. You enjoy your job and your personal life. You have a good relationship with your flying partners. In general, life seems to be treating you well. Then, during a medical checkup, your doctor notices something and orders some additional tests. You are diagnosed as having a potentially serious health problem: a lump in your breast, an irregular PAP smear, an HIV-positive result on a blood test, a spot on your lungs in a chest X-ray, a heart problem.

Immediately, your life has changed. For now, of course, you can go to work as usual, function normally, and you still look the same as before. "But how long will that last?" you ask yourself. Medication and medical procedures to fight the disease may, for a time, affect how you look. The unfortunate, all-too-persistent "glamor" image of flight attendants, which equates personal worth with physical attractiveness, is an added pressure if treatment affects your appearance. Although you can work, you worry about losing your job, and your health insurance, if the company finds out. You want your co-workers' support, but you're afraid if they find out, even though your illness is not contagious, they will shun you.

This scenario gives a small glimpse into part of what chronically ill flight attendants go through. It's a scenario our sisters and brothers living with chronic disease know all too well.

If a Flying Partner Has a Life-Threatening Illness

If you know a flying partner has a chronic illness, you may feel awkward about how to act toward her/him. Your reactions may be: • I don't know what to say to the person, • when I do say something, it sounds stupid, • it's depressing to be around her/him, • I'm afraid I may "catch" the illness, even though I know it's not contagious, or in the case of HIV disease, not contagious through casual contact, • I'm afraid I might have to do extra work on a trip, but I feel guilty about saying anything, • the person is a constant reminder of my own mortality and vulnerability.

Source: Flightlog, January–March 1992, p. 4 (Association of Flight Attendants, AFL–CIO).

EXHIBIT 10–6

Confidential Membership Survey
Concerning Life-Threatening Illnesses

Dear Colleague,

The primary purpose of this questionnaire is to determine, on a totally confidential basis: • how many among us are living with a life-threatening illness, • how many among us are caring for someone in this situation, and • what services the union should consider providing to assist members in maintaining their livelihood.

We are seeking to assess the overall impact of critical health issues among our members in order to identify topics which might be addressed in union publications or other forums. Please take a few minutes to complete this survey and return it by May 1, 1992.

Thank you for your interest and concern.

In Solidarity,

Dee Maki, National President

1. Are you reluctant in any way to work with someone who has been diagnosed with:
HIV/AIDS? Yes ❑ No ❑
Other life threatening illness? Yes ❑ No ❑

2. When you are working with someone with a critical illness, what are your primary concerns? *(check all that apply)*
❑ I prefer to avoid interaction with her/him.
❑ I am concerned about the ill person's appearance.
❑ I never seem to know what to say to them.
❑ I find it depressing to be around people who are ill.
❑ I'm afraid I might get it.
❑ I'm concerned the person won't do her/his share.
❑ I worry I may have to perform emergency first aid.
❑ I worry whether they can perform their safety duties.
❑ I worry about their well being.
❑ Other_____

3. Is someone close to you suffering from a life-threatening illness?
Yes ❑ No ❑
If yes, does this illness affect your: Spouse/domestic partner ❑
A family member ❑ Friend(s) ❑ Co-worker(s) ❑ ? *(check all that apply)*

4. Are you presently or have you been a care-giver for someone who is critically ill?
Yes ❑ No ❑
If yes, is this person your: Spouse/domestic partner ❑ Child ❑
Parent ❑ Sibling ❑ Friend ❑ Other ❑ _____

5. Have you ever been diagnosed as having a life-threatening illness?
Yes ❑ No ❑ (If no, go to question 10.)

6. What was the diagnosis? *(Please be specific)*_____

7. How recently was the diagnosis confirmed?_____

8. Are you currently receiving treatment for your illness?
Yes ❑ No ❑
If yes, what type of treatment(s)?_____
If no, why not?_____

9. Have you communicated that you are suffering from a life-threatening illness to: Your partner ❑ Your family ❑ Your friends ❑ Your co-workers ❑
The company you work for ❑ ? *(check all that apply)*

10. Have you utilized AFA's Employee Assistance Program (EAP) as a resource to help you cope with your illness or the illness of someone close to you?
Yes ❑ No ❑ If no, why not?_____

11. If available, would you utilize a long-term, union-based support system focused on helping you deal with your illness, bereavement, or the care of someone close to you who is ill? Yes ❑ No ❑

over

EXHIBIT 10–6 (continued)

If yes, which of the following services would you utilize?

a. Support Groups *(Check all that apply)*

❏ Exclusively for **AFA** members with critical and terminal illness.

❏ Exclusively for **AFA** members who care for someone with a critical or terminal illness.

❏ Exclusively for **AFA** members who are coping with bereavement.

b. Buddy Network

❏ An **AFA**-member buddy who would volunteer to provide you with extra help and support during your illness.

❏ An **AFA**-member buddy who would volunteer to provide you with extra **help** and support during the time that you are caring for someone who is ill.

If no, why not?_____

Demographic Information   *(Please check those areas which apply to you)*

Female ❏   Male ❏   Lineholder ❏   Reserve ❏ Number of years as a flight attendant:_____

Carrier size: Major ❏ National ❏ Regional ❏

Married ❏ Permanent domestic partner ❏ Single ❏

Do you consider yourself: Heterosexual ❏ Homosexual ❏ Bisexual ❏

Please fold, staple, stamp and return completed surveys by May 1, 1992.

Place 29 Cent
Stamp Here
Post Office will
not deliver
unless stamped

AFA Special Projects Coordinator

Association of Flight Attendants, AFL-CIO

1625 Massachusetts Avenue, NW

Washington, DC 20036

Source: Flightlog, January–March, 1992, p. 4 (Association of Flight Attendants, AFL–CIO).

to lay off present employees on a temporary or permanent basis. Indeed, with a smaller labor force, the management could also save on the number of foremen needed to supervise the work of its employees.

Production standards are thus directly related to the staffing of jobs or to the question of how many employees are needed to carry out a specific plant assignment. But even when contractual commitments or past practices obligate the company to assign a certain minimum number of workers to a given operation at all times, significant economies can be realized by management if it is able to impose higher production standards upon this inflexible crew.

If the interest of management in production standards is understandable, however, it is no less understandable that employees and their union representatives have an equal interest in ensuring "reasonableness" and "fairness" in this phase of the firm's operation. Before the advent of unions, employers could require employees to produce as much as management directed. Failure to meet these production standards could result in the summary dismissal of the employee. At times, employees suffered accidents, psychological problems, and a generally shortened work life in meeting the standards of the employer. And although modern enlightened management does not normally impose production standards that employees cannot reasonably attain, unions and employees are nonetheless still vitally concerned with the amount of production that an employee must turn out in a given length of time because of the patent ramifications of job opportunities and union membership.

There is no simple solution to the problem of how much an employee must produce to hold a job or to earn a given amount of pay. At times, the determination of a solution is purely subjective in character; a supervisor's individual judgment is the criterion adopted to resolve the problem. To this, unions argue that the judgment of employees or labor union officers is as good as that of the management representatives.

More sophisticated methods of determination are available, but these techniques, too, are hardly so perfect or "scientific" as to end the controversy. Such techniques fall under the general title of time and motion studies. That is, having been shown the most efficient method of performing a job, so-called "average" employees, who are presumably working at average rates of speed, are timed. From such a study, management claims that the typical employee in the plant should at least produce the average amount in a given period. Where incentive wage systems are in effect, as we know, the employee receives premium pay for output above the average. However, production standards are important even when employees are paid by the hour, since failure to produce the average amount could result in employee discipline of some sort—ranging from a reprimand to discharge, with intervening levels such as a suspension or a demotion to a lower-paying job. Unions are far from convinced that time and motion studies constitute the millennium in the resolution of the production standards problem. They claim that the studies are far from scientific, since they still involve human judgment, and that employees who are timed are often far better than average, so that their rate of speed is consequently unrealistically fast.

With few exceptions (most notably in the garment industries), unions have pressed for an effective means of review of employer establishment of production standards, rather than toward seeking the right to establish such standards initially. Organized labor has generally believed that employee and union institutional interests are served as effectively, and without the administrative and political complexities of initial standard establishment, if there is a union opportunity for challenge of the management action, either through arbitration or by the exercise of the right to strike during the contractual period in the event of unresolved production standards disputes.

Some unions have historically preferred the right to strike to arbitration in this area. The United Automobile Workers has, for example, steadfastly refused to relinquish its right to strike over production standards disputes, and although the UAW now agrees to arbitration on virtually all other phases of the labor agreement, it is adamant in its opposition to the arbitration of standards. The international neither distrusts arbitrators nor challenges their professional competency. Rather, it believes that a union cannot properly prepare and present a case in arbitration that can successfully challenge production standards. It contends that the problems are so complicated, the proofs so difficult to assemble, and the data so hard to present in satisfactory form that arbitration is not the proper forum for resolving production standards disputes. In essence, it claims that employers have an advantage in any arbitration dealing with production standards, and the union does not intend to turn to this process because it would jeopardize the interests of its members.

On the other hand, most unions have now agreed to the arbitration of production standards. Beyond reflecting the general acceptance of the arbitration process itself, this course of action has behind it a highly practical reason: Frequently, production standards are protested by only a small group of employees in the plant. For example, the employer may have changed the standards in one department (because of improved technology, equipment, or methods) but left unaltered at least temporarily the standards in all other departments. Without arbitration, the only way in which the affected employees could seek relief would be for the entire labor force to strike—at times, a politically inopportune weapon for the union to use, because the employees in the other departments are satisfied and do not care to sacrifice earnings just to help out employees in a single department. Arbitration avoids this situation, while still allowing a final and binding decision on the grievance of the protesting employees.

There is, however, probably no area of labor relations in which management and organized labor still stand any further apart than in production standards. There is no magical solution to such controversies when they arise. Standards lie at the heart of the operation of the plant and are vital to the basic interest of the employees and unions. To say that they should be established "fairly" and "reasonably" is to recognize only an unrealizable ideal, since in the give and take of day-to-day operations deep and bitter conflicts are still bound to arise. The stakes are very high, and as long as management seeks efficiency and the union seeks to protect the welfare of its members, there exists no easy way out of the problem. Certainly nothing approaching a panacea for it has yet been discovered by the parties to collective bargaining.

TECHNOLOGICAL CHANGE

"I essentially hoped to shuffle off to a quiet demise," declared AFL-CIO president Lane Kirkland a while ago, "without ever having learned what a computer is all about or the intricacies of microwave transmission or low-frequency transmission or cable TV and satellite TV and all of those things. But I am aware that a revolution is going on."[15]

An *unparalleled* revolution, he could have added. In both the factory and the office, technological change is affecting employment needs so greatly that it is now estimated that some 45 million existing jobs in the United States (more than 40 percent of all jobs, indeed) will be directly touched in the next decade.

Not long ago, many observers thought that the industrial robot, characterized by mechanical arms connected to reprogrammable computers, might soon affect a significant percentage of these jobs all by itself. A 1981 study conducted at Carnegie-Mellon University concluded that contemporary robots had the technical ability to perform millions of factory jobs and that some time after 1990 it would be technically possible to replace *all* manufacturing workers in the automotive, electrical equipment machinery, and fabricated metals industries—some 7.9 million—with robots.[16] At about the same time, the General Electric Corporation launched an ambitious program that was ultimately expected to lead to the replacement of half of its 37,000 assembly-line employees with robots. And with robots seemingly getting cheaper all the time—their average unit price dropped 20 percent in 1988 from the previous year, for example, to about $40,000—it was not hard to find industrial analysts as recently as 1990 who expected as many as 100,000 robots (up from 25,000 in 1990) to be in use by the year 2000.

Today, such dramatic estimates are no longer viewed as realistic. A combination of some amount of robot unreliability and a managerial inability to mesh robots smoothly with workers and other equipment has put to rest the once common thought that robots would soon surpass $10 billion in annual worldwide sales and revolutionize the world of work almost overnight: Depending on how "robot" is defined, worldwide sales are currently around $2 billion a year and seem to be holding at approximately that level. Even at that, however, industrial robots that can efficiently paint, weld, seal, assemble, and package all kinds of products and make such service-sector contributions as delivering meals to patients in hospitals and polishing retail store floors are now increasingly in evidence, as is a commensurate fear on the part of workers and their unions that major job displacement will be the consequence.

The robot hardly stands alone, moreover, as a form of changing technology significantly affecting the work force. Examples abound to show the impact of other forms of automation—broadly defined as a system of automatic devices that integrate the entire productive process—as well. At the Port of New York Authority waterfront, for example, where over 85 percent of all general cargo now moves in containers, fewer than 10,000 workers now handle the same volume of freight that 30,000 did two decades ago. In its last years, before being broken up into smaller independent companies in 1984, the American Telephone & Telegraph Company cut some 120,000 jobs from its payrolls, at least primarily because of automation. In railroading, the automatic dispatching of freight cars has made the human dispatcher about as visible as the steam locomotive. And job obsolescence has already been the fate, too, of thousands of workers even in retail trade, as symbolized by one mail-order house in which a computer now handles over 100,000 tallies each day, keeping an automatic record of the 12,000 items sold by the employer in the process. Nor has governmental employment been immune from automation's inroads: The 450 U.S. Treasury Department clerical employees who were not long ago replaced by a single computer that can accommodate the half a billion checks issued by the federal government every year are far from unique among the casualties of technological change in that sector.

Not all of the jobs involved are, of course, unionized ones. Retail trade is, as we know, hardly a hotbed of organized labor, and (although the Treasury clerks in the above example happen to have been union members) clerical work, too, is clearly far more nonunionized than it is unionized. But the fact remains that the blue collar worker in mass-production industry—automobiles, steel, electrical, and other bastions of collective bargaining—has been the most visible victim to date of the new era of rampant technological change. The robot and other computer-based automation have a natural affinity for these sectors and, whatever the future brings, job totals here have already suffered most notably.

In the typical automated radio manufacturing establishment, for example, only two employees produce 1,000 radios per day, where standard hand assembly called for a labor force of 200. Fewer than twenty glass-blowing machines have for some time produced almost all the glass light bulbs used in the United States and, still having time on their hands, all the glass tubes used in radio and television sets (except for the picture tubes). New technology has already eliminated thousands of automobile industry jobs, with robots—costing a mere $6 hourly to operate and able to do the work of two $20-an-hour human workers—ever more tempting given the financial problems of that sector. And in steel the inroads of technology have combined with foreign competition to cut the 500,000 production workers of two decades ago down to only about one third of that figure. The steel industry itself has in recent years come back from the brink of near extinction; but the sight of steam once again billowing from the smokestacks of USX and Bethlehem brings no joy whatsoever to the thousands of permanently displaced workers still living in steel towns who are not being allowed to participate in the resurgence.

For all of these labor-displacement and related skill-rating effects, there are clearly some offsetting advantages. The employer implementing the changes presumably benefits, as in steel, either by gaining a competitive edge or by closing a competitive gap. The increased productivity that is created raises national living standards immensely: The average family income in the United States, at constant dollars, is now expected—for example—to reach an impressive $33,000 annually by the year 2000, up from less than two-thirds of that figure today. Jobs are invariably made safer, with materials handling and other relatively dangerous occupational aspects either considerably minimized or eliminated altogether. Product quality is frequently improved, since the automatic machine has little room for human error. And even an improved national defense can be said to have been generated, with modern warfare now so dependent upon the most advanced technology.

Most importantly, it can be argued with considerable justification that everyone, in the long run, benefits from scientific progress. There are infinitely more people working in the automobile production and servicing industries (even now) than there ever were blacksmiths, for example. And the number of employees associated with the telephone industry vastly exceeds the highest labor force totals ever achieved by the town-crier profession.

All these arguments, however, are of small consolation to the employee actually being displaced or threatened by technology. Just as logically, the employee can echo the irrefutable statement of Lord Keynes that "in the long run, we are all dead." And one can often balance the fact that technology has generally improved working conditions by pointing to undesirable features of the problem that have an impact upon the workers: greater isolation of employees on the job, with less chance to talk face to face with other workers and supervisors; a greater mental strain, particularly since mistakes can now be much more costly; the deterioration of social groups, since it requires considerably less teamwork to run the modern operation; and the fact that jobs in the automated plant (or office) are fast becoming much more alike, with less on-the-job variety also often the case, and attendant psychological and social implications stemming from this situation.

But most worrisome of all to the industrial worker is the threat of displacement, or at least of severe skill requirement downgrading, through *future* technological change. The results of one employee survey with which the authors are personally familiar showed that almost three quarters of all respondents, asked whether they believed that "automation is a good thing for workers," replied in the negative (and many of them added that the new methods constituted a "real job threat"). Such findings have been echoed in countless other studies.

The fears appear to be well grounded. If technological change undeniably creates new jobs and even industries, the possibility remains that at the present time, it is destroying more jobs than it creates. Even placing all government and private estimates at their rock-bottom minimums, it is likely that 20,000 jobs are eliminated *each week* in this manner. And however many of the displaced are ultimately reabsorbed into the employed labor force, the increasing skill requirements of an automated world leave little room for at least the unskilled worker to join their ranks; at the time of this writing, with a national rate of unemployment seemingly inflexibly fixed above 7 percent, the rate for unskilled workers has steadily exceeded 25 percent in recent years.

Thus, while by far the greatest organizational problem of unions involves the organization of the white collar sector in the face of the automation-caused changing complexion of the work force, within the current arena of collective bargaining, organized labor—both as the blue collar worker's representative and for its own institutional preservation—has inevitably been forced toward the promotion of *measures minimizing job hardship for blue collar workers.*

Accordingly, unions have in recent years pushed hard, and with much success, for several devices geared explicitly to cushioning the employment impact of technological change. Some of these—SUB, pension vesting, severance pay, extended vacation periods, extra holidays, and early retirement provisions—have already been discussed as "economic supplements" (see Chapter 8). They have frequently been negotiated to satisfy goals other than adjustment to automated change: A desire for greater leisure purely and simply sometimes motivates vacation and holiday demands, for example, and severance pay implementation or liberalization may be triggered by, say, a union wish to protect workers unable to work because of permanent disability. In addition to these devices, several that tend to be more directly related to technological change deserve attention:

1. *Advance Notice of Layoff or Shutdown.* Such advance notice, impracticable for management in the case of sudden cancellation of orders and various other contingencies, is far more feasible where technological change is involved, since many months may be required to prepare for the new equipment and processes. An increasing number of agreements now call for notice considerably in excess of the few days traditionally provided for in many contracts, with most of the liberalizations now providing for six to twelve months.

Managements independently have often agreed with the advisability of such liberalization—to maintain or improve community images, to dispel potentially damaging employee rumors, and, frequently, because of a desire to develop placement and training plans for displaced workers. Very often, in fact, the actual notice given by management exceeds that stipulated in the contract. There seems to be little doubt, however, that unions have been instrumental in inserting longer advance-notice provisions in some contracts—as in portions of the meatpacking, electrical, and electronics industries—that might otherwise not have modified traditional practices. Such certainly appears to have been the case in recent General Electric and Westinghouse negotiations, where the companies agreed to give six months' notice before shutting down product lines (and sixty days' notice before installing robots). Bargaining in the telephone industry has resulted in comparable contractual obligations for the employer, and for the same reason.

2. *Adoption of the "Attrition Principle."* An agreement to reduce jobs solely by attrition—through, in other words, deaths, voluntary resignations, retirements, and similar events—by definition gives maximum job security to the present jobholder, although it does nothing to secure the union's long-run institutional interests. As a compromise, it has appealed to many employers as an equitable and not unduly rigorous measure. Managements have proven particularly amenable to this arrangement when the voluntary resignation rate is expected to be high, when a high percentage of workers is nearing retirement age, or when no major reduction of the labor force is anticipated in the first place (and the number of jobs made obsolete by automation is consequently small to begin with). In other cases, unions have been the major force behind introduction of the principle—usually, however, with some modifications more favorable to the union as an institution placed upon it. Thus, the current agreement between the Order of Railroad Telegraphers and the Southern Pacific Railroad places an upper limit of 2 percent upon the jobs that can be abolished for any reason in a given year. Good faith is obviously required in such cases, however: If employers later feel that the upper limit is too severe for them to live with, given a bleak economic climate or other adverse conditions, they could understandably be tempted to encourage additional workers to leave by implementing unreasonable working conditions or otherwise lowering the employee satisfaction level in violation of the spirit of the agreement.

In recent years, many railroad workers have received the protection of the "Attrition Principle," as have newspaper printers, printing-press workers, and postal service employees, among others.

3. *Retraining.* An expanding but unknown number of bargaining relationships now provides opportunities for displaced employees to retrain for another job in the same plant or another plant of the same company. The same protection is also increasingly being extended to employees for whom changes in equipment or operating methods make it mandatory to retrain in order to hold their current jobs. Often, such retraining opportunity, which is most commonly offered at company expense, is limited to workers who meet certain seniority specifications. General Electric workers, for example, must have at least three years of continuous service in order to qualify. At other times, preference but not a promise for retraining is granted senior workers, as in one Machinist union contract that provides that such employees "shall be given preference for training on new equipment, provided they have the capabilities required."

Where such provisions have significantly mitigated displacement, not unexpectedly, they have been implemented by companies whose operations have been expanding in areas other than those causing the initial displacement. "Retraining for *what?*" is a pertinent question when such expansion is not in evidence or at least is not highly likely. Lack of employee self-confidence or lack of worker interest sufficient to meeting the new skill requirements have also been known to make the retraining opportunity an essentially valueless one for employees permitted to utilize it. The 52-year-old with a quarter-century's experience as a blast furnace operative and the grizzled veteran of two decades on the automobile assembly line often have little optimism that they can successfully be retrained for jobs in the sales, health, clerical, and other fields where positions *are* being created. And they frequently have no greater amount of interest in finding out in any event. Thus, for example, when General Motors and the UAW cooperated a few years ago in a venture to train laid-off employees at two California automobile facilities for jobs in data processing (as well as aerospace), there were few takers: Only 1,522 of the 5,400 eligible workers signed up; many of the others thought that they might be rehired when GM and Toyota jointly began building new cars in the area and preferred to take their chances in this direction.

Nor can the United States government, it would seem, realistically be expected to do much to help the retraining efforts. Even the $3.5 billion Job Training Partnership Act, which took effect in late 1983 and was expected to train some 100,000 displaced workers (in addition to 1 million disadvantaged teen-agers and adults), was widely perceived as a very modest effort in view of the numbers of people covered, the fact that only 70 percent of the monies would actually go for training, and—again—the immobility, real or imagined, of those displaced.

It appeared that retraining for positions outside the employer's operations, however appealing its theory, would remain in practice anything but a powerful answer to the job losses caused by technological change.

4. *Restrictions on Subcontracting. Subcontracting,* the term that stands for arrangements made by a company (for reasons such as cost, quality, or speed of delivery) to have some portion of its work performed by employees of another company, can obviously have major work-opportunity ramifications for the first company's employees. There is probably no completely integrated company in the nation, and some measure of subcontracting has always been accepted by all unions as an economic necessity. But when the union can argue that union member employees could have performed the subcontracted work, or that such work was previously done by bargaining unit employees, it can be counted upon to do so. And when disputes do arise over this issue, they are, as Chapter 4 has pointed out, often of major dimensions. In the face of automation-caused job insecurity, there has been an observable recent trend toward union control over many types of subcontracting; the battle has tended to move from open interunion competition to the union-management bargaining table.

So thorny is the subcontracting problem that more than 75 percent of all major contracts still make no direct reference to it in a special contractual section, and thus situations such as those depicted in Exhibit 10-7 constitute minority ones. But an increasing number of contracts are incorporating into various of their other sections (ranging from union recognition clauses to seniority articles) or in separate "memoranda of understanding" certain limitations on the procedure.

The limitations are of several kinds: (1) agreements that subcontractors will be used only on special occasions (for example,. "where specialized equipment not available on company premises is required" or "where peculiar skills are needed"); (2) no-layoff guarantees to current employees (as in "no Employee of any craft, which craft is being utilized by an Outside Contractor, shall be laid off as long as the Outside Contractor is in the plant doing work that Employees in such craft are able to do"); (3) provisions giving the union veto power over any or all subcontracting; and (4) requirements that the company prove to the union that time, expense, or facility

EXHIBIT 10–7

ARTICLE 19　SUBCONTRACTING

Section 1. General

1. Whenever a contractor or subcontractor performs work on Company premises which would ordinarily be performed by employees covered by this Agreement, the Company will include a provision in the applicable contract requiring the contractor to pay (1) not less than the rates of pay provided for in this Agreement for the same character of work, and (2) one and one-half (1 ½) times the employees' regular rate of pay for hours worked in excess of forty (40) hours per week.

Section 2. Maintenance Subcontracting

1. Whenever the Company contemplates contracting out any type of work normally performed by maintenance employees it shall inform the President, Chairman of the Grievance Committee and the affected Shop Steward of its intentions prior to making a decision to award the contract.

2. It is further agreed that the Union retains the right to examine any existing or new subcontracting agreement for the purposes of checking wage scales and the specific work contracted.

3. The Company shall not subcontract the work of any maintenance employee when the total number of maintenance employees falls below:

a. 22 percent of the total active permanent workforce (excluding short-term disability, LTD, laid-off employees, and summer employees). For example, if the total hourly active workforce is 160, then the Company may not subcontract if the maintenance force falls below 35 (22 percent of 160). The maintenance force shall be counted in the same manner as the permanent workforce.

b. For the purposes of this paragraph Maintenance employees shall exclude Storehouse Clerks and Salvage Section.

4. The Company will provide the Union quarterly reports summarizing subcontracting performed in the prior three (3) months plus a three month projection of anticipated major subcontracting projects, including a review of total workload.

5. The Company further agrees:

a. The purchase requisition will require designation of whether outside repairs or construction services will be required.

b. Contractors will not perform a significant amount of work outside the original scope of a job unless an additional subcontract notification is submitted.

c. The Company will submit a list of service contracts to the Union by January 31 of each year.

d. The Company will notify the Union as soon as practicable of any outside vendors called in for trouble-shooting that are not on service contracts.

considerations prevent it from allowing current employees to perform the work.

As Exhibit 10-8 illustrates, subcontracting has for some time been an area of large controversy in collective bargaining, and in a time of wide-

EXHIBIT 10–8

Source: Public Employee magazine, November 1985, front cover.

spread worries over jobs it can realistically be expected to spread. It seems a safe prediction, indeed, that management will fight even more vigorously to preserve its work assignment ability as foreign competition and cost pressures become more intense, and that organized labor will continue to push for limitations on the employer's subcontracting flexibility. Only when more adequate solutions to the problems of technological change are formulated can one expect the conflict in this area to abate.

5. *Other Measures.* Unions have also unilaterally attempted to minimize the administrative, institutional, and other problems of technological change through increasingly successful, if still limited, bargaining table campaigns for (1) shorter workweeks, often with a prohibition against overtime work when qualified workers are on layoff or where the overtime would result in layoffs; (2) the requirement of joint labor-management consultation prior to the introduction of any automated change; (3) the overhauling of wage structures with job upgrading to reflect the "increased responsibility" of automated factory jobs; and (4) special job and wage provisions for downgraded workers, to minimize income losses suffered by such workers, or to offset them entirely. In addition, unions have in some cases sought to facilitate new employment through the development of their own training, placement, and referral services. And, perhaps more visibly, they have often waged highly ambitious political lobbying campaigns (both on the international and AFL-CIO levels) for the following: a vast array of employment-generating public works programs; far-reaching tax programs and expanded Social Security benefits (to increase consumer purchasing power and lessen the burden on those most likely to be displaced); and innovative federal and state training programs.

As judged by short-run goals—the insertion of the various contract provisions within labor agreements and, in the latter case, the enactment of the lobbied-for legislation—unions have achieved a considerable measure of triumph (if less in the relatively penny-pinching governmental years of the past decade than earlier). And the fact that they have frequently been aided in such campaigns by increasingly social-minded employers in no way detracts from this success. Although union aggressiveness and creativity have varied widely, there can be no denying that many unions have considerably alleviated the burdens of technological change for many workers.

Yet neither singly nor in combination have these measures, or the host of other automation-adjustment methods cited earlier, provided anything approaching a full solution for the basic problems with which they deal. The displacement and displacement threats continue, now actually in accelerated form, as the march of technology continues to prove that it is both a blessing and a curse for society. Indeed, a case can be made that a vicious circle is involved: Virtually all these measures increase labor costs for the companies concerned, giving the employer even further motivation for automating, and often thus causing the represented employees to lose jobs all the more rapidly.

There appears to be rather general agreement among all segments of our society on at least three relevant points, however. First, most of us concede that technological change is a product of society. It is not caused only by individuals, single firms, or groups of firms, but rather is an expression of our cultural heritage, our educational system, and our group dynamics. As such, unlike other problems affecting collective bargaining, it requires not only a private (labor-management) solution but a supplementary public (government) one. Second, we are essentially in agreement that no single group should bear the entire burden but that we should all bear it by making sure that the benefits of the increased productivity allowed by technology are shared by all. Without such a philosophical basis, automation and other such changes would mean that some would make spectacular gains, and others would shoulder the full burden. We do not want automation to divide the nation into "haves" and "have nots." Third, we share general unanimity that this is a time for daring innovation in social dynamics and social engineering and that, although the problem is great, we fortunately have within our capacity the power to deal with the issues within a system of free enterprise. Since old methods will not work, we must innovate and pioneer.

The increasing attention being given to the consequences of technology at the bargaining table (and by the bargaining parties in the public arena) can thus be viewed as recognition of a great but not necessarily insurmountable challenge.

PLANT CLOSINGS

If, as noted above, there has been something of a trend to liberal advance notice on the employer's part in the case of both layoffs and the closing of some product lines stemming from technological change, few labor-management contracts require much advance notice when an entire plant is to be permanently closed. According to the Bureau of Labor Statistics, only about 10 percent of all agreements contain such a provision. Even these, moreover, usually call for little more than a month or so in the way of notification.

Managements have some very rational reasons for wanting to keep their shutdown intentions confidential. Employees who realize that even with the best performance on their part they will lose their jobs might well engage in excess absenteeism, tardiness and even, at the extreme, vandalism (presumably in an attempt to get even). Customers, concerned about future replacement parts, could take their business elsewhere. Bankers might prove unwilling to extend further credit. Stock market considerations, too, may dictate playing it close to the vest when a shutdown is contemplated. Historically, most of organized labor could be said not only to have understood all of this but to have been relatively sympathetic to these managerial considerations.

Yet, as plant closings have accelerated in the past dozen or so years—especially in such hard-pressed older industries as automobiles, rubber, steel and meatpacking—unions have changed their attitude. They have become quite active in attempting to block the closings, especially when they have viewed the latter as mere vehicles for switching jobs to plants with lower wages in the middle of union contracts, as has in fact often been the case.

Initially, labor turned to the courts. It challenged management closing actions there on the grounds that under Section 8(d) of Taft-Hartley neither party can force the other to modify an existing contract before it expires. But while it won two major federal appeals court rulings on the subject, in 1979 and 1982, these decisions were both reversed in 1984 by a new conservative majority on the National Labor Relations Board. In cases involving respectively the Milwaukee Spring Division of the Illinois Coil Spring Company (268 NLRB 87) and the Otis Elevator Division of the United Technologies Corporation (269 NLRB 162), the labor board held that employers need not bargain over the transfer of work unless a labor contract required them to do so. Moreover, said the board, there was no need to bargain at all if the plant move was due to factors other than cutting labor costs.

Lobbying hard for protective legislation on the subject in the face of such board unfriendliness, unions were finally rewarded four years later when Congress enacted a significant plant closing law.

Under the provisions of the Worker Adjustment and Retraining Notification Act of 1988 (known, appropriately enough, as WARN), companies with 100 or more full-time employees must give their workers and communities at least sixty days notice of shutdowns and major layoffs when

- a plant closing would cost fifty or more full-time employees at a single site their jobs;
- a layoff is planned of six months or longer that would affect at least fifty workers who constitute at least one third of the work force;
- a six-month or longer layoff is planned of 500 or more workers even if these constitute less than one third of the work force.

Employers who violate the law, which became effective in February 1989, cannot expect to get off easily. They will be liable for one day's pay plus the cost of employment benefits for each day that notice is not given to each worker. They will also owe the local community up to $500 a day for each day that the required notice is not forthcoming, with a limit of $30,000. Notification to the local government gives the latter a chance to persuade the firm not to shut down.

Some loopholes are included in the law, and these could make it to some extent less effective. Plant closings or layoffs resulting from business activities that could not be "reasonably foreseen," including natural disasters, are exempt from the notice requirement. Also exempted are "faltering companies" that have reasonable grounds for believing that a notice of closing would prevent them from obtaining capital that they need to stay in business. And of the total U.S. labor force only about 49 percent of employees are covered because of the limitation of WARN to companies with at least 100 employees. For those workers who are excluded, unions can be expected to push now for notification requirements at the bargaining table.

But even with its limitations, the plant closing measure by any standard constitutes a giant step in the direction of protecting both worker and public interests. It avoids psychological trauma to workers who report to work only to find padlocked doors and suddenly abolished jobs. Notified of a shutdown, employees have the opportunity to seek other employment and training for new jobs. And cities and even states can, with notification, try to locate ways of keeping the firm in business, presumably to the benefit of all concerned.

A full four years after the law's implementation, there was agreement in both management and labor union quarters that employers were generally complying with WARN. Fewer than twenty lawsuits alleging violations had been filed, and even in most of *these* situations it appeared that some confusion as the exact requirements of the law rather than a direct employer intent to evade had been the trigger. In fact, overcompliance (on the part of managers who were not subject to WARN but who thought that they were) seemed to be far more common than undercompliance. Nor did employers appear to be finding the requirements of the new law particularly burdensome: WARN had been described by one qualified observer, in the context of causing trouble to business, as a "nonevent"[17] And most other experts seemed to share this opinion. If it was accurate, major progress in worker rights had been achieved at little or no cost to managements. (*Case 12, the last one in the book, focuses on a plant closing*.)

A CONCLUDING WORD

The mutual accommodations to the hard issues of collective bargaining that the parties have displayed in regard to wages, employee benefits, and institutional issues are no less in evidence when one inspects the current status of the administrative issues in our labor relations system. Management has increasingly recognized the job-protection and working-condition problems of the industrial employee and has made important concessions in these areas. At the same time, however, there has been reciprocal recognition on the part of unions that the protection of the employee cannot be at the expense of the destruction of the business firm. The axiom that employees cannot receive any protection from a business that has ceased to exist appears to have been fully appreciated by all but the extreme recalcitrants of the labor movement, and workable compromises have usually been possible with respect to the areas of seniority, discipline, and most of the various other dimensions discussed in this chapter no less than in the case of previous topics.

Clearly, there is considerable room for future progress, and, on occasion, the conflicts between the parties on the administrative issues can be very serious. Production standards and subcontracting remain highly visible sticking points. And strikes do, of course, at times result. There should be no illusion that the sensitive matters of collective bargaining are adjusted without painful struggle. Even standing alone, however, this chapter demonstrates rather irrefutably that managers and unionized employee representatives have increasingly recognized each other's positions. It offers additional evidence of the growing maturity of the American labor relations system, a theme that in one way or another has marked so much of this book.

DISCUSSION QUESTIONS

1. It has generally been agreed that the increased use of the seniority concept in industrial relations has lessened the degree of mobility among workers. What can be said (a) for and (b) against such a consequence?

2. "The typical labor agreement's disciplinary procedures contain as many potential advantages for management as they do for unions and workers." Comment.

3. Jack Barbash has commented that "management's perception of technological change is producing an offensive strategy; the union's perception is in general producing a defensive strategy." Confining your opinion to automated changes, do you agree?

4. The several devices noted in the "Technological Change" section of this chapter constitute the major existing avenues for minimizing employee resistance to such change. Can you suggest other measures that might be utilized in an attempt to realize this goal?

MINICASES

#1 The Dangerous Knife

The Northwest Electronics Corporation has a rule against the possession of dangerous knives on company property and over the years it has disciplined (generally by discharging) more than a few of its approximately 5,000 employees for having violated it. In all such cases until now, however, the knife was visible (more than once because it was being brandished).

Recently, plant security guard Ralph Von Strasser, suspecting the possession of a knife by a female worker, unilaterally entered and searched her locker and her purse and discovered that his suspicions were in fact warranted since the dangerous knife was in the purse. As the woman made ready to leave the premises by the front gate at quitting time that afternoon, she was escorted to the security office and asked to empty her purse. She was not informed why this request was being made. Refusing to honor it, she took her purse and went out the gate.

She was informed when she showed up for work on the following morning that she had been discharged for "refusing to obey the legitimate order of a plant security officer." The case wound up in arbitration.

Had you been the arbitrator here, would you have sustained the discharge, and why or why not?

#2 Vocal Criticism by an Employee

A woman who owned 49 percent of a company's common stock became ill and had her son, who happened to work for the company as a stock boy, represent her at the company's annual meeting.

During the meeting, the son expressed several strong criticisms not only of management policies but also of three of the firm's top executives. Subsequently, the management discharged the son, contending that his "attitude toward work had changed considerably" and that he had begun to act "more like a manager than an employee."

Stalemated in the grievance procedure, the case went to an arbitrator. At the hearing, the union admitted that the son-employee had been "vocal in his criticism" and that he had "challenged the competence" of the various managers. But the union sought to have the discharge reversed on the grounds that the son had registered "complaints and criticism not as an employee but as a representative of his mother."

Did the son's actions at the meeting constitute in your opinion proper grounds for discharge?

NOTES

[1]Carl Gersuny, "Origins of Seniority Provisions in Collective Bargaining," in *Proceedings of the 1982 Spring Meeting, Industrial Relations Research Association*, April 28–30, 1982, p. 520.

[2]*Gulton Electro-Voice, Inc.*, 266 NLRB 84 (1983).

[3]*Atwater Mfg. Co.*, 13 LA 747.749, as quoted in Frank Elkouri and Edna A. Elkouri, *How Arbitration Works*, 3rd ed. (Washington, D.C.: Bureau of National Affairs, 1973), p. 611.

[4]*Taracorp Industries*, 273 NLRB 54 (1984).

[5]*Grievance Guide*, 4th ed. (Washington, D.C.: Bureau of National Affairs, 1972), p. 30.

[6]Elkouri and Elkouri, *How Arbitration Works*, p. 641.

[7]*New York Times*, September 20, 1980, p. 19.

[8]Joseph F. Follmann, Jr., *The Economics of Industrial Health* (New York: AMA-COM, 1978), p. 75.

[9]Eula Bingham, "The New Look at OSHA: Vital Changes," in *Proceedings of the 1978 Annual Spring Meeting, Industrial Relations Research Association,* May 11–13, 1978, p. 488.

[10]*Ibid.*

[11]AFL-CIO Dept. of Legislation, *The People's Lobby: AFL-CIO Report on the 98th Congress,* March 1985, p. 22.

[12]*American Federationist,* April–June 1982, p. 16.

[13]*Wall Street Journal,* January 17, 1992, p. A7A.

[14]*Time,* September 16, 1991, p. 28.

[15]*New York Times,* November 15, 1981, Sec. E, p. 3.

[16]Sar A. Levitan and Clifford M. Johnson, "The Future of Work: Does it Belong to Us or to the Robot?" *Monthly Labor Review,* September 1982, p. 11.

[17]T. S. Lough, "WARN: The Rights, Duties, and Obligations of Employers, Employees, and Unions," *Labor Law Journal,* May 1991, p. 294.

SELECTED REFERENCES

Bacow, Lawrence S., *Bargaining for Job Safety and Health.* Cambridge, Mass.: MIT Press, 1980.

Bluestone, Barry, and Bennett Harrison, *The Deindustrialization of America.* New York: Basic Books, 1982.

Bourdon, Clinton C., and Raymond E. Levitt, *Union and Open-Shop Construction.* Lexington, Mass.: Heath, 1980.

Chapman, Paul K., *Trouble on Board: The Plight of International Seafarers.* Ithaca, N.Y.: ILR Press, Cornell University, 1992.

Denenberg, Tia Schneider, and R. V. Denenberg, *Alcohol and Drugs: Issues in the Workplace.* Washington, D.C.: Bureau of National Affairs, 1984.

Donovan, Ronald, and Marsha J. Orr, *Subcontracting in the Public Sector: The New York State Experience.* Ithaca, N.Y.: New York State School of Industrial and Labor Relations, 1982.

Gersuny, Carl, *Punishment and Redress in a Modern Factory.* Lexington, Mass.: Heath, 1973.

Hall, Francine S., and Maryann H. Albrecht, *The Management of Affirmative Action.* Santa Monica, Calif.: Goodyear Publishing Co., 1979.

Katz, Harry C., *Shifting Gears: Changing Labor Relations in the U.S. Automobile Industry.* Cambridge, Mass.: MIT Press, 1985.

Koven, Adolph M., and Susan L. Smith, *Alcohol-Related Misconduct.* Dubuque, Iowa: Kendall/Hunt, 1984.

Lofgren, Don J., *Dangerous Premises: An Insider's View of OSHA Enforcement.* Ithaca, N.Y.: ILR Press, Cornell University, 1989.

Mintz, Benjamin W., *OSHA: History, Law and Policy.* Washington, D.C.: Bureau of National Affairs, 1984.

Nelkin, Dorothy, and Michael S. Brown, *Workers at Risk: Voices from the Workplace.* Chicago: University of Chicago Press, 1984.

Quick, James C., and Jonathan D., *Organizational Stress and Preventive Management.* New York: McGraw-Hill, 1984.

Redeker, James R., *Employee Discipline: Policies and Practices.* Washington, D.C.: Bureau of National Affairs, 1989.

Thomis, Malcolm I., *The Luddites: Machine-Breaking in Regency England.* New York: Schocken Books, 1972.

Tobin, John A., *A Positive Approach to Employee Discipline.* Wheaton, Ill.: Hitchcock, 1976.

Trice, Harrison M., and Paul M. Roman, *Spirits and Demons at Work* (2nd ed.). Ithaca, N.Y.: ILR Press, Cornell University, 1978.

Westin, Alan F., and Alfred G. Feliu, *Resolving Employment Disputes Without Litigation.* Washington, D.C.: Bureau of National Affairs, 1988.

Wokutch, Richard E., *Worker Protection, Japanese Style.* Ithaca, N.Y.: ILR Press, Cornell University, 1992.

Seniority: The Case of the Bypassed Senior Employee

In matters of promotion, employers stress qualifications and ability and unions emphasize seniority. The conflict is usually resolved by contractual language that contains both factors as the selection basis for promotion. However, in most contracts, seniority governs only when the senior employee has qualifications relatively equal to those of a junior service employee who also bids on an available promotion or when the senior employee has the ability or the qualifications to perform the work. In a comparatively small number of labor agreements, the employer must automatically promote the senior employee even if that worker has no demonstrated qualifications, experience, or ability for the job. Under these circumstances, the employer is obligated to train the senior employee. More commonly, however, contracts provide for a trial period for a given length of time after the employee is selected for the job in the light of the contractual system established to fill job vacancies. In the trial period, the employee has the opportunity to demonstrate fitness for the job. The employee may be disqualified if during the trial period, he or she does not perform the job in a proper manner.

Seniority issues presented in the following case include whether the senior employee should have had a chance to prove his qualifications for the job; whether the senior employee had the right to the job because he had qualifications to perform it, despite the fact the junior service employee had superior qualifications; and how contract negotiations impacted on the application of the seniority provisions contained in the agreement.

As is common, the Union objected when the Company bypassed the senior employee, awarding the job to the junior service employee. The Union supported the employee's grievance, asserting that "to this Union, and to all unions, seniority is a sacred right." As you read the case, pay particular attention to the way the Arbitrator handled the evidence presented. Determine whether you believe he handled the Union's "sacred right" statement in a proper manner.

GRIEVANCE AND LABOR AGREEMENT

After Harry R. Stull was denied his bid as Flexo Operator Assistant on the No. 2 Flexo machine, he filed Grievance No. 78-40, dated December 6, 1990. It states:

Harry Stull was not given the job of Flexo Assistant. He feels he should be given the job because of his seniority and experience in the printing area. Adjustment sought is that he be given the job of Flexo Assistant.

Having failed to settle the dispute in the Grievance Procedure, the Parties submitted it to arbitration for its final and binding determination. Material to the case are the following provisions of the Labor Agreement:

Article 6—Seniority

Section 10. An employee may bid for the job opportunity by writing a bid on the forms provided by the Company. Any employee promoted or awarded a bid job, who during the trial period not to exceed forty-five (45) working days (unless extended by the Company) proves incapable of properly performing the duties or requests removal within thirty (30) working days, will be returned to the employee's former position and those affected by the move shall be returned to their former jobs. An employee who completes the trial period shall be considered qualified.

Section 11. Promotion will be made on the basis of seniority and qualifications, and when all factors that constitute qualifications are relatively equal, seniority will prevail.

Section 12. An employee may apply for a future job vacancy paying a lower base rate or the same base rate including a job in the same classification. Once assigned the employee shall not be eligible to bid down or laterally for a period of twelve (12) months from the time of accepting the job bid.

Memoranda of Agreement

17. (C) Article 6, Section 11

Relatively equal qualifications shall be defined as those qualifications learned in one (1) working day or less and enabling the employee to acceptably perform all aspects of the job.

BASIC QUESTION

The basic question to be determined in this arbitration is framed as follows:

Under the circumstances of this case, did the Company violate the material provisions of the Labor Agreement? If so, what should the remedy be?

BACKGROUND

On November 16, 1990, the Company at its Cincinnati, Ohio, plant posted a notice to fill a vacancy as Flexo Operator Assistant on the No. 2 Flexo machine. Grievant Stull and nine other employees bid for the job. Austin Downs, who has less seniority than the Grievant, was awarded the job. Whereas Stull started his employment on November 5, 1977, Downs was hired on September 4, 1980. It was the selection of the junior service employee that generated this dispute.

For about ten years before he bid on the job, Stull was classified as Rotary Die Cut Assistant and Operator on the Ward Die Cut machine. As of July 2, 1990, the base hourly rate of the Operator on the Ward Die Cut, a manual-fed two-color printer that prints and cuts cartons as they come out of the machine in flat forms, was $8.65.

Prior to being selected for the job in question, Downs was classified as Flexo Operator Assistant on the No. 1 Flexo, having served in this classification since May 31, 1989. Beside the No. 1 and No. 2 Flexo machines, the No. 3 Flexo is also involved in this dispute. As of July 2, 1990, an Operator Assistant assigned to any of the three Flexo machines received the same base rate, $8.30 per hour. Of these three machines, however, the No. 2 Flexo generates the highest incentive earnings. In addition, Stull testified that the incentive earnings on the No. 2 Flexo exceed those on the Ward Die Cut by about $30–$40 per week. That is why, Stull said, he bid on the No. 2 Flexo, even though the base rate on the Ward Die Cut is higher than that of the No. 2 Flexo.

In other words, whereas Downs bid laterally from the No. 1 to No. 2 Flexo in terms of the base rate, and the Grievant bid down, both employees sought higher incentive earnings. Article 6, Section 12, authorizes employees to bid down or laterally after serving in a job for a period of 12 months. Under this criterion, both Stull and Downs were eligible to bid on the No. 2 Flexo as Operator Assistant.

When an employee bids down or laterally, his bid is handled under the standards incorporated in Article 6, Section 11, the provision that deals with employee promotions. Jim Meeks, Plant Personnel Manager, said that

> though Section 11 deals with promotions, it has been used to award bids which involved a lateral or downward movement in terms of the base rate.

Thus, if Stull's grievance has merit, it must meet the selection criteria incorporated in Article 6, Section 11.

Unlike the Ward Die Cut, the Flexo machines not only print and cut cartons but also fold and glue the cartons. The three Flexo machines operate in the same manner except that the No. 2 Flexo contains an automatic feed system and the No. 1 and No. 3 are manually fed. Apparently, this is the reason why the incentive earnings on the No. 2 Flexo are higher than those on the No. 1 and No. 3.

After Downs was selected for the position in question, the job he vacated on the No. 1 Flexo was posted for bid on November 27, 1990. Stull did not bid on that job, explaining that the incentive earnings on the No. 2 Flexo are higher than on No. 1. However, on February 15, 1991, an Operator Assistant vacancy was posted for the No. 3 Flexo. Stull bid on it and was selected on February 26, 1991. This was the job that the Grievant held at the time of the arbitration. He said that he had bid on this job because the incentive earnings on the No. 3 Flexo are higher as compared with the No. 1 Flexo.

With respect to his current job, Stull testified that he did not receive any special training. For two hours on two days, another Operator Assistant worked with the Grievant on the No. 3 Flexo. Stull testified:

> He did not tell me anything. He just stood there watching me, or did some off-bearing.

As to his work as Operator Assistant on the No. 3 Flexo, Roger Gell, Production Superintendent, testified:

> Stull has not yet qualified on the job. He is not completely familiar with the job. He still is not familiar with all his responsibilities.

Considerable testimony was offered concerning the 1988 contract negotiations that resulted in the adoption of the current Labor Agreement. These negotiations are material because the Parties adopted the aforecited Memoranda of Agreement and particularly that language that relates to the promotion provision, Article 6, Section 11. This new language, cited as Paragraph 17C in the Memoranda, defines "relatively equal qualifications" as contained in the promotion provision.

In the 1988 negotiations, the Union proposed on June 2 that the qualifications criteria be stricken from Article 6, Sections 4, 5, and 11. Sections 4 and 5 deal with the layoff and recall of employees, and Section 11 relates to promotions. If the Union proposal prevailed, layoffs, recalls, and promotions would be based on strict seniority. The Company did not accept the Union proposal, and the qualifications criteria remain in the current Labor Agreement as they did in the previous contract.

On June 18, the Union proposed the addition of a new Article 37. This proposal established a time limitation for the qualification of employees assigned to a series of jobs. Lowell Hunt, Union President, explained that the Union was dissatisfied with the qualification program because the Company at times did not qualify employees after they received a new job within a reasonable length of time. To deal with this problem, the Union proposed that the Company be required to qualify an employee after he served on a job for a specific length of time. Twenty-seven jobs were covered by the Union proposal. Under the program, a Flexo Operator Assistant would be qualified within 60 days.

The Company did not agree to the Union proposal, and it, too, is not incorporated in the current Labor Agreement. Under the instant contract, any employee promoted to or awarded a bid job is afforded a maximum 45-day trial period (unless extended by the Company) during which time he may be disqualified should it be determined that he is not capable of performing the duties of the job.

On June 25, the Union proposed that certain unskilled jobs be awarded solely on the basis of seniority under Article 6, Section 11. It proposed that the current language of the promotion provision be retained, except that the following be added:

However, all jobs as outlined in Section 4(a) of this Article will be open and seniority will prevail.

Thus, for these jobs, the qualifications criteria would not apply. Twelve jobs were to be covered by this language. Flexo Operator Assistant was not included in the jobs listed by the Union.

The Company rejected the Union proposal, and, again, it is not included in the current Labor Agreement. Meeks explained the reason for the Company's action, testifying:

We did not want to be tied down to those listed unskilled jobs. There could be other unskilled jobs.

On the same day, June 25, on which the Union proposed the exception of the unskilled jobs from any qualification test for the purpose of promotion, the Company made a proposal dealing with the application of the promotion provision that was accepted and incorporated in the Memoranda of Agreement. Under this provision, found in Paragraph 17C of the Memoranda, "relatively equal qualifications" contained in Article 6, Section 11 are defined

as those qualifications learned in one (1) working day or less and enabling the employee to acceptably perform all aspects of the job.

POSITION OF THE PARTIES

The position of the Union is that the grievance should be granted, and the Company requests that it be denied. During the arbitration, however, the Union said that the remedy to be afforded the Grievant should not necessarily be the awarding of the job, but that he be given an eight-hour trial period on it. Such an opportunity, the Union claims, is contemplated by Paragraph 17C of the Memoranda of Agreement.

ANALYSIS OF THE EVIDENCE

Article 6, Section 11: Comparative Qualifications

Before relating Paragraph 17C of the Memoranda of Agreement to the circumstances of this dispute, we shall first test the merits of Stull's grievance under Article 6, Section 11. Indeed, if the grievance has merit under the promotion provision standing alone, there would be no need to determine the applicability of Paragraph 17C.

Article 6, Section 11, establishes a qualification contest between a senior and junior service employee who bid on the same job. Obviously, the provision does not award a promotion solely on the basis of seniority. If it did, there would have been no need for the Union's unsuccessful attempt to change its language to make seniority the exclusive factor for promotion during the 1988 negotiations.

Not only does the promotion provision tell us that a promotion will be based on seniority and qualifications, but it also says that seniority will prevail only

when all factors that constitute qualifications are relatively equal.

Some collective bargaining contracts state that promotions will be made on the basis of seniority and ability or qualifications. That is, if the senior employee is qualified or has the ability to perform a job, he will receive the promotion even if a junior service employee has superior qualifications.

Instead of a promotion program, based only on seniority and qualifications, the language states that seniority will prevail when the qualifications are "relatively equal." In other words, the comparative qualifications of the senior and junior service employees must be evaluated. If the evidence demonstrates that the senior bidder's qualifications are relatively equal as compared to the junior service employee, the senior employee has the contractual right to the promotion. On the other hand, the senior employee may not claim the job should the evidence demonstrate that he does not have qualifications relatively equal to the junior service bidder.

This analysis makes unacceptable the Union argument that the Grievant had the right to the job in question based on the proposition that he had the minimum qualifications to serve as Operator Assistant on the No. 2 Flexo. On the Grievant's behalf, the Union said:

Stull had the minimum qualifications to fill the job. Since he had the minimum qualifications, he had the right to the job.

It is true that there are some similarities in the operation of the Ward Die Cutter and the No. 2 Flexo. Though William Grove, classified as a Flexo Operator on the No. 2 Flexo for several years, testified that there are some differences between the two machines, the thrust of his testimony is that they are essentially similar in operation. The Grievant was, of course, assigned to the Ward Die Cut for many years, and in light of these Ward Die Cut and No. 2 Flexo similarities, the Union claims that the Grievant presented "minimum qualifications for the No. 2 Flexo."

Even if we assume that the Grievant had the minimum qualifications to operate the No. 2 Flexo, based on his experience on the Ward Die Cut, it would not be proper to grant the grievance on this basis. It would not be proper because Article 6, Section 11, by express or implied language does not say that the senior employee has the contractual right to a job based only upon seniority and qualifications. To accept the Union's argument would eliminate from the promotion provision the qualification contest between the senior and junior service employees. On this issue, what the Union really requests is that the Arbitrator rewrite the language contained in the provision and read the provision as if the Parties agreed to a promotion program under which the senior employee has the contractual right to a promotion because he has the qualifications for the job. How can the Arbitrator possibly grant such a Union request and remain faithful to a most fundamental arbitration principle forbidding any arbitrator to legislate new contractual language? If the Parties believe that it would be prudent and fair to award a promotion to a senior employee based on his qualifications to perform a job, and independent of comparing his qualifications with those of a junior service employee, such a provision must be established at the bargaining table and not in arbitration.

Union Precedents

To support its position in this proceeding, the Union cited two arbitration precedents. One involved the Union and another of the Company's plants, this one in Columbus, Ohio. In that case, decided on May 12, 1990, Arbitrator Edes granted the grievance, holding that under the material contractual language and the facts of the dispute, the senior employee had the contractual right to a job. However, the material provision of the labor agreement in effect at Columbus is quite different from that in the instant dispute. Whereas Article 6, Section 11, establishes a qualifications contest between a senior and junior service employee, the language in the Columbus contract states:

> Journeymen having qualifications as both a Machinist and a Mechanic will be eligible to bid on the job posted.

In other words, in contrast with the instant Labor Agreement, the language in the Columbus case does not compare qualifications. All that it says is that employees qualified in the two crafts have the right to bid on a posted job. Unlike the Arbitrator's responsibility under the instant Labor Agreement, Arbitrator Edes was not obligated to compare the qualifications between the senior and junior service employees. While granting the grievance, he stated:

> I am fully persuaded on the entirety of the evidence in this case that Kazee was sufficiently qualified to perform the work of the Mechanic classification.

The second cited case involved the Container Manufacturers Institute and Glass Bottle Blowers Association. At that time, in 1980, the Company was a member of the Institute, but it since has withdrawn and negotiates its own contracts with the Union. In the 1980 contract, the Institute and the Union changed the promotion provision to read:

> Seniority plus ability shall govern in the case of promotions.

Before the adoption of this language, the promotion provision stated:

> Seniority dates shall govern in cases of promotions where qualifications are relatively equal between employees.

In other words, in the 1980 contract, the Parties wiped out the comparative qualifications criteria, and agreed to award promotions on the basis of seniority and ability. No longer would the senior employee be denied a promotion because the junior service employee had superior qualifications. All that the senior employee had to present was his ability to perform the job.

For reasons previously made clear, this is not the promotion system under the instant Labor Agreement. To repeat, for purposes of promotion, seniority governs only when the senior employee's qualifications are relatively equal to those of the junior service employee.

In short, the two cases supplied by the Union as precedent cases do not apply to the circumstances of this case because they contain promotion language which is quite different from that contained in Article 6, Section 11, of the instant Labor Agreement.

Application of Article 6, Section 11

With the meaning of Article 6, Section 11, made clear, the question now is whether Stull had qualifications relatively equal to those of the successful bidder, Downs, for the No. 2 Flexo job. If the evidence demonstrates that he did, the Grievant has the contractual right to the job because he is senior to Downs.

As the record shows, whereas the junior service employee was assigned to a Flexo machine and was classified as Flexo Operator Assistant between May 31, 1989, and the date of the posting, November 16, 1990, approximately eighteen months, the Grievant was never classified as a Flexo

Operator Assistant. Granted some similarities in operation between the No. 2 Flexo and the Ward Die Cut machines, it would not be proper to find that Stull had relatively equal qualifications for the job in question as compared with the junior service employee. This would still be the case even if we assume that Stull had the minimum qualifications for the job as the Union contends.

It is recognized that under the circumstances of a particular case a senior employee's qualifications may be relatively equal to those of a junior service employee even though the latter had operated the machine involved in a job bid and the former had not. This would be a proper finding when the senior employee had served on a machine so like the one in question that it could be said with reasonable assurance that the senior employee could step in and perform the job as effectively as the junior service employee. Under these circumstances, the senior employee would transfer the skills gained on the similar machine to the one in question and operate it as effectively as the junior service employee.

In the light of the evidence, however, it may not be said with reasonable assurance that Stull could step in and operate the No. 2 Flexo as efficiently and effectively as the junior service employee. Even the Union witnesses stated that there are differences between the Ward Die Cut and the No. 2 Flexo. As a matter of fact, as later discussion will demonstrate, there are significant differences between the two machines.

In short, given the differences between the two machines, it would strain the concept of "relatively equal" to the breaking point to find that Stull had relatively equal qualifications to operate the No. 2 Flexo as compared with the junior service employee. To find their qualifications relatively equal would ignore the fact that Downs actually had served as a Flexo Operator Assistant for about 18 months and equally would ignore that the Grievant had never been so classified prior to the posting of the job.

Paragraph 17C of Memoranda of Agreement

Up to this point, the evidence shows that Stull's grievance has no merit under the terms of Article 6, Section 11. What remains is to determine whether Stull has the contractual right to the job based on Paragraph 17C of the Memoranda of Agreement. Does the proper application of this provision establish his right to the job where in its absence his grievance under Article 6, Section 11, standing alone, lacks merit?

Paragraph 17C of the Memoranda defines the concept of relatively equal qualifications for purposes of Article 6, Section 11. It states that such concept is defined as those qualifications learned in one working day or less and enabling the employee to acceptably perform all aspects of the posted job. What the provision means for practical purposes is that a senior employee's qualifications are deemed to be equal to those of a junior service employee under circumstances where the senior employee can learn on one shift the qualifications of the posted job so as to enable him to perform all aspects of the job in an acceptable manner.

Scope of Provision

Before applying Paragraph 17C to the circumstances of this dispute, one matter concerning the provision must be resolved at the outset. In the view of the Company, the provision applies only to unskilled jobs. Since the operation of Flexo No. 2 involved skilled work, the Company argues that the provision is not applicable to this dispute. In this regard, Meeks testified:

> Paragraph 17 C evolved from the Union's listing of unskilled jobs. Flexo Operator Assistant was not on the Union listing. It was the Company's understanding that the provision relates only to unskilled jobs since the provision evolved from the Union's proposal to make listed unskilled jobs subject solely on seniority.

Earlier the chronology of the 1988 contract negotiations was presented. Of significance here was the Union's proposal made on June 25. At that time, the Union proposed that 12 unskilled jobs, not including Flexo Operator Assistant, be awarded solely on the basis of seniority. The Company rejected the proposal, and it is not included in the current Labor Agreement.

In any event, it was on the basis of such Union proposal that the Company claims that Paragraph 17C relates solely to unskilled jobs. It claims that this provision of the Memoranda of Agreement "evolved" from the aforesaid Union proposal. *This Company argument is not acceptable because Paragraph 17C does not state that it applies only to unskilled jobs.* All that it states is this:

> ...to acceptably perform all aspects of *the job*. [Emphasis added]

If the Parties intended that the provision apply only to unskilled jobs, they would have inserted the word "unskilled" into the provision. To explain why the Company did not place the word "unskilled" in the provision, Meeks said that the Company did not want to be "tied down" to those unskilled jobs listed in the Union proposal. Whatever may have been the reason for the Company's failure to propose that Paragraph 17C be limited to unskilled jobs, the fact remains that the language contains no such limitation on its scope of application, and it would be highly improper for the Arbitrator to place such a restriction into the provision.

Paragraph 17C was the Company's proposal. The Company drafted the language that subsequently was incorporated in the Memoranda of Agreement. Arbitrators have consistently held that should there be any doubt or ambiguity as to the construction of contractual language, it shall be construed against the party who proposed it. As Arbitrator Kahn stated, typically, in *Wurlitzer Company* (44 LA 1196, 1201):

> The Company, as the drafter of this ambiguous restriction, had an obligation to make clear to the Union, during the negotiations, that it intended such a major limitation on IX-K's use.

It must be held that Paragraph 17C applies to all posted jobs, including the one involved in this dispute.

Application of Provision

With this matter resolved, we are now prepared to apply Paragraph 17C of the Memoranda of Agreement to the specific facts of this case. Stull's grievance would have merit should it be determined that within one shift he could learn the qualifications of the Flexo Operator Assistant job so as to enable him to perform all aspects of the job in an acceptable manner. Under such circumstances, he would then possess qualifications relatively equal to those of Downs within the meaning of Article 6, Section 11.

Some evidence indicates that Stull could meet the requirements of Paragraph 17C. About six years ago, Grove was assigned to the 0-34 Partition machine. As in this case, a job was posted for a Flexo Operator Assistant on the No. 2 Flexo. Grove bid on the job and received it. He asked his foreman when he would be qualified on the No. 2 Flexo. Grove testified:

> He [the foreman] told me that he did not have to qualify me on the No. 2 Flexo. He said that I was already qualified. He said I was qualified on the Flexo because I was qualified on the Partition machine. I received no special training. I just started to work with the Operator.

Grove also said that the Grievant could have qualified as a Flexo Assistant Operator within eight hours, testifying that

> anyone who had prior knowledge on the presses could do this. All presses are the same.

In addition, we have available the experience of the Grievant when he bid and received the Flexo Assistant Operator job on the No. 3 Flexo. As the record shows, he was awarded the job on February 26, 1991. Stull testified that he had received no special training on the job, and another employee worked with him for only four hours. He said further that this employee did not even actually train him but "just stood around and watched me."

On the surface, it would appear that the declarations offered by Grove and the Grievant should be sufficient evidence to demonstrate that Stull could fulfill the requirements of Paragraph 17C. That is, within one shift he could learn the job in question so as to enable him to perform all aspects of the job in an acceptable manner. Before reaching this conclusion, however, other matters must be considered.

Just because Grove's foreman immediately qualified him on the Flexo based on his experience on his prior machine does not necessarily mean that Paragraph 17C should be applied in the Grievant's favor in this dispute. That event occurred several years ago, and before the adoption of this provision. Grove's testimony, though material, does not prove conclusively that the Grievant in this case meets the requirements of the provision. In the final analysis, the Arbitrator must apply the criteria contained in the provision in the light of the circumstances of this case. It would not be proper to regard Grove's experience as proof positive that the Grievant in one working day could learn the qualifications of the job in question so as to enable him to perform acceptably all aspects of the job.

In addition, Grove's testimony is somewhat contradictory. At one point in his prior testimony, he acknowledged differences between the Ward Die Cut and the Flexo. Then he told us that all "presses are the same" in the sense that an employee could move from machine to machine and within eight hours be able to learn qualifications of the job so that he could perform all aspects of it in an acceptable manner. Indeed, not only did Grove originally concede differences between the Ward Die Cut and the Flexo machines, but the differences were spelled out in detail by the Production Superintendent. It was, of course, the Grievant's previous experience on the Ward Die Cut that the Union argued was sufficient for Stull to meet the requirements of Paragraph 17C.

Without contradiction, Gell spelled out differences between the two machines. Whereas the Ward Die Cut is fed manually, the No. 2 Flexo (the posted job) contains an automatic feed capability. Unlike the Ward Die Cut, the Flexo involves considerable set-up time, from 3/4 of an hour to 1 and 1/2 hours. In other words, the set-up on the Flexo is more complicated than that of the Ward Die Cut. Moreover, the Flexo contains a supply tank of glue and a glue feed, an assembly not contained in the Ward Die Cut. That the glue function of the Flexo is an important attribute of the machine is made clear by the fact that the Company receives complaints from its customers concerning glue-related problems. Whereas the Flexo contains folding arms, such an assembly is not on the Ward Die Cut. On the Ward Die Cut, there is only one stacker. On the Flexo, there are stackers along with hold-down wheels and a counter rejecter.

These differences between the two machines were not made evident on the diagram drawn by the Grievant to establish the kindred nature of the two pieces of equipment. But the differences are not minor. They are substantial and compelling in character. They place in proper perspective Stull's testimony relative to his assignment to the No. 3 Flexo on February 26, 1991. Such testimony appears to suggest that without any training whatsoever he was able to perform all aspects of the job in a capable manner. It would seem that he did not even need eight hours for that purpose. Instead, he was a fully qualified Operator Assistant from the minute he was assigned to the job.

If this is so, how do we account for the following testimony offered by Gell, and *not refuted or contradicted by any Union witness*. Gell testified:

> Stull is not yet qualified. He is not completely familiar with the job. He still is not familiar with all his responsibilities.

Naturally, the Arbitrator understands that Gell had a motivation to present testimony that would not be favorable to the Grievant. After all, the Company denied his bid in the first place. By the same token, the Arbitrator also understands why the Union witnesses presented testimony favorable to the Grievant since the Union's fundamental position in this dispute is to minimize qualifications and maximize seniority for purposes of promotion. However, what corroborates the testimony of the Production Superintendent is his unrefuted and objective description of the significant differences between the two machines in question. In the light of these compelling differences, it is credible that as of the date of the arbitration—about six weeks after the assignment of the Grievant to the Flexo No. 3—he still was not fully qualified on the job.

Since Stull was not fully qualified after about six weeks on the Flexo job that he claimed on February 15, 1991, it is not possible to conclude that within one working day he could have learned the qualifications of the job in question to enable him to perform acceptably all aspects of the job. Thus, the Grievant could not meet the requirements of Paragraph 17C of the Memoranda of Agreement. Since he could not, it may not be held that his qualifications for the posted job were relatively equal to those of the junior service employee.

Opportunity to Demonstrate Qualifications

During the arbitration, the Union argued that the Company did not comply with the requirements of Paragraph 17C of the Memoranda of Agreement because it did not permit the Grievant to demonstrate his qualifications. In the Union's view, under the provision, when an employee shows a potential to perform a posted job he is entitled to an eight-hour trial period to demonstrate whether within that period of time he can learn the qualifications of the job to enable him to acceptably perform all aspects of the job.

The selection of the successful bidder was made by Gell and Meeks on the basis of the employment records of the two employees. Stull was not given an opportunity to demonstrate his qualifications on the job. In this regard, the Union argued:

> We feel strongly that the Company should not make a determination on the basis of pieces of paper. We are not requesting an 8 hour trial period for all employees. But we are requesting a trial period of 8 hours when an employee has a potential to do the posted job. He should be given an opportunity to prove his qualifications.

In the case at hand, even if this position of the Union has merit, a problem to be dealt with below, it would not be practical to afford the Grievant the trial period that the Union requests. By the time this Award reaches the Parties, Stull will have been on the Flexo No. 3 job for approximately 10 weeks. Under these circumstances, it would likely be that he could step in and perform the Flexo No. 2 Operator Assistant job on a fully qualified basis. Thus, a trial period at that time would not prove anything. It is impossible to turn the clock back as if a trial period would occur in the absence of the experience of the Grievant as a Flexo Operator Assistant.

On the other hand, if it is held that the Grievant had a contractual right to the trial period requested by the Union, there would be a basis to grant his grievance and direct the Company to place him on the Flexo No. 2 as an Operator Assistant. Under these circumstances, the Company would have violated the terms of Paragraph 17C of the Memoranda of Agreement.

In any event, on this issue, and with full deference to the Union, the provision does not call for an opportunity or trial period for an employee to prove his qualifications. *There is no language in the provision to establish such a state of affairs.* The only trial period mentioned in the Labor Agreement is the one spelled out in Article 6, Section 10. Such trial period becomes effective only after an employee is awarded a job based on the criteria contained in Section 11.

If the Parties intended that a trial period be provided, they would have adopted express contractual language to provide for such an opportunity. If the Union intended that Paragraph 17C should call for such an opportunity, the Union was obligated to make that intention clear at the bargaining table. Just as the Company desires the Arbitrator to read into the provision the unskilled job limitation, the Union here desires the Arbitrator to put into it a condition not provided for by its terms. Just as the Arbitrator refused to limit the provision to unskilled jobs, he must of necessity reject the Union argument for a trial period. It is interesting that in this case both Parties urge the Arbitrator to amend an agreement reached at the bargaining table!

As a matter of fact, the record of this case does not demonstrate any discussion at the bargaining table concerning a trial period. Though Hunt testified that the Union intended and/or understood the provision to provide for such an opportunity, he did not testify that the matter was discussed. Meeks said that the Company

> never agreed to give an 8 hour training period to any employee who had some ability to do a job.

Certainly, if a condition were not even discussed, let alone not being incorporated into a labor agreement, the Arbitrator should not read such a condition into its terms. This is not the first time, nor will it be the last time, when a party to collective bargaining leaves the bargaining table with its own understanding and/or intent of what negotiated language means. For purposes of arbitration, such privately held intent or understanding has no evidentiary value. To have standing in arbitration, an intent or understanding must be communicated to the other party at the bargaining table. After all, negotiators of labor agreements are not in the business of mind reading.

Conclusions

For reasons expressed, the grievance shall be denied. Given the qualifications of the two employees involved, and the character of the job involved, it cannot be held that the Grievant had qualifications relatively equal to those of the junior service employee under the terms of Article 6, Section 11. Paragraph 17C of the Memoranda of Agreement does not convert an otherwise meritless grievance to one of merit because under the circumstances of this case it was not reasonable to believe that the Grievant in one working day could have learned the qualifications of the job in question to enable him to perform acceptably all aspects of the job. Since Stull did not meet the requirements of Paragraph 17C, it may not be held that his qualifications were relatively equal to those of the junior service employee.

Let it be clear, however, that the Arbitrator has decided this dispute under the particular facts of this case. He certainly does not hold that Paragraph 17C of the Memoranda of Agreement has no future application. Should the facts of a case demonstrate that a senior employee can learn the qualifications of a job within one working day so as to enable him to perform acceptably all aspects of a job, the Company must award the job on the basis of seniority. Should it fail to do so, the Company would violate the Labor Agreement and an appropriate remedy would be directed.

One final comment is in order. The Union said:

To this union, and to all unions, seniority is a sacred right.

No one need instruct this Arbitrator as to the importance of seniority to the well-being of employees. It is recognized that the labor movement has done much to protect the job rights and job security of employees on the basis of seniority. As a matter of fact, over the years, this Arbitrator has granted many grievances because employers have violated the seniority rights of employees established in collective bargaining contracts.

That is, of course, the essential point. Though the Arbitrator understands the character of seniority, and its benefits to employees, he is necessarily bound by the agreements reached at the bargaining table regarding its application. If seniority is a sacred right to employees and unions, the Arbitrator by the same token finds sacred his faithful observance to the terms of a labor agreement and the evidence of a particular case. In this case, the material provisions of the Labor Agreement and the evidence do not permit the use of seniority as the basis of the decision. If they did, be assured that the Arbitrator would have granted the grievance and directed an appropriate remedy.

QUESTIONS

1. Why did the Arbitrator rule that the precedent cases presented by the Union were unpersuasive?

2. What reasoning did the Arbitrator use to hold that the Grievant was not entitled to the opportunity to prove his qualifications for the job?

3. Do you agree with the Arbitrator that the grievance did not have merit even though the Grievant may have had the qualifications to perform it? Explain your answer.

4. What impact did the contract negotiations have on the decision?

Employee Discipline

The next two cases deal with employee discipline. No issue in labor relations exceeds the importance of this area to all concerned. As a matter of fact, almost 50 percent of all arbitration cases concern discipline, and most involve discharge. To the employee, needless to say, the job is his or her most important asset. Take away the job, and the employee and family life collapse with tragic consequences. No wonder that unions elect to arbitrate discharge cases even when considerable doubt exists as to their merits. But to the employer, discipline under proper circumstances is necessary to maintain an efficient labor force. Failure to enforce rules of conduct could result in chaos within the firm.

You are the arbitrator in Case 10. In disputes involving employee discipline, the employer bears the burden of proof. The employee does not have the responsibility to prove that he or she did not commit the offense that resulted in discipline. Instead, the employer must present clear, convincing, and sufficient evidence to prove that the employee is guilty of the offense.

In discipline cases, the employer may present two types of evidence: direct and/or circumstantial. Direct evidence means that a person(s) actually observed the disciplined employee commit the offense. In contrast, circumstantial evidence relates to a chain of events that proves that the employee engaged in the conduct that resulted in the discipline. Circumstantial evidence, however, would not normally stand if the defense presents a theory consistent with the facts reasonably indicating that another person may have committed the offense.

In Case 10, the Company discharged an employee for theft. To prove its case, it presented both circumstantial and direct evidence. As you read the case, establish the character of the circumstantial and direct evidence that the Company used to prove the employee's guilt.

In addition, in cases of discipline, credibility of witnesses frequently becomes a problem. As you will learn in this case, two supervisors testified that they saw the Grievant holding the stolen property in his hands. However, the Grievant denied the supervisors' testimony.

In short, your problem is to determine, based on the record, whether the Company presented sufficient, clear, and convincing evidence proving the employee committed the theft for which he was discharged. To put it another way, did the Company meet its burden of proof?

Case 11 is surely one of the strangest cases in the annals of arbitration. A comparatively small telephone company was privately owned by its president. For about one year, the employer paid an employee full wages and fringe benefits even though he did not require the employee to work! Then the employee was discharged, the company alleging that his productivity was deficient and that he was psychologically unfit to work. Despite the odd character of the dispute, the arbitrator attempted to apply sound arbitration principles as the basis of his decision. As you read the case, try to determine the real reason why the employer paid the employee even though the latter was not required to work.

Employee Discipline:
The Case of the Stolen Bins

CAST OF CHARACTERS

Gest	Grievant
Boles	Supervisor, 2nd Shift
Arco	Process Operator
Ikes	Supervisor, 3rd Shift
Sarrin	General Supervisor
Kane	Plant Manager
Rado	Refinery A
Karco	Refinery B
Reis	Process Helper
Olds	Process Helper
Basto	Maintenance
Lash	Employee
Will	Union Steward

GRIEVANCE

Effective August 31, 1986, Donald Gest was terminated, charged with being involved in the theft of Company property. In protest, the Union filed Grievance No. 9-86, dated September 9, 1986, requesting reinstatement with back pay and contractual rights.

On October 3, 1986, the Company denied the grievance in Step 4 of the Grievance Procedure. Failing to settle the dispute, the Parties convened this arbitration for its determination.

LABOR AGREEMENT

Article 13—Settlement of Disputes

1. *Intent:* It is the desire of the parties that the procedure involved in this Article shall afford an effective means of settling all questions, disputes, and grievances arising as to interpretation of the provisions of this Agreement and its application.

2. *Discharges:* The Union, upon request, having been informed fully concerning the reasons for discharges, may submit the same for review in the manner provided for the submission of grievances. When an employee is discharged for just cause and an investigation made pursuant to the Union's request discloses the cause to be insufficient to warrant discharge or the facts leading to such discharge shall have been unsupported by proper evidence, such employee shall be reinstated to his position with uninterrupted seniority and with pay allowed for the period of his suspension. In cases meriting such action by agreement between the Company and the Union, such employee may be reinstated without pay allowance. Unless the provisions of this Article are invoked by the Union within 3 working days of an employee's discharge as to such employee, they shall be deemed waived.

ISSUE

Under the circumstances of this case was Grievant Gest discharged for just cause? If not, what should the remedy be?

BACKGROUND

Events of Saturday, August 30, 1986: Within the Plant

At 10:40 P.M., August 30, 1986, Dale Boles, Supervisor, 2nd Shift, received a phone call from Leo Arco, Process Operator B, advising him that two Delavel Bins were missing from the Parts Room. Each bin was about 3 feet high and 4 feet long, weighing 40 pounds when filled with parts and 25 pounds empty. After receiving the call, the supervisor went to the Guard House, located at the Main Gate, meeting Don Ikes, Supervisor, 3rd Shift, who was to relieve him at 11 P.M. They instructed the guard to shut the parking lot gate, effectively sealing the plant. Boles telephoned Dale Sarrin, General Supervisor, advising him of the situation. Since it was 11 P.M., the end of the second shift, Sarrin instructed Boles to open the gate to permit the second shift employees to leave.

Thirty-eight employees worked the second shift on the day in question. Tom Kane, Plant Manager, testified that of that number, six employees were assigned to jobs who could be away from their work stations without attracting attention. They were Tim Rado, Refinery A; Leo Karco, Refinery B; Herschel Reis and Darrell Olds, Process Helpers; T. Basto, Maintenance; and Grievant Gest, Outside Forklift Driver. Those employees worked in the Refinery area in which the Parts Room is located. As the Outside Forklift Driver, Gest, hired about ten years ago, hauls skids and pallets and moves chemicals, and waste materials to a large dumpster located near the contractor gate. The Parties stipulated that three employees drove small forklift trucks within the warehouse, and Gest was the only employee assigned to the large forklift. According to Gest, however, other employees have driven the large forklift truck without permission. Boles declared that other employees operate that vehicle when Gest does not report to work. Kane said there have been two or three complaints about unauthorized employees using the large forklift truck.

At 9:40 P.M., Boles testified, a Process Helper wanted to know where Gest was. The supervisor said he searched the plant for about ten minutes and could not find him. At another time during the shift, Boles testified, he saw the large forklift truck outside the Parts Room, but did not see Gest. He said this was "unusual" because Gest would not have any duty to perform in the Parts Room.

According to Gest, he did not park his forklift truck outside the Parts Room. Instead, he claimed, he parked it outside the Control Room, which is about 20 feet from the Parts Room. At the time in question, Gest testified, he brought a pallet of chemicals to the Control Room to exchange for an empty pallet. To explain his absence from the forklift truck, he said that he left the vehicle for a minute or two to perform some duties within the Control Room. He denied that he went into the Parts Room that night.

Employees Clocked Out

Boles testified that at 11 P.M. about ten employees were in the Guard House to clock out. He and Ikes declared that Gest was not in that group. The supervisors declared that Gest drove his van to the Guard House from the parking lot and then clocked out. According to their observations, he was the last employee to clock out.

Gest testified that he was relieved by Ted Lash shortly before 11 P.M. He showered, went to the Guard House to clock out, and saw the two supervisors standing around the Guard House. After he got into his van, Gest discovered that he had left his watch in the Guard House. He returned in his van and retrieved his watch. He testified that he clocked out the first time he was in the Guard House, and not the second time when he went back to get his watch. For the night in question, Gest's time card showed he clocked out at 11:06 P.M. At that point, he requested and was granted permission to leave by the supervisors.

Events on Durkee Drive: Supervisors' Version

Starting at the Main Gate is Durkee Drive, a road that employees use to leave the plant. Boles and Ikes related the following events after Gest began to drive down the road. After he traveled about 700 feet, Gest stopped at the side of the road. After another automobile passed him, Gest turned off the van's lights. Getting into Ikes's pickup truck, the two supervisors and a guard drove down the road with their lights off. When about 100–150 feet from the Grievant, Ikes turned on the lights of the vehicle.

Boles testified:

We saw Gest standing at the passenger side of the van holding the parts bin in his hands. He was facing us. At that time he dropped the bin to the ground, opened the passenger side door, took out a jacket and put it on. We walked up to him, and asked what he was doing. He said he got cold driving, and stopped to put his jacket on. When Ikes asked about the bin, Gest replied "It was just there."

As to these events, Ikes declared:

When about 100 feet from Gest's van, I put on my lights and saw him with the bin in his hands. At this point, he dropped it to the ground, and put on his jacket. When I asked about the bin, Gest replied: "I did not know it was there; it was just there."

Both supervisors testified that the parts were scattered on the ground.

Gest's Version

As to the events on Durkee Drive, Gest related the following:

I was driving down the road and it was chilly. My jacket was on the passenger seat and the window was open. I stopped my van, shut off the lights, went around to the passenger side and opened the door, got my jacket and put it on. I rolled up the passenger window. I saw the bin laying in the ditch beside the road. I did not pick it up because I did not want to get dirty.

When the supervisors arrived at the scene, one of them asked Gest, "Where is the other bin?" He replied: "I am not aware of the other bin." All three looked at the bin lying in the ditch. They unsuccessfully searched for the other bin.

With the permission of Gest, Boles searched the van by looking in the driver's side door, but did not discover the other bin in the vehicle. According to the supervisors, the side doors on the passenger side of the vehicle were open. In contrast, the Grievant testified that they were closed.

Subsequent Events

After Gest departed, the supervisors picked up the parts and drawers that were scattered on the ground, placed them in the bin, and returned to the plant. Before doing that they discovered a hole in the perimeter wire fence enclosing the plant. According to Ikes, the hole was 50–100 feet from where Gest had stopped his van and was located about 1,250 feet from the Parts Room. Kane, who inspected the hole during his investigation of the case, testified that it was not a newly cut hole, but an old one, the wire prongs being rusted. He said that the hole was about 3 feet high and 3 feet wide, and that when the hole was peeled open it was of sufficient size to push the bin through it and large enough for a thin man to crawl through.

When Boles returned to the plant, he and Sarrin searched for the other bin. They found it in the large dumpster, all smashed up. The dumpster was located about 1,140 feet from the Parts Room.

When Sarrin advised Kane of the events at 1:30 A.M., Sunday, August 31, he told the supervisor to suspend Gest when he reported to work for his 3 P.M. shift. At 2 P.M., Sunday, August 31, 1986, a meeting was held attended by Kane, Boles, Gest, and Union Steward John Will. When requested to explain the circumstances, Gest told the group that it was a cool night and he had stopped the van, had gotten out of it, gone to the passenger side, and opened the door. He had, he said, taken out his jacket and put it on. That is when the supervisors confronted him. Gest also said that at that time he did not see the bin in the ditch until it was pointed out to him by the supervisors. He denied that he had stolen the bin. When requested by Kane, Boles related the events essentially the same way as he testified in the arbitration, telling the group that he saw Gest holding the bin. At the close of the session, Kane suspended Gest pending investigation. Subsequently Gest's suspension was converted to a discharge.

POSITIONS OF THE PARTIES

Company

The Company claimed that it supplied sufficient evidence proving that Gest stole at least one of the bins. Although it conceded that no one actually saw the Grievant remove the bins from the Parts Room, it believed that circumstantial evidence demonstrated that the Grievant committed the theft. It said that Gest had the means, opportunity, and the time to transport the bins across the plant without attracting attention.

In this respect, it stressed the following. The large forklift is required to move the bins. Gest was assigned to that vehicle. For some time during the shift, he disappeared and could not be located. Supervision saw the large forklift parked near the Parts Room. On Durkee Drive, the Grievant stopped his van at the precise spot where the bin was found.

Aside from the circumstantial evidence, the Company claimed it presented direct evidence proving the Grievant committed the theft. Thus:

> We presented two reliable witnesses who testified they saw Grievant holding one of the bins in his hands. No reason exists to doubt that testimony.

Union

On its part, the Union asserted that the circumstantial evidence presented by the Company was not sufficient to prove Gest committed the offense. Other employees had access to the large forklift. Plant Manager Kane testified that five other employees could be away from their jobs without attracting attention. He also said that "there have been complaints that unauthorized employees have used the large forklift." Another employee could have pushed the bin through the hole in the fence.

It also argued that the Company did not present sufficient direct evidence showing how the bins came to be located in the ditch and dumpster. Even Kane declared:

> We do not have direct knowledge how the bin got outside the plant. We do not have direct knowledge how the other bin got into the dumpster. We know who committed the theft, but we do not know how it was done.

The Union also pointed out that the guard who accompanied the two supervisors did not testify in the arbitration. On this point, it said:

> It was quite interesting that the guard who was supposed to observe the alleged act did not testify and was not present at the hearing.

Finally, the Union declared:

> In no way does this Union condone theft of Company property. But here the Company did not prove its case against Gest. Its evidence falls far short from that needed for them to prove the charge. The Company is using Gest as a scapegoat. It would be a travesty of justice to find him guilty.

The Case of the Employee Who Was Paid and Not Required to Work

CAST OF CHARACTERS

Hall	Discharged Employee
Jones	A Union Witness
Thomas	President of Company
Fells	Superintendent

GRIEVANCE AND LABOR AGREEMENT

In protest against his discharge, effective October 1, 1975, Hall filed a grievance dated October 2, 1975. It states:

In reference to letter received by aggrieved employee Sept. 30, 1975 from employer stating that his job would be terminated Oct. 1, 1975 for violation of Paragraph 2, Page 1, of Contract. Aggrieved employee has not violated Paragraph 2, Page 1, of Contract and has no knowledge of why he is accused of doing so or for what reasons the Company has for stating that his job would be terminated Oct. 1, 1975.

He requests that he be reinstated to his regular and/or normal job with full seniority and made whole for any and all monies and benefits due him in accordance with terms and conditions of contract.
The employer has not found proper cause to discharge aggrieved employee.

Having failed to settle the dispute in the Grievance Procedure, the Parties convened this arbitration for its final and binding determination.
Material to the dispute are the following provisions of the Labor Agreement:

Paragraph 2

The Union agrees that its said members will individually and collectively, at all times perform loyal and efficient service, comply with the terms and working conditions of this Agreement, use their influence and best efforts to protect the property of the Company and all its employees to such ends.

Paragraph 3(b)

Subject to the provisions of this Agreement, the Company shall have the right to schedule and assign work, to hire, promote, recall, demote, suspend, transfer, lay off and for proper cause to discharge employees.

Paragraph 16

The arbitrator or arbitrators shall have no authority to add to, subtract from, or modify any provision of this Agreement, or to rule on any questions except the ones submitted for arbitration.

BASIC QUESTION

The basic question to be determined in this arbitration is framed as follows:

Under the circumstances of this case, was Grievant Hall discharged for proper cause? If not, what should the remedy be?

BACKGROUND

Grievant Hall was hired by the Company on June 6, 1966. On August 4, 1974, he broke a leg while riding a horse. Though the Labor Agreement does not contain a sickness-accident program, paying employees for non-work-related accidents or sickness, employee Jones said that it was the policy of the Company to pay employees about six or seven weeks' pay when they were disabled as a result of such circumstances.
Some time in September 1974, Hall called Thomas, President of the Company. The Grievant testified that two weeks prior to the call he had received four days' pay, and a week before the call, he did not receive any pay. He testified that the purpose of the call was to discuss the problem with Thomas.

According to the testimony of Thomas, at one point in this phone conversation Hall said to him:

The only reason I work for a S.O.B. like you, is because I have a wife and children to support.

As to this event, the Grievant denied that he made the aforecited statement attributed to him by the Company President. Hall testified that he said to Thomas:

I have a wife and two children who depend on me and that is why I work.

Hall declared that Thomas replied:

If you don't like to work for me, why don't you work for a good guy?

On or about October 14, 1974, Hall reported to work though he still had a cast on his leg. Fells, Superintendent, assigned him to driving a truck. However, at times, Fells said, the Grievant buried cables, using a vibrator and a back-hoe. On November 18, 1974, Hall buried cables for nine hours.
The next day, November 19, 1974, Fells called the Grievant and told him to bring his truck in for repairs. He did so and had a conversation with the Superintendent. Hall testified that he told Fells that work was falling behind, and asked for another truck. Fells refused. Instead, Fells told the Grievant to go home and wait until he was called back to work. In this regard, Hall testified:

Fells told me that my truck needed repairs. He told me to go home and wait until I was called.

Also, Fells told the Grievant that he would get full pay for all the time he did not work. As events turned out, the Company paid the Grievant his full pay and fringe benefits from November 19, 1974 until October 1, 1975, on which date he was discharged. In other words, for about one year, the Company paid the Grievant although he did not work. During this period of time, Hall periodically executed a Daily Time Report. On this report, he would write: "Waiting on truck." These reports were sent to Fells, who approved them, and the Company paid the Grievant although he did not actually perform work for his employer.
Thomas explained the reason for such a state of affairs. He testified:

I heard for a long period of time many complaints from my customers. This indicated to me that Hall was not working. Also, after he called me in September 1974 and said "the only reason I would work for a S.O.B. like you, is because I have a wife and children to support," I assumed that he did not want to work for me. I decided that we would be better off to leave him on the payroll and not have him work. I did not want any more customer complaints. He was impeding the progress of other employees. But the precipitating cause for this action (pay and no work) is that he simply did not want to work for me. It was in the best interest of the Company for us to take a $20,000 loss by paying him for not working than to assume the risk of having him work.

In addition, Thomas said the reason why the Grievant was not discharged on November 19, 1974, was that "I was not certain about the problems of terminating an employee."

Superintendent Fells also explained why the Company paid the Grievant though he did not perform any work. He said:

> We were unhappy with him because of his work performance. We did not think we were getting the job done. It was our judgment that he was not producing enough. He took too much time on a job.

During the period of time in which the Grievant was paid though he did not perform any work, there was no contact between the Grievant and the Company except the sending of his paychecks by the Company, the acceptance of them by the Grievant, and the filing of periodic Daily Time Reports. The Company did not call or write him, nor did Hall come to the Company, or write or phone.

In any event, effective October 20, 1975, the Grievant was discharged. Thomas wrote him:

> Mr. Hall:
>
> Paragraph 2 in the contracts (sic) reads:
>
> The Union agrees that its said members will individually and collectively, at all times perform loyal and efficient service, comply with the terms and working conditions of this Agreement, use their influence and best efforts to protect the property of the Company and all its employees to such ends.
>
> It is because you have violated these terms of this contractual agreement, you are hereby terminated effective October 1, 1975.

Thomas disclosed the circumstances which prompted him to discharge the Grievant. It so happened that an employee of the Company had a son with some degree of mental deficiency. The employee asked Thomas to hire his son. Thomas did not hire the young son because he feared that he might have an accident. In the light of this event, Thomas said:

> I had a man [Grievant] who was not working and drawing full pay. The boy could probably have performed more work than Hall. After serious thought, I wrote the termination letter.

During the processing of the grievance, Thomas made two offers to settle the dispute. On October 15, 1975, he offered to pay the Grievant his full wages until July 1976, at which time Hall would qualify for early retirement. Under the applicable early retirement provisions of the Labor Agreement, the Grievant would then receive $210.00 per month for life. The offer was refused by the Grievant.

A second offer was made in the middle of December 1975. Thomas proposed that he would return the Grievant to his job provided that Hall visit a psychological social worker weekly. Such treatment, Thomas explained, would be at the Company expense. Hall refused this offer. In the Company brief, Thomas stated:

If I could have come up with any other new and better ideas to help this man, I would have done so. As I explained at the hearing, we are operating with a Humanitarian philosophy of business management, and we care for the people who work for us.

ANALYSIS OF THE EVIDENCE

Strange Character of Case

To say the least, this is a very strange case. In the quarter of a century of the Arbitrator's experience, he knows of no situation in which a company paid an employee and did not require that person to perform any work. The fact that this was done for about one year underscores its extraordinary nature. It was not a situation where the Grievant was physically disabled and received accident benefits. For about five weeks before his discharge, Hall was working, though he had a cast on his leg. Also, in February 1975, Hall was released by his doctor, demonstrating that his leg was fully healed. Thus, during the year or so in question, Hall was physically qualified to work, and received full pay and fringe benefits, but the Company did not require him to work.

In any event, the uniqueness of the dispute should not serve to mask its substantive issues. As the Company's termination letter demonstrates, Hall was discharged on the grounds that he violated Paragraph 2 of the Labor Agreement. Under this provision, the Union agreed that its members will perform loyal and efficient service for the Company. Should the evidence demonstrate that Hall violated his obligations under this provision, it would follow that his discharge was for "proper cause" under the terms of Paragraph 3. Of course, if Hall engaged in conduct that offended his obligations as an employee, he could be discharged for "proper cause" without reference to Paragraph 2.

Grievant's Work Performance

As Company testimony demonstrates, one charge against the Grievant was that he did not satisfactorily perform his job. Fells testified that Hall "was not producing enough," and that he "took too much time on a job." Thomas said that he received customer complaints about the Grievant. In other words, when the Grievant was actively working for the Company, he failed to produce satisfactorily. His productivity did not measure up to acceptable standards.

As a threshold observation, it may be stated that an employer may properly discharge an employee under such circumstances. An employer must produce satisfactorily, or face the consequences. Indeed, the Arbitrator has sustained the discharges of employees who failed to meet reasonable production standards. Professional arbitrators have recognized that to keep a job, an employee must satisfactorily meet reasonable standards of productivity.

Thus, the first question to be determined is whether or not the evidence demonstrates that the Grievant produced satisfactorily. In this respect, the Company has the obligation to provide competent and convincing evidence to prove that Hall did not measure up to reasonable production standards. As countless arbitration decisions demonstrate, in a disciplinary case the employer bears the burden of proof. In short, the employer must supply convincing evidence that the employee committed the offense for which he was discharged. It is up to the employer to prove the employee "guilty," and not the employee who must prove himself "not guilty." This is a rock-bottom principle of arbitration, and so familiar that no citation of arbitral precedent is necessary.

Quality of Company Evidence

Applying this principle to the circumstances of this case, the conclusion is inescapable that the Company failed to prove that the Grievant did not produce satisfactorily. All that the Company supplies in this respect is the judgment of its two officials that the Grievant failed to produce adequately. With respect to the customer complaints against Hall, Thomas testified that he received two phone calls from the Company's customers complaining about the Grievant. He said:

> These two complaints were from women who complained that the Grievant was in the coffee shop. I probably got these calls in 1974.

Note that the Grievant was employed by the Company for about nine years. Even if the complaints were fully justified, the occurrence of two complaints of this nature in a nine-year period does not demonstrate that the Grievant was not a satisfactory employee. Beyond this, the Company apparently did not regard these two complaints to be of much consequence because it did not call them to the attention of the Grievant.

In addition, the judgment of the Company officials that the Grievant was taking too much time on his jobs and/or did not produce enough is not backed up by objective evidence. Note the testimony of Fells:

> It is our *judgment* that he was not producing enough. He was taking too much time on his jobs.

Though the judgment or opinions of supervision deserve consideration, they are not of much evidentiary value unless supported by objective evidence. Any supervisor can testify that in his opinion or judgment an employee is not doing his job. In this respect, the Company has not provided any evidence whatsoever to support the judgment or opinions of its officials.

Daily time sheets are filled out by the employees, and these documents are inspected by the Superintendent. Such time sheets show the kinds of jobs performed by the Company's employees and disclose the time spent on such jobs. In other words, there exists objective evidence to demonstrate the productivity of the employees. However, before the Company discharged the Grievant, no reference was made to such documents. Fells testified: "I did not examine his time sheets before we discharged him."

Progressive Discipline

Added to these considerations, the record shows that at no time did the Company ever warn the Grievant that his production was not satisfactory. During his nine years of service, Hall did not receive any warnings, reprimands, or suspensions. In fact, Fells testified that his work was "average," [*] and that "I never told him that his work was taking too long."

It is a matter of common sense that when an employee falls below par, the worker should be counseled, warned, reprimanded, and even suspended before discharge takes place. This is what is meant by progressive discipline, a system used by employers to rehabilitate an employee. In cases of this sort, where the allegation is made that an employee fails to meet reasonable standards of production, the employer first counsels the employee in the effort to improve his or her performance. If such counseling, fairly given, fails to correct the employee's deficiencies, the next step is to implement discipline. Normally, the employee is first warned orally and/or in writing. If this does not induce the employee to improve production, the next step is a suspension. When all this fails, the employer then discharges the employee on the grounds that all efforts to rehabilitate the employee have failed.

In this case, even if we assume that the Grievant did not meet production standards, the Company made no effort to rehabilitate him. As a matter of fact, at no time did the Company even tell the employee that he was not producing satisfactorily. Clearly, it is a matter of common sense that when an employee does not turn out a "fair day's work" the employer calls this to his attention. If the employer does not do this, how does the employee know that his work is not satisfactory? In the absence of counseling and/or warnings, the employee has reason to believe that his or her work meets production standards.

In any event, in this case, the evidence simply does not support the charge that the Grievant was not doing his job. All that we have in the way of evidence is the unsupported opinion of the two Company officials. Beyond this, the Company did not offer a scintilla of evidence to prove the charge. Indeed, the very fact that the Company never counseled or warned the Grievant discloses that his work was satisfactory. In short, in the light of

---

[*] In all fairness, in the light of the general testimony of Fells, when he described the work of the Grievant as "average," he was apparently making the assessment in reference to the quality of the Grievant's work rather than about its quantity.

the available evidence, it would be absolutely improper to sustain the discharge of the Grievant. Such a decision would be totally unwarranted given the state of the evidence and would fly in the face of settled and recognized principles of the arbitration process.

Psychological Fitness of Grievant

In addition, the Company argues that Hall is psychologically unfit to return to work. With respect to this feature of the case, Thomas says:

> Offered early retirement of $210.00 per month, he refused. Offered his regular job provided he would see a psychological social worker on company time and at company expense, he refused this also.
>
> Still he persists he wants to come back to work for a man he intensely dislikes. This is not the behavior of a rational man; rather, it is the behavior of a very neurotic man. In the interest of the company and its customers, I can and will not gainfully employ anyone too sick to do an adequate job, whether it be physical or psychological.
>
> Hall has not always been willing to follow instructions from the company in the past. The only possible explanation for the fact that he could take full pay for doing absolutely no work for almost a year, and rather dutifully stay around Dover, because he was "waiting on truck" as ordered, and never in the entire time communicate with me is an indication of the seriousness of his neurosis.
>
> What alternatives do I have where an employee is physically healthy, but is not at all well psychologically? We accept the responsibility of taking care of our employees from their time of employment to their death. However, when one is sick, should that man get full pay? I think not, in fairness to our other employees, the company owners, and the telephone customers.
>
> Termination was my last alternative, only because I could not think of any other options to offer Hall.

Under proper circumstances, an employer may properly terminate an employee for reasons of psychological or mental unfitness to hold a job, or under proper circumstances, an employer may require an employee to be treated for mental or psychological disorders as the prerequisite for holding a job. In this case, the Company relies upon these propositions to justify the discharge of the Grievant.

To support its position, the Company says that Hall demonstrated irrational and psychologically unsound behavior because he accepted pay for about one year without performing work. It argues that this state of affairs "is an indication of the seriousness of his neurosis."

Certainly, this feature of the case demonstrates its rare and unusual character. Here we had an employee receiving full pay and fringe benefits, and the Company did not require him to work. As noted earlier, the Arbitrator has never been confronted with such a situation, and it is probably unique in labor relations. To conclude on this basis, however, that the Grievant is psychologically unsound to work is unwarranted. The bottom line is that the Grievant did exactly what the Company told him to do. On November 19, 1974, the Company told the Grievant to "go home and wait until he was called back to work." He was told that while he waited for the call he would receive full pay and fringe benefits. If it is held that it was strange behavior on the part of the Grievant to accept such payments, it was just as strange for the Company to have permitted this state of affairs to occur.

At any time, the Company had the power to stop this unusual condition. At any time, it could have directed the Grievant to return to work or discharged him as it eventually did on October 1, 1975. True, the Grievant testified that he felt "uncomfortable" when he received pay without working. But what was Hall supposed to do? He did not have the authority to work without receiving such permission to work. It was the responsibility of the Company to direct him to work. In the absence of a call to work, should he have refused payment and thereby lose the source of income to support his family? Should he have quit his job, and thereby forfeit his contractual rights gained over nine years of service? Should he have quit his job and taken his chances on getting another job given the fact that jobs are scarce because of the current national problem of unemployment? Clearly, if the Company was willing to tolerate this strange state of affairs, it was to be expected that Hall would accept payment. Indeed, it would be an irrational act on his part to refuse payment or to quit his job. In short, the Arbitrator finds that the Grievant's acceptance of payment does not demonstrate irrational behavior or show that he was psychologically unfit to hold his job, or that he required psychological or psychiatric treatment.

In support of the Company's argument herein considered, the Company also argues that Hall

> still insists he wants to come back to work for a man he intensely dislikes. This is not the behavior of a rational man, it is behavior of a very neurotic man.

Even if for the sake of argument we may assume that the Grievant does not like Thomas,[*] this does not make Hall a psychological cripple unable to hold his job. Many employees do not necessarily like their employers, but they still work for them given the realities of life. We do not have a society or an economy where employees are free to quit their jobs just because they do not necessarily like their employers. A man has to work, and he subordinates his resentment of his employer to the necessity of earning a living.

*Apparently the Company concludes that the Grievant "intensely dislikes" Thomas because of the nature of the phone conversation of September 1974. Without exploring in depth the character of this Company argument, the fact that the Grievant vented his anger about being denied sick pay (with or without justification) does not necessarily show that he "intensely dislikes" Thomas. It is not uncommon for employees to say things in anger about their supervisors. This does not necessarily prove that the employees harbor a deep-seated and irreversible hatred of their employers. Indeed, in the course of human events, we all say things in anger (even between husband and wife) that do not reflect a permanent dislike for one another. In fact, the venting of anger, some say, is a healthy psychological therapeutic device.

Apparently the Company regards the workplace as some sort of idyllic society wherein each member plays his or her role with contentment and where peace and harmony prevail. To the contrary, in the real world, frictions develop in the employer-employee relationship, and there does not exist a condition of love and contentment between employees and employers. Conditions develop in which employers resent employees, and employees resent employers, but still they tolerate each other. No one has as yet devised a system wherein the workplace would be converted into some sort of idealistic community in which love characterizes the employer-employee relationship. In any event, it would be a masterpiece of error to hold that the Grievant is psychologically unfit to hold his job even if it is true that he may not like Thomas.

Beyond these observations, the Arbitrator finds nothing in the record to demonstrate that the Grievant is psychologically unfit to hold his job. He testified in the arbitration in a rational manner; spoke clearly; and was in full control of his behavior. He was tuned into reality and did not demonstrate the behavior of a psychological cripple. He worked for the Company for nine years, and nothing in the record demonstrates irrational behavior while he was on the job. If it is true that the Grievant was psychologically unsound, there would have been evidence of irrational behavior while he was on the job. No such evidence was supplied by the Company.

For nine years, he had a spotless disciplinary record. At no time was he warned, reprimanded, or suspended for any employee offense. Indeed, the charge that he did not produce enough and/or took too much time to do his work was not proved by the evidence.

CONCLUSIONS

In arbitration, we base decisions on facts and evidence. We do not make decisions based upon suppositions or unsupported allegations. Indeed, the published and unpublished decisions of this Arbitrator demonstrate that he has frequently sustained discharges of employees. In those cases, he found on the evidence that employees engaged in offensive conduct of a serious nature and that the employers proved that the employees had committed the offenses for which they were discharged.

In the case at hand, the Company did not prove that the Grievant was deficient in his obligations as an employee. The evidence does not support the charge that he did not perform his work satisfactorily. The evidence does not support the charge that he was psychologically unsound in the sense that he cannot hold his job. For these reasons, the Arbitrator shall grant the grievance. In the final analysis, the Company has failed to prove that it discharged the Grievant for proper cause within the meaning of the Labor Agreement.

QUESTIONS

1. Now that you have read the case, what do you believe to be the real reason why the employee was paid for not working?

2. What evidence did the arbitrator use to show that the employee was not a psychological cripple?

3. How did the arbitrator deal with the charge that the employee's productivity was not sufficient?

4. Why do you believe that the employee refused the two offers made by the company to settle the grievance?

Plant Closing The Case of the Silent Sale

You are the arbitrator in this case. In a very few instances, when unions make economic concessions, employers in exchange agree not to move or close the plant during the term of the labor agreement. More frequently, employers agree to notify the union before closure.

These were the circumstances that prevailed in this case. In exchange for concessions, the employer agreed to notify the union should it decide to close the plant. Such advance notice would provide the union with the opportunity to present reasonable alternatives to closure. During the period of the contract, the employer sold the plant to another company. On the day of the sale, the plant was closed permanently, resulting in the loss of 159 jobs. When the employer was negotiating the sale of the property, it did not notify the union of those events. In light of the circumstances of this case, you must decide whether the employer violated the agreement requiring that it notify the union before closure. To arrive at your decision, certain problems require consideration, such as: Did the employer close the plant before the sale? Did the employer have knowledge that the purchase would close the plant? If it had such knowledge, should the employer have disclosed that information to the union? Would the union have had a reasonable alternative to closing available had it been notified that the plant might close?

FILING OF GRIEVANCE

Effective August 15, 1984, the URSA Corporation sold its Komo Division to Barnes Industries. Sold were Trojan, Inc., Inwood, Indiana, manufacturer of electric harnesses for household and office equipment; and another plant located in Ohio. On the same day, the Trojan plant was closed permanently. Prior to the shutdown, URSA did not provide notice to the Union. A grievance was filed, dated August 23, 1984, which stated:

> Local 770 grieves and protests the sale and closing of the Inwood, IN, plant on or about August 15, 1984, without proper notice to the Union. Local 770 maintains the sale and closing of the plant, without proper notice, has violated the memo of understanding between the parties dated 3/9/83. Local 770 requests the company immediately return the work, reopen the plant, reinstate the affected work force and make our membership whole for all losses.

On August 25, 1984, the Company denied the grievance, stating:

> URSA did not make the decision to close the facility but sold assets to Barnes Industries on August 15, 1984. Therefore, there is no contract violation and this grievance is denied.

LABOR AGREEMENT

ARTICLE 10

Section 5

> The Arbitrator may interpret the Agreement and apply it to the particular case presented to him; but he shall, however, have no authority to add to, subtract from, or in any way modify the terms of this Agreement or any agreements made supplementary hereto.

Memorandum of Understanding—March 9, 1983

> In the event the Company, in its sole discretion, determines that it is advisable to close the plant, the Company will notify the Union and afford them the opportunity to present reasonable alternatives.

ISSUE

Under the circumstances of this case, did the Company violate the Memorandum of Understanding? If so, what should the remedy be?

BACKGROUND

Contract Negotiations

In the negotiations which resulted in the current Labor Agreement, dated March 1, 1983, the Company negotiated concessions in wages and benefits. According to Moore, a member of the Union Negotiating Committee, Mills, Vice President of URSA, told the Union Committee that because of the competition, the profit situation, and the general state of the economy, the Company could close the plant if concessions were not secured. Concessions were granted by the Union Committee, but the membership refused the proposed contract and a strike began on March 1, 1983.

Negotiations continued during the strike. On March 2, Mills sent a letter to Union members, including the following statement:

Is it possible for Trojan to move?
Yes, we are attempting thru our negotiations with you to save our Inwood jobs. The competition took many jobs away already. They would take more if we stay uncompetitive. Before Trojan loses *all* of its business, it would be *forced* to move to a low labor rate area. (Emphasis in original)

On March 9, 1983, the strike ended and the Labor Agreement was adopted. According to Clark, Union Steward and Recording Secretary, the Union accepted a cut in wages and benefits amounting to $1.25 per hour. Before the concessions, Moore, classified Group Leader, earned $5.69 per hour. Under the new Labor Agreement, the rate for the same job was reduced to $5.16 per hour.

In exchange for the concessions, the Union requested the Company to agree that it would not close or move the plant during the effective period of the contract, which was scheduled to terminate on February 18, 1986. Clark said the

Union members wanted something to protect their jobs in exchange for the concessions.

In any event, the Union was not successful in securing that kind of assurance for continued employment. Instead, the Parties adopted the aforesaid Memorandum of Understanding.

Before the new contract went into effect, the bargaining unit contained 85 employees. As of August 14, 1984, the number had increased to 159, and the plant operated on a two-shift basis. Clark testified that the Company earned a profit for the first quarter 1984, the first profitable quarter in the previous sixteen months. She said Mills provided this information during employee meetings, and also testified he "bragged that the Company was making profits."

Sale of the Plant to Barnes Industries

Dane, URSA Chief Financial Officer, related the circumstances that resulted in the sale of Trojan to Barnes Industries. In 1983, URSA experienced losses of several million dollars. As a result, it sold the Glass Products Division, which operated in California, Oklahoma, Ohio, and Pennsylvania, to a French firm, effective December 31, 1983. Of URSA's $100 million in annual sales, Glass Products Division accounted for $80 million. Funds resulting from the sale were assigned to creditors, but URSA was still liable for $5 million in unpaid bills.

With the sale of the Glass Products Division, attention was attracted to the financial condition of URSA. In late May 1984, several firms expressed an interest to purchase Komo Division, including Barnes Industries, of Miller, Indiana. Discussions were held between URSA and Cook, Chief Executive Officer, Barnes Industries. In July 1984, a letter of intent to sell was signed.

After that time, discussions continued between Cook and his attorneys and URSA representatives. Cook insisted that both plants be operated as going concerns. Eventually a Sales and Purchase Agreement was executed by the two corporations. Section 11, Paragraph B of the document stated:

> The assets and property that are the subject hereof and the business conducted by the Trojan and Komo divisions are going concerns and shall not have been adversely affected in any material way.

Section 12, Paragraph A provided:

> Between the date hereof and the closing date, Komo will cause the businesses of the Trojan and Komo operations to be continued in a prudent manner in the ordinary course and substantially in the same manner as heretofore conducted and will take any and all steps necessary to maintain the businesses in their present form and mode of operation.

In addition, Barnes Industries prohibited URSA from discussing the sale with any URSA employee. When Dane asked the reason, the buyer said it did not want URSA making any promises of what might occur after the sale. Section 10, Paragraph I of the Sales and Purchase Agreement stated:

> The supervisors, agents, officers or Directors of URSA and Komo have made no representation to any employee of the Trojan and Komo operations or any other person as to Barnes Industries' intended disposition of the Trojan and/or Komo operations.

Discussions also involved the status of the URSA multiemployer pension plan. As provided by the law, the withdrawal from a multiemployer plan involves a financial liability. In URSA's case, the amount would be $340,000. Under the Sales and Purchase agreement, Section 10, Paragraph A, URSA assumed the liability unless within 60 days of the sale's closing, Barnes Industries voluntarily assumed the obligation.[*] The same area of the document indicated that Barnes Industries would not assume, honor, or perform the Labor Agreement between Trojan and the Union.

On August 9, 1984, Cook requested that an inventory be held in the Inwood plant on August 15. On the same day, by phone, he told Dane that the Trojan plant would be closed effective August 15, 1984. Dane said he was "stunned" because "we felt Barnes Industries would continue to operate both plants."[**] Cook also told Dane not to tell employees, including Ellis, Plant Manager at Trojan, of the closing of the plant.

When Dane conveyed that information to Glenn, URSA Chief Executive Officer, Glenn contacted Cook, telling him of the advantages of operating the Inwood plant and the disadvantages of closing it. At that time, Cook said he would reconsider the decision to close the plant after consulting with his attorneys.

Events of August 15, 1984: Plant Sold and Closed

Under the terms of the Sales and Purchase Agreement, the closing of the transaction was established at 10 A.M. (EDST) stating:

> The term "closing date" or "closing" as herein used shall be deemed the hour of 10 A.M., EDST, on the 15th day of August, 1984, at the offices of URSA, Carmel, Ohio, or at such other place or date mutually agreed upon by the parties.

Pursuant to this agreement, URSA and Barnes met on August 15 in Carmel, Ohio, for the formal signing of the closing papers. In the morning, Cook told Dane he believed the plant would be closed. About 155 minutes later, Dane called Ellis, advised him of the closing, and instructed him to permit Barnes's personnel access to the plant. At 1 P.M. (EDST), the closing of the transaction was completed, and the necessary documents signed.

Events at Trojan

On August 9, 1984, as noted, Cook requested that an inventory be taken at Trojan on August 15. On the morning of August 14, 1984, Ellis posted the following notice:

[*]As it turned out, URSA assumed the liability. Payment was to be made each quarter. At the time of the arbitration, URSA had not paid any of the obligation.
[**]Whereas the Inwood plant was closed, the plant located in Ohio continued to operate.

> Due to circumstances beyond our control, I herewith advise each of you that we will shut down at 12:30 A.M. 8/15/84, (after conclusion of 2nd shift today), for purposes of taking an inventory. At present, we expect this will take the remainder of the week.
>
> Those employees that will be needed to assist with the inventory will be personally contacted by myself prior to 3:30 P.M. today.

At 4 P.M. on the same day, the Company met with the Union Committee. At that time, Evans, Director of Personnel, advised the Union that the plant was in the process of being sold. Union President Morgan testified that Evans said it was a "silent sale" and that as far as he knew the employees should report to work the following Monday. When asked what effect the sale would have on the employees' jobs, Evans responded that the purchaser had several options—operate the plant on a *status quo* basis; continue to operate, but not honor the Labor Agreement or recognize the Union; or close the plant.

At 10 A.M., August 15, 1984, Morgan visited the plant, noted that tractor-trailer trucks were at the loading docks; and later on that afternoon, when she was in the plant (with Evans's permission) Morgan observed that machinery was being dismantled and finished products loaded into boxes.

On August 17, 1984, the Company sent a letter to all Trojan employees, stating:

> This letter is to confirm that the assets of Trojan and Komo have been sold, effective August 15, to Barnes Industries. Although both units are solid, profitable operations, they did not fit into the long-range plans of URSA Corporation, and their sale will enable the Company to restructure its long-term debt.
>
> Throughout the negotiations for this transaction, we understood that Barnes planned to operate both the Trojan and Komo facilities. However, we were notified very recently by management of Barnes that it has now decided not to operate the Trojan facility. Therefore, the plant which was closed August 15 for inventory is no longer the property of URSA and apparently will not reopen under the new owner.
>
> This letter is your official notification that your employment with Trojan as a unit of URSA Corporation was terminated effective August 15, with the sale of the unit's assets to Barnes Industries.
>
> A summary of the effects of the termination regarding insurance coverage and conversion rights, pension, vacation pay, etc., will be forwarded to you in the immediate future.

Negotiations on Effects of Closing

On August 22, 1984, the Parties met to negotiate terms regarding the effects of the closing on the bargaining unit employees. At that time, the Union proposed a number of economic and noneconomic proposals. Agreement was reached on various insurance items, vacation pay, and letters of recommendation for employees seeking new jobs. In addition, the Company agreed not to contest unemployment compensation claims, to provide the Union with a current mailing list, to furnish employees with copies of their personnel records at 20 cents per copy, and to distribute to employees the proceeds of the profit-sharing plan.

No agreement, however, was reached on the Union's proposal for a severance pay program, which called for 40 hours of pay for each year of service. In addition, the Company refused to pay each eligible employee 80 hours of pay in lieu of notice of closing as provided in the Memorandum of Understanding. Morgan testified that the Union told the Company it was entitled to such notice, but the Company replied that the plant was sold for economic reasons and that Barnes Industries, and not the Company, closed the plant.

POSITIONS OF THE PARTIES

Basic to the Company position is that it did not close the Trojan Plant. It asserts that the plant was sold to Barnes Industries, the plant being closed by the purchaser of the property. "It was Barnes," the Company says, "and not us who closed the plant. We had nothing to do with its closure." It also contends that Management could not advise the Union of the impending sale because under the terms of the Sales and Purchase Agreement, Barnes Industries forbade any disclosure of the impending sale to anyone. If it disclosed the information, the Company feared that Barnes would refuse to purchase the property. Also, it argues that not until August 15, the date of the actual sale, did the Company know for sure that Barnes would close the plant. On August 9, after being told closure would take place, Glenn persuaded Cook to reconsider closing the plant. Under all these circumstances, the Company concluded that it did not violate the Memorandum of Understanding.

On its part, the Union asserts the Company violated the Memorandum of Understanding. It contends that the Company should have notified the Union of the impending sale so that it might have presented reasonable alternatives to closure. It stresses testimony offered by Union President Morgan that Plant Manager Ellis tried to raise sufficient money to purchase the plant when he heard of the closing. (Morgan's testimony in this respect, not mentioned previously, was not challenged or refuted by the Company. It did not cross-examine Morgan on this portion of her testimony, nor did it present Ellis as a witness). Morgan testified that Ellis tried to raise the money, but did not have time to do so. She said he had told her that if he had had six or seven days he might have raised the necessary money to purchase the plant.

In short, under the circumstances of this case, the Union claims that the Company violated the Memorandum of Understanding because it was not notified of the impending closure of the plant. In its post-hearing brief, it requests that the Company pay eighty (80) hours pay to each of the 159 employees who lost their jobs because of the closing of the plant.

Mock Negotiation Problem

The purpose of this problem is to familiarize students with the negotiation of a labor contract. The problem is strictly a hypothetical one and does not pertain to any actual company or union. It is designed to test in a practical way the student's understanding of the issues of collective bargaining studied during the semester and the strategy of the bargaining process. The strategy and techniques of negotiations are treated in Chapter 5, and the issues of collective bargaining are dealt with primarily in Chapters 7 through 10. Before the actual mock negotiation, the student should carefully reread these chapters.

PROCEDURE AND GROUND RULES

1. Class will be divided into labor and management negotiation teams. Each team will elect a chairperson at the first meeting of the team.
2. Teams will meet in a sufficient number of planning sessions to be ready for the negotiations. Each participant will be required to engage in necessary research for the negotiation.

3. In the light of the following problem, each team will establish *not more* than eight items *nor fewer* than six that it will demand. *All demands must be based on the problem. No team will be permitted to make a demand that is not so based.* For purposes of this problem, a union wage demand and all fringe issues, if demanded, will be considered as only *one* demand.

4. Each team should strive to negotiate demands that it believes to be most important. This requires the weighing of the alternatives in the light of respective needs of the group the team is representing.

5. Compromises, counterproposals, trading, and the dropping of demands to secure a contract will be permitted in the light of the give and take of the actual negotiations.

6. Each team should strive sincerely and honestly in the role playing to do the best job possible for the group it represents. This is a *learning situation* and to learn there must be sincere dedication to the job ahead.

7. *Absolutely no consultation with any of the other teams, regardless of whether company or union, will be permitted. Each team must depend entirely upon its own resources.*

8. Chairpersons should coordinate the planning of each team, decide on the time and place for planning sessions, and assign work to be done to members of the team. Chairpersons, however, are not to do all the talking in the actual negotiations. To maximize the learning situation, each member of the team should positively participate in the negotiations.

9. There must either be a settlement of all issues in the negotiation or a work stoppage. *No extension of the existing contract will be permitted.* It is a question of either settlement or work stoppage.

10. Someone on each team should keep track of the settlements. Do not write out the actual contractual clauses agreed to. It will suffice only to jot down the substance of agreements.

11. There will be a general discussion of the problem after the negotiation. Each team chairperson will make a brief statement to the entire class as to the final outcome of the problem.

Herein follows the problem on which the demands will be based and which provides the framework for the negotiations. *Read the problem very carefully to size up the situation. Base your demands only on this problem.*

Representatives of the Auto Products Corporation of Indianapolis, Indiana, and Local 5000, United Metal Workers of America, are in the process of negotiating their collective bargaining contract. The current contract expires at the close of today's negotiations. *(Instructor should set the date of the mock negotiation, and the exact clock time that the contract expires.)* The negotiations cover the Indianapolis plant.[*] Auto Products also owns a plant in Little Rock, Arkansas, but the southern plant is not organized and

[*]The location of the plant may be shifted to your own area to provide more local relevance.

is not a part of the current negotiations. The current contract, which covers only the Indianapolis plant, was negotiated for a three-year period. *The time of the negotiation is the present, and, accordingly, the parties are conditioned by current elements of economic trends, patterns of collective bargaining, and labor relations law.*

The Indianapolis plant has been in business for sixty-one years and has steadily expanded. At present, 3,800 production and maintenance employees are in the bargaining unit of the plant.

Except for the years of the Great Depression, the financial structure of the firm has been relatively good. Here are some financial data from the Indianapolis plant for the fiscal year preceding these negotiations:

Net sales	$200,825,900
Material costs	79,250,000
Direct labor costs (includes fringe benefits and reflects layoffs in previous fiscal year)	72,635,000
Other variable costs	13,265,000
Fixed costs	5,500,000
Total expenses	170,650,000
Income before taxes	30,175,000
Net income after taxes (federal, state, county, municipal)	9,400,000

In the past, the experience has been to distribute about 65 percent of net profits in dividends and 35 percent has been held as retained earnings. Last year the company borrowed $6.3 million from the Hoosier National Bank. The rate of interest on the loan was 8.2 percent. The proceeds of the loan were used to expand the Little Rock plant. The loan is scheduled for liquidation in ten years.

The company manufactures a variety of auto accessories. These include auto heaters, oil pumps, fan belts, rear-view mirrors, and piston rings, and in the last year the company has also started production of auto air conditioners. About 65 percent of its sales are to the basic auto companies (General Motors, Ford, and Chrysler), 25 percent to auto-repair facilities, and the rest to government agencies. The plant operates on a two-shift basis. A 10-cent-per-hour premium is paid to employees who work the second shift.

The employees of the company were unionized in 1937, as a result of the CIO campaign to organize the mass-production industries. In August of that year, the union was victorious in an NLRB election. As a result of the election, certification was awarded, on August 17, 1937, to Local 5000, since which time Local 5000 has represented the production and maintenance workers of the company. The first collective bargaining agreement between the company and Local 5000 was signed on November 14, 1937.

Only one contract strike has taken place since the union came into the picture. It occurred in 1940; the issues were the union's demands for a union shop, increased wages, and six paid holidays. The strike lasted six weeks. When it terminated, the union had obtained for its members a 4-cent hourly wage increase, retroactive to the day of the strike (the union had demanded 7 cents), and four paid holidays. The union failed in its attempt to obtain any arrangement requiring membership in the union as a condition of employment. Also, the current contract does not include a "checkoff." At the time of these negotiations, all except 400 workers in the bargaining unit are in the union.

The average wage for the production workers in the Indianapolis plant is $10.17 per hour. Of the 3,800 employees, there are 175 skilled maintenance employees (electricians, plumbers, carpenters, mechanics, and tool and die makers), and their average rate is $12.49 per hour. The existing contract contains an escalator (COLA) clause providing for the adjustment of wages in accordance with changes in the Consumer Price Index. There is no "cap" on the amount of the increase. It provides for a 1-cent increase in wages for each 0.4-point increase in the CPI. The escalator arrangement is reviewed on a semiannual basis. The current wage rates include the increases generated from the escalator clause and the annual improvement factor. During the term of the three-year contract, workers received a 50-cent increase in wages: 20 cents from the operation of the escalator clause and 30 cents from the operation of the annual improvement factor (a 15-cent increase on the anniversary date of the contract in each of the past two years).

The Little Rock plant was built five years ago. It started with a modest-size labor force, but during the past three years the southern plant has expanded sharply, and it now employs about 1,500 production and maintenance workers. Efforts to organize the southern plant have so far been unsuccessful. The union lost an NLRB election last year by 300 votes. Of the 1,500 employees, 1,300 cast ballots, with 800 voting against the union and 500 voting for it. The average wage in the Little Rock plant is $8.12 per hour. Currently, 450 employees in the Indianapolis plant are on layoff. It is no secret that one reason for this has been the increase of output in the Little Rock plant. Another reason was the decrease in sales at the Indianapolis plant. In Little Rock, essentially the same products are made as in Indianapolis. Of the 450 on layoff, reduction in sales caused by the state of the automobile industry accounts for 300, and the remainder is attributable to the southern situation. There is talk in the plant that some laid-off employees will never be recalled to work. Of the 450 laid-off employees, 75 have exhausted their benefits under the Indiana Unemployment Compensation Act. The present contract does not provide for a supplementary unemployment benefit program.

In general, the relations between the management and the union have been satisfactory. There have, of course, been the usual disagreements, but all in all, relations have been quite harmonious. However, last month there was a wildcat strike, the first one since the union came into the picture. It occurred in the Oil Pump Department, and the alleged cause was the discharge of the steward of the department on the grounds that he shoved a supervisor while he was discussing a grievance with him. The union disclaimed all responsibility for the strike, and its officers stated that they did all they could to get the workers back to work. However, the employees in the Oil Pump Department picketed the plant, and the incident, which lasted two days, shut down all production in the plant for these two days. There is a no-strike clause in the contract that states:

There will be no strikes, slowdowns, or other interruptions of production because of labor disputes during the contract period. Employees who engage in such prohibited activity are subject to discharge.

The company threatened to sue the union for damages under the Taft-Hartley law, but management finally decided not to go to court after the employees returned to work. No employee was disciplined because of the strike; however, at present, the steward remains discharged, and the union has demanded that he be returned to his job. Under the contract, the company has the right to discharge for "just cause." The steward is 64 years old and was one of the leading figures in the earlier years of the union. He is known affectionately by his fellow workers as "Old Joe."

The existing contract contains a standard grievance procedure and provides for arbitration for all disputes arising under the contract, except production standards, which management has the unilateral right to establish. During the last contractual period (three years), seventy-five written grievances were filed by employees protesting "unreasonably" high production standards. As required by the contract, the company negotiated the production standard grievances, but the union did not have the right to appeal to arbitration or to strike over them. In three cases sparked by the production standard grievances, the company reduced the standards. In all other cases, the company denied the grievances. The management rights clause states in effect that the company retains all rights except as limited by express provisions of the labor agreement.

Provided in the contract are a series of fringe benefits: eight paid holidays; a pension plan similar to the one negotiated in the basic automobile industry; and a paid vacation program wherein employees receive one week's vacation for one year of service, two weeks for five years, and three weeks for twenty or more years of service.

A medical insurance program covers the entire bargaining unit. However, the program does not cover employees laid off for more than 30 consecutive days. Of the 450 employees on layoff, 80 percent have been laid off for more than thirty consecutive days. It covers physician and hospital services, including emergency room treatment. It provides "first dollar coverage"—no deductions are assessed against the employee before insurance kicks in. Reflecting national trends, the costs of the medical insurance program have been mounting: $2,040 per employee in 1988 and $2,750 per employee at the present time. The Company pays the entire cost of the plan.

Under the corporate pension program, employees with twenty or more years of service may retire at age 65 and receive full benefits, though retirement is not required of anyone. The average age of the employees in the plant is 39. About 8 percent are over 65 years of age and have more than twenty years of service. The average benefit for the last fiscal year was $433 per month.

The total cost of the fringe benefit program for the last fiscal year amounted to $4.40 per hour.

The current seniority clause provides for promotions based on length of service and ability. That is, seniority governs when the senior employee has qualifications reasonably equal to those of junior employees who bid on the job. During the contract period, twenty-one grievances were filed by employees who protested against the company's filling jobs with junior service employees. The company's position in these grievances was that the junior employees had far more ability than the senior employees. Five of these grievances went to arbitration, the company winning four and the union winning only one. Promotions are bid for on a departmental basis.

The seniority area of the existing contract provides for plantwide application of seniority credits for layoffs and recalls, provided that the senior employee has the necessary qualifications to perform the available work. During the recent period in which layoffs occurred, the company, as required by the contract, laid off many junior employees rather than senior employees because of the plantwide system. Supervisors have complained to management that, in many cases, the junior employees who had been laid off were more efficient than the senior employees who had to be retained because of the plantwide system.

Also, the current contract provides that an employee whose job goes down, or whose job is preempted by a more senior employee, may bump any junior employee in the plant, provided that the preempting employee has the qualifications to fill the job. During layoff periods, the company became aware that this situation caused a great deal of expense because of an unreasonable amount of job displacement. Also, the current contract does not contain a temporary layoff clause. This means that displaced employees may exercise their bumping rights based on their plantwide seniority regardless of the length of the layoff. Supervisors have complained to the management that employees should be laid off without regard to seniority when the layoff is for a short period of time.

The existing contract provides for "superseniority" for stewards and other union officials. This provision protects the stewards and union officials only from layoffs. There are sixty stewards in the plant. Last year, stewards spent, on the average, about ten hours each per week on grievance work, for which they were paid by the company. There are no limitations on stewards for grievance work. Supervisors have complained that some stewards are "goofing off," using "union business" as a pretext not to work. All the stewards deny this. In fact, the stewards claim that it is the unreasonable attitude of supervisors that provokes grievances and complaints. Also, the stewards claim that there cannot be a true measure of their time on the basis of the number of written grievances (a total of 450 grievances, including the production standard complaints, were filed during the last three years), since a good share of their time is spent discussing grievances on an oral basis with employees and supervisors before a written grievance is filed. There is no record to show how many of these oral discussions ended problems without written grievances being filed.

Last year, because of an unexpected order from the government, the plant worked Saturday and Sunday overtime for a period of two weekends. Under the existing contract, the company has the right to require overtime. About 200 employees refused to work overtime and did so only because the company threatened to fire them if they refused. These 200 employees have been raising a lot of trouble in the union about this overtime affair. Also, the company has the right to select the employees to work overtime. Some employees have claimed that supervisors are not fair, giving their personal friends the opportunity to earn the extra money and discriminating against the other employees.

For many years, by custom, each skilled tradesperson has worked only within his or her trade. Five months ago, the company required a mechanic to do a job normally performed by a plumber. The employee and union filed a grievance, and the case went all the way to arbitration. The arbitrator sustained the position of the union on the basis of the "past practice" principle.

Some maintenance people have been affected by the current layoff, with twenty-five laid off. They charge that the company has been subcontracting out skilled work that could be done by them. Last year, for example, the company subcontracted out electrical work while three electricians were on layoff. The subcontract job lasted six days. Under the current contract, there is no restriction on the company's right to subcontract.

The present contract, as stated, was negotiated for a three-year period. Both sides have indicated that in the future they may want to move away from this long-term arrangement for a variety of reasons. However, there is no assurance of whether this attitude indicates the parties' sincere position or is merely an expression of a possible bargaining position.

Automation has been a problem in the company for several years. About 250 workers have been permanently separated because of automation. Union and management meetings to deal with the problem during the past several years have proved fruitless. Previous discussions have centered on the rate of automation, the problem of income for the displaced employees, and the training of employees for the jobs created by automation. All indications are that the next wave of automation will cost about 390 bargaining unit jobs. The 250 employees who have been permanently separated are in addition to the 450 employees who are currently on layoff because of the southern situation and the drop in sales.

There has been considerable controversy over the problem of temporary transfers. Under the existing contract, the company may not transfer an employee to a job not in his or her job classification.

There are also problems regarding other working rules. These now include a fifteen-minute rest period every four hours; a stipulation that no supervisor may perform bargaining unit work regardless of circumstances; paid lunch periods of twenty-minute duration; and paid "wash-up" time for ten minutes prior to quitting time. The company contends that these "working rules" are costing it a lot of money. Whenever this issue has been brought up in the past, the union has refused any change.

Company records show that 60 percent of the workers have seniority up to ten years; 30 percent, between ten and twenty years; and 10 percent, more than twenty years. About 20 percent of the bargaining unit are women, and 15 percent are blacks. Some black employees have complained that they have not been given equal opportunity to get better jobs. Of the 175 in the skilled trades, only 8 are black. They have threatened to file complaints against both the company and the union under Title VII of the Civil Rights Act and Taft-Hartley. They have retained an attorney for this purpose.

Two final issues appear to be involved in the current bargaining.

First, a number of employees have told the union leadership that it is high time that at least one union representative was offered a seat on the nine-person company board of directors. These workers, who are particularly vocal ones as it happens, feel that this matter deserves considerable priority.

Second, the company's president tends to favor the imposition of a two-tier wage system, whereby all workers hired after the new labor agreement is signed would receive pay rates well below those of the current employees. He has publicly declared that "two-tiering could well be the salvation of this company."

*A*uthor Index

Subject Index